Mao's Great
Revolution

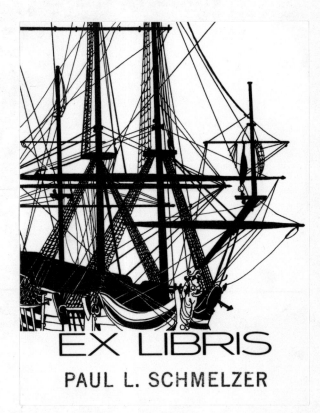

Also by Robert S. Elegant

China's Red Masters
The Dragon's Seed
The Center of the World
A Kind of Treason
The Seeking

Mao's Great Revolution

ROBERT S. ELEGANT

THE WORLD PUBLISHING COMPANY

NEW YORK AND CLEVELAND

Published by The World Publishing Company

Published simultaneously in Canada
by Nelson, Foster & Scott Ltd.

First printing—1971

Library of Congress catalog card number: 72-124282

Printed in the United States of America

WORLD PUBLISHING
TIMES MIRROR

For L. Ladany, without whose
inspired guidance and carping criticism
this book would have been written much
more easily—and even less accurately

Contents

BOOK THREE

The Subsiding Waves

Introduction

In the year 2293 B.C., shortly before the ascension to the Dragon Throne of the Great Yü and 1,742 years before the birth of the sage Confucius, who illuminated the manners, morals, and government of men with the light of reason, the heavens poured rain and the rivers burst their banks, not only inundating the low-lying rice-fields, but lapping at the highest mountain peaks. The Great Yü, son of a humble farmer, subsequently ascended by virtue and genius the greatest heights to which any mortal might aspire. He actually attained semi-divinity, for he later ruled *Tien Hsia,* "all that which lies under the heavens," the land most men today call China and the Chinese themselves call *Chung-kuo,* the Central Realms. When the primordial floods threatened to destroy all mankind, the Great Yü devoted all his manifold powers to the task he was *obliged* to undertake.

By exercise of transcendant industry and intelligence for 18 years, the future Emperor turned back the waters and bestowed renewed life upon mankind. Still, his work was but half-completed, his full responsibility as yet undischarged. In order to preserve all mankind, who lived in *Tien Hsia,* from a repetition of the catastrophe, the Great Yü turned his powers to a new task. He conceived—and constructed by the massed labor of his diligent and willing compatriots—great dams to control the rising and the ebbing of the waters for all time thereafter. Men say that the enormous barrages of wicker, stones, and earth which still hold back and channel the rivers of the Chengtu Basin in Szechwan Province, the most fertile and populous of all China, are the handiwork of the Great Yü, renewed and replenished innumerable times by the industry of his descendants, the great Han race. For his accomplishments, he became Emperor, founding the Hsia Dynasty in 2265 B.C.

The legend differs significantly from the Biblical tale of the great flood. The Chinese Noah, who was far greater than Noah in ability as much as virtue, did not blindly obey God's command. His trumph was a triumph of the *human* will. Nor did he content himself with preserving the different species of beasts. The Great Yü decisively reversed the course of nature and immutably fixed its future course—for the benefit of *all* mankind, who were his subjects in the Central Realms. Man had proved himself supreme over the supernatural—and man was Chinese.

The Emperor Yü, no more than his multitude of successors, even unto the "Great Leader, the Great Teacher, and the Great Helmsman," Chairman Mao Tse-tung of the Communist Party of China, excluded the unfortunate non-Chinese. All recognized that other peoples existed, though they were regrettably deficient in virtue and knowledge beside the *central* people. China's leaders have always been willing to extend to the barbarians the blessings of Chinese virtue and knowledge, *providing* the "outsiders"—as the Chinese call barbarians*—were willing to acknowledge Chinese superiority and behave after the Chinese manner.

The truly great and truly magnanimous race, which founded the world's oldest living civilization, was further invariably ready to accept —and adapt to its own needs—certain customs and material devices of the outsiders. However, the race was *not* willing to acknowledge, even to itself, the extent of its cultural debt to the outsiders. Even today, educated Chinese bridle at any suggestion that Chinese civilization would not have burst forth in the magnificent flowering of the Han Dynasty in the second century B.C. if it had not been for the contribution from the "Western Regions," which stretched all the way from the Pamirs in Central Asia to Rome on the Mediterranean. Particularly during the present time of turmoil and troubles do such men react most hostilely to the suggestion that traditional Chinese civilization was not wholly autarchic.

It makes little difference to their attitude whether they are Communists, the nominal rulers of all the continental territories of four million square miles, or Nationalists, who claim such dominion, but actually rule only the 14 thousand square miles of Formosa. Men who candidly acknowledge China's debt to the outsiders are reviled as traitors or, even worse, deracinated. The Communists, for their part, assert that the doctrines of Marxism-Leninism, irrefutably Western in origin, have been so

---

* An alternate term, used before the twentieth century, was *yi* (夷), which literally means "barbarians." The term is not in colloquial use today, nor does it connote "beasts"—as sensitive early foreign visitors felt because the same word *is* used for flying rodents.

transformed by the supreme genius of Chairman Mao Tse-tung that they are today a uniquely transcendant and uniquely *Chinese* expression of man's capabilities. The Communists are, as ever, not only willing, but anxious to share their unique wisdom with those outsiders who are sufficiently enlightened to follow the Chinese way. But China remains today, as she has always been, an exclusive world of her own, rather than a nation.

The immensity of the concept of China as the Central Realms is matched by the immensity and diversity of the land, as well as the magnitude of a population numbering between 700 and 800 millions. The all-embracing concept is also matched by the immensity, diversity, and obduracy of the multitudinous problems which confront the titular rulers of the Central Realms. Four hundred years are but a season in history— as the impatient descendents of the great Yü would *like* to reckon time when they remember that he "served the people" for over 150 years, more than 3,000 years in the past. Only 400 years ago, the few outsiders who penetrated to their heart and learned their ways acknowledged with unfeigned awe that the Central Realms were the most advanced, most prosperous, most virtuous, and happiest realms on earth. The outsiders could quite understand—even if they could not themselves accept the concept—why the Chinese considered themselves not merely unique among mankind, but *the* center of *all* civilized mankind.

Yet today, the inhabitants of the Central Realms are among the more retrograde, pinched, bedeviled, and unhappy peoples of the earth. China has been radically transformed in the brief space of the historical winter by the malignity of nature, the rapacity of the outsiders, the myopia of her leaders, and the inflexibility of her customs. It is, therefore, hardly remarkable that her people feel themselves oppressed by maleficent natural and human forces, while her rulers, despite their assertions of infallibility, are deeply perplexed by the apparently intractable problems of governing the vast realms that are truly a world—in themselves and unto themselves. It is hardly remarkable that the Chinese—always committed to the proposition that no obstacle can resist human, *i.e.*, Chinese, ingenuity and industry, as the floods yielded to the Great Yü—are ever more inclined to essay solutions which appear to other peoples excessively radical and sometimes quite irrational.

Despite their brilliant early technical achievements, the Chinese became complacent after the Mongol Conquest of 1254 A.D. and the restoration of the Chinese Ming Dynasty in 1389. Since they possessed all knowledge, all virtue, and all material necessities well into the sixteenth century, they saw no need to change their customs or their thinking. The civilization which had once eagerly accepted new ideas and new artifacts came to consider both mere gadgets. The Japanese, hampered by neither overweening pride nor lithic stability become inertia, could adapt to the demands of Western industrialization without rending the fabric of their race and culture. The Chinese could not.

The knowledge that they were *the* Central Realms allowed them to accept lesser innovations of lesser peoples, but forbade their acknowledging the existence of superior knowledge or, even, equal peoples. Besides, acquiring and utilizing "outside" knowledge would require fundamental change. The massive superiority of their own unique greatness made the Chinese slow to adjust to the purely material superiority of the West—if not wholly incapable of such adjustment. Even though conservatives objected, Chinese leaders felt they need merely take over the *practical* devices the West had created, from cannon and clocks to steam engines and surgical techniques, just as they had used other "barbarian" devices. The Chinese could apprehend neither the necessity nor the possibility of altering the fundamental character of their society. They could not realize that Western technology was an organic growth from the soil of Western social, economic, and political organization. One of the more advanced Chinese thinkers of the nineteenth century expressed the *liberal attitude* when he wrote in an *Exhortation to Learn* (from the West): "Western knowledge for [practical] application; Chinese knowledge as the [immutable] basis!"

The character of the land and the character of the people acted upon each other. Because she had rejected the essential foundations of Western techniques and because the resources of the soil appeared inexhaustible, China remained an overwhelmingly agricultural nation. Almost 90 percent of her people toiled on the land. Although some areas had been cultivated continuously for more than four millennia, the soil had retained some vigor because of the universal use of organic fertilizer. Since it was more than four thousand miles from Canton in the far southeast to Urumchi in the far northwest, so the Chinese felt little concern for their chief—if not quite their only—resource, agricultural land. No matter that no more than one-third of China's four million square miles could be cultivated efficiently.

By the mid-nineteenth century, much of the potential of the land was exhausted, despite heroic efforts to "cultivate the swamps, the forests, and the mountains," sustained by the ingenuity and industry the Han race devoted to its traditional, intensive agriculture. Population had increased geometrically after the repeal of the head tax in 1711 by the excessively benevolent Manchu Emperor Kang Hsi. Rebelling against the burden of humanity laid upon her, the earth itself turned against the Chinese. Pestilence, floods, droughts, and famines scythed the population, and undercut the Manchu *imperium*. Revolts erupted across the land, as they had during the declining phase of each previous dynasty. Manchu power was sapped by more than 100 separate revolts from 1841 to 1849; from 1849 to 1861, six major insurrections tormented the Dynasty. Moreover, the impatient and aggressive West would no longer be denied its "right" to trade freely with a nation-world which had never even considered the possibility of open and equal commercial exchanges with other nations—in large part because it *knew* that no other equal nations existed.

From 1839 to 1945, foreign nations tore at the fabric of China with their vastly superior implements of war. Not only European and American nations but Japan as well, participated in the ostensible attempt to impose "equality of trade" by force. They acquired large "concessions" within China, where "extraterritorial rights" negated Chinese law; they made formal colonies of extremities of the great sub-world; they manipulated Chinese governments by arms and gold for their own political and economic gain; and they seized the management of the Chinese Maritime Customs (as well as much internal taxation) in order to "repay" the debts they had imposed upon China. Chinese felt themselves, as they truly were, second-class citizens in their own nation. In the space of a century and a half, China had fallen from the heights of unique superiority into the slough of political and psychological despond the Marxists described as semi-colonialism.

The Manchu Empire had been destroyed by Western-oriented revolutionaries in 1911, just five years after the abolition of the Civil Service Examinations cut the last feeble roots of the two-thousand-year-old Confucian civilization. The successor Republic of China was a state of chaos, rather than progress or stability. While the common people suffered, impotent to affect their own fate, a small number of Chinese, later denounced by the Communists as "bureaucratic capitalists," made common cause for common profit with foreign interests. Their depredations were sanctioned by the lingering Confucian *ethos,* which considered duty to one's clan-family the highest responsibility and service to the common good a secondary responsibility. There was, in any event, no coherent nation which might claim their allegiance. Warlords ruled the disintegrated sub-world, each supreme for a time in his own small realm and each dedicated primarily to his own self-aggrandizement. All China was a devastated area where the strong looted and the weak suffered.

The Communist Party, founded in July 1921, was dedicated to making China once more strong and predominant in the world. The Communists' drive to power, exacerbated by the Japanese invasion in the 1930s, negated whatever chance the Nationalist Government might have had to re-create a powerful nation characterized by social and economic justice after the Nationalists came to power in 1928. The Nationalists were equally hampered by internal divisions they could not heal. Parliamentary democracy, however attenuated, was never given the opportunity to prove or disprove its validity for China.

The Communists came to power in 1949 after a bitter Civil War, which the United States attempted—vainly and naïvely—to mediate. The Soviet Union gave the final impetus to Communist victory by turning over to the armies of General Lin Piao great quantities of Japanese military supplies captured in Manchuria. The Communists, during the following 20 years, sought by a variety of means to make the nation-world called China strong enough to resume her dominant place among the other nations. They also sought, with somewhat less ardor, to improve the material and spiritual condition of the masses. Their varied and ingenious approaches are portrayed in the course of this narrative. None has yet succeeded.

For the world—as much as for China—a fundamental question remains. It is the single issue which has dominated Chinese development during the past 400 years: Can the Chinese accept the fact that they are not the Central Realms, but an equal nation among other equal nations, a great power, destined to become even stronger by possession of a formidable nuclear arsenal, but, nonetheless, only one great power among other great powers? If the Chinese can, finally, make that quintessential psychological adjustment, the agony China has imposed upon herself and the world will finally begin to abate. A new cycle will begin in the evolution of the world's largest, oldest, and, in many ways, most vital nation. It may be excessively optimistic to discern indications of a great catharsis of the Chinese spirit and mind as a consequence of the Great Proletarian Cultural Revolution. Such indications are, nonetheless, apparent.

Hong Kong—Vienna—Los Angeles
August 1967—September 1970

BOOK ONE
The Clouds Gather

I

Morning on Mount Lu

The black limousines rolled over the green, river-veined plain. Army lorries loaded with supplies and troops chased each other among the staid official automobiles in a robot game of tag. The traffic converged on the cleft in the pine-cloaked mountains rising abruptly at the edge of the river flatlands. Spear-straight from the city of "Nine Rivers," Kiukiang, to the jagged heights called Mount Lu, the road was a joyous playground for the laughing youths at the wheel of their mechanical toys. Surfaced only that spring with black asphalt, the road was also impressive evidence of the new force created ten years earlier with the proclamation of the People's Republic of China. Despite the Communists' great energy, it was a rare monument. The land was so vast and its needs so great that the regime had built few paved highways. It had, instead, concentrated its efforts on the packed-earth byroads and single-track railways essential to opening the great expanses of China.

The young, inexperienced drivers were exhilarated by the flat, gleaming road. From time to time their older passengers leaned forward and spoke softly to check the youths' exuberance. Some of these elders wore the uniforms of People's Marshals, bestrewn with gold leaves and bright red trimmings in the Russian manner. Most wore the self-consciously austere Liberation Suits of "senior cadres" of the Chinese Communist Party. Buttoned to their high-necked, folded collars, the tunics were beautifully tailored. They were also light-weight, for the steamy summer of the Yangtze Valley hung oppressively over the plains in July 1959.

Only the dry coolness of Mount Lu could restore the energy sapped by the humid heat. Yet the passengers did not come to relax, for the new road had not been built for the pleasure of the 200-odd men and women

3

who ruled the world's most populous nation. After nearly a full decade of stewardship of the nation, the Central Committee of the Communist Party of China was meeting in extended Plenary Session. They came to Mount Lu to scrutinize the past and set the course for the critical decade to come—the decade that would determine the fate of China.

Although the manner of life, like their dress, was ostentatiously austere, these men had seen glittering visions—and lived to transform many of these visions into reality. Princes of the Communist hierarchy, they commanded the labors of more than half a billion souls. But they all paid deference, some gladly, some grudgingly—to the greatest visionary of them all, Chairman of the Communist Party Mao Tse-tung. He was the reason for their presence at Mount Lu and the focus of their thoughts. They had come to consider the spectacular successes—and failures—of Chairman Mao's policies. Only a year earlier, his leadership had culminated in the Great Leap Forward, history's most audacious endeavor to transform the physical shape of a nation and the hearts of its people in a historical instant.

Some of the Communist leaders were devoted—flesh, bone, and spirit —to Mao Tse-tung. Others felt his genius had faltered under the mundane, but immense difficulties of ruling the vast nation. The majority of the Central Committee were puzzled and fearful, for they neither enthusiastically supported the Maoist way nor resolutely opposed it. The Great Leap Forward had created catastrophe, instead of the brilliant new society it had sought. Yet the actors in the curious drama unfolding at Mount Lu in the summer of 1959 were not unduly perturbed, for they had faced apparent disaster many times in the past—and had triumphed.

Though they were unaware, the Communist leaders stood at one of the great forks of Chinese history. By summer's end, the Eighth Plenary Session of the Central Committee elected by the Eighth National Congress of the Communist Party of China in 1956 had clearly become one of those rare historical events that, in the Chinese term, "demarks epochs."

It was the last time the leaders of the world's most populace nation would meet in obstensible amity. Bitter strife would soon become overt. Just seven years later, the consequences of Mount Lu would thrust China into the greatest turmoil she has known in this century—the Great Proletarian Cultural Revolution. No sense of foreboding hung over the deliberations. The Communist chieftains were beyond such fancies. But, their conclave was as crucial as the smoke obscured battle that fixes the fate of a continent. Rising from the Eighth Plenary Session At Mount Lu, torrents of violence would roll across all China from 1966 to 1969 in the home of the Great Proletarian Cultural Revolution. These torrents would sweep away the existing structure of the Communist Party, crack its ideological foundations, and, for a time, leave China without government or purpose.

Almost the entire cast of the subsequent drama was assembled at Mount Lu—the stars, the character actors, and the supporting players. Only the great chorus of the "masses" was invisible, waiting in the wings of the vast stage called China. Mount Lu, prologue to the tragedy of the Cultural Revolution, merely indicated the violent hatreds and hidden jealousies. Unloosed in 1966, those passions would impel the Communist leaders to strive to destroy each other. The entire country would fall into chaos Peking itself described as "total anarchy."

Supported by a few zealots and many opportunists, Chairman Mao Tse-tung would denounce his associates of four decades in language a Shanghai longshoreman or Shansi mule-driver would consider coarse. Caught up in their patrons' quarrels, millions of Chinese would attack each other—first with fists, clubs, and knives; later with rifles, machine guns, and field pieces. The Central Government of the People's Republic would be paralyzed by fratricidal strife, and the Communist Party of China would disintegrate. Bands of frenzied adolescents called Red Guards would, for an extended time, dominate the spirit and the institutions of the People's Republic. Their own moving spirit was the spirit of vengeance, though they strove toward perfect, mass participatory democracy. Only the People's Liberation Army, itself shaken by dissension, would remain an effective instrument of authority.

Striving to make China a predominant and respected world power, the Maoist clique would, first, make the country an object of amazement and, later, total incredulity to the outside world. The great goals would be abandoned. One overriding problem would ultimately dominate the country—preserving a semblance of authority in order to preserve the political entity called China.

Portents abounded at Mount Lu. But no one could have foreseen the still incalculable consequences. Even the ultimate sources are still obscure, since the final reasons for men's actions are as tangled as mangrove roots entwined beneath a tropical swamp. Therefore, one can only speculate.

Perhaps the Great Proletarian Cultural Revolution was predestined by the harshness a middle-class Hunan farmer named Mao Jen-sheng showed his son, Tse-tung, at the end of the nineteenth century. Perhaps his colleagues in the Communist Party made the cataclysm inevitable when they censured Mao Tse-tung for indiscipline in the 1920s. Still, the root cause may not have been merely the character of Mao Tse-tung, but the interplay between himself and his "Deputy Commander-in-Chief and closest comrade-in-arms," Field Marshal Lin Piao. Perhaps the upheaval began with the bankruptcy of a family textile mill during the First World War—and the consequent adversity suffered by the adolescent who was to become Deputy Chairman Lin of the Communist Party of China.

The exact moment a new epoch begins is normally as difficult to fix as its ultimate cause. The crystallization of events that produced the Great Proletarian Cultural Revolution can, however, be marked with some precision.

The time was July and August of 1959. The place was Mount Lu, a mist-enfolded range in northern Kiangsi Province, high above the silver-red undulations of the Yangtze River. The actors were the rulers of one-quarter of mankind: the Political Bureau and the Central Committee of the Communist Party of China.

The stage was itself as symbolic as the actors. The entire Chinese landscape is imbued with racial memories. The race that inhabits the ancient land is, itself, old almost beyond reckoning, and its unbroken history has been tumultuous. Mount Lu is even more heavily laden with memories of great and tragic events than most of the history-saturated land.

Even before the eleventh century, statesmen, scholars, officials—and others who were merely rich—had fled to Mount Lu to escape the oppressive summer of the plains. One great poet-official of the Sung Dynasty celebrated the mountains' manifold enchantments in a line that has passed into the common consciousness: "No man can ever look upon the true face of infinite Mount Lu!" Each man sees a different image of the mountain and reality, while no man comprehends the essence of either, he implied.

The procession continued after the eleventh century. Princes of the Blood, who enjoyed much deference but little power, and powerful Imperial mandarins, qualified to rule by rigorous examinations in the Confucian Classics, were borne upward in carved and gilded palanquins. During the first decades of the twentieth century, swinging with the balance of power, the passengers were as often plump European businessmen or pale American missionaries as rich and powerful Chinese. The sweating coolies under the shafts of the palanquins were a race apart from their scented burdens in sleek silk or starched linen.

For two months in the summer of 1959, the Red mandarins took the newly paved road from Kiukiang in German Mercedes and Russian Zis limousines. Their plain, soft-collared tunics mocked the gorgeous mountain pines that enfolded the road where it wound upward. The road ended at Kuling, a resort town compressed into the narrow cleft between two steep hills. Kuling lay beneath slopes dominated by three monumental buildings with curving eaves capped by vermilion tiles: the Library, the Great Hostel, and the Grand Temple of Mount Lu. There the Central Committee met.

Sightseers rode still higher in bamboo sedan-chairs—up a steep stone stairway into the clouds that perpetually draped the slopes like a white scarf on the shoulders of an indifferent beauty. Had the Communist officials gone higher, they would have reached the Great Grove of Temples—more than 300 shrines and pavilions built in the fourth century A.D. Emerging from that forest of devotion onto the winding Road to Pay Respect to the Spirits, they would have come to the Terrace of Ascension, whence, fable relates, a poet of antiquity had flown to heaven on a white deer. A perfect moon-disk pierced the wall beyond the Terrace. Framed by the moon-gate stood a great rock, which gave root to a gnarled fir revered as one of the oldest trees in all China. Looking from the rock across the rolling clouds, innumerable poets have sung the immutable beauty of Mount Lu, which incarnates the grandeur of the four-thousand-year-old civilization of China.

It was a fitting stage for the battle between the enduring values of old China and the creed of destruction called Maoism. Chairman Mao Tse-tung had come to Mount Lu to beat down the swords raised against his policies and his pre-eminence. Confident as always that his truth would prevail, Mao gave vent to his ardent romanticism as he contemplated the ancient landscape on July 1, before the confrontation. His verses called "Ascending Mount Lu," are heavy with classical allusion:

> The mountain springs from the broad riverside.
> Soaring from vast groves of encompassing trees,
> I gaze upon the world—a single, total scene.
> I know not where, beyond this world, one finds Paradise.
> We must create *our* Utopia by diligently tilling the fields.

On September 9, 1959, after his triumph over his enemies, the Chairman praised the indomitable fir in an inscription on a photograph taken by his wife:

> As darkness thickens, I look upon that eternal tree,
> Still standing proud among the roiled clouds.
> Heaven created here a miracle of the spirit,
> Illimitable splendor on this perilous peak.

The symbolism was baldly obvious. Like the fir, Mao Tse-tung stood firm after the wild seas of his enemies had subsided. But Mao betrayed his foreboding, the Chinese feel, by acknowledging that he stood on "this perilous peak."

People's Marshal Chu Teh, too, chose verse. Like Mao Tse-tung, his junior by seven years, Chu Teh—Generalissimo of the Communist armies against both the Japanese and the Nationalists—favored the literary and personal styles of old China. Chu Teh was 73 in summer 1959. He was no longer in the mainstream of affairs, although he was still a vice chairman of the People's Republic and a member of the Political Bureau of the Communist Party. The grizzled, broad-faced veteran still enjoyed the great affection he had always evoked among both troops and civilians. His prestige rivaled Mao's, though the Chairman evoked not affection but respect, awe, and fear. That summer Chu Teh was, above all, eager to reconcile the potentially fratricidal differences within the Party. His verses, entitled "Ascending Mount Lu with Chairman Mao," asserted hopefully:

> Mount Lu reveals the rivers' banks
> And Kuling, where we stand supreme,
> While the gentle rain and winds of harmony
> Caress the Pavilion of the White Deer.
> The curtain of clouds lifts,
> And the fog parts to reveal the blue skies.
> We are supported by multitudes of the faithful;
> Though quarrels brought us to this mountain range,
> We are met here to pledge our unity,
> Joining our hearts to build the future.

Generalissimo Chu was not primarily a particularly brilliant field commander. He was a paternal figure, an organizer his generals vied to serve. Having cast aside the personal ambition that made him the leading warlord of southwest China, he had adopted the Communist creed—abandoning his concubines and his opium pipes. He had also demonstrated total personal devotion to Mao Tse-tung and on one occasion had accepted the prospect of certain death at the hands of Mao's chief rival rather than betray his leader. Although his steadfastness had guaranteed Mao's ascendancy, Generalissimo Chu Teh was, seven years later, to be viciously assailed by impassioned Maoists with the apparent sanction of the Chairman himself. The tidal wave of the Cultural Revolution swept over not only institutions but the network of personal relationships among Communist leaders that gave those institutions life.

At Mount Lu, before the deluge, Mao Tse-tung bore himself with the remote dignity of a traditional Confucian emperor. His resemblance to that earthly divinity, set far above daily affairs, had been inadvertently enhanced by events following the Great Leap Forward in 1958. Determined at that time to prove that Mao ruled not by divine right but by their common consent, military leaders, regional pro-consuls, and senior officials had pitted their united will against him. They had prevailed.

Threats and entreaties had forced him to abdicate the largely ceremonial office of Chairman (President) of the People's Republic. Mao had, however, remained Chairman of the Communist Party. The Party was the brain that controlled the People's Government, the People's Liberation Army, and the multitude of "small units and people's associations"—the nerve fibers and the muscles that moved the vast organism called China. Mao still wielded great power, despite the fact that his command over daily decisions had diminished. Later his detractors would equate Mao Tse-tung with that stubborn Empress Dowager whose insistence upon antiquated policies contrived the Manchu Empire's collapse in the first decade of this century—and the Maoists would reply with violent indignation. But, at Mount Lu, Mao Tse-tung remained the single commanding figure. Even if diminished, his prestige remained supreme. His aura of personal power still struck awe into all but his closest associates.

In the eyes of many members of the Central Committee of the Communist Party, however, his aura was fading. They had already checked Maoist excesses by elevating the Chairman to an eminence where he would "concern himself primarily with doctrinal matters." The great mandarins of Communist China came to Mount Lu to chart a new route into the future, since profound crises had frustrated Maoist efforts to create a wholly new nation by expunging the old ways of life and thought exemplified by tradition-laden Mount Lu.

The chieftains still deferred to the Chairman, but a significant minority was profoundly dissatisfied with his political romanticism. A few exceedingly powerful men were the nucleus of dissatisfaction that long summer on Mount Lu. Their detailed objections to specific deeds done in Mao's name had already been expressed in previous meetings and had been circulated in writing to thousands of "senior cadres." Still, they cloaked their ultimate defiance of the revered Chairman by laying the blame not on his conceptions but on faulty execution by subordinates, a thin pretense. For it was, ultimately, impossible to question Mao's policies without implicitly attacking Mao himself, for the man and his doctrines were indivisible.

The dissidents felt they had no choice. They were deeply alarmed by the volatile extremism Mao had displayed since the establishment of the People's Republic of China in 1949. Mao Tse-tung had been a brilliant political strategist and a crafty general of guerrillas through three decades of struggle for power, but, the malcontents felt, he was strikingly less effective as chief of the conventional state China was becoming.

The men who doubted dared not call themselves an opposition, since such intra-Party "factions" were prohibited. Perhaps they did not even think of themselves as a united opposition. But no one could prohibit private discussions where men said flatly that Mao Tse-tung, still the supreme authority over grand policy, was leading the nation down the road to disaster. Visionary theories, they declared, had displaced concern with reality.

His sycophants apostrophized the Chairman as: "The greatest political genius of modern times, who has brought Marxism-Leninism to its apogee . . . shaped and perfected by the concrete conditions of the Chinese revolution." The dissident faction felt his style was anachronistic, better suited to a traditional Confucian emperor than the leader of a modern state within the Socialist brotherhood of nations.

Mao's ultimate purpose was the creation of a perfect new social order which would produce unmarred harmony and ideal virtue among, first, the Chinese people, and, soon thereafter, all mankind. That world-wide, all-embracing Utopia was to be guided by the canonical Thought of Mao Tse-tung. Mankind would not come to the Maoist Utopia via heavy industry and thriving agriculture, the "state of material abundance" that Karl Marx had seen as prerequisite to his Utopia of "pure Communism." The Maoist road led through heart and spirit. Cultivated through intensive study of the sacrosanct doctrines of Maoism, the perfect Communist man would know neither psychological nor economic conflict. Men of almost unbelievable—and, the opposition felt, unattainable —virtue would be the foundation stones of the Maoist Utopia. Each would work unstintingly for the common good, disregarding personal welfare for the "collective welfare." Mankind's creativity would flower in unprecedented abundance to create a new Golden Age.

China's specialists in the modern technology of industry, administration, and arms had grown up under Mao's tutelage as guerrilla fighters. In the process they had passed beyond his simplistic faith. They could believe in neither the perfect Communist man nor in Mao's second great purpose—making China once again predominant among nations by moral force. Men tempered by ten years of immediate responsibility for governing China considered both the Chairman's goals and his means naïve.

Yet Maoism had already shaped external as well as internal policy. Obsessed with his own vision of Utopia and the way thither, Mao Tse-tung had already broken with Moscow, doyen of the world "Socialist brotherhood." He had characteristically disregarded the inconvenient fact that the Soviet Union was China's *only* source of the economic, military, and diplomatic support she so badly required. Since China could not immediately build the heavy industrial base Karl Marx considered essential to alter human nature, the Maoist argued that the hearts of men must be transformed *first*. The dissidents felt Mao was not behaving like a true Marxist.

Instead, he was behaving like a Taoist monk intoxicated by his own mysticism, or an Imperial sage-official seeking to re-create the mythical Golden Age Confucius had eulogized in 500 B.C. Mao did not merely lack understanding of modern industrial and military power; he was incapable of presiding over an efficient modern administration. The Central People's Government in Peking displayed the full panoply of ministries, boards, bureaus, and special offices appropriate to a modern government. But that government was not permitted to function in a systematic manner.

Instead, the life of the People's Republic of China was periodically disrupted by intermittent upheavals called "campaigns." Each campaign strove for a single, specific purpose, whether it was quadrupling steel production in a single year or total "reform" of the remaining "bourgeois elements." Each campaign demanded the full attention of all administrators and almost every individual Chinese. Each campaign superseded all other Party and Government business during its often brief, but always intense, life. Each succeeding campaign superseded—and quite often negated—the preceding campaign.

The most recent and disruptive Maoist campaign was still formally in progress in the summer of 1959, though in practice it had already been mitigated. The Three Red Banners had first loomed on the horizon in summer 1958. They were: the General Line of the Party, which meant, the malcontents whispered, merely the whims of Mao Tse-tung; the Great Leap Forward, which meant attempting impossible feats of industrial and agricultural production through the utilization of *unlimited* human labor, which even teeming China did not possess; and, finally, the Great People's Communes, "a totally new organization of human society" that would, the Maoists contended, at once bring China to the ultimate Utopia of true Communism and, the Maoists implied, re-create the Golden Age idealized by Confucius.

To call the consequences of that campaign disastrous would be a deplorable understatement. Intense human suffering evoked widespread resentment against the Communists, while the dislocation of normal economic processes wreaked chaos on industry, agriculture, and commerce. Having welcomed the Communists as liberators only ten years earlier, the people of China were, by the summer of 1959, muttering darkly that they had simply exchanged one form of servitude for another. The corrupt, brutal, and inefficient Nationalist regime had given way to a more onerous and more capricious administration dominated by a man who had parted company with reality.

However, a countercurrent ran strong. The pragmatists within the Communist structure—a clear majority—had already checked many excesses and were determined to re-create rational systems of administration and economic interchange. Many Red mandarins endorsed the common people's complaint that the rule of Mao Tse-tung promised not peaceful prosperity but anguished deprivation; not progress toward Utopia, or even moderate comfort, but a descent into the maelstrom.

II

The Actors

When the chieftains came to Mount Lu, active dissatisfaction had already coalesced around a man second only to Chairman Mao Tse-tung and Generalissimo Chu Teh in the affection and respect he commanded from civilian "cadres," the People's Liberation Army, and the Chinese masses. As he alighted from his black limousine and strode into the gaudy conference chamber, the gold-decked uniform of a People's Marshal set off his strapping, dark-browed presence. When he strolled down the main street of Kuling, past souvenir shops in "Western-style" buildings, his bemedaled figure drew stares of awe. He was Peng Teh-huai, Vice Premier and Minister of Defense of the People's Government and China's premier serving soldier.

Marshal Peng had followed his own road to eminence. Even after enrolling under the Maoist banner in the late 1920s, he had maintained his independence of thought and action. Despite his differences with the Chairman, Peng Teh-huai had commanded the "Chinese People's Volunteers" in the Korean War and still controlled all China's armed forces. He had also established close liaison with the leaders of the Soviet Union. He was a moderate, sympathetic with the anti-Stalinist "revisionism" of Soviet Premier Nikita S. Khrushchev. He was an internationalist who truly believed in the Socialist commonwealth of nations directed from its proper capital in Moscow.

Advocating centralized power within China because they controlled the Party, the Maoists customarily assailed their internal opponents for "establishing independent kingdoms." If there was indeed an "independent king" in Communist China, he was People's Marshal Peng Teh-huai. With his strong, semi-autonomous power base in the People's Liberation

12

Army bolstered by his personal prestige, Peng possessed great freedom of action.

Peng's rise in the face of Mao's intermittent disapproval emphasized a reality obvious to the Party leadership, though not to the outside world. Mao Tse-tung was by no means an absolute despot. He functioned as a domineering chairman of an unruly board of directors, which was the Politburo and the Central Committee of the Communist Party. Therefore he was forced to tolerate Peng's irritating independence. Mao himself had, in a poem of praise, given Marshal Peng Teh-huai his favorite nickname: "Great General Peng"; and so he was called, sometimes even to his face.

Before his confrontation with Mao Tse-tung at Mount Lu in August 1959 the Great General had hazarded both prestige and position by openly soliciting support for his criticism of the Maoist "General Line" of the Party. Although his respectful criticism was generally acknowledged as valid, he secured no more than muttered approval from most of his shamefaced colleagues. Fear of the wrath of Mao Tse-tung prevailed in their hearts over fear that the Chairman's errors would land the ship of state on the rocks.

The Maoists secured their position. The garrison company of Mount Lu, secure in its comfortable assignment for almost a decade, was tumbled out of its barracks at midnight and shipped away. The replacements owed personal loyalty to the Great General's chief rival, People's Marshal Lin Piao, who had made his career almost as much by devotion to Mao Tse-tung as by his brilliance as a field commander. Lin Piao was already undermining the Great General's control of the People's Liberation Army by insinuating his own officers into influential positions. Though Lin Piao's coup was hardly complete at Mount Lu, Great General Peng no longer enjoyed the unrivaled control of the army he had exercised just one year earlier. Rather than compromise, Chairman Mao and fifth Vice Chairman of the Communist Party Lin Piao were prepared to split the People's Liberation Army, which was the chief buttress of Communist power. Although it was outwardly an abstract controversy over high policy, personal rivalries were readily apparent, even in the first phase of the power struggle.

Regardless of their misgivings regarding Maoist policies, most of the Red mandarins refused to commit themselves to a losing battle. Great General Peng obtained only three endorsements for the long critique he presented to the Central Committee in mid-July 1959. His chief advocate was Huang Ke-cheng, Chief-of-Staff of the People's Liberation Army, his personal appointee. The second supporter was Chang Wentien, a vice minister for foreign affairs and former ambassador to Moscow. Chang possessed the broad culture most of his colleagues lacked.

He had been a leader of the so-called international, or pro-Russian, faction in the 1930s. He had, however, fallen to the second echelon by 1959, retained chiefly to maintain a balance within the Central Committee and to placate Moscow. During the Cultural Revolution, Chang Wen-tien was to be accused, among other crimes, of plotting in the sabotaging of a chartered Air India plane carrying Chinese delegates to the Bandung Conference of 1955. The third adherent was a lesser figure: Chou Hsiao-chou, First Secretary of the Communist Party in Hunan, the ancestral province of both Mao Tse-tung and Peng Teh-huai. He was, half derogatorily, called the Housekeeper because he looked after the Chairman's home province.

Great General Peng was counting on the support of a majority of the Central Committee. His colleagues were, like himself, distressed by the suffering inflicted upon the people through the vain attempt to make China a major power overnight. Chief among those who had secretly encouraged the Great General to his quixotic effort was Liu Shao-chi, 61 years old in 1959 who had suceeded Mao Tse-tung as Chairman (President) of the People's Republic of China in April of that year.

Liu Shao-chi was a compromise candidate. He was acceptable to the practical men who feared the Chairman's collision course with history, while the Maoists could tolerate him as the man who had been the Chairman's executive officer for many years. Chief-of-State Liu Shao-chi was also second in the Party hierarchy. No one knew his precise views on the crucial issues to be raised at Mount Lu, for he had always avoided explicit commitment.

A gray and furtive figure, Chairman Liu had been an unobtrusive administrator for the secular demigod—Chairman Mao. He therefore knew well the suffering that extremist policies had inflicted as well as the ultimate impossibility of enforcing those policies. Like Mao and Great General Peng, Liu was a native of Hunan, that seedbed of revolutionaries, though his temperament was quite unlike their fiery ardor. He had been a quiet man of the underground, a clandestine manipulator, who once he had won power, had become a champion of "Socialist legality" and order. He had written both the Communist Party Constitution and the definitive handbook for Party members called *How To Be A Good Communist*. Despite his eminence, the quiet, gray-haired man, homely with his blunt, jutting nose, was known affectionately to his fellow mandarins and the Chinese people as Comrade Shao-chi.

Beside Liu Shao-chi stood Teng Hsiao-ping, Secretary-General of the Communist Party, known as the Organizer. Teng, too, was physically unattractive—stocky and short, with hair bristling in a crewcut and a permanent smirk limned on his square face. His personality was no more prepossessing than his appearance. The 57-year-old organization man was abrasive toward his friends, ruthless toward his enemies, and persistently self-assertive. But the Organizer, Teng Hsiao-ping, was the indispensable man of the Communist Party. Comrade Shao-chi, the First Vice Chairman of the Party, was Mao's executive officer, but Teng Hsiao-ping controlled the day-to-day functioning of the 18-million-strong apparatus of the Communist Party that actually ruled China. The Organizer knew all the levers of power and could, therefore, manipulate them as he believed best for China—and himself.

The unstable relationship between Comrade Shao-chi and the Organizer became a determining factor in the Cultural Revolution. Nearly as crucial were Comrade Shao-chi's relations with the First Secretary of the North China Bureau of the Communist Party, who was also Mayor of Peking. Peng Chen stood higher than the Organizer in both the hierarchy and Liu Shao-chi's affections. His breezily confident demeanor at Mount Lu showed that he knew his own value and his own strength. It was in 1959 quite inconceivable that the skillful *apparatchik* would be the first major victim of the Cultural Revolution.

At Mount Lu, Peng Chen stood within the inner circle as eighth-ranking member of the Politburo. He was responsible for the capital and the metropolitan provinces. Even more important, he controlled the directorates of culture, education, and propaganda. His comrades called him Mr. Mayor, half in respect and half in jest. It was easy to joke with the big, heavy-set man of 57 from the northern frontier province of Shansi. Although his entire adult life had been spent in the murky half-world of "underground work," he appeared open and candid. His career had prospered under the patronage of Comrade Liu Shao-chi. Both were essentially civilians, skilled in subversion within "enemy areas," but both championed "Socialist legality" once they attained "legitimate" power.

Both the graying Chairman of the People's Republic and the blunt frontiersman with the big, bald head were invariably mentioned when men speculated in whispers on probable successors to Chairman Mao. Their prospects may have invited Mao's enmity, for an emperor rarely feels affection for his likely heirs. Besides, both Comrade Shao-chi and the Mayor had established "semi-independent kingdoms" at the center of Communist power. Together with the Organizer, they controlled the civilian apparatus of the Party, though they lacked military support.

Yet they vacillated at Mount Lu.

A strong-minded, impassive Hunanese called Chou Yang attended the Mount Lu Plenum as an alternate member of the Central Committee. Although his formal rank was insignificant beside that of the others, Chou Yang held a pivotal position in the machinery of power. His character was so imposing that men thought him tall and were surprised anew to find that he did not tower above them. He was a professional literateur and critic, with a reputation independent of Party sponsorship. Chou Yang, later to be excoriated as "the Backstage Boss of the anti-Party Black Gang on the literary front," was directly responsible for managing the arts as Deputy Chief of the Communist Party's Propaganda Bureau. His immediate superior was Lu Ting-yi, a functionary with no claim to literary achievement. Above Lu Ting-yi was the Mayor, Peng Chen. But the Backstage Boss, in direct charge of the press and the arts, immediately controlled Communist China's culture. Since the 1940s, he had employed all his influence to propagate Mao Tse-tung's "line on art and literature."

Typical of the writers among whom he moved in Shanghai in the 1930s, Chou Yang's temperament and background nonetheless set him off from his fellow Red mandarins. Son of a rich landholding family, the Backstage Boss remembered his traditional obligations to his sisters and brothers after he attained power in the People's Republic. He had been criticized for that fraternal solicitude long before the Mount Lu Plenum, just as he was later to be attacked for his unorthodox concern for "people's artists." Young intellectuals repeated with relish the story of Chou Yang's reprimand of the Party Secretary at the Central Conservatory of Music. That functionary had permitted China's most eminent pianist to risk injuring his hands by "participating in the collective labor of breaking stones." Chou's kindness to promising youths was a byword among writers and artists.

The Backstage Boss was urbane. He had known the world beyond the provincial Communist movement during his education in Japan and his sojourn in the United States from 1946 to 1948 as a subtle propagandist for the Communists. He bestowed intellectual respectability and artistic validity upon the propaganda apparatus. No other functionary possessing equal power could also claim true literary achievement. Editor of *The Literary Gazette,* the organ of the League of Left-Wing Writers, he had also translated *Anna Karenina* and other Russian novels in the 1930s. He was, as well, a prolific commentator on aesthetics. He was never an original thinker or a creative artist like the deposed non-Communist Minister of Culture, novelist Mao Tun. He *was* a faithful servant of Mao Tse-tung, the foremost public advocate of the Chairman's thesis that "art is neither more nor less than a major weapon in the revolutionary class struggle."

Later the Maoists were to discern deliberate sabotage in Chou Yang's advocating "living literature about real people" instead of the stereotyped morality tales the unsophisticated Communist chieftains preferred. He argued that it was pointless to flood the country with the works of Mao Tse-tung and accounts of brutal landlords defeated by a coalition of oppressed peasants and good Communists. The masses, he said, would not read such arid stuff—and propaganda could not be effective if it were ignored.

But the Backstage Boss knew when to stop. Immediately after the Mount Lu Plenum he commanded writers to "form a united battle-front." He exhorted: "We must oppose the fanfares of the rightists and struggle for a rich literary and artistic harvest. The rightist opportunists attack the Three Red Banners: the General Line of the Party, the Great People's Communes, and the Great Leap Forward. We must support the Three Red Banners and constantly hymn their praises!"

Neither his protestations of orthodoxy nor his great services were to help Chou Yang when the fundamentalist fury of the Cultural Revolution overwhelmed China. The Backstage Boss, his immediate superior, Lu Ting-yi, and their joint superior, Mayor Peng Chen, were to be replaced by a forceful administrator whose interest in literature was a late —and forced—growth.

The subsequent Director of the Propaganda Bureau of the Communist Party and fourth man in the hierarchy was another Hunanese. Tao Chu was known as the King of the South because of his stringent rule of the Central–South China Region after 1961. The King of the South was primarily qualified for the task the Maoists assigned him during the Cultural Revolution by his devotion to Lu Hsün, China's leading author of the twentieth century, whom he imitated in manner, dress, and even hair style.

A pivotal figure later in the Cultural Revolution, Tao Chu played a minor role at Mount Lu. Fifty-eight years old in 1959, he was only ninety-fifth in the hierarchy, and his primary concern was the day-to-day administration of his fief. Initially he had attempted to enforce Mao's Utopian programs literally, but eventually he had begun to moderate his policies in the face of popular dissent. While he inclined toward the organization men of Comrade Shao-chi, he had no quarrel with the idealists of Chairman Mao Tse-tung.

The genial and quick-witted King of the South wished neither to make enemies nor to become enmeshed in abstruse doctrinal disputes. His hair bristling in the crewcut affected by his idol, Lu Hsün, and his tunic only half-buttoned, he moved casually through the Mount Lu Plenum, avoiding commitment. He was confident that his day would come, and in the interim he was fully occupied with the delicate task of ruling the restless South. He could not know how short would be his ascendancy—barely five months between his rise and his fall.

Great General Peng Teh-huai's faction can, for convenience, be called the right wing. The Great General enjoyed the sympathy—though not the open support—of much of the Central Committee and most "working-level cadres." Those officials charged to shape immalleable human beings and the obdurate material world according to the visions of Mao Tse-tung resented their impossible task.

But they feared the wrath of Chairman Mao. They, therefore, preferred less hazardous passive resistance to the public confrontation that Great General Peng proposed. Assessing his order of battle for the most important engagement of his life, Great General Peng looked in vain to the silent majority in the center, aligned with Comrade Liu Shao-chi and the Organizer Teng Hsiao-ping. The organization men gave loyalty to the pair who controlled the Communist apparatus. Chiefs and deputy chiefs of the central bureaus of the Communist Party, as well as hundreds of provincial functionaries, opted for watchful waiting and devious obstruction. They would not directly oppose Mao Tse-tung and his Utopian fantasies until they had first been attacked as "the men in power in the Party who follow the capitalist road."

One protagonist at Mount Lu defied classification—and still slips, quicksilver-like, from exact classification. He was Chou En-lai, then as now third in the Party hierarchy and Premier of the People's Government. Chou En-lai endured because he was indispensable and because he was as adroit as any courtier. He would be attacked during the Cultural Revolution, as he had been attacked in the past; he would be caught on the wrong foot by Mao Tse-tung's commands, as he had often been caught in the past. But he would survive to speak for reason. The dark-visaged Chou, his mobile actor's face always expressive, was 61 years old at Mount Lu. He was known as the First Minister of Great Peace in tribute to his skill in compromise.

Chou En-lai is often described as the Chinese leader best informed on the outside world. He was that, though the implication of great expertise in foreign affairs is exaggerated. The First Minister's knowledge of foreign lands is, at best, uneven. He returned from four years of study in Europe in 1924, and, until establishment of the People's Republic in 1949, he saw nothing of other countries except the Soviet Union. Thereafter, he traveled amid the stultifying dignity of official state visits. The fact that he does indeed know more of the external world than do other Chinese Communist chieftains demonstrates the profound ignorance of his colleagues, rather than the profundity of his own knowledge.

Chou was indispensable not because of his presumed expertise in foreign affairs but because of his administrative ability and his personal corps of capable administrators. He would execute any policy, protesting only when implementation was quite impossible. Besides, he was a valuable symbol of rationality for display to the outside world. The extremist Maoists therefore kept the moderate Chou En-lai. Chou never wholly lost his credit with the opposition—even at the maddest moments of the upheaval. Like all "practical" men, they recognized that it is sometimes necessary to say one thing while believing quite otherwise.

The group centered around Comrade Liu Shao-chi was complacent at Mount Lu, while First Minister of Peace Chou En-lai was elusive. The left was assertive, though represented by an outwardly unimpressive figure: Field Marshal Lin Piao, 51 years old, was the youngest of the senior hierarchs. Though his manners were not polished, he had won advancement by concealing his ambition behind a veil of humility. He had avoided ideological conflicts for passages at arms from the time he entered the Communist movement through the Socialist Youth Corps at barely 16. Lin Piao's chief published work avoided sweeping pronouncements or grand designs. His detailed critique of irregular warfare discussed not only principles but homely details like soldiers' footgear. Yet his brilliant performance on the battlefield had won him an honored place among men compelled as much as American university professors to display their intellectual attainments by the injunction: "Publish or perish!"

Because of his delicate health, Lin Piao attended the Mount Lu Plenum only sporadically. He was, moreover, busy building Maoist strongpoints in the People's Liberation Army, while his rival, Minister of Defense Great General Peng, concentrated upon the doctrinal dispute. Having for decades ranked just below the Great General, Lin Piao yearned to be first in the Chinese military. He therefore undermined Peng Teh-huai and gave total allegiance to Chairman Mao Tse-tung, who held the prize in his grasp.

By carefully sidestepping controversy Lin had made friends and patrons, rather than enemies of the hierarchs. Aside from a few senior generals who had seen his true face, the Communist chieftains considered him a polite young man—and no threat to themselves.

Lin was known as the Invalid, for he suffered many ailments. He had been wounded at the battle of Pinghsing Pass in 1937 and apparently again in Korea, where he seems to have been the first commander of the "Chinese People's Volunteers." When Great General Peng Teh-huai succeeded him in Korea, their rivalry became virulent. Lin Piao's penchant for the offensive had swept the surprised American armies down the mountainous peninsula. When General of the Army Douglas MacArthur recouped with his flanking attack at Inchon, Lin was driven back in retreat. Peng Teh-huai came to Korea to stabilize the Communist lines and fight the war of position Lin Piao disdained.

The conflicting approaches of the two People's Marshals were confirmed by their battles against the United States. Long after the Korean armistice, Lin Piao still believed that Western technological superiority could be broken by a "forward strategy"—constant guerrilla assaults by proxy outside China's borders. His contingency plan in the event of invasion was defense-in-depth, depending primarily on guerrilla and civilian resistance. Great General Peng, on the other hand had learned respect for the firepower of highly mobile American troops. Encouraged by his friends among the Soviet military, he wished to transform the People's Liberation Army into a modernized, technologically skilled force to meet scientifically armored American units on equal terms.

The burly Great General Peng and Lin Piao differed not only politically and strategically but also physically. Pale and unhealthily chalky, Lin was slight, short, and ungraceful in movement. He was, withal, China's most dashing field soldier and the darling of the activists of the People's Liberation Army. As much as his aquiline nose and the black bar of his eyebrows, his spirit had won him a second half-affectionate, half-derisive nickname—Eaglebeak. But most Chinese called him the Disciple because of his ostentatious devotion to Chairman Mao.

When the Disciple became Minister of Defense in September 1959, he chose as Chief-of-Staff of the People's Liberation Army an officer who had won reputation not on the battlefield but in the police station. An improbable commander, General Lo Jui-ching was known throughout China as the Security Policeman—and he was much feared. He was not in the front rank at Mount Lu; his forte was suppressing dissent rather than making policy. Because of his detachment, the tall, wiry officer from Szechwan, in the far southwest, appeared the ideal man to "reform" the Liberation Army.

A specialist in countering espionage and heresy and only 53 at Mount Lu, General Jui-ching had pursued a remarkably consistent career. The cautious son of a landlord family, he had studied law at Sun Yat-sen University in Moscow after graduation from the Whampoa Military Academy, where he had come under the influence of Political Commissar Chou En-lai and met his classmate, Lin Piao. In the Soviet Union and at a clandestine school in France, he underwent special training in secret-police techniques. He served as a political commissar and administered the counterintelligence apparatus in the Communists' Yenan redoubt in the 1930s. After 1949, Lo Jui-ching became Minister of Public Security, Commander-in-Chief of the 400 thousand men of the National Public Security Corps, and concurrently Director of the Public Security Bureau of Peking itself. He retained those posts, controlling the apparatus of repression, until his peculiar talents were required in the People's Liberation Army.

His mouth was twisted in an unvarying slight grin as a result of a face wound. The Securityman was by inclination at odds with the "professional soldiers" who supported Great General Peng, for he was a dedicated servant of the ideologues. The mission assigned him in September 1959 was simple and direct: to purge the Liberation Army of "professional arrogance" and bring the military establishment under the absolute control of Chairman Mao's operational commander, People's Marshal Lin Piao.

It was not merely surprising but astonishing when the Securityman, Lo Jui-ching, converted to the doctrines of the "professional generals," became the second major victim of the Cultural Revolution.

Those men who stood staunchly behind Mao Tse-tung, whatever his excesses, had little choice, since their fate was inextricably intertwined with the Chairman's. One of the men of Mount Lu had been indispensable to Mao for years; although his formal Party rank was not high, he was as close to Mao Tse-tung as any man could be. A former professor and literateur, Chen Po-ta had for decades been Mao's intellectual *alter ego,* his chief speechwriter, and his counsel on doctrine.

Like Lin Piao, Chen Po-ta originally evoked more affection than apprehension, an affection tinged with condescension. Even his physical appearance disarmed suspicion. Squat and chubby in his ill-cut Liberation Suit, Chen peered at the world through thick, black-rimmed lenses. At 55, he owed his position neither to administrative ability and force of personality nor to a devoted following. He was, quite simply, Mao Tse-tung's man.

No political activist, Chen Po-ta, almost alone among the senior leadership, was truly an authority on the complex doctrine called Marxism-Leninism. Since he combined complaisance verging on sycophancy with that expertise, he was an ideal servant to the imperious Chairman who had never quite mastered the arcane intricacies of doctrine. He required a professional guide through the intellectual labyrinth. Like a brilliant lawyer who finds legal justification for his client's desires rather than pointing out their essential illegality, Chen manipulated doctrine to suit Mao's needs.

He first won the Chairman's approbation by a coruscating public defense of Maoist positions in 1930, when Mao was under strong attack from the Shanghai-based "international faction" of the Party. Once established, the relationship hardly altered. Every informed Chinese knew that the inspiration was Mao Tse-tung's, while the theoretical justification was Chen Po-ta's. Chen Po-ta was therefore known as the Ghostwriter or the Private Secretary.

The Ghostwriter provided the ideological weapons with which Mao Tse-tung beat back his enemies' attacks at Mount Lu. When the Cultural Revolution began seven years later, he received his reward. The man who had never openly coveted power was elevated to the fifth position in the hierarchy and was appointed Chairman of the Maoist

Task Force Directing the Great Proletarian Cultural Revolution. His closest collaborator became Madame Mao Tse-tung.

Mao's wife, the vengeful Fury of the Cultural Revolution, was in the background at Mount Lu, as she had been for the preceding 20 years. The Chairman apparently insisted that his fourth wife, a second-rate actress called Chiang Ching who bore him two daughters, play a wholly domestic role during the years of his unchallenged pre-eminence. He was, after all, a Chinese of the old school in his personal life.

Chiang Ching, who began life as Li Chiang-yun and subsequently took the self-consciously romantic stage name of Lan Ping, "blue drift-weed," was at Mount Lu to look after her husband and perhaps to serve tea to the wives of other leaders. She did not join the deliberations of the Central Committee. Since she had never risen to the first rank, even in the leftist film industry, she was disparagingly known as the Starlet. She had never enjoyed the public acclaim that should have been tendered the wife of the Chairman, her youthful attractiveness had passed, and her face was already fixed in the deep lines of dissatisfied middle age.

When the storm of the Cultural Revolution broke, Mao Tse-tung finally turned to Chiang Ching. Driven to bay, Mao quite logically concluded that she was one of the very few he could trust implicitly. She had no choice but to serve him faithfully, since her fate rested entirely upon his own. Madame Mao Tse-tung undertook the reform of literature and art, in particular of the stage, though she was far better qualified for the job by her marital status than by her own undistinguished professional career. Gathering a cadre of ambitious young writers and critics, the Starlet set out to remake the all-important propaganda machinery in the Maoist mold.

Finally given her head in 1965, the Starlet attained sweeping power and displayed vengefulness that frightened even the hardened veterans of four decades of "revolutionary struggle." She was more than the Madame Defarge of the Cultural Revolution—she not only counted the victims, but chose them.

The Starlet depended primarily upon those literary careerists the Chinese contemptuously call "the young opportunists." But she also drew support from one of the oldest and most ruthless Bolsheviks of them all: Kang Sheng, a native of Chiang Ching's home county in harsh Shantung Province, was called the Lord High Executioner. The title described his metier—and the technique he taught the execution squads that enforced rigid discipline on Communists and meted out measured terror to the enemy. Either a sharpened bamboo slip or an ordinary dagger would serve, he taught, for the quick blow to the larynx, which killed instantly and bloodlessly. During the years of struggle, he had often been proved correct by his diligent students.

Though a member of the Central Committee and an alternate member of the Politburo at Mount Lu, the 56-year-old Kang Sheng played a minor role. He had fallen from favor soon after the establishment of the People's Republic for being too closely allied with the "international faction," which acknowledged the final authority of Joseph Stalin in the Kremlin over Mao Tse-tung in the Chinese countryside. Besides, the nearsighted Executioner, his sharp features fixed in a perpetual half-sneer, had risen rapidly within the Communist Party, actually outranking Mao himself for a time. He was therefore dispatched to the shadows for a number of years, being "sent down to the countryside" to perform manual labor and learn humility. He was too well educated, too independent, too menacing, and too ruthless for even the implacable Mao Tse-tung to keep by his side.

The Executioner's chief published work defined his single-minded purpose in life. It was called *On the Development, Form, and Present Responsibilities of the Struggle Against Traitors*. Having been chief of the Organization Bureau of the Communist Party and an alternate member of the Executive Committee of the Communist International in the 1930s, Kang Sheng was tempered in the bitter quarrels of the world-wide movement and looked down upon the rustic Mao Tse-tung. Nonetheless, Mao used his special talents. Seeking to impose his absolute temporal and spiritual authority upon the Party, through the Rectification Movement of 1942, the Chairman had called upon Kang Sheng. He had been rewarded for his skill in the use of terror with re-election to the Politburo, but again lost his position in the early 1950s.

This truly sinister figure rediscovered his metier at the outbreak of the Cultural Revolution, when his talents were once again required. He would stand to the end beside the Starlet and the Chairman. Like the Ghostwriter, Chen Po-ta, he was indispensable to the dissension-riven Maoist faction. By that time he had, of course, been purged of all idealism and even of ideological conviction by the fires of revolution. His only purposes, it appeared, were to survive—and to punish.

The Mount Lu Plenum was the first confrontation, and it temporarily postponed the total violence of the Great Proletarian Cultural Revolution. The chief actors had already taken their places.

Foremost was Mao Tse-tung, the embittered and enfeebled Chairman, supported by his ambitious Disciple, Lin Piao. The first open challenge was hurled by Great General Peng Teh-huai, supported by his few followers. Comrade Liu Shao-chi, Chairman of the People's Republic, and the Organizer, Teng Hsiao-ping, Secretary-General of the Chinese Communist Party, stood for "Socialist legality," moderation, and nonalignment. The Mayor, Peng Chen, was to rally the opposition forces, only to be crushed by the Maoists' first major counterattack. He was to be preceded into obscurity by the Securityman, Lo Jui-ching, initially selected by Lin Piao to "rectify the armed forces." He was to be followed by the King of the South, Tao Chu, who soared high with the formal proclamation of the Cultural Revolution and fell to oblivion within five months.

Chou En-lai, the First Minister of Great Peace, was a largely rational human being tossed by the waves of unreason. Generalissimo Chu Teh remained the national father-figure, removed from the immediate strife. On the left were the Ghostwriter, Chen Po-ta, the Lord High Executioner, Kang Sheng, and the Starlet, Chiang Ching, awaiting their hour of deceptively great, but finally spurious power.

The first open confrontation at Mount Lu ended in apparent victory for Mao Tse-tung. But the Maoists met growing passive resistance. Imbued with a stubborn will of its own, the apparatus of the Communist Party and the People's Government administered the nation largely as it wished—virtually ignoring Mao Tse-tung's directives. Seven years after Mount Lu undermined the unity of the Communist Party, the violent struggle for the soul of China began. The proceedings at Mount Lu foreshadowed the later unrestrained violence which altered the lives of all leading Communists, "touched the souls" of most Chinese—and irrevocably altered the essential character of the People's Republic of China.

III

The First Confrontation

The Red mandarins seated themselves in the Great Temple, blinking in the semi-darkness after the sun's glare on the vermilion tiles without. Even before the Eighth Plenary Session convened at Mount Lu in the summer of 1959, the Central Committee had foreseen the confrontation between Great General Peng Teh-huai and Chairman Mao Tse-tung. The delegates pondered their own feelings—and the Great General's decision to force an open contest. They knew he was encouraged by the concerted opposition that had compelled Mao's resignation as chief-of-state only eight months earlier. They knew too that he had drawn confidence from protracted consultations with foreign Communist leaders.

Peng Teh-huai spent the late spring and early summer of 1959 in the Soviet Union and Eastern Europe, where he conferred with reigning Marxist leaders and won Nikita Khrushchev's approval of his opposition to the Great Leap Forward and the Great People's Communes. The alarmed European Communists, for their part, saw in Mao's "fanaticism" not only a challenge to their own power, but a threat to the Communist bloc. Peng Teh-huai had, the Maoists later charged, been behaving like an independent satrap rather than a loyal subordinate by conducting personal diplomatic negotiations, despite his foreign allies and the vulnerability of supreme power. Still, the Great General's prospects were poor, for he had overlooked the trenchant maxim: "Do not shoot at a king unless you aim to kill!" He sought not to overthrow Mao Tse-tung, but only to moderate Maoist excesses. He should, perhaps, have realized that his painstaking critiques of Maoist policies would be considered a personal assault by his old chieftain, but a certain freedom of discussion had always obtained at the apex of the Party. Peng apparently expected to stimulate open debate on policy, rather than personality.

But he was challenging a man who could not distinguish between abstract discussion and personal affront. Mao Tse-tung had been surprised by the revulsion that forced his resignation in December 1958. Veteran of scores of intra-Party feuds and victor in most, he had rallied with accustomed resilience. While his opponents relaxed, Mao had packed the Central Committee with his own sworn followers. As long as Comrade Liu Shao-chi and his centrists withheld their hands, Great General Peng Teh-huai had little hope of securing an impartial hearing, much less carrying his point. Preliminary skirmishes had already demonstrated that Maoist strength, though diminished, was still superior to the ill-organized opposition.

The Great General's preliminary indictment of the Great Leap Forward was distributed in his *Position Paper* of July 14, 1959. It opened with a ritual apology for his temerity. Peng Teh-huai compared himself to "that simple man Chang Fei," the impulsive general depicted in one of Mao Tse-tung's favorite novels, *The Romance of the Three Kingdoms.*

"Like Chang Fei," Great General Peng said, "I am crude and have no tact at all. . . . If what I say is wrong, please correct me." Peng did not remark on an ominous parallel. Chang Fei had been slain for *his* temerity.

The Great General's *Position Paper* affirmed that "the achievements attained during the Great Leap Forward of 1958 are firm and undeniable." He accepted official, inflated statistics (later revised by the Party) to demonstrate his support of the principle of the Great Leap Forward. "This is not only a great achievement for our own country," he explained, "but will exert the strongest positive influence on the development of the Socialist camp for many years to come."

Peng then turned to negative aspects, noting that: "Some capital construction in 1958 was too hasty or too ambitious. Much capital was, therefore, tied up unproductively, while some essential projects were delayed. This error basically derived from lack of experience. We did not understand the problem thoroughly, and, when we finally understood, it was too late." He hastened to balance his criticism: "However, these projects were, after all, essential to national reconstruction. In the next year or two—perhaps a little longer—they will gradually yield returns."

The Great General sought to guide the future, rather than to avenge the past. He suggested that plans for 1960 be approved only after "seeking to understand our true circumstances by examining the facts."

Nonetheless, he inescapably implied that all leaders had ignored reality in the frenzy of the Great Leap Forward. Asking that many scheduled projects be canceled or reduced "for the time being," he noted: "We must lose something to get something. Otherwise, widespread signs of serious disharmony [between Party and people] will grow greater and last longer. If we do not break the present stalemate caused by general [popular] passivity, we will be severely hampered in our effort to surpass Britain in the next four years."

The Great General had touched an exposed nerve. Grandiose Maoist propaganda had promised in 1958: "We will surpass Britain's industrial production in five years' time!"

The Maoists were vulnerable on all fronts. They had themselves contrived the spectacular failure of the Great Leap Forward. Their policies had thrown the economy into disorder and had demoralized the Chinese people by demanding ever greater prodigies of work in return for constantly decreasing compensation.

Peng's *Position Paper* doggedly probed all the sensitive nerves, while carefully alternating praise with criticism. He lauded the Great People's Communes, that "totally new" Maoist organization of society. The Communes were, he declared, "a movement of great significance which will not only enable our peasants to free themselves completely from poverty, but will provide the correct way to speed up the building of Socialism in the period of transition to true Communism."

"Nevertheless," he added, "there has been a period of confusion regarding the system of ownership, while some shortcomings and errors appeared in our actual execution of the plan. This is, of course, a serious phenomenon." He was actually understating the peasants' hatred of the People's Communes that made them hardly more than serfs bound to the land and to toil.

Another major effort of the Great Leap Forward had been the construction of tens of thousands of miniature steel plants, "backyard blast-furnaces." They were to double steel production in a single year and to disperse industry for defense. "We built many small, native-style [i.e., primitive] blast-furnaces, which were really not necessary," Peng Teh-huai declared. "Substantial resources, both material and financial, were thus dissipated, and much manpower was wasted. We sustained a considerable loss."

The Great General sought again to balance criticism with praise of "positive aspects" of the Great Leap Forward:

"A preliminary geological survey of all China has been carried out on a huge scale," he noted. "Many technical personnel have been trained, while the broad masses of cadres have been tempered and have learned to improve themselves in the course of the movement." But, he added, "great sums of money have been spent, amounting to 2 billion *yüan* [approximately $1 billion U.S.] and, even in this respect, there have been losses, as well as gains."

Peng's summation of the experience of the Great Leap Forward and the lessons to be learned was the heart of his *Position Paper*. "The essential question," he advised, "is whether we can actively and positively mobilize the broad masses to continue the Great Leap Forward into the future. That question is critical when we consider the disproportions [of income and privilege] between workers and peasants, between the different social groups in the cities, and between the different categories among the peasants."

No matter how he tried to balance his assessment, the disasters wrought by the Great Leap Forward unavoidably dominated his discussion by their own weight. He could not avoid "emphasizing losses over gains," as Mao Tse-tung himself later complained.

"Objective examination of the errors of the Great Leap Forward," the Great General said, "will enable us to turn the passive situation into an active one in certain important respects. It will help us to understand the economic laws of Socialism even more penetratingly. It will allow us in due time to readjust imbalances, and it will give us understanding of the true meaning of 'balance'."

Peng's criticism of Maoist policies—and Mao Tse-tung himself—was no longer veiled and discreet. It was explicit and direct. Neither as a Chinese patriot nor a dedicated Communist, determined to correct mistakes before they produced total disaster, could he refrain from criticism that would infuriate the Chairman.

He did not assuage Mao's fury when he added, "We have not handled the problems of economic construction as successfully as we dealt with questions of quelling Tibet and shelling Quemoy." The Tibetan Autonomous Administrative Region was in endemic revolt. Shelling the Nationalist-held islet of Quemoy in the mouth of Amoy harbor on alternate days was hardly a satisfactory substitute for conquering that insignificant —but highly irritating—piece of real estate. Nikita Khrushchev, Mao Tse-tung's *bête noir,* had warned of the folly of risking war with the United States over Quemoy, and the Chairman had received that unsolicited advice with rage.

Stoking the fires of Mao's anger, Peng observed:

> The objective situation at the present time is that our country is poor and blank, while there are still many people who do not have enough to eat. Last year, there was an average of only eighteen feet of cotton cloth for each person, just enough for a shirt and two pair of trousers. The people urgently demand a change in present conditions. . . . It is

necessary—and entirely correct—to seize this opportune moment to institute policies which will satisfy the fundamental demands of the broad masses of the people. We must speed up our rebuilding. We must alter the poor and blank outlook of our country as rapidly as we can. We must create a still more favorable international situation.

The Great General's oblique allusion to the international situation was actually a scathing criticism of the Maoists. China had come to the verge of an abysmal break with the Soviet Union. She had yet to attain her primary international purposes—the "liberation" of Nationalist-held Formosa, let alone islets like Quemoy, and the testing of her first atomic bomb.

"The habit of exaggeration has become universal," Peng declared, returning to domestic issues hardly less explosive than international policies. "Everybody originally felt—on the basis of a totally unwarranted estimate of grain output—that the problems of food had been solved, and that their attention could be freely directed to industrial development." Yet industry too had suffered because of "grave superficiality" in plans for iron and steel production. Practical problems, he said, had been ignored; words substituted for reality; and "unbelievable miracles were reported in the press." The total effect had "done tremendous damage to the Party's prestige [and credibility]."

His further cautious criticism drove the Maoists from anger to fury. The Communist Party had promised to attain the Utopia of true Communism almost immediately. "Some comrades became dizzy with apparent success," Peng asserted. "Petty bourgeois fanaticism become prevalent." Peng confessed that he was himself "no exception to the general error of only assigning tasks and targets, but not considering the concrete measures necessary to fulfill those tasks."

"It is not easy to get a true picture of a situation," he conceded. "Despite the Wuhan Conference [which forced Mao to resign as chief-of-state in December 1958] and other conferences this year [1959], we have still not been able to determine the realities of the overall situation."

The greater the truth, the greater the injury—to the Maoists. The Great General wrote:

I was, like many comrades, bemused by the achievements of the Great Leap Forward and the enthusiasm of the mass movement. Left-extremist tendencies developed to an unprecedented extent; we wanted to enter Communism with a single step. Our minds were swayed by the dream of being the very first [ahead of the Soviet Union] to attain [true] Communism. We forgot to seek objective truth from actual facts. We confused strategic planning with concrete measures; long-term policy with immediate steps; the whole with the part; and the big [read, ultimate] collective [life of final Communism] with the small [read, transitory] collective [life of the People's Communes].

Great General Peng in effect declared that Chairman Mao had himself deviated from true Marxism. He was charging the Chairman with following personal intuition rather than the "scientific truth" of the time-tested ideology. No accusation could have been more devastating, particularly since it had already been expressed by Moscow. Peng Teh-huai provoked a mortal confrontation with Mao Tse-tung; it could only end with his own—eclipse—or the Chairman's.

"For instance," Peng wrote, "the slogans raised by the Chairman, such as GROW MORE, PRODUCE MORE, AND REAP MORE! and CATCH UP WITH BRITAIN IN FIVE YEARS! were strategic and long-range policies. But the cadres made the mistake of demanding that goals and quotas fixed for as much as a decade later be fulfilled in just one year—or even a few months. Such demands, which ignored reality, alienated the masses from the Party."

That was a spectacular understatement of popular antagonism and disillusionment.

"In the view of some comrades, PUTTING POLITICS IN COMMAND! was a substitute for everything else," he wrote, stating the essence of his disagreement. The slogan PUT POLITICS IN COMMAND! was the wellspring of Maoist dogma. The inherent power of the Chinese people, "correctly" directed politically, was to accomplish miracles of material and social progress—regardless of "bourgeois" economic and psychological laws. Peng asserted, pressing hard:

> Those comrades forgot that PUTTING POLITICS IN COMMAND! was aimed at raising the political consciousness of labor; at improving both the quantity and quality of production; and at giving full play to the enthusiasm and creativity of the masses *in order to speed our economic construction.* PUTTING POLITICS IN COMMAND! is no substitute for basic economic principles, still less for the concrete measures necessary to run successful economic enterprises.

Peng Teh-huai had touched a mortal weakness. If "objective" economic needs took precedence over political demands, China could only achieve gradual progress. The Thought of Mao Tse-tung, hailed as the apogee of human wisdom, was, he implied, no substitute for the "objective laws" of nature and society.

Bitter controversy between Maoists and non-Maoists at the start of the Cultural Revolution in 1966 centered upon the same issue. The

Maoists would insist that politics must command all, even if agricultural and industrial production declined. The non-Maoists would maintain that PUTTING POLITICS IN COMMAND! was intended to stimulate production in order to make China a major industrial and military power.

Great General Peng concluded the *Position Paper* on an optimistic note that still infuriated the Maoists:

"By overcoming the concrete problems which appeared during the Great Leap Forward," he declared, "the target of catching up with Britain in five years can still be basically accomplished during the next four years." He thus clearly—and correctly—implied that the Great Leap Forward had actually *delayed* economic and social progress.

The *Position Paper* was prelude. Peng's remarks to the Plenum at Mount Lu were even more pointed—and were, quite patently, aimed directly at Mao Tse-tung. The situation created by Maoist excesses, he declared, was "so disastrous that only the good nature of the Chinese people has prevented bloodshed. . . . Lower cadres informed Chairman Mao only of what was possible and apprised him only of successes. Dizzy with success, it is easy for one to turn a blind-eye and a deaf-ear to evil or disadvantageous phenomena."

Peng called the Great Leap Forward "a rush of blood to the brain . . . a high fever of unrealism." He described economic policies as "blunder after blunder," while the Party's own statistics showed that the people's rice ration had decreased steadily from 1953 to 1956—and sharply in 1958. He warned that continuing lack of sufficient food could provoke riots worse than those of 1957, when suppression followed the brief flowering of free speech.

"If the Chinese workers and peasants were not so decent and well-behaved," Peng asserted, "a Hungarian Incident would have exploded in China. It might even have been necessary to call upon Soviet troops to suppress a bloody uprising." The Great General's assessment was accurate, but his tactics were faulty. He cast doubt on the steadfastness of the People's Liberation Army and implied that the detested Russians might still find it necessary to apply their "correct" solutions to China's internal problems.

Most of the charges and countercharges made at Mount Lu were later revealed verbatim by the contending parties during the frenzies of the Cultural Revolution. One major source of controversy, however, has not yet been thoroughly illuminated, perhaps because it is so critical. By reading a multitude of innuendos, nuances, and half-revelations, one can deduce a reasonably accurate outline of the critical debate on foreign policy and defense—touching on issues almost as important as the polemics on internal affairs. Moreover, Defense Minister Peng Teh-huai was directly responsible for the Chinese military establishment, and he had just concluded protracted discussions with the Russians.

The Liberation Army, dispersed across the face of China, had always been assigned a variety of primarily political and economic missions. The troops could, therefore, not attain full military effectiveness, and were in addition deprived of supplies of modern weapons by Soviet reluctance to arm a Communist Party that became daily more hostile to Moscow.

The Maoists dismissed the generals' fears that China could not defend herself. Guerrilla tactics, they argued, would not only defend the People's Republic, but would spread the revolution abroad. Maoist doctrine on "people's war" asserted that native insurrections, supported and inspired from Peking, would sweep the world clear of capitalism. A modern, mechanized army was, in their judgment, not merely unnecessary, but actually disadvantageous. Such a "professional" force would draw excessively on China's limited industrial production and would further threaten the supremacy of the Party.

Great General Peng argued that Maoist policies were acutely dangerous. Contemptuous antagonism toward Moscow and constant challenges to Washington, he stressed, could force confrontation between China and either—or both—the great powers. China had, after all, not yet developed the nuclear weapons she must eventually possess. The Defense Minister pointed out that his troops had become a political security force. He contended that China must be defended by highly trained soldiers equipped with modern weapons and motivated by professional *esprit*.

The Great General could not convince most delegates at Mount Lu that China's domestic and foreign perils required them to imperil their own futures. But his attack forced the aloof Mao Tse-tung to a direct reply. The squat figure of the Organizer, Teng Hsiao-ping, his heavy features meticulously devoid of expression, nodded ceremonially. The Chairman mounted the podium and tossed back the shocks of hair sprouting from his temples. The vehement rejoinder was the most impassioned and most defensive speech Mao had delivered in many years. Although most delegates felt the outcome was already determined, Mao Tse-tung himself knew that his power as chairman of the board of the Communist Party of China was imperiled. Therefore, he declaimed:

> Comrades, I am not going to mince words! There is never any point in mincing words, particularly not if we are discussing a "great and catastrophic muddle." I shall speak to you with painful directness. This is good. The more directly and painfully we discuss this "great cata-

strophic muddle," the better it will be. We must all give these matters our closest attention.

In the course of our debate, some people have derided our efforts as "battering our heads against a stone wall." But many other comrades insist that we must press on. They believe that we must keep up our attack on the seemingly impossible.

A man can only move a step at a time. He can only chew a mouthful at a time. If he wants to swallow an entire plateful in a second, he can't. One must chew meat mouthful by mouthful. One doesn't get fat simply by eating a mouthful. But eating several pounds of meat a day will make you fat in less than a year. The great differences between the Commander-in-Chief and myself did not develop in one day and one night. The differences between myself and the Commander-in-Chief will not be settled in one morning.

The Chairman sounded eminently reasonable. Speaking in the homely folk metaphors he adored, he appeared to be inviting open discussion in the old tradition of intra-Party democracy:

Among the several hundred millions led by our cadres, 30 percent, at the very least, are positive activists. Perhaps 30 percent of our people are negative and obstructionist, including former landlords, rich peasants, counterrevolutionaries, evil elements, and hidebound bureaucrats. But the poor and lower-middle-class peasants of the mainstream represent 40 percent.

How many people are there in that first, activist 30 percent? I'd say about 157 million. They truly want to create People's Communes, to eat in common messhalls, and to increase the degree of their *collective* life. They are remarkably activist, and they want to get on with things.

Now, how can you say that this mass desire is petty bourgeois madness? These people are not representatives of the petty bourgeoisie. They are the poor farmers and the lower-middle-class farmers. They are the proletariat and the semi-proletariat. The additional 40 percent who want to go along are also with us—and only 30 percent are opposed. If you add the 30 percent of our people who are activists to the 40 percent who want to go along, you end up with 70 percent of the nation—or 357 million men and women. Can so many people be afflicted with madness at one time?

It is true that, for a few months after the Spring Festival [the Lunar New Year in February 1959] some people were not happy—but that is all changed now. After first showing unsmiling faces at being forced to dine on thin sweet-potato soup, both cadres and the peasantry have learned the advantages of the Communes.

The Chairman openly acknowledged that some errors had been committed, but he insisted that the regime was now well on the way to correcting all its mistakes. He indignantly rejected the charge that the People's Communes and "the current of common ownership" had actually exploited the masses by depriving them of their own property. He extolled the Great Leap Forward as an "enormous schoolhouse" which had taught the people and the cadres that "our Party is great, enlightened, and correct."

His verbal arrows all aimed at one target—refuting Great General Peng's charge that the Chinese people had turned against the Communist Party because of the suffering inflicted by the Great Leap Forward. He admitted:

Yet, even the activists ask: "How long will it go on? One month, two months, half a year, one year, three years, five years—even ten years?" Some comrades say "protracted war" is the only way—and I agree with them. These comrades are, after all, the majority.

You all have ears, so please hear me out! No matter how painfully and directly I speak, no matter how hard my words may appear, please welcome them! Unless we talk frankly of hard and controversial issues, what is the point in talking at all?

We must speak of specific issues, no matter how knotty they may be. Regardless of whether it is a temporary lack of vegetables, or the shortage of barber's scissors, or, perhaps, that we lack soap. For example, if we have sometimes miscalculated . . . if market conditions and supply are very tight and most of the masses also feel tense, and the hearts of most of our Party comrades know great tension, I still maintain that there is no real tension.

I am also tense at times. To say that I am not would be a lie. After all, if you are tense for half the night and then take a tranquilizer, you will not be tense for the rest of the night.

There are people who say that we have lost touch with the masses. But I say that this is, at most, a temporary phenomenon and that the masses are still on our side. There was a period of one, two or, perhaps, three months after the Spring Festival when this was true. But I know that we and the masses are now cooperating very well indeed. We must not throw cold water on the mass movement. We can only encourage them. Comrades, your hearts are good. If things are sometimes difficult, we must not lose heart. We must still advance.

Mao's speech was, as always, liberally larded with historical citations and analogies. Graphically demonstrating his preoccupation, almost all those analogies were drawn from *Chinese* history rather than previous

Marxist experience. He touched every responsive string in his emotional appeal for support.

"I am," he affirmed, "absolutely convinced that *all* the people can study and learn about politics and economics." He then cited several historical figures who had been illiterate or semi-literate, but had nonetheless proved first-class leaders. His defensiveness was obvious. Mao was implicitly refuting charges that he himself lacked formal education in either Chinese history or the subtleties of Marxism. Passing beyond his personal defense, Mao asserted again and again his confidence in the great wisdom of the unlettered masses. Then the Chairman moved from the defensive to the offensive—and to threats—as he declared:

> I shall continue to batter my head against the stone wall—and I will finally break through. In my early youth, I learned one thing: "If people did not harm me, I would not harm them, but if they harmed me, I would strike back harder." Anyone who injured me found that I paid him back in ample measure. I have still not abandoned that basic principle. . . . I have listened for some weeks to attacks on me. Now is the time to counterattack. I urge you comrades to listen to me. Whether you approve or disapprove is your business. If you disapprove . . . if you believe I have erred, I shall make a self-criticism.

The Chairman had ostentatiously displayed his humility. He had ceremoniously acknowledged his subordination to the collective will of the Central Committee. Then he exhorted:

> But all comrades must be steadfast at this critical moment. *Peng Teh-huai emphasized losses rather than gains.* Such emphasis is nothing less than wavering. Worse, it is stealthy, destructive criticism. The rightists have arisen again—in a new guise. If unrestricted, public criticism of all aspects of the Great Leap Forward were permitted, our nation would collapse within a year's time. If imperialism did not return to impose itself upon us, the people themselves would arise and overthrow us. If you want to publish such newspapers, the kind that each day print only bad news, it may not even take a year—but perhaps only a week or so—before our eclipse. If we Communists go, ours will no longer be a Socialist country, but a petty bourgeois country.

The Chairman reminded his followers that their fate too was in the balance. Speaking with intense emotion, he drove his point home:

> If that sort of thing happens and we must be eclipsed, I shall take my leave of you. I shall go back to the countryside and lead the peasants

in overthrowing the government. If your Liberation Army does not go with me, I will unfurl the Red Flag once again and raise my own army. But I am certain the People's Liberation Army would be on my side.

A sickly silence greeted the open threat. Mao Tse-tung had wielded his most powerful weapon. The Central Committee knew that it could endure neither emotionally nor politically without the heroic figure of the Chairman. Even the Party chieftains would feel themselves bereft should he leave them, while the masses, despite their obvious dissatisfaction, still revered the father-figure. Without Mao Tse-tung, there could be no People's Republic of China.

The Central Committee voted on August 16, 1959. Great General Peng Teh-huai and his "anti-Party clique," the final resolution declared, had "aimed at splitting the Party." Condemned in the document, which was not made public until eight years later, Peng was stripped of his offices in September 1959. The Party formally dedicated itself to a renewed Great Leap Forward. The moderation imposed in the early part of 1959 was, officially at least, repealed. The Maoists' triumph appeared total.

The ringing reaffirmations of the Mount Lu Resolution could not quite camouflage the new mood of the Party. Mao's "victory of annihilation" was by no means total. The practical decision of Mount Lu directed a pause in intellectual repression and economic exploitation. Peng Teh-huai, who had dared to speak out, was sacrificed to unite the Party. But he had made his point. Extremist policies were checked.

Comrade Liu Shao-chi and his men of the center had withheld their hands. They had not wanted to contrive Mao's fall, but they certainly did not wish the Maoist mania to rage on unchecked. Great General Peng Teh-huai went, and Mao's Disciple, Lin Piao, took his place as Minister of Defense. Chief-of-Staff Huang Ke-cheng went, and the Securityman, Lo Jui-ching, took his place.

The Great General accepted his degradation with apparent resignation, though his failure to commit an act of total self-abnegation irritated the Maoists. In his ritual confession he said:

I *do* still feel the Chairman has been somewhat excessive in his speech, and I still retain some reservations. I cannot accept the Chairman's allegation that my *Position Paper* sought to muster men and assemble horses for a private revolt. Nor can I acknowledge that I was ambitious and hypocritical. However, I agree—with some reservations—to my dismissal from office. Free of official duties, I will be relieved of much care. In any event, these are many people who are more capable than

I am, and I should properly make way for them. After the Mount Lu Plenum, my career as a Hai Jui is finished.

Hai Jui had been a popular hero of the Ming Dynasty in the sixteenth century who was dismissed from office for championing the common people against the rapacious Imperial Court and its corrupt officials. Great General Peng was not to rise to power again. But his career as a Hai Jui had just begun.

IV

The Upright Mandarin

Peng Teh-huai suffered personal defeat at Mount Lu. His critique of Maoist excesses was formally rejected, and he was himself degraded. The barracks-room style of his righteous anger did nothing to advance his cause. Defiant in defeat, he told the Central Committee: "In Yenan, during our previous quarrel, you raped my mother for 40 long days. I have now toyed with your mother for only 18 days at Mount Lu, but you will not permit me to go on."

His support evaporated. The Party's Secretary-General, the Organizer Teng Hsiao-ping had slipped away, complaining that his acute rheumatism required immediate treatment. Comrade Liu Shao-chi, still the unchallenged Chairman of the People's Republic, had skillfully effaced himself. Although he acknowledged vaguely the "problems in relationships between the leaders and the masses," Liu dissociated himself from the Great General.

Shortly after the Mount Lu Plenum, Nikita Sergeyevich Khrushchev, the flamboyant ruler of the Soviet Union, spent five days in Peking to attend celebrations of the tenth anniversary of the People's Republic of China on October 1, 1959. Fresh from talks with President Dwight David Eisenhower, Khrushchev was abubble with the "spirit of Camp David." He told the Chinese bluntly that attempting the violent destruction of the capitalist camp "under the leadership of American imperialism" was both dangerous and futile.

Speaking in the cavernous Hall of the National People's Congress in Peking, the Soviet leader employed the forthright peasant locutions that had won him amused affection at home. He called the Maoists "stupid

38

for desiring to test the might of American imperialism by military force."

Yet Khrushchev failed signally to convert the Chinese to his policy of "peaceful competition with capitalism" and hastened the breach between Peking and Moscow that startled the world six months later. Feeling himself once more wholly in control of China, Chairman Mao Tse-tung "sternly repulsed" the Soviet proposals. With the monumental insensitivity that finally contrived his own downfall, Khrushchev asked to see his old friend, Great General Peng. He carried gifts in return for those Peng had given him early in the year. He further inflamed Mao Tse-tung by describing Peng Teh-huai as the "most promising, most courageous, most upright, and most outspoken leader within the Communist Party of China."

Such a crude display of alien favor hardly helped Peng's cause among the xenophobic Chinese. Abandoning hope of rehabilitation while his enemies, the Chairman and his Disciple, ruled, the Great General disdained compromise. Instead, he continued to press his case against Maoist policies. He traveled widely, assessing what the Maoists characterized as "temporary difficulties owing to natural catastrophes and the cessation of Soviet aid." Still associated with the Higher Party School, he disseminated his findings in the first of a series of formal critiques after Mount Lu.

"If we follow the standards established by international experience," Peng wrote, "we have but one choice—to reorganize the leadership of the Communist Party in order to rectify mistakes in our general policies."

From 1959 through 1961, the Great General made five reports criticizing decreasing production and inefficient distribution. His personal prestige ensured their circulation to provincial Party committees, as well as the Central Committee. Insisting "the general line of the Party must be altered," Peng too gave way to the Chinese impulse toward versifying. One stanza was widely quoted:

> Grain lies scattered on the ground,
> And potato-plants wither all around.
> All men and women, too, are busy making steel,
> While only striplings and small girls till the soil.
> Where will we find next year's meal?
> How can the starving masses still toil?

Although degraded, Peng Teh-huai was not transformed into the unperson he might have become in the Soviet Union. Chairman Mao chose not to show open vindictiveness toward the Great General beloved by the people. It was the Chinese style to avoid imprisonment, exile, or execution of senior miscreants. The Chinese people were told only that Peng Teh-huai had left office. His iniquities were not fully publicized until the bitter revelations of the Great Proletarian Cultural Revolution.

Somewhat like a democratic politician in opposition, Peng was reasonably free to travel and to visit old friends and associates. While still a member of the Central Committee, the Maoists later charged, he intrigued to regain power and undermine the Chairman's authority.

Peng prepared a second *Position Paper* of 80 thousand words. Not available in full, his second *Position Paper* analyzed the concrete evidence of disaster all Chinese plainly saw. His policies were slowly gaining ground, but Peng Teh-huai's personal cause was lost at the Tenth Plenary Session of the Central Committee in September 1962. After distributing his second *Position Paper,* he told the Committee, "I can keep silent no longer. I want to be a Hai Jui!"

His alternating acceptance and rejection of the symbolic role dramatized Peng Teh-huai's true role as the Hai Jui of the Communist regime. Since that "upright Mandarin," his career blighted by his conscience, was a folk-hero of the Chinese masses, the Red mandarins could not ignore the portentous appearance of their regime's own Hai Jui.

In the late sixteenth century, the Ming Emperor had made Hai Jui governor of Nanking and ten surrounding prefectures. He was the court's chief representative and the common people's chief recourse against injustice. Finding that the landlord gentry, supported by a retired prime minister, were exacting usurious rents and exploitive taxes, Hai Jui championed the people's rights. But the exploiters' influence at court reversed his reforms. After offering a memorial of protest to the Emperor, Hai Jui resigned. He died disgraced, in poverty.

The identification of Great General Peng with Hai Jui would have stung even a regime that was not hypersensitive to criticism through historical analogy. Accustomed to systematic suppression of free expression, the Chinese people were remarkably acute in comprehending such oblique protest. If Peng Teh-huai was Hai Jui, Mao Tse-tung was the callous Emperor and his obtrusive cadres were the wicked officials. Calling Peng Teh-huai Hai Jui was therefore to condemn the Maoist *imperium.* Moreover, Peng Teh-huai, like Hai Jui, still had many friends at Court.

The Maoists' were not angry solely because they felt guilty. The dissidents had actually conspired to make Peng Teh-huai a living symbol of rational resistance to Maoist excesses. The Great General evoked not only popular affection but official respect for his stubbornly independent concern for the "masses." He was an ideal rallying point for the dissatisfied.

Throughout his career, Peng had embodied a powerful non-Maoist tendency within the Communist movement. Greatly senior to the Disciple, the Great General had always been a substantial barrier to the younger man's ambition. Mao Tse-tung and Lin Piao were therefore united not only by their master-disciple relationship but by the common threat posed by Great General Peng. They used their rival's own character to destroy him.

Like both Chairman Mao Tse-tung and Comrade Liu Shao-chi, Great General Peng was a native of Hunan, the central province that was both China's granary and the seedbed of her revolutionaries. Like Mao, born in Hsiangtan County, Peng Teh-huai was imbued with that county's spirit of perpetual rebellion. Something in the soil of Hunan nurtures the hot red peppers that flavor provincial dishes—and the fiery temperaments that make the Chinese political stew so piquant. The cottage in Shaoshan village, where Mao Tse-tung was born, has been restored as a secular shrine—at the end of a new railway spur. No shrines have to date been erected to either Comrade Liu Shao-chi or Great General Peng.

Mao Tse-tung was shaped in the mold of the traditional revolutionary. Constant clashes with his harsh, avaricious father bred the habit of rebellion. Disdain for his father impelled him to disdain alike material possessions and the bourgeois values that exalted possessions.

Peng Teh-huai responded still more aggressively to boyhood circumstances still more harsh. He too became a revolutionary.

Though the son of a prosperous farmer, he learned early that the world was not shaped for his own comfort. His mother died in 1903, when he was six, and his new stepmother hardly coddled the boy she called "a stone in her rice." When his stepmother responded to his deliberate harassment with contemptuous neglect, Teh-huai grew openly rebellious. He lashed out bitterly at his father, who was more concerned with his new family than the malcontent son of a dead marriage. Finally, Teh-huai vented his resentment on his grandfather's widow, whose matriarchal authority was sustained by tradition and by her own strong character.

In 1909, two years before the collapse of the Manchu Dynasty, filial piety was still *the* cardinal social virtue and *the* foundation of the Confucian social system. The Pengs solemnly resolved that the 11-year-old boy be sent forth from his father's home. His stubborn recalcitrance had shown him unworthy of the family's continuing protection.

Yet to abandon him wholly would have been a violation of the social ethos more flagrant than his own consistent disobedience. He was, therefore, placed under the protection of his dead mother's prosperous brother. But resistance had become a habit; young Peng Teh-huai was too proud and too resentful to exchange obedience for comfort. His uncle could only see that he did not starve. Barely 12 years old, Teh-huai was entangled in a snare of his own weaving. By his defiance of family authority, he had automatically rejected the total system of values upon which Chinese civilization rested. As a youth without a family, he was without fixed position in a hierarchical society.

Peng worked awhile as a cowherd's assistant and a bunker-boy in a coalmine. The work was backbreaking, and the recompense infinitesimal. Finally tamed by menial labor and the economic distress that followed the republican Revolution of 1911, Teh-huai asked his rich uncle to take him in.

His mother's brother was twice pleased. He had been uneasy at neglecting his nephew; and his own daughter would soon be marriageable. His nephew had, he felt, outgrown his youthful rebelliousness. He had also displayed an aggressive spirit that promised well for his future. Teh-huai was equally pleased. For two years, he lived in his uncle's home in the traditional state of semi-adoption of a daughter's prospective bridegroom, though he did not take his uncle's name.

During his free and joyous companionship with his pretty young cousin, he absorbed his first systematic education. His mind was quick, and he was enterprising. A secure bourgeois future appeared his—when his resentful idealism contrived fresh disaster. The day the hungry poor of his village looted the hoarded grain stores of a usurer-merchant, Peng Teh-huai was in the front ranks. He was forced to flee. The revolutionary had entered upon his career.

When Peng Teh-huai again left the only real home he had known, he was, at 16, old enough to follow the one calling that required neither capital nor family backing but only a strong body and a resolute spirit. In 1913, he joined one of the numerous roving bands of soldiers that tormented China under ambitious "generals" who were distinguished chiefly by greed and ambition. The soldiers were alternately free-lance bandits or "bandit-suppression" troops, depending upon the political situation and personal allegiances.

His new life suited Peng Teh-huai. His aggressiveness found a congenial outlet adapted to the milieu. His superiors' lives and fortunes depended upon the competence of their subordinates, but competence was rare among the ne'er-do-wells who filled the ranks. Peng Teh-huai was competent. He possessed combative instinct and a quick mind, two essential qualities in his new profession. At 18, he was given command of a platoon in the army of the chief warlord of Hunan Province. With the imminent collapse of all semblance of constitutional government in Peking, the warlord era had begun. Peng was a small star in a minor constellation, but he was a rising star in the stormy Chinese political firmament.

The next ten years shaped his character. He grew to manhood in the military service. Skirmishes and marches, plots and counterplots, glancing defeats and small successes were the threads that wove the fabric of his daily life. If he did not quite know for whom he fought, he was learning to fight well. He attended military schools that put a cutting edge on his professional skill. He moved rapidly up the ladder. Soon he no longer fought solely for personal advantage. He was endowed with respectability and purpose by his commanding general's alliance with the Nationalist armies which ostensibly campaigned for the unification of China rather than personal aggrandizement.

However, Peng Teh-huai's life was not dominated solely by patriotic dedication during the early 1920s. Just three years older than the century itself, he was known for his meticulously tailored uniforms and the self-confidence of his heavy tread and decisive manner. Although his swarthy features were stolid in repose, they glowed with enthusiasm as he talked, gesturing grandly with large, well-shaped hands.

He enjoyed a well-earned reputation as a lady's man. Ting Ling, China's foremost woman writer, who had herself engaged in many a passionate passage-in-arms, later remarked, "Something about Peng Teh-huai, though it's hard to say exactly what, is very exciting to us females!" In 1926, Peng married a young middle-school graduate, a cultured lady in a nation where few boys and fewer girls achieved secondary education. Peng had come a long way from his family's insular, self-satisfied materialism.

Life was pleasant for a rising young officer in an army that was winning more battles than it lost. Nevertheless his restless spirit drove him to compulsive self-examination and self-education. Like his mentor of later years, Generalissimo Chu Teh, he pondered the greater purposes of his actions. Remembering too well for complacency his years as a young, drifting laborer, he was not content with mere self-gratification. The new-model Nationalist Army had been born as a "people's force," but he saw it quickly take on the faults of the old warlord troops as it destroyed their power.

He might have been watching a garish carousel. Each time the music stopped, a new set of riders would scramble for the vacated seats, and the carousel would again whirl dizzyingly. It always remained in exactly the same place.

Peng Teh-huai read the self-searching political writings of China's liberal thinkers. Though they offered some of the abstract answers he sought, they raised innumerable practical questions. He was forced to the conclusion that his colleagues—the heirs of Dr. Sun Yat-sen, the founder of the Nationalist Party—actually differed from the warlords more in words than deeds. He shortly glimpsed a totally different system of thought in the widely circulated translations of the Russian anarchist Kropotkin; and in Bukharin's *ABC of Communism* he found a concrete expression of Kropotkin's idealism. The rigidity of Marxism greatly attracted Peng, and so many of his contemporaries, for they were pragmatic men who desired immediate and preferably absolute solutions to China's manifold problems.

From 1924 to 1927, the fledging Communist Party, legitimized by its reluctant alliance with the Nationalists, was allowed to propagate its views. Already turning from Western liberalism toward the extreme Russian experiment for inspiration, China's radical thinkers took up the translations of Marxist tracts and Russian novels that were widely available. In almost all Peng's reading, the influence of Soviet thought was dominant. Finally, a translation of Kautsky's *The Class Struggle* came into his hands and, shortly thereafter, its parent work, *The Communist Manifesto*.

The young officer read *The Communist Manifesto* with the same sensation of soaring enlightenment many Europeans had felt in 1848. In the third decade of the twentieth century, neither China's industrial development nor her social thought had advanced beyond the Europe of a century earlier. Peng Teh-huai had found the absolute answers he sought—decades after those answers were first advanced.

Peng Teh-huai, like Generalissimo Chu Teh, came to Communism through the soldier's trade; he had not taken up arms to realize Communist ideals. His closest friend was a fellow officer who was already a Communist. In March 1928, almost a full year after the decisive split between the Communists and the Nationalists, his political mentor sponsored Peng's application for membership in the Communist Party. If he were interested solely in personal advancement, as the Maoists later charged, Peng could hardly have chosen a less auspicious moment to enlist under the Red Banner.

In April 1927, Nationalist Generalissimo Chiang Kai-shek had turned decisively against the uneasy alliance between Nationalists and Communists ordained by Moscow. Shaken by Chiang's attacks and by conflicting and irrelevant orders from Moscow, the Communist movement was disintegrating. As if already determined to be a Hai Jui, Peng Teh-huai joined the Communists at the moment of their greatest disarray.

In July 1928, Peng led his battalion in revolt and established a small "Soviet Area" at Pingchiang in the remote mountains of northeastern Hunan. Like other local commanders scattered through eastern China, he was adrift between contending factions of the Communist Party. He nonetheless confirmed his allegiance by an aggressive military attack. He later recalled:

I had heard about the defense of Chingkangshan [by the fugitive commanders, Mao Tse-tung and Chu Teh], and, after the uprising failed, I led about a thousand men to join the mountain soldiers. By this time our forces had grown. I had a thousand men, and our peasants were flocking to the mountains, so that we had between four thousand and five thousand men altogether, and a considerable number of rifles and bayonets. But we were still weak compared to the enemy. They said publicly that they had 60 thousand well-trained and well-equipped troops. They may have had about 45 thousand! . . . The enemy had good leaders. Their officers were all *Kuomintang* [Nationalist] officers . . . but we defeated them, first in hundreds of skirmishes and later in battles. It was the first time the *Kuomintang* used radios; we did not even have telephones. Nevertheless we drove them away. Actually we never had radios at all until the siege of Changsha in [July] 1930. Even if we had had radios, we would not have known how to use them.*

Although it may not have appeared so at the time, Peng Teh-huai's attack on Changsha was decisive to his personal career. His action endorsed the strategy of Mao's arch-rival, another Hunanese called Li Li-san. In control of the legal "Party Center" in Shanghai, Li believed in 1930—as Mao himself was to contend after 1958—that the capitalist world was ripe for revolt. Arguing that exploiting China was essential to the survival of "capitalist imperialism," Li determined to shake the tree of history so that capitalism would come tumbling down. He contended that the loss of key cities to the Communists would force the capitalists to retreat from China. Deprived of the ill-gotten fruit of its exploitation of China, he concluded, the capitalist system—already beset by worldwide depression—would collapse.

Mao Tse-tung at that time followed a completely different course. He wanted to build firm bases of Communist power in rural China before attempting to take the cities, and he foresaw no quick victory.

When he marched on Changsha, the capital of Hunan, Peng Teh-huai could hardly have foreseen the consequences of his implicit opposition to Mao Tse-tung. The Chairman was merely one leader of the obscure "rural faction," half-dishonored by Moscow's half-repudiation. However, Mao never forgot an injury, intentional or inadvertent. Nor could Peng have foreseen the final irony. After 1958, Peng strove to restrain

* *Journey to Red China* by Robert Payne. London: Heinemann, 1947, pp. 37, 38

Mao Tse-tung, who believed he could transform China and "liberate" all the oppressed peoples by attacking throughout the underdeveloped world, much as Li Li-san had wanted to liberate China by attacking cities like Changsha. Peng later recounted:

> We occupied Changsha for ten days in 1930. It started with our anniversary meeting at Pingchiang! . . . [Nationalist] troops arrived, but we routed them about six *li* [two miles] away, and then decided to follow them. We had nothing to lose, and they were very frightened. Changsha was defended by five regiments—a total strength of about 30 thousand. To attack Changsha with our 10 thousand* was technically impossible —the city was difficult to attack, for it favored the defenders—but our morale was high, and we were bitterly determined to show the warlords that peasants could muster enough force to get through.
>
> We got through. We fought a nasty engagement on the Nanling River, 15 *li* from Changsha, and attacked with bayonets, since our main weapons were bayonets. It was costly. We had between two and three thousand casualties. There was fighting along the approaches to Changsha the whole day and part of the night, and even when we entered the city, there was still fighting going on outside. It was a hard war, and in 10 days [Nationalist General] Ho Chien was bringing so large a force against us that we evacuated.

Peng Teh-huai had thus inadvertently made his choice. The consequences were long delayed. During the turbulent 1930s, Peng rose rapidly, in part through the sponsorship of Generalissimo Chu Teh. The two warlords-turned-Communists shared not only a common background but a common largess of spirit. They were tolerant men, irritated by the constant intra-Party intrigues of "professional politicians" like Mao, who were so unlike the "professional soldiers." But they followed Mao because he provided firm leadership.

Despite Peng's often outspoken opposition, Mao needed the Great General. Upon the establishment of the People's Republic in 1949, Peng was appointed Deputy Commander of the People's Liberation Army. Generalissimo Chu Teh was the largely inactive Commander-in-Chief. Other honors and greater responsibilities followed. The Great General became satrap of the Northwest Military and Administrative Area. He led the "Chinese People's Volunteers" during the grinding battles of position of the last two years of the Korean War—and learned to respect modern weapons in American hands. He enunciated his program for "liberation" of Southeast Asia in late 1953. He supplied the equipment

---

* Peng appears to exaggerate the enemy's strength, as he does his own.

that gave the Vietminh victory at Dienbienphu. He finally became Minister of Defense.

Nonetheless, Great General Peng was moving unavoidably toward the moment when—like Hai Jui or Martin Luther—he could no longer be silent. The Mount Lu Plenum forced him to denounce the excesses of Maoism. Thereafter, his course was set. During the crucial years from the summer of 1959 to the beginning of the Great Proletarian Cultural Revolution in the autumn of 1965, Peng Teh-huai followed the model of Hai Jui. Two antagonistic forces contended for the soul of the Communist Party of China—romantic Maoism and mundane pragmatism—and each commanded a large number of adherents. The Great General was the symbol and the inspiration of the realists.

V

A Bright View
from the Tower

Governments manifest themselves in three chief aspects: the reality of
power; the image of power officially projected; and the reality most men
accept—or pretend to accept. The reality and the accepted consensus
control the life of the nation, while the official image imperfectly recon-
ciles the two.

During the six years from the Maoist victory at Mount Lu until the
first tremors of the Great Proletariat Revolution, most men believed that
Chairman Mao Tse-tung controlled the apparatus of power. Some who
knew better pretended to believe.

Mao transcended humanity. His demi-deification followed traditional
Chinese as well as new Marxist practices. The Chairman was tendered
ritual forms of address and adulation prescribed for the Emperor, who
had been called the Son of Heaven. Denying any power greater than
man, Marxism indulged in the secular deification of its great men.
Technically brilliant, though grisly, the mummification of Vladimir Ilyich Lenin and Joseph Stalin had preserved the supermen's material
forms. They would have been worshiped as demigods had Marxist
theology permitted. In his own lifetime, Mao Tse-tung was exalted even
higher. The cult of his personality and the Maoist directives emanating
from Peking testified to his absolute supremacy. The Mount Lu Plenum,
it appeared, had given the Chairman total power and fixed his infallibility.

The few men who knew the reality of power in China knew better
than to reveal the truth. In reality, Great General Peng had largely won
his points by sacrificing himself. The machinery of the Communist Party

48

and the People's Government Mao Tse-tung had created were more powerful than Mao himself. They had transformed the man into a semicelestial being, far above mundane affairs of state, for like the Confucian Emperor, Chairman Mao no longer concerned himself with "minor matters." The organization went its own way, while rendering elaborate obeisances to "the Great Commander-in-Chief," Mao Tse-tung.

The new order was characteristically Chinese. As the sage Confucius had directed, the "proper forms of ritual" were directed towards divinity, while professional administrators managed practical affairs. The compromise permitted the recovery of the economy and popular morale after the Great Leap Forward. The arrangement was devised by Chairman Liu Shao-chi of the People's Republic and his chief lieutenant, Secretary-General Teng Hsia-ping of the Communist Party, the Organizer. But the courage of the Mayor of Peking, Peng Chen, made the arrangement possible.

The secret history of Communist China from 1960 to 1966 was a magnificent rescue operation. Pragmatic leaders and technical advisers struggled, with gradually increasing success, to find a way out of the economic and psychological morass into which the Great Leap Forward had precipitated the people. They simultaneously resisted further Maoist excesses and rehabilitated the nation. Inherent Chinese pragmatism deviously bypassed the rigid state ideology—as it had tempered Confucian dogmatism in the past. The first major effort to restore sanity was directed by the Mayor in late 1961. For his pains, he was later pilloried as an arch-villain of the Great Proletarian Cultural Revolution.

The secret conference in November 1961 at the Chang Kuan Lou— the Tower of the Auspicious View—in the Peking Zoological Garden looms in retrospect almost as high as the Eighth Plenum at Mount Lu two years earlier. The Mayor commanded 20 of his closest associates to search the records of the three disastrous years of the Great Leap, 1958 through 1960, in order to find a rational road to the future through full understanding of the errors of the past—just as Great General Peng Teh-huai had advocated.

The seminar was organized by a slender newspaperman called Teng To, whose decades of devotion to the Mayor had previously earned him the posts of editor-in-chief of *The People's Daily,* the organ of the Central Committee, secretary of the Secretariat of the Communist Party's Peking Municipal Committee, and alternate secretary of the Secretariat of the North China Bureau. Mayor Peng Chen was, of course, first lord of all the press and First Secretary of both the Peking and North China committees. Teng To was not only a faithful follower of the Mayor, but a gifted satirist. Like so many men vilified during the

Cultural Revolution, he was stubbornly devoted to the public welfare. He sinned by refusing to subordinate his clear view of reality to Maoist fantasies.

Even the Mayor's protection was not strong enough to retain the editorship of *The People's Daily* for Teng To after he protested in print against the catastrophic illusions of the Great Leap Forward and the Great People's Communes. But the Mayor found his chief lieutenant shelter within the Peking Municipal Committee and gave him control of that Committee's publications, the magazine *Front Line* and the newspapers *The Peking Daily* and *The Peking Evening News*. Teng To's journals became a platform for the pragmatists and rivals to the national organs, *Red Flag, The People's Daily,* and *The Liberation Army Daily*.

The Young Editor of the legal "underground press" was a curious and unstable blend of traditional qualities and revolutionary fervor. Former acquaintances remark of the writer who dared question not only the omniscience but also the sanity of Chairman Mao: "He was a most reasonable chap, by no means a firebrand. He reminded me of a typical moderate Chinese scholar. He saw all sides of the question." Despite his long career as an agitator, Teng To retained the detachment that should characterize reporters and scholars. He had not only been the Communists' leading journalist, but had, as well, published scholarly historical studies laden with heavy sociological emphasis.

Teng To met Peng Chen when he was auditing courses at Peking University in 1935. The Mayor and Comrade Liu Shao-chi were directing the "underground movement" in North China. Shortly after joining the Communist movement, Teng To was interrogated by the Nationalist Security Police; upon his release, he vanished into "underground work," traveling throughout China under Peng Chen's direction. But the sharp-featured intellectual was torn between scholarship and propaganda. He published his first book in 1936, when he was just 25. Issued by the Commercial Press from the political sanctuary of Shanghai's International Settlement, the work was entitled *A History of China's Redemption from Calamities*. It was followed by numerous articles analyzing Chinese history from the Marxist viewpoint and by two further books: *The Institution of Slavery in Historical Chinese Society* and *The Devious Development of Capitalism in Modern China*. It was all good, orthodox Marxist historiography. The imprint of true scholarship delighted the largely self-educated Mayor Peng Chen, who was in the process of forming his personal circle of intellectuals. Teng To, therefore, won rapid advancement in the Mayor's domain.

In 1938, because of their alliance with the Nationalists against the Japanese, the Communists were permitted to publish their own newspaper in the wartime capital, Chungking. Teng To was named editor-in-chief of *The New China Daily* and became the public voice of the Communists in Nationalist territory. He was thus raised to prominence among Communist delegates in Chungking, including the First Minister of Peace, future Premier Chou En-lai. Since *The New China Daily* was the chief vehicle for transmitting the Communists' viewpoint to foreign diplomats and correspondents, the Young Editor was a major figure. He was charged with evoking foreign sympathy for his comrades sequestered in the hills of the Northwest.

When appointed First Secretary of the North China Bureau, the Mayor needed his protégé's services urgently. The Young Editor was transferred to the Shensi-Chahar-Hopei Border Area. As chief of the Border Area's Propaganda Department and publisher of the *Shen-Cha-Ho Daily,* as well as chairman of the Border Area Association of Writers, Teng To controlled literary, academic, and artistic endeavors in the Communist stronghold in North China.

Unmarried till "liberation" in 1949, the Young Editor enjoyed the flirtations of a society contemptuous of "bourgeois restraints" on relations between men and women. Attractive and intense, but intriguingly casual, he made many conquests. His tastes were, in general, remarkably "bourgeois." He was a noted gourmet, like so many natives of Peking where the best chefs from every province of the nation of gourmets offered their infinitely varied cuisine—in return for gold and renown.

After the Communists took Peking, the Young Editor indulged his connoisseurship of traditional Chinese art. Delighting in displaying his treasures, he gave one formal party solely to celebrate acquiring a famous Sung Dynasty (A.D. 960–1278) scroll. It was all cosily bourgeois and mildly decadent, hardly good "proletarian" dedication to the austere "masses" life style Chairman Mao preached, but did not practice. However, the Mayor's patronage and the Young Editor's own usefulness normally excused his peccadillos. Besides, many Communist leaders allowed themselves similar pleasures. The rabid anti-intellectualism and anti-aestheticism of the Great Proletarian Cultural Revolution had not yet ordained the destruction of "every aspect of the old society."

Teng To worked hard for his privileges. He was active in a number of international "friendship societies" and writers' associations. He also pursued his studies as a member of the faculty of the Sociology Department of the Academia Sinica, China's foremost research institution. While serving as both publisher and editor of *The Peking People's Daily,* the Party's organ, he wrote finely honed essays and composed verses in the classical style. His verse lacked polish, but breathed intense personal feeling unusual in that petrified form.

Teng To was relieved as editor-publisher of *The People's Daily* in 1959 for refusing to follow the Maoist line. His enemies methodically besmirched his character. *Red Flag* accused him of conducting an illicit love affair with a violently anti-Maoist girl, who had studied philosophy at the Chinese People's University until the brief freedom of speech afforded by the Hundred Flowers Movement of 1957. The 23-year-old student, a "fighter" of the Liberation Army at 13, demanded that the Communist regime be "rent assunder." She added with stark simplicity: "When I am finished speaking, I am ready to go to jail!" The Young Editor, already married to an attractive, well-educated girl, had tried to protect the firebrand—whether for political or personal reasons.

His own valedictory poem, published in *The People's Daily* in July 1959, later evoked horror among the Maoists:

> I have driven my pen hard for two decades;
> My labors clearly were no dream of idle shades.
> Having covered reams, this poor author tires;
> With his comrades, he stands between the fires.
> Please reckon, then, both my sins and my great feats,
> And let me depart, knowing that life's cycle repeats,
> That despised today, tomorrow I'll be brave.
> If I am proud, I have earned the right.
> I shall later raise a tidal wave
> To sweep the nation and touch—heaven's height.

But Peng Chen immediately found Teng To a place in his personal organization. If the Mayor was indeed creating an "independent kingdom" in North China with Peking as its center, Teng To, who had implicitly threatened Mao himself, was obviously Minister for Culture and Public Relations.

The Mayor's men sought no publicity for their deliberations in November 1961 in the Tower of the Auspicious View. Under the Young Editor's direction, they concealed themselves by display, meeting in the much-visited Zoological Gardens in Peking's western district. The conspirators were camouflaged by the throngs swarming among the cages. A few steps north of the pool where seals and walruses sported lay the zoo's most popular exhibit. The great carnivori roared on Lion-Tiger Hill, an artificial eminence behind broad moats. Just north of Lion-Tiger Hill stood the pavilion called the Tower of the Auspicious View. The two-story structure, ornately painted in red and green beneath the traditional eaves of palace architecture, had been built as a public restaurant, but the Communists used it only for special gatherings. On November 10, 1961, the Mayor's task force filtered unnoticed into the building for the nine-day seminar which documented the catastrophic errors of the Great Leap Forward. The Mayor's personal secretariat had diligently searched confidential Communist Party records all the previous year for concrete evidence, and had marked many specific miscalculations that led to economic and political disaster.

The Mayor set the tone of the seminar in opening remarks that prejudged the investigation, while the roaring of the great cats ominously rumbled in the background:

> Many failings and errors have been evident in the work of the past few years—and many great problems have arisen. What is the reason? Although there have been natural calamities, they were not the chief reason. The fundamental cause has been our losing touch with the masses, as well as the preconceived judgments which forced our policies to depart from actual, objective conditions in China. Now, where did this ill wind arise? We must search the basic Party documents for the answer. We must *dare* to search the basic documents so that we can discuss the problems intelligently.

Small working groups examined specific problems: agricultural and industrial failings; the performance of cadres; the distortion of statistics; the execution of directives; popular morale; and the dolorous state of "culture," the portmanteau term meaning propaganda and indoctrination, as well as *belles lettres* and the graphic arts. The evidence was voluminous, and the Mayor's directions were clear. The "preconceived judgments" were Chairman Mao's, for he had decreed "the general line of the Party." The Mayor's candor demonstrated his trust in his subordinates—as well as his own self-confidence, for he was "aiming his spear" directly at Chairman Mao. Emboldened by their leader's candor, the working groups were soon calling back and forth to each other with glaring examples of error.

"Listen to this one," they shouted from room to room.

"Old Mao is just too old," they confided, shaking their heads. "What a mess they made of *this* Commune. *That* program was a pipe dream. It sounds like the ravings of a man with brain fever. Old Mao's arrogance got us all into this mess!"

The criticism was perhaps emotional, but it was certainly justified. The Great Leap Forward had produced the near collapse of the economy, a crisis of morale throughout the nation, and a major erosion of the Party's authority. All senior Communists, except the most purblind zealots, knew how violently things had gone awry. They also knew the true source of the catastrophes the Maoists blandly attributed to "natural calamities and the treacherous withdrawal of Soviet economic aid." The men in the Tower of the Auspicious View were, for the first time,

systematically examining the extent of the catastrophe and *proving* that
the responsibility should be laid at the Chairman's feet. The Maoists
were quite right when they later called the Mayor's detailed analysis a
"bill of indictment" against Chairman Mao—a bill, they charged, drawn
with the assistance of the Soviet Union, which was "whipping up an international anti-Chinese upsurge" by openly attacking Maoist doctrine
on every major question of domestic development and foreign policy.

The Chang Kuan Lou investigation was thorough. Teng To called for
"examination of problems of policy and directives that are obviously
contrary to—or, at least, widely divergent from—the spirit of the instructions issued by a number of sessions of the Party's Central Committee." He was, the Maoists later claimed, "waving the Red Flag to oppose
the Red Flag." The Maoists' own words were cited against them, and
their repeated deviations from the consensus of the Central Committee
were meticulously analyzed. The "conspirators" studied high-level directives and their implementation. They catalogued voluminous reports
from "lower levels" that criticized the general policy and offered concrete evidence of specific failures.

The meetings in the gaily painted pavilion took on a festive, almost
carnival air. The Peking Municipal Committee smelled victory—and
rejoiced. The Young Editor was forced by illness to spend much time
resting in a back room. The others did themselves well: "Despite the
country's economic difficulties," the Maoists charged, "they had flour
and wheat, chicken and duck, fish and meat. Every day, they played
mahjong, bridge, and billiards until two or three in the morning. After
their meals, they strolled in the park, watching the monkeys climb trees,
the bears prance in their cages, and the peacocks spread their tails."

The work was, nonetheless, done well. The indictment was devastating and the recommendations comprehensive. The Mayor advocated
measured progress consonant with China's resources, as opposed to the
headlong "leaping" of Mao Tse-tung. Peng Chen's was not so much a
policy as an anti-policy. It was, however, eminently practical.

The Great People's Communes were characterized as "strange phenomena set up on sudden impulse, which were really a fantasy." The
critics noted that "production had *not* increased during the stage of the
Co-operativization Movement [1955–57], but the really grave problems
arose when the People's Communes were established. With the Great
Leap Forward, the strength of the State was weakened and grain output
decreased." The conclusions were devastating and undeniable.

They were also farsighted. Transcending immediate difficulties, the
investigators addressed the chief problem of the future. Unless the
Communists could train a "generation of revolutionary successors" that
was both highly competent and highly motivated, all their efforts would

be in vain. The Mayor's task force therefore concentrated much attention on education:

> During the past few years, education has been spurred on blindly. It has developed too fast. Too much has been demanded too fast. Pedagogy has become detached from the economic base of our society. . . . Manpower and material resources have been wasted profligately. There have truly been "three increases" in education in 1958. The number of schools increased; the labor quota [of "production work" demanded of students] increased; and political activity increased. But the quality of education declined.

The commission audaciously and accurately blamed Chairman Mao's zealotry. "The basic levels of the Party," they reported, "should not be blamed exclusively for the upsurge of these problems. The wind blows from the higher to the lower levels. . . . The leadership was feverish. . . . Subjectively defying the objective laws of nature and society, the leadership overturned the balance of teaching." The Maoists had planned to produce "intellectuals with proletarian minds by combined study and work." The indictment observed: "Schools can not run productive factories efficiently since they possess neither technical skill nor managerial experience."

That apparently mild and indirect assertion totally repudiated Maoism. The Maoists strove to produce a "perfect, new Communist man," who would be equally skilled "as an intellectual and a laborer, a peasant and a soldier, an artisan and a manager." His *primary* qualification would be his perfect "redness," or devotion to the Marxist-Leninist ideology as perfected by Chairman Mao. The Mayor's investigators were undermining the entire foundation of Maoist doctrine when they insisted that specialists must control education—and all other areas of endeavor.

Directed ostensibly at educational failings, the comprehensive indictment of Maoist errors actually touched every fundamental weakness of the new Chinese society. It also anticipated the chaos of the Cultural Revolution, when student Red Guards first "administered" schools and subsequently forced them to close for four years. "Pedagogical reform should be . . . under the leadership of those *few* teachers and specialists who are expert in their work," the Chang Kuan Lou report asserted. "The students may, of course, make suggestions. But reforms should not —and cannot—be carried out by making the students the chief arbiters of curricula and techniques—*the error that occurred in 1958.*"

"When rating students, close attention should be paid to their political consciousness," the Maoists had directed, "and, then, secondarily, some attention should be given to their studies in the classroom."

The dissidents retorted: "Such regulations demand redness at the expense of expertise." "During the past few years . . . we have given undue importance to politics, while neglecting studies. Teachers' enthusiasm has been dampened, while students have been encouraged to disregard the substance of their courses!"

"Unceasing class struggle" was the Maoist design for the entire social structure. "Because the struggle between the two roads of capitalism and Socialism is constantly pursued among students," the seminar's report pointed out, "we have fallen into the error of nurturing constant criticism and repudiation. All problems, even those which have nothing to do with class struggle, are treated as examples of the struggle between the two ways!"

Having committed the ultimate heresy of belittling "class struggle," the task force condemned selection of students for higher studies because of political reliability and "good class background," which meant "peasant and worker" rather than "bourgeois" families. It praised Chinghua University, a non-Maoist stronghold, for stressing academic achievement over political merit. One investigator pointed out:

> Chinghua is more intelligent in dealing with this question. The University pays particular attention to the cultural qualification of candidates for admission. The high academic standard of its graduates demonstrates the validity of that approach. The University even seeks out some candidates for admission who have poor [i.e., Nationalist, anti-Communist, or bourgeois] backgrounds, but are distinguished in their studies. Other universities dare not accept such students.

The total indictment of Maoist failure in education summed up:

> History itself has contrived the objective circumstances which determine that the children of workers and peasants cannot, at present, do well in universities. If their entry into universities is overemphasised and we adjust our standards to their low level, we will, quite strangely, be improving education by destroying education. It will be like encouraging the growth of wheat by pulling up the stalks.

Having made its fundamental points by charting the educational quagmire which was the Mayor's special concern, the investigators surveyed the economic quicksands of the Great Leap Forward just as thoroughly. It is only necessary to illuminate the high spots to demonstrate why the criticism was so scathing. The Great Leap Forward, the Mayor's task force asserted, was "largely high-sounding talk, which has produced innumerable problems during the past few years because everything was undertaken on too large a scale." Thus they defined the Maoists' single greatest error.

"Too much work has been done on water conservation, and manpower has been wasted," the seminar declared. Earth-and-stone dams constructed by the massed labor of 100 million men and women collapsed under the pressure of the rising waters. China simultaneously suffered drought and flood—and the leaching of hundreds of thousands of acres after vain attempts to reclaim saline fields.

The Chang Kuan Lou seminar characterized the "Anti-Rightist [purge] Campaign" as "excessive." "The anti-rightist policy has not been clearly defined, while its methods are simplistic and crude. . . . There are, in any event, rightists at the top, just as there are leftists and rightists at the bottom." Seeking to crush opposition to Maoist excesses, the Anti-Rightist Campaign had deprived China of desperately needed skills, while actually stimulating fervent opposition among technicians and managers.

"Many of the problems arising during the past few years," the report noted, "have come directly from the Party Central Committee."

One trusted lieutenant of the Mayor all but identified Chairman Mao by name when he summed up the Great Leap Forward: "It is said that when one horse runs in front, ten thousand horses follow. Now, ten thousand horses have followed the one in front—and they have all broken their legs. . . . During the years from 1958 to 1960, many people behaved as though they were under the influence of drugs."

He added, "As soon as the steel-manufacturing campaign was ordered, everything else was put aside. The raw materials and equipment needed by other industries was consumed by steel-manufacturing, making it impossible to plan or maintain normal production." The Maoists had ordered 100 million Chinese to manufacture steel in crude "backyard blast-furnaces." The nation was cannibalized for "scrap metal" to feed those furnaces. Millions of useful articles—pots and pans, doorknobs and window frames, tools and agricultural implements—were consumed by the fires. The impromptu blast furnaces poured out somewhat more than three million tons of "steel" that could only be used for ballast, paperweights, and sinkers.

The Maoists believed they would do miracles by concentrating on key ideological and economic projects. Instead, they had cast China into chaos by attempting to perfect all projects at once. Excessive—and all but mindless—concentration upon crash projects had blasted the Chinese economy and broken popular morale. Suffering great deprivation, the people turned away from the Communists. Starting where Great General Peng Teh-huai left off, the seminar at the Tower of the Auspicious View documented the disaster from official Party records.

The conference in the Tower broke the barriers. Thereafter, the Mayor's associates—and the increasing force of his allies—spoke ever more openly. Comrade Liu Shao-chi startled the Central Committee in early 1962 by comprehensively criticizing the policies of Chairman Mao Tse-tung. "China has been brought to the verge of collapse during the past few years. Normal conditions will be exceedingly difficult to restore," he asserted. More circumspect than the Mayor, he argued: "To criticize Chairman Mao is merely to criticize an individual like any other senior comrade. It is not to criticize the Party itself!"

But Comrade Shao-chi's rapier thrust deeper than the Mayor's saber strokes. Direct criticism of Mao Tse-tung was no longer *lèse majesté*. Cleverly circumventing the Chairman's instructions, the non-Maoists greatly increased their power during the four years that intervened between the investigation in the Tower of the Auspicious View and the Maoists' counterattack in the autumn of 1965. They discreetly enlisted like-minded cadres at all levels of the apparatus. The levers that controlled the machinery of the Communist Party lay under the hands of the Mayor, Peng Chen, Comrade Liu Shao-chi, and the Secretary-General, the Organizer Teng Hsiao-ping. The new alliance worked generally for the benefit of the people.

The moderates had learned much from tilting against the windmills of reality on Chairman Mao's orders. They proved the converse of Lord Acton's observation, "Absolute power corrupts absolutely!" Responsibility in adversity sobers, *if* it does not first make one mad. They had learned the great difference between reality and the vision of Utopia. Their recovery was hastened not only by the catharsis of confession, but by the violent shocks they experienced as one after another of the Maoists' grandiose plans collapsed. The moderates' domestic policies and their discreet publicity acknowledged major errors of the past.

Peking still paid lip service to the Three Red Banners: the General Line of the Party, the Great Leap Forward, and the Great People's Communes. But the ritual praise deceived few. The practical bureaucracy that in effect ruled China regarded those experiments as proven failures. Power was exercised with the conviction that man was, after all, an economic animal. Peking used material incentives to increase agricultural and industrial production instead of relying upon the sacred writings of Chairman Mao to arouse "unquenchable" spiritual fervor.

The Great People's Communes were denatured. First, the Great Production Brigade and, later, the Small Production Team became the basis of agricultural life. The Small Production Team was hardly more than the old Chinese village, with a degree of not totally unwelcome cooperation enforced upon different clans. Peasants were permitted to farm private plots and to sell their private produce in "free markets."

Production increased and the State's exactions were reduced, so that the rural populace gradually recovered from the ordeal of the Great Leap Forward. To lessen the burden on farmers, the State imported about five million tons of grain a year. The reserve food was intended for emergency relief and to feed the armed forces. Imports of grain permitted exports of rice that commanded a significantly higher price on the world market. It all made economic sense.

The "new economics" also directed China's industry. Capital investment was, somewhat paradoxically, sharply reduced. The pragmatists understood their unique problems. During the Great Leap Forward vast quantities of goods and billions of man-hours had been lavished upon impossible schemes. The first need was to restore stability.

Tens of thousands of "backyard blast-furnaces" were dismantled. They had, at great cost, produced steel resembling Swiss cheese, largely because no one had remembered that impurities in the firebrick contaminated the product. The practical men concentrated on developing the basic industry the Communists had either inherited from the Nationalists or built with Soviet aid before 1958. Acknowledging that the fantastic claims advanced during the Great Leap were fallacious, they no longer imposed unattainable production quotas. Individual managers were given greater independence in running their enterprises. Workers and management were stimulated to greater efforts by the promise: "More pay for more work!"

Gradual, nondoctrinaire progress was under way. Instead of steel for machine tools and weapons, the Chinese industrial machine concentrated on consumer goods like bicycles, thermos bottles, radio sets, and small, semi-mechanized agricultural implements. The farmers' increased incomes bought those goods. The direct benefits to farmers thus stimulated essential agricultural production.

The pragmatists recognized that agriculture rather than industry must remain the basis of the Chinese economy for some time to come. Foreign Minister Chen Yi, chief lieutenant of Premier Chou En-lai, assigned the highest priority to mechanizing agriculture. But, he admitted, full mechanization could not occur for "twenty to thirty years." Chen Yi even rejected the slogan PUT POLITICS IN COMMAND! It was, he said, even more important to be expert in one's trade than red in one's convictions. The practical, nondogmatic approach had achieved formal approval. The Chinese people recovered their spirit gradually after the battering of the Great Leap. Better morale made for further material progress in a perfect, progressive symbiosis.

The *non*-Maoists—not yet *anti*-Maoists—had taken matters into their own hands. Their policies were hardly liberal in Western terms or even by the standards of the evolving "Socialist nations" of Eastern Europe.

They were, however, far removed from the unremitting intellectual and economic repression practiced by the Maoists. The non-Maoists, the practical men of affairs, performed the near miracle of regenerating China's economy and reducing political tensions.

Ironically, their visible success was later exploited to defend Maoist excesses by ignorant or self-serving "foreign friends." The apologists argued that economic progress and popular well-being justified intellectual repression. Those benefits had actually been achieved by the non-Maoists, who permitted a degree of intellectual and economic freedom as a calculated device to stimulate production.

Veiled attacks on Maoism became common. The parallels between Great General Peng Teh-huai and Upright Mandarin Hai Jui were merely whitecaps on the waves of criticism rising against the Chairman. Historical analogy and oblique ridicule discredited the extreme Maoist position; publicists argued forcibly that China required not more direction but less.

The Maoists later charged their enemies with conspiring to "restore capitalism." But apparently no organized conspiracy operated. The nation-wide upwelling was an almost spontaneous alliance of like-minded men. Few as yet wished to depose Mao Tse-tung himself. The image of the benevolent demigod was too useful. Their aims were less grandiose. Above all, they wanted to make the system work, and they were prepared to take grave risks to succeed.

The Communist Party's chief of propaganda for Kiangsi Province demonstrated how *apparatchiks* could evade orders for major "campaigns" they considered either unenforceable or counterproductive. Until 1960, a "campaign" had been a total effort with radios, newspapers, magazines, theatrical troupes, publishing houses, and the entire propaganda machine devoting *all* efforts to expounding the new goal. The Kiangsi Provincial Committee simply began to sidetrack impractical campaigns. Instead of mobilizing the great resources at his command, the chief of propaganda would instruct his deputy to publish Peking's latest announcement on an inside page of *The Kiangsi Daily*. He would then report to the Party Center that the campaign had been conducted "with fanfare—with beating of drums and dancing." Business would then proceed as normal.

Seeking the possible, the dominant non-Maoists turned China into a more pleasant country. Neither depressed living standards nor fundamental industrial and agricultural insufficiency could be sharply improved immediately. But rough social justice succeeded remission of the Maoists' impossible demands on men and nature. The administrators

distributed the still inadequate fruits of the land equitably, and almost
everyone enjoyed at least a bare sufficiency. By the beginning of 1966,
most of the Chinese people were better off than they had been since the
disruptive cycle of civil and foreign wars began 140 years earlier. China
appeared to have weathered the great storm of Maoist excess.

The pragmatists had achieved no miracles. They could point to no
more than minimal economic advances; reconstruction, rather than
rapid progress, was their chief accomplishment. Animal-power and manpower were still the chief sources of energy. In the countryside and even
within the great cities, most goods still moved on the backs of men and
beasts, in man-pedaled tricycles, or on carts pulled as often by men and
women as by animals. Consumer goods were more readily available, but
they were available in no great quantity or variety. The attempt to create
modern heavy industry overnight was postponed. Even partially effective
mechanization of agriculture was not likely for two to three decades.
The pragmatists' economic accomplishments were gratifying. They were
not spectacular.

However, the Maoists were still strong. The non-Maoists could
more easily reshape economic policy than compulsive "thought-remolding." The Chinese people were still subjected to abrasive demands for
intellectual conformity. Having failed to remake the physical shape of
China to their own desire, the Maoists sought to force every Chinese
individual into their own ideal mold. No knowledge of the outside
world—or even China's own past—was officially permitted that did not
exalt the sacrosanct Thought of Mao Tse-tung as the apogee of human
evolution.

Yet even "thought-remolding" was in part a ritual performance to
placate the Maoists. The Central Committee dutifully issued directives
designated to create the "ideal Communist man," but orders from Peking
were as often as not ignored in the provinces. The "working cadres,"
supported by the non-Maoists at the Party Center, avoided the dogmatic
excesses that had poisoned their relationship with the Chinese people
during the "leaping" years.

Chairman Mao Tse-tung had lost immediate, effective control of
China. But he was by no means reduced to a powerless cypher during
the moderates' romance from 1961 to 1965. The practical men wished
to make him wholly a ceremonial figure, honored and exalted, but unable to interfere with their reconstruction of China. The Chairman had
no intention of sitting complacently behind the altar like an unmoving
Buddha-figure while his visions were destroyed and his policies mocked.
Compliance had never been his way.

VI

The Chairman

Mao Tse-tung rarely distinguished between personalities and policy, nor did he easily surrender his views to others'. Any objection to his political desires was a personal affront. In the early 1960s, the Chairman felt deeply aggrieved personally and mortally imperiled politically. His most trusted associate, Comrade Liu Shao-chi, had turned against him.

Born 35 miles apart in Hunan Province, the pair had worked in harmony for three decades. Their talents and personalities so complemented each other that, until the spring of 1958, it was inconceivable that they would ever fall out.

Chairman Mao Tse-tung of the Communist Party was a domineering extrovert, obsessed with grandiose theories and transcendent policies. He left to others the picayune details of administration and the finicky compromises necessary to manage men. Despite his conviction of his own genius and his brief exposure to sophisticated Peking University, he felt most at home with bluff farmers.

Chairman Liu Shao-chi of the People's Republic of China was uneasy in the public prominence forced upon him with the presidency in April 1959. He was a creature of the back alleys. His original métier was clandestine subversion and devious conspiracy. He possessed an aptitude for handling tedious administrative and personnel problems. Disdaining the limelight, he had been content to remain the hardworking, methodical chief-of-staff to his intuitive, brilliant commander-in-chief, Mao Tse-tung.

Their contrapuntal personalities had produced harmonious efficiency. They had been "as close as lips and teeth," as the Chinese say, from 1932 when Comrade Shao-chi became Labor Commissioner of Mao's

62

personal redoubt, the Kiangsi Soviet Area. He had himself linked Mao's "rural faction" and the Moscow-oriented Shanghai Central Committee. Shortly thereafter, Liu became "director for the Nationalist-controlled areas." While Mao Tse-tung built the rural Soviet Areas, Liu weakened the enemy's society in preparation for military attack from Mao's secure bases.

The last public demonstration of their unity was played out before a large audience in the fall of 1960, shortly before policy disagreements were transmuted into personal antipathy.

The great Soviet turbo-prop had just landed at Peking's Tungchiao Airport. The four double propellors pinwheeled slowly to a halt; open doors pitted the elongated fuselage of the IL-114, perched like an enormous stork on its stiltlike landing gear. A stout man in a loosely cut tunic strolled confidently through the flower-bedecked throng that opened before him. The turbo-prop had brought home the Chinese delegation to the Conference of 81 Communist Parties convened in Moscow in September 1960. The Marxist chieftains had come together to reconcile acute Sino-Soviet differences over doctrine and policy.

Instead of seeking reconciliation, the Chinese had bitterly denounced the "modern revisionism" of First Secretary Nikita Sergeyevich Khrushchev of the Communist Party of the Soviet Union for major errors of external and internal policy. They had attacked Khrushchev's concept of "peaceful competition with capitalism"; they had insisted upon the Maoist doctrine of "world-wide liberation through people's wars." They had rejected Khrushchev's contention that material abundance was *the* absolute precondition for attaining true Communism; they had insisted upon Mao Tse-tung's thesis that social reorganization could create the perfect "Communist man" and thus achieve true Communism.

The Chinese delegation had almost provoked an open break between the world's most powerful Communist regimes. Liu Shao-chi was its leader. His deputies were Secretary-General Teng Hsiao-ping, the Organizer, and the Mayor, Peng Chen.

Stout, with wings of black hair framing his domed forehead, Chairman Mao Tse-tung came to Tungchiao Airport to welcome home the men who had so faithfully done his bidding. The trio thus honored was only six years later to be denounced publicly as "the leaders of the black anti-Party gang, anti-Socialist agents of Soviet revisionism and American imperialism, determined to restore capitalism in China."

While the crowds cheered, the two Chairmen clasped hands. Mao, burly, high-colored, and ebulliently self-confident; the slender Liu, gray of hair, complexion, and clothing, his manner self-effacing and his features undistinguished except for a jutting nose.

Holding almost all real power in the world's most populous nation, the pair still appeared to exercise that power in complete harmony. Yet everyone in the inner circle knew that the Chairmen were not at one regarding the Great Leap Forward and the Great People's Communes, even though disagreement had been temporarily sunk in common obedience to the Communist Party's absolute discipline. The Central Committee had moderated extremist policies, while still acclaiming Mao's theoretical genius. "Democratic centralism" appeared to have prevailed. Even the shock of Mao's precipitate "resignation" from the chair of the People's Republic in December 1958 had been softened by the appointment a few months later of Liu Shao-chi, his closest associate, to the vacant post. But their previous fruitful cooperation was rapidly coming to an end. From 1961 onward, Comrade Shao-chi would dourly resist the Chairman's constant pressure for further internal repression and external adventures.

Standing on the tarmac in the bright sunlight, Mao seemed to tower over Comrade Shao-chi, though he was actually only a few inches taller. The force of his personality, founded upon total self-confidence, reduced the stature of all other men. The great round face wore its tufted tonsure like the laurel wreath that crowns a demigod. Approaching his sixty-seventh birthday in the autumn of 1960, Mao was already acclaimed "the most brilliant Marxist-Leninist of modern times . . . the world's greatest contemporary thinker and political genius." Later, he accepted without demur frenzied adulation that made even those encomiums sound pallid.

The Chairman was convinced that he, alone in all the world, saw the shape of the future clearly, and that he alone could shape the ideal world he envisioned. His conviction of infallibility could kindle imperious passion, but his patient cunning matched his implacable will. He would not rashly commit his depleted forces to the climactic battle, but would first conduct persistent guerrilla skirmishes. He would marshal his troops cautiously for a total assault upon a Communist Party that opposed his vision of Utopia and the road thither.

The Chairman's character was admirably suited to the "protracted struggle" he foresaw in the early 1960s. The obvious misgivings of his old comrades confirmed his belief in his own visions; he had always proved himself by overcoming dissent. He had never acknowledged a superior. Only rarely—and then only under duress—had he accepted equals. Since adolescence, he had encouraged sycophants like the Disciple, Lin Piao; the Starlet, Chiang Ching; and the Ghostwriter, Chen Po-ta. He wanted followers, not advisers.

The dominant theme in Mao's life was assertion of his own will. He was almost pathologically independent. Perhaps only self-assertion could free him from the psychological straitjacket of the Confucian tradition —and from the domination of his grasping, self-willed father. The elder

Mao personified the morally corrupt and politically decadent tradition the young Mao saw in the subsiding Manchu Dynasty during the two decades following his birth on December 26, 1893. The elder Mao also personified the self-seeking new petty bourgeois class that gorged itself like maggots on decaying Imperial China.

The Mao family displayed no true distinction—scholarly, commercial, military, or official—in all the generations listed on the sacred ancestral tablets. But fortunes were changing. After serving in the provincial army, the elder Mao had returned to his native Shaoshan village with enough capital to purchase nearly four acres and set himself up in a small way as a moneylender and pig trader. The spoils of war thus provided the basis for his eldest son's education; the Imperial troops took booty from both the established classes they protected and the rebel bandits they fought. Mao Jen-sheng became a "rich-peasant," that class which, second only to landlords and "bureaucratic-capitalist lackeys of foreign imperialism," his son later hated most fiercely.

Retrospective exaltation of the families of Asian Communist leaders is widespread today. Premier Kim Il-sung of North Korea has canonized his father and his grandparents, his brothers and uncles, and particularly his mother. She is revered as "the mother of all Korea," in a cult akin to Maryolotry. Although the cult of Mao Tse-tung transcends the adulation accorded any other Communist leader, his family has, in contrast, never been hallowed. Not even his two younger brothers who were "martyred" by the Nationalists have been hailed as secular saints. His father was obviously not fit for Communist canonization, even if he had not roused his son's bitter resentment. His mother—that pale woman who took refuge in Buddhist temples from the strain of keeping peace between her strong-willed husband and her hot-tempered son—has been ignored.

In the small village school, the child Mao Tse-tung received a perfunctory education in the Confucian classics from an unsuccessful candidate for the academic degrees which were prerequisite to appointment to state office. His attendance demonstrated both the family's new affluence and its heightened aspirations. After the Boxer Rebellion and the foreign occupation of Peking in 1900, the Manchu Dynasty—and the Confucian Imperial system itself—endured barely another decade. Portents of "imminent" collapse are obvious to historians, but, at the time, mastering the Confucian classics still seemed to be the single road to official rank and the coveted academic degrees. The elder Mao, a man of traditional China, was, in any event, firmly convinced that classical studies would make his son's career and greatly enhance the standing of the entire family.

A prototypical economic man, Mao Jen-sheng considered his son not only a future mandarin, but an immediate source of free labor. Tse-tung therefore worked in the fields and was early initiated into the business. He ran errands and learned bookkeeping on the abacus and was constantly reproached for laziness and wastefulness by his avaricious and frugal parent. After one bitter lecture, the angry youth cast aside the cardinal traditional virtue of "filial piety" to upbraid his father for exploiting the poor. Threatened with a beating, he dashed to the village pond and threatened to drown himself if his father came a step nearer. It was his first open act of rebellion. He was later reported to have remarked, "From that time onwards, I learned to use staunch resistance to oppression in order to protect myself!"

The apocryphal tale has a certain inner consistency. His threat of suicide foreshadowed his threat at Mount Lu to "return to the mountains and raise a new guerrilla army"—unless his opponents yielded. Eager for knowledge, Mao fought with his teachers. Eager for independence, he could not cajole his father to send him to the "modern" primary school at Tungshan, 20 miles from his home village. He won always by frontal assault; compromise was not merely alien but abhorrent to him.

The spirit of the times nurtured his rebelliousness. Staid, successful men like his father might still believe that the Imperial-Confucian system was only passing through another of the upheavals that had periodically interrupted its triumphant progress through the millennia. But young men and adolescents knew that change was total. Endemic since the mid-1800s, rebellions against the Manchus had altered radically by 1900. The rebel leaders no longer sought the Dragon Throne for themselves. Most wished, rather, to displace the monarchy with Western parliamentary democracy. Some Chinese advocated Socialism and anarchism, while even dedicated royalists championed a new limited monarchy. All the revolutionaries were determined to alter China's essential character so that she could meet the powerful West on equal terms. Some, even then, looked beyond equality to restoring China's domination over the entire known world.

If the times were confusing, they were also stirring. Not even the remote village of Shaoshan was undisturbed by the fighting and riots spreading all across China. Even mature men questioned the moral and ethical foundations of the Confucian system. The young Mao apparently began reading outside the Confucian classics after the abolition of the Civil Service Examinations in 1906. He would have been an exception among intelligent youth if he had not begun to ponder the future of the nation and to evolve his own idealistic schemes for its redemption.

At the age of 13, five years before the Revolution of 1911 destroyed the Manchu Empire and substituted an unstable republic, Mao Tse-tung was forced to leave the local primary school. Although his two younger brothers were allowed to continue their schooling for a few years, the eldest son was put to work full-time in the fields and in the family business. His younger sister was given barely more formal education than their illiterate mother.

Tse-tung showed his contempt for his father's money-grubbing by open-handed generosity with beggars and creditors, which infuriated his father. Yet his reaction was equivocal when political action touched him directly. A local uprising of impoverished peasants, encouraged by the powerful, secret Society of Elder Brothers, seized his father's rice shipments. He considered, he later admitted, that his father was hard and unfeeling, but he did not really approve of the peasants' taking the law into their own hands.

The future Communist hero made his first major break with family and the Confucian tradition at the age of 16. He enrolled in the Modern Tungshan Primary School in the home district of his mother. Mao Tse-tung arranged his admission in secret and was initially supported by a loan from a friendly neighbor. His father could well afford to dispense with his labor and to maintain him at school, and eventually Mao Jen-sheng was forced to approve and provide a subsistence allowance for his son. He would otherwise have lost much prestige.

The "modern" school, which offered courses broader than the petrified Confucian classics, became a battleground for Tse-tung as much as a place of learning. He had been inflamed not only by the injustice and disorder he saw around him as the Manchu Dynasty collapsed, but by his favorite romantic tales of legendary Chinese heroes in the old popular novels he loved to read. Already half-convinced that he alone knew truth, Mao was expelled despite the sympathy of the principal, who had waived formal requirements to admit him. He forced his expulsion by a particularly violent argument with his teachers, who acknowledged that his beloved novels were *based* upon history but maintained that they were *not* "true history." The academic discussion had deteriorated first into personal invective against the teachers and schoolmates who did not support him, and finally into a furniture-throwing match.

Six years older than most of his classmates, Mao had found his year at Tungshan trying. Nonetheless, he longed for education. In the late winter of 1911, the year of the revolution, he secured admission to the First Middle School of Changsha, the capital of Hunan.

Still supported by the "oppressive" father whose indulgence he later claimed he had forced "by struggle," Mao briefly attended the middle school. His studies were interrupted by the overthrow of the Empire through the premature revolt in Wuhan, Central China's industrial complex. After the republican victory, Mao served as a private in the revolutionary army for about six months. But the man who was later to become the apostle of armed—indeed, militarized—Communism did not find life in the ranks congenial.

In his subsequent idleness, he read voluminously in Chinese translations of Western works that were just becoming available. He was not yet a Communist, nor even a Socialist, for those first few works were largely products of nineteenth-century liberalism. Although his own thoughts were still fixed on personal advancement, his reading did discover the existence of a vast world of "Western learning" old China had ignored.

He seems to have been motivated by personal ambition as much as by thirst for learning when he begged money of his father to attend a law school that promised to transform its students into "modern mandarins," the new equivalent of the scholar-officials who had ruled the Empire. Disrupted by turmoil as the local warlords destroyed the Republic of China, Mao's education was equally chaotic. The tall, slender youth of 20, distinguished by a great shock of black hair and a strident voice, left law school after one month. He briefly dropped in on courses ranging from soapmaking and commerce to police administration. He, quite literally, had no idea where he was bound, for the society into which he had been born was dissolving around him.

Mao found in himself no affinity for either commerce or administration. Though, as he later said, he would have liked to become rich, he finally entered the First Provincial Normal School in Changsha in early 1913. Quite remarkably, he remained with his class until graduation in the spring of 1918, when he was 24. That teacher-training course, classified as "secondary schooling" by the authorities, was the first and only systematic formal education he ever received. He also broadened his outside reading—and, once again, clashed with authority.

Again conflict rose out of his obdurate insistence upon the infallibility of his own opinions. Each time he found a stirring new book, he adopted its theses as his own, maintaining that they were the only absolute truth. His proselytizing of his schoolmates was often violent, and he was several times saved from expulsion only by the intercession of two teachers whom his eager spirit entranced. One of those teachers eventually became a respected elder of the Communist Party. Mao subsequently married the other's daughter, putting away the "village wife" his parents had chosen for him.

Like any confused and ardent young man, Mao Tse-tung sought sympathetic associates. After a number of false starts, he founded the New Man's Study Society, its declared purpose to seek "China's salvation." Several members later rose with him to the heights of the Communist Party. Some were denounced during the Cultural Revolution.

Mao's thinking was still far from Marxist. Indeed, he looked to the inspiration of the military heroes of China's past rather than to new ideologies for "salvation" of a country riven by internal power struggles and foreign exploitation. Nonetheless, he avidly read *The New Youth,* a magazine founded by Chen Tu-hsiu, who would later become the first Secretary-General of the Communist Party. Chen sought to inculcate China's intellectuals with totally new attitudes—after convincing them that they must reject the past and all its values.

Mao's first published work, an article appearing in *The New Youth* in 1917, stressed not ideology but physical fitness and military valor. "Our nation is wanting in strength," he wrote. "The military spirit has not been encouraged. . . . The principle aim of physical education is military heroism." Mao repeatedly displayed a predilection for military solutions. Though never a willing soldier, he felt that the ultimate source of power was force.

Mao Tse-tung's first stirring of political sophistication followed a year of employment as an assistant in the library of Peking National University, the nation's premier institution of higher learning. A Peking in ferment after the upheaval of World War I turned Mao into a revolutionary—and directed his rebellious spirit toward Communism. It did not, however, give him any further formal education. The university was a center of radical thought and action, stimulated by Dean of Letters Chen Tu-hsiu, editor of *The New Youth* and already a Communist. Other faculty members not only built the theoretical bases of Marxism in China, but formed the organizations that soon coalesced into the Communist Party.

In 1919, restive students of Peking University ignited the great mass demonstrations, called the May Fourth Movement, which forced the warlord government to retreat from its subservience to Japanese ambitions. Even more important, the students proved that mass action was a powerful political weapon in a chaotic China.

Mao Tse-tung made a small name for himself in Peking writing essays on "political and social questions" in a number of minor journals, but only later in Shanghai was he finally converted to Communism.

After being imprisoned by the Peking government for allegedly inciting the May Fourth Movement, Dean Chen Tu-hsiu had sought refuge in the International Settlement of Shanghai. There, Chen Tu-hsiu made Mao a Communist—instruction the future Chairman repaid by later branding Chen a "Trotskyite traitor."

After the conversion, Mao Tse-tung's life, for the first time, began to assume definite form and to display definite purpose. In 1920, after having supported himself as a laundryman in Shanghai, Mao returned with the troops of a "leftist" warlord to Changsha to become director of the primary school attached to his alma mater, the Changsha Normal

College. At that time he married Yang Kai-hui (the Changsha professor's daughter), and their home in the suburbs became the center of the radical movement in Hunan Province.

The movement was soon directed into specifically Marxist channels through the creation of branches of the Socialist Youth League and the Communist Party of China, which still had no national structure. Mao Tse-tung was not the formal leader; he was foremost among the founders of front organizations like the Marxist Study Society and the Cultural Writings Society. Members of these societies formed the nucleus of the Hunan Branch of the Communist Party of China, when that nation-wide body was formally established by the eight-day First National Congress held in the French Concession of Shanghai in July 1921.

Mao was one of 12 delegates to the Congress, which represented no more than 400 members of various Marxist groups scattered throughout China—perhaps 100 of them Party members. Although he was elected to no major office, he startled the delegates by his plea for greater attention to the peasantry, who made up roughly 85 percent of the Chinese population. He argued against concentrating upon the minuscule "industrial proletariat" as the "revolutionary nucleus"—despite most stringent advice to the contrary offered by representatives of the Communist International from Moscow to the tyro Chinese conspirators.

The fledging Communist Party of China ignored Mao and reluctantly accepted Moscow's directive that the revolution must be based upon the industrial proletariat. The Central Committee formally ordered Party members to concentrate their efforts on two important tasks: studying Marxism, the doctrine they honored much but understood little; and organizing the working class of the cities. Theory and reality were soon out of joint. The nation was overwhelmingly agricultural, the "proletarian laboring class" was minute, and self-conscious "proletarians" were almost nonexistent. Despite personal reservations, Mao obeyed the directive, submitting for the first time to external authority. In 1922 he appears to have first encountered Liu Shao-chi, who was to become his most trusted associate—and finally his most bitter enemy.

As First Secretary of the Party's Hunan Branch, Mao dutifully devoted himself to the two tasks formally laid down by the First Party Congress: further study of Marxism and proselytizing new members, supplemented by organizing labor unions. He developed a brilliant talent for using "respectable fronts." He even drew the American-sponsored Y.M.C.A. into a "mass education movement," which preached Communist doctrine in simple texts ostensibly designed to further adult literacy.

Moscow was, at the time, trying to ride two horses simultaneously—

the Nationalist Party of Dr. Sun Yat-sen and the Communist Party of Dr. Chen Tu-hsiu. Since the Communist International felt that the "proletarian revolution" in China was still a long way off, it seemed only logical to press the Communists to collaborate with the Nationalist "bourgeois revolution" before going on to their own revolution. Moreover, the policy would presumably ensure the Soviet Union a dominant position no matter which Party prevailed.

Extended negotiations, in which Mao Tse-tung played only a secondary role, led to a reluctant union of the two parties in 1924. Having been elected a member of the Central Committee and chief of the Organization Bureau of the expanding Communist Party in mid-1923, Mao Tse-tung was designated an alternate member of the Central Executive Committee of the *Kuomintang* (Nationalist Party) when the two parties joined forces under the aegis of Moscow.

Serving in Shanghai, Mao Tse-tung faithfully directed the Communists to concentrate on the "industrial proletariat"—and just as faithfully cooperated with the Nationalists. Only when the national interests of the Soviet Union, expressed through the Comintern, blatantly clashed with the national interests of China did he protest. He was, actually, derided by some fellow Communists for excessive loyalty to the *Kuomintang*.

When he retired to his native village of Shaoshan in 1925, Mao for the first time began to study in earnest the latent political force of the peasantry he had championed four years earlier. During the next two years, his concern with the "revolutionary potential" of the peasants, as opposed to the workers, intensified to the point where he was for a time denied publication in the Party organ, *The Guide*. Secretary-General Chen Tu-hsiu, on the other hand, still espoused the Moscow line, maintaining that the farmers were "small peasant proprietors with a keen sense of private property" and were therefore unlikely revolutionaries. Despite differences, Mao was able to publish his first serious theoretical work, *An Analysis of Chinese Social Classes,* in 1925 and, the same year, was made chief of the Communist Party's Peasant Bureau.

His moment came when the Nationalists, under Chiang Kai-shek, broke with the Communists after their joint conquest of Shanghai in March 1927. For both the Communist Party and the 34-year-old Mao Tse-tung, 1927 was a year of decision.

The rising leader made his first move at the Fifth National Congress of the Communist Party, held in April in the industrial center of Wuhan, where Communist influence was still dominant despite crises in relations with the Nationalists. Mao introduced a resolution demanding that the Party sponsor land reform. Rebuffed, he returned to Hunan to write his *Report on the Hunan Peasant Movement,* which is today acclaimed as *the* seminal document of the Chinese revolution. Tension between Nationalists and Communists increased as rapidly as tension between Mao Tse-tung and the regular leadership of the Communist Party.

Muzzled by the leadership, Mao Tse-tung was revenged by the events set in motion by the Nanchang Rising of August 1, 1928, when Communist officers seized the city and held it for a few days. The rebellion forced a total break between the Communists and the Nationalists, for Nationalist leader, Generalissimo Chiang Kai-shek had already made the rupture inevitable by attacking his Communist allies in Shanghai in April 1927.

After the Nanchang Rising failed, Chen Tu-hsiu, the Secretary-General with whom Mao had been in constant conflict, was removed by a rump meeting of the fugitive Central Committee. Although Mao is reported to have presided at that session, he was unable either to impose his will or to win major office. His revenge had borne little fruit but revenge itself. Unchastened, he compulsively returned to Hunan to organize the Harvest Rising of September 1927—now hailed by Maoists as the decisive first step toward the conquest of China.

At the time, the Harvest Rising appeared a dismal failure. Accompanied by a few bewildered followers, Mao Tse-tung was a harried fugitive in the hills. Captured by government forces, he escaped by subterfuge and finally ended up at Chingkangshan, a remote mountainous area in Kiangsi Province. There he set about building his own forces in collaboration with Chu Teh, the former warlord general converted to Communism in Europe and later generalissimo of the Chinese Communist armies for several decades.

Chu Teh, the elder by almost eight years, at first appeared the dominant member of the pair, and the peasants called the Communist forces the Chu-Mao Army. But Mao rapidly asserted his political supremacy. He became Chairman of the First Soviet Area in China and leader of the "rural faction," which stood against the Moscow-oriented Shanghai Central Committee. He was, once again, in the congenial state of opposition to established authority.

Once again, Mao Tse-tung followed his own course, sustained by absolute self-confidence. For the first time, he commanded his own military forces in his own "independent kingdom" in the mountains, which became the Kiangsi First Soviet Area. He joyously defied the Moscow-oriented official Central Committee, that almost impotent body which had fled to the International Settlement of Shanghai where foreigners continued to provide refuge for Chinese rebels. The complex relations between the two Communist centers uncannily presaged the beginning of the Cultural Revolution, when Mao held Shanghai and his enemies Peking.

The Shanghai Center in the late 1920s and early 1930s displayed kaleidoscopic changes of leadership and policy. One strategy promised to precipitate the "imminent, world-wide collapse" of capitalism by capturing China's chief cities. The "Li Li-san line" maintained that imperialism would collapse if deprived of the markets and raw materials of China. The fledgling Red Army set out to seize China by attacking the old walled cities, striking twice at Changsha, the capital of Hunan. The costly failure of the second attack, led by Great General Peng Teh-huai, discredited the Li Li-san Line and the Shanghai Party Center. The scattered battalions of the Red Army were gradually brought under the dominant influence of Mao Tse-tung's "rural faction" by intrigue, violence, and deceit.

Mao asserted his pre-eminence in 1932 in Juichin, the capital of the Kiangsi Soviet Area. For the first time, Communist officials who actually ruled fixed areas met in the First Congress of Soviet Representatives. Though not yet claiming sovereignty over the Communist Party, Mao alone exercised real power. His "Chinese rural faction" still paid formal deference to the "international [Russian], proletarian faction" led by the Shanghai Central Committee and the Communist International, but he disregarded Shanghai in administering his "independent kingdom." The ever flexible First Minister of Great Peace, Chou En-lai, accompanied by the ineffective Secretary-General of the Communist Party, made the "underground" pilgrimage to attend the Congress, which elected Mao Tse-tung Chairman of the Kiangsi Soviet People's Government and Generalissimo Chu Teh Chairman of the Kiangsi Soviet People's Military Affairs Committee. The mission from Shanghai tacitly acknowledged Mao's victory. The Chairman had firmly established the first strong territorial base of Communist power in China. He had also confirmed his own conviction of omniscience—and his contempt for the opinions of others.

Small success brought great danger. The Kiangsi Soviet Area expanded through a finely calculated policy that nicely balanced propaganda, terror, land reform, and opportunity for the "oppressed masses." A series of Nationalist "Extermination Campaigns" finally forced upon the Communists the agonizing decision to flee. The goal of their Long March of 1934–35 was Shensi Province in the remote northwest. A small but active Communist underground awaited them; Nationalist power was almost nonexistent; and the Soviet Union was only a few hundred miles away. The immense force required to break the Communist hold on Kiangsi did little credit to Nationalist arms. A sledgehammer had come down on a walnut. But its hard shell was not crushed. The walnut simply rolled away—far out of reach in Yenan.

Enforced retreat from his stronghold did not initially enhance either Mao's reputation or his power. While the Disciple, Lin Piao—commanding the "First Army Group," an effective force of no more than 20 thousand—gave absolute loyalty to the Chairman, other soldiers like Great General Peng Teh-huai and even Chen Yi found it hard to believe that withdrawal was the path to victory.

Nonetheless, Mao seized power during the retreat later celebrated as the victorious Long March. At Tsünyi in mountainous Kweichow Province of the deep south, Mao's column was cut off from communication with many members of the Central Committee. There in January 1935, he forced his election as Chairman of both the C.C.P.'s Political Bureau and Central Committee. Mao Tse-tung had finally attained formal supremacy, although a lesser figure retained the hollow title "Secretary-General." Mao's ascendancy had characteristically been contrived by intimidating a small group of his "senior comrades."

The new Chairman's chief rival, Chang Kuo-tao, was read out of the Party in 1938 by a conference packed against him. The Chairman was firmly established as *the* single supreme leader beyond effective challenge—a position he was to maintain for two decades. In the informal atmosphere of Yenan, Mao functioned as chairman of the board rather than dictator. Even had he formally possessed absolute power, he could not have exercised it. Scattered over large areas of northwest China, the chief Communist armies and cells, of necessity, enjoyed a large measure of autonomy. The Chairman re-ensured his own supremacy in Yenan, however, by purging the Shensi Communist underground, which had originally welcomed him.

The Communists fought their internal struggles in the face of open Japanese invasion, which began in 1937 and compelled the second period of cooperation between Nationalists and Communists. While Mao agreed to reunite Communist forces with the Nationalist Government against the common enemy, he pressed relentlessly toward his ultimate goal—the conquest of all China for Communism. Mao Tse-tung and Chang Kuo-tao, his chief rival, had disagreed on the Nationalist alliance. The Chairman felt that Communists must always act: first, to further their own power; second, to resist the Japanese; and, a distant third, to collaborate with the Nationalists. Chang Kuo-tao had insisted that the struggle against the Nationalists must be suspended in order to give all attention to resistance to the Japanese.

All the while consolidating his power and plotting to extend his sway, Chairman Mao was building a reputation as a theoretician. Ideological authority was an essential cachet for a man who aspired to lead not only China but, in the fullness of time, the entire Communist world. The faithful Ghostwriter, Chen Po-ta, assisted in the composition of six major theoretical works—among them *On Coalition Government, On Practice, On Protracted War,* and *Problems of War and Strategy.*

Mao's personal life at the time was not unhappy, for he had already taken a third wife to replace Yang Kai-hui, who had been executed by the Nationalists. In his mid-forties, Mao Tse-tung was reaching toward the height of his powers, political and personal. In 1940, the Starlet, Chiang Ching, came to share his bed as his fourth and last wife.

By the early forties, Mao Tse-tung had put his personal ideological stamp upon the Chinese Communist movement. Not content with undisputed political ascendancy, he demanded absolute conformity to his views. The first great Party Rectification Campaign, the Movement to Order the Winds, swept the Party in 1942. With the exception of a few articles by Marx, Stalin, and Lenin, and one by Comrade Liu Shao-chi, the approved texts were all from the pen of Mao Tse-tung, all inspired and polished by Chen Po-ta. All cadres were compelled to study these texts—just as the mandarins of the Empire had memorized the Confucian classics and the commentaries appended thereto by the emperors.

When the war ended in 1945, no man questioned the Chairman's absolute authority within the Communist Party—or his primacy over the 70 million Chinese already ruled by the Communists. Alternate battles and negotiations with the Nationalists finally brought him to the position he had sought all his adult life. When the Nationalists fled to exile on Formosa, Mao Tse-tung stood in the Emperor's place atop the Gate of Heavenly Peace in Peking on October 1, 1944, and formally proclaimed the establishment of the People's Republic of China. "Today," he told the cheering throngs, "the Chinese people stand erect!"

But he had just begun breaking the Chinese people to his will. The Land Reform Movement of 1950–53 smashed the old structure of Chinese society through the execution of millions of "landlords and other evil elements."* Just as he had forced the Chinese Communist Party into the mold of his own will, Mao Tse-tung was pressing the Chinese nation to that same mold. His vision of the future of China—and the role of a resurgent China in the world—was fixed. It remained only to shape his human material for the great mission he envisioned.

While still consolidating his power over China, the Chairman looked outward. He left China for the first time in 1950, visiting Moscow as the guest of Joseph Stalin. He returned with promises of military assistance and a loan worth $600 million—at 6 percent. He was also promised

---

* The exact figure has never been established, but the purge claimed the lives of at least 2 million men and women, according to Communist figures. An estimate of 10 million is not excessive, though 20 million, the figure advanced by some commentators, is probably high.

military* and economic assistance, eventually totaling at least $4.5 billion. Aside from a second and briefer trip to Moscow in 1957 for the fortieth anniversary of the Soviet revolution, the Chairman has never since traveled abroad.

Within China, things went well. The Communists skillfully rode the wave of enthusiasm for their dynamic regime. Almost the entire population welcomed effective central government after the inept rule of the Nationalists. The Communists set out to repair the widespread disruption of a century of strife, capped by the Japanese invasion and the Civil War of 1945–49.

But the Chairman was still not content. China was gradually advancing under the so-called New Democracy, Socialist in neither its premises nor its administration. Mao demanded accelerated movement in the "correct" ideological direction. In 1955, the First Minister of Great Peace, Premier Chou En-lai, pointed with pride to great progress in both agriculture and industry. Immediately thereafter, Mao discerned a "high tide of enthusiasm for collectivization in the countryside." The Chairman was determined to begin the Socialization of China—despite the opposition of his senior executives.

Mao's motives were theological, not practical. Blessed with the first efficient central government in a century and a half, the Chinese people were reasonably content during the first years of Communist rule. The end of strife alone would have ensured economic progress, even if the regime had not inherited a tremendous, half-completed infrastructure to build upon. Railways, factories, bridges, dams, and even major new ports had all been blueprinted or half-begun under the Nationalists before disorder set in. The roadbeds of some railways were laid, but the bridges and culverts were not in place; elsewhere, bridges and culverts had been built, but the roadbeds were not laid. The efficient Communists utilized popular support—and Soviet technical assistance—to "reconstruct" the nation.

Communist China had also ascended a peak of international influence and prestige she had not known for more than two centuries. At the Bandung Conference of Afro-Asian Nations in the spring of 1955, Premier Jawaharlal Nehru of India sponsored Premier Chou En-lai of China, only to be eclipsed by the witty and charming Chinese. More and more, the nations of Asia looked to China as the model for the future.

Still the Chairman was not content. He had not striven for more than three decades in order to preside over a comfortable bourgeois nation that would create peace and prosperity by measured progress. He was

---

* Lin Piao said in May 1969, that initial Korean War loans alone had totaled 1.46 billion rubles—about $1.5 million.

determined to realize his obsessive personal vision of the ideal China. The great potter in Peking once more laid his hands upon the malleable clay of the Chinese people.

Collectivization of agriculture began in 1955, depriving the peasants of the fields allotted by land reform. In 1956, remaining private commerce and industry were nationalized. Sensing some diminution of enthusiasm, which he ascribed to his cadres' errors, the Chairman invited criticism late that year. He was convinced that he had already won the hearts of the Chinese people and had totally "remolded" their thinking. Hoping to revive enthusiasm, he proclaimed: "Let a hundred flowers blossom! Let all schools of thought contend!" But free speech was an ephemeral bloom, enduring only through May of 1957.

The popular reaction was violent. Communist-educated youths as well as older intellectuals rejoiced in the invitation to denounce the regime. Not all were as heated as those who asserted that a new form of slavery had been imposed on the Chinese people, but all the strident and voluminous criticism was sharp and biting. The intellectuals—the managers, technicians, teachers, writers, and artists—rejected the Chairman's intellectual and temporal authority. His immediate response was greater repression. If the "bourgeois-tainted" intelligentsia would not serve him, he would create his own "proletarian" intelligentsia.

In 1958, once more reveling in the fight against apparently insuperable odds, Mao simultaneously proclaimed the Great Leap Forward and the Great People's Communes. He had, finally, challenged not only the Chinese people but also the Chinese Communist Party. His ultimate failure to conquer the Party led directly to the Great Proletarian Cultural Revolution.

While domestic strife welled, China's international position deteriorated. The Chairman was indignant at Moscow's refusal to acknowledge his ideological primacy after the death of Joseph Stalin—and was angered by Moscow's grudging support for the development of Chinese nuclear weapons. He was infuriated by the denunciation of Joseph Stalin and by most of Nikita Khrushchev's doctrines, which he characterized as "modern revisionism."

Convinced that Khrushchev had betrayed the basic principles of Marxism-Leninism, the Chairman ordered his followers to attack Moscow in public, as well as in private. The primary issues were: first, foreign policy and relations among Communist parties; second, the "correct" process of development of Communist societies.

Mao insisted that "monopoly capitalism" could only be overthrown by violence, conspiracy, and ultimate warfare between the Communist bloc and the "imperialists." He derided Khrushchev's doctrine of "peaceful competition" as an illusion and, worse than an illusion, a betrayal of "proletarian, revolutionary internationalism." Only through the "era of final imperialist wars" foreseen by Lenin, he maintained, could the Socialist bloc triumph. He cited, with much satisfaction, the victories the Communists had won as a consequence of the two world wars: the establishment of the Bolshevik regime in Russia in 1917 during World War I and the establishment of the People's Republic of China after World War II.

The Chairman was equally vehement regarding relations among Communist parties. He insisted that policy and doctrine must flow from a single center, while the Soviet leaders were being forced, against their own inclinations, to allow semi-autonomy to foreign Communist parties and regimes. Mao declared himself willing to submit to the authority of Moscow—as long as Moscow publicly acknowledged the absolute primacy of his own doctrines.

Questions of internal development were heroically abstruse. Faithful to the vision of Karl Marx, the Soviet leaders argued that "Socialist societies" must pass through many stages before reaching the paradise of "true Communism." "Material abundance" created by thriving industry and agriculture, they contended, was the essential prerequisite to the "withering away of the State" and the appearance of the new "Communist man." Only when the material base had been perfected would all men live in a new society, which was free of both conflict and coercion. Only under conditions of "material abundance" would they work not for material reward, but solely for the joy of creation.

Since they knew that they could not create material abundance for decades—perhaps centuries—the Maoists stressed the prior creation of the "new Communist man." After the spiritual regeneration of mankind had occurred, they contended, material abundance would be automatically created by a work force that toiled joyously for the common good.

Abstruse issues narrowed to a single practical point. If the Chinese accepted Russian doctrines, they would interminably occupy second place in the Communist world. Voluntary submission to Moscow would also surrender Mao's assertion of ideological primacy. Since the Chinese had, quite consciously, chosen Communism as the instrument that would restore China to her former pre-eminence in the world, they could not yield.

The Chairman therefore forced the quarrel. The Russians gradually withdrew assistance to Chinese industry in general—and to the production of conventional and nuclear weapons in particular. Nikita Khrushchev had no desire to create a major new military and industrial power which contested both his ideological and his temporal pre-eminence. Moscow and Peking became rivals rather than allies.

By late 1959, Great General Peng Teh-huai had been censured at

Mount Lu for soliciting support from the Soviet Union and the Communist nations of Eastern Europe, and even the faithful Comrade Liu Shao-chi was suspect because of the close relations between the Chinese Communist Party and Communist Party of the Soviet Union. Mao Tse-tung believed the Soviet Union was not only withholding material assistance, but was directly intervening in China's internal affairs.

The split with the Soviet Union shocked the substantial position of the Chinese hierarchy, which was truly dedicated to the solidarity of the international Communist movement. But Comrade Liu Shao-chi, Chairman of the Chinese People's Republic, faithfully followed Mao Tse-tung —as did the Organizer Teng Hsiao-ping, the Mayor Peng Chen, and Premier Chou En-lai the First Minister of Peace. At international Communist conferences, they pressed the quarrel with the Russians to the breaking point.

At home, adulation of Chairman Mao attained heights of extravagance never scaled by sycophants elsewhere. Both Maoists and non-Maoists joined wholeheartedly in the paean, for the cult suited the purposes of both groups. Somewhat paradoxically, the adulation actually assisted the moderates. With the Disciple, Lin Piao, as its high priest, the cult effectively transformed Mao Tse-tung into a "semi-celestial being" —and at the same time removed him ever further from the daily administration of China, lest mundane cares distract him from planning the transfiguration of all mankind. Even when he wished to interfere, his power to do so was severely limited by the institutional structure. It was later reported, perhaps apocryphally, that the Chairman had complained, "I feel like a man attending his own funeral. No one consults me on Party or State business anymore." The apparatus went its own way. The Disciple, for his part, labored to exalt Mao in order to raise himself. But even Lin Piao did not wish his aging sponsor to interfere too closely with his own campaign for supreme power.

Besides, Mao's personal powers appeared to be failing. Though his physical and psychological debilities still remain close state secrets, he may have been suffering from Parkinsonism, a disease characterized by periodic disabling attacks. He displayed the outward physical symptoms of that syndrome: "block movement," like a mechanical toy; wandering attention; and difficulty in initiating physical movements. He also appeared to withdraw periodically into the senile dementia of Parkinsonism, isolating himself for extended periods. His disability was apparently compounded by the latent paranoia he had displayed for many years. It was characteristic of the disease that he trusted only patent subordinates like the Disciple, the Starlet, and the Ghostwriter and distrusted his equals, the old Bolsheviks of the Chinese Communist Party.

Mao's opponents, moreover, seriously underestimated his vindictiveness. The fiery Hunanese, Mao Tse-tung, revealed himself as even more dangerous than the calculating Georgian, Joseph Stalin. His ego was far greater than Stalin's, though his patience was not as great. Stalin was essentially a realistic *apparatchik,* and his goal was absolute personal power. Mao Tse-tung was a total idealist, and his goal was Utopia. He was, therefore, a force markedly more injurious to both his associates and the Chinese people. He would allow neither institutional nor humanitarian considerations to turn him aside from his mission—perfecting all humanity.

Unlike Stalin, the manipulator, Mao was bored by trivial intrigue within the Party. Unlike Stalin, who depended only on himself, Mao depended on others, notably the Disciple, to carry on the fight for him. He stood above the strife. Their methods were, also, totally opposed. Stalin seized the apparatus of the Communist Party of the Soviet Union in order to gain absolute personal power. Mao finally broke the Communist Party of China in order to pursue his vision of the ideal Chinese state—and the ideal world order.

The Chairman truly wished to decentralize the administration of both the Party and the People's Republic. Hating the "bureaucratic tendencies" that crushed the *true* Communist spirit, he wished to give the "masses" greater power. He thus created his own dilemma. He exercised his authority through the centralized Party apparatus, but he endeavored to reduce the power of the apparatus and to decentralize administration —thus inevitably depriving himself of power. He believed that he could rule through a unique moral force exerted directly upon the souls of the devout—like a Pope or a traditional Confucian Emperor.

Because of this paradoxical approach to government and because of his hubris, the Chairman was vulnerable to ridicule. The moderates openly used the propaganda apparatus of the Party itself to attack Mao Tse-tung and his extremists. That apparatus was, after all, effectively under non-Maoist control. With the blessing of Mayor Peng Chen, the Czar of Chinese culture, the non-Maoists' sharp pens slashed at Mao Tse-tung in a series of parables entitled *The Three Family Village* and *Chats At Swallow Mountain*—printed in *The Peking Daily** and distributed throughout the nation in pamphlets as well. The Young Editor, Teng To, the historical dramatist Wu Han, and the venerable playwright Tien Han composed most of the sketches. But hundreds of disillusioned writers, editors, and educators labored "to prepare public

* The organ of the Peking Municipal Committee of the Communist Party, directed by Teng To—not to be confused with *The Peking People's Daily,* organ of the Central Committee of the Communist Party.

opinion" for new policies. The propaganda machinery of the Party deliberately discredited the Chairman's Utopian visions. Selected extracts illuminate not only the non-Maoists' concerted campaign, but also the thinking of most reasonable Chinese during the early 1960s. An article entitled "Big Talk" by Teng To declared:

> Some persons are very eloquent. They can talk on and on without even stopping to catch their breath. Their speeches truly flow without pause, just like a cataract. However, after listening to their speeches, we try to digest them in order to understand their real meaning. But we find that we can hardly ever remember what they talked about. . . . They themselves do not really know what they are talking about—even after half a day of non-stop talking. Their explanations further confuse things —or are really no explanation at all. Such is the nature of Big Talk . . .
>
> It cannot be denied that Big Talk is unavoidable under special circumstances, and, consequently, it is, in a certain sense, essential. However, it will be terrible if Big Talk becomes universal—if it comes into play at every turn and is even considered a special kind of concrete accomplishment. It will be even worse if future generations are taught nothing else—if they are trained to become experts in spouting empty talk.

The cap obviously fitted so well the Maoists wore it—even against their will. By their violent reaction, the Maoists acknowledged the Young Editor's acute criticism of their leader's visionary meanderings and the empty ideological "education" being given the "successor generation." Like the Monkey King, the hero of a popular allegorical novel of the fourteenth century, the Maoists were fitted with a cap they could not remove. Like the Monkey King, they found that the cap contracted and bound their temples in a ring of agony.

"Is Shrewdness Dependable?" from *Chats At Swallow Mountain,* observed most pointedly:

> Man's wisdom is definitely not unlimited. The desire to possess unlimited wisdom—or the assertion that one man does indeed possess absolute wisdom—is but the wishful thinking of a fool, for his grand purposes can never actually be attained. . . . Some persons are too fond of showing off their abilities. They think that they are wise, and they have no respect for the masses. Regardless of how diverse are the problems they may handle, they always want to assert their own ideas over all others'. They attempt to overcome all other ideas by surprise and bluster; they refuse to accept the good ideas of the masses beneath them. If persons with such shortcomings do not wake up and smartly rectify their own mistakes, they will undoubtedly pay dearly for their faults one day.

Teng To had hardly bothered to veil his contempt for Mao Tse-tung and the coterie of Maoist sycophants who hailed the Chairman as "the greatest genius of contemporary times." It was no secret that Mao cavalierly disregarded the opinions of the "masses" of working cadres responsible for executing his unworkable policies. Nor was it any secret that he was dedicated to "grand purposes [which] can never actually be attained."

The Young Editor's most cutting and most candid satire, entitled "A Special Treatment for Amnesia," was published in 1962 in *The Peking Evening News:*

> There are many people in the world who are sick. . . . Among their ailments is one called amnesia. . . . Men suffering from this disease . . . often go back on their word and repudiate their promises. Their behavior inevitably rouses suspicion that they are only capable of playing the fool and are, therefore, totally unworthy of trust. . . . It appears to many that the case of one such amnesiac has now become rather serious.
>
> We still cannot predict how the victim will behave when his disease reaches its most serious stage. He will, probably, either become wholly crazy or lapse into simple idiocy.
>
> The disease, after all, induces not only forgetfulness, but gradually leads to abnormal displays of pleasure or anger; to difficulty in expressing oneself in words; to a propensity toward losing one's temper; and, finally, to total insanity.
>
> If treatment is not rendered at an early stage, the victim will inevitably become a maniac or an idiot. When the above symptoms are marked, the person suffering from amnesia must promptly take a complete rest. He must not talk to anyone or conduct any business. If he insists on talking or managing affairs, he will cause untold trouble.

Again, no great perspicacity was required to discern that Teng To had openly attacked the sacrosanct Chairman. Mao already displayed a number of curious traits: irrational distrust of subordinates; difficulty in expressing himself in public; and outbursts of rage alternating with depression, neither rising from sufficient external cause. The mental ailment Teng To delicately called "amnesia" could explain the Chairman's actions at least as well as could the orthodox conviction that he was inspired by the greatest wisdom ever granted a human being. The Young Editor was, moreover, quite openly demanding that Mao Tse-tung retire before he caused greater catastrophe.

The satirist even dared suggest that Mao must be disposed of if he would not yield of his own. With deliberate exaggeration, the Young Editor wrote:

> Modern Western medicine treats the acute stage of this disease, amnesia, in a particular way. A specially made club is employed to hit the patient on the head. That treatment induces a state of shock, and, thereafter, he is given medicine to restore consciousness.

If Teng To was not advocating shock treatment for the Chairman—political as well as medical shock treatment—in his absurd description of the method of "modern Western medicine," he was making no point at all.

The essays were scathing in their comments on the pressing economic and political problems created by the debacle of the Great Leap Forward. The great dynasties of the past, the Young Editor noted, had always been very careful to "conserve labor power." He was drawing an obvious contrast with the lavish, wasteful, and finally counterproductive employment of the labor of hundreds of millions of Chinese—a resource the Maoists treated as inexhaustible. He knew that Maoist bungling had actually created the virtually impossible—a labor shortage in teeming China.

The Three Families Village went beyond satire to openly advocate internal policies directly contrary to the Maoists'. With the usual Chinese passion for categorization, the pragmatists' agricultural policy was described as the "three freedoms and the one guarantee." The three freedoms were: free markets, individual (free) plots for peasants, and independent (free) management of enterprises. Individual households would further be guaranteed that only a fixed quota of their produce need be delivered to the State, while the rest would be allotted for their own consumption or sale for profit. The moderates thus advocated direct reversal of the Maoist policy through which the People's Communes seized almost all production for the "collective" and the State.

The pragmatists' external policy was described as "three accommodations and one reduction." That meant, according to the Maoists: "deemphasizing struggle against and stressing accommodation with the [American] imperialists, the [Soviet] modern revisionists, and reactionaries everywhere, while reducing our support for militant revolutionary movements abroad."

The pragmatists, in sum, looked toward a less stringently controlled economy and toward relatively peaceful relations with the outside world. The Maoists demanded controlled exploitation to crush individual initiative, a policy sustained by incessant ideological indoctrination. The Maoists further demanded unwavering hostility to almost every other nation, hostility expressed by sponsoring violent, subversive "liberation movements" in the underdeveloped countries.

The barrage of satire affected not only public opinion but Maoist sensibilities. Hypersensitive to the function of propaganda in the government of men, the extremists realized that they were rapidly losing effective power. They concluded that they would be destroyed if they did not resist—and they resisted mightily from 1960 to 1965.

The Chairman assigned the Disciple, Lin Piao, to lead the counterattack. Lin's chief weapon was the Chinese People's Liberation Army. In 1959 he had made the Securityman, Lo Jui-ching, chief-of-staff to reshape the Liberation Army by purging senior officers and by sweeping reorganization. The militarization of China had begun. Having taken power by the sword, the Chairman could, it was manifest, rule only by the sword.

Lin Piao had won Mao Tse-tung's confidence by his youth and his apparent lack of personal ambition. The new chief-of-staff enjoyed Lin Piao's confidence because he was a professional policeman rather than a professional soldier. The enemy within the military was the "professionalism" exemplified by Great General Peng Teh-huai, the conviction that strictly military requirements must take precedence over the political and economic functions Maoism assigned the Liberation Army. The Securityman possessed a noteworthy record of suppressing dissent. From his military power base, Great General Peng had intervened in many vital nonmilitary matters. Lin Piao was determined that the army would still intervene, but only in the interests of Mao Tse-tung, Maoism —and Lin Piao.

The intense controversy was, in the early 1960s, largely concealed from the "masses." Similar conflicts in the past had not been revealed until their resolution. The Liberation Army had previously been subjected to purges. Nonetheless, the power struggle following the Mount Lu Plenum was the most virulent since the founding of the People's Republic.

Lin Piao's personal ambition, thitherto assiduously concealed, leaped joyously to the assignment of making the army a perfect Maoist weapon against the opposition. The "remolded" People's Liberation Army would re-establish the unassailable primacy of the Thought of Mao Tse-tung. The Disciple's own triumphant reassertion of the Chairman's authority would establish his own pre-eminent claim to succeed the Chairman.

Lin Piao was dealing with an organization that was both greater and less than a conventional Western army. Growing from guerrilla forces that were a people in arms, units of the Liberation Army had developed strong allegiances to specific localities and a powerful tradition of semi-autonomy. The Communists' adherence to a fixed ideology had, however, united the disparate units. As Mao Tse-tung's doctrinal authority declined, that unifying factor had been weakened and natural divisive tendencies had grown. The Disciple's first problem was to reverse the trend without destroying either the morale or the structure of the essentially regional People's Liberation Army.

From 1960 to 1965, many senior commanders were reassigned. Generals and colonels who gave primary loyalty to Lin Piao rose, while the adherents of Great General Peng Teh-huai were relegated to lesser posts. Young officers who displayed proper enthusiasm for Chairman Mao—and Defense Minister Lin—were assured of rapid advancement. The Liberation Army was to be totally "remolded" according to the word of Chairman Mao—as interpreted by his disciple, Marshall Lin Piao.

Lin Piao strove first to re-establish the canonical Thought of Mao Tse-tung as *the* single doctrine of the Liberation Army. Acting always "on behalf of Chairman Mao," he exhorted the soldiers to "living study and living use of the Thought of Mao Tse-tung." The non-Maoists strove to neutralize Mao's political power by transforming the Thought of Mao Tse-tung into an abstract theology. Lin Piao sought to frustrate them by transforming the Thought into a field manual of practical action —and making the Liberation Army China's *chief* political force because it exemplified the practical application of the Thought.

The physical threat was obvious behind the spiritual fervor. Monopolizing guns and ideology, the army would be supreme. Defense Minister Lin Piao would be first in the nation—under the aloof demigod, Chairman Mao. The Disciple further intrigued vigorously to bring quasi-governmental organizations like the Young Communist League and the Trade Union Federation under his personal control. Mao Tse-tung had apparently sanctioned the Disciple's extension of his personal power. Lin did not threaten his supremacy while his mentor lived; it seemed he would insure continuity of doctrine and policy when the master died. After 1959 the Disciple enhanced his prestige and power by pressure, cajolery, and intrigue.

Lin Piao's attempt to assert the absolute supremacy of the Maoist minority failed because it was, rather uncharacteristically, too cautious. Passive resistance prevented his attaining his first objective, absolute control of the Liberation Army. Local loyalties to old commanders and old techniques were too deeply rooted to be destroyed in a half decade. The civilian resistance commanded many resources: the senior cadres and the administrative functionaries of the Communist Party; the essential—and always disaffected—intellectual class; and, above all, the "masses," who were weary of the constant "class struggle" demanded by the Chairman. The loose alliance of those forces proved too strong for the Maoists.

The Disciple's strategy was also upset by events abroad. The Maoists believed the forces of "capitalist imperialism" were demoralized and disunited. They therefore sponsored "people's wars"—spearheaded by local guerrillas and supported by mass propaganda campaigns throughout the world—concentrating upon disputed territories like South Vietnam. That strategy, they argued, would at once make China secure and gain general victory for Communism abroad. But Great General Peng had warned at Mount Lu that Mao's militant foreign policy would actually accomplish the opposite. Growing American intervention in Vietnam, "the focus of the world-wide liberation struggle," was actually proving the opposition's point in the early 1960s.

Instead of sending the imperialists scurrying in retreat, Chairman Mao's war by proxy stiffened American resolution. As Great General Peng Teh-huai had warned, the "forward policy" increased the danger of attack on China. Rent by doctrinal strife and power struggles, the People's Liberation Army was in no state to confront American power. Not quasi-guerrillas but a modern, technological army, the opposition argued, was essential to adequate defense. Proxy wars abroad, they added, would endanger China, while failing to attain their goals.

In May 1965, Lo Jui-ching, appointed chief-of-staff to purge the People's Liberation Army, espoused the viewpoint of the "professional soldiers," who were the Disciple's enemies. A long article from his pen— "Commemorate the Victory Over German Fascism! Carry the Struggle Against U.S. Imperialism Through to the End!"—urged preparations for defense-in-depth like that the Russians had mounted against the Germans. He further advocated modernization of the Liberation Army, particularly the all-important and highly technological antiaircraft forces. The bitter debate was, at least in part, conducted in public. Lin Piao himself refuted the professionals' theses in his first major ideological article, "Long Live the Victory of People's War!" published in September 1965.

The Disciple argued that "people's wars" abroad, crowned by inevitable victory, were the best defense of China. He reassured the fainthearted, promising that such wars would not be fought by Chinese soldiers but by "local patriots." Yet the Securityman's defection demonstrated that the Maoist resurgence was faltering badly within the Liberation Army.

The Maoists asserted with bravado, "The East Wind Is Prevailing Over the West Wind!" But the Maoist East Wind was actually dropping. The pragmatic and inherently conservative functionaries of the

Communist Party, supported by the intelligentsia, were not only beating down the Maoist challenge, but were decisively increasing their power. The Maoists found themselves no longer striving primarily to re-establish their absolute authority in order to realize the Chairman's Utopian visions. They were, instead, fighting for political survival.

The Chairman and the Disciple therefore grasped the initiative by ordering a major counterattack on wholly new terrain in 1965. Their flanking attempt to control the military—and through the military the nation—was a failure. The Maoists therefore launched a frontal assault on the center of enemy strength. Their objective was the apparatus of information: the editors, writers, scholars, and teachers who manipulated public opinion. The attack commanded by Lin Piao was mounted by the band of young, ambitious literateurs the Starlet had recruited to make herself Czarina of Chinese culture.

BOOK TWO

The Storm

VII

The Revolt of the Scribes

The Temple of Tranquillity was an old Buddhist landmark of western Shanghai. As the coastal megalopolis expanded under Communist rule, the surrounding district became a hub of trade and transport. The Graveyard of Tranquillity opposite the temple was transformed into a People's Park, where families strolled during their few off-days—and urchins begged or stole. The Square of Tranquillity resounded with the rattle of trams and the throaty exhaust of buses on the six roads converging into the wide plaza. Shops and stalls catered to all needs: foodstuffs, spices, and snacks; clothing from shoes to overcoats; books, magazines, and newspapers; pots and pans; umbrellas and thermos bottles.

Queues formed before the newspaper kiosks as early as 6:00 A.M. when major events were in progress, and by eight all newspapers are generally sold out. During the two months of the Hundred Flowers Movement in the spring of 1957, when the regime permitted relatively free expression, eager readers clamored in the Square of Tranquillity every morning.

Even during normal periods of minimum disclosure, the Shanghailanders searched their newspapers anxiously. They had of necessity become expert in discovering the true meaning concealed by official jargon. Periodicals and broadcasts conveyed the orders of a regime that had virtually cast aside the pretense of consulting popular wishes. In the sixties, the latest pronouncement could, quite literally, mean life or death for citizens of the "last great bourgeois stronghold"—continued residence in Shanghai or transportation to remote rural areas to "work for national reconstruction." Sixteen years of Communist rule had not eradicated but enhanced the Shanghailanders' urban shrewdness. As crisis compelled the authorities to erratic candor, the Shanghailanders read their newspapers with even greater avidity.

On November 10, 1965, the newspaper kiosks of the Square of Tranquillity were besieged as they had not been since May and June, 1957. Anxious hands snatched the newly printed sheets of the *Shanghai Wen Hui Pao,* the organ of the extreme left. Rumor, as always, fed on the secrecy of the rigorously closed society. Rumor had for five years retailed diverse accounts of the struggle between Maoists and moderates begun by Great General Peng Teh-huai, though actual events at Mount Lu were known only hazily. But the Maoist daily had begun a revealing new "campaign." On that chilly November morning, the *Wen Hui Pao* finally began to tell the commonalty of the climactic struggle that would determine their fate.

The open battles of the Great Proletarian Cultural Revolution, the grand climacteric of the Chinese People's Republic, began that November morning in Shanghai. The barrages and the counterbarrages opened with a single shot entitled "On the New Historical Play, *Hai Jui's Dismissal From Office."* The article itself made weary reading. Elsewhere the long, turgid disquisition would have been interred in the deserved obscurity of a second-rate academic quarterly. Its Marxist cant, tainted with neo-Confucian pedantry, was garnished with chopped logic and hysterical denunciation.

The canny Shanghailanders, however, were alerted by the prominent display given the "academic essay"—and by its extraordinarily virulent invective. The attack on *Hai Jui's Dismissal From Office* would thus have commanded attention even if that historical hero had not already been identified with Great General Peng Teh-huai. It was clearly an "important statement." Even though Chinese literary critics sometimes speak with vehement self-righteousness that would embarrass an Old Testament prophet; even though the Marxist experiment in the perfection of mankind has always been addicted to gutter vituperation; even though the Chinese language often transforms abstract discussion into personal diatribes by its remarkable capacity for abuse, the critique transcended the normal shrillness of modern Chinese diction. Foreboding intensified when men realized that the playwright who was the target was much more eminent than the critic who trained the gun and pulled the lanyard.

The critic was a literary scavenger in his mid-thirties, who had clambered to dubious eminence as a hyperorthodox Maoist critic over the political corpses of better-known writers. He had first gained serious public notice when the Communists began devouring their literary children in 1955. Yao Wen-yüan, son of a distinguished "left-wing writer" of the 1930s, had endeared himself to the extremists by attacking *The*

Dream of the Red Chamber, a popular novel of the seventeenth century. Thereafter, ambition directed his pen to the service of the Party's absolutist bigots. They were determined to destroy all writing but their own, and all thought but their own. Yao Wen-yüan's slaughter of reputations had already won him the nickname, the Literary Assassin. Encouraged by the Starlet, Yao would become ever more vehement and ever less scrupulous as the Cultural Revolution widened. The Great Revolution gave him constant opportunity to exercise his instinct for the jugular.

Yao's target was Wu Han, 57 years old in 1965 and one of the regime's chief intellectual adornments. The leading authority on the Ming Dynasty (1368–1644), he was not only a scholar but a dramatist of note. He had been rewarded for his devotion to the Communist cause by a vice mayoralty of Peking and the patronage of Chairman Mao himself. After a decade of silence imposed by Mao Tse-tung's direct instructions to "serve the people as an administrator," he had begun writing again in 1959, just before the Mount Lu Plenum.

Wu Han was obsessed with Hai Jui, the "Upright Mandarin" of the Ming Dynasty. In June 1959, when the skirmishes "between the two lines" had just begun, he published an article in *The Peking People's Daily* called "Hai Jui Scolds the Emperor." In September 1959, after the decision had been handed down from Mount Lu, that newspaper published his second article praising the same hero. Wu Han was largely responsible for the popular identification of Great General Peng Teh-huai with Hai Jui.

Performed in February 1961, Wu Han's play *Hai Jui's Dismissal From Office* won acclaim for its "moving portrayal of the feudal official who sacrificed himself on behalf of the oppressed masses." The literary atmosphere in the early 1960s was hospitable, and Wu Han became the most prominent of the many authors under the protection of the powerful moderate faction who criticized Maoist excesses through historical analogy and allegory. Wu Han's prominence obviously made him the most useful stalking horse for the Maoists. Eventually the reverberations of the Assassin's attack on Wu Han shook every remote reticulation of the network of institutional and personal relationships that controlled China.

However poets preen themselves for their earth-shaking lines, it is truly remarkable that the collapse of an authoritarian regime should have begun with a literary controversy. Literature has, of course, played a part in political conflict, but in China—under mandarins or commissars —reverence for the written word has ordained that novels, plays, and essays should be major political weapons. The innovating Chinese had, after all, conducted the first great politically inspired burning of books in the second century B.C. The Manchu Dynasty had consolidated its power not only by banning seditious works, but by compulsory study of its new canon. The Maoists followed tradition faithfully—destroying their opponents' works and glorifying their own.

The Chinese leaders' ingrained fear of free expression was exacerbated by the Hungarian Revolt of 1956. Convinced that the Petöfi Club of militant writers had ignited the explosion in Budapest, the Maoists were determined to prevent a revolt among Chinese scribes. But the genesis of the Hungarian Revolt merely confirmed the Maoists' chronic fear. Since 1949, an unending literary inquisition had been the constant obligato to political and economic "campaigns."

One specific absurdity of the inquisition is worth noting, not because it was unusual, but because it was typical. Two dramas had been abused because of their totally opposite appraisals of Yung Chen, the hapless last Emperor of the Ming Dynasty.

The first, *Rising in Official Rank,* had attacked Yung Chen for his apathy, corruption, and ineffectiveness, which had left China defenseless before the Manchu invaders. Discerning an intentional parallel between Mao Tse-tung and the defeated Emperor, Peking banned the play and punished its author.

Shortly thereafter, a film called *The Peach-Flower Fan* also came under scathing criticism. Yung Chen was presented therein as a pathetic victim of circumstances who had endeavored to preserve the nation as best he could. The protracted resistance of his loyal followers, based in the end on Formosa, was depicted as a heroic drama exemplifying noble patriotism. But, Peking asserted, Yung Chen really represented Generalissimo Chiang Kai-shek. *The Peach-Flower Fan* was therefore a "poisonous weed"—vile propaganda attempting "to prepare public opinion" for the restoration of the Nationalist regime.

Since the Chinese people were accustomed to such clearly schizoid behavior, the Literary Assassin's vicious attack on Wu Han occasioned no surprise. The timing was another matter. The dominant pragmatists and their publicists had become overconfident because they controlled the legal apparatus of government. Forgetting the Chairman's character —obdurate, mercurial, vindictive, and quixotic—they complacently behaved as if they were secure in power. The propaganda machinery had from 1959 to 1965 produced numerous articles defending Wu Han and pointing out the analogy between Hai Jui and Great General Peng Teh-huai. The non-Maoists were, however, totally wrong in believing that Chairman Mao would yield without a fight. Launched with Yao Wen-yüan's assault on Wu Han, Mao's counterattack became the Great Proletarian Cultural Revolution.

What, however, had Wu Han written to arouse such vehement condemnation from one faction and such great approbation from the other? What, precisely, were the Assassin's charges against Wu Han?

Hai Jui's Dismissal From Office manifested no great departure from normal Communist morality plays, which recalled the evils of the old "feudal-bureaucratic system" and by contrast illuminated the blessings of the new era. Before the Cultural Revolution undertook to "destroy the past," the Communists had deliberately encouraged pride in China's ancient glory, and certain figures from Chinese history were regularly presented as precursors—albeit flawed—of absolute Communist virtue. Wu Han had used both techniques.

Celebrated amid general decadence as a "clean and upright mandarin," hero Hai Jui was assigned to Yingtien (Nanking) in the summer of 1569 as governor of ten prefectures west and north of the present city of Shanghai. His domain along the Yangtze River was noted for its fertile soil and its rapacious landlords.

Wu Han's Hai Jui champions the impoverished peasantry against the landlords and their henchmen among the corrupt mandarins. He orders the landlords to "return the land" they had stolen from the peasants by manipulating the Ming Dynasty's chaotic tax and land-tenure systems. The brutally exploitive landlords naturally resist with all their wiles and influence. Led by a retired prime minister, the unholy trinity of usurers, landlords, and officials appeals to the Imperial Court itself.

Defending his decree, Hai Jui reminds the Emperor of his fundamental duty: The Throne must cherish the poor masses, rather than encourage their exploitation by the "bureaucratic landlords." Hai Jui is triumphant. The miscreants are punished, and the peasants once more enjoy their patrimony. In a melodramatic final scene, Hai Jui raises his great seal of office over his head and declaims, "A virtuous man stands with his head reaching the sky and his feet firmly on the earth!"

Wu Han's drama improved on imperfect reality. The playwright did not choose to depict his hero's later disgrace or his death in penurious exile. Since omission of inconvenient facts was encouraged by the regime, Wu Han could not really be faulted for rewriting history in his play. All in all, it was a commendable tale of a heroic patriot fighting for the people at his own peril, a foretaste of the Communists' greater deeds to come. The Capital Opera Troupe of Peking, the country's foremost theatrical group, staged the play in 1961. The performance directly challenged Chiang Ching, who was just beginning to assert herself as *the* arbiter of the arts. The Starlet's chief concern was the stage, and the Capital Opera Troupe was her immediate preoccupation. Wu Han not only aroused the Starlet's personal antipathy, perhaps unwittingly. He also consciously criticized times present in his drama of times past.

By 1965, "the struggle between the two lines" had become so acute that it required no particular ingenuity to draw an indictment against

Wu Han. Yao Wen-yüan, declared in his critical article: *"Hai Jui's Dismissal From Office* is not a fragrant flower, but a poisonous weed. . . . Its distortion of history implants evil ideas . . . and seeks to stimulate the rebirth of capitalism." Hai Jui's condemnation of wicked officials and his admonitions to the Emperor, the critic charged, were both direct criticisms of the Maoist regime. Hai Jui had called for "return of expropriated land to the peasants" and "remedying their grievances." Exalting Hai Jui as an example of correct behavior, the Assassin asserted, actually condemned the Great People's Communes that had converted individually owned plots into "collective property."

"Do we want the People's Communes to 'return the land'?" the assassin inveighed. "Can it be said that the 500 million peasants who are pushing forward with great resolution along the Socialist road should be required to learn such 'return of land'? . . . If we are required to learn 'to remedy grievances' today, we must ask: Which, after all, are the classes who have grievances—and how can their grievances be redressed?"

Yao Wen-yüan cut to the heart of Wu Han's position:

> Where will it end if we today laud such "righteous, great men" in the abstract? Would we not, then, be praising as "upright persons" those who, with scornful frowns, coolly defy the proletariat? Would we not be accepting their selfish concept of "self-respect" to demand the "return of land and remedying of grievances"? Would we not, then, actually be arguing that "today's bureaucratism" should be opposed and that present-day "officials should be dismissed"?

The Assassin asserted that Wu Han's was a "bourgeois, rather than a proletarian class-viewpoint." Although contemporary nuance and historical allusions, garbled by neo-Marxist logic, were obscure in the diatribe, the main point was clear. Wu Han *had* written the play just after the Mount Lu Plenum, suddenly resuming his literary career after a decade of silence. The timing was taken as *prima facie* evidence that the playwright had been encouraged by the non-Marxists—and that he had sought to help them consolidate their power.

The political purposes the Assassin discerned were half-proven by the drama itself. Extolling Hai Jui for demanding "return of land and remedying [the] grievances" of peasants, Wu Han had made his analogy unmistakable. The Great People's Communes had deprived the peasants of their small "private plots," just as the usurious Ming landlords had stolen small holdings. Wu Han had, further, praised Hai Jui for "saving the people from dying of starvation." That was hardly a tactful observation when Maoist excesses had led to acute privation for the masses.

Yet in his subsequent compulsory "self-examination" (read, confession), Wu Han refused to acknowledge that he had attacked Mao Tse-tung and championed Great General Peng Teh-huai. After all, he said, Hai Jui had triumphed because the Emperor condemned the wicked exploiters. But the obvious parallel admonished: If the Maoists' demonstrated failures were not now set right, the oppressed people might take matters into their own hands.

Wu Han, too, had friends at court, and they rallied to his defense. *The People's Daily* preceded its reprint of Yao's article with a temperate introduction. The moderates who controlled the chief organ of the Central Committee tried to divert the controversy from politics to pure scholarly inquiry. *The People's Daily* declared:

> We are of the opinion that Hai Jui and the play, *Hai Jui's Dismissal From Office*, actually involve the problems of how to deal with historical characters in plays; what viewpoint should be adopted in the study of history; and what forms of art should be used to reflect historical characters and events. The views of our thinkers are at variance regarding these problems. . . . We plan to start a debate on the play, *Hai Jui's Dismissal From Office*, and other problems. Readers among historians, philosophers, writers, and artists are welcome to participate in this debate.

Deliberately designed to avert the purge the Maoists planned, the literary debate lasted several months. Learned academicians defended Wu Han, dwelling on obscure criteria for reading historical records and evaluating their economic data. All proved their objectivity by finding minor points to criticize in both Wu Han's play and his essays, but the final judgment was in his favor.

Even his opponents qualified their disapprobation and pointed the moral—as did a letter from a Shanghai editor: "Wu Han wants us to study Hai Jui's quality of daring to wage struggle. Will he kindly tell us what is the opposite aspect? Who is the Emperor of today? Who is the retired Prime Minister? Who is the hypocrite? The reading public has the right to ask these questions."

Summing up the debate, the editorial board of *The People's Daily* came down cautiously on Wu Han's side. After perfunctory criticism, the appraisal ended: "Although peasant uprisings had erupted in many places in the days of Hai Jui, yet the Soochow-Sungchiang area was still rather peaceful. The Ming Dynasty was not yet on the eve of its downfall. Judged by the principal aspects, *Hai Jui* should be affirmed."

The "academic debate" was to become the vortex of a maelstrom of political controversy that engulfed the Communist party and the entire nation. Moderate writers protected by senior hierarchs were later stigmatized as "the black, anti-Party gang." Ranking members of the Central Committee were themselves later purged. The Maoists characteristically contended that the issues transcended the fate of individuals. But the character of the middle-aged intellectual called Wu Han was central to the drama of the Great Revolution.

The questions remain: Why did Wu Han, after ten years' silence, begin writing again in 1959? Why did he choose Hai Jui as his hero? Wu Han's shifting attitude during the first decade of the Communist regime reflects not only Maoist suppression of intellectuals, but radical changes in the regime itself. It was Mao himself who had originally enjoined Wu Han to put aside his pen and "serve the people" as an administrator.

Not yet transformed into the drably monumental capital of the People's Republic of China, old Peking in mid-1949 was the wellspring of a people on the march. Having just welcomed the Communists with spontaneous enthusiasm, intellectuals and commonalty alike cheered the People's Liberation Army as it rolled up the old way of life in China. One summer evening, the man riding the crest of the wave of the future summoned an unlikely visitor to his austere quarters in the Imperial City, where the Emperor's Court had once paraded its splendors. Mao's guest was a 40-year-old vice mayor of Peking called Wu Han, the leading historian of the Ming Dynasty. Though not yet a member of the Communist Party, Wu Han was a brilliant intellectual jewel in the Communists' crown, and he had already been rewarded with public office for his earlier "underground work"—in part, in order to attract other intellectuals to the cause.

Chairman Mao did not summon Wu Han to discuss immediate political issues. He was concerned with the historian's spiritual development, as demonstrated by an obscure matter of Ming Dynasty history. Wu Han had just published an essay celebrating the Taoist Monk Peng, a leader of the uprising that overthrew the *alien* Mongols and established the *Chinese* Ming Dynasty in the fourteenth century. The heroic monk had then retired to a quiet life of study, Wu Han wrote. He implied that Peng would be the model for his own actions after the "victory of the people." Since Nationalist tyranny had been overthrown, there was no further need for intellectuals to concern themselves with politics. Wu Han therefore planned to return to his studies.

The omniscient Chairman Mao was much disturbed because the essay revealed Wu Han's "bourgeois thinking." His visitor, he pointed out, exemplified the problem of the "class-viewpoint" of intellectuals. If the historian were truly "proletarian" in his thinking, Mao explained, he would not give way to his "individualistic desire" to retire to his library. He would not wish to withdraw from public affairs, but rather to "serve the people" with all his energy and ability. The historian's plans, Mao said gravely, revealed "a very selfish manner of thought, a negative, poisonous, Taoist manner of thought, setting yourself outside the masses and above social classes."

Wu Han later reported that his conversation with Mao Tse-tung totally altered his plans. He no longer felt that he "transcended social classes" or that he should retire to his library. Wu Han wrote in 1950:

> In accordance with the instructions of Chairman Mao, I read *The State and Revolution* by Lenin and the *Selected Works of Chairman Mao,* and I comprehended the Thought of Mao Tse-tung. I studied the history of the Communist Party and reports on land reform. I understood exactly what leftist and rightist deviations really were and how victory was brought about by the leadership of Chairman Mao. . . . I continued to study Marxism-Leninism and the Thought of Mao Tse-tung, and I no longer praised the Monk Peng. Instead, I worked in the city government of Peking.

Wu Han had, under duress, become a bureaucrat rather than a scholar. His essay continued:

> When I talked with Chairman Mao, he told me something remarkable about Monk Peng. He said the political error had not been committed by the Monk himself, but by the historical record. I therefore carefully reread *The Daily Chronicle of the Ming Dynasty.* Therein, I found that, some years later, the Monk Peng was captured and slain by Ming troops. The new information showed that he had not retired, but had remained a revolutionary to the end. I have, as yet, found no other historical material regarding the Monk Peng, and it is still not clear to me why he turned against the uprising. But, during the following decade, I devoted myself to my administrative duties and wrote little.

Wu Han expressed no misgivings because the monk he had chosen as his model had been slain by the men he had helped bring to power. A decade and a half after his conversation with the Chairman, Wu Han came under attack. Presumably he then understood—without further reference to historical records—why the Monk Peng, after fighting to establish the Ming Dynasty, had become its enemy.

Wu Han's fate, too, transcended individual concerns. His career was the career of an entire generation of leftist intellectuals who had served the Communists well. His life was also the life of thousands of originally sympathetic intellectuals who turned against the Maoists. He became a major symbol, for he exemplified the tragedy of the Chinese Communist revolution.

"You could not tell from either his appearance or his demeanor," a former student remembered, "that Wu Han had struggled hard to become a teacher and writer after his birth as the grandson of a tenant farmer. He hardly appeared a passionate man who had risked everything to serve the Communist underground during the struggle against the Nationalists."

Wu Han's medium height, placid manner, and stocky build, made him appear a typical, apolitical professor. The student recalled:

> He dressed simply, spoke so slowly that men thought he had a speech impediment, and appeared wholly unemotional. His placid features were dominated by a towering forehead which seemed to occupy more than half the distance from his chin to his hairline. His eyes were calm behind their silver-rimmed glasses, and only two outward characteristics revealed the intense nature within: the full, sensual lower lip and the deep caliper-lines which ran from his nose to the corners of his mouth when he smiled or frowned.

All in all, the symbol was a man of neither outstanding presence nor distinctive history. He was just another Chinese intellectual, who had displayed somewhat greater courage and somewhat greater industry than most under the Nationalist regime.

Born in the southern coastal province of Chekiang in 1909, Wu Han remembered that his grandfather was a tenant farmer who was able to accumulate ten *mou* (somewhat less than two acres) of land and divide it among his five sons as a meager patrimony. His own father was just barely qualified to teach primary school after the Revolution of 1911 swept away the Chinese Empire. The teacher was rarely more than one step ahead of the class, for he had himself received only primary schooling. He spent much time helping Wu Han's grandfather roll firecrackers to supplement the family income.

After Wu Han's birth, his father somehow continued his middle-school education, all the while teaching primary school. He was finally qualified for a position his son described vaguely as "an official government post." The Maoist account of Wu Han's life deliberately denigrated him, since *all* the Chairman's enemies were to be proved "traitors by family and class background" as well as personal character. Wu Han's enemies described his father as a policeman "who exploited the common people." The playwright's deliberately vague description of his father's occupation lends credence to the Maoist account, though the discrepancy is critical only in a "classless society," obsessed by class differences into the third generation. In any event, the elder Wu quickly lost his official post—whether through incompetence or political misfortune is not recorded. "Thereafter, he spent his time," Wu Han recalled, "grumbling and drinking all the day." Despite hard times, the youth went to middle school—at the cost of one-third of the family income. When he expressed a desire to attend university in Shanghai, he was told that there was no more money.

Casting about for alternatives, he hit upon the free course of the newly established Whampoa Military Academy at Canton, where Generalissimo Chiang Kai-shek was commandant and the First Minister of Peace Chou En-lai was political commissar. Had his scheme worked, Lin Piao would have been among his schoolmates. But the Wu family could not raise the fare to Canton. His frustrations ended when his mother sold her remaining ornaments* to pay for his university education, first in nearby Hangchow and later in Shanghai, at the liberal Chinese People's University. Life was hard for the Wus, but they were patently "bourgeois"—or their son would have received no schooling at all.

When he was a sophomore, family funds ran out. But Wu's luck held. A class paper on Chinese culture brought him a small sum from an academic journal and—more important—the approbation and patronage of the president of the university, Professor Hu Shih, a Ph.D. of Cornell University and one of China's leading liberal thinkers. A champion of reform and Westernization, Professor Hu was already famous for his critical and linguistic writing; he later bacame Nationalist Ambassador to Washington.

But Hu Shih was dismissed for his liberal views in the early 1930s, and Wu Han followed him to Peking. He lived by working as an assistant in the library of Yenching University, as Mao Tse-tung had in the library of Peking University a decade earlier. Sustained by his small salary and Hu Shih's patronage, Wu Han entered Chinghua University's History Department as a sophomore. Occasionally he was fortunate enough to sell an article to a literary journal; for a time he supported his younger brother and sister, who were also studying in Peking. In 1934, at the age of 22, he was graduated and appointed an assistant instructor at Chinghua.

Wu Han advanced rapidly in the academic world before the Japanese invasion forced the universities to flee to Kunming in Yunnan Province in the far southwest in 1938. There, China's first-rank universities combined to form the Southwest United University. By this time Wu Han was a senior member of the History Department—but, he recalled, he lived in a half-ruined house next to a small, noisy market. The window frames were covered with torn paper, and the blue sky showed through

---

* The family's portable bank account, in the manner of many peasants who prefer to invest their wealth in tangible gold and silver bangles for their women rather than trust intangible figures on paper.

the cracks in the roof. The structure was crumbling around him. Bits of plaster occasionally dropped into his rice bowl. One of his greatest trials in 1943 and 1944 was the leaky bucket of the well which was his only source of water. It was so battered that half the time it came up empty—and one day it came up with no bottom at all.

While teaching, studying, writing, and doing most of the housework for his ailing wife, Wu Han operated an "underground" printing press. He published banned books like *On the New Democracy* and *On Coalition Government,* both by Mao Tse-tung, and *The War in the Liberated Areas* by Generalissimo Chu Teh. Since he had also organized a secret pro-Communist discussion and propaganda group, he considered himself "a good revolutionary." Yet he later confessed in his compulsory "self-examination" that he had retained a "bourgeois view of the world." He apparently did not realize that manual labor ennobled the intellectual, teaching him the "proletarian world-view" so that he could become "one with the proletariat." To the contrary, he resented the time menial tasks took from his studies and his political work.

Regardless of the state of his soul, Wu Han's political activities served the Communists. He was even more useful when he returned to Peking in 1946 as chairman of the History Department of Chinghua University. A committed activist by 1947, he fled from Nationalist arrest, traveling secretly to Yenan. Thus he openly declared his allegiance to the Communist cause.

Prevailed upon by Mao Tse-tung after the Communist conquest, Wu Han became convinced that he must dedicate himself to the "great affairs of state" instead of to scholarship. He was a model functionary. "Between attending meetings and dealing with administrative matters," he wrote, "I reached a point where my day was so full that, by evening, when I had a bit of free time, I was totally exhausted. Since I was too tired to know what I was doing, the evening and night passed without study."

On the rare occasions when his two young children found him at home, they would beg him to tell them well-loved and well-remembered stories. One night he was so tired that his memory failed completely and the children had to finish the story for him.

Perhaps it was the same night, he mused later, that he had written a letter to his old friend, the dramatist Tien Han, also to be pilloried by the Maoists. Deciding to deliver the letter himself, Wu Han looked at the address he had copied from his address book. He found he had not only miswritten the characters but had mistaken the street. Carrying the letter in his hand, he spent several hours hunting for the house, whose location he knew almost as well as his own. If exhaustion was the mark of a good Communist official, Wu Han was outstanding indeed.

In 1959, his life again changed completely. He once again began writing prolifically; but in none of his subsequent "self-examinations" did he explain this abrupt reversion, though in retrospect, the reason appears clear.

Wu Han had truly worked hard for the cause, traveling to Moscow and Berlin for Communist conferences and serving on "international friendship associations," which were conduits for Chinese propaganda abroad. His offices were many, and his services to Mao Tse-tung were great. In 1957 the tide turned against the "rightists," members of the various "democratic parties," which, in theory, participated in the "coalition government." Those "democratic personages" were foolish enough to offer honest criticism—at Mao Tse-tung's own invitation to "let a hundred flowers blossom." By that time a loyal member of the Communist Party, Wu Han was in the forefront of the counterattack ordered by the Chairman. The freedom of comment for which he had fought Nationalist suppression apparently no longer mattered to him.

He had accepted another absolute standard: the will of the Communist Party. He was vociferous and skillful in excusing Maoist repression. He wrote:

> My own attitude toward these men [the "rightists"] is entirely different from that of their defenders. I am opposed to them chiefly because their attitudes have attempted to dispense with and to destroy the leadership of the Communist Party—and, because they have opposed the Socialist direction of events. We must consider all incorrect opinions from the viewpoint of the masses, and we must criticise them thoroughly. *All* expressions of opinion which violate the standards of Socialism are wholly false.

Wu Han thus explicitly sacrificed both scholarly objectivity and political morality. He recognized only one truth—the truth, however inconsistent, expressed by Chairman Mao and the Party center.

This total devotion endured through March of the critical year 1959, when Wu Han wholeheartedly entered a literary controversy to defend the orthodox Maoist position. The details were obscure and involved. But the issue was clear, for it touched upon the infallibility of Mao Tse-tung. The Chairman had published an essay praising Tsao Tsao, the archetypical villain of Chinese history. Wu Han's defense of Mao's position uncannily foreshadowed the defense he was to offer almost seven years later on his own behalf.

Wu Han asserted that the Tsao Tsao of history and the Tsao Tsao of art—that is, the man who was the embodiment of evil to traditional China—were two entirely different persons. The traditional image of

Tsao Tsao projected through the centuries by artists and Confucian historians might endure. Nevertheless, Chairman Mao was wholly justified in praising the actual Tsao Tsao, the real historical figure the Chairman had discovered beneath the debris of centuries of calumny. That historical Tsao Tsao had truly served China, despite his later reputation for treachery. Nowhere did Wu Han publicly reflect upon the Chairman's curious affinity for the Machiavellian intriguer who had conquered a dynasty.

Wu Han's transformation from slavish apologist for the Chairman to subtle critic came in the three months preceding the Mount Lu Plenum. In March 1959, he justified Mao's praise of Tsao Tsao. In June 1959, he began writing about Hai Jui. The subject was delicate and provocative, though Great General Peng Teh-huai had not yet been openly identified with that "upright mandarin." Wu Han's abrupt transformation has never been fully explained, in part because most of the available information comes from Maoist sources.

It may have been opportunism. In June 1959, the Chairman's star appeared to be falling. Yet Wu Han was not primarily an opportunist or a careerist. Perhaps the Party's intellectual paladin could finally no longer deceive himself. Perhaps his "proletarian consciousness," so painfully acquired on the Chairman's direct orders, could no longer explain away Maoist excesses. He saw all around him the disastrous effects of the Great Leap Forward and the Great People's Communes on the Chinese economy—and the consequent suffering inflicted on the Chinese people. Perhaps the man who had been an honest liberal could no longer stomach the outright lies and the distortions of both present and past reality he was required to endorse.

The precipitating factor may have been a sudden combination of all three elements. In any event, Wu Han's abrupt reversal was characteristic of the mercurial temperament of the Chinese intellectual. After June 1959 his writing consistently protested the Maoist course toward disaster. His meaning was barely veiled by allegory—certainly because he had been assured of protection from on high.

By no coincidence, scores of other writers soon joined in relaying the same message to the Chinese people. Their protests were encouraged by the senior hierarchs, who felt, along with Great General Peng Teh-huai, that Mao Tse-tung *might* remain, but his fantasies *must* be restrained. Protected by powerful "senior cadres," the suppressed writers of China spoke up. From 1959 to 1965, oblique attacks on Maoism were the mainstream of serious Chinese writing. The message was obscure to outsiders, but quite clear to Chinese readers. The Chairman was systematically—if indirectly—ridiculed by the Communist press.

The Maoists' initial response was slow, for their enemies controlled the propaganda apparatus. But they remembered only too well that the Hungarian Revolution had begun in the Petöfi Writers' Club. Feeling power slipping from their fingers, they finally concluded that only Draconic measures could recoup their position. The "bombardment" of Wu Han—and all that he represented—in late 1965 was the first barrage of the Maoist counterattack. On January 1, 1966, the Maoist-controlled ideological journal *Red Flag* thundered that Chinese society "must be reorganized in every respect" in the coming year.

The Furies remained muted, but the conflict within the Communist Party of China which led to the Great Proletarian Cultural Revolution had begun. The non-Maoists, who also controlled the legal Party apparatus, were slow in manning their defenses. Even when the opposition mounted sallies to spoil the Maoist counterattack, it was still complacent. The non-Maoists were apparently convinced that the battle would be short and their final victory certain.

VIII

The Mayor at Bay

If Wu Han's had been a lone voice crying against injustice, the Maoists would still have discerned a vast conspiracy. They could not believe that one Quixotic individual would tilt alone against the Great Wall of authority. Even if Wu Han's sudden obsession with Hai Jui had not coincided with the revolt of Great General Peng Teh-huai, the Maoists would have sensed a plot. Like medieval inquisitors, they could smell out heresy—even where it did not exist. They could even create heresy by altering doctrine after the protestant had revealed his soul. They could not acknowledge to themselves that a single brave man might be compelled by conscience to speak out. Open heresy could only prove that the "bourgeois class enemies" were "in collusion to restore capitalism."

Because they themselves used literature solely to manipulate the people, the Maoists were convinced that their enemies were attempting to "alter the climate of public opinion in order to prepare the masses for the recrudescence of capitalism." By Maoist definition—which differs significantly from Marxist definition—all art directly reflects social turmoil. Every play, essay, or novel was therefore a fusillade in the "class war." All previous literary inquisitions had revealed the machination of the Maoists' own particular devil, "the class enemy." Bourgeois conspirators had invariably been uncovered, invariably seeking to overthrow "proletarian power" with their pens.

Wu Han hardly put the Maoists to the trouble of inventing a conspiracy. He was chosen as the initial target of their cultural counterattack because he was most prominent among the writers who questioned Maoism and its policies. His political associations and his numerous sympathizers demonstrated that he was no solitary protestant.

106

Exacerbated by personal rivalry, differences regarding policy had spawned a non-Maoist force within the Political Bureau. The nucleus was Peng Chen, Mayor of Peking, and Wu Han, his vice mayor. Peng Chen was First Secretary of the Peking Municipal Committee of the Communist Party; Wu Han was a subordinate secretary. The Mayor was director of all cultural activities; Wu Han was a prominent intellectual "activist." Peng Chen was, further, eighth in rank in the Political Bureau and was one of four chief aspirants to succeed the Chairman. The others were Comrade Liu Shao-chi; Premier Chou En-lai; and Field Marshal Lin Piao.

Peng Chen came from the northern province of Shansi, noted for its canny mule traders and its yellow *loess* soil, scarred with hundred-foot-deep ravines worn by erosion and cartwheels. The Mayor was, with less affection, sometimes also called the Medieval Hero because he displayed a striking affinity for a semi-feudal epoch. He was tall, burly, and vigorous, the image of the figure Westerners call a "typical northern Chinese." His big, square face, with its generous nose, was frank and open beneath a receding hairline. He had spent most of his adult life in the shadow world of "underground" conspiracy.

In early 1966, while attacks on Wu Han and the "literary black gang" mounted, the 64-year-old Mayor was at the height of his power. Ruling not only his "independent fief" of Peking but also the North China Region, he dominated literature, education, the graphic arts, and the drama—indeed all "culture." His nominees controlled the Propaganda Bureau of the Central Committee, which, in turn, controlled every organ of the press, the radio, the stage, the schools, and the cinema. He was answerable only to Comrade Liu Shao-chi and Chairman Mao Tse-tung.

Even if Peng Chen had not been Mayor of Peking and, *ex officio*, publisher of the capital's newspapers that obliquely criticized Maoism, the attack on his deputy would have been ominous. Ultimately the Mayor was responsible for *all* propaganda, including *The Peking People's Daily*, the organ of the Central Committee. Moreover, Wu Han was his man—as was the Young Editor, Teng To. Shooting at the playwright Wu Han and, shortly thereafter, at the satirists, the Maoists were clearly aiming at the Mayor. They attacked him in public only as "the behind-the-scenes leader of the anti-Party black gang" because the rigid etiquette of Chinese purges reserved identification by name until the miscreant had been thoroughly discredited.

The Maoists charged in the Party's closed sessions that Peng Chen—backed, they implied, by Comrade Liu Shao-chi—had organized a great conspiracy "to overthrow Socialism and restore capitalism." The accusation was far-fetched, but the Mayor and his followers had undeniably extended their power and implemented non-Maoist policies. Contending over policy, the hierarchs staked their personal careers. Abstract differences regarding policy became stark conflicts for individual survival, and the bayonets of personal animosity were drawn from the concealing scabbards of ideology. Peng Chen, of course, realized how hazardous it was to encourage his publicists to ridicule the Chairman. Having come to power as much by the word as by the gun, the Communists respected and feared the power of the word.

Though they appear complacent in retrospect, the Mayor's coterie had every reason for self-satisfaction at the beginning of 1966. The catastrophies wrought by Maoism had been largely reclaimed, and the Maoists' weapons had been blunted. However the Maoists fulminated, the practical men felt they held actual power through their legitimate control of the Party apparatus. Bemused by "Socialist legality," the non-Maoists therefore responded negligently to the first challenge. They behaved like independent princes who held impregnable positions, rather than an insurgent minority called to account by their acknowledged master.

On February 3, 1966, the Mayor mounted his defense by convening the Group of Five Directing the Cultural Revolution, a new body created to oversee a new movement, on the surface little different from the innumerable "campaigns" that had shaken China since 1949. The term "Cultural Revolution" was then unknown to the general public, which was still tormented by two continuing Ideological Rectification campaigns. The great mass of cadres heard of the Cultural Revolution for the first time when they received the directive promulgated to the entire Party by the Group of Five on February 7, 1966.

The Mayor's directives, called the *February Theses,* vividly demonstrated how circumstantially mortal battles for power begin in the tortuous milieu of Marxist theology. Neither side could foresee the outcome. The debate within the Communist Party over the "two lines" had surged and ebbed ever since the Mount Lu Plenum, and the non-Maoist pragmatists had usually emerged victorious.

The Maoists obviously possessed a clearer appreciation of the coming battle. They observed that the Literary Assassin's attack on Wu Han "signaled the imminent emergence of China's Great Proletarian Cultural Revolution." They further ascribed* remarkable prescience to the Mayor and his adherents:

> Because of their keen counterrevolutionary sense of smell, the handful of top Party persons in authority taking the capitalist road [Comrade Liu Shao-chi and the Organizer, Teng Hsiao-ping] and the Peng Chen

* In an article in *The People's Daily* of June 11, 1966, signed "Jen Li-hsin." Often attributed without proof to Chairman Mao himself, the pseudonym at the very least carried high authority.

counterrevolutionary revisionist clique felt a foreboding that the torrents of the Great Proletarian Cultural Revolution pouring across the entire country would sweep over the positions they occupied in the fields of ideology and culture. That group was fearful of losing its hold on the crucial centers of power—Party and governmental power, financial and cultural power. They were afraid that their dream of restoring capitalism would be shattered once and for all. Therefore, the article by Comrade Yao Wen-yüan caused Peng Chen, the Party tyrant, to explode with anger.

Peng Chen had deeply resented the Assassin's attack on Wu Han in the organ of the Communist Party's Shanghai Municipal Committee, *Wen Hui Pao.* He reprimanded the leftists for violating Party discipline by "failing to consult the Propaganda Bureau of the CCP Central Committee." He was technically correct.

"Wu Han is now very nervous," the Mayor was informed. "He knows that this criticism and repudiation have strong backing." Peng Chen reportedly replied with anger: "Never mind where it comes from. To hell with it. I am only interested in the truth. Everyone is equal before the truth."

The Mayor's self-righteousness had overcome his misgivings, although he sensed that Chairman Mao himself was the "strong backing" his enemies invoked. His calm riposte in February was couched in the ritualistic language of Party polemics. While it ignited the terrible battle for the control of China, the initial debate was abstract. The *February Theses* addressed themselves to "the problem of academic criticism." The Maoists had charged Vice Mayor Wu Han with specific literary and historical errors, and his champions were content to fight on the same narrow front. They hoped to blunt the attack by feigning compliance with the Maoist line. They hoped to divert the assault from the true citadels of their power by pretending that the controversy was scholarly and aesthetic rather than political.

The *February Theses* therefore acknowledged that China "was engaged in a gigantic struggle in the *ideological* sphere between Marxism-Leninism and the Thought of Mao Tse-tung, on the one hand, and bourgeois ideas, on the other." But the non-Maoists did not rush to the confrontation. They sought to contain the "gigantic struggle" by ordering it "carried out *under close direction,* seriously, positively, and prudently . . . over an extended period of time." * Delaying tactics had, they knew, often triumphed in the past.

The Mayor also sought to muddle the issues by citing Chairman

* Emphasis supplied.

Mao's "doctrine of opening wide to all opinions," and he asserted: "Without construction, there can be no destruction!"—an inversion of the Maoists' declaration, "There can be no construction without destruction!"

The non-Maoist rebuttal subtly appealed to the "working cadres," who preferred reason to dogma because they had known the frustration of enforcing unenforceable Maoist policies. The non-Maoists, in addition, attempted to muster the pragmatic cadres against the extremists by ordering all Party units to organize new executive organs under moderate control. The *February Theses* were the last full statement of the moderate views dominant within the Communist Party from 1961 to 1965. Believing they had brought the old tiger to bay, the non-Maoists behaved as if mere ritual obeisance to the Chairman's pre-eminence would suffice. The *Theses* repeatedly stressed "gradual reform" rather than headlong change and technical expertise rather than ideological purity. "We must," they asserted, "beat the other side not only politically, but must surpass them by a wide margin *academically and professionally.*"*

The directive was a remarkable display of political prestidigitation by men assigned to plan their own destruction. They tried to allay the threat by "reserving for future discussion" those divergent opinions that might remain "unresolved" after peaceful debate. In naïve hope of diverting the storm, Article 4 directed comrades "not to attack each other." The Maoists had, of course, already launched their attack.

The non-Maoists' defensive strategy was outlined in the *February Theses* in two parts—a general survey of China's culture problems was followed by specific instructions.

"The criticism of Wu Han's *Hai Jui's Dismissal From Office* and the resultant discussions . . . on the appraisal of historical figures and viewpoints and methods of historical research have accomplished much by enlivening thinking—and by lifting the curtain [on the intra-Party controversies]."

China, the appraisal declared, was engaged in a "struggle in the *academic* sphere to eliminate bourgeois, reactionary, and mistaken ideas. . . ." Recognizing that "this large-scale debate is bound to spread to all *academic* spheres," the *Theses* emphasised: "While studying and struggling simultaneously, we must train a red-and-expert academic force and *gradually and systematically* solve all problems in this area." It was, the non-Maoists stressed, necessary to "take adequate account of the *duration, complexity, and enormity* of this struggle. . . . We should seriously

* Emphasis supplied.

and uninterruptedly persevere in this struggle for a *prolonged* period of time." *

The non-Maoists quoted Holy Writ voluminously. The Chairman, they noted, had in 1957 called for: "Full expression of all kinds of opinions, including anti-Marxist opinion—so that, in the course of the struggle between contradictions and by putting facts on the table and reasoning things out, reactionary and mistaken ideas may be analysed and criticised, truly refuted and destroyed."

The opposition thus perfected the techniques of evasion that became a high art during the Cultural Revolution, citing Mao's words to justify anti-Maoist actions.

"We must insist on seeking truth in the facts themselves," the Mayor's *Theses* asserted tendentiously on the basis of Mao's own directive, "and we must uphold the principle that everyone is equal before the truth. We must convince the people with facts. We must not behave like scholar-tyrants who act arbitrarily and try to overwhelm people by power alone."

Seeking survival and ultimate triumph through apparent compromise, the *February Theses* directed "the gradual reform of old intellectuals," re-education, rather than elimination. "We must welcome those who have made mistakes and even those who still cling to reactionary academic viewpoints. . . . We must permit them to correct their mistakes. We must solemnly resolve to act leniently." The jargon hardly veiled a startling appeal for freedom of thought and expression.

Regarding men like Wu Han who treat history from a bourgeois view of the world [*Weltanschauung*] and have committed political mistakes, discussion in the press should *not be confined to political matters,* but should go fully into the various *academic and theoretical* questions involved.** If opinions still differ at the end of the discussion, they should be shelved for discussion in the future.

The press should exercise great care in naming those selected for major criticism. If they are prominent men, the responsible leading bodies [of the Party] must first approve. Actors who have performed in bad plays must, for example, not be asked to make public self-criticism in the press during the present controversy. Their mistakes may be solved on later occasions.

---

* The curious language is the Communists' own translation into English, though I have supplied emphasis.

** The Maoists sought a direct *political* confrontation, while the non-Maoists sought to transform the confrontation into an *intellectual* debate.

All Communist Party units were ordered in Peng's *Theses* to "organize forces of revolutionary academic workers . . . to engage in struggle and construction at the same time." The *Theses* warned against excessive stringency in "thought-remolding" and ordered formation of "mutual aid teams and co-operatives of academic workers of the left" to conduct the Cultural Revolution.

The summation elaborately justified the conciliatory approach:

> Even some men who have demonstrated by their performance through decades that they are staunch revolutionary leftists could not avoid making occasional erroneous statements or committing a few big or small mistakes on certain issues—because they had not totally eliminated their old ideas—or because they possessed incomplete understanding of the problems involved. . . . Such revolutionaries may be assisted by study and rectification to set their thinking in order and to distinguish right from wrong, thus enhancing their resistance to error. When they correct their past mistakes, they will be all right. . . . They must not grapple with each other. Mutual attacks would only hamper our forces' *scholarly criticism** of the bourgeoisie and their own self-improvement.

The Mayor thus ordered defensive action he judged appropriate to the threat. But in the process he committed several major strategic errors because he failed to appreciate the Chairman's determination and vindictiveness.

"The key point in *Hai Jui's Dismissal From Office*," Mao had already observed in December 1965, "is the question of dismissal from office. The Ming Emperor dismissed Hai Jui from office, and in 1959, we dismissed Peng Teh-huai from office. Peng Teh-huai is also a Hai Jui."

The Mayor did not repudiate Wu Han, but merely reprimanded him —and expressed confidence that Wu Han would reform. He planned to placate the Maoists with offhand reassurances, as if they were but importunate children. He acted as if the extreme left posed no real threat. He treated Mao Tse-tung as if he were already a spent force. Above all, he underestimated the boundless ambition of the Disciple Lin Piao.

The Mayor's own character probably hindered his appreciation of the Master and the Disciple, who lived as much for the struggle as for the victory. Having finally matured under responsibility, Peng Chen could not understand men perpetually dissatisfied with peace. Like his mentor, Comrade Liu Shao-chi, the Mayor came from a different milieu. Like Comrade Shao-chi, he was essentially a civilian. He knew the secret

* Emphasis supplied.

apparatus of the cities rather than the "armed struggle in the country-side" which obsessed Mao Tse-tung. The Mayor's reaction to the assault upon his protégés revealed generous loyalty, simplistic confidence in the ill-defined concept of "Socialist legality"—and a touch of *hubris*.

Peng Chen's refusal to turn his back on Wu Han was, perhaps, commendable. It was not wise. He should have learned more of the art and the necessity of self-preservation from his own long experience in a political movement so often characterized by fratricidal betrayal. He erred even more deeply by expecting his own sponsor, Comrade Liu Shao-chi, to protect him as he had protected his subordinates. Yet, in February 1966, Peng Chen had every human and political reason to count upon Comrade Shao-chi's loyal support. They had worked in intimate association for more than three decades. The Chairman of the People's Republic had been the chief catalyst in the transformation of the son of a poor Shansi farmer into a Communist potentate.

Peng Chen's avid quest for education had been hampered by his family's poverty and by political turmoil. He was ten years old when the Republic of China was proclaimed in 1912. He was 20 years old in 1922, when he finally graduated from higher-primary school, having been exposed to six years of elementary education that should normally have been completed at the age of 12. Even given the disruption in China's educational system under the warlords, he should have finished the course when he was no older than 16. Thereafter, he progressed rapidly through a new "normal school," which offered an incongruous mixture of modern and traditional courses. After this brief and desultory education, he became a teacher in a Shansi primary school.

Even before graduation, Peng Chen had taken two decisive steps. He had married a young girl from his native village, a match arranged by his parents in the traditional manner. More important for his future, he had joined the fledgling Socialist Youth League in 1923. The course of his life was fixed. By 1926 he was a member of the Communist Party. He began his lifelong association with North China when he was as-signed to Tientsin, the chief port of the region, 65 miles from Peking. He later served briefly elsewhere, but North China dominated his career until his downfall.

In 1927 Peng suffered his first serious emotional blow. His wife died the painful and undignified death of dysentery. He pursued an arduous and bleak existence, solaced only by his immersion in Party work and the vision of the bright future he and his comrades would create. The attractive second wife he took a few years later was a "female comrade," who eventually became deputy chairman of the Peking Municipal Women's Association.

The Mayor-to-be had demonstrated his talents as an agitator among students and workers of Taiyüan, the capital of Shansi. At the same time, Comrade Shao-chi was serving as a labor organizer in the coal mines of central Kiangsi Province. It sounded very impressive to be secretary of the Taiyüan Workers' Union while in one's early 20s, even if the position was strenuous and frustrating and carried little real power. Nonetheless, their positions placed Peng Chen and Liu Shao-chi in the mainstream of a Communist movement which concentrated on the industrial proletariat. The Chinese Party Center obeyed directives issued by a Comintern that neither understood conditions in China nor was primarily concerned with the fate of the Chinese Communist Party. Moscow placed its stake on the Nationalists, reorganized into a disciplined, totalitarian party by Comintern advisers. Since Moscow's scenario called for using the Nationalists and then "casting them aside like a squeezed lemon," the Communists were forced to cooperate with Chiang Kai-shek. But the Nationalists squeezed first, outlawing and dispersing the Communists.

In 1928, after Communist ranks had been scythed by Nationalist persecution and internal purges, Peng Chen was abruptly appointed to the Party's clandestine Hopei Provincial Committee. He once more found himself operating in the Tientsin-Peking area, after having been diverted by the brief Nationalist-Communist alliance.

Since senior Communists in the North had been eliminated by Nationalist repression, Liu Shao-chi was sent to North China to rebuild the dispirited, disorganized Party apparatus. There, in 1929, the two men first entered into an intimate association which would endure until they were both purged.

Comrade Shao-chi, too, had suffered personal distress. He had, a few years earlier, married the daughter of an elder statesman of the Party. Finding life with the humorless Iron Bolshevik arduous and joyless, Mrs. Liu had diverted herself with extra-marital affairs and finally had eloped with her lover. Liu Shao-chi despaired. As a Chinese chronicler remarked, "Myriad bitterness beset his soul, and he talked constantly about suicide." Impressed into service as a go-between, the family friend Peng Chen brought the couple back together through cajolery and threats.

The political landscape in the late twenties was clouded by Moscow's preoccupation with the purge of Trotskyites—and by the C.C.P.'s disunity. Li Li-san, director of the Chinese Organization Bureau, therefore sent Chou En-lai to Tientsin to reorganize the North China Bureau. In late 1929, Comrade Liu Shao-chi was posted to Harbin as First Secretary of the Manchurian Party Bureau, while Peng Chen was given orders to revive the labor movement. He expressed his enthusiasm in words that foreshadowed the slogans of the Cultural Revolution: "We must all go down among the working masses in order to learn what is essential. All intellectuals should pass through 'proletarian transformation.' "

The Mayor's opportunity for "proletarian transformation" was brief. In 1930 he was arrested for murder. The deposed First Secretary of the reorganized Hopei Provincial Committee had refused to accept Party discipline, and his followers incited the rank-and-file to revolt against the new leadership. Formally sentenced to "liquidation" by the new Provincial Committee, two rebels were shot outside a church in the French Concession of Tientsin. The leaders' widows denounced the killers. Peng Chen was arrested along with other leaders of the Hopei Committee—though they had sent professional executioners to do the deed.

Peng was sentenced to serve "10 years or more" in the Western District Prison of Tientsin. Conditions were hardly arduous, while security was quite lax. Nationalist sources admit that Peng Chen directed Communist subversion from his cell. He was, moreover, released in 1935, with at least five years still to serve. The Maoists later tried to link his release to a group, acting under Comrade Shao-chi's instructions, who had escaped their cells by formally repudiating Marxism so that they could serve the Communist cause at liberty. Whether he compromised with the Nationalists or simply bribed his way out, Peng Chen emerged from five years' imprisonment utterly dedicated to the cause and still vigorous. He was a big man, and he possessed a big man's strength.

Peng Chen renewed his intimate association with Comrade Liu Shao-chi—once again First Secretary of the North China Bureau—as if the five years had been a fleeting interval. Peng became director of the Organization Section specially charged to develop the "student movement." Both Peng and Liu were active on various campuses in Peking, easily evading the lax surveillance of the Nationalist Special Police. A medical student at Peking University later recalled that he knew their faces well in 1935 and 1936 "because they were always around the campus." But he did not know who they were until the pair stood forth in their true identities during the second period of Nationalist-Communist cooperation against the Japanese.

Peng Chen hastened that cooperation. The Japanese were pressing to wrest control of North China from a Nationalist Government that appeared quiescent, though it was perhaps playing for time. The impatient Communists feared that Japanese conquest would impede their own ultimate conquest of power. "Foreign imperialism" was, in their eyes, an even more formidable opponent than the regime of Generalissimo Chiang Kai-shek. They therefore sought to enhance their own power legitimately—and counter the Japanese threat—by making common cause with the Nationalists. On December 9, 1936, the students of Peking demonstrated in the streets, shouting prepared slogans: DESTROY

JAPANESE IMPERIALISM! END THE CIVIL WAR BETWEEN THE COMMUNISTS AND THE NATIONALISTS! WE OPPOSE A DIVIDED LEADERSHIP!

Peng Chen had organized the "spontaneous" demonstrations in Peking and the itinerant "Chinese People's Liberation Vanguard," which awakened opinion by staging demonstrations throughout the country. Describing the December Ninth Movement for an audience of Peking youth 13 years later, he made much of his own deeds:

> At that time, the reactionary Nationalist government and the Japanese imperialists had already concluded a treaty which sold out China. The Nationalist army and the Nationalist Party had already withdrawn from the northern provinces, and T. V. Soong [Chiang Kai-shek's brother-in-law, who was a power in South China] had already asked, "If Chiang Kai-shek can sell out, why can't I do the same?" But two great forces were operating to change the history of China. Together, they frustrated the Nationalist policy of capitulation. Those forces were: the Chinese Red Army's Long March of 25,000 *li* [8,000 miles] from Kiangsi to Shensi to build a new base to oppose the Japanese—and the December Ninth Student Movement, which aroused the masses of the entire nation in a general campaign to OPPOSE JAPAN AND SAVE THE NATION.

Peng's *hubris* here led him into major error. He was unwise to equate his success in the pacific student movement with the Chairman's triumphant leadership of the Red Army's *Anabasis*. His words were duly noted—to be later used against him. The Mayor compounded his error. He failed to render the mandatory absolute adulation to Mao Tse-tung, and he implicitly denigrated the Chairman's "class background." In 1949 he told the Peking audience:

> Some people say that Mao Tse-tung is an intellectual sprung of the intellectual classes—and that, therefore, our revolution was led by an "intellectual element." The first part of that statement is correct, but the second is wrong. It is correct that Chairman Mao is an "intellectual element," but that does *not* mean that the "intellectual element" is capable of leading the revolution. . . . Chairman Mao is an intellectual who has united with the workers and peasants. He is an intellectual who arose armed with Marxism-Leninism. He is the vanguard of the proletariat. He is not an "intellectual element" who belongs to any class other than the proletariat. We must study Chairman Mao and, above all, we must study his own "proletarianization," his theories, and his Sinicized Marxism-Leninism.

A decade and a half of "arduous struggle" lay between Peng Chen's first great success with the December Ninth Movement of 1936 and his indiscreet speech in November 1949, shortly after the proclamation of the People's Republic of China. They were hard years, but they were happy years of ambition finding fullfillment. Distinguished by his role in the December Ninth Movement and by the friendship of Liu Shao-chi, Peng Chen became First Secretary of the North China Bureau in 1939, when Comrade Shao-chi was transferred. He still struggled in the "underground," directing subversion, propaganda, and passive resistance in the areas under Japanese occupation. In 1941, an intra-Party clash bestowed further power on the rising leader, who was already attracting his own devoted following—*the* essential to greater power.

The Lord High Executioner Kang Sheng, the Communists' director of intelligence, was relieved in 1941 as deputy principal of the Central Party Academy in Yenan, the guerrilla capital. The Executioner lost his job because he would not base the entire curriculum on the Thought of Mao Tse-tung. Just beginning to reveal his overwhelming narcissism, Mao had determined that *his* revolution should do reverence to both his person and his transcendent doctrines. Kang Sheng refused to displace orthodox Marxism-Leninism with "Mao Thought."

On Comrade Shao-chi's recommendation, Principal Mao Tse-tung gave the vacant post to Peng Chen, who enjoyed great independence. Mao Tse-tung, consolidating his absolute power, left day-to-day administration of the Party Academy to his deputy. Thus Peng was responsible for training the new generation of Communist leaders. He gladly catered to the Chairman's obsessions.

Nonetheless, the Executioner Kang Sheng proved an adept professional survivor. When the Cultural Revolution sanctified the Thought of Mao Tse-tung, Kang Sheng was a stalwart of the dwindling Maoist clique, while the orginally pliable Peng Chen was finally condemned to oblivion.

In 1941, however, the future Mayor appeared secure from the enmity of the man he had displaced. Mao at that point sought civilian leaders to balance the power of his semi-autonomous generals, and Peng Chen answered his needs.

As deputy principal of the Party Academy, the future Mayor supervised the intensive indoctrination of future Communist leaders. He controlled the Lu Hsün Academy of Art, named for China's foremost contemporary writer, and several other vital schools. His devoted following increased steadily, and he was gradually consolidating his control over propaganda, literature, and the arts.

In 1942, Peng Chen's group of "cultural activists" responded with alacrity to the Chairman's command to "order the winds" and reform all Communist thinking. The Thought of Mao Tse-tung was made the sacred canon of the Party, and Peng Chen was among its chief propagators. All heretical thought was to be crushed by the Rectification Campaign, and Peng Chen was chief among the inquisitors.

Peng's overweening pride was nurtured by his rapid advancement. In 1945, shortly before the Japanese surrender, the Seventh National Congress of the Communist Party formally confirmed Peng Chen's membership in the Central Committee. His next appointment clearly designated him one of the most important figures in the movement. He was named First Secretary of the Northeast (Manchurian) Bureau, a vital position his mentor, Comrade Liu Shao-chi, had held earlier. Altered political conditions made the post much more important than Peng's previous First Secretaryship of the North China Bureau. Since the Communists were massing their armies for the final assault on the Nationalist regime, the regional bureaus were major power centers, rather than the mere coordinators of subversion they had been in the 1930s. Moreover, Manchuria, China's major industrial complex, was critical to the Communists' grand strategy. Supported by the Russian occupation forces, the Chinese used the Northeast as the base for the conquest of all China.

Despite the post's immense prestige, the immense responsibility it entailed proved a stumbling block rather than a stepping stone for Peng Chen. The circumstances of his appointment awakened the enmity of powerful rivals. Mao Tse-tung was determined that the broad Manchurian plains should prove his strategy of first winning over the peasantry by "land reform" and then "encircling" the enemy-held cities from the Communist-held countryside. The Chairman originally wished to award the First Secretaryship to Kao Kang, a native of rural Yenan who had already proved himself among the peasantry. Urged by the persistence of Comrade Liu Shao-chi, Mao Tse-tung finally agreed that Peng Chen was instead the man for the task. Kao Kang became his deputy.

Mao, however, rejected Comrade Shao-chi's recommendation that Peng Chen also be appointed Political Commissar of the Manchurian Democratic Allied Armies, which were then under the command of Lin Piao. Instead, Lin Piao was made both Commander-in-Chief and Political Commissar. The Mayor was technically the superior, since the Party Bureau formally controlled the military. Therefore, the appointment aroused the enmity of both Kao Kang and Lin Piao. Although Kao Kang fell from grace and reportedly committed suicide a few years later, the Disciple Lin Piao cherished his grudge. In 1966, he presided with relish over the Mayor's degradation.

The task, inauspiciously begun, moved rapidly toward disaster. Peng Chen was required to transform Manchuria into a military base. He concentrated on the "proletariat" of cities half-stripped of their industrial plant by Russian looting. He enjoyed little success, harassed as he was by uncertain Russian cooperation and the cities' occupation by Nationalist troops arriving in American airplanes. In the countryside, "land reform" was largely neglected, even though it was the Chairman's obsession. Peng Chen provided a sufficiency of neither recruits nor food for the Communist troops.

Kao Kang drove the stiletto into his chief's vulnerable back in a formal report to the Political Bureau:

> Our work in Manchuria must immediately change its entire emphasis. We must deeply penetrate the rural areas and arouse the rural masses. By thorough-going "land reform" we can vastly increase our source of troops. Our leading cadres must vacate their quarters in comfortable foreign-style buildings. They must, indeed, get out of the cities entirely. They must alight from the railroad carriages, take off their foreign-style leather shoes, don Chinese-style cloth shoes, and go into the villages.

Since he had failed to "establish a secure base in rural Manchuria," Peng Chen was relieved of his post. His eclipse was brief. In 1948 he was appointed deputy chief of the Organization Bureau of the Central Committee. Comrade Liu Shao-chi was the chief of the Bureau, whose function was to control, strengthen, and enlarge the Party's ranks.

After the establishment of the People's Republic in 1949, the Mayor's star again rose rapidly. He became Vice Premier for Politics and Law, directing all the pertinent ministries, and First Secretary of the Peking Municipal Committee of the Party. In June 1950, he was raised to the Political Bureau, the inner circle of 21 that ruled China. In March 1951, he became Mayor of Peking and Vice Chairman of the Oppose-America Assist-Korea Association, which rallied support and funds for the "Chinese People's Volunteers" fighting in Korea. Again under Comrade Liu Shao-chi as chairman, Peng Chen was a leading member of the Chinese delegation to ceremonies that year in Moscow which marked the anniversary of the October Revolution in the same year.

Peng once again became First Secretary of the North China Bureau, in 1956 when the regional bureaus of the Communist Party—abolished when the People's Republic was set up—were reactivated to check the power of the semi-autonomous generals. When the Eighth National Congress of the Chinese Communist Party met in September 1956, the Mayor was appointed Secretary of the Secretariat, the body responsible for day-to-day administration.

He also became a world traveler, making state visits to the Soviet Union, Eastern Europe, North Korea, and North Vietnam. He ventured into the non-Communist world to attend ceremonies celebrating the forty-fifth anniversary of the Communist Party of Indonesia in Djakarta in May 1965. Demonstrating his loyalty to Mao Tse-tung, the Mayor had earlier clashed with Nikita Khrushchev at an international Communist conference in Budapest in 1960.

"If Lenin could rise from his grave," the Mayor then declaimed, "he would grab by their ears all these men who are distorting his word and he would teach them how to recognize the truth of what is going on." The Mayor continued to press the Maoist view on the "revisionist" Soviet leaders during a series of visits to Moscow in company with Comrade Shao-chi and Teng Hsiao-ping, the Organizer, the last in 1962.

If his praise of Maoism was more impressive than his observance of Maoism, the Mayor's personal life was exemplary. When the time came for the ritual vilification of his character, the charges were feeble, despite extensive Maoist investigation. While citing numerous *political* crimes, the Maoists initially could only charge the Mayor with the *personal* sin of sanctioning the wasteful construction of a club for senior officials.

Casting wide, the Maoists finally found a young nurse who had looked after the Mayor. She protested that he disregarded the convenience of others because he had customarily summoned her in the early morning hours. Since most senior leaders followed Chairman Mao's own practice and worked chiefly during the night, the accusation was hardly sensational. The nurse indignantly added that the Mayor was addicted to ping-pong and card games, charges that somehow failed to horrify.

"His bed was higher than most beds in China," the nurse went on, "because of his passion for display." She recalled that the Mayor had refuted her condemnation of the Manchu Dynasty for "oppressing the masses and yielding to the imperialists." The Manchus, he had said, also remitted the onerous head tax and unified the nation.

The total effect was not quite what the Maoists sought. The nurse had portrayed a busy man who willingly conversed with a young lady whose intelligence was less than penetrating. Many Chinese might consider his condescension undignified, but good Communists could hardly condemn the Mayor for his willingness to "instruct the masses." Besides, many objective historians would agree with the Mayor's assessment of the Manchus. His real sin could not, of course, be publicized. He reasoned for himself and drew his own conclusions—in defiance of the Maoist dogma.

The Mayor's destruction was deemed essential because he was both heretical and effective. He dared to question Maoist dogma, and he rallied the non-Maoist opposition. If he survived in power the Maoists could not regain power. His influence was too great in three vital spheres: Peking and the surrounding provinces of North China; the Communist Party Apparatus; and the propaganda machinery, which shaped all men's thinking.

Moreover, external events were pressing. The timing of the first Maoist counterattack in November 1965 and the *February Theses* in

1966 definitely indicates reaction to American moves in Vietnam. The great Chinese debate on defense policy in 1965 was apparently precipitated by massive American intervention in that year. The protracted pause in the bombing of North Vietnam from Christmas 1965 through January 1966 also appears to have encouraged the extremists, who argued that American imperialism was "a paper tiger," fierce in appearance but so fragile that its claws and fangs would shred in the gales of the "people's struggle." The bombing pause allowed the Maoists to contend that the paper tiger was already dissolving amid the "winds and waves of people's war" and that Mao's thesis of "the inevitable victory of people's war" was being proved by the failure of American resolution.

Resumption of the bombing in late January, on the other hand, appears to have renewed the pragmatists' fears that Maoist foreign policy invited American attack.*

In any event, the internal struggle quickened in February 1966. The Maoists later charged that anti-Maoist field marshals had planned a military *coup d'état* in late February. The available evidence regarding a military plot to support the Mayor is obscure and inconclusive, though circumstances were undoubtedly ripe.

Defense Minister Lin Piao had worked from 1959 to 1965 to build a firm power base within the People's Liberation Army from which to attack the non-Maoists who controlled the Communist Party. Resistance within the army was led by adherents of deposed Great General Peng Teh-huai and the Bandit General Ho Lung. "Professional soldiers" argued that Maoist policies were provoking attack, while making China vulnerable by depleting her military strength. Their chief convert was the Securityman, General Lo Jui-ching, appointed chief-of-staff after Mount Lu to purge the army. Since senior field marshals were the moral basis for the resistance, the anti-Maoists *may* have responded to the Maoist counteroffensive in the winter of 1965–66 with an abortive attempt to seize Peking and North China by arms.

The non-Maoists' February riposte—political and, perhaps, military —was ineffective. The division of the Communist Party of China into a Maoist "Shanghai Center" and an anti-Maoist "Peking Center" was all but total. The Maoists were openly attacking to regain their lost power. The anti-Maoists were defending entrenched positions they considered impregnable. The Maoists pressed their assault vigorously. Lacking either a sense of imminent danger or a coordinated policy, the non-Maoists remained ineffective.

* I owe the suggestion of the connection between the bombing pause and the beginning of the Cultural Revolution to Dr. Alice Langley Hsieh. I am, however, responsible for the perhaps excessive simplification of her subtle and thoroughly documented thesis.

IX

The Starlet on Stage

Secure in their legitimate control of the Party apparatus, the Mayor's Group of Five believed it had been duly appointed to conduct the Cultural Revolution, which was still only an intra-Party debate. Neither the Chinese people nor the outside world had any idea that a Cultural Revolution was in the making. The *February Theses* were not published, nor was the devastating movement yet given its full, resounding title: the Great Proletarian Cultural Revolution. The Mayor's offhand response to the Maoist resurgence demonstrated both his ignorance of the magnitude of the threat and his overwhelming self-confidence.

Peng Chen had good reason to believe he could pigeonhole the attacks on Vice Mayor Wu Han and the Young Editor Teng To. The conference in the Western Hills outside Peking that had produced the *February Theses* of 1966 appeared to be no more than another episode in the unremitting struggle that had shaken the Communist Party since the Mount Lu Plenum. The Maoists issued sweeping decrees, but the non-Maoists interpreted them "in the light of local conditions." Real power, they seemed to feel, had already passed, leaving Chairman Mao Tse-tung an ornamental fountainhead of abstruse philosophy. The non-Maoists could not conceive that the new spasm was a serious threat to their entrenched positions and "legal" power.

But the counterattack became a major threat to their vulnerable flanks when the People's Liberation Army entered the fray. On New Year's Day, 1966, the chief political commissar had raked the *status quo* in *Red Flag,* the Party's ideological journal, demanding total reform of the regime. "All bourgeois influence must be extirpated," he had warned. The threat of the gun had altered the battle of words.

122

A new alliance entered that battle. The Disciple Lin Piao found a puissant—and most unlikely—ally in the Starlet Chiang Ching, who directed the Forum on Literature and Art in the Liberation Army in February 1966 in Shanghai. Ostensibly a discussion on ideology and art, the 18-day Forum actually drafted the operational orders for the Great Proletarian Cultural Revolution. Literature and art were the first battlefield chosen for the Maoists' reconquest of power. The field commanders were the ailing 58-year-old First Vice Premier and Defense Minister of the People's Government, Lin Piao, who was also Fifth Vice Chairman of the Communist Party, and the 56-year-old retired actress, who presumably spoke with the authority of her husband. Their weapons were as yet words, but the pair held in reserve the mystical charisma of Chairman Mao and the guns of the Liberation Army.

Had they known Mao's wife better, Mao's enemies might have feared the vengeful Starlet more. But her attempt to manipulate the theater, art, and literature of People's China initially appeared no more than a nuisance. Chiang Ching had played the role of an unobtrusive housewife since her marriage to the Chairman in 1940. When she began meddling with opera and motion pictures in the early 1960s, she did not appear a formidable danger. Against the Starlet, the non-Maoist Establishment could rally hundreds of writers, directors, actors, and playwrights who were directed by the Party's Propaganda Bureau itself. The Starlet's challenge to the Mayor's powerful apparatus of culture, therefore, appeared initially no more than self-therapy for her professional frustration.

Besides, Chiang Ching was a woman. Disarmed by their own prejudices, the moderates refused to consider a female a serious threat. Under feudal princes, Confucian mandarins, Nationalist bureaucrats, and Marxist commissars alike, Chinese society had been male-centered. Woman's place had been markedly inferior in both custom and law. Eager to exploit the resentment of hundreds of millions of Chinese women, the Communists had emancipated them by decree. Yet the strictures of millenia-old customs were extraordinarily tenacious.

Moreover, statutes could not expunge prejudice based on memory of four women in power—three empresses and a concubine—all authoresses of disaster. Throughout Chinese history, female ascendancy had signaled calamity. Deeper than ideology, Chinese custom demanded that women be humble in public, though they might rule autocratically within their homes. Not only conservatives mouthed the old couplet: *When a dynasty is disaster bound, portents must abound! When the hen rules the roost, the Court's doom is unloosed!*

Despite some splendid exceptions, women normally attain power by marriage in bourgeois society. It should, theoretically, have been otherwise in People's China, but it was not. Male dominance persisted. The hierarchy was adorned by no significant number of female commissars. The few women who held high positions were almost all wives of "senior comrades." Their influence was largely restricted to "women's and children's organizations," though most had qualified for power by long service to the cause.

China's two first ladies remained wholly outside the political arena until the critical 1960s, when "the two lines" championed by their husbands, Chairman Mao Tse-tung and Chairman Liu Shao-chi, came into conflict. Chiang Ching and Wang Kwang-mei were in Chinese eyes the harbingers of the doom of the Communist dynasty. Irrational foreboding chilled many Chinese when women openly entered the power struggle and played leading roles.

The two ladies were superficially distinguished by no particular malignity. Chiang Ching had been a lively, even flighty, habituée of leftist cinema circles whose erratic love affairs had, at least on one occasion, delighted the yellow press. In the early 1960s, she was the frumpish, bespectacled fourth wife of the Chairman. Her brief and decidedly unmeteoric motion-picture career had earned her the mocking nickname the Starlet and had imbued her with deep resentment.

The meticulously groomed Wang Kwang-mei, 12 years younger, was either the second or third wife of Comrade Shao-chi. She was called— without intent to flatter—the Campus Belle, because of her glittering social career as a student at Western-oriented Fujen and Yenching Universities in Peking. She had studied English as an undergraduate and later theoretical physics, but her demeanor was unmistakably *haut bourgeois*.

When the Great Proletarian Cultural Revolution rent the veils of Party secrecy to reveal the intrusive roles the two ladies had played since 1962, the Chinese gave them a new nickname. Delicately translated as "the Consorts," *Niang Niang* actually means "the Concubines."

If a literal-minded Maoist playwright had required two characters to typify the contending parties in the Cultural Revolution, he would have *invented* the Starlet and the Campus Belle. For the Maoist "rebel revolutionaries," aflame with hatred of established authority and determined to destroy "all the old ways of life and thought," there was Chiang Ching, the daughter of a poor farmer whose widow had been a maidservant. For the non-Maoist "men in power following the capitalist road," there was Wang Kwang-mei, daughter of a Nationalist official and factory owner. The bitter elder woman was born in 1910 in a China still under the titular rule of the Manchu Dynasty, which collapsed the following year. The privileged younger woman was born when her parents were vacationing in the United States in 1922, a year after the founding of the Communist Party had begun a new era.

Even a playwright who was not ideologically motivated might have used the pair. The somewhat obvious symbolism of their roles in the Cultural Revolution was relieved by anomalies which demonstrated their common humanity. Chiang Ching, the "daughter of the masses," was fascinated by that most stylized of the arts, the petrified Peking Opera, unaltered for centuries. Wang Kwang-mei, the daughter of privilege, concerned herself deeply with the problems of the depressed peasantry. The Starlet, that stern champion of Maoist austerity, was before her marriage a self-indulgent bohemian. The Campus Belle, sprung of "decadent bureaucratic capitalists," had displayed exemplary feminine virtue by any standard, Communist or bourgeois.

The Starlet played the more compelling—and startling—role in the Cultural Revolution. Except for her implacable ambition, the future scourge of China had not been discernible in the amorous butterfly who flittered about the motion picture colony of Shanghai three decades earlier. But the vengeful bitterness she later displayed arose from constant professional and personal bitterness. Comparison of recent pictures with one showing the happy Maos before their cave home in the yellow hills of Yenan in the early 1940s indicates that life with the Chairman was not conducive to preservation of either physical beauty or good temper. The first shows a plump woman in her early thirties with glossy hair, attractive despite her baggy Liberation suit and the slightly protruding teeth revealed by her half-smile. Almost the only remaining characteristic is her protruding teeth, for even the shape of her face has altered. Her neck is scrawny under the scarf tucked into her well-tailored tunic. Though her trim slacks display her concern for her appearance, the Starlet's eyes glitter behind utilitarian, metal-rimmed glasses. She appears more likely to shriek imprecations than to arouse desire or tenderness.

Chiang Ching was born Luan Shu-meng, the daughter of a struggling farmer-shopkeeper in Chucheng in mountainous Shantung Province on the northern coast. After her father's death, when she was eight, her mother worked as a maidservant, but found life as a menial in a rich household insupportable—psychologically and materially. Mother and daughter soon moved to Tsinan, the provincial capital, where her maternal grandfather was a clerk in a junior high school. A meager, provincial town by the standards of Peking, Shanghai, or Canton, Tsinan was a commercial metropolis, a veritable artistic and intellectual center to the small girl from the country. Besides, her grandfather's patronage provided opportunity. She continued her formal studies through the tenth grade. Since few Chinese of either sex acquired even elementary school-ing, she thus transcended her "proletarian background" to become a "petty bourgeois." By Chinese standards she was also an intellectual—like almost all the Communist leaders who later destroyed Chinese society in order to destroy the bourgeoisie and "reform" the intellectuals.

The next phase of her life was marked by her first change of name—as was each subsequent phase. Adopted by her grandfather upon her mother's death, she was called Li Yün-ho and soon thereafter Li Ching-yün.* She was a strapping, vivacious girl who, as early as her fifteenth year, knew her own mind well. Opportunity, however, was severely limited.

The abundance of apocryphal tales and the fog of Party secrecy obscure her biography, but her adolescent associates seem to have called her "the Great Miss Lee," a cruel nickname earned by her pretentious air. Some accounts relate that the Starlet's mother had wished to sell her to a prosperous family, where she would work as an unpaid maidser-vant and perhaps eventually marry one of the sons. The Dickensian quality of life in China during the tumultuous 1920s is further reflected in the report that she was abducted by white slavers, who forced her to perform at local fairs before becoming a gilded prostitute. Her grand-father reportedly redeemed her with the aid of influential friends. In any event, her orphaned girlhood was stormy.

Her grandfather wished her to return to senior high school, but she insisted that her future was on the stage. Yielding with grace, the old man arranged her admission to the Tsinan Experimental Drama Acad-emy. The troupe presented "modern" plays, both foreign and Chinese, in *pai hua,* the spoken language, rather than the stylized, half-incompre-hensible language of the traditional theater. It was a bold venture initiated by free spirits and condemned by conservatives. Time acceler-ated fantastically for the girl; she moved from early Victorian squalor and Dickensian perils to Edwardian enlightenment and Shavian emanci-pation.

The Chinese intelligentsia borrowed from abroad to replace out-moded Confucian aesthetic and moral standards which, they felt, had contrived national disaster. Young writers and actors gravitated toward the extreme left, for the Nationalist Party was conservative and bureau-cratized by power. In the Tsinan Experimental Troupe and later as an auditor and library clerk at Tsingtao University, the Starlet associated with young men and women naturally inclined toward the Communist cause.

* *Li* was her grandfather's surname. *Yün-ho* means the "crane of the clouds." *Ching-yün* means literally "blue clouds," though the word *ching,* which recurs in her "Party name," Chiang Ching, denotes "blue-green" or, generically, "the color of nature."

Her complex amours began in that atmosphere of disdain for traditional restraint. Among her first lovers was a well-born young Nationalist
Party member who became a Nationalist official—the better to serve the
Communist underground. She lived in Tsingtao, the largest and most
cosmopolitan city of Shantung, from 1929 to 1934. Though she rejoiced
in playing an occasional dramatic role, she was not content. Her lover
soon left her, while professional success eluded her. Failing to conquer
even the small world of Tsingtao, she longed for greater worlds to
conquer. In her early twenties, she was moved by neither intellectual
curiosity nor ideological commitment—except a general, unthinking
inclination toward things modern, Western, and "progressive."

The Starlet fretted in North China while her future husband, 17 years
her senior, was patiently building a power base in the isolated First
Soviet Area in Central China. In 1934, Mao Tse-tung was forced to
abandon his mountain redoubt and order the Long March that finally
brought him to sanctuary in the northwest. In the same year, the Starlet
set out for Shanghai, the most glittering and most corrupt city of Asia.

The megalopolis on the mudflats was the sophisticated playground
and counting house of foreigners and the new, Western-oriented *haut
bourgeoisie;* a stronghold of traditional, extra-legal secret societies; and
the clandestine base of the Moscow-oriented Central Committee of the
Chinese Communist Party. Chiang Ching won her passage to Shanghai
neither by talent nor by love. Opportunity came in the person of a
successful motion-picture director who was visiting his old friend, her
avuncular admirer, the Dean of Letters of Tsingtao University. Her
importuning wrung from the director a vague promise of employment in
Shanghai. Finally she was "on her way to greatness."

"The Great Miss Lee" sloughed her old identity, her old friends, and
her old name. She took the self-consciously romantic stage name, Lan
Pin, replete with literary allusions. *Lan* means simply "blue." The small
water plant called *pin* is inelegantly known as "duckweed" in English.
The spray of tiny blue flowers is rootless, and a Chinese couplet says:
"The wind is born in the depths of the earth, but blows strong from the
petals of the blue-green* *pin.*" Rootless, Lan Pin drifted aimlessly
about the Shanghai film colony for the next four years, taking minor
roles and minor lovers.

The leftist Tien Tung Studio, which paid her the equivalent of $14 a
month, was supported by a wealthy fellow-traveler for one year before it
was closed down. Its organizers, writers and directors, were later vilified
during the Cultural Revolution, for the vigorous spirits who were the
vanguard of the "left literature and art movement" of the mid-1930s

---

* Again, *ching,* blue-green or the color of nature, which reappears in *Chiang
Ching.*

also led the intra-Party resistance to Maoist aesthetics in the early 1960s. They included the eminent playwright Tien Han, who wrote the words of the Communist National Anthem, Chou Yang, the Backstage Boss, and other men who subsequently controlled the Party's Propaganda Bureau. Personal revenge and political expediency may have fused when the Starlet destroyed the men who had given her only one satisfactory role.

In "The Talk of the Town," Chiang Ching played a country girl first entrapped and finally ruined by sinful, capitalist Shanghai. Her performance is described as "adequate" by those who have seen the film. All prints have now vanished, as have her other films—a gesture that may have been prompted by the conservative Mao's reluctance to allow his wife to display herself in public, or by his desire to wipe out all record of her merely "adequate" performances.

Suppressed in 1935, Tien Tung was succeeded by the Lien Hua Studio—financed by the same angel and run by the same artists. The simple artifice sufficed, for the Nationalists were strangely lax in controlling Communist propaganda. For Lien Hua, the Starlet gave her best performance. In "Wang Lao Wu," she was a young girl who married a middle-aged confirmed bachelor. Whatever small fame she won came from that role. It was her single triumph.

Chiang Ching also staged a colorful personal drama at the time. After various casual amours, she had met, lived with, and finally married a bright young assistant director called Tang Na. When she left him for a more influential director, Tang attempted suicide. His unsuccessful attempt was splashed over the scandal sheets, bringing the Starlet notoriety, but not the stardom for which she yearned.

One major thread of the Starlet's life is obscure. Her amours were complex, and her enemies have delighted in retailing lurid rumors. In this respect, she may be much maligned since she may have pledged herself to only two or three men before her alliance with the Chairman. She may, on the other hand, have pursued the career of cold self-seeking so rancorously ascribed to her. Above all, obscurity surrounds the children she may—or may not—have borne to Tang Na and other lovers in Shanghai.

One highly reliable informant recalls a long association with a youth who claimed to be the Starlet's son. Resentful of his anomalous position and moved by the same "spirit of rebellion" that flared so bright in his mother, the young man was perpetually in trouble with the Communist authorities. Living on the fringe of the world of letters, just as his mother had 30 years earlier, he was denounced as a "rightist and reactionary." From time to time he found himself in "preventive detention," but his release was as often ordered by unknown authority. To that extent, at least, the Starlet seems to have watched over a feckless son.

The putative child—or children—of her youth appear to have been only incidents to the ambitious Starlet. She left Japanese-occupied Shanghai late in 1937 for one more assault on the heights of stardom. Her destination was Chungking, the Nationalist capital astride the gorges of the upper Yangtze River. The Political Department of the National Military Affairs Commission, which directed all propaganda, was seeded equally with Nationalists and Communists at the time and had been ordered to produce "national defense" literature, plays, and motion pictures. Despite her scrabbling for introductions and her ostentatious activity on behalf of the Communist Sino-Soviet Friendship Association, the Starlet was as disappointed in Chungking as she had been in Shanghai. Her single role was a peasant's wife in "China's Sons and Daughters."

Only one resort remained open to her. In mid-1938 Chiang Ching left for Yenan. The Nationalists permitted such travel, though they did not approve. The passage from Chungking in the far southwest to Yenan in the northwest was even more arduous than the journey from Shanghai to Chungking through the Japanese lines. Encouraged by the Communist representatives in Chungking to migrate to the cave-city, where "the new China was in the making," ardent neophytes traveled painfully by bus, by truck, and on foot across the primitive hinterlands. Removal from her birthplace of Chucheng to Tsinan, the capital of Shantung, had been a voyage from an eighteenth-century village into the twentieth-century's intellectual and material excitement. The Starlet's journey to Yenan carried her backward in time. She haggled with greasy proprietors of flea-ridden country inns and rode ramshackle buses topheavy with luggage, trade goods, and livestock. But she was drawn onward by her vision of an abode of opportunity where her dedication and talent would finally win the recognition she had been denied by both insensitive capitalists and prejudiced leftist intellectuals. Besides, she knew that there were 18 men for every woman in Yenan.

The Starlet found a primitive community hewn from the yellow hills. True egalitarianism prevailed, and Chairman Mao himself cultivated his own tobacco patch—not chiefly seeking "proletarianization" by manual labor but because he was an inveterate chain smoker. Despite her left-wing associations and her small reputation, the Starlet was an intruder among men and women bound by a decade of shared hardship. She was accepted as another novice in the ranks, but no more.

Lan Pin, as she was still known, was required to prove herself and to "remold" her thinking. She was accordingly enrolled in the Lu Hsün Academy of Art to study Maoist aesthetics between her performances in propaganda plays. Written for simple "peasants, workers, and soldiers," the morality plays presented simple characters: the good Chinese and the bad Japanese; the good proletarian and the bad capitalist; the good peasant and the bad landlord. The plots were equally stark. The virtuous suffered hardship and torture at the hands of the evil, but in the end triumphed—with the assistance of that reliable *deus ex machina,* the valiant Communist Party. At the Marxist-Leninist Institute, the Starlet learned a smattering of the doctrine she had espoused. The courses were almost as unsophisticated as the plays produced by the Lu Hsün Academy of Art, named for modern China's most sophisticated social satirist.

The Starlet was dismayed when the new promised land did not spontaneously recognize her worth. The same intellectuals who had thwarted her ambitions in Shanghai dominated the artistic milieu of Yenan. Both her schools were directed by the Mayor, Peng Chen, and administered by the leftist writers and directors the Starlet had hated for their "personal prejudice" in Shanghai and Chungking. She enjoyed minor success on the propaganda stage—and delighted in the attentions paid a vivacious, attractive young woman in a harsh community largely deprived of femininity. But her goal—becoming China's leading actress —was as remote as ever.

Despite the ostentatious puritanism of Yenan, everyone from the Chairman and his Political Bureau to the latest arrival mingled in loud camaraderie at public dances. Despite the assertive austerity of Yenan, love affairs bourgeoned. The Chinese never accepted the early Leninist argument that sexual intercourse was no more significant than drinking a glass of water to satisfy a different physical need, but the self-conscious bohemianism of rebels against the bourgeois conventions sanctioned extra-legal liaisons. They had already rejected the terms "husband" and "wife" for the word *ai-jen,* which literally means "beloved." Profane love had not yet been displaced by sacred love for Chairman Mao.

The Starlet availed herself of the opportunities open to a young, attractive woman in bleak Yenan. Her first lover was, characteristically, a "senior comrade" who was influential in the theater. She was, therefore, stricken professionally as well as personally when she was supplanted by a better-known and better-looking actress, an old Shanghai rival. In her bitterness, she laid her plot to scale the pinnacle of Yenan society.

Her objective was Chairman Mao Tse-tung himself. Yenan was a small place, and the Starlet arranged frequent "chance encounters" with the Chairman. When he lectured at the Marxist-Leninist Institute, she sat pertly in the first row, nodding vigorous agreement. Rising to ask questions, she registered fervent enthusiasm. Mao was at first startled by the Starlet's persistent adulation. But he was never one to question flattery. He was gratified by the admiration of the young woman who possessed an artistic reputation—however small. Moreover, the Starlet's devotion to the theater created a community of interest with the poetaster who considered himself *the* final authority on Chinese literature. Proving her own profundity by echoing Mao's views, Lan Pin created a unique intellectual intimacy.

The Chairman was a lonely man, for his dignity inhibited the easy liaisons permitted lesser figures. His third wife, companion of the Long March, had departed for "medical treatment" in the Soviet Union when the couple were already estranged. Like the Chinese bourgeoisie he despised, Mao was inclined toward younger women. The Starlet, almost 20 years his junior, exerted a strong sensual appeal. Since he could not compete openly, she conducted the campaign—and both triumphed.

One summer night in 1940, the pair tacitly acknowledged their liaison. The Starlet failed to return to the dormitory of the Lu Hsün Academy. Shortly thereafter she was transferred to the Archives Section of the Military Affairs Commission of the Communist Party. Mao was *ex officio* chairman of that Commission, and its headquarters were near his cave home. The physical liaison was accomplished. The happy couple had still to win Party approval.

The Communists were intentionally vague about marital arrangements, in part because they wished to free women of their legal and social status as chattels by giving them complete equality with men and in part because Chinese men had always been free to take many wives and concubines. The Chairman's first wife was the young country girl selected by his parents; he married his second wife in a legal ceremony; and his third wife, whom the Starlet succeeded, was apparently not bound to him by formal ceremony. In Yenan, woman, declared wholly equal to man, had the same right to select and discard her partners— within the limits of blatant promiscuity.

The Chairman's choices were more circumscribed than an ordinary comrade's. Restricted by his eminence, he required the consent of his peers to a new liaison that was likely to be protracted—if not necessarily permanent. Some colleagues were disturbed by the informal "marriage" of the Chairman and the Starlet, while others approved. Their motives were mixed. Some "senior comrades" feared the influence of a woman of dubious reputation who was, at that point, not even a Party member. Others sought to enhance their own positions by fervent support. One such advocate was the Lord High Executioner Kang Sheng, who had, coincidentally, been born in the same small Shantung village as the Starlet. He was advanced during the Cultural Revolution, while many opponents of the match were degraded.

Dwellers in Yenan during the crisis vividly recall Mao's efforts to prove the Starlet a suitable consort. One remembers the Chairman's pleading his case from cave to cave through the dark Yenan night, lighting his way with an oil lantern. However it was done, it was finally done, perhaps, as one apocryphal story relates, by a bounteously pregnant Starlet's announcing to a group of senior cadres: "Comrades, I have something to tell you. Chairman Mao and I are living together as husband and wife."

The Starlet's legitimization was conditional. She retired into seclusion more appropriate to the consort of a Confucian emperor than the common-law wife of the leader of a movement sworn to "emancipate" women. Either because Mao Tse-tung so wished or because his colleagues insisted, the mercurial Starlet was banished to the hearth. She did not even perform the ceremonial functions expected of the wives of bourgeois politicians, such as inspecting schools and nurseries or presiding over charitable drives. But the Party could hardly prevent her exerting great influence with the family circle to which she soon contributed two daughters. Her domestic influence grew into political power —exerted first through her husband and, later, directly in the name of her husband.

With her marriage she once again changed her name. The Chairman himself chose to call her *Chiang Ching,* literally, the "green-blue river." Chinese scholars can find a multitude of explanations for his choice. But it is most likely that Chiang Ching derived directly from a Tang Dynasty couplet the Chairman admired: *The melody fades away and there is no one to be seen. A few distant peaks across the river glow green.* She was, thereafter, known as Chiang Ching, but she never knew the serenity of the idealized landscape.

The irreverent Chinese continued to call her the Starlet, later adopting the less flattering sobriquet, the Concubine. She played the secluded consort of the great man with grim resignation. Even before "liberation" in 1949, however, the power-hungry Starlet deviously sought power over the theater. In 1950 she was somewhat mollified by appointment to the Motion Picture Guidance Committee of the Ministry of Culture. But her influence was slight until the early 1960s, when the battle between the extremist Maoists and the moderates raged through the Communist Party's inner councils.

The Starlet emerged in 1962 as the champion of the orthodox Maoist line in music, the graphic arts, literature, and the theater. She fought a bitter battle against stubborn resistance for control of the Capital Opera Troupe, the premier company presenting traditional Peking operas. She demanded total submission in every technical and artistic detail, for she was determined to reshape both traditional and modern works to her views.

She insisted, for example, upon completely remaking the opera called "Sha Chia Pang," which glorified victory against the Japanese. She expunged the original's historically accurate emphasis upon subversion and guerrillas. Clandestine "illegal activity" was, after all, Comrade Liu

Shao-chi's preserve. In her revised version, victory was won by the regular Communist troops of the Eighth Route Army. Conventional armed force rather than "underground work" was Mao Tse-tung's forte. The emphasis upon regular units, of course, also gratified Field Marshal Lin Piao. He and the Starlet were in 1963 forming an alliance for mutual defense—and aggression.

Not content to alter fact, the Starlet systematically perverted the manner of the highly stylized Peking Opera. Hosts of fervent aficionados were deeply offended, for they loved the classical dramas as the Spanish love the ritual of the bullring or the Russians the old ballet. Her six "model dramas" were anathema to the audience. Her harsh recasting of form and content was a Phyrric victory. Every battle she won created myriad new opponents.

The Starlet and the Disciple attacked in February 1966, when "the two lines in art and politics" met in open conflict. Chief advocates of the pragmatic line were the "Peking Center" of the Communist Party under the Mayor, Peng Chen, tacitly encouraged by Comrade Liu Shao-chi. Chief advocates of the dogmatic line were the "Shanghai Center" under Lin Piao and Chiang Ching, supported by the prestige of Chairman Mao himself. In November 1965 the Starlet had loosed hostilities with the assault on the playwright Wu Han by Yao Wen-yüan, the Literary Assassin.

While the Mayor sought to divert the attack through his *February Theses,* the Disciple and the Starlet convened their Forum on Art and Literature Within the Armed Forces. One side thundered from Peking, the other from Shanghai.

Chinese Communist obsession with literature may appear inexplicable to outsiders. Totalitarian regimes have, of course, always rigorously manipulated all media of expression because they feared the latent force of suppressed public opinion. Most Communist regimes, however, have accepted Karl Marx's dictum that there is "not necessarily" a direct correlation between social development and artistic expression. They have, quite pragmatically, normally used art and literature as means of social control. Yet Mao Tse-tung maintained that art and literature were not merely weapons of the revolution, but were also direct evidence of the state of the revolution.

The first source of Mao's heresy against orthodox Marxism was his belief that not material abundance—that is, not economic productivity —but a "high level of ideological consciousness" was the basic condition for attaining true Communism. The perfect Maoist man was to create perfect Communism, rather than material abundances' breeding the new Marxist man who worked spontaneously for the common good because he transcended both material incentives and conflict with his fellows. Since China's hopes of attaining material abundance were slight, the ideal new human being was to be created by spiritual means, his soul exalted by perfect comprehension of Maoism instilled by study of the Maoist classics and Maoist literature. The Chairman was further impelled to lay primary stress on the social function of literature by traditional Chinese reverence for the written word. He knew that the Confucian classics had shaped the character of his people and their governments. He was determined to transform both people and administration through his own classics.

The Maoists were therefore determined to create "Socialist" art and literature—at once to demonstrate their progress and to compel that progress. Karl Marx had declared that "proletarian art" could not be forced, but must spring from true Communism. The Starlet was determined to force the growth of a Maoist culture in which true Communism would develop. She possessed a sophisticated appreciation of the total impact of the channels of information and entertainment—in sum, propaganda—in shaping a nation. She was, however, naïve in believing that she could create a new force of artists—read, propagandists—from peasants, workers, and soldiers. But she had little choice, for the "professional intellectuals" had already repudiated the Maoists.

The Starlet attacked vigorously when the battle became overt in early 1966. She knew the true prize at stake in the controversy that superficially appeared to be no more than an aesthetic debate of theological intensity. The non-Maoists, on the defensive, advocated restraint, discipline, and "professional skill," sustained by strict intellectual and aesthetic standards. The aggressive Maoists contended that literature must be created by the raw vigor of the resurgent masses guided by the sacrosanct Thought of Mao Tse-tung. Art and education, they insisted, must be mighty weapons in the "unending class struggle." The Maoists' ultimate weapon in the ostensible debate on aesthetics, literature, and pedagogy, however, was the People's Liberation Army that they believed to be securely controlled by the Disciple Lin Piao. The final objective of their assault on literature, education, the stage, music, and the graphic arts was to "seize power" from the non-Maoist opposition.

Therefore, the Forum on Literature and Art in the Armed Forces was a major battle. The Starlet presided over the 18-day conference, which began on February 2, 1966. She selected all the participants, and she drafted the ten-point conclusion that totally repudiated all established forms and organizations:

   1) An acute class struggle has been fought on the cultural front since liberation. 2) A revolution has taken place in drama and all the arts

during the past three years, producing many fine works of art which serve the workers, peasants, and soldiers. 3) The enemy is plotting to corrupt the armed forces through literature and art. 4) The People's Liberation Army must play an important role in the Great Proletarian Cultural Revolution. 5) The myths surrounding the literature and art of the 1930s,* as well as Chinese and foreign classical literature, should be shattered. 6) Democratic practices should be upheld in literary and art works.** 7) Mass literary and art criticism should be promoted. 8) Revisionist [*i.e.,* non-Maoist] literature should be criticised and repudiated. 9) Revolutionary realism and revolutionary romanticism should be combined in imaginative writing. 10) Literary and art cadres should be re-educated, and literary and art forces should be reorganized.

The report of the February Forum anointed Chiang Ching as the sole aesthetic and propaganda arbiter of the Liberation Army and the nation. The Disciple ordered:

> All the Army's documents concerning culture should be sent to her. . . . We should always seek her opinions on improving literary and art work in the armed forces. . . . Our association with her has convinced us that Comrade Chiang Ching possesses a profound understanding of Chairman Mao's Thought. She has made a prolonged and brilliant investigation of the problems of literature and art, and has already gained rich personal experience. . . . Undertaking arduous work while she was in poor health, she has enormously enlightened and assisted us. . . ."

The February Forum itself complained ominously that the absolute primacy of Mao Tse-tung's dicta on literature and art had been ignored by the Party. It offered a remarkable confession of failure—and an extraordinary remedy:

> During the 15 years since the founding of the Chinese People's Republic, literary and art circles have fundamentally failed to follow the guidance of Chairman Mao's works. The present dictatorship of the anti-Party, anti-Socialist black line is diametrically opposed to Chairman Mao's Thought. The black line in literature and art combines bourgeois concepts, modern revisionist [Soviet] ideas, and the standards of the 1930s. Specific expressions of the black line are theories like "truthful writing, the broad path of realism, deepening realism, refusal to consider [prole-

---

* In effect, a declaration of war against the leftist intellectuals who had frustrated her ambitions during the period.
** That is, control should be exercised by the "masses" through their all-wise leaders, the Maoists, rather than by "professional intellectuals."

tarian] subject matter decisive, mid-level [typical] characters [rather than staunch proletarians], and opposition to the smell of gunpowder." But the true spirit of the age is now sweeping across the land in a broad offensive.

The Forum reported:

Under the irresistible impact of this offensive, the Peking Opera, which was formerly the most obdurate enemy stronghold, has been radically revolutionized, both in ideology and in form [by Chiang Ching herself]. That transformation has inspired revolutionary changes in all literary and art circles. Peking operas based upon contemporary revolutionary themes like *The Red Lantern, Sha Chia Pang, Taking the Bandits' Stronghold,* and *Raid on the White Tiger Regiment**; the ballet, *The Red Detachment of Women;* the symphony, *Sha Chia Pang;* and the sculpture-group called the Rent Collection Courtyard [depicting the misery of exploited peasants in the bad old days] have been approved by the broad masses of workers, peasants, and soldiers, and have been acclaimed by Chinese and foreign audiences.

The vindictive Starlet obviously delighted in commanding the "offensive." Besides ordering the Liberation Army to "remold" the arts, the February Forum reopened bitter, but obscure controversies of the 1930s, when the Starlet had been humiliated by the men who dominated "left-wing literature," the same men who in 1966 controlled the Party's propaganda apparatus. Nor was her venom exhausted in revenge. Even Joseph Stalin was reprimanded by the new Czarina of Maoist culture.

"Stalin . . . uncritically accepted the legacy of the classical writings of Russia and Europe," the Forum judged. "The consequences were very bad." Only Mao Tse-tung among Marxist-Leninists, it was clear, truly comprehended the "struggle on the literary and art front," while his infallible doctrines were "correctly" interpreted only by his wife. The Starlet raised her own literary legions.

"We must place the weapon of criticism of literature and art in the hands of the masses, the workers, peasants, and soldiers," the Forum commanded. "We must make criticism more and more militant. . . . We must reform style; we must encourage short popular articles; we must make criticism of literature and art into *daggers and hand grenades.*** We must use those weapons to great effect in close combat—within 200 meters."

The Disciple and the Starlet combined strategies. The so-called Lucky

* Chiang Ching's "model dramas."
** Emphasis supplied.

General had consistently advocated hand-to-hand combat to overcome the enemy's technological superiority. Moreover, the Forum's military language was by no means entirely metaphorical. The Maoists meant exactly what they said. They *would* storm the enemy's strongholds—regardless of the cost in aesthetic values, public order, or human life. Political power was their sole objective.

The report of the Starlet's Forum prescribed:

> We must strive enthusiastically by every possible means to project heroic images of workers, peasants, and soldiers. . . . We must describe revolutionary war clearly: *We are just and the enemy is unjust.** Our writing must depict our arduous struggles and our heroic sacrifices, but must also portray revolutionary heroism and revolutionary optimism. While describing the cruelty of war, we must not exaggerate its horror. While describing the hardships of our revolutionary war, we must not exaggerate the suffering caused.

We are just, and we *will* win! We will suffer, but not *too* much! What better way to recruit ambitious or idealistic adherents than by promising them arduous struggle and total victory—without excessive suffering?

The Starlet clearly set forth her two-phase strategy for winning control of all propaganda: "On Comrade Lin Piao's suggestion, the General Political Department [of the People's Liberation Army] has printed and distributed *Mao Tse-tung's Lectures on Literature and Art* [delivered in Yenan in 1942] to all literary and art workers in the armed forces," the Forum reported. "This book is to be read constantly—while comprehensive review and examination will occur every May. This procedure must be enforced vigorously—and indefinitely."

Such was Phase I of the Starlet's strategy. The gospel of Chairman Mao according to Chiang Ching was to control the Liberation Army. The Army was to direct all culture. That was Phase II.

> Literary and art workers of the armed forces should participate most actively in the affairs of local [civilian] associations of writers and artists. Their work should be placed for publication in local [civilian] newspapers, magazines, and publishing houses, as well as with film studios for adaption to the screen. Control [of their output] must be enforced . . . while the Party Committee of the General Political Department of the Armed Forces should provide stringent leadership over all literary and art work.

The thought of Mao Tse-tung was to direct the gun, and the gun was to rule Chinese culture. The Mayor's effort to divert the struggle into academic debate had failed.

* Emphasis supplied.

On April 10, 1966, the Maoist minority of the Central Committee sitting in Shanghai issued a directive flatly repudiating Peng Chen's *February Theses*. Distributed to every major unit of the Communist Party, as well as the General Political Department of the Liberation Army, the document made its point in a few forceful sentences:

> Persistent resistance—or intransigent opposition—to Marxism-Leninism and the Thought of Mao Tse-tung is the dividing line clearly demarking Socialist literature and art from capitalist literature and art. . . . The *responsible departments of the Central Committee and the overwhelming majority of local Party Committees have never possessed adequate understanding* of the class struggle on the literary and art front. They have not engaged in that struggle with sufficient vigor. They have not seriously and thoroughly implemented Chairman Mao Tse-tung's concepts on literature and art or obeyed his directives. *These grave malfeasances must be altered rapidly and radically.**

The climactic struggle between pragmatists and extremists, which would torment all China, was openly engaged. Direct personal confrontation between Comrade Liu Shao-chi, Chairman of the People's Republic, and Chairman Mao Tse-tung of the Communist Party was inevitable.

X

The Other Chairman

The confrontation was inevitable, for the two Chairmen advocated antagonistic solutions to every major problem facing the country. The mutual trust sprung of three decades of collaboration might have withstood the great debate within the Communist Party from 1960 to 1965, but neither political nor personal confidence could survive the brutal assault on the fundamental principles and key personalities of the legal apparatus of the Communist Party mounted by the Maoists in May 1966.

Supported by Comrade Liu Shao-chi, the Mayor held his own until early May. His *February Theses* had been rejected by the Maoist minority of the Central Committee sitting in Shanghai. His writers and editors were subjected to fierce verbal attacks directed by the Starlet Chiang Ching and the Disciple Lin Piao. For a while, however, Comrade Shao-chi's protégé and chief supporter retained both position and power.

Then on May 16, 1966, the rump Shanghai Central Committee issued a circular deposing Peng Chen and his adherents. The action was patently illegal, for the majority of the Central Committee had not debated the issue—much less voted. It was almost as patently directed against Comrade Shao-chi as much as the Mayor. Both relied on their entrenched "legal" positions to withstand the Maoists' frontal attack. Chairman Mao had, after all, been forced to his wild assault because the moderates held actual political power—and because he and Chairman Liu could no longer agree on any substantive issue. Since Liu was supported by the great majority of "senior and working-level cadres," the Maoists could only regain effective power by staging a coup within the Party.

139

Comrade Liu Shao-chi, Mao's junior by five years, was a man of middle height, slender in build and restrained in movement. He was the model *apparatchik,* dedicated to the apparatus above personal interest. His white hair rose in a gentle crest above his pale face, distinguished chiefly by a jutting, slightly bulbous nose; his physical appearance reinforced the impression of drabness conveyed by his furtive demeanor. He was the author of a thousand and one intrigues in Nationalist territory during almost three decades of civil war. Self-effacement had become so ingrained that he seemed almost incapable of asserting either his personality or his views. He was not a classic hero, a profound thinker, or the creature of unbounded ambition. But responsibility could compel him to transcend his limitations.

Comrade Shao-chi had been compelled to understand the true condition—and the true needs—of the Chinese people. That knowledge, in turn, compelled him to the anguished decision that popular welfare must take precedence over the visions of Mao Tse-tung. He was sustained by the Party Center and the practical administrators throughout China. Because he had drafted the organic laws of the Party and the State, he was determined that "Socialist legality" would guide the great apparatus he controlled.

Before the Great Proletarian Cultural Revolution, Liu Shao-chi was a man in the shadows. Although he performed the ceremonial functions of the chief-of-state, his personal history was deliberately obscured. Since the Cultural Revolution, his enemies' attacks have provided much information. A fairly consistent picture emerges from those virulent attacks; it is by no means an unattractive picture.

The most comprehensive account is a chronology prepared by the "rebel revolutionary" Red Guards: *Down with Liu Shao-chi—The Life of the Counterrevolutionary Liu Shao-chi!* Curiously, it confirms the impression derived from his public words and deeds. Comrade Shao-chi was attacked by the "rebel revolutionaries" for precisely those qualities which endeared him to most Chinese—respect for law, moderation, and recognition of reality. He was, in addition, a ruthless *apparatchik* who undoubtedly slew his thousands. Yet Comrade Shao-chi appears to have suffered less than most of his fellow players in the melodrama of Communist conspiracy from egotism so great it eclipses reality.

Comrade Shao-chi was condemned for licentiousness in his personal life. His detractors credited him with so many liaisons—legal, quasi-legal, and extra-legal—that they themselves became confused. The chronology lists the Campus Belle, Wang Kwang-mei, as either Liu's sixth or seventh wife—a remarkable total even for a peripatetic activist. On at least three occasions, his critics charge, he drove his wives to nervous breakdowns. Once perhaps, twice possibly, but three times hardly—unless, of course, he attracted neurotics. However, he lived in amity with the Campus Belle for more than 20 years, and he and she both refused to testify against each other, as had so many husbands and wives in China and the Soviet Union.

Liu Shao-chi's licentiousness was complemented by a sin of equal gravity in the eyes of his enemies—excessive concern for his children. He closely supervised the education of his three sons and two daughters besides spending much time in their company. Moreover, he was "too concerned" that they should marry happily. Even his advising his eldest son to work diligently, after having educated himself thoroughly, was denounced as "promoting careerism." His enemies themselves asserted that he told his children: "Do not concern yourself with personal advancement, but work hard for the welfare of the people. Personal advancement will follow if it is merited."

He was also accused of avarice. The hearsay evidence centered on curiously diverse objects: a gold shoehorn and a gold belt buckle, a smoked bear's paw, a box of dried beef, a bag of oranges, steamed chickens, and a radio set.

In the incongruous apposition of a surrealistic painting, the gold shoehorn and belt buckle constantly disappear and reappear in the critical chronicle. Originally wrought from gold provided to finance his underground activities, those precious objects seem to have taken on a perverse life of their own. They were constantly deposited and withdrawn from various "bourgeois" banks; they were presented to his "various wives" and then demanded back.

Liu accepted the smoked bear's paw, a great delicacy, from cadres during a tour of the northwest. The dried beef was presented by an "Indonesian comrade." The bag of oranges symbolized his self-indulgence when, as Political Commissar of the New Fourth Army in 1941, he "dined on steamed chicken daily—and even ate oranges." The radio set he gave to his father-in-law, the Campus Belle's bourgeois parent, displayed unseemly family feeling, which flouted proper "class feeling."

The "rebel revolutionaries" brought no other charges against the man denounced as "the number one individual in power in the Party following the capitalist road . . . the chief agent of imperialism . . . China's Khrushchev. . . ." Other disgraced leaders were charged with constructing luxurious clubs, embezzling funds, and staging orgies, but Liu's life revealed no such vile secrets to the muckraking Red Guards. The depravity of the second most powerful man in China symbolized by a golden shoehorn. What manner of man was this?

Ruthless with his foes, he had trusted too much in his colleagues. He had, therefore, committed major tactical errors. He had antagonized the vindictive Lin Piao by disputing his strategy and his authority. He had alienated the implacable romantic, Mao Tse-tung, by denying his Utopian visions. He had, moreover, organized the Communist apparatus so that it responded to his will rather than Mao's. He had thus become *the* chief threat to the power-obsessed master and disciple.

Liu Shao-chi was in no way touched by genius, and he had not planned to challenge Mao. His origins were identical with those of most Communist leaders, almost all sprung of the petty bourgeoisie. Like Mao Tse-tung, Comrade Shao-chi was the son of a well-to-do farmer of Hunan Province, born in 1898 in Ninghsiang County near the capital of Changsha. Unlike Mao's, his family was descending the economic and social ladder during the decline of the Manchu Dynasty. Earlier generations had been local gentry, for his landlord grandfather owned 120 *mou,* almost 20 acres. His father was a "rich-peasant" like Mao's, but he lacked the ruthless drive of the elder Mao. The Lius were nonetheless better off than the Maos and more accommodating. The youngest of two girls and four boys, Comrade Shao-chi was given not only love but understanding. He was eager for "modern education to help the nation," and his secondary schooling was financed by his eldest brother, a battalion commander in a warlord army.

Although he could not join Chou En-lai and other "worker students" in France, young Liu Shao-chi entered the Socialist Youth League in 1920 and the Communist Party in the winter of 1921–22. He studied in the Soviet Union from mid-1921 to mid-1922, when Lenin's New Economic Policy permitted limited free enterprise based on material incentives—concessions granted to prevent economic collapse. Having formed a close liaison with the Soviet Communist Party early, Liu immersed himself in the Chinese labor movement. He organized the Coal Miners' Union at Anyüan in Kiangsi Province and led the first major strike of the Chinese labor movement. Later the Maoists, on the one hand, denounced the strike as a failure that "cost many lives" and, alternately, asserted that Mao Tse-tung rather than Liu Shao-chi had led the miners to victory. At the time, the movement was pleased by Comrade Shao-chi's performance, and he became Vice Chairman of the All-China Federation of Trade Unions in 1925.

The Nationalist-Communist coalition of 1924 allowed Communist labor organizers to walk in the sunlight, and Comrade Shao-chi was a traveling delegate to the unions of the coastal metropolises of Shanghai and Canton as well as the inland Wuhan industrial area. He later complained that the restrictions imposed on Communist labor agitators by membership in the Nationalist Party all but nullified the advantage of legalization. He blamed his difficulties on the Secretary-General, who had reluctantly obeyed Moscow's orders that the Chinese Communist

Party subordinate itself to the Nationalists. In 1927, for example, the Comintern's chief representative rejected a Communist request to divert five thousand rifles from a shipment to the Nationalists. The Comintern did not wish the Communists to "dissipate their strength" in independent action.

Despite his resentment, Comrade Shao-chi collaborated with the Soviet Union throughout the Chinese revolution, for he approved Moscow's emphasis on the urban proletariat. From 1925 until the break with the Nationalists in 1927, Liu was a highly effective labor leader.

On May 30, 1925, the British fired on a Chinese crowd in Shanghai. Liu helped to organize the strikes and the boycott of British goods that displayed labor's political strength. In 1926 he established the Wuhan Federation of Trade Unions, which exercised great influence in the major Central-China industrial area. He was also heavily involved in organizing the "street unions" of Shanghai, which were backed by armed People's Militia. Like the Minister of Peace Chou En-lai, Comrade Shao-chi barely escaped execution when Chiang Kai-shek turned on the Communists in April 1927 and slaughtered the Militia.

Just after the final break with the Nationalists in August 1927, Liu's wife bore his first child, a daughter. Personal joy was but an incident in the life of the revolutionary. In late 1927, not only Communists but moderate Nationalists either went "underground" or fled China. While Mao Tse-tung led the Autumn Harvest Rising, Comrade Shao-chi made for Moscow.

The Sixth National Congress of the Chinese Communist Party convened on June 18, 1928, in Moscow—the only possible venue. Even the International Settlement of Shanghai, the Communists' customary refuge, was denied them by Chiang Kai-shek's understanding with the foreign powers. Although representation was obviously restricted, the battered Party considered a National Congress essential.

The Moscow Congress honored Liu Shao-chi, electing him to the Central Committee and appointing him director of the Labor Bureau. Mao Tse-tung was at the time struggling in arduous obscurity, exiled in the hills of Kiangsi. Comrade Shao-chi's role in the Congress confirmed his predilection for the regular Party apparatus and "Socialist legality," not yet blasted by Joseph Stalin. Mao Tse-tung was a virtual outcast from the Chinese Communist Party and the Comintern.

Returning from the Soviet Union in 1929, Comrade Shao-chi once again went "underground," this time in Manchuria. The Russians, the Japanese, and Chinese warlords were contending for domination of the major industrial and communications center. Comrade Shao-chi assisted the Russians as an outrider for the invading forces of Field Marshal Vasili Blyukher, Soviet commander-in-chief in the Far East, who had earlier trained the Nationalist-Communist armies under the *nomme de guerre* General Galen.

Although Liu's chief effort was to be concentrated on Manchuria and the adjoining North China Region for almost a decade, reconciliation between the Shanghai Center and Mao Tse-tung's "rural faction" diverted him for a time. He was smuggled into the Kiangsi Soviet Area in 1932 to become Commissioner of Labor and Chairman of the All-China Federation of Trade Unions. The outward harmony between the two Chairmen then sealed remained unbroken for three decades.

The abusive Red Guard chronicle makes tantalizing references to Liu's personal life at the time. His first wife having died "in anguish of a nervous disorder," his enemies reported, he remarried in the early 1930s. His second wife was captured by the Nationalists and executed. During the Long March he purportedly married a third wife—his fourth if the "village wife" of his youth is included. The personal account is confusing, undocumented, and scurrilous.

But his political spoor is clear. As Commissioner for Supply on the Long March, he was closely associated with Great General Peng Teh-huai. At the Tsünyi Conference of January 1935, he loyally supported Mao Tse-tung's bid for power and was himself re-elected to the Central Committee.

The highly critical chronicle prepared by the Chingkangshan Fighting Corps of the Fourth Peking Hospital offers its version of Liu's "corrupt" personal life. However unreliable, it is a sterling example of both the charges and the inimitable Red Guard style:*

> At the end of the year 1935, Liu married Hsieh Fei, a native of Kwantung of a poor family [by this count, his fourth wife] at Wayaopao in Shensi. At the time of their marriage, Liu Shao-chi hoodwinked Hsieh, saying that if he were ever untrue to her she could shoot him. Hsieh Fei asked Liu Shao-chi to give relief to her few nephews (dependents of a martyr), but Liu bawled her out, saying: "Those people are not your parents. Why take trouble to look out for them?"
>
> Liu Shao-chi always wanted Hsieh Fei to dress well, to wear makeup, to put on a red dress and high-heeled shoes. He expected Hsieh Fei to wear gloves, even in the summer, because she had cut her little finger while harvesting when she was young, and there was an unsightly scar left on that finger.

* The translation is not my own but that of the invaluable Press Translation Unit of the American Consulate-General in Hong Kong. I have left even its most grotesque locutions unchanged because they convey the flavor of the barbarous Chinese original.

The Maoist morality held it sinful to neglect nephews by marriage who came of "revolutionary, proletarian" background—and equally sinful to care for parents-in-law who were bourgeois. Regardless of her "class origin," it was sinful to dress one's wife well.

Despite such personal sins discovered after the fact, Mao Tse-tung demonstrated his great confidence in Comrade Shao-chi by appointing him First Secretary of the North China Bureau in the spring of 1936. He operated independently in "enemy-occupied territory," that is, the Nationalist areas. Working with the Mayor, he organized the December Ninth Movement. The student demonstrations not only compelled the Nationalists to resist the Japanese but hastened the second Nationalist-Communist alliance, which ended when the final Civil War erupted in 1946. Nonetheless, the Red Guards found much to complain of in Liu's behavior at the time. Their *Chronicle* recounted:

> When Liu Shao-chi made his way from Yenan to the White Area, the organization gave him more than one *catty* [1.3 pounds] of gold to cover expenses. For convenience of transport, the gold was made into one pair of gold bracelets, one necklace, and one belt-buckle. These articles were deposited with the bank after he arrived at the White Area. Later, when Liu Shao-chi returned to Yenan, he was so corrupt as to embezzle the belt-buckle and the gold shoehorn [later] made with Party dues collected and money donated by front organization in the White Area.

Comrade Shao-chi in the mid-thirties formed ties with his later followers. He secured the release of "70 comrades" imprisoned by the Nationalists. He directed them to confess their errors and to promise to oppose Communism. Since the Party desperately needed competent conspirators, it was a logical, even brilliant stroke. Liu was later attacked for "encouraging renegades." Returned to Yenan in April 1937 to attend an Enlarged Meeting of the Political Bureau he had just entered, Liu was acclaimed. But, the Red Guards later charged: "Liu Shao-chi brought the gold belt-buckle with him when he departed; Hsieh Fei [his wife] also took the gold left in the bank in the White Area and handed it to Liu. After Liu returned to Yenan, he embezzled the gold belt-buckle and the gold shoehorn. We have no idea whatsoever of how he disposed of the other articles."

Between alleged peculations, from 1938 to 1942, Comrade Shao-chi was Political Commissar of the New Fourth Army, an independent force operating in Central China. He also composed major theoretical tracts, including *On Inner Party Struggle, Liquidate Menshevik Ideas in the Party,* and *How To Be A Good Communist,* which was later violently denounced. In 1942 the text used for the *Cheng Feng* (Ordering the Winds) Movement, the first great ideological purge, was 22 canonical *Documents on Ordering the Winds*. Most were written by Mao Tse-tung, but the source book included articles by Lenin and Stalin, as well as Liu's *How To Be A Good Communist*.

In 1943, Comrade Shao-chi was elevated to the Secretariat of the Central Committee. The 13 men of the Political Bureau stood in the same relationship to the five-man Secretariat as the British Cabinet to the War Cabinet during the 1939–45 War. Nominally responsible to the Central Committee, the two "leading organs" actually ruled absolutely. Comrade Shao-chi had come to the pinnacle of power.

He could for the first time draw his family around him, reclaiming children previous assignments had forced him to leave to the care of strangers. His personal life was complicated, however, by the rapid succession of two new wives—at least according to the Red Guards' *Chronicle* of his licentiousness. The Red Guards also asserted that he continued to oppose the Chairman's policies and was again playing criminal tricks with the ineffable golden shoehorn.

> His wife wanted to study Chairman Mao's *On New Democracy*, but Liu Shao-chi asked her to read Tsao Yü's *Thunderstorm* and another novel called *The Travels of Mister Derelict*. He talked nonsense, saying, "The Chairman's writings are not cultural works, and you won't be able to understand them!" Liu Shao-chi handed the gold belt-buckle and the gold shoehorn, which he had embezzled, to his new wife for safe custody. Later, after he divorced her, he took away the gold shoehorn and falsely accused her of stealing his gold belt-buckle.

Victory in 1945 raised Comrade Shao-chi to new heights. The Seventh National Congress of the Communist Party convened in Yenan with 755 persons in attendance. Comrade Shao-chi, who was chief among the drafters of the new Party Constitution, presented the draft to the Congress. His *Report on the Party Constitution* was also later used against him, even though he and Chairman Mao were then in perfect rapport in demanding that the Party be administered by "democratic centralism." Mao Tse-tung had written:

> When the heterogeneous tendencies of the petty bourgeoisie are introduced into the Party's administration, we call that phenomenon extremely democratized thought. Such thought is basically incompatible with the militant responsibilities of the proletariat, for, objectively viewed, it is a kind of counterrevolutionary thought. All persons who permit themselves to indulge in that kind of thought serve the counterrevolution.

Comrade Shao-chi vigorously sustained Chairman Mao's demand for absolute obedience to central authority. Noting that much autonomy had unavoidably been granted local guerrilla commanders, he served notice that independence was at an end.

Anti-democratic, dictatorial tendencies and the phenomenon of extreme democratization are the two extremist phenomena in the Party's internal life. However, the phenomenon of extreme democratization, when checked and reprimanded, often gives rise to dictatorial tendencies. On the other hand, when dictatorial tendencies encounter difficulties, they often undergo transformation into the phenomenon of extreme democratization.

The confusing jargon has been deliberately preserved in my translation. In essence, it displayed the fear that opposition—left or right— would unite against the Party Center, which meant Chairman Mao Tse-tung. Comrade Shao-chi was Chairman Mao's faithful advocate. Indeed, he was the indispensable executive officer to the mercurial Chairman. While Mao pondered grand policy, Liu ran the Party machinery.

He was: First Vice Chairman of the Military Affairs Commission, Mao *ex officio* Chairman; member of the Standing Committee of the Political Bureau; and Secretary of the Secretariat. When the Chairman and Chou En-lai, the First Minister of Great Peace, flew to Chungking to negotiate with Chiang Kai-shek from August 28 to November 11, 1945, Liu was supreme in Yenan. Because Comrade Shao-chi apparently lacked both charisma and ambition, he was wholly trusted. He used his authority, the Maoists later charged, to advance his own followers—in opposition to the Disciple Lin Piao.

Early in the year [the Red Guard *Chronicle* charges], Liu Shao-chi outrageously attacked Lin Piao in the northeastern [Manchurian] theater of war. He was as nonsensical as to say the Chairman Mao's strategic thought of "encircling the cities with the countryside" was not applicable in the Northeast. However, Comrade Lin Piao firmly adhered to Chairman Mao's correct line and refused to carry out the erroneous line. As a result the whole of the Northeast was smoothly liberated.*

The clash with the Disciple was provoked by Liu's support for his protégé, the Mayor Peng Chen, just appointed First Secretary of the Party's Northeast Bureau. Moreover, the *Chronicle* conveniently chose

* Translation by the Press Translation Unit, American Consulate-General, Hong Kong.

to ignore the fact that Lin Piao's Manchurian Democratic Allied Armies were armed, equipped, and guided by the Soviet Occupation Forces, and that Manchuria was finally conquered by taking the cities with Russian help, though a few Nationalist garrisons brought in by American aircraft held out for some time.

As First Secretary of the Northeast (Manchurian) Region for many years, Comrade Shao-chi had built the secure base from which the Disciple's forces staged the attacks that routed the Nationalists and conquered China. His power within the Party was therefore unchallenged—as was his devotion to Moscow.

When his eldest son left to study in the Soviet Union, Comrade Shao-chi advised:

> Apply yourself to study and pay no attention to events at home. . . . Grasp the Soviet experience thoroughly through study so that you may return home to participate in construction. The Soviet Union is, at present, the only country with experience in Socialist construction, and other countries must in the future take the Soviet road in such construction. It is, therefore, necessary to learn not only technique but also the method of management. . . . By bringing back all Soviet experience and utilizing it in conjunction with the unselfish aid given by the Soviets, our construction will not take as long and will require less effort."*

Thus Comrade Shao-chi was second only to Chairman Mao. When Nationalist forces took Yenan in the spring of 1947, Chairman Mao and Chou En-lai moved westward with the army. The Working Committee of the Central Committee, under Comrade Liu Shao-chi, Generalissimo Chu Teh, and the Mayor, went east to govern the second chief Communist area. The divided command ended with Communist victories on the battlefield, and in 1948 the Working Committee was dissolved into the reunited Party Center. Comrade Shao-chi was still the powerful second man, while his followers controlled the Party's six regional bureaus.

Faithful to the Soviet Union and the dictates of Mao Tse-tung, Comrade Shao-chi heartily supported Moscow against the revolt of Marshal Josip Broz Tito of Yugoslavia in 1948. His polemic, *On Internationalism and Nationalism,* was the first extensive statement of the Chinese international position, the "policy of leaning to one side" that Chairman Mao would follow until the rage of frustration impelled him to break with Moscow.

"Tito's anti-Soviet stand," the homily warned, "will lead to Yugoslavia's becoming a dupe and the victim of aggression by American imperialism. It will destroy Yugoslavia's independence and make her a colony of imperialism."

* Translation by the American Consulate-General, Hong Kong.

Liu expounded the conventional Marxist rationale. To the bourgeoisie nationalism was an expression of their "class interests." Unsated with the fruits of their exploitation of their own domestic working class, the "bourgeois ruling circles" were eager to exploit the foreign proletariat. Bourgeois nationalism inevitably led to imperialism. "Proletarian nationalism," was quite another matter. Socialist nations wished only to extend the hand of friendship to the proletariat of other nations.

While a capitalist nation *must* become imperialistic, he pointed out, it was quite *impossible* for a Socialist nation to indulge in self-aggrandizement at the expense of other nations. The laws of history decreed that all Socialist nations *must* cooperate for common good. So had Karl Marx written—and so Comrade Shao-chi reaffirmed.

The irony must today ring almost as loud in Liu's own ears as in Chairman Mao's, particularly after the Czech invasion of 1968. But Liu's devotion to Moscow remained constant. In the summer of 1949, just before the founding of the People's Republic, Comrade Shao-chi made his third trip to the Soviet Union, visiting his son and daughter, who were studying in Moscow. He encouraged his son to marry a Soviet girl, to the later ire of the Red Guards. With him went his new wife, the Campus Belle, Wang Kwang-mei. He was later denounced for telling his children: "You have another new mother. Wang Kwang-mei is young and beautiful. You will certainly grow to love her."

Comrade Shao-chi's infatuation with the Soviet Union continued, the Red Guards charged, even after the People's Republic was founded on October 1, 1949, and he became Vice Chairman of the Central People's Government, Vice Chairman of the People's Political Consultative Conference (theoretically comprised of representatives of all political groups), Vice Chairman of the National Committee of the Sino-Soviet Friendship Association, Honorary Chairman of the All-China Federation of Trade Unions, and Vice Chairman of the World Federation of Trade Unions.

He was also blamed for coddling Soviet experts because he reportedly told Chinese technicians working with them: "After the coming of the Soviet technicians, all Chinese cadres must ensure their solidarity with those experts. The Chinese cadres must shoulder the entire responsibility if the relationship and that solidarity are not as perfect as they should be. If the blame for lack of solidarity lies with the Chinese cadres, they must be given three strokes of the cane. If the blame lies with the Soviet side, the Chinese cadres must still receive three strokes of the cane." China desperately needed both Soviet expertise and material aid. Besides, the independent Chinese had for generations dismally failed to work effectively with other foreign "experts."

Comrade Shao-chi continued to press for the closest cooperation with the Soviet Union, even after he became Chairman of the Standing

Committee of the National People's Congress, the showcase "legisla-
ture," and Chairman of the People's Political Consultative Conference,
with the Mayor as his Vice Chairman. Even after Nikita Khrushchev
denounced Stalin at the Twentieth Congress of the Communist Party of
the Soviet Union in 1956, Comrade Shao-chi continued to urge cooperation with the "modern revisionists." He counselled Chinese students in
the USSR: "You have been sent to the Soviet Union to learn techniques,
not to concern yourself with foreign relations or to fight against revisionism. What is the point of quarreling with them? Would it not be bad for
China if they should ask you to leave the Soviet Union because of your
contentiousness?"

His position was eminently practical. China's economic interests were
more important to Liu Shao-chi than ideological controversies. Indeed
he was *too* practical. His pragmatic advice invaluably complemented the
Chairman's visionary enthusiasm—until the Chairman abandoned all
practical counsel.

As early as September 1949, Liu had promised that the transition to
Socialism and Communism would be gradual—and nonviolent. His
reasoned program at once allayed fears of precipitate social revolution
and laid the foundation for the eventual revolution. According to the
Red Guard account, Comrade Shao-chi even told the capitalists of
Tientsin: "Capitalism should be developed to a certain extent, even if
this means that exploitation* by capitalists is increased. I hope that
those of you who are at present exploiting only one thousand workers
will be able to exploit two thousand or even 20 thousand workers."

Devoted to rational, gradual economic development, Comrade Shao-
chi declared: "While it is necessary to carry out Socialism in the
countryside, it is basically not possible to realize collectivization without
concomitant industrial development." His 1954 report on the Draft
Constitution of the People's Republic of China added: "For a considerable time to come, the Socialist economy will co-exist with the capitalist
economy. . . . The State will protect by law the ownership and means of
production and other forms of capital controlled by capitalists."

Comrade Shao-chi's gradualism was eventually criticized as deliberate
defiance of Chairman Mao. Liu argued, for example, that material
incentives were necessary to increase production: "Although piece-work
is not a very satisfactory system, it is still one way to stimulate activism
in production." While stressing the need for material progress, Comrade
Shao-chi deprecated Maoist emphasis upon "unremitting class struggle."
Because the "exploiting classes" had been wiped out and "the stormy

---

* The Red Guard attack deliberately used the pejorative term "exploit,"
whereas the original statement used a term meaning "employ" or "utilize."

period of the revolution has passed" he advocated not "direct action by the masses" but "proper and fair legislation."

Liu added, "with the exception of individual diehards who still attempt to resist, the overwhelming majority of the national bourgeoisie has accepted Socialist transformation economically and has gradually become workers in both name and fact. . . . The capitalists have surrendered their factories and . . . have submitted to Socialist transformation. The capitalists of today are capitalists of a new type." In 1957, he asked: "If our economy is not as flexible and diversified as capitalism, but is characterized chiefly by rigidity, how can we talk about the superiority of Socialism?"

In sum, Liu Shao-chi championed gradual economic progress under the rule of law, rather than the disruptive "campaigns" and purges by which Mao Tse-tung ruled.

The Chief-of-State also took a measured view of foreign affairs. "Even within the U.S. ruling circles," he asserted, "there are some soberminded men who have gradually come to see that the policy of war is not necessarily profitable to the United States." The Red Guards commented bitterly that Liu Shao-chi's quest for economic progress within China and peace abroad were "merely reprints of Khrushchev's Peaceful Transition [to Communism] and Peaceful Competition [with capitalism]."

Because he was nondoctrinaire, Comrade Shao-chi attained the zenith of his power after the failure of the Great Leap Forward. The Second National People's Congress made him Chairman of both the People's Republic of China and the Government's Military Affairs Commission in April 1959. He undertook the assignment of salvaging the Chinese economy and restoring popular morale.

The Red Guards charged:

> After he became Chairman of the State, Liu Shao-chi constantly blew his own trumpet, saying that he was busy and that his responsibilities were heavy and that he was required to handle all the affairs of the country. Wang Kwang-mei was even so brazen-faced as to tell her children, "Daddy is very busy. He has no time for rest. Chairman Mao has now washed his hands of the practical affairs of the State and handed all of them over to your father. You must not disturb him."

Despite wifely pride, the Campus Belle's admonition was not far from the literal truth. Her husband was truly responsible for the administration of both the State and the Party.

In 1959 Comrade Shao-chi remained loyal to Chairman Mao, and refused to join Great General Peng Teh-huai's assault at Mount Lu. Still seeking harmony, he is reported to have jested: "Rather than allow Peng Teh-huai to usurp power in the Party, it is better for me to do so." He told the Military Affairs Commission: "In order to grasp the policies of the Party you must swing left and right, just as in piloting an airplane to Moscow you must make many deviations before you can reach your destination. . . ." On October 1, 1959, the tenth anniversary of the People's Republic, he expressed his general policy: "The first decade has been devoted to reform. The second should be devoted to reconstruction."

Liu Shao-chi was both pragmatic and ruthless. He would use all possible means to increase production. In 1962 he remarked:

> The peasants exploit our weaknesses on the question of food grain. We must exploit their weaknesses in turn, for example their desire for piece-goods, salt, kerosene, matches, insecticides, chemical fertilizer, farm implements, electric power, and the like. . . . The prices asked by the peasants in the free market are very high, but we sell them manufactured goods at cheap prices. With the exception of manufactured goods bartered to the peasants for farm produce, we should sell manufactured goods to them at higher prices.

Although he affirmed the value of the Thought of Mao Tse-tung, the Maoists felt that his enthusiasm was insufficient. When Lin Piao asserted that the Thought of Mao Tse-tung was the apogee of Marxism-Leninism, Liu Shao-chi answered: "It is unscientific to say that the Thought of Mao Tse-tung is the climax of Marxism-Leninism. Can it be said that Marxism-Leninism cannot be developed any further?"

By 1962 the quarrel over ideology and policy was open and bitter. In September the Central Committee enacted harsh new repressive measures. Partial recovery from the Great Leap Forward having been attained, the Chairman had decreed intensification of economic and doctrinal tension. The informal sanction for peasants to work private plots and market their product in free markets was severely curtailed. A Socialist Education Campaign was ordered to bring the masses—and the cadres—back to strict devotion to the Thought of Mao Tse-tung.

Neither the executives of the Party Center nor the "working level" cadres fully enforced the new repression. The cadres in the provinces knew that they could drive the Chinese people just so far. They had convinced the pragmatists of the Central Committee that pressure must be leavened with restraint. Economic repression was, by and large, either diverted or rendered token compliance. The Socialist Education Campaign in the Countryside and the Four Purifications Movement in the cities were directed primarily toward improving relations between the Party and the people—and only secondarily to breaking the masses to the Maoists' will. Loyal to Mao Tse-tung as far as he could be, Comrade Shao-chi was being gradually pushed toward the non-Maoist camp.

He was forced to speak out, noting that the "so-called temporary difficulties of the Great Leap Forward had been brought about 30 per cent by natural calamities and 70 per cent by man-made disasters." He explained in conciliation:

> In saying that the situation was very favorable, the Chairman was discussing the political situation, since the economic situation cannot be described as very favorable. *Indeed it is most unfavorable.* During the past year, the Central Committee has underestimated the gravity of the situation. We have not seen our problems clearly, although our present financial and economic difficulties are great indeed, for *our economy is on the brink of collapse.**

He documented his general criticism:

> Our losses in manpower, fertility of the land, and natural resources have been so heavy that it will be difficult to restore them even in seven or eight years. We are still unwilling to face reality, and we tend to discount our difficulties for fear that presenting a true picture of our predicament would make our cadres lose confidence. Such an approach is obviously not true bravery. It is definitely not the demeanor of a revolutionary or a proper Leninist. . . . Any method which serves to revive the activism of the peasants and to increase production is good enough for the transition period.

Urging tactical retreat in industry, as well as agriculture, Comrade Shao-chi ordered that individual production quotas should be fixed by a realistic appraisal of capability rather than an optimistic assessment of possibilities. "The construction of all projects which cannot make money or yield immediate economic results should be halted," he suggested. "All present enterprises which cannot make money or actually run at a loss should suspend operations and stop paying wages."

Comrade Shao-chi's remarkable ability to abandon petrified thinking was summed up:

> Those who are unable to till their land may ask others to till it on their behalf or put it out to lease. The peasants are free to dispose of

* Emphasis supplied.

their surplus product [after taxation and "deliveries to the State"]. They can take it to the free market for disposal; sell it to the State at a high price; or barter it for manufactured goods to the State. In this way, the peasants can be encouraged to show greater activism in production; the market can be enlivened; and the difficulties of the State can be solved in part. . . . The circulation of commodities is not limited to the adoption of one form of distribution or restricted to one channel. Diverse forms may be adopted, and the free market is one of them.

These heretical suggestions that dogmatic policies be adapted to economic reality aroused Mao Tse-tung's bitter anger. The Chairman was implacably committed to his vision of the ultimate perfection of man. "Class struggle," he insisted, must not merely be endured, but must actually be incited in order to purify society. Comrade Shao-chi believed that material incentives would stimulate gradual progress toward attainable economic goals. Progress would bring harmony out of discord—and, further, productivity out of harmony. Both Chairmen espoused the Marxist analysis and prognosis of social development. Mao, however, maintained that the foundation of the Marxist Utopia could be laid in a historical instant, while Liu contended that rational progress would reach that goal in time.

The pair also differed radically on the use of coercion. Comrade Shao-chi believed that coercion should not be abandoned but must be moderated—lest it become an end in itself. Chairman Mao wished to apply such intense coercion that coercion ultimately became unnecessary. He took the logic of Marxism to the point where it became wholly illogical because it excluded humanity. Comrade Shao-chi accepted the "lower cadres" contention that the Chinese people could not be driven but must be led to Utopia. Socialist Education to him meant measured inducements and persuasion rather than pressure so intense it created popular opposition, as iron becomes steel in the crucible.

The two Chairmen differed equally on foreign policy, though both were determined to avenge the humiliation and exploitation China had suffered from the intrusive West. Mao was determined to sweep away the old world order with the iron broom of "people's war"—guerrilla warfare and subversion, directed from Peking, which would make Chinese influence predominant throughout the world. Less grandiosely, Liu worked to make China a great power by creating conventional industrial and military strength to arm her vast population. Since he had no choice, he was willing to wait. Already experiencing intimations of mortality, Chairman Mao was impatient. The Chairman's foreign policy was based on passionate intuition; Comrade Shao-chi's was based on external realities rather than visceral reactions. Comrade Shao-chi applied cold reason to the Maoist argument that China could not attain Communism until all the oppressed countries of the world had been "liberated" and had attained Communism. He could not endorse Mao's rationalization that domestic failures were due to international conditions or the attempt to compensate for internal difficulties by external victories. He argued against China's undertaking hazardous new adventures abroad while she was crippled by domestic problems. Noting that the withdrawal of Soviet experts in 1960 had severely hampered economic progress, Liu asked: "Since we are preoccupied with our own affairs, how can we provoke U.S. imperialism and Soviet revisionism by aiding the struggles of the peoples of the world?" He thus expressed the basic fears of most of the Chinese leadership, particularly the military.

The Chinese hierarchy grew restive under the lash of the Chairman's obsessions. They knew far better than outsiders how the "cult of personality" and one man's dictatorship could terrorize a party and a nation. In 1964, Liu Jen, Second Secretary of the Peking Municipal Committee and First Vice Mayor of the capital, openly warned the staff of the Peking Friendship Hospital, which had been called the Sino-Soviet Friendship Hospital until the Sino-Soviet rift.

"You have not experienced intra-Party struggle," he said in a lecture, "but I was in the Soviet Union during the Stalin era. At that time, no man dared speak candidly to any other person, while groups of more than two or three never dared to chat in public." The Vice Mayor's next words unmistakably singled out Mao Tse-tung: "In the fall of 1964, I had a long chat with Peng Chen about the problem. I told him that, seeing the way things were going, *they* would soon create another Stalinist situation."

Vice Mayor Liu Jen had been nurturing his apprehension for some time. As early as 1959, he had clashed with the Disciple Lin Piao, newly named Minister of Defense.

Lin Piao told Liberation Army political commissars that the primary and overriding subject of all instruction within the armed forces must be the Thought of Mao Tse-tung. Having coined his personal credo, LIVING STUDY AND LIVING USE OF THE THOUGHT OF MAO TSE-TUNG!, Lin Piao had promoted himself by promulgating the slogan. Vice Mayor Liu Jen had resisted the Disciple's self-glorification. He had insisted upon the principle, "Education must be the pursuit of fundamental knowledge, based upon the systemic study of the development of human society!"

Supported by men like Liu Jen who feared a new terror, Comrade Shao-chi inspected actual conditions throughout the country, while Chairman Mao remained aloof in Peking. He thus inadvertently gave the Red Guards another stick to beat him with. Peking had ruled that no cadre might receive any gift at any time—an unmistakable admission of corruption among the sea-green incorruptibles. While inspecting Manchurian lumber sites, Comrade Shao-chi had accepted a preserved bear's paw from local cadres, and later a box of dried beef from an Indonesian Chinese. Normal etiquette forbade his returning such gifts, which were trivial beside the wholesale corruption of the middle and lower cadres. After the tangled tales of the golden shoehorn and belt buckle, the bear's paw and the dried beef were the last speculations ascribed to Liu Shao-chi.

Through 1965, Comrade Shao-chi both implemented moderate policies to rebuild the economy and consolidated his control of the Party and State apparatus. He acted according to "Socialist legality," for he legitimately directed both the Party Center and the Party branches. The Secretariat was controlled by his protégés: the Organizer Teng Hsiao-ping was Secretary-General, while the Mayor Peng Chen was his deputy. The Securityman Lo Jui-ching, Chief-of-Staff of the Liberation Army, and Lu Ting-yi, chief of the Propaganda Department, were members of the ten-man Secretariat, along with five other moderates. Of his close associates, only the Lord High Executioner Kang Sheng later turned extreme Maoist, and even his position was equivocal until the Cultural Revolution.

Comrade Shao-chi's chief error was his failure to woo the Liberation Army, probably because he felt the Party would continue to control the gun. Despite Lin Piao, the Army appeared subject to the pre-eminent influence of the moderates. The Securityman had been won over to the professionals' view that China's strategy should be defensive rather than offensive. Wherever they looked, the Liu faction saw that they occupied impregnable positions.

They had not reversed dangerous Maoist policies completely, although China was not directly involved in Vietnam. Indeed, Foreign Minister Chen Yi made it quite plain in September 1965 that China had no intention of using her own troops in Vietnam. He warned that an American invasion of China would result in general war, but the obverse was also true: Nothing less than invasion would evoke armed response from Peking.

As the year 1965 closed, morale and production had largely recovered from the Great Leap Forward, though China could boast no spectacular progress. The people were reasonably happy and reasonably well fed. They were even beginning to trust the Communists again.

Lulled by his belief in "Socialist legality" and his apparently impregnable position, Comrade Shao-chi failed to understand the magnitude of the danger inherent in the attack upon playwright Wu Han in November 1965. Maoist pressure mounted in the spring of 1966, but was applied directly against the Mayor rather than Comrade Shao-chi. Like the Soviet hierarchy in the 1930s, the Chinese moderates appeared incapable of appreciating the Chairman's determination to destroy them. A complacent and undeniably naïve Liu Shao-chi was therefore earnestly administering the Communist Party's permanent offices in Peking when the Chairman summoned his minority of the Central Committee to his "temporary revolutionary base" in Shanghai in May 1966.

The Maoists built up their strength by wooing regional and provincial satraps—a slow task, only partially successful—and by deploying military units loyal to Defense Minister Lin Piao. They also extended their attack on the literary front after the Starlet's February Forum on Art and Literature within the Armed Forces. Young Editor Teng To, spokesman for the Mayor, was their main objective at that time. Soon after Wu Han's purgatory, the Young Editor and other writers associated with the Peking Municipal Committee were "exposed for their calumny of Chairman Mao." All their works, the Maoists alleged, deprecated Chairman Mao and the sacred Thought of Mao Tse-tung by innuendo, by inference, and by historical analogy. The newspapers and the magazines of the Peking Municipal Committee, the Maoists asserted, had been "cultivating poisonous weeds under the direction of the anti-Party, anti-Socialist black gang of demons and monsters."*

In mid-May 1966, the Maoists attacked the Mayor head-on. The rump Central Committee in Shanghai refuted the Mayor's *February Theses* and stripped him of all his offices, including the first secretaryships of both the North China Regional Bureau and the Peking Municipal Committee of the Communist Party. The moderate majority of the Central Committee was simply ignored. The *May Sixteenth Circular,* illegally promulgated from Shanghai, was the first barrage of the Maoists' renewed attack on their enemies.

Immediately distributed to every major branch of the Communist Party, the *May Sixteenth Circular* opened an "attack on all fronts." The engagement was no longer limited to the "literary battlefield." The *Circular* commanded a purge of all "bourgeois elements" and formally initiated the Great Proletarian Cultural Revolution, which would throw all China into disorder. All moderation and all balance, all caution and all pragmatism were to be cast aside. Economic realities were ignored by the campaign to PLACE POLITICS IN COMMAND! Ideology—and only ide-

---

* So reads the official translation. The words rendered as "demons and monsters" literally mean "ox-ghosts and snake-spirits."

ology—was to rule. The absolute personal authority of Chairman Mao Tse-tung was to be restored, and the perfect new Communist man of his visions was to be created in a few months' time.

Even abstract truth was arraigned. The *May Sixteenth Circular* asserted:

> Just when we began the counter-offensive against the wild attacks of the bourgeoisie, the authors [the Mayor *et alia*] of the *February Theses* raised the slogan: "Everyone is equal before the truth." This is a bourgeois slogan. Completely denying the class nature of truth, they used this slogan to protect the bourgeoisie and to oppose the proletariat, to oppose Marxism-Leninism and the Thought of Mao Tse-tung. . . . *There is absolutely no such thing as equality before the truth.**

Still Comrade Shao-chi was not unduly perturbed by the indiscriminate attack against "counterrevolutionary revisionists," although the *Circular* added: "Some are still trusted by us, and are, further, being trained as our successors. There are Khrushchev-type persons who still nestle beside us. . ." Still administering Party headquarters in Peking, he did not reject the degradation and expulsion of the Mayor and the entire Peking Municipal Committee.

Yet the deed hardened concerted opposition, an unprecedented development which shocked the opportunists and the dogmatists. The Mayor was unanimously supported by his subordinates—as he had, courageously and without precedent, supported them. The normal rush to save one's self by betraying one's comrades did not occur. The Peking Municipal Committee stood fast as a group.

In April 1966, when the Mayor's fate was all but sealed, First Vice Mayor Liu Jen had persistently defended his chief and his associates. He declared: "The only mistake Peng Chen made in the *February Theses* was correcting leftist excesses. Peng Chen took the responsibility of giving Chairman Mao the raw material on those leftist mistakes. After all, Chairman Mao's spirit is essentially one of uniting to oppose the enemy." Such tenacious loyalty aroused foreboding among the Maoists. Even in late May 1966, when they were all under direct attack, the Mayor's associates refused to save themselves by repudiating him.

For the first time in its history, a major organ of the Communist Party of China resisted *en masse* "correction by higher authority"; every member of the Municipal organ was expelled *en masse*. As startling as their unanimous defiance of a Central Committee directive, however flawed legally, was the resultant suspension of *every* publication of the

* Emphasis supplied.

Peking Municipal Committee. The peremptory action of a segment of the Central Committee under the spell of Chairman Mao and manipulated by a small group of extremists led by the Disciple thereby established a hazardous precedent. It was the most flagrant breach of "Socialist legality" since the founding of the People's Republic. The subsequent defiance of the Peking Committee was as mortal a blow to Party discipline as was the *May Sixteenth Circular* to "Socialist legality."

Nonetheless, Comrade Shao-chi still went along, betraying his protégé Peng Chen. A compromise candidate was installed in the Mayor's place as acting First Secretary of the Peking Committee and the North China Region. Since he was not a member of the Maoist inner circle, he was acceptable to the non-Maoists. He was, for the time being, minimally acceptable to the Maoists as well, though he would during the Great Revolution be purged—and ultimately restored to favor. The legitimist Liu Shao-chi did not protest this gross breach of "Socialist legality." Although the mass expulsion of the Peking Municipal Committee must have shaken his confidence in its efficacy, he still controlled the Party apparatus.

Moreover Comrade Shao-chi had begun to build his defenses. He organized Work Teams of the Cultural Revolution to carry out the purge in the manner *he* ordered, since it was his proper function as administrator of the Party headquarters to direct the new campaign. The public phase of the Great Proletarian Cultural Revolution thus began under the apparent direction of its chief victim.

But a major new force had entered the battle. For the first time, the People's Liberation Army issued direct orders rather than obeying the Central Committee. The military's organ, *The Liberation Army Daily,* became the Maoists' chief voice. *The Army Daily* no longer echoed superior publications like *The People's Daily,* the organ of the Central Committee, or *Red Flag,* the Party's ideological journal. Instead, the military newspaper chided those publications and in fact ordered *The People's Daily* to reverse itself on at least one memorable occasion. Words were backed by force—and the threat of force. Soldiers were on the move throughout China; troops loyal to Lin Piao marched on Peking after securing Shanghai. The replacement of a guard company had been a determining factor at the Eighth Plenum of the Central Committee at Mount Lu. The threat of Lin Piao's guns was to be decisive at the Eleventh Plenum, which formally launched the Great Proletarian Cultural Revolution.

By that session, the military had already deposed certain key members of the Party's Propaganda Bureau, all protégés of the Mayor. Still Comrade Shao-chi held on, secure in the belief that he too had friends within the Army. It was a major miscalculation. Like the amorphous "opposition" to Joseph Stalin, he played for time. But, like that opposition, he waited too long to organize his resistance. He was apparently still mesmerized by Chairman Mao. Like the Soviet opposition, he was incapable of comprehending his leader's total recklessness. He certainly underestimated the influence of the Disciple, had he fully understood Lin Piao's implacable drive for power and vengeance, he might have acted quite differently.

As late as June 1966, Liu Shao-chi apparently believed he could contain the struggle for power within legal limits. He ignored the fact that those limits had already been violated by the Maoists' illegal dismissal of the Mayor. The struggle was already moving out of the party's councils into China's chief universities. The Communist Party's fratricidal battle was focused on the campuses where the movement had begun 50 years earlier. His own Work Teams of the Cultural Revolution moved onto the campuses of Peking in mid-June, initiating the interim period called "the 50 days of Liu Shao-chi." The other Chairman, it appeared, was finally moving effectively to reassert "Socialist legality"—and save China from anarchy.

XI

The Siege of the Campuses

Across four million square miles from the icy Manchurian steppes along the Ussuri River in the extreme northeast to the jagged crevasses drenched with green tropical growth in Yunnan in the extreme southwest—and even on the high and windy Tibetan plateau—Communist leaders were "mobilizing soldiers and assembling horses." The population watched, bewildered by their masters' preparation for strife. China came more than once to the brink of open civil war between the followers of the two Chairmen, some bound by personal loyalty and personal interest, others still pondering their true allegiances. Although a conventional civil war was fought only briefly in a few provinces in 1968, June and July of 1966 witnessed the first major battles of the political war that was to provoke almost universal civil disorder.

The struggle ranged from the six powerful Regional Bureaus of the Communist Party to the headquarters of divisions and corps scattered through the 13 Military Regions. Battle was met in radio stations, printing houses, and newspaper offices, as well as the headquarters of the Public Security Corps, the ubiquitous network of guard troops, police, and agents. Yet the contention was limited to a few thousand senior policymakers and administrators in the early summer of 1966. Peking was the major and Shanghai the secondary battlefield. Traditional Maoist tactics were reversed, for the two great cities contended to conquer the countryside. Peking was on the defensive, troubled by shifting alliances, threats and counterthreats, constant anguished consultations, and ceaseless rumors. The Shanghai minority under Chairman Mao successfully intimidated the legitimate Party Center in the capital.

The first violent skirmishes of the Cultural Revolution were fought on Peking's campuses, which had been centers of decisive political influence since the fall of the Manchu Dynasty. Despite the Mayor's degradation, the entire Peking Municipal Committee still resisted the Maoist assault, relying upon its strongholds in the universities. Awakened at last from his torpid complacency, Comrade Shao-chi was invading the campuses with his Work Teams of the Cultural Revolution. Seedbeds of the "successor generation" of new revolutionaries, the universities provided ideas, recruits, and stimuli for political change.

Foremost was the Peking National University, called *Pei-ta,** short for *Pei-ching Ta-hsüeh,* as the University of Pennsylvania is called Penn or the University of California at Los Angeles U.C.L.A. China's first modern institution of higher learning, Pei-ta had always been a political cockpit. Doctrines and organizations bred in the Pei-ta classrooms and dorms had dominated twentieth-century culture, directly effecting sweeping social and political changes.

In summer 1966, Pei-ta outwardly appeared a sanctuary of peace in the tumultuous capital of People's China. Enclosed by an arc of low, traditional buildings with upturned eaves, a pastel 13-tier pagoda was reflected in twin lakes at the center of the campus. Four-story buildings among green groves housed dormitories, classrooms, and laboratories. The gray-green Western Hills rose hazily on the horizon, where the eternal yellow plains of the north marked the verge of vast, age-old agrarian China. It was in every external aspect an ideal site for the untroubled pursuit of pure knowledge.

Yet many great storms that transformed the nation had risen out of that tranquil setting. Founded in 1898 by the Reformer Emperor, Kuang Hsü, to "alter the nation," Peking University had survived the wrathful counterreformation commanded by his aunt, the reactionary Empress Dowager, Tzu Hsi. From 1917 to 1919, Pei-ta nurtured not only Marxism but also the Literary Revolution that destroyed the elided Classical style and the Confucian state ideology that had dominated the nation for two millennia. Politics and literature were inseparable, for officials had qualified by composing *belles lettres* essays.

The New Literature Movement culminated in the May Fourth Movement of 1919. Student riots forced a venal government to risk war with Japan by rejecting an ultimatum that would have destroyed Chinese sovereignty. Students and activist professors became a major force, for they had discovered that mass demonstrations are a powerful political weapon. The classes of 1914 to 1921 produced most of the founders of

---

* The term is pronounced *Bay-dah,* despite the conventional transliteration which confuses pronunciation for all but the initiate.

the Chinese Communist Party. Chairman Mao himself was no more than an assistant in the University Library, but China's two chief Marxist theoreticians were senior professors. The Party's First Secretary-General was Dean of the Faculty of Letters. Any realistic appraisal of Pei-ta's power compelled the Communists to pay the University close attention.

Not only the bright young men of the Communist Party but the intellectual leaders of the Nationalists as well came from Pei-ta's faculty and student body during the 1920s. Active in propaganda and literature as well as in politics and technology, Pei-ta men fostered a "modern" national consensus among the intelligentsia. Although the officers of the Nationalist-Communist forces that defeated the warlords in the 1920s were educated at the Whampoa Military Academy, the administrators and theoreticians were largely products of Pei-ta and other civilian universities.

Student protest against "imperialists and Chinese exploiters" moved the Chinese people to some degree of unity. In the 1930s, student demonstrations forced the reluctant Nationalist government to resist the Japanese. The Mayor Peng Chen and Comrade Shao-chi personally organized student cells. From Pei-ta the Mayor recruited the activists of the December Ninth Movement of 1936, which culminated in the Nationalist-Communist alliance against the Japanese.

The University was equally active during the Communists' final drive to power in the late 1940s. Cavorting in grotesque costumes to depict "American imperialists and Nationalist oppressors," students had roused the intelligentsia's ardor for the Communist cause. Thousands of students streamed to the "liberated areas" to contribute their skill and passion to shaping a new China in the Communist mold. Their conspiracies, their labors, and their demonstrations brought doom to the Nationalists and power to the Communists.

After the establishment of the People's Republic in 1949, Pei-ta was shaken by literary and philosophical debates arising directly out of major controversies within the Party. In 1957, Chairman Mao proclaimed: "Let a Hundred Flowers blossom! Let all schools of thought contend!" and the University again revolted against oppression. Students denounced the regime's dogmatism and deliberate suppression, protesting the stifling of economic and intellectual life. Shocked by the intense resentment thus revealed, the Communist Party ruthlessly counterattacked. Students were "sent down" to the countryside to learn "true proletarian consciousness through manual labor." The Communists had learned that the intelligentsia, exemplified by Pei-ta, would not be their "docile tools."

The Maoists had by 1958 decided to dispense with the "old-fashioned, bourgeois-tainted intelligentsia," but Peking University remained a contentious center of experiment. Its classrooms were packed with "workers, peasants, and soldiers," whose academic qualifications were abysmal, but who were presumably pure ideologically. Since even the most extreme Maoists realized that they could not dispense with Pei-ta, they sought to alter its nature. The University was directed to "produce a new generation of educated proletarians."

There was no real agreement within the Party on educational policy. Antagonistic factions contended for control of the University. The pragmatists largely prevailed because the students supported them. The moderates of Comrade Shao-chi, after all, opposed Maoist anti-intellectualism, were inherently civilian-oriented, and were men of the book rather than the gun. The University's economists, technicians, managers, and scientists had, therefore, overseen the gradual recovery from the Great Leap Forward in the early 1960s.

As Pei-ta went, so would go the other universities of the nation. Only slightly less influential was neighboring Chinghua University, seven miles beyond the northwest quarter of Peking. The domed central hall stood at one end of a broad prospect; at the other, a traditional Chinese arch was supported by Ionic columns, an incongruous combination of East and West. Lacking Pei-ta's rigorous intellectual prestige, Chinghua boasted outstanding work in science and engineering. Despite traditional rivalry, students of Pei-ta and Chinghua united against tyranny, joined by American-founded Yenching University. In China the universities of Peking were the intellectual, political, and social equivalent of Britain's Cambridge and Oxford or America's Ivy League. They were not merely the plexus of China's "old boy net"—under Communists as well as capitalists—but a prime mover of political change.

The Disciple Lin Piao, a product of the Whampoa Military Academy and later president of the Anti-Japanese Political and Military Academy in Yenan, maneuvered to control the universities as he had already infiltrated the Communist Youth League and the Federation of Trade Unions. Aggressively plain-spoken himself, Lin Piao resented the polished products of the civilian universities. He joyously used the same "strategy of annihilation" that had prevailed over both the Japanese and the Nationalists. In time his strategy proved of little avail, but his opening attacks were meticulously planned and brilliantly executed.

Memories of past political struggles were almost tangible among the brick walls and winter-blasted lawns of Pei-ta's campus on May 26, 1966, when the small Maoist faction began its guerrilla offensive against the non-Maoist majority. The Mayor and the Peking Party Committee had already been dismissed by the *May Sixteenth Circular*. His "old cadres," who controlled the administration and dominated the faculty, had already been shaken by the general Maoist assault on academia. They were brought under direct attack as a plump, middle-aged instructor in the Philosophy Department posted an indictment thereafter acclaimed as "the first great-character poster of the Great Proletarian Cultural Revolution." Nieh Yüan-tze, a bespectacled lady of uncertain years, was a protégé of Chiang Ching. The poster had been tested as a weapon in the Hundred Flowers Movement, when the campus blossomed with "great-character posters"—until the Maoists suppressed freedom of expression.

Fighting desperately to regain power in the late spring of 1966, the Maoists employed the weapon of the minority. Thus began "the battle of the posters." Nieh Yüan-tze's was the precursor of tens of millions which spread over China like an irrepressible tropical growth. If the Cultural Revolution was initially fought with words, the "great-character posters" were its machine guns. The heavy artillery was the press and radio; the mortars, Red Guard tabloids; and the small arms, "face-to-face accusations in mutual criticism meetings." The posters were called *ta-tze pao,* literally "big-ideograph papers," because the Chinese characters were writ large for easy reading.

The Mayor and the entire Peking Committee still persisted in their defiance. The target of the "first great-character poster" was "Peng Chen's agents on the campus," the president and administrative officers who also controlled the university's Party committee. Some were true scholars, while others were *apparatchiks,* but all were supporters of the moderates. Almost all had won advancement through political intrigue rather than the equally bitter academic intrigue common to Western universities. They could therefore expect no mercy from the Maoists.

Nieh Yüan-tze's poster was unquestionably dictated from above by the Starlet and the Disciple. The Maoists later said Chairman Mao himself had bestowed his *imprimatur* five days after its appearance. The Maoists claimed that the first poster was an expression of spontaneous indignation, but the "great-character poster" that began the Cultural Revolution was both too audacious and too specific to give credibility to their claim.

> Counterattacking the sinister black gang which has frantically attacked the Party, Socialism, and the Thought of Mao Tse-tung is a life-and-death struggle. . . . Mass meetings and great-character posters are the masses' best weapons in the battle to denounce the counter-revolutionaries.
>
> Now is the time for all revolutionary intellectuals to go into battle . . . to resolutely, thoroughly, and totally wipe out all monsters and demons and all counterrevolutionary revisionists. . . .

Why are you so afraid of great-character posters and mass denunciation meetings? By "guiding" the masses to avoid mass meetings and great-character posters . . . are you not supressing revolution, preventing the masses' making revolution, and opposing their making revolution? We will not permit you to do so!

You prate about "strengthening the leadership and standing fast at one's post." That slogan displays your true colors. . . . It is not absolutely clear what "posts" you want to hold fast and whom you wish to retain? Have you not revealed exactly what kind of people you are and what evil tricks you are still playing—as you still desperately resist. You want to "stand fast" to sabotage the Cultural Revolution. We warn you that ants cannot stop the wheels of a car or mayflies topple a giant tree. You are only day-dreaming!

Now is the time for all revolutionary rebels to go into battle! Let us unite and hold high the Great Red Banner of the Thought of Mao Tse-tung! Let us rally round the Party Central Committee and Chairman Mao! Let us smash all the taboos and plots of the revisionists!

The president of Pei-ta learned of the poster's appearance while attending a meeting of the Peking Municipal Committee. Formally—if illegally—deposed, that body was still in session. Despite Comrade Shao-chi's tepid and equivocal attitude, the Peking Committee insisted that it still held legitimate authority. Mao Tse-tung's personal fiat, the Mayor argued, could not sweep aside "Socialist legality." He demanded that the full Central Committee judge his case, for he knew that the non-Maoists commanded a legitimate majority. The Shanghai group was, he asserted, but a handful of opportunists mesmerized by Mao's evil genius, Lin Piao.

The president of Pei-ta rushed back to the campus to rally his supporters. The administration in solid phalanx denounced Nieh Yüan-tze and her collaborators as "opportunists and liars."

But the Maoist attack could not be turned, much less broken, by such feeble sallies. On June 1, 1966, Madame Nieh's text was broadcast to the entire nation by Radio Peking, and the Great Proletarian Cultural Revolution had begun. The battle was fairly met. All study and research was suspended at the Pei-ta campus while the contending factions covered every wall with thousands of "great-character posters." Soon no verticle surface remained unpapered, and walls of straw matting were raised to display the diatribes.

The "rebel revolutionaries" met stiffening opposition from students and teachers aghast at the new purge. Work Teams of the Cultural Revolution dispatched by Comrade Liu Shao-chi from the legal Party Headquarters to control the fighting were commanded by his wife, Wang

Kwang-mei, the Campus Belle. Their instructions were vague, largely because their masters were indecisive. Still, they bolstered the administration's resistance to the violent Maoist attacks. But Comrade Shao-chi's Work Teams soon realized that the enemy was skillfully organized and directed.

Official periodicals the Maoists had seized by force of arms soon denounced the president of Peking University by name, in contrast to the usual procedure of reserving identification until the purge had been accomplished. On June 8, 1966, the ideological journal *Red Flag* formally proclaimed the Great Proletarian Cultural Revolution, revealing Maoist determination to scourge the entire nation. The ideological magazine edited by the Ghostwriter, Chen Po-ta, Mao's political secretary, issued a stark order: "Crush all the men following the capitalist road who have wormed their way into power within the Communist Party!" The pragmatists were excoriated for "opposing Chairman Mao." They were reprimanded for their liberal domestic policies, and for advocating "compromise with enemies abroad" rather than "people's wars of liberation"—like the struggle in Vietnam.

Chanting students swarmed through Peking, waving placards bearing opposing slogans. Most of the activists supported the Maoists, for the moderates' organization was tumbling. Liu Shao-chi was still "administering the headquarters of the Communist Party," and Mao Tse-tung was still in refuge in the south. The Maoists had brilliantly organized their psychological campaign; they called for "rebellion" against the bureaucrats who "suppressed the masses and defied Chairman Mao." The moderates denounced personal dictatorship and the "cult of personality." Both autocratic Chairmen—Mao Tse-tung and Liu Shao-chi—appealed to the students to rally to the cause of liberty. Both charged their wives to lead the struggle on the campuses. The Starlet had entered the fray in February. The Campus Belle had been active for years in support of her husband. Public scandal had already flowered from the deep-rooted enmity between the two ladies during the preceding years.

Feminine pique, as well as conflicting interests, lay behind that enmity. The sunny, well-educated, and cosmopolitan Campus Belle was everything the bitter, ill-lettered, and insular Starlet was not. Madame Liu, the Chinese said, was a "nail in the eye" of Madame Mao. The Starlet, who had attained her position so arduously, deeply resented the Campus Belle, to whom everything was given freely. Moreover, the Campus Belle was feted at home and abroad, while she herself lived in gray seclusion. The Starlet felt she should stand in the limelight as China's true first lady.

The personal enmity was manifest when the Campus Belle was vilified by the Starlet's Red Guards for walking arm-in-arm with President

Sukarno of Indonesia and for flaunting her clothes and her jewelry. In Rangoon, Wang Kwang-mei had appeared in a pink silk dress with a matching parasol—a costume hardly designed to win the Starlet's approbation. She had further offended by asking Chiang Ching whether she should wear a costly pearl necklace—and ignoring her advice not to indulge in "bourgeois display."

In her flair for fashion, as in so many other respects, Wang Kwang-mei was the antithesis of the bitter country girl Chiang Ching. Born in 1922 in San Francisco,* the Campus Belle grew up in Tientsin, the commercial capital of North China, just a few hours' ride from Peking. She chose her parents well—by bourgeois standards. Her father had collaborated with the "Northern Warlords" for economic advantage before the Nationalists unified the country in 1928. He not only held lucrative official posts, but grew wealthier through commerce. Her maternal uncle was managing director of the Heng Yüan Spinning Mills, one of North China's largest enterprises. The Wangs and the Tungs, her mother's clan, were among the leading families of Tientsin, the *haut bourgeoisie*. They maintained close economic, social, and cultural ties with Western businessmen. The Campus Belle was almost unique in her "class origin" among the Communist hierarchy, most of whom were born of petty bourgeois or middle-class farm families. She paid dearly in the end for her early advantages.

Life was pleasant and stimulating for a rich man's daughter in the cosmopolitan city. Her every childhood wish was fulfilled and often anticipated by devoted servants in soft slippers. She was sent to an expensive girls' school. The burly driver of her limousine was as much bodyguard as chauffeur, for the wealthy young Miss Wang was an obvious lure to kidnapers. Occasional foreign travel with her indulgent parents spiced the pleasant routine. She developed strong and rather old-fashioned filial devotion—a quality that later excited the wrath of the Red Guards.

The smooth pattern of her life was hardly disrupted by the Sino-Japanese conflict, which began in earnest in 1937. While China was fighting Japanese invasion, she attended Fujen University and then Yenching University. Both were located in Peking, and both were Western-oriented, the former Catholic-sponsored, the latter American-sponsored. The front line had already moved far beyond Peking, where the Japanese sought to maintain normal administration through quisling governments, and Communist agents were active on the campuses through the apparatus created by Comrade Shao-chi and Peng Chen in the mid-1930s. Wang Kwang-mei's conversion to Communism was ac-

* *Kwang-mei* means "the light of America," while her youngest brother, born in London, was called *Kwang-ying,* "the light of England."

complished with her accustomed serenity. Unlike many schoolmates, she was moved neither by resentment of her parents nor by anger at society. She was inspired by detached idealism and ardent patriotism.

The Communists deliberately appealed to the nationalistic pride of young Chinese who saw their nation rent by foreign invasion after suffering decades of humiliation at foreign hands. Since the Nationalists had been unable to stem the Japanese incursion, the Communists asserted that only they could "save the nation." The Campus Belle was engrossed by her social career and her studies, English as an undergraduate and, later, physics. She did not become a zealot. She did not join classmates in the stealthy journey to Yenan to enroll in the Communist ranks.

But the Campus Belle was a serious young lady, despite her pleasure in parties and self-adornment. She was a delicate, soft-skinned girl with finely shaped hands and ankles. Her manner was demure, and her spirit was troubled by neither adversity nor doubt. When the war ended in 1945, she was already half-converted. Her first participation in politics was an implicit decision for the Communists. Her road to Yenan led through the Temple of the Thousand Sleeping Colonels. The 24-year-old Campus Belle used her excellent English as an interpreter for the Communist delegation at the Peking headquarters of the American mission led by General of the Army George C. Marshall, which sought to reconcile Nationalists and Communists. Negotiations dragged on inconclusively, since both sides considered talking merely a screen for fighting. In 1947, General Yeh Chien-ying, the chief Communist negotiator, persuaded the Campus Belle to commit herself and come to Yenan.

Since her reception was arranged by friends within the hierarchy, she was warmly welcomed as a valuable recruit and made the trip without discomfort. Her course was utterly different from the struggle the Starlet had endured in order to reach Yenan and make her mark there.

Marriage to Liu Shao-chi was a natural, untroubled consummation. Vigorous at 45, he was already second only to Chairman Mao in the hierarchy. His life had been an unending conspiratorial struggle recorded in his drawn features and his furtive air, but he had already emerged into the sunlight. Comrade Liu Shao-chi's previous wife had already died, and the Party offered no objection to the match. The suspicion that plagued the Chairman and the Starlet had passed. Wang Kwang-mei and Liu Shao-chi lived the conventional tale of a woman and a man: they met, they loved, and they married. They came to Peking less than two years later, and the People's Republic of China was formally established on October 1, 1949. Mao Tse-tung was Chairman and Liu Shao-chi Vice Chairman.

The Campus Belle slipped into quiet domesticity in the Chungnanhai (South Lake) District within the Imperial City, where senior Communist leaders lived. She cared for Comrade Shao-chi's young daughter by his previous marriage and herself bore him two daughters. Unlike "female comrades" distinguished by personal accomplishments, she rarely appeared in public during the first decade of Communist hegemony. Both Chairmen relegated their wives to the seclusion traditionally considered proper for the consorts of Chinese rulers.

The pattern was broken in the early 1960s, when the Starlet and the Campus Belle were elected to the National People's Congress of 1964. Membership in the parliament, in theory the supreme authority of the State, formally acknowledged the new roles they had already assumed in the struggle within the Communist Party.

Uncharacteristically, Madame Liu Shao-chi took the more dramatic and more active part at the outset. While Madame Mao Tse-tung attacked the Peking Opera, the Campus Belle went to the "masses." In 1963 she was "sent down" to live among the peasants, China's chief source of power and chief problem. Her assignment was part of a concerted campaign to relieve the deprivation and demoralization that followed the Great Leap Forward. The Liu administration urgently required reliable, firsthand information on actual circumstances in the great agricultural hinterlands where 80 percent of China's population lived and labored.

Recognizing that the People's Communes had alienated the rural population, the pragmatists were determined to regain the peasants' confidence. Otherwise production would not increase nor would the State acquire a significant portion of the yield, though need for capital was acute. With the cancellation of Moscow's aid as a result of the Sino-Soviet quarrel, Peking was forced to rely upon its own resources. Only a resurgent agriculture could restore popular morale, remedy acute food shortages, and provide the capital to revitalize the economy. Of course, only a rebounding economy could maintain the Communist *imperium* over China.

The doctrinaire Maoists, who were still drafting formal ideological pronouncements, offered a characteristically impractical solution based upon a characteristically unrealistic assessment. They asserted—and believed—that, neither unrealistic programs nor high-level maladministration but, "natural calamities," compounded by withdrawal of Soviet aid, had caused "temporary difficulties." The Maoists contended that floods, drought, typhoons, and inefficiency at the working level, rather than massive errors of judgment, had produced the catastrophic failure of the Great Leap Forward and had generated massive resentment against the Great People's Communes. The Chairman specifically put the blame on the "excessively low ideological level of working-level cadres and the masses." The explanation deluded few Chinese—aside from purblind Maoists.

The characteristic Maoist solution was a new campaign of repression designed to extirpate such evil tendencies among rural cadres and the masses as political and economic corruption, disorganization, and ideological deviation. Since failures of the human spirit rather than material phenomena had frustrated their design for mastering man and nature, the Maoists commanded total spiritual regeneration of the Chinese people. Peking ordered the Great Socialist Education Campaign in the countryside in 1963; the Four Purifications Movement was first to purge evildoers.

The moderates approached the "rural problem" in a wholly different spirit. They felt so securely in control that, after performing the ritual obeisances to Chairman Mao, they conducted both movements as "underground campaigns." There was so little "fanfare" that the outside world knew almost nothing of the scope planned for these movements— while both rural and urban masses were disturbed as little as possible. The moderates wished to base agricultural policy upon material and psychological reality, rather than the Chairman's determination to impose moral perfection upon all men and women. They realized that they could not depend upon information supplied by local cadres who systematically falsified reports to mollify a distant and wrathful Peking. Totally reliable agents were essential to determine what was *actually* happening in the countryside.

Since conflict within the Chinese Central Committee was intense, the leaders required agents bound to them by the strongest ties of kinship, obligation, or common interest. Comrade Shao-chi used his wife and his protégé, Peng Chen; Chairman Mao used his wife and his protégé, Lin Piao. Conditioned by the Confucian system of nepotism and mutual protection, China's rulers had for millennia instinctively turned to such individuals in moments of supreme crisis.

In November 1963 the Campus Belle was sent to the Tao Yüan (Peach Garden) Great Production Brigade in a People's Commune 150 miles from Peking to see how matters really stood. She called herself Tung Tu, adopting her mother's surname to remain incognita, although nearly everyone knew she was wife to the powerful Chairman of the People's Republic. Her instructions from Comrade Shao-chi were simple: "Do not proceed from rigid preconceptions. Since everything derives from actual, fundamental reality, we must solve problems as they actually are—rather than as we imagine them to be!"

Superficially it was an incongruous assignment. The delicate city-bred beauty was ignorant of rural life and was personally fastidious. Yet the time was critical, since the peasants were close to the political, psychological, and economic breaking point; direct participation by Lui Shao-chi's wife demonstrated his overwhelming personal concern and, at the same time, provided an instrument he could trust absolutely—in judgment, discretion, and loyalty.

Hostile Red Guard publications subsequently portrayed a selfish, pampered woman who lived apart from the common people and insisted upon a new road's being built to the village to serve her comfort. Yet the Red Guard's detailed changes half-refuted their own accusations. The worst personal charge they could conjure up was: "She always wore white gloves to protect her hands!"—a practice hardly unknown among farm women. Their worst political charge: "She formed a coterie of anti-Party elements," who gave personal loyalty to her rather than to Mao Tse-tung. The comprehensive criticism that she had behaved in a "disgusting bourgeois fashion" was refuted by the Red Guards' admission of the influence she gained among the farmers. Besides, the new road opened the Peach Tree Commune to the outside world, conferring an enormous economic advantage.

The intended vilification in fact portrayed a woman who immersed herself in the life and problems of the peasants who were the matrix of Chinese society. She appears finally to have been accepted—despite natural suspicion of one who was both a fine lady and a powerful commissar. The peasants were impressed as much by her sharing their labor and hardship as they were by her concern with their problems. A plaque was erected by the village upon her departure. It read:

> During the Four Purifications Campaign, Comrade Wang Kwang-mei lived for five months in the small hut of the old poor-peasant Liu Yu-shen. Her quarters were cramped, and she had neither a table nor a chair to use when she had to perform clerical work. Instead, she quite happily spread her papers on the *kang*.* Comrade Kwang-mei worked hard until 11 or 12 every evening. When she had a free moment during the day, she would carry water from the well or sweep out the courtyard. She always worked hard and diligently. Her life was as meagre and deprived as our own. She ate together with the other comrades, following the Principle of Three-Togetherness. She behaved with much courtesy toward all of us and was very concerned about our needs—she rejected no one. Comrade Wang Kwang-mei's revolutionary spirit and outstanding performance made a deep, enduring impression on the broad masses of the comrades of the Commune!

Knowing who she was, the peasants obviously felt it politic to express their approbation fully. But the inscription would hardly have breathed

---

* The large earthen platform, heated by a small internal fire of millet stalks and twigs, which serves the farmers of North China as both bed and table.

simple sincerity, unblemished by Party jargon, had she not behaved well. If the farmers found her congenial, the Campus Belle for the first time understood the nature of the life of the rural masses. She had obeyed the Chairman's dictum, "Go among the masses and learn from the masses!" Her impressions, however, were greatly at variance with Mao Tse-tung's own conception of the state of the peasantry. The Peach Garden Production Brigade, she found, was really a traditional Chinese village—the age-old harshness of existence hardly altered by the formal Communist superstructure imposed by the People's Commune.

The Campus Belle's lengthy report, *Experiences at Tao Yüan,* was the basis of the formal *Later Ten Conditions on Agriculture* issued by the Party in 1964. That document was a substantial revision of the *Earlier Ten Conditions on Agriculture* drafted by Mao Tse-tung himself. Implicitly contradicting the Chairman's assumptions, the *Later Ten Conditions* outlined a non-Maoist policy toward the farmers. In essence Wang Kwang-mei's *Peach Garden Report* was no more than an acknowledgment of reality—as was the policy it fostered. The practical men of Peking sanctioned the "Three Freedoms and One Guarantee" the peasants already enjoyed, which was what the peasants wanted. Since 1960 local cadres had tolerated limited "free [private] markets, individual [free] plots, independent [free] management of economic enterprises, and guaranteed [*i.e.,* fixed and reasonable] crop allotments for the State."

The Maoists denounced the Three Freedoms and One Guarantee as "anti-Socialist." The extremists wanted a regimented peasantry, bound by rigid production quotas and arbitrarily altered "deliveries to the State." The doctrinaire Maoists objected to communities of independent farmers, free to grow their own crops on their own plots and to sell them on the open market. The ideologues said, quite correctly, that such groups were "petty bourgeois, not proletarian." The Maoists, rather paradoxically, wished to reverse the basic conception of the Great People's Communes. Originally conceived to decentralize economic responsibility and reduce bureaucracy, the Communes were to be restored as a means of imposing the central bureaucracy's absolute control.

The *Later Ten Conditions on Agriculture* and the new direction given the Socialist Education and Four Purifications Campaigns, in turn, reversed the Maoist course. Instead of concentrating upon studying the Thought of Mao Tse-tung, the rural population was allowed to get on with its work. Instead of rigid control of production and distribution, the peasants enjoyed relative freedom. The battle for political supremacy underlying the controversy over agricultural policy presaged the pitched battles of the spring of 1966, when the non-Maoists maneuvered to turn the Great Proletarian Cultural Revolution to their own ends, as they had turned the Four Purifications Campaign. Through the engagements of the spring of 1966, Comrade Shao-chi and the Campus Belle sought to divert the thrust of the Cultural Revolution and to maintain their policies and their power. The campuses of Peking, rather than the villages of the countryside, were the battlefield.

Wild and occasionally ludicrous confusion ruled the capital of the world's most populous nation that spring. The Chairman of the legally elected Central Committee had enrolled the volatile students to break the will of the majority of that Committee. Debates raged back and forth, punctuated by threats, confinement, and violence.

The hardest battle was fought at Chinghua University, Peking's second institution of higher learning, where the Maoist organization was initially more powerful. The Campus Belle herself led the Work Team, which exerted intense psychological and somewhat less intense physical pressure against the Maoists. The Work Team was supported by influential faculty and students from the President, who was also Minister of Higher Education in the People's Government, and the Campus Belle's stepdaughter Liu Tao, Comrade Shao-chi's child by an earlier marriage, to Ho Peng-fei, the son of the Bandit General Field Marshal Ho Lung. The battle was fought on the campuses throughout June and well into July. It ended in a draw—with an exchange of "strongholds." The Maoists generally prevailed at Pei-ta, while their opponents "seized" Chinghua.

The Campus Belle spent 40 days at Chinghua directing the fight against the "rebel revolutionaries." The Starlet and the Ghostwriter Chen Po-ta, supported by the King of the South Tao Chu, pleaded the Maoist case. Emboldened by the decline of authority, students on both sides defied their elders. Fistfights and suicides, street fighting and abductions created an atmosphere of anarchy. The old days of student power and free speech seemed to have come again. Eager to vent their resentments, many students supported the Maoists who urged them: "Dare to make revolution and be good at making revolution! Dare to create disorder!"

The Maoists withheld their chief assault, as Lin Piao harassed the enemy with guerrilla tactics before the main onslaught. Although his Work Teams were badly directed, Liu Shao-chi still held much power. Despite his failure to defend his closest associate Peng Chen, the new Peking Municipal Committee was inclined toward Comrade Shao-chi. He still controlled the central apparatus, as well as most provincial Party branches, and he was, it appeared, supported by the Party's Secretary-General, the Organizer Teng Hsiao-ping.

The moderates, at long last, rallied their forces outside Peking. Their emissaries traveled throughout the country to woo local leaders. Among others, they enrolled two formidable supporters: Liu Lan-tao, First Secretary of the Northwest Bureau, which controlled China's nuclear facilities; and Li Ching-chüan, First Secretary of the Southeast Bureau, with its seat in Chengtu, the capital of the "independent kingdom," where, behind their mountain walls, more than 70 million Szechwanese produced much of China's rice. Both Regional First Secretaries were old adherents of Comrade Shao-chi; both sat high in the Party's central councils; and both shared common interests with the legitimate, civilian apparatus.

The Maoists, too, were recruiting adherents, chief among them the King of the South, Tao Chu, First Secretary of the Central–South China Bureau, which presided over major industrial and communications facilities. The non-Maoists appeared to the advantage, for they commanded the majority of the Central Committee and the great mass of "middle and lower cadres." The division was acute, for the struggle for power and principle was quite clearly the most critical in the history of the People's Republic.

But the civilians had ignored the Maoist maxim: "Power grows from the barrel of the gun!" They still believed that the Central Committee rather than the Liberation Army would shape the future of China. Chief-of-Staff Lo Jui-ching was a non-Maoist who had already agreed that the civilian police must be strengthened, while the Liberation Army stayed outside the struggle. The moderates had already worked out a loose agreement with General Wang En-mao, satrap of the New Dominion of Sinkiang, who controlled China's uranium mines as well as her nuclear and rocket ranges. They had reached an understanding with a number of field marshals and senior generals, who no longer commanded troops directly. But they could not muster many generals who commanded divisions, corps, or armies. Their inability prevented open civil war—and severely limited the moderates' effectiveness.

The Maoists used the gun. Their field commander was Defense Minister Lin Piao, who had indoctrinated the Liberation Army with the Thought of Mao Tse-tung—as interpreted by Lin Piao. His generals had sworn loyalty to the "Chinese people and Chairman Mao," with the Communist Party a poor third. Since the beginning of 1966, the Army's propaganda organs had been the chief voice denouncing the moderates. While the non-Maoists maneuvered politically, Lin Piao was moving troops. He ordered no armed assaults, and no shots were fired. But in mid-June, soldiers took up positions at all vital installations in Peking— even at key street corners.

The naked threat of armed force was unusual, though not rare, in Party history. With the Central Committee split between the Shanghai and Peking Centers, it seemed only armed force could resolve the stalemate. As early as May 15, 1966, rumors swept Peking that the Mayor had already been arrested by soldiers. Actually, the Shanghai Center had just dismissed him from office (Mao Tse-tung was scheduled to speak in Peking that day, but had prudently remained in the South.) Since armed soldiers controlled the offices of the Peking Municipal Committee, the Mayor retreated to his private quarters. He was guarded by "blue-coated cadres," his shadowy secret police. From his home, the Mayor governed the city of Peking and the North China Bureau of the Party as best he could. Though virtually abandoned by Comrade Shao-chi, the Mayor's faction defied the Shanghai minority.

In early June the Shanghai Center dispatched troops to Peking to stiffen the wavering garrison. Under the command of the Disciple's faithful executive officer, General Yang Cheng-wu (Yang the Gun), the troops' mission was brutally simple. The ideological organ, *Red Flag,* was then controlled by the Ghostwriter, but other national organs of publicity remained under Liu Shao-chi's agents. Yang the Gun seized national communications. Troops occupied the offices of *The People's Daily,* Radio Peking, and the New China News Agency. By that bloodless coup, Comrade Shao-chi lost his channels to the "masses" and the outlying cadres.

Liu's supporters had but one recourse against the usurpation of power; they determined to convene a plenary session of the Central Committee. The moderates counted four of the six great regions in their camp. Only East China and Central–South China inclined toward the Maoists.

Early in July, Central Committee members began arriving from the provinces. By mid-July, 51 full members of a total of 97, and 38 alternate members out of 96 had gathered in Peking. Comrade Shao-chi and the Mayor, still tenuously allied, were trying to assemble an overwhelming majority to beat down the Chairman's challenge to legal authority—as they had in December 1958 when Mao resigned as chief-of-state. By mid-July, Comrade Shao-chi, counting his majority, was ready to convene the plenary session with or without Mao Tse-tung, who still lurked in the South. The Party's Secretary-General Teng Hsiao-ping possessed formal authority to summon the Central Committee. Comrade Shao-chi, the extremists charged in retrospect, had plotted to depose Chairman Mao; in truth he did not seem to seek the overthrow of the Chairman so much as the preservation of the legitimate supremacy of the civilian majority by preventing a military coup.

The next phase of the struggle is murky. The Organizer Teng Hsiao-ping apparently equivocated, playing for personal power. The Disciple Lin Piao reportedly encircled Peking with his personal troops. Foreigners were restricted to Peking itself and denied their usual "right" to travel ten kilometers beyond the city limits. The Securityman Lo Jui-ching, Chief-of-Staff of the People's Liberation Army, reportedly ordered units from the northwest to Peking to counter Lin Piao's forces. Despite the endeavors of Lo Jui-ching and General Wang En-mao, the confused division commanders obeyed the direct orders of the Minister of Defense to stay at their posts. The plenary session of the Central Committee, which Liu Shao-chi had ordered, was abruptly canceled on July 20, 1966 as the Organizer had refused to act. Having consolidated the South, the Chairman and the Disciple were finally ready to storm Peking. The moderates' influence within the Army had proved insufficient to thwart the *coup d'état*.

On July 1, 1966, the theoretical journal *Red Flag* began calling the list of victims. The Ghostwriter, Chen Po-ta, who was editor-in-chief, announced the relief of the Backstage Boss, Chou Yang, deputy director of the Propaganda Bureau, protégé of the Mayor and old antagonist of the Starlet. On July 10, Peking's Central Broadcasting Station revealed that Lu Ting-yi, director of the Party Propaganda Bureau and the Government's Minister of Culture, had been replaced by the King of the South, Tao Chu. Hundreds of lesser figures fell in journalism, education, publishing, the theater, and the cinema. They were all charged with: "Plotting with the black, anti-Party, anti-Socialist gang to restore capitalism." On August 2, the Securityman Lo Jui-ching was publicly replaced as Chief-of-Staff by his deputy, Yang the Gun, to ensure Lin Piao's direct control of the military. The revolution was devouring its children with relish.

All the men dismissed had been standard-bearers of the orthodox line in literature, art, and culture for a quarter of a century. Even the Securityman had been installed as Chief-of-Staff—in succession to the nominee of Great General Peng Teh-huai—to suppress both pragmatic and "professional" tendencies in the armed forces. They all had to go, not because they were "anti-Socialist agents seeking to restore capitalism," as the Maoists charged, but because they had aligned themselves with the legitimate majority of the Central Committee.

China was thereafter ruled by two chief agencies, neither deriving its power from the consent of the governed. The first was "the coercive power of the State," exercised by the police, the courts, and the military. The second, equally important, was the propaganda apparatus. Education, journalism, painting, the theater, the cinema, the radio, and publishing—all the systematic external influences upon men's minds—were only instruments of political power. Their sole purpose was to implant the convictions and reactions the Party prescribed. The psychological doctrines of I. P. Pavlov were paramount. Like experimental dogs, the

Chinese people were to be "conditioned" to react automatically as their masters desired.

The fiercest and most destructive "struggle" was met in the Propaganda Bureau. The Maoists' chief target was the Backstage Boss Chou Yang, a respected critic and long the Party's most eminent spokesman on literature, who had thwarted Chiang Ching's ambitions in Shanghai in the 1930s. Chou Yang's example of "bourgeois, feudalistic" transgressions served as a warning to other malefactors. Hundreds of thousands of words of accusations cast a ray of black light into the involuted, Kafkaesque world inhabited by the hierarchs of Chinese Communism. Some displayed the ponderous, minutiae-obsessed pedantry of third-rate Ph.D. dissertations; others were so vehement, vile, and sweeping in condemnation they would offend the delicacy of a Shanghai longshoreman. The polemics revealed not only the dark corners of Chinese Communism, but the literary and artistic ideals the Maoists envisioned. The extremists' ultimate purpose was to use the arts to create a subspecies of humanity who were "coals in the furnace of the revolution," as one "model soldier" recorded his most profound desire.

The Great Proletarian Cultural Revolution was the means to that end. In July *The People's Daily* characterized the new movement:

It is a revolution which will completely eradicate all old ideology and culture, all the old customs and mores, which, springing from exploitive social systems, have poisoned the minds of the Chinese people. In our eyes, the eyes of the proletariat, individuals can find the most profound significance in their lives . . . in immersing themselves in the revolution—in surrendering their own, finite, individual being to the infinitely splendid cause of Communism.

Seeking utter subjugation of the individual will to its "collective" will, *i.e.,* the will of Chairman Mao, the Maoists considered literature solely "a weapon of class struggle." Ironically, the Backstage Boss had expressed that doctrine most forcibly, most baldly, and most frequently. But he was a professional writer. He was degraded because he rejected the abysmal aesthetic standards of Chairman Mao.

The model Maoist author was a former construction worker who earned his rice as a farmer and wrote in his spare time. He was called Hsü, though his name is not important, for he was a symbol rather than an individual. He was the spokesman of the silent "masses."

"The heroes portrayed in his stories," the New China News Agency observed, "are loyal to the revolutionary cause and devoted to the interests of the people of the collective—without any thought of self." A sterling short story by Comrade Hsü exemplified the new genre: ". . .

the commander of an Army company which sets off explosive charges rushes forward, heedless of his own safety, to save a companion-in-arms. He is always enthusiastic about undertaking the most arduous, difficult, and dangerous tasks, and he takes immense pains to master the art of shot-firing."

Lest his Baroque imagination and bounding originality make his writing incomprehensible to the "masses," Comrade Hsü imposed automatic self-censorship. "When he has an idea for a short story," the New China Agency explained, "he often outlines it to the other members of his commune to get their opinion. He constantly revises his ideas before putting them down on paper. Once he has written his first draft, he again asks the peasants for their criticism."

The Backstage Boss was not amused by such straightforward tales. He encouraged fiction that would evoke human response from reasonably literate human beings, instead of staccato barks of approval from semi-literate Party hacks or the nervous applause of frightened peasants. The Maoists' Pavlovian arrogance, in contrast, held that subtlety was not merely wasted but counterproductive. Any man could be compelled to think and act as his masters directed—if sufficient pressure was exerted and the conditioning was sufficiently prolonged.

Nosing among the literary carrion of the 1930s, the Maoist jackals* led by the Literary Assassin, Yao Wen-yüan, recalled that Chou Yang had advocated "national defense literature" instead of "mass literature of the national revolutionary war." The first encouraged sincere collaboration with the Nationalists against the Japanese invaders. The latter made propaganda for the Communists' ultimate conquest of power.

The more recent sins of the Backstage Boss were glaringly apparent. He had "opposed Mao Tse-tung himself." He had objected to "the cult of the individual" and "strangling the people's initiative." He had advocated "literature for all the people" rather than the "proletarian class" alone. He had imprudently remarked: "Talking about Mao Tse-tung every day does not necessarily mean understanding Mao Tse-tung's Thought!"

But Chou Yang's chief sin was his insistence that propaganda must be effective. He was no liberal thinker, but a professional Communist propagandist. He was astute enough to realize that the simplistic, bombastic fiction his opponents advocated would not advance the Communist cause—largely because the "masses" would either snicker at its simplicity or reject its aridity. The Backstage Boss was also less xenophobic and more literate than most cadres. He did not reject useful foreign models. He encouraged fiction concerning recognizable human

* The style is infectious, particularly when it is so manifestly appropriate.

beings, rather than the stereotyped "heroes of the revolution" and "black-hearted oppressors" the Maoists publicized.

The violent assault on the moderates' literary strongholds was the opening phase of a battle that was "complex and confused," as the Maoists put it. Undermining the propaganda apparatus, and destroying men like the Backstage Boss and the Securityman, cleared the land for the siege of the structure of the Communist Party itself.

While Peking swirled with rumor and his opponents slowly awakened to their peril, Chairman Mao relaxed. He avoided Peking because his strength lay in the South and the preparations for Lin Piao's *coup d'état* were not yet complete. He also bewildered his opponents by his apparent unconcern.

The Maoist press recounted Mao Tse-tung's idyllic days. On July 16, 1966, the 72-year-old Chairman, it was reported, swam nine miles in 65 minutes in the turbulent Yangtze River. That speed could have won him Olympic gold medals—even if he had not paused to float on his back and instruct the accompanying "masses" in natation and doctrine. The First Secretary of the Hupei Provincial Committee swam with Mao and displayed natatorial prowess as impressive as the Chairman's. He was later purged, presumably for political error, not for competing with the Chairman.

On July 17, the Chairman received delegates to the Conference of the Afro-Asian Writers Association. The man they met in Shanghai hardly resembled the jolly, stout Chairman who had reappeared in May after seclusion that began in late November 1965. His tunic hung loose on his emaciated frame, and his jowls were slack. He exchanged individual greetings with the delegates, most of them veterans of similar conferences. But a Japanese writer later recalled: "Chairman Mao seemed to have difficulty in remembering my name, although he had met me many times before!" The Japanese, however, insisted that the man he had seen was indeed Chairman Mao Tse-tung.

Since all China was arumor that Mao was ill or newly convalescent, his ostentatiously strenuous recreations continued. On July 18, two days after his epic swim, he stopped in the Central China industrial complex of Wuhan to cheer the masses by showing himself hale and hearty. A hiatus of ten days thereafter appeared in reports of the Chairman's activities. He finally arrived in Peking on July 28. Four airplanes deposited him, the Disciple, and the Maoist minority of the Central Committee at Tungchiao Airport. The situation was so precarious that plans for a whistle-stop progress by train had been canceled. After nine months' seclusion in the South, Chairman Mao was finally ready to confront his enemies. Behind him stood the Disciple's troops.

While the two factions girded themselves for the climactic Eleventh Plenum of the Central Committee, already once postponed, student mobs surged through the streets of Peking once more. The climax of mob intimidation came on July 29, just after Mao's arrival. Hundreds of thousands of enthusiasts chanted their loyalty to the Chairman and demanded the destruction of his enemies. In that atmosphere, the Central Committee of the Communist Party of China began its Eleventh Plenary meeting on August 1.

Although the Party Constitution provided for a National Congress every five years, the Central Committee had been elected by the Eighth National Congress in 1956, for legalistic niceties had been abandoned years earlier. The Eleventh Plenum also disregarded the legal forms prescribed for full sessions of the Central Committee.

The men and women who finally sat down to determine the fate of China had been winnowed by Lin Piao's troops. They numbered less than half the 193 full and alternate members of the Central Committee. they sat under the guns of the Disciple's troops, and they were assailed by the shouts of his mobs. The gun was taking control of the Communist Party of China.

XII

The Disciple

The hand holding the gun seemed frail. Lin Piao, Minister of Defense and faithful servant of Chairman Mao, commanded the shock units of the People's Liberation Army that staged the bloodless *coup d'état* against the Communist Party and the People's Government. He looked slender and weak, but he was a man of great force. His control of the Liberation Army seemed total, though later events clearly showed that it was flawed. The alliance of the exalted Chairman Mao Tse-tung and Defense Minister Lin Piao constituted a powerful new force that dominated the Eleventh Plenum—and the life of China—for the next three years.

The alliance was shaped by common interest. At 72, Mao Tse-tung was displaying suspicion so acute it verged upon paranoia. Lin Piao, 58 in 1966, escaped the Chairman's distrust of his contemporaries. The Chairman did not fear Lin Piao, because the younger man could, quite obviously, wait for supreme power. Besides the Disciple had always been deliberately self-effacing—indeed almost obsequious—before his elders. Mao Tse-tung required a vigorous young successor to carry on his policies. Lin Piao, pledged to personal loyalty, also possessed the personal prestige essential to a crown prince. The Chairman further required a field commander for his campaign to reconquer power. Lin Piao possessed the formal rank and, apparently, unchallenged control of the Army. The ambitious Disciple required no less than a revolution to destroy the older hierarchs who blocked his road to supreme power. Those joint needs bound the old Chairman and the younger Disciple even more closely than the mutual trust presumably born of long collaboration.

The pair disposed of two major forces outside the formal institutional structure. Mao Tse-tung was: "the Great Helmsman, the Great Teacher, the Magnificent Commander-in-Chief, the greatest genius of contemporary times, the Saving Star of the Chinese people, and the Red, Red Sun in Our Hearts." His charisma had been transformed into a unique force by the adulation orchestrated by Lin Piao since 1959. It appeared that the "docile masses" considered the Chairman's personal prestige beyond question, indeed, beyond discussion. Lin Piao nominally ruled the People's Liberation Army of almost three million, the nation's most powerful "coercive force." Although Comrade Shao-chi controlled the Party apparatus, which was the legal center of power, the alliance reckoned that their combined weight could "seize Party power"—or crush the Party. Both were, moreover, impatient to break the party center which had rejected Mao's visions and thwarted Lin's ambition.

The golden boy of Chinese Communism has been given many nicknames. Heavy black eyebrows bristling above his aquiline nose justified the sobriquet "Eaglebeak." He was also called the Invalid because of his ill health; he had been wounded in 1937, perhaps again in 1950 in Korea, and is reportedly tubercular. He was also known as the Lucky General, though his victories were won by meticulous planning and dashing execution. His self-bestowed title was "Comrade Mao Tse-tung's closest comrade-in-arms and his best disciple." Since 1966, the Chinese have called him the Disciple, as well as *Tai-tze,* the Crown Prince, and other less laudatory nicknames referring to his sycophancy toward the Chairman.

Their close collaboration had been cemented in 1934 after the weight of Nationalist numbers forced Mao's "rural faction" to abandon the Kiangsi First Soviet Area and flee to the far northwest. The young Lin Piao had sustained Mao Tse-tung and Generalissimo Chu Teh on the eight thousand-mile Long March—which became the central myth of the Chinese Communist movement—a feat that ranked with the Anabasis for courage in adversity.

The retreat was forced by the Fifth Extermination Campaign mounted by Chiang Kai-shek against the mountain redoubt. The Workers' and Peasants' Red Army, grown more than a hundred thousand strong, broke through Nationalist cordons. The columns struggled against wild terrain—over rivers, between gorges, across prairies, and through mountains. They carried machine tools and printing presses, to produce their best weapons: guns and political tracts. They were harried by Nationalist and provincial troops—and by tribesmen whose lands they crossed. Their ranks were riddled by battle, disease, and accident, but all the leaders arrived safe in the northwest, even acquiring new adherents in the latter stages of the Long March.

The brilliant strategems of the young Lin Piao and his First Red Army Group provided a shock force 10 to 20 thousand strong. It may have been the margin of survival. Looking in his rumpled uniform less like a dashing general than a bright young clerk on a weekend excursion into the countryside, Lin Piao repeatedly appeared at critical moments to frustrate an ambush or resolve a wasting battle. He won his elders' affection by his demeanor, truly "filial" in the traditional manner. Only Great General Peng Teh-huai disliked Lin Piao, perhaps out of professional jealousy, perhaps because he perceived the Disciple's true character. Mao Tse-tung was, however, enraptued as much by Lin Piao's doctrinal orthodoxy as by his tactical brilliance.

Lin Piao's actions have been revealing, but the Disciple's heart is closed. Therefore no one can assume that he was moved *solely or primarily* by expediency and ambition to his role in the Great Revolution. He had been Mao Tse-tung's true disciple for almost three decades —since he was just 20 years old. All he knew of social and political thought, all he comprehended of historical processes, all he understood of the great world—he had learned from the Chairman. One of the few hierarchs sprung from the urban middle-class, he appears to have been moved as much by his dedication to the Chairman's mystical visions as by his yearning toward power—despite the ruthless ambition he revealed when he cast aside his mock humility to command the ruthless Great Revolution.

Generalissimo Chu Teh and Great General Peng Teh-huai are revolutionaries from an old Chinese novel, but Lin Piao is a wholly modern man. Until seduced by the lure of power, he was an engineer-in-arms, a professional paragon who seemed beyond doubt or hesitation. His thorough preparation for battle made the planning of the German General Staff seem almost extemporaneous. The only human weakness he showed was the inability to sleep before a major battle, which drove him to pace the earthen floor of his field headquarters, usually a simple peasant's house. But even Napoleon was restless before battle. The Disciple was no less ambitious than Napoleon, another bourgeois who captured a revolution.

The Disciple's personal history was more characteristic of Nationalist than Communist generals. He was born in 1908, the second of six sons of a family that owned a small textile mill in Huangan, a county seat of 50 thousand in Hupei Province near Wuhan, the triplet industrial cities of Central China. The collapse of the Manchu imperium in 1911 created severe economic dislocation, as well as political turmoil, in the Wuhan area. Machine-made textiles ruined the market for the products of the Lins' simple looms. The First World War subsequently stimulated native industry by diverting the great powers from exploitation of China, but only the big capitalists benefited, while small enterprises like the Lins' suffered. The Disciple's father was bankrupt, but his education found him employment as a purser on steamships plying the Yangtze River. He apparently felt himself fortunate in becoming an employee of the "bureaucratic, imperialist capitalists" who had ruined him, but the young son learned early to hate "capitalism and imperialism."

Lin's mother brought up her sons, cheered only by her husband's occasional visits. Her task was not easy. Lin Yu-yung—the fierce cognomen Piao, meaning "lynx," came later—was bright and self-willed. Vehement in his protests against the traditional morality that impeded modern development, he was *too* precocious. He began mouthing "revolutionary ideas" at 11.

An apocryphal tale relates that Mao Tse-tung came late in 1919 to Huilungshan, where the Lins lived, as an itinerant schoolmaster seeking a meager living and knowledge of China. He gave the village children elementary schooling in an abandoned temple—and fanned their spirit of rebellion. Lin Piao attended that school, it is said, until the local authorities padlocked the doors. Alarmed by Mao's "modern doctrines," they posted an old text on the gate: "When the students rebel, the country cannot know peace!"

But the seed of rebellion was already implanted in the Disciple, who later deployed the Red Guards, his "little generals of disorder," to make the ultimate revolution throughout China. After studying basic writing and revolution under Mao Tse-tung, Lin Piao yearned for a "modern education." Although his family could provide only the barest financial assistance, they could manage without his labor when, at 14, he qualified for high school. With his parents' reluctant blessing, the Disciple set out for Wuchang, one of the three industrial cities of Wuhan, to enter the Kungchin Middle School. From 1921 to 1924 he lived in an atmosphere of revolt against all established mores. A part-time worker in a cotton mill, he was engrossed by "social questions."

The triplet cities, which had ignited the revolt against the Manchus, were a fertile field for political agitators. The factories employed the "industrial proletariat," which the Communist International exalted as the moving force of the Chinese revolution. But the Communists' message was received more eagerly by students and teachers, than by workers. The discontented youth of Wuhan were thus forced to political maturity. The Disciple joined the Nationalist Party and was active in the Social Welfare Club, a student organization responsive to the cultural and political tides from the West. Lin Piao rejected traditional China, which had bankrupted his family—and had so ineffectually allowed itself to become the prey of the rapacious West.

Although he joined his contemporaries' philosophical discussions, Lin Piao felt little affinity for abstractions. He was interested in politics in their most concrete aspect—the use of arms. He joined the Socialist Youth League after coming under direct Communist influence at a student conference in Shanghai early in 1925. The great labor demonstrations of 1925, called the May Thirtieth Movement and directed in part by Comrade Liu Shao-chi, convinced him that only radical solutions could "save the nation." In October 1925 he enrolled in the Fourth Class of the Whampoa Military Academy, graduating in 1926.

The first three classes graduated after only three or four months, but the fourth underwent almost a full year of training. They studied military tactics under the Japanese-trained Commandant Chiang Kai-shek and "General Galen," the pseudonym of Marshall Blyukher, who later commanded the Soviet Far East Armies. The Director of the Political Section, Chou En-lai, was guided by the Comintern agent Mikhail Borodin. The Soviet Red Army was the model for organization and tactics; stressed equally with techniques of arms was "mobilizing the masses" through propaganda and front organizations. Since the Nationalists had found the outside support they needed only in the Soviet Union, the *Kuomintang* was reorganized by Comintern advisers as a totalitarian, disciplined party. Whampoa was itself a politicized military academy, producing political subalterns who in time became political generals.

Honor student Lin Piao learned at Whampoa that generals ultimately depend upon politicians. He realized that a nonpolitical Chinese general was a futile creature. He applied his lessons throughout his career, most spectacularly when he depended on the Red Guards—rather than on troops—to mount the first great onslaught of the Cultural Revolution.

Upon graduation in 1926, the Disciple joined the Communist Party and was commissioned in the "Nationalist Revolutionary Army." Belying his apparent frailty, he became a company commander at 19 and, briefly, an acting battalion commander in the Revolutionary Army massed to seize control of China from the warlords. When the Northern Expedition, preceded by Communist political agitators, marched out of Canton in June 1926, the Nationalist armies truly offered careers open to talent. Growing with each victory, the armies mustered few officers with even a year's formal professional education. The Northern Expedition promised Lin Piao a brilliant future.

When the Nationalists and the Communists split, the Disciple was torn by conflicting allegiances. He chose the absolute doctrines the Communists offered. He was also moved by personal loyalty to Chou En-lai, who had recruited him into the Communist Party at Whampoa. He was, however, more concerned with results than with dogma. Agitation directed by Political Commissar Chou En-lai had proved as effective as the Nationalists' military prowess against the warlords' underpaid, underfed, unwilling, and ill-trained forces. Moreover, his division commander, Yeh Ting, whose daughter Lin Piao later married, was a secret member of the Communist Party.

When Lin Piao joined the Communist Party, he had discerned no conflict of interest in his simultaneous membership in the Nationalist Party. Although Stalin himself said the Communists would use the Nationalists and "cast them aside like a squeezed lemon," the moment of truth was still a distant abstraction when the Northern Expedition began. The Comintern had ordered protracted cooperation with the Nationalists to complete the "bourgeois revolution" before the Communists themselves seized power. Some Chinese Communists already feared that Moscow really sought a dependent "bourgeois" China rather than the victory of the weak and recalcitrant Communist Party. Such subtleties escaped the Disciple, who was prematurely forced to choose between Nationalists and Communists.

Generalissimo Chiang Kai-shek did not wait to be tossed aside. He began to harry the Communists even before the Northern Expedition marched, but the Comintern insisted that the Chinese Communists continue to give him wholehearted cooperation. In April 1927, after taking Shanghai, a stronghold of "imperialist capitalism," Chiang Kai-shek chose new allies—the great capitalists of China's most Westernized city and the chieftains of the Red Band, China's most powerful extra-legal secret society. The new alliance slaughtered the Workers' Militia organized by Comrade Liu Shao-chi and Chou En-lai.

Despite the open assault, the Comintern still insisted upon continuing "cooperation." Moscow had a large investment in the Nationalists. A joint Nationalist-Communist government formally "governed" all China from Hankow, one of the Wuhan cities. Dominated by Communists and the anti-Chiang "left-wing" Nationalists, the Hankow Government was close to Moscow. But it was largely impotent. By the summer of 1927, Communist officers felt themselves in immediate personal, as well as political, peril. Cooperating with the "bourgeois revolutionaries" was obviously not the prelude to the conquest of power. The Comintern's inept efforts to gain maximum advantage for itself finally breached the relationship between the Communists and the "left-wing" Nationalists.

Communist generals made one last desperate cast for power. On August 1, 1927, they led a revolt at Nanchang, capital of Kiangsi Province. The leaders were the later Generalissimo Chu Teh, then commandant of the Nanchang Branch of the Whampoa Military Academy; Yeh Ting, Lin Piao's immediate superior; and the Bandit General, Ho Lung. The Red troops were soon driven from Nanchang.

The Disciple was fully committed to the Communists. He led his battalion into hiding with Generalissimo Chu Teh in northern Kwangtung Province during the winter of 1927–28, finally joining Mao Tsetung in his mountain redoubt at Chingkangshan in May 1928. His subsequent rise was even more rapid than it would have been in the Nationalist Army. His first command was a battalion of Chu Teh's Twenty-Eighth Regiment, exactly half the Workers' and Peasants' Red Army at the time. In 1929 he was given command of the Red Fourth Army.

The Communists avoided standard nomenclature that would reveal their numbers, preferring unit designations that exaggerated their strength. Their deviousness has proved almost as troublesome to historians as it was to the Nationalists, for the size of early Red units is almost impossible to determine. It is, however, unlikely that the Disciple's Fourth Army ever exceeded 8 thousand, or that more than 15 thousand men formed the First Army Group he led on the Long March.

Lin Piao had already become not only a general but a member of the Central Executive Committee of the Provisional Chinese Soviet Republic. Mao Tse-tung's admiration for Lin Piao was solidified by the young soldier's performance on the Long March. Great General Peng Teh-huai commanded the opposite arm when Lin Piao's forces closed the pincer to win the battle of Tsünyi in late 1934. At Tsünyi in January 1935, Mao Tse-tung was elected Chairman of the Central Committee of the Chinese Communist Party. Between them, the Disciple and Great General Peng thus assured the pre-eminence of the man who Lin Piao later manipulated to attain power—and Peng Teh-huai confronted to preserve "principled" government. But that irony was 20 to 30 years away when the Communists reached Shensi Province in October 1935.

The Disciple was appointed president of the Chinese Workers' and Peasants' Red Army University, the chief training school for cadres. In 1937 the University was renamed the Anti-Japanese Political and Military Academy—which was exalted as the model for *all* China during the Great Revolution. Lin's reputation was high in July 1937, when the Sino-Japanese War formally began, and during the consequent second period of Nationalist-Communist cooperation he was given command of the 115th Division of the "Eighth Route Army." The Communist forces took that name to sustain the fiction that they were a loyally subordinate unit of the Nationalist Government in Chunking. Again terminology confused reality. Each of the four Communist divisions numbered almost a hundred thousand men operating over vast stretches of territory.

Lin Piao took first honors in the war. His 115th Division won China's first major victory against the Japanese. In September 1937 he defeated the Japanese Fifth Division at Pinghsing Pass in northeastern Shensi.

The Japanese troops let themselves be trapped in a narrow defile, largely because they were contemptuous of the Chinese military. The Disciple later observed in his first major political-military treatise that the enemy's greatest weakness was his arrogance in underestimating Chinese resistance. The Japanese unit was "annihilated," which in Communist terminology means put out of action; and the conquest of Shansi Province was delayed for several months. It was hardly a decisive victory, but it was the first significant victory of Chinese arms.

The Disciple's later critique of the battle spared none of the participants—the Japanese, the Nationalists, or the Communists. His brusque style avoided the customary flourishes of Chinese prose and rarely slipped into stereotyped Marxist rhetoric. It was the product of a tough-minded general rather than a theoretician. It was, characteristically, concerned as much with immediate tactics and logistics as with grand strategy. The Disciple was a painstaking technician who wrote:

> One good method is to harass the enemy's flanks while he is attacking the camps of allied [*i.e.,* Nationalist] troops . . . whose discipline is entirely too lax so that they [the Nationalists] do not even stick to the fixed plan of battle they themselves insist upon. While you fight—the allied army stands by and listens. They boast continually that they will win decisive battles, but, in practice, they make elaborate preparations and fail to execute them in battle. Or, if they finally *do* fight, they fight without much resolution.
>
> The [Japanese] enemy fears night attacks, because his tactics are useless after dark. In order to sustain a protracted war we must study the techniques of night attacks. . . . We must also make greater efforts to develop our technical skill, paying special attention to the education of common soldiers, squad, platoon, and company commanders. Although our troops have progressed greatly in the last year, their technical training has not been made uniform. In the future we must stress this kind of education.

Lin's thesis on Pinghsing Pass outlined the strategic and tactical precepts he has constantly followed throughout his career. Lightly equipped troops were to get as close as possible to a superior enemy, preferably at night, so that they could neutralize his greater firepower. Only "protracted warfare" could defeat the enemy totally by sapping his resources and his resolution, while the "people's forces" were constantly replenished by popular support. The Disciple later offered the same guidance to the ungrateful —and unheeding—Viet Cong.

Lin harried the Japanese for the next half year—until his wounds equired treatment in the Soviet Union. The voyage was also political, for he was designated the Chinese Communist Party's representative in Moscow. He is, again apocryphally, reported to have taken part in the defense of Leningrad, and he presumably learned some Russian. The Disciple returned to China in 1942, just in time for the First Rectification Campaign to impose the Thought of Mao Tse-tung on the Chinese Communist Party. He became vice principal of the Higher Party School in Yenan, with the Mayor his co-equal vice principal. Mao Tse-tung was himself principal.

As the war against Japan slowed down, the Chairman began preparations for the war against Chiang Kai-shek. Lin Piao was elevated to the Central Committee by the Seventh Party Congress, which met in Yenan from April 23 to June 11, 1945, to organize the conquest of power. The Russians had occupied Manchuria during the last weeks of the war, and Lin Piao was ordered to recast the guerrillas of the Manchurian People's Forces into the conventional army that would begin the final conquest of all China. The nucleus was renamed the Manchurian Democratic Allied Armies when it took in deserters from pro-Japanese Chinese units. After prevailing over the region's First Secretary, the Mayor, in 1946, Commander-in-Chief Lin Piao became Political Commissar as well. Liberally equipped by the Russians, his forces broke out of Manchuria in 1948 to take Tsinan, the capital of Shantung Province, and begin the final rout of the Nationalists.

During the Civil War, the Disciple established himself as the Communists' chief military strategist, though his shoulders appeared frail for their burden. A Chinese interpreter for the American "observer teams" mediating between Nationalists and Communists in 1947 was shocked to find that the Disciple, just closing 40, moved and talked "as if he might fall apart at any moment." The Nationalist representative, General Tu Yi-ming, called his slight, stooped antagonist "little brother" because he had been his senior at the Whampoa Academy. Lin Piao would not be baited into losing his temper or altering his bargaining position. Taunted with his troops' numerical inferiority, he replied with the countryman's proverb: "One spark can consume a hundred miles of prairie!"

Despite his "bourgeois" origins, Lin Piao was truly concerned for the peasants' welfare—and their political potential. His constant use of homely farmers' maxims—in imitation of the Chairman—convinced many Chinese that he lacked true culture. His few classical allusions, the tokens of true learning, were drawn from a meager stock. Chinese intellectuals felt he was virtually unlettered; his limited formal education was revealed by his lack of traditional learning.

Even acute observers felt that the Disciple lacked both intellectual curiosity and humility, despite his ostentatious deference to superiors and his courtesy to all men. He recalled a student who reads his assigned lesson and then lays his books down. He possessed a general knowledge of the Marxist canons, but no deep understanding. His intellect, the observers concluded, was narrow, though his pungent, detailed military critiques were used as textbooks and he was justly described as "a scholar in warfare." With their bone-bred respect for erudition and a good presence, many Chinese were shocked because Lin Piao "looked and talked like a village carpenter."

His negotiations with the Nationalists revealed that he was not a simple man. His open demeanor hardly reflected a frank, direct personality. His evasive answers, often flatly misleading, were the despair of the American mediators. Since the Disciple desired no peace, he would fix a conference and discover, sometimes 15 minutes before the appointed time, that he was too ill to attend. When he did appear, he would propose precisely the same conditions rejected at the preceding session. He always spoke temperately, but never agreed.

His behavior portended Communist tactics in later direct negotiations with the United States. In 1947–48, however, the Americans were only "conciliators," lured by the chimerical hope of reconciling the contending sides and bringing peace to China. The Disciple's purpose was, of course, quite different. His only goal was the conquest of China for Communism.

Despite the conciliatory manner that cloaked his obduracy, Lin Piao was jealous of his prerogatives and sullen when slighted. His anger was dramatic. His bushy eyebrows would knot over his "eaglebeak" nose, and his chalk-white pallor would pale further so that his black beard seemed to bristle under his close-shaven cheeks. However, his temper was at his own service; it was another negotiating device. But he put aside dignity when it served his ends. A non-smoker, the Disciple profusely thanked an American colonel for a carton of Old Golds and a tin of chocolates, though offended by such niggardly presents. Chinese etiquette requires that gifts to generals be lavish, and General Lin Piao was quite conscious of his position. But it was not politic to reveal his true nature.

After the farcical negotiations had won the Communists time to mobilize, the Disciple's army of about 800 thousand, assisted by the Second Field Army of the Bandit General, Ho Lung, "liberated" vast areas of Central and South China, finally taking Hainan Island in the extreme South in April 1950. Initial cautious preparation followed by dashing execution secured vast areas and consolidated Lin Piao's reputation.

Although it has never been definitely established, the Disciple appears to have led the bulk of his Fourth Field Army into Korea as the

"Chinese People's Volunteers" in 1950 to sweep the Americans from the North. Again, his rash courage reportedly exposed him to wounds that forced his replacement. The nature of the war had, in any event, by that time changed from rapid maneuver to the attrition of positional warfare. He was succeeded by Great General Peng Teh-huai, his chief rival.

After the establishment of the People's Republic and his brief adventure in Korea, the Disciple's political career moved forward as rapidly and as smoothly as his personal life. Both were, however, slightly marred, the first by persistent illness and Great General Peng's seniority, the second by a marital contretempts. Lin had met a young girl student at his Anti-Japanese Military and Political Academy in Yenan. She was called Liu Hsi-ming, while her Party name was Chang Mei, literally the "beautiful [Miss] Chang." They were married in 1937, and she accompanied him to the Soviet Union the following year.

The marriage was not made in heaven, though blessed by that earthly divinity, Chairman Mao. In the Soviet Union, in 1941, the beautiful Miss Chang bore a daughter, Lin Tou-tou, who was still known by that childhood name when she became an activist in the Cultural Revolution. The Disciple's marriage to her mother ended in divorce about the time he returned to China in 1942. Shortly thereafter, he married Yeh Chun, daughter of his first division commander, Yeh Ting. That marriage has endured. Yeh Chun was finally elevated to the Political Bureau at the end of the Cultural Revolution—primarily as a symbol of her husband's power. Lin Piao has limited himself to two wives, while China does not gossip about his extra-marital affairs—the surest indication of his faithfulness.

The major impediment to the career assured by Lin Piao's brilliance and his prudence was his continuing bad health. Illness hampered him from 1949 through 1958, and the official press repeatedly published messages wishing him a speedy return to health. He was frequently hospitalized, probably for tuberculosis aggravated by wounds. Nonetheless, his pivotal role in the Civil War assured his appointment to the chairmanship of the Central–South China Administrative Area in December 1949. That post, in turn, assured his domination of the area for the next decade. He was also First Secretary of the Chinese Communist Party's Central–South China Bureau until its abolition in the administrative reorganization of 1954.* He continued to amass responsibility—and power.

Appointed one of the nation's seven vice premiers in 1954, he became First Vice Premier in 1955. He was in that year also raised to the

---

* The Regional Bureaus were later re-established.

Political Bureau and created a Marshal of the Chinese People's Republic. He was listed third among the original ten marshals, with only Generalissimo Chu Teh and Great General Peng Teh-huai ranking above him. Following the Eighth National Congress of the Communist Party in September 1956, he became a vice chairman of the Central Committee. He was fifth among five vice chairmen—an indignity he quickly corrected. After the Mount Lu Plenum and his appointment as Defense Minister in 1959, his public appearances became more frequent.

Throughout his ascension, Lin Piao deliberately worked to transform Chairman Mao into a "semi-celestial being"—and to make himself *the* authoritative interpreter of the Chairman's philosophy. The dominant slogan of the Cultural Revolution, admonishing "living study and living use of the Thought of Chairman Mao," is invariably attributed to the Chairman's "best student." It is often displayed in his own spiky calligraphy.

Lin Piao's personal history after 1959 is the history of the "conflict between the two lines within the Communist Party." He demanded that the People's Liberation Army function as a political instrument rather than a purely military force. He derided "professional generals" like Peng Teh-huai. He deprecated nuclear weapons as "paper tigers" and asserted that the People's Republic possessed its own "spiritual atomic bomb"—the great masses of the Chinese people. He campaigned under the slogan PUT POLITICS TO THE FORE!, an echo of Mao Tse-tung's exhortation PUT POLITICS IN COMMAND! During the preliminary skirmishes of the early 1960s, the Disciple was ever more closely identified with the Chairman and the Messianic spirit of Maoist orthodoxy.

The commander of the Hunan Military District declared in 1963: "A series of guiding principles, policies and measures, formulated by the Central Military Committee and Marshal Lin Piao upon the basis of the Thought of Mao Tse-tung, should be implemented in actual work so that they become the unvarying conscious responses of us all!" By mid-1965, not only military but civilian publicists unremittingly proclaimed: "Comrade Lin Piao has creatively developed and applied the Thought of Mao Tse-tung."

On September 3, 1965, a 30-thousand-word article entitled "Long Live the Victory of People's War!" asserted the Disciple's personal authority as a major theoretician. Lin Piao restated and expanded Mao Tse-tung's doctrine of "people's war." He declared that the Maoist strategy of the "countryside's encircling the cities" was the universal principle that would bring "proletarian" victory throughout the world. He further advised the Vietcong to fight a "protracted war depending upon your own resources," rather relying on either the North Vietnamese or the Chinese. Although such assistance would of course be forthcoming, he stressed that a "people's war" could only be won by the people themselves. His article also reasserted the Maoist doctrine for defending China through a "forward policy" of attacking potential enemies abroad by proxy. The "professional generals," on the other hand, contended that the country must prepare a "defense-in-depth," supplemented by modern weapons, against the American or Soviet attacks the "forward policy" might provoke.

The Disciple had spent his life preparing for the opportunity that opened in 1966. When his moment came, he seized it. After maneuvering to outflank the moderates in the spring, he was ready to seize power in the summer. Lin Piao dominated the Eleventh Plenary Session of the Central Committee of the Chinese Communist Party held during the first half of August 1966. It was a strange gathering. Only half the duly elected members were present in a hall "guarded" by Lin's troops, who had virtually occupied Peking. The proceedings were dominated by the threat of their guns—and by the raucous enthusiasm of the "revolutionary students" packing the galleries. Throughout the meeting, Lin Piao spoke in the name of his chief, Mao Tse-tung, whose own remarks are still recorded only in part.

Chairman Mao did, however, wander out on the evening of August 4 to exhort crowds gathered outside the Imperial City: "Make revolution! Manage the great affairs of State yourselves!" The incident was hushed up—perhaps because his erratic behavior revived persistent doubts concerning the state of his health, perhaps because he should not have "met the masses" without sanction. *The People's Daily,* reporting in massive red headlines, "Chairman Mao Goes Among the Masses," was hastily recalled. A substitute edition diminished the untoward incident to insignificance.

If Maoist control of the Eleventh Plenum was ensured by the coercion of troops and "rebel revolutionary" students, the coup was facilitated by the vacillation of the Party's Secretary-General Teng Hsiao-ping. Apparently unable to make up his mind which side would win, but half-convinced it would *not* be the moderates, the Organizer withdrew his support from Comrade Liu Shao-chi. The Maoist victory went unchallenged. The Disciple forcefully told the rump Central Committee what lay ahead for China. The full available text, apparently authentic, threatened nothing less than a total purge of the Communist Party of China.

The Disciple declared flatly there are "only two kinds of people in respect to the Thought of Mao Tse-tung." He recognized only absolute loyalists and enemies. "Some people," he explained, "oppose the Thought of Mao Tse-tung and deride the study of the Thought of Mao

Tse-tung." Having divided all China into two parts, the Disciple promised retribution against those who opposed him. "There are also people," he added, "who always try to please everyone by doing nothing and participating in nothing and hoping to offend no one . . . who try to retain cordial relations with all and thus get more votes for themselves in elections." Such temporizers, he warned, were just as bad as men who actually attacked the Thought of Mao Tse-tung. Chilling words followed:

Therefore, we demand a general examination, a general realignment, and a general reorganization of the ranks of cadres. In the light of the five-point principles governing the cultivation of revolutionary successors by the Great Proletarian Cultural Revolution as stated by Chairman Mao, *we* have proposed three criteria to which the Chairman has agreed:

1. To hold high the red banner of the Thought of Mao Tse-tung. Those who oppose the Thought of Mao Tse-tung are to be dismissed from their posts.

2. To engage in political-ideological work. Those who upset the political-ideological work of the Great Proletarian Cultural Revolution are to be dismissed from their posts.

3. To possess revolutionary zeal. Those who do not possess revolutionary zeal are all to be dismissed from their posts.

The Disciple made the absolute, but general threat ominously specific:

We are going to dismiss a number of people, promote a number of people, and keep some in their posts. There will be a general organizational adjustment. . . . As for those who are incorrigible, they must be relieved of their posts. Unless we do so, we shall not break the present stalemate. We know that it would be just such people who would carry out subversive activities, and then trouble would flare up.

He paraded his familiar mock-humility again:

Recently my heart has been quite heavy. *I am not equal to my task and may fail in my duties.* I may make mistakes. But I am doing the best I can to diminish my mistakes. I shall rely on the Chairman, on the entire body of my comrades on the Standing Committee [of the Politburo], and on my comrades of the Cultural Revolution Group* [just appointed to direct the purge]. With Chairman Mao as the axle, we are the millstones [grinding fine]. We must do everything in accordance with

* Literally, "The Small Group Directing the Great Proletarian Cultural Revolution." I have also used an alternate translation: The Task Force Directing the Cultural Revolution.

the Thought of Mao Tse-tung. There is no other way. There cannot be two policies or two Proletarian Headquarters. . . . Only the Chairman can command, and we must closely follow his every command. . . . I have no special talents, but I rely on the wisdom of the masses, ask the Chairman for instructions whenever I undertake any task; and execute all actions according to his order. *I never interfere with him on major matters, nor do I trouble him with minor matters.**

Thus humility was, for the moment, cast aside. Lin Piao was plainly telling the Central Committee that *he* was in command, *his* power sanctioned by *his* unique comprehension of the Chairman's doctrines, by the unique confidence of the Chairman reposed in *him*—and by the power of *his* troops.

Noting that the Great Proletarian Cultural Revolution had already been diverted briefly, the Disciple defined the basic task: "to work in the spiritual sphere by transforming people's ideas. . . . Should we promote material incentives as the revisionist countries do, we would be bound to retrogress and revert to the old order. Revisionism would be bound to reappear. . . . We will win on the spiritual front! We will also win on the material front!"

The orders were plain, and the rump Central Committee was obedient. Manipulated by the Maoists and cowed by the Disciple's troops, the Eleventh Plenary Session, which was by no means plenary, formally passed the *Sixteen-Point Directive Regarding the Great Proletarian Cultural Revolution.*

The masses were ordered into battle against the Chairman's enemies, who were also the Disciple's enemies. They were further commanded to "create an entirely new society." A massive purge of cadres and organizations was forecast, since China would be administered as was the "non-exploitive" Paris Commune of 1871. Universal suffrage among the proletariat would choose working men and women, who would, simultaneously, be legislators, judges, and administrators. Total reform of education would ensure "destruction of the entire old structure of society and culture." Countryside and city would become a seamless uniformity, while all distinction between manual and intellectual labor would be abolished.

Scientists were, however, told that they would be safe from the tidal wave of revolution—*if* they continued to "serve the nation" devotedly. Laborers and peasants were also promised immunity, since a purge of the working force would hamper production. The immediate target of the Great Proletarian Revolution was the Communist Party and unregenerate remnants of the urban bourgeoisie who "still persisted in

* Emphasis supplied.

their evil ways." The Eleventh Plenum, in effect, resolved to destroy the managerial and technical "middle class" by "totally destroying the old civilization" that had nurtured that class. The proletariat was to rule— under the Chairman and the Disciple.

In addition to reaffirming all the disruptive Maoist policies diverted by the moderates during the early 1960s, the Eleventh Plenum raised the People's Liberation Army above the State. The Army, the *Sixteen-Point Directive* provided, would "deal with its own problems."

That dispensation was a tribute and an act of submission to Lin Piao. The professional soldier who was the son of an impoverished bourgeois family, already hailed as the single authoritative interpreter of the Thought of Mao Tse-tung, was further acclaimed as "Chairman Mao's closest comrade-in-arms." The rump session elected him *sole* Deputy Chairman of the Central Committee of the Communist Party, making him the second man in all China and heir-apparent to Mao Tse-tung. The five vice chairmenships were abolished; Comrade Liu Shao-chi, who had been second, was relegated to eighth place in the hierarchy. The Organizer Teng Hsiao-ping retained his seventh ranking as a reward for betraying Comrade Shao-chi, but his position was precarious. Other major realignments completely destroyed opposition within the Party Center. The Disciple, it appeared, had triumphed unconditionally in Peking.

Lin Piao, the faithful soldier who never expressed an opinion or breathed a thought that diverged from Mao Tse-tung's, had finally come into his reward. He was, until the spring of 1967, the master of a disintegrating nation. He accelerated the chaos by mobilizing the adolescent Red Guards as his own shock troops of the Great Proletarian Cultural Revolution.

XIII

The Little Red Book

Beyond counting, multitudes of red banners danced in demoniac frenzy over the hundred-acre Plaza of the Gate of Heavenly Peace. Diffused by the fine dust from Central Asia, the pink radiance of the sun rising over Peking on August 18, 1966, kindled the clouds of red bunting. Almost every one of the million-odd young Chinese who jammed the Plaza wore a bright crimson armband, flaunting in flowing script: *Hung Wei Ping*— "Red Guard."

A new force was born in China, so new that even its creators did not fully understand its nature.

The youths and maidens wearing those armbands hardly knew what the words meant. Nor were they quite sure what they tremulously awaited as they chorused that old favorite "The East is Red" and the spontaneous new hit song introduced only three days earlier, "Sailing the Seas, We Depend on the Helmsman." They beat time with booklets covered in fire-engine-red plastic, the red sea rising and falling "like waves of blood," as one unwittingly prophetic bystander observed. The refrain crashed out from a million throats: "Mao Tse-tung is the red, red sun in our hearts!"

The booklets flipped open at a signal, and the Red Guards chanted in unison selected texts from *The Quotations of Chairman Mao*. All were aggressively militant, not to say military.

"We must distinguish between our friends and our enemies: We must defend our friends and crush our enemies. . . . Without a people's army, the people have nothing. . . . The revolutionary war is a war of the masses. It can be waged only by mobilizing the masses and relying upon the masses."

198

The war chants reverberated from the massive red brick walls of the fifteen-century Gate of Heavenly Peace. Beside an enormous portrait of Mao Tse-tung hung red banners indited in great gold characters: HAIL THE CHINESE PEOPLE'S REPUBLIC! HAIL THE GREAT UNITY OF THE COMMON PEOPLE OF THE WORLD! The soaring eaves of the double-tiered roof shone pale yellow in the morning haze. Among the frenzied throngs towered a white marble obelisk, the Memorial to the Heroes of the Revolution and the Civil War, its cracked base covered with neck-craning enthusiasts. The obelisk's solid Edwardian contours were as anachronistic as the pillared façades of the Great Hall of the people and the People's Revolutionary Museum flanking the Plaza. They symbolized victory and solidity, peace and established power. Yet the greatest revolution of all was rising to transform China by first breaking China.

It was almost ten before the multitudes were rewarded for their patience. They had waited all night, sustained only by cold rice and bread supplemented by bits of pickled vegetable. They had resorted frequently to the temporary public toilets on the perimeter of the Plaza. Their long wait was finally at an end.

Remote as the wooden figures on a spire clock, a procession appeared in the deep shadows of the upturned eaves. As he emerged into the sunlight, half-leaning on his smaller companion, the leading figure raised his hand in a slow, angular gesture. His ponderous head turned from side to side like a clockwork doll. All restraint vanished from the throng. A million Chinese were in that instant transported beyond the frenzy of anticipation to the fulfillment of true rapture.

"Mao Chuhsi! Mao Chuhsi! Mao Chuhsi!" the crowd chanted, "Chairman Mao!" until the words ran together in an ecstatic cataract: "Chuhsi Mao Chuhsi Mao Chuhsi Mao Chuhsi . . ." The torrents of sound swelled and broke to rise and swell and break and rise and swell and break, time and time again. Girls jumped high into the air, tears streaming down their contorted faces. Youths bounded about and pummeled each other in their transport. The red banners cavorted as if tossed by gales from the northern steppes. The little red books rose and fell in the demented rhythms of storm-borne breakers.

The wave of emotion was not merely overwhelming. It was transcendent. Individual identity, and all individual feeling, were submerged in the torrent of mass emotion.

The object of the frenzy was minuscule in the distance and walked with a mechanical, shuffling gait. But his every feature, his every expression, and his every gesture, were intimately familiar to the throng through hundreds of millions of portraits, photographs, and motion pictures; his every sacrosanct Thought was ingrained in their souls by constant "living study and living use." The sanctified Chairman Mao was the focus of all the frustrated yearnings of a generation promised infinite "proletarian" blessings. They were assembled to be promised even more spectacular hope—and to be offered new butts for the vast resentment bred by more than a decade and a half of Communist rule. Like a Renaissance king appealing to the burghers to support him against the wicked nobles, Mao Tse-tung had appealed to the "proletarian revolutionary masses" to unite with him against the wicked "bourgeois bureaucracy" of the Communist Party.

Though it was deliberately inspired, the hysterical response was genuine. The stage management was precise. At the peak of emotion, a group of enraptured adolescents was ushered before the benignly smiling figure. A teen-age maiden pinned on his revered arm a red brassard bearing the flowing characters: RED GUARD.

She was the daughter of an old comrade, but Mao Tse-tung asked her name.

"I am called Sung Ping-ping!" she replied.

The Chairman inquired gently, "Does *Ping-ping* not mean 'refined and gentle?'"

When she agreed, the Chairman asked with great concern, "Do you not wish to do battle?"

The rest of the tale is best told in her own words:

> When I went down again, my heart simply would not stop its furious beating. Over and over again I heard in my ears the voice of *my* Chairman Mao asking: "Do you not wish to do battle?" That sentence moved me deeply, and I realized that I was too far removed from what the Chairman wished me to be. Since the beginning of the Cultural Revolution, I had dared too little. When I beheld Chairman Mao and spoke to him and pinned the red brassard around his venerable arm, I knew boundless joy and an overwhelming sense of duty. My determination to dare to rebel became overwhelming. I will certainly not fail the Chairman's expectations. I will do battle! I will create disorder! I will carry through the Great Proletarian Cultural Revolution to the very end!
>
> Before Liberation, the old revolutionary generation, depending on Chairman Mao and their guns, broke through the mountains and the rivers and shook Heaven itself. With their revolutionary power, they forged a new China. Thus political power grew out of the barrel of the gun.
>
> *Will to do battle!*—that profound truth has come to us from the past. It endures today—as it will in the future.

The maiden declared that she changed her name from *Ping-ping,* meaning "Refined Gentleness," to *Yao-wu,* meaning "Will to Battle."

The million zealots gathered in the Plaza of Heavenly Peace did indeed go into battle. They were to wage total war against "the men in power in the Party following the capitalist road." All the failures of past decades, the disasters and suffering wrought by the wildly romantic visions of Mao Tse-tung were blamed on the pragmatic non-Maoists who had tried to alleviate deprivation and hardship.

The Maoists could not rest content with their stunning victory in the intra-Party struggle—won by force and intimidation. Formally proclaiming the Great Proletarian Cultural Revolution, they moved to purge the Communist Party and the People's Government root and stock. Their still imperfect victory at the Party Center would otherwise have been in vain. They knew they had taken only a few critical positions in Peking. The regional, provincial, and local apparatus of the Party and the Government was still in the hands of their moderate enemies.

The Red Guards were ordered to "destroy the entire old civilization." Only by destroying all that existed could they level the ground for the earthly paradise toward which Maoism yearned. The instructions were taken with painful literalness by the rampant Red Guards. Perhaps they were intended to be taken literally.

The resurgent Maoists might have avoided the subsequent disorder that negated their initial victory if they had paused to consolidate their gains in August 1966. They might have gradually plucked their enemies from the power structure by deceit, false charges, and show trials as Joseph Stalin had in the 1930s. Their dilemma was rendered acute by their ideological motivation. If they had contented themselves with formal victory, with a realignment of the Political Bureau like so many that had gone before, they would merely have prepared the way for a new *embourgeoisement*. The Cultural Revolution would not have "touched all men's souls." The new era of mankind the aging Chairman envisioned would not have come to birth. The Disciple's drive toward supreme power might have been thwarted. Lin Piao, therefore, ordered his characteristic "strategy of annihilation." At the moment of victory, the Maoists struck harder on a wider front with a new force, the Red Guards.

The political *coup* had been brilliantly managed. Overawed by soldiers and students, the rump Central Committee had done the Disciple's bidding.

Lin Piao had been elevated from fifth vice chairman to sole deputy chairman of the Communist Party. While the pliant First Minister of Great Peace, Premier Chou En-lai, retained his third position, Comrade Liu Shao-chi, who had been second to Mao, was dropped to eighth place. The Organizer Teng Hsiao-ping retained his seventh position in the hierarchy, but he would retain his reward for betraying Comrade Shao-chi only briefly. Tao Chu, chief of Central–South China as First Secretary of the Regional Party Bureau, became the fourth man in the Communist Party. The highly efficient and occasionally ruthless administrator was given control of all "propaganda and cultural work," the realm of decision where the Mayor Peng Chen had reigned. Just beneath the King of the South stood the Ghostwriter Chen Po-ta, the Chairman's personal confidant and ideological adviser. Next came the wispy figure of Kang Sheng, the Lord High Executioner, an old Bolshevik already once discredited and once rehabilitated.

The Ghostwriter was appointed chief of the Task Force Directing the Cultural Revolution, the Starlet Chiang Ching, his first deputy, and the Lord High Executioner Kang Sheng, his "adviser." The Task Force was studded with the Starlet's protégés, including the Literary Assassin Yao Wen-yüan, who had fired the first shot. That small group commanded the violent campaign to create a perfect new Maoist world by destroying the old world. In the beginning, they met little resistance to their purge of hundreds of senior officials in the Party's Provincial Committees, Regional Bureaus, and Central Bureaus. The Government, an appendage of the Party, could mount no effective resistance. The masses were apathetic—and largely ignorant. The Task Force, idealists and opportunists alike, was in command in the high summer of 1966. Their great task was, at that moment, just begun.

The Maoists had mobilized the Red Guards for a specific mission. The "little generals of disorder" were to sweep the moderates from power and to terrorize the intellectuals, technicians, and managers who supported the moderates. Despite the absence of organized opposition to their *coup de main,* the Maoists were determined to intensify their attack and to enlarge its scope enormously. While they had seized the central control panel, they in fact exercised real power over niether the Party Center nor the provincial apparatus. Remembering the attrition of their power since the Mount Lu Plenum in 1959, the Maoists were determined to crush the passive resistance of the "working-level" cadres. They sought not merely the seats of power and the trappings of power, but the total transformation of China. They could not transform the nation unless they first remade the Communist Party.

Inclination and self-interest commended the same tactics. "Local power-holders" had to be displaced from positions they had held for decades. The Red Guards were flung against the entrenched "men in power in the Party following the capitalist road." The Red Guards were totally new. Their only ties with the Communist Establishment were emotional—and their dominant emotion was detestation.

* * *

In the beginning, an eager youth had to pass many tests to join the Red Guards. Flaming indignation against the bureaucracy and total devotion to the secular demigod called Chairman Mao were essential, but they were not, in themselves, sufficient qualification. The original adolescent recruits were qualified by "class, family, and personal background." They were sons of the proletariat with "spotless political records." The greatest number were high-school students ranging from 14 to 19, rather than older, more sophisticated college students. The most ardent had not done well in their studies. The specific resentment of "unfair and prejudiced" teachers was easily fanned into general wrath at the social system that sustained those teachers. Deliberately stimulating youth's normal rebelliousness, the Maoists chose their vanguard from the most unruly youth. They ordered: "Dare to rebel, for rebellion is good! Dare to create disorder! Dare to make a total revolution—and excel at making revolution!"

It was a peculiar rebellion, even for a nation accustomed to meticulously organized "spontaneous" demonstrations. The rebellion was directed by the most regimented segment of a regimented society.

The People's Liberation Army organized the Red Guard. The Army provided the communications and transport that, among other feats, flew 100 thousand youths from remote areas to the capital for the first "mass rally" on August 18, 1966. The enfeebled figure of Mao Tse-tung appeared on the Gate of Heavenly Peace in the simple khaki uniform of the People's Liberation Army, wearing red collar flashes and a red star on his soft-crowned cap. It was his first appearance in military uniform since the Communist conquest of China.

The Liberation Army remained in the background when the frantic adolescents went into combat. The military did not appear to lead the forces assaulting "the entire old civilization." Although they had used the threat of armed force, the Maoists did not wish troops to openly attack the offices and officials of the Communist Party. They were, in the first place, not quite sure of the troops' loyalty. Moreover, they feared that armed attack would generate armed resistance—and, perhaps, ignite the fuse of civil war. They were confident that their new shock troops could destroy their enemies, while the Army remained a threat in the shadows.

The Maoists proclaimed an ideological confrontation—a great "spiritual contest" they would, paradoxically, fight by force and intimidation, as well as "persuasion." Their target was not only the intelligensia, the urban "bourgeoisie," and the "men in power within the Party following the capitalist road"—but "the souls of the masses." Their chief weapon was the doctrines of Chairman Mao, "the greatest living Marxist-

Leninist, the greatest genius of modern times." The Thought of Mao Tse-tung fell into three chief categories: 1) glorification of Chinese valor, ingenuity, and industriousness, which would prevail over both man and nature; 2) denunciation of domestic "class enemies" and the international foes, Soviet revisionism and American imperialism; and 3) a strategy for the conquest of power at home and abroad. Because of its homespun quality, the doctrine was highly pertinent to certain conditions in China. Still, it promised too much and offered too little, for it went beyond reason. The Maoists were convinced that intensive indoctrination with the Thought would destroy their enemies, and make their adherents totally obedient. Not only buildings and trees were hung with banners inscribed with the sacred quotations, but bicycles, locomotives, trucks, and ships. The concrete expression of devotion was the little red book each Red Guard carried and, almost incessantly, read aloud. The little red book was an insignia, a pledge of devotion, and a major weapon.

Speaking to the enraptured throng in the Plaza of Heavenly Peace "on behalf of Chairman Mao and the Party Center," Lin Piao issued his first order of the day to his Red Guards. The heir-apparent spoke in the regional brogue of his native Hupei Province, so thick that many of his words were only half-intelligible. His virulent tone and his violent commands contrasted with the chalky pallor of his face and its curious immobility. His body was slender within his loose olive-green tunic, and clear-framed spectacles bestrode his acquiline nose. He appeared no virile paladin of the new order, but the invalid he was. He declared:

> We firmly support your proletarian revolutionary spirit of daring to break through, daring to act decisively, daring to make revolution, and daring to rise in rebellion!

Thunderous shouts drowned his voice. The Disciple raised his eyes from his text and paused briefly. Mao Tse-tung shuffled stiffly to his side and peered amiably over his shoulder.

> The Great Proletarian Cultural Revolution is aimed with exact precision at eliminating bourgeois ideology, establishing proletarian ideology, remolding men's souls, revolutionizing their ideology, digging up the roots of revisionism, and developing the Socialist system.
> *We will strike down* those men in authority who are taking the capitalist road! *We will strike down* the reactionary, bourgeois academic savants! *We will strike down* all bourgeois royalists! We will staunchly resist any suppression of the revolution! *We will strike down all demons and monsters!*

Again, torrents of cheers overwhelmed the voice booming from a hundred loudspeakers. The Disciple looked up, as if mildly surprised. The Chairman nodded like an indulgent uncle accepting thanks for a birthday present.

> We will *energetically eradicate all* the old ideas, the old culture, the old customs, and the old habits of the exploiting classes. We will *totally transform all* those parts of the social superstructure which do not harmonize with the Socialist economic base. *We will sweep away all vermin and clear away all obstacles!*
>
> We will vigorously establish proletarian intellectual authorities, our own academic savants. *We will vigorously establish* the *new* ideas, the *new* culture, the *new* customs, and the *new* habits of the proletariat. In a word, we will strive with the utmost energy so that the Thought of Mao Tse-tung achieves *complete ascendancy* . . .

Finally growing animated, as if kindled by his own rhetoric, Lin Piao uttered his summing-up in shrill and menacing tones while hysterical cheers interrupted his words.

> It is imperative to act resolutely, to arouse the masses boldly . . . to strike at the handful of ultrareactionary rightists. . . . *We must launch fierce attacks* on bourgeois ideology, on old customs, and on the influence of old habits! We must *totally topple, smash, and expose* the counterrevolutionary revisionists, the bourgeois rightists, and the reactionary bourgeois academic savants. *They must never be allowed to rise again!**

The *Sixteen-Point Directive Decision of the Central Committee on the Great Proletarian Cultural Revolution* laid down the general strategy of the Maoist forces. The subtle document had been forced through the Eleventh Plenum. It mobilized the extremists, while lulling the moderates by concealing their total peril. The *Directive* nonetheless anticipated neither the stubborn resistance that finally forced the Maoists to destroy the Communist Party nor the wild wilfullness that soon carried the Red Guards beyond control.

The *Directive* declared that China had reached "a new stage in the Socialist revolution," which required a total transformation of public opinion by "the destruction of the entire old civilization." Mao was quoted as having observed, as early as September 1962: "To overthrow political power, it is always necessary to labor first of all to prepare the proper climate of opinion . . ."

* Emphasis supplied.

The "masses of workers, peasants, soldiers, revolutionary intellectuals, and revolutionary cadres" were exhorted to use "great-character posters and great debates" to express their own opinions. They were instructed to "argue things out, expose and criticize thoroughly, and launch resolute attacks on the overt and hidden representatives of the bourgeoisie."

The *Directive* divided all Party organizations into four categories: 1) those whose correct leadership wholly supported the Maoists; 2) those where the leadership, weak in understanding, was fearful of change; 3) those where the leadership had committed many mistakes and was therefore particularly fearful of correction; and 4) those totally controlled by the "class enemy." Aside from "stubborn, incorrigible enemies," who would be crushed, all leaders who "reformed by harkening to mass criticism" would be pardoned.

Cautioning against confusing "internal contradictions," which were susceptible of resolution, with irreconcilable contradictions, the *Directive* warned that the "class enemy" would label loyal Maoists "counter-revolutionaries." It envisioned new organizations, called "Cultural Revolutionary Groups, Committees, and Congresses," to implement the Maoist line in every "unit"—meaning factories, farms, schools, economic enterprises, and Party branches. Quite obviously planning to use a purged Communist Party, the *Directive* called the Revolutionary Committees "an excellent bridge to keep our Party in close contact with the masses."

The *Directive,* however, projected a new, parallel structure of power, for it promised selection of the Revolutionary Groups, Committees, and Congresses "by a system of general elections like that of the Paris Commune" of 1871. The ultimate Utopian goal was thus revealed.*

At the outset, the purposes appeared attainable, if not entirely rational. Educational institutions were to be reformed by "overthrowing bourgeois academic savants" and giving students the commanding voice. The concrete reforms called for shortening courses; increasing their "practical" content; intensifying their ideological emphasis; combining study with labor; and encouraging students to "make revolution."

"Class enemies" were to "be criticized by name in the press" only with the consent of higher Party authority. Scientists, technicians, and administrators in research and productive enterprises were not to be touched, as long as "they are patriotic, work energetically, are not opposed to the

---

* The influence of the ideal represented by the Paris Commune was to be dominant for a brief time. The theoretical goal of the Cultural Revolution, as formulated by the Chairman's ideological mentor, the Ghostwriter, is discussed at length in Chapter XVI.

Party or Socialism, and maintain no relations with *any* * foreign country." Those essential men were to be allowed to "reform" themselves
"under guidance."

The *Directive* clearly marked the chief target—the apparatus that
shaped public opinion. "The cultural and educational units and leading
organs [of publicity] of the Party and the Government in the large and
medium cities are the points of concentration of the present Proletarian
Cultural Revolution." The *Directive* thus indicated further that both the
Communist Party and the People's Government would endure and rule
—*as they did not*. It also excluded the countryside from the "disorder"
of the Cultural Revolution—*an exemption not long sustained*. Farmers,
it indicated, were already being "reformed" by the Socialist Education
Campaign. Since the economy was not to be disrupted, the "proletarian"
working-class was also exempted—*but that immunity was also brief*.
The Maoists had obviously planned their revolution meticulously, but,
as obviously, they had not really foreseen that their "total revolution"
was to be truly total. They were soon to find that no group could be permitted to abstain.

Exempting agriculture and industry from attack by the Red Guards,
the *Directive* stressed the need to increase production. The Cultural
Revolution, it maintained, would stimulate economic activity, a dubious
proposition that was later proved wholly erroneous.

The People's Liberation Army was also granted immunity, since the
military would carry out necessary reform through their normal political
apparatus. The *Directive* made no provision for the Group Directing
the Cultural Revolution within the Armed Forces, a later, unexpected
growth.

The sweeping *Directive* was thus marked by a degree of restraint. The
Maoists preached "total revolution," but ordered only that their immediate enemies be attacked. Lest there be any misunderstanding, *The
People's Daily* a few days later precisely delineated objectives and
tactics:

> The torrents of the Great Proletarian Cultural Revolution are pound-
> ing at every kind of obstructive force. . . . The Party organization of
> every area and every unit must unconditionally pursue the mass line and
> accept supervision and criticism by the masses. On no account may such
> organizations use any pretext whatsoever to reject or to suppress criti-
> cism by the masses [as had the Peking Municipal Committee]. . . . If
> the Party organization of any area or any unit acts contrary to the cor-
> rect guidance of the Party Central Committee headed by Comrade Mao

* Emphasis supplied. The prohibition, implicitly directed primarily at the
U.S.A. and the USSR, expressed the comprehensive Maoist xenophobia.

Tse-tung or to the Thought of Mao Tse-tung, why should it not be criticized, why should it not be opposed?

It is good indeed that great numbers of revolutionary students are arising to wage the revolution and to oppose the bureaucratic overlords. . . . They have the right to hold demonstrations on the streets and the [unconditional] right of assembly, association, public speech, and publication. They dare to use Mao Tse-tung's Thought to criticize the errors of the Party Committees of their own schools and Party Committees at higher levels. Such are precisely the tactics which can straighten out the leadership of all Party Committees. As for the diehards of the right, as for those bureaucrats who are intractable, their utter collapse is a very good thing indeed.*

A truly new force had arisen in China. The night the long knives were drawn against the Communist Party in the provinces lasted almost three years. The ultimate victim was all lawful order.

The spiritual regeneration of a nation was to be accomplished by a "revolution that touches the soul of every man." Symbolic actions against the material environment were necessary to accomplish spiritual transformation. One such action was undertaken by Red Guards on the afternoon of August 24, 1966, less than a week after the first great rally in the Plaza of Heavenly Peace. The Maoists reported the incident in their own words in the *domestic service* of the New China News Agency:

> PEKING, August 25—On the afternoon of 24 August, *a revolutionary fire was ignited on the campus of the Central Institute of Arts to destroy the sculptures of Buddha, the niches of Buddha, and sculptures of emperors, kings, ministers, generals, scholars, beauties, and demons of Greek and Roman origins or of ancient, feudal China.* The revolutionary teachers and students of the Institute said excitedly: "What we have destroyed and crushed are not only a few sculptures, but the entire Old World!"
>
> The masses of revolutionary students and teachers of the Central Institute of Arts together with the revolutionary students and teachers of other fraternal schools and institutes of higher learning such as the Peking Normal College and others, who came to support them and join their rebellion, were in high spirits. They cast out from their classrooms, studios, and storerooms *the sculptures of the Goddess of Mercy, princes, and the fierce-looking gods Shu Yu and Yu Lu which they had collected*

---

* The translation, though awkward, in this case conveys the flavor better than would a more polished or idiomatic rendition into English.

*from various temples in China; the stone horses and tigers they had col-
lected from Imperial tombs; the sculptures of King David of Israel—
the "hero" David in the Bible; the "Goddess of Love and Beauty"—the
Venus of Greek legends; Apollo, and others purchased abroad.* All these
were burned and smashed in broad daylight.

During the past 10 years or more, the revolutionary students and teachers of the Central Institute of Arts were under the bad influences of
feudalism, capitalism, and revisionism, and worked only on the dead,
the foreign, and the ancient. Today they have stood up in the stormy
Proletarian Cultural Revolution under the bright light of Mao Tse-tung's
Thought. They want to liberate themselves and sweep away all harmful
elements with their own hands and remove all the obstacles in their way.

Trampling the sculptures under their feet, the students and staff members of the Central Institute of Arts indignantly denounced those persons
who were in power at the Institute who took the road of capitalism and
used these "old masters" to corrupt and poison the youths and attempt
to restore capitalism. That was a frenzied counterrevolutionary crime.

During the 10 years or more since liberation, the Central Institute of
Arts, under the control of a handful of anti-Party and anti-Socialist
rightists, followed the system of bourgeois institutes in the West and
carried out the same kind of education in art given by the European
bourgeoisie. Those rightists and the reactionary academic "authorities"
held those ancient and European "old masters" in high esteem and made
replicas of those sculptures, distributing them to other parts of the country. They thus created a very bad influence. *They kept the students in
their studios all day long, forcing them to worship emperors, goddesses,
and Buddha and ordering them to study and copy those sculptures more
than a thousand times.* From enrollment to graduation, the students
were forced to crawl before these "old masters" and worship them.

Now the revolutionary storm sweeping away all old ideas, old culture,
old customs, and old habits [the Four Olds] of the exploiting classes has
swept the whole country. *The use of dead foreigners and ancient dead
people to enslave and torture the revolutionary teachers and students is
no longer allowed to persist.*

*Shouting indignantly, the revolutionary teachers and students said: "Let
these 'old masters' of bourgeois art go back to God! We must crush them
and trample them under our feet so that they will never stand up again!"
Beating gongs and drums joyously, the revolutionary teachers and students raised their axes, picks, and iron spikes and struck at the heads of
the sculptures of emperors, goddesses, and Buddha.* In a short time, the
"corpses" of sculptures fell to the ground. *A revolutionary fire was ignited by the revolutionary masses to reduce to ashes those hard-to-crush
wooden sculptures of Buddha. The fire burned vigorously in the wind.*

In no time, all the monsters and demons which had been enthroned in art studios for thousands of years were burned up completely.

With revolutionary fire burning in their hearts, the teachers and students of Peking Normal College presented *a portrait of Chairman Mao* to the revolutionary teachers and students of the Central Institute of Arts. When the color portrait of Chairman Mao was displayed before the masses, it attracted the attention of the emotion-filled masses. Thousands of Red hearts flew to their beloved leader Chairman Mao. Immediately, shouts of "Long Live Chairman Mao!" and a chorus of "Sailing the Seas, We Rely on the Helmsman" soared from the campus.*

Pure "proletarian art" was poster-portraits of Chairman Mao, which displaced Michaelangelo's "bourgeois" *David*. A purpose transcending the violent repudiation of millennia-old Chinese and Western aesthetic standards guided both destruction and replacement. Public vandalism served both as catharsis and inspiration to further destruction by its example of "mass participation and mass emulation." Maoist psychologists based their tactics on the teachings of I. P. Pavlov. The Red Guards and the masses were to be "conditioned" by their own deeds.

Not just ancient works of art were to be destroyed, but the "old academic authorities [savants] of bourgeois art" as well. The learned professors exalted and embodied those traditions of both East and West which the Maoists denounced *en bloc* as "the rotten old world." Maoist attacks on the "old academic authorities" were politically justified, for the savants were the protégés of the non-Maoists who had ruled China since the early 1960s. By humiliating the professors, the Red Guards were also attacking their "masters behind the scenes," the moderates entrenched within the Communist Party.

In Shanghai, the humiliation of an aged former official of the Manchu Dynasty emboldened the Red Guards, convincing them that they were truly "smashing the old world." A literal translation of a personal account may least prejudicially describe actions that occurred tens of thousands of times in one form or another:

In my neighborhood in Shanghai there had lived for a long time a *Hsiu-tsai.*** In August, 1966, he was 88 years old, and the neighbors all looked upon him as a living fossil—a relic of the Manchu Dynasty who possessed great knowledge of China's traditional culture. Since his age was very great, his character was undoubtedly quite unbending—and he was not conversant with the thought of the new age. In truth, consider-

* Emphasis supplied.
** The first or "bachelor's" degree under the old Civil Service System, the *Hsiu-tsai* qualified the holder for lower government office.

ing the vast alterations in Chinese society during the past 90 years, it would be almost impossible for any individual to comprehend and accept them all, particularly an individual who had received his education in traditional Chinese culture under the Manchus.

Because his years were so great, his children, grandchildren, and great-grandchildren all insisted that he remain at home, without participating in any kind of work. Regardless of the season, he normally wore a traditional Chinese gentleman's long-gown, only varying its weight according to the temperature. Each morning and each afternoon, he would take a stroll in the vicinity of his home. Passers-by, particularly pert children and youths, looked upon him as a most peculiar phenomenon. They mocked him and hooted at him. They said that he was, after all, not a living person of modern times, but a figure who had stepped out of the pages of history. Although his queue had been snipped off at the time of the Revolution of 1911, he wore his hair very long, much like the hippies of the Western world.

When the Red Guards' Movement to Destroy the Four Olds began, this 88-year-old *Hsiu-tsai* came immediately to their minds as a fitting object for "destruction."

The Red Guards flocked to his house with leering faces. They screamed and shouted outside the gate, demanding that he bring out all objects which exemplified the "Four Olds" so that they could be burnt on the street corner. Perhaps because he remembered the violence attendant upon the clipping of his queue in 1911, the old gentleman was immediately and effusively cooperative. He produced a number of fine scrolls bearing lines from ancient poems inscribed in excellent calligraphy—so that they might be burnt on the street corner.

Most of the bystanders, who were his neighbors, had known him from their earliest years, and they felt that he was most co-operative. They all began to clap their hands, chiefly to make the Red Guards feel satisfied that they had already won the "glory of victory"—and to induce them to cease attacking that figure out of the history books. But the Red Guards reckoned that he must still possess many other objects exemplifying the "Four Olds," and they rushed in to search his house.

They saw two scrolls hanging on the wall of his parlor. They were couplets composed by a famous general and patriot of the Sung Dynasty who had steadfastly resisted the Mongol invasion. Because they were written in the General's own hand, those originals from the 12th century A.D., were extremely valuable. Besides, the calligrapher was a great hero, particularly to the people of Southern China. Both artistically and historically, they were truly priceless scrolls.

When the Red Guards wanted to burn those scrolls, the old *Hsiu-tsai* finally got his back up. He said the scrolls were a legacy left by a hero of China's past. He explained that they were not merely rare, but incalculably precious. The Red Guards were not impressed!

The old *Hsiu-tsai* then said that he would be glad to present those priceless objects to the National Museum. He asked the Red Guards to bring their leader to him so that he could make a formal presentation.

The Red Guards shouted indignantly: "What is a leader? We are all leaders. We are all the Red Guards of Chairman Mao. When we say do something, you must do it. Who would dare to come and give *us* orders?"

The old gentleman's anger flared to match theirs. He answered: "Chairman Mao also writes old-style poetry. Why don't you go and destroy his Four Olds?"

The Red Guards dragged him out into the street and popped a dunce cap on his head.* They beat him and, on his breast, they hung a placard which read: OLD DECAYED FILTH! On his back they hung another: VOMIT OUT SUCH POISON OF THE PAST!

He was then paraded through the streets, handled none too gently. To the spectators it looked like a funeral procession. But the Red Guards chanted and beat drums as if they were great heroes and the saviours of the world, while the old gentleman was their vanquished enemy.

I later heard, though I am not certain, that the old gentleman died a few days later. No one knows exactly why he died or what injuries he may have suffered, but rumors nonetheless began to fly. Still the death of an 88-year-old man is hardly a surprise.

As for the two scrolls by the General of the Sung Dynasty, they were burned on the street corner.

It was "a great victory for the Thought of Mao Tse-tung."

Such great victories were celebrated across all China immediately after the proclamation of the Great Proletarian Cultural Revolution and the formation of the Red Guards. Peking's official translation of their war chant, "The Battle Song of the Red Guards," describes the temper of resentful adolescents marching against a civilization:

We are Chairman Mao's Red Guards,
We steel our red hearts in great winds and waves.
We arm ourselves with Mao Tse-tung's Thought
To sweep away all pests.

* The dunce cap has a special meaning for the Chinese, since traditional superstition holds that the spirits of criminals wear such caps in Hell. The Red Guards constantly used this traditional and superstitious form of degradation in their fight against superstitious tradition.

We are Chairman Mao's Red Guards,
Absolutely firm in our proletarian stand.
Marching on the revolutionary road of our forebears,
We shoulder the heavy task of our age.

We are Chairman Mao's Red Guards,
Vanguards of the Cultural Revolution.
We unite with the masses and together plunge into the battle
To wipe out all monsters and demons.

Refrain:
Dare to criticize and repudiate, dare to struggle,
Never stop making revolutionary rebellion.
We will smash the old world
And keep our revolutionary state red for ten thousand generations!

Such was the spirit the Red Guards' adult manipulators, the generals of Lin Piao, inculcated.

In September the Disciple struck to remove the great majority of functionaries of the Communist Party. *The People's Daily* sounded the tocsin for battle between two generations of Communists. Youths threatened to "destroy" their parents. The contrived struggle between maturity and youth reflected the fundamental struggle for supremacy between the established Communist Party and the "mass organizations" the Disciple had hastily created.

An open letter from the adolescent "Red Guards of Peking" warned parents that they would be "destroyed" if they did not bow. Although obviously inspired, the brutal language was the authentic voice of adolescents running amok with the blessing of the Disciple and the Starlet:

Daddies and Mamas:
Your sons and daughters have all risen in the new revolution. They are all engaged in rebelling and they have all joined the Red Guards! Everyone calls you "old revolutionaries." But we want to tell you a few things: Among you old revolutionaries, some people are just muddling and confusing the revolution! How long do you think you can get away with just muddling along?

The threat clearly included all "old revolutionaries"—even those as eminent as the Chairman of the People's Republic, Comrade Liu Shao-chi. The "old revolutionaries bound by old inhibitions" were informed that their children's loyalty was given to "the laboring masses, who are the mothers and fathers of us all!" They were further informed: "The time has come for you to rise in revolt!" If they did not join the Witches' Sabbath, they would be "plucked out as revisionists."

"Who says that children cannot rebel against their own parents and strike them down?" the open letter demanded. "We will do so!"

The Disciple was building his personal power on the fanaticism of youth. Mobs of frantic adolescents ran wild through the streets of China —and overran the structure of the Communist Party.

Outsiders called it the Children's Crusade, because that term was dramatic and evocative. But the Red Guards, at least 20 million at full strength, were quite different from the pathetic raggle-taggle that set out to liberate the Holy Land in the thirteenth century. For all their "spontaneous" appearance on the political scene, they were the creation of the People's Liberation Army. They were—initially, at least—marshaled and deployed as efficiently as the Disciple's troops had been commanded in battle.

Two mass meetings demonstrated both the intensity and the objective of the assault. The first convened amid torrential rainstorms on the morning of August 29, 1966, in Harbin, a grim industrial city and the capital of Heilungkiang Province.* The atmosphere was as gray and foreboding as a Manchurian winter's day, but the Red Guards struck fire by their vehement oratory and violent chanting. The lowering skies echoed the demand of the "rebel revolutionaries": "Burn down the Heilungkiang Provincial Committee of the Chinese Communist Party! Bombard the headquarters of the counterrevolutionary black gang within the Communist Party!"

Lin Piao's threats had become harsh reality. Official after official, senior Party leader after senior Party leader—almost the entire hierarchy of Heilungkiang—were condemned as "traitors belonging to the black, anti-Party gang." They were to be "weeded out" of office, their places taken by—no one at all. The total purge provided no replacements to operate the Party apparatus. Moreover, it was nation-wide. The rally attended by "revolutionary cadres" was called "the first wave of a fierce attack on demons and monsters of all kinds *everywhere in China.*"

The Third Secretary of the Party's Manchurian Regional Bureau and the First Secretary of the Heilungkiang Provincial Committee were reluctant participants. Their presence demonstrated that the first mass rally was neither a localized phenomenon nor a spontaneous aberration. The Party Center, the headquarters in Peking newly captured by the

---

* Literally, "Black Dragon River," the Chinese name for the Amur River.

Disciple, had commanded the "bombardment of the Heilungkiang Provincial Committee."

The shrill voice of the girl student who spoke first declared that the meeting was to be an inspiration and a model for Red Guards throughout the nation.

Inspired by the Thought of Mao Tse-tung, a stormy and violent struggle is being carried out throughout China. It is the Great Proletarian Cultural Revolution initiated by Chairman Mao. Hundreds of millions of workers, peasants, and soldiers all over the country have risen against the representatives of the bourgeoisie who have wormed their way into the Party. The rebel revolutionaries have already achieved one victory after another in defeating the black gang, thereby gradually expanding and consolidating our Socialist State. The countless misdeeds and crimes discovered during the past three months can be used as good lessons by negative example for the broad masses throughout the country.

Revolutionary comrades of the Great Cultural Revolution, our primary target is clear. We must bombard the command headquarters and drag out the leaders of the black gang in the Heilungkiang Provincial Committee. If these careerists are not dragged out, how can the revolutionary masses of our province possibly carry out the struggle successfully? If the demons and monsters are allowed to hold their present entrenched positions, the revolutionary cause will suffer serious setbacks. . . .

The "revolutionary storm" had just broken, but resistance was already forming. It was not just the "men in power," the first targets, who began to muster defenses but students and workers appalled by the impending destruction. The formal resolution of the Harbin Rally anticipated the resistance to Red Guard excesses that would soon rise. It was, even on August 29, 1966, apparent that the extremists would not sweep unopposed to victory.

Red Guard organizations are mass organizations of the Great Cultural Revolution. Not just anyone can easily become a Red Guard. . . . Recently some landlords, rich peasants, and counterrevolutionaries, as well as bad and rightist elements, supported by the royalists, have put on red armbands and called themselves Red Guards. How can those rotten eggs possibly qualify as Red Guards?

Most despicably, those bad elements, using their red armbands as weapons, have utilized devious and vicious tricks to oppose the . . . revolutionary masses and to conduct widespread undermining and sabotage. . . . The rally puts forward the following proposal to thwart the evil elements:

First, thoroughly purge the Harbin Red Guards to ensure that they are true representatives of the Thought of Mao Tse-tung—a contingent possessing high class-consciousness and composed of the children of workers, poor and lower-middle peasants, revolutionary martyrs, revolutionary soldiers, and revolutionary cadres. Stiffened by that revolutionary backbone, the Red Guards will be the vanguard of the Great Proletarian Cultural Revolution. They must sweep out the landlords, rich peasants, and counterrevolutionaries, the rightist elements who have wormed their way into the ranks of the Red Guards.

Second, student participation in revolutionary activities must, first, be arranged and, later, managed in a disciplined manner by well planned organizations. Each and every red rebel team and Red Guard organization must, therefore, plan all revolutionary actions in a united manner.

Thus Harbin set the pattern for the nation. Urged to "rebel," the Red Guards were required to accept rigid discipline. The Disciple demanded their effective subordination to the military.

The Peking Mass Rally three days later revealed that Lin Piao's plan for a quick "victory by annihilation" was going awry. The second of the Eight Great Rallies of the Cultural Revolution was hastily convened on the evening of September 1. Though only half a million "rebel revolutionaries" were assembled in the Plaza of Heavenly Peace, Hong Kong Communist newspapers delayed publication by several hours to carry the news.

The leading players of the August 18 Mass Rally, which had begun the Cultural Revolution, performed again—in slightly different roles. Instead of appearing on the vast, remote stage of the Gate of Heavenly Peace, the leaders of China rode through the Plaza in a cavalcade of motor cars, trundling Mao Tse-tung before them like a stuffed mascot.

Four men shared the leading automobile with the silent Mao. They were all soldiers: the Disciple himself; the Bandit General, Ho Lung; General Hsieh Fu-chih, the professional soldier who controlled the repressive machinery of the Ministry of Public Security; and Yang Cheng-wu, Yang the Gun, acting chief-of-staff of the Liberation Army.*

The Disciple Lin Piao, already named Defense Minister, First Vice Premier of the People's government, and sole Deputy Chairman of the Communist Party, stood forth as Chairman of the Communist Party's Military Affairs Commission. Mao Tse-tung had held that latter position since the mid-1930s. The manner and content of Lin Piao's brief speech, "delivered on behalf of Chairman Mao," openly asserted his domination —and the primacy of the Liberation Army. The Red Guards were

---

* Both the Bandit General and Yang the Gun were later swept into oblivion.

further exalted by their designation as "the powerful reserve force of the People's Liberation Army."

The rally demonstrated that the Red Guards were almost as much the creatures of the Starlet as the Disciple. She was tendered unprecedented public honor. The Starlet rode in the second automobile with the First Minister of Peace, Premier Chou En-lai, the Disciple's civilian administrative assistant, and she was publicly hailed as Deputy Director of the Task Force of the Cultural Revolution.

Her eminence set rumor loose. His wife, men whispered, obviously manipulated the enfeebled Chairman. Since Mao was still silent, suspicious Chinese believed he suffered either mental or physical debility. Before the "revolutionary storm," the Starlet had formed her personal following, even more vociferous and extreme than the Disciple's henchmen. She would soon assert her own power over the Red Guards.

The rally further revealed that the Great Revolution was already "encountering difficulties." The Disciple and the First Minister of Peace spoke briefly to denounce growing opposition in Party cells, administrative organs, and economic enterprises. The Red Guards were exhorted to prepare for a protracted campaign, since "the class enemy" would not yield gracefully.

Largely bereft of adult support within the Party, the Disciple was forced to rely upon the fanatic enthusiasm of the young Red Guards. But even in September, the Red Guards were getting out of hand. The adolescent "shock troops" were hardly a disciplined instrument like the Liberation Army. The Disciple, who had never previously committed his forces without the most elaborate preparations, had mustered his shock troops hastily and thrown them into battle precipitately. Lin Piao feared that he might lose command, for the Red Guards literally obeyed the injunction "Dare to rebel!" Were they not the darlings of Chairman Mao, the "true representatives of the revolutionary masses?" Their commander felt it necessary to caution his unruly youth troops.

"Use persuasion rather than force!" Lin Piao ordered. "Do not lift your hands to strike people!"

The hazardous experiment in mass psychology went astray. The Disciple could not, on the one hand, urge the Red Guards into action with vicious invective and, on the other, exercise absolute control to restrain them. The assault on the "old civilization" was beginning to display its totally disruptive violence.

Nonetheless, the First Minister of Great Peace, Premier Chou En-lai, ordered the Red Guards to "carry the revolution to every part of the country." They were to displace untrustworthy organs of the People's Government and the Communist Party. Students would spread out from Peking to the hinterlands to create the new Utopia. At the same time,

Chou said, "all revolutionary college students and large numbers of high-school students from all parts of the country" would come to Peking to "see Chairman Mao"—and be inflamed by the spirit of the Cultural Revolution. Abandoning almost everyone over 25, the Maoists spoke as if youth would truly rule China.

Implicitly contradicting his admonitions against aggression and violence, the Disciple reaffirmed the Red Guards' primary mission—terrorizing provincial officials. "The main target of the attack," he reiterated, "is those persons in power who have wormed their way into the Party and have now taken the capitalist road."

The strategist who had counted on instantaneous victory was realizing that the battle had just begun.

XIV

Destroy the Old World

Before setting out, a Long Marcher should adjust his cloth-wrapped parcel on his back so that one end of the cloth goes over his right shoulder and the other around his waist on the right side. He should sling his canteen-strap over his left shoulder, so that the water-bottle hangs on his right side. He should, further, secure both the parcel and the canteen by a belt or a length of string for comfort on the march. Next comes his knapsack, which should be 40 centimeters long and 30 centimeters wide, its straps crossing just below his shoulders. His pace should be four kilometers an hour, but he may proceed more slowly at first. . . .

The Red Guards were re-enacting in miniature in the autumn of 1966 the eight-thousand-mile Long March of the Red Army in 1934 and 1935. The instructions ran for five pages in the *Canton Red Guard Journal.* The Disciple Lin Piao was determined that his shock troops would maneuver under precise discipline. He further issued a 25-page atlas "for use in exchanging revolution experience," the official euphemism for the destructive Long Marches of the Red Guards.

Like any good military manual, the painstaking instructions to the insurgent adolescents assumed that the readers were, by and large, idiots. The People's Liberation Army, having organized the Red Guards, continued to oversee their peregrinations. Official reception centers were established in major cities under Army officers called "political advisers." Transportation was assigned, as were quarters and rations at destinations. The chief railway station of Peking was reserved solely for the millions of Red Guards who attended the Eight Great Mass Rallies.

The Liberation Army Daily was not indulging in metaphor when it hailed the Red Guards as "the powerful reserve force of the People's Liberation Army." It was intended that their "disorder and rebellion" would be stringently controlled by the Army.

The guerrilla general, who had become the second man in China by intimidation, used the Red Guards as his private political army. The single most powerful force in the country, the People's Liberation Army, had been his personal fief as Minister of Defense since 1959. But the army had been systematically "corrupted" by the Securityman, Chief-of-Staff Lo Jui-ching, appointed to purge non-Maoist officers. Besides, Lin Piao did not wish to wage open war against the Chinese people, but a limited war against the opposition. He therefore hurled his Red Guard guerrillas at the structures of the Communist Party, the People's Government—and all fundamental institutions of Chinese society. He was, however, driven by the same compulsion that has driven other generals fighting other political wars. He longed for the "total victory" that is the Holy Grail of all generals.

The Disciple, the field commander, and his mentor, Mao the grand strategist, ordered a massive assault on the institutions built by 18 years of Communist rule—and on the intellectual and social remnants of the past. Their assault troops were the Red Guards. Their objective was the "four olds—old habits, manners, custom, and culture," in sum really the entire extant civilization of China. The Mao-Lin faction decided to burn down the house in order to smoke out their enemies. Utopia would rise "on the ashes of the old society."

But the opposition was entrenched in "local strongholds" everywhere in China. The initial attacks had combined the chief aspects of Peking Opera and traditional Chinese battles. The Disciple was using tactics proved in the distant past and the recent present to demoralize his enemies. Fierce display of weapons, igniting firecrackers, clanging cymbals, and firing cannon before a traditional Chinese battle sought to break the enemy's will by demonstrating the immensely superior force he opposed; tens of thousands of guerrilla pinpricks had broken the nerve of Japanese and Nationalists opponents during the long struggle for power. The first Red Guard terror sought the same results, but failed. Despite much shouting of criticism and blowing of bugles and chanting of slogans, the "stubborn bourgeois element within the Party" was not sufficiently terrorized by the Children's Crusade.

On September 15, 1966, the Third Great Mass Rally assembled a million "rebel revolutionaries" in the Plaza of Heavenly Peace. Lin Piao issued new orders. It was time to alter his tactics. As he had done in his formal battles, he concentrated his attack upon the center of enemy resistance.

The Disciple ordered the Red Guards to "bombard the headquarters" of his opponents within the Communist Party everywhere in China. The men who still dared resist would be broken by frontal assault.

In the gathering dusk of the Peking autumn, the Disciple spoke "on behalf of Chairman Mao," who was again present, but again did not speak. Lin Piao praised the Red Guards for creating consternation among "the handful of men in power who take the capitalist road"; for terrifying the "reactionary bourgeois scholarly authorities"; and for paralyzing the "blood-suckers and parasites."

"You have done well!" The Disciple's tone and manner marked him as the master of China. "The present movement's main target of attack is *now* those men within the Party who are in power and who are taking the capitalist road. You must bombard their headquarters."

Minister Chou En-lai struck a note of caution. He emphasized the necessity to maintain production in order "to advance the revolution" —and admonished the insurgent adolescents not to interfere with industry or agriculture. Nascent fear that Red Guard violence might escape control was reflected by *The People's Daily*'s subsequent instructions:

"Production must not be interrupted. The Cultural Revolution in the factories and rural areas should be carried out in connection with the original arrangements for the Four Purifications Movement." Since the general urban public was sufficiently terrorized, the Maoists wished to concentrate Red Guard violence directly on the "power-holders" within the Communist Party. They still believed they could avoid injuring the economy, since it was not necessary to attack workers and peasants.

In mid-September, the Cultural Revolution had encountered greater resistance than was anticipated, yet it was still proceeding as planned. While the Red Guards were exhorted to "destroy the old civilization in order to establish the new civilization," a new administrative structure was being constructed to displace the People's Government. The "Groups and Committees of the Great Cultural Revolution" were quietly established in colleges, schools, factories, and Communes throughout China. They were to be the basis of "true proletarian rule," inspired by the Paris Commune of 1871. But the Communist Party itself was originally not marked for destruction. The Revolutionary Committees would manifest "extensive democracy," which the Party would guide under "democratic centralism."

By the end of September, a totally new strategy was forced on the Maoists. They would if necessary destroy the Communist Party itself. The "reasoned approach," the calculated use of limited terror, was failing. The non-Maoists entrenched in the Communist Party—and, for want of more attractive objects, in the affections of the masses—were too strong and too determined. By the end of September, the rampages of the adolescent Red Guards had become a spectacle of mindless, indiscriminate terror. The Red Guards had, in part, escaped central control, but, equally, the Maoists were compelled by circumstances to press the total, vicious assault on all stable institutions.

Although it may appear somewhat absurd, the total offensive was not wholly Quixotic within its own particular context. The Maoists had been frustrated time and time again by the most tenacious civilization and the most stubbornly conservative race on earth. Although they had striven since 1949, they had failed to smash the world's oldest living culture. They had neither created the ideal China they envisioned, nor made their own power absolute. Since they did not recognize universal "human nature" but only "class nature," they could not acknowledge that their enemy was the essential character of the human being. Instead, they concluded that their ambition was frustrated by the "bourgeois thought patterns" of the unregenerate "bourgeois elements" within and without the Communist Party. They therefore determined to destroy the old culture by force in order that a new "proletarian class nature" might burgeon. The decision was rigorously logical within their own philosophical framework, however ludicrous it may appear to non-Maoists.

The peregrinations of the newly hatched Red Guards were essential to the grand Maoist design. The adolescents would not only "remold" their own nature by enduring hardships and "learning from the proletariat," but would inspire the masses by their sterling example. Transferring the shock troops was also a tactical necessity. The "vigorous attack" on the entire established order could not be mounted by youths in their native areas. The "revolutionary rebels" were still restrained by ingrained respect for officials, teachers, and parents who had brought them up.

Since every city and town was to be invaded by "outside" Red Guards, all China was astir with the movement of earnest youths and maidens wearing the crimson armband in the autumn of 1966. Whether to Peking to draw inspiration from mass rallies at which the silent Chairman Mao was exhibited like an animate idol or to the provinces to "make revolution," millions of Red Guards stalked across the vast nation like hordes of enraged soldier ants. They traveled by railroad, bus, and airplane until the transportation system began to collapse under their weight. Then they were ordered to emulate the heroic Long March on foot.

In the beginning, an efficient system provided food, lodging, and specific assignments to the errant Red Guards the insular Chinese called "foreigners" when they were 50 miles from their homes. Their assignments varied: "reforming" schools; ridiculing Party officials; humiliating professors; and destroying all objects and manifestations of the "old civilization"—to the accompaniment of choral readings from *Quotations*

From Chairman Mao; staging propaganda playlets; and composing "great-character posters" attacking "bourgeois diehards." From September through December 1966, the Red Guards' "campaign" was the emotional heartbeat and the chief administrative activity of the People's Republic of China. Sometimes they were orderly, but determined. Sometimes they were frivolous or venal. Often they were violent and cruel, with the special relish of youths exacting vengeance upon the unsatisfactory world of their elders' creation—and upon their elders, too.

The Red Guards came close upon midnight in early October to a Nanking home. Mrs. Yang was the widow of a senior member of the Democratic League, one of the splinter "democratic parties" that had previously propped the façade of "coalition rule." Ten young men trooped into her anteroom and read aloud the rump Central Committee's *Sixteen-Point Directive* commanding the "destruction of the old world." Having been briefed from dossiers, they knew the family's history well. The Yangs, the adolescents declared, were a nest of rightists, a virulent "bourgeois infection." They then searched for "decadent objects," which might be anything from a reproduction of a Western painting or a non-Maoist book to Nationalist flags or propaganda.

Mrs. Yang had learned to bow before the wind, unlike those foolhardy householders who resisted, verbally or physically, and were beaten or killed for their courage. She assured her inquisitors that she was eager to destroy any bourgeois artifacts they might find.

She felt reasonably certain that she possessed no incriminating objects, except letters and photographs from her daughter, who had fled to Hong Kong three years earlier. She had not been able to bring herself to destroy those mementoes. The Red Guards did so for her. They then carried away every piece of furniture, even the old lady's bed and small radio. All her belongings, except for a few garments, were adjudged "bourgeois objects of pleasure." They did not, however, molest her further because she had not opposed their search. Later, two families of workers were quartered on Mrs. Yang. They helped her buy a few essential pieces of furniture with money her daughter sent from Hong Kong.

Perhaps harassing elderly "bourgeois elements" helped create an earthly Utopia. But many other antics appeared only perverse "self-education." Girls wearing tight trousers were restored to modesty with razor blades, while boys or girls wearing long hair were "proletarianized" with scissors. Colorful clothing, pointed shoes, or bright make-up, whistling Western songs, and reading nonrevolutionary novels—all non-Maoist diversions were forbidden. The "revolutionary rebels" severely punished all those outward manifestations that mark young rebels in the West.

Homes were purged of "reactionary objects"—reproductions of Western or traditional paintings, non-Maoist literature, jewelry, and classical, popular, or jazz records—all ornaments, in sum, except portraits of Chairman Mao and Deputy Chairman Lin, and all objects that touched non-Maoist intellectual or emotional chords. The total ideological purification also cleansed public buildings, and even the streets—in its own way. The ideal human being was the hard-working farmer or laborer. The entire physical environment was, therefore, to be transformed to harmonize with his presumably austere and simple needs.

All "bourgeois luxuries" were destroyed. The signboard of the Wing On Department Store in Shanghai was toppled because its name, Eternal Peace, offended revolutionary militants. Wing On was, thenceforth, to be known as the People's Department Store. Morrison Road in Peking became People's Road because it recalled "foreign imperialism." Signs that evoked the classic Chinese tradition were also pulled down in the assault on "the four olds." The Moon Terrace Tea Shop became Food Shop Number Two, and the Moon and Pine Pavilion became Food Shop Number Three.

Zeal often outdistanced even the magic carpet of Maoist logic. Shanghai's Peace Hotel, so called after the city's "liberation" in 1949 because Cathay Hotel was repugnantly "imperialist," was again renamed because the word "Peace" was "revisionist." But the Fragrant Shrimp Restaurant, faintly evocative of the classical tradition, was renamed the Peace Restaurant. One becomes two and two becomes one—as Mao Tse-tung teaches. Hundreds of East-Is-Red streets appeared—and scores of Anti-Revisionism alleys and Anti-Imperialism roads.

One of the first casualties of the paralysis of authority and the proliferation of "revolutionary" street names was the Chinese Postal Service. China's most faithful civil servants were hindered by Red Guards or condemned to wander about with packets of letters they could not deliver. That dislocation of communications may seem minor amid the total disruption of the Cultural Revolution, but it was not.

The Postal Service was among the most efficient institutions in China. The Mongol Dynasty (c. 1280–1368) had stationed relays of swift post-horses and built straight roads to maintain rapid communication throughout their enormous Empire. After half a millennium, the Postal Service was re-created in the nineteenth century by the Chinese Maritime Customs, organized and administered by foreigners. In the twentieth, letters mailed in Japanese-occupied Shanghai were delivered to the provisional capital of Chungking on a regular schedule, and even the Civil War did not disrupt the service. Like secular heralds, the postmen were immune to harassment as had been the sacred heralds of ancient Greece.

The breakdown of the Postal System demonstrated the "destruction of the old civilization"—and the disintegration of order. Letters from

Shanghai to Chungking took six to eight weeks. They had normally taken a week—and, even during the wars, no more than two or three. Drab-uniformed postmen wandered bewildered through the maze of "revolutionary" streets, wondering in which of dozens of East-Is-Red streets, Anti-Imperialism alleys, or Anti-Revisionism roads they might find the particular Mr. Wang or Mrs. Li they sought.

Their patient, frustrated plodding typified the Cultural Revolution as much as the public rampages of the Red Guards. Like everything that smacked of the past, the Postal Service was to be "remade"—regardless of social or economic effects. It was as much a relic of the old imperialism as were the buildings on the riverfront Bund in Shanghai.

"The tall buildings along the Bund, which was once the center of the Imperialists' criminal activities aimed at plundering the Chinese people," Peking reported, "have also been the targets of the revolutionary rebels, who have made a clean sweep of every vestige of imperialism. They removed the bronze lions placed in front of the entrances of buildings by the imperialists and took away the foreign signs on the walls."

Major vandalism of buildings was unusual, but the total purge of every physical, emotional, or spiritual aspect of China that evoked the old days and the old ways was unremitting. Nothing in the physical environment was to distract from total attention to the greatness of Chairman Mao and his "closest comrade-in-arms and best disciple, Deputy Chairman Lin Piao." No diversion was to impede the ceaseless study of the sacred Thought of Mao Tse-tung.

The Soviet Embassy in Peking was besieged by shouting Red Guards after its address was contemptuously altered to Anti-Revisionism Street. Violinists and pianists, once honored as proof of the *Chinese* genius for Western arts, were humiliated and beaten. Sometimes their fingers were broken. Not only was the Great Museum of the Central Academy of Arts in Peking stormed by the puritanical Red Guards, but, elsewhere, scenes of equally barbaric absurdity were enacted with hatchets and torches.

A mock trial convened in Canton before the tomb of the Seventy-two Martyrs of the Revolution against the Manchus. The accused was the Statue of the Goddess of Liberty that marked the tomb. The verdict was foregone. The Red Guards posted signs reading: TO THE DEVIL WITH YOU, GODDESS OF LIBERTY! DEMOLISH THE GODDESS OF LIBERTY!

The replica of the Statue of Liberty in New York Harbor was reviled because it was foreign. Her contours not only recalled the contemptible —yet feared—American imperialists, but harked back to the Nationalists' Republic of China. The judgment was vehement:

As criminal evidence of imperialist aggression against China, the Goddess of Liberty exhudes the rotten stench of the bourgeoisie. We are determined to smash it to bits. All things called "liberty, equality—and fraternity" are merely [empty] slogans camouflaging shameful bourgeois misdeeds. In the old society, the great laboring masses possessed only the "liberty" to be exploited and oppressed by their masters. Now *we* are the masters in our own house! We will no longer permit the Goddess of Liberty to maintain her sway over the masses. We will certainly not give the bourgeois revisionists liberty. We will thoroughly smash the Goddess of Liberty! We will bury the old world! We will build a new world and preserve China for the proletariat!

Little Revolutionary Fighters, each wielding his little hammer, climbed upon the inscribed tablet commemorating the Seventy-two Martyrs. As Peking reported:

In a moment, the torch in the hand of the Goddess of Liberty, which had been exhuding the rotten bourgeois stench, was smashed to pieces by the Little Revolutionary Fighters. In another moment, the arm of the statue was broken to pieces. When the hammers fell on the head of the Goddess of Liberty, prolonged applause rose from the multitude. Many of the onlookers could not restrain themselves from shouting at the top of their voices: "Long Live Chairman Mao! Long Live the Great Proletarian Cultural Revolution!"

In Chengchow, students at the Honan College of Traditional Chinese Medicine were foremost in the fray. The archetypical students of "the old culture" proclaimed themselves the scourge of the "old civilization." They demanded that the city's cinemas be renamed East-Is-Red Theater, Workers, Peasants, and Soldiers Theater, and Red Banner Theater. "Wielded by revolutionary workers, the iron Broom of the Revolution" swept a broad swathe through Chengchow. At the State-owned Number Four Cotton Mill, the "rebels" smashed "architectural ornaments—dragons' heads, dancing storks, and the Chang-ou," a mythical beast in flight to the moon—all because of their "feudal flavor." They took down all pictures of women and children in their dormitories—and substituted portraits of Chairman Mao. They burned their playing cards, "bad books," and "bizarre clothing." The brand name of the mill's cloth was changed from "Phoenix Terrace" to "Worker, Peasant, and Soldier." For good measure, Tsai's Dumpling Shop scrapped the signboard that had stood for decades. Old Tsai's place was given a proper revolutionary name: "East Wind Dumpling Shop."

In Canton, even the language was purged, while industrial measurements were no longer inches and feet, but centimeters and meters. Despite the likely future benefit, the alteration immediately impeded production. Objects were no longer to be called by either direct translation or transliteration of foreign words. A sofa was no longer a *shafa,* and ordinary round nails were not to be known as *yang-ting,* meaning *"foreign* nails"—as opposed to old-fashioned, square Chinese nails. In the north, where they had been known as *yang-huo, "foreign* fire," matches were to be called by the southern term, *huo-tsai,* literally, "fire-kindling." Spanners could no longer be called *shi-ba-na,* nor ball-bearings *bei-ling,* while cotton waste was no longer *way-shi.*

Such vagaries were comic relief to the drama of terror, for violence was universal. Hundreds of particular Red Guard attacks on individuals and groups, many ending in death, can be documented. But no full account of their depredations against life and property can be presented, because the scope was too widespread and the actions too diverse. The Red Guards were, in the beginning, acting under specific orders. Even when discipline broke, they executed their primary mission—paralyzing the Communist Party and its "counterrevolutionary elements." They were to "sweep out" everyone opposed to the new order Mao Tse-tung envisioned—and everyone who did not bow to the dominance of the Disciple, Lin Piao.

The first object lesson was wrought upon the meager possessions and the persons of the dwindling middle class. The first victims were the "intellectuals"—teachers, managers, technicians, writers, and artists who had departed from the "proletarian way of life." Specific "targets" had almost all been designated in advance. Red Guard leaders referred to detailed orders, treasuring their written instructions like insanely methodical midget accountants. The power-crazed adolescents, most between 14 and 20, humiliated and harassed their elders. They destroyed and mocked; they burned and killed.

An old term returned to currency, *yu-chieh,* meaning "to parade through the streets." Victims, including senior officials, marched through cities wearing great dunce caps and bearing placards reciting their crimes. Not all submitted docilely. Those who resisted humiliation were beaten into acquiescence. Soldiers stood by to prevent interference with the Red Guards and, presumably, to curb unsanctioned excesses. But the Red Guards were, by and large, set free of all China. Striking gongs, beating drums, and clashing cymbals, they marched through every city—and most towns and villages. Often they rode State trucks or commandeered pedicabs, heedless of the sweating "proletarian" pedaling the cumbersome vehicles.

The Red Guards carried many different weapons, most commonly clubs, steel bars, broad leather belts, and long knives. Mesmerized by the gongs and drums that resounded and thundered by day and by night, they invaded homes, shops, public buildings, factories, temples, and museums. Loudspeakers mounted on buildings and automobiles urged them on.

Exhorted to "make a new world by destroying the old," the adolescents compiled with delight. They broke the doors and windows of homes marked by their advance men. Piles of furniture, books, and pictures were doused with gasoline and made gaudy bonfires. Altars and religious statues were smashed, as were churches and temples themselves, while the Red Guards systematically looted shops selling "luxury items."

In some places, confiscated art treasures were sequestered in guarded warehouses for export; in others they were destroyed. Public monuments and massive sculptures were everywhere defaced and smashed. In Peking, the adolescents threatened to gut the exquisite Summer Palace more thoroughly than had foreign invaders in 1861. But the Liberation Army posted guards with submachine guns. After the first frenzied days, troops patrolled the capital's major museums, the villas of high officials, the road to the airport, and the Imperial City, where both Chairman Mao and Comrade Liu Shao-chi lived.

Not only Chinese but foreign observers witnessed both torture and executions. Men and women were thrust into the glowing ashes of their possessions. Others were tied to their door frames and beaten to death. In the Central China industrial complex of Wuhan, long queues of men and women marched under guard along the main streets by day and by night. All wore dunce caps and placards, while some had blackened faces, the traditional mark of the stage villain. Only their guards returned.

Asked by his foreign charges whether the captives were being confined in prisons or concentration camps, a China Travel Service guide asked simply, "Do you think that there are that many jails in China?"

Pressed harder he snapped, "Can't you guess for yourself?"

Foreigners were even allowed to mingle with crowds lynching "class enemies." They were merely instructed not to take pictures. In some cities, travelers heard repeated fusillades lasting more than thirty minutes.*

Terror paralyzed the Communist Party apparatus in the beginning. Party Secretaries were deprived of all authority, for the Red Guards took their orders ostensibly only from the new Revolutionary Commit-

---

* These events occurred before rival factions of Red Guards, intermixed with local "power-holders,' fought pitched battles with machine guns, and even field pieces, against each other and against Liberation Army troops.

tees—and actually through military channels. The First Secretary of one town near Canton was marched through the streets wearing a gigantic dunce cap and a placard listing his "crimes." Though the ritual humiliation was standard practice, that town is of particular interest because a fugitive later described the precise division of the assault into three distinct phases. He was speaking of the early period, when discipline generally prevailed.

During the first stage, the adolescents tested knowledge of *Quotations From Chairman Mao.* During the second stage, "class enemies" were paraded through the streets and attacked at mass meetings. Labeled "ogres with the souls of oxen, monsters with the spirits of snakes," they were compelled to denounce themselves. During the final stage, the "criminals," having confessed their sins, were transported for punishment. Terror was an end in itself, and terror was meticulously orchestrated.

In Canton, the Great Revolution began in measured stages. Even before the Red Guards appeared in mid-August, every household was required to possess "the three jewels"—a portrait of Mao Tse-tung, the four volumes of his *Selected Works,* and the little red book called *Quotations From Chairman Mao.* Portraits were snipped from newspapers when stores ran out of posters. Precise rules governed display: "First, no black frames or cracked frames; second, no swords or daggers hung nearby; and, third, always higher than family photographs."

Personal photographs were not prohibited, but ancestral tablets were removed from doorposts as "relics of feudalism"—so that revolutionary slogans could be posted. All "feudal customs" were proscribed: the paper models of automobiles, houses, and utensils burnt at funerals to provide for the soul's needs; coffin burial, for cremation was ordered; all traditional holidays, including the ancient Harvest Festival and its gooey mooncakes; and even cultivating flowers, keeping birds, or collecting stamps.

"Destroy-the-old teams" searched houses to enforce regulations. When a search team found a costume-jewelry bracelet once distributed by Civil Air Transport, the Chinese Nationalist airline, the entire family was arrested as spies. Canton Red Guards' searches led to bitter incidents. One woman of "landlord background" defended her possessions with a cleaver. She was beaten to death in the roadway before her front door. The son of a Party official condemned as a "black-gang element" killed the classmate who led the attack on his father's house. On one short lane, there were eight suicides in one autumn evening.

Schools were in chaos. Teachers began by joining in the "struggle to root out the influence of the anti-Party black gang." But, quite soon, almost all were denounced as "lackeys of the black gang." Students insulted and beat them. The teachers wore the dunce caps and placards reciting their crimes, while senior students took over classes—until all the schools closed. The "temporary suspension of classes according to plan" was to last three years—not at all according to plan.

Antagonism was methodically provoked. Although the Red Guard was not mustered in public until mid-August 1966, the nucleus had formed in June and July. The "core elements" were vigorously selected. Generally no more than teen-agers, they possessed "pure backgrounds," for they were the children of workers, soldiers, and peasants with un- smirched political records. One school of two thousand qualified only 20 initially. The elect paraded their self-importance, arousing the resent- ment of the excluded majority. By late September, when almost anyone could become a Red Guard, internal antipathies were fixed.

Clashes between "foreign" and local Red Guards starting in late September 1966 forshadowed the widespread factional fighting of the following year. In Canton, local Red Guards fought pitched battles with the arrogant youths from Peking; yet the continuing destruction and assaults on the "bourgeois elements" were hardly affected. Amid the debris and the smoke of "bourgeois possessions," the "little generals of disorder" chanted the texts of Mao Tse-tung. A few decades earlier, the Buddhist and Taoist clergy had performed similar—though less destruc- tive ceremonies—to exorcise devils.

The Red Guards were casting devils out of the paradise-to-be of China. Their enemies, the "men in power in the Communist Party following the capitalist road," were the "demons and monsters." The inquisition was directed against tens of thousands of conscientious officials who gave obedience to the legitimate apparatus of the Party and the State. Manipulated by military "advisers," the Red Guards attacked those malefactors, first verbally, then in "great-character posters," and, finally, physically. The assault began at the lower levels, but soon senior provincial and regional Party secretaries were paraded through the streets. They were frog-marched to "mass criticism meetings," to be reviled by thousands of screaming youngsters. The First Secretary of the Tientsin Municipal Committee died after three days of mistreatment.

Such tactics sought to paralyze the administrative machinery and to terrorize non-Maoists into surrender. The Communist Party was to be purged more thoroughly than ever before. Out of the shouting, the fury, and the destruction a new China was to emerge. All men were to be innately "good"—and automatically obedient to Maoist commands— because all "bourgeois influence" would have been violently extirpated. "Proletarian class nature" was to imbue every living Chinese. The secular inquisition was to purify an entire nation by "touching every man's soul"—and by destroying even brick, mortar, and paint that retarded revolutionary progress by recalling the past.

As the seventeenth anniversary of the establishment of the People's Republic of China on October 1, 1966 approached, the purge of senior cadres intensified. Comrade Liu Shao-chi and the Organizer Teng Hsiao-ping were obviously in disgrace. Only two of the Six Regional Bureaus of the Communist Party had not been "criticized." Hardly a single province remained where senior members of the hierarchy had not undergone violent "public criticism." The dogmatists of Lin Piao had apparently attained their first objective. The normal machinery of the Communist Party ceased to function after its battering by the Red Guards. Yet opposition to the extremists was simultaneously mounting in every province. The Communist Party was totally divided against itself. The ranking leaders were calling for each other's blood.

The Red Guard terror had weakened the "citadels of the bourgeoisie within the Communist Party," as the Disciple had softened his enemies by guerrilla harassment and artillery barrages. The "class enemy" had been compelled to "reveal himself" by his resistance to the youthful irregulars. Still, Lin Piao could not indefinitely withhold his main attack. Becoming aware of their peril, his enemies were strengthening their defensive positions in the provinces. *The Liberation Army Daily* directed: "The enemy must be completely surrounded by a vastly superior force."

By October 1, the Disciple's new strategy was operational, although only a few among the high-ranking leaders had been formally dismissed. The Communists had customarily allowed an "opposition element" to remain in office—if not in power—until he was wholly discredited. The Disciple followed the custom in Peking, since he could not dismiss the great majority of China's highest-ranking officials. Yet the pressure of time forced his hand; he abruptly dismissed major provincial figures before they could become impregnably entrenched.

Possessing much strength, if poor cohesion, the moderate faction finally engaged the dogmatists in open battle for the soul of China. They contended that the extremists' domestic and foreign policies were quite simply bad for China. Ever expanding repression at home and unremitting support of revolution abroad, they argued, could neither succeed in their purposes nor benefit the Chinese people. More interested in rice than guns, more concerned to maintain an ordered society than to pursue grandiose visions, the pragmatists began closing their ranks.

They were not only attracting mass support, but were finally utilizing their great tactical advantages. They did, after all, still control the Party organization, and the Party was temporarily paralyzed, but by no means broken. Before the Cultural Revolution, their position had been so commanding that they could at will ignore Peking's orders. The apparatus of publicity, the first instrument torn from the hands of the moderates, had been notorious for passive resistance and active disobedience. Since the opposition was finally coalescing, the Disciple could only consolidate his position by breaking the Party in the provinces. The aroused opposition was using both local organizations and local loyalties to frustrate his grand design. The terror had failed to stun the "class enemy" into surrender.

By October, the battle arrays were drawn up. The Maoists openly "criticized" the first secretaries of four of the six Regional Bureaus of the Communist Party. Only two were immune from attack: the Manchurian Regional Bureau, the Disciple's private preserve, which was already purified; and the Central–South China Bureau, the fief of the King of the South Tao Chu, elevated in August to fourth place in the hierarchy.* The First Secretary of the East China Bureau and the First Secretary of the Southwest Bureau came under intense public attack. Their effective resistance at the time presaged their later removal amid bloodshed.

After meticulous preparation, the Maoists had seized the Party Center and had ordered the Red Guards to mount a total attack on their enemies in the provinces. But the Maoists were shaken by the opposition they provoked. Ever stronger measures became necessary, as the two sides contended for the future of China. The fate of every Chinese hung on the outcome of the battle.

* The acting First Secretary of Central–South China, who had first swum the Yangtze with the Chairman and later succeeded Tao Chu, was to fall with his sponsor, the King of the South, a few months later.

XV

Little Generals of Disorder

The adolescent shock troops were intoxicated with rage that was but half-induced by the diatribes, the martial songs, the chanted slogans, and the ever rising crescendo of gongs and firecrackers. They had finally found the mystic unity of purpose consistently promised and as consistently denied them by their authoritarian masters since 1949. The natural idealism of impatient youth was finally recognized as the chief positive force in Chinese society—and that idealism was offered a most congenial expression, destruction of the oppressive institutions that had frustrated youth's aspirations. Anarchism in all its perfect purity was their overwhelming ideal. They would "remake the world" by transports of violence, rather than hard work. They had been given license for the retribution of total destruction on their elders' oppressive institutions by the one individual they had been conditioned to respect.

Acknowledging no being superior to Chairman Mao Tse-tung, the Red Guards, nonetheless, believed that their hatred was divinely inspired. Since they were the scourge of their demigod, the punishment they inflicted would purge China of evil. As assured as medieval inquisitors, they knew that the devil of revisionism was formidable and the struggle against heresy unending. They believed passionately that, "armed with the invincible Thought of Mao Tse-tung," they would in the end destroy the agents of the devil, "the demons and monsters, the class enemy, the black, anti-Party, anti-Socialist gang in league with American imperialism and Soviet revisionism."

The secular arm stood watchful—but still quiet—behind the newly consecrated inquisitors. Although it too was consecrated to the holy cause of "protecting to the death Chairman Mao and the Thought of

233

Mao Tse-tung," the People's Liberation Army was not required to move openly while the Red Guards attacked. Although violence was to be done—and, above all, to be seen to be done—the Maoist encyclicals* ordered: "Struggle by persuasion, not violence!" But the Red Guards restrained their violence within the prescribed limits only in the beginning.

At the start, there was little need for the Liberation Army to intervene decisively—either to support the Red Guards or to curb their excesses. Even as the movement grew increasingly violent, the "little generals of disorder" were executing precisely the mission assigned them by the Disciple's strategy. The resentment of a frustrated generation was deliberately directed against the men and the apparatus they believe to have betrayed their hopes and circumscribed their lives. The "little generals of disorder," intoxicated by their unprecedented freedom, attacked the entire structure of the Communist Party, the entire Chinese Establishment that blocked Lin Piao's road to power. The "power-holders," the Red Guards believed, were the blackest heretics and renegades. They had betrayed the sacred truth of Mao Tse-tung, which gave freedom to the masses; they were responsible for all repression and deprivation. They were to be "rooted out and crushed."

Nonetheless, the "little generals of disorder" were initially no more than mannikins who danced when the Maoists pulled the emotional strings. Their freedom was an illusion, for their deeds were scrutinized and controlled by the constant military presence in the shadows. Their own accounts demonstrate how restricted was their scope in the beginning—and how rapidly the force developed a will of its own.

The first defectors began trickling out of China in the late autumn of 1966. Much emotion was recollected—though hardly in tranquillity—on quiet verandas in Hong Kong. Some still raging with divine anger, others stuttering in fear, youths recounted their deeds and explained why they had chosen to flee the overwhelming catharsis of the Great Proletarian Cultural Revolution. Perhaps their tales should be discounted because they were the faint of heart. But escape from China required great perseverance and courage, while their willingness to discuss their experiences with foreigners showed no mean spirit. Having lived all their lives amid suspicion, violent retribution, and *agents provocateurs,* they could not know that their names would not be reported to Peking—and they themselves pursued by vengeance even in Hong Kong, while their

---

* The religious parallels and theological terminology that occur throughout this account—and particularly in this chapter—may offend some readers. I should like to apologize for any such offense, while noting in exculpation that no other vocabulary could truly convey either the emotion or the reality. The Maoists themselves, of course, constantly employed similar analogies.

families were punished in China. Some were moved by mercenary motives, and all certainly needed the small sums paid for their stories, as much in charity as inducement. But the risks were great and the rewards small.

Most appeared determined to hazard their lives to tell the outside world what they had seen and done in China. Curiously, they had come to trust foreigners more than Chinese. Their attitudes reversed traditional xenophobia—and, particularly, the violent anti-American feeling the Maoists had implanted. Moreover, their accounts were corroborated. The professional skeptics who interviewed those defectors found their tales of the terrible autumn of 1966 borne out—some immediately, some much later—by both official Communist statements and by the thousands of tabloids Red Guards published *within* China. The evidence weighed so heavy one simply had to accept the totality, while remaining cautious regarding details.

They were the vanguard of the disillusioned, a group that ultimately included almost all their fellows. They were, perhaps, the craven and inconsistent, but it could be argued with equal force that they were the most sensitive and courageous. They were, certainly, the most fortunate. Two chief sources of disillusionment were apparent in the accounts of dozens of youths from places as distant as the northeastern tip of Manchuria to Kwangtung in the deep south: the *indiscriminate* violence they wreaked; and the opposition of the "masses" they believed they served.

It had all started as a bit of a lark. After all, classes were out, and they were to remain out for the next three years. What better opportunity than joining the Red Guard to see China free, while wielding great power?

The defectors had been appalled to learn that their battle cry was their literal purpose. They were, after all, accustomed to Communist hyperbole, which set a great distance between words and reality. But the youths discovered that the Maoists meant exactly what they said when they commanded: "Destroy the old civilization!" The skylarking adolescents also discovered that they had little heart for the extirpation of every significant aspect of the culture and the society that had bred them. Despite constant propaganda excoriating the evils of traditional Chinese civilization, all had derived personal pride and drawn spiritual sustenance from being *Chinese*. Even the Maoists had played on the theme of *Chinese* greatness when it suited their purposes—as it frequently did. The more intelligent among the Red Guards therefore began to wonder what would remain after their ravages. As time passed, they feared no foundation whatever would exist for the construction of the "great, new *Chinese* civilization" the Maoists promised.

Equally disillusioning—and even more dismaying—was the counter-violence their own violence evoked. The Maoists had bestowed a singular accolade, dubbing the Red Guards "the judges of the old world." They found that they were in truth "the arbiters and critics of the old world"—and, however reluctantly, the executioners as well. Some were sickened by their own violence. Others were shocked by the resistance of the masses. The Red Guards had been told that "the laboring masses," the rural and urban proletariat, had been "cheated, deceived, misled, and exploited by the black gang." Yet those very masses, the quintessential Chinese people for whom the Red Guards fought, resisted their campaign with forthright denunciation and violent deeds.

The local "working-level cadres" had formed ties of sympathy and mutual interest with the people they governed, just as had the Imperial county magistrates, "the mother and father officials," before them. Ten thousand Hai Juis suddenly appeared, more devoted to human welfare than abstract doctrine. On most occasions before the Great Revolution, the "black gang" had defied the Chairman's dogmas for the immediate benefit of the masses. It was, therefore, not remarkable that peasants, workers, the People's Militia, and local Party members should rally around their own local officials. Instead of enjoying public acclaim as the vanguard of a great popular movement, the Red Guards met concerted popular resistance. New gangs armed with makeshift weapons formed Red Self-Defense Corps to resist the "little generals," the title recalling the early days of Chinese Communism as much as the term "Red Guard" itself. Some men with pawky senses of humor called themselves Scarlet Sentinels. The horrified "Red Guards of Chairman Mao" soon found that the harder they pushed, the more stubborn became the opposition of the masses.

No one, within China or without, knows how many men, women, and children died or were injured in the terrible autumn and winter of 1966–67. Nor can anyone assess those casualties—or the higher casualties of late 1967—accurately until Peking reveals its estimates. Suicides, assassinations, and deaths from wounds probably numbered tens of thousands. The Disciple himself hinted at the extent of suffering when he said, consolingly, that the casualties were "less than those of the Civil War." Such sensational aspects have, quite naturally, attracted most attention abroad. The record may, perhaps, be balanced by the less dramatic tale of a 26-year-old Red Guard who was notably unenthusiastic. His experiences were not necessarily typical, but they were more representative than the brutality of the small core of ruthless zealots. Yet the group that rejoiced in atrocities was at least 5 to 10 percent of the Red Guards—one to two million persons.

He must be called Wu Ming-shih—literally, "Mr. No Name," the Chinese equivalent of John Doe. A slight figure with heavy glasses and a disconcerting habit of cracking his knuckles nervously, Wu had actually decided to leave China in 1958. That was the year of the Great Leap, when the doctrinaire Communists began to cut down trees in order to increase the cultivated acreage in his native Kwangtung Province. He escaped when the turmoil of the Cultural Revolution provided the opportunity. Wu offered a higly critical, but apparently dispassionate account of the Cultural Revolution—and his own role therein.

"Anyone," said Wu, perched on the edge of a bamboo sofa on a Hong Kong veranda, "should have known that cutting down the groves would result in floods, droughts, and erosion. Anyone with any sense should have known that food supplies would be diminished—and not increased as the Communists promised us. I saw it, though I was only 18 in 1958 at the time of the Great Leap Forward.

"But the Communists either didn't know or didn't care—even then!"

He sipped a glass of Chinese tea, straining the leaves through his teeth, and continued after reflection:

> The Red Guard Movement, when I got into it, was much the same thing. Looking at it from the inside, it seemed to make about as much sense as cutting down the trees. We made an awful lot of noise, and we wasted a lot of time and energy. As for accomplishments, I saw none. The Red Guards didn't accomplish much of anything at all for the men who started the movement. And they certainly didn't do anything for the people of China. But they did do a lot of harm in their own way. After a while, I came to the conclusion that we were cutting down people—just as the Communists had cut down trees eight years earlier!

Wu's account reveals the movement in an oblique light. He told of the mobilization and deployment of the Red Guards of a small rural county in the northwestern part of Kwangtung, China's southernmost province. His story was the more credible for its lack of histrionics. It was the story of a *routine* Red Guard unit.

In manner and experience, Wu Ming-shih, the rural southerner, contrasted sharply with Wang Chao-tien, the 19-year-old from the extreme northern city of Manchouli, whom the Nationalists on Formosa publicized widely because he was the first Red Guard to fall into their hands. Wu was nervous to the point of diffidence and would speak only of things he himself had seen. Wang was an easily recognizable type in any society, the swaggering juvenile delinquent, compensating for mistreatment and disregard, inflicted in his case by Communist China, rather than a bourgeois society. He initially reveled in the Red Guards' sanction of his willful destructiveness but defected when discipline was enforced. He was also drawn by the material lure of the outside world.

Even on Formosa he defied the authorities, deliberately missing appointments, and becoming a well-known menace on the Honda he demanded. Attaining such notoriety was no small feat on an island where traffic is, to say the least, eccentric. Wang, the teen-ager, his broad lips twisted in a disparaging grin and his narrow eyes alight with tentative malice, was the type the outside world imagined when it thought of the Red Guards—Mao Tse-tung's lost generation. Wu, seven years older, diffident and frightened, was the type of the old China that endured in large numbers, even among the Red Guards. Wang was boastful, but Wu was appalled by his own actions.

Yet their separate accounts did not so much contradict as complement each other. Their stories demonstrated an obvious fact. Like all Chinese Communist campaigns, the climactic Great Proletarian Cultural Revolution was intense in some places and mild in others; some operations were meticulously planned, and others were quite haphazard. The indisciplined violence Wang Chao-tien discussed with relish was apparently no more typical than the somewhat aimless meandering Wu Mingshih recounted. Since the violence has already been reported in detail, the second aspect now merits greater attention.

Wu was an instructor at a rural school in northern Kwangtung. He was teaching irrigation techniques when he first heard the term "Great Proletarian Cultural Revolution" in June 1966 from *The Peking People's Daily*. In August, he learned of the existence of the Red Guards in the same manner. In obedience to the newspaper's instructions, the First Secretary of his school's Communist Party Committee formed a Red Guard unit of about 100 members at the end of August 1966. Wu saw no evidence of outside direction of those 80 students and 20 young teachers until the middle of September, when 14 Red Guards from Peking stopped in his village on their return journey from the southern metropolis of Canton. They had been sent to direct the organization of the Red Guards of Canton, but Wu's rural People's Commune was both too small and too remote to merit more than passing attention from the Peking "hard bones of the revolution."

The Peking detachment was energetic during its brief stay, though Wu asserted that they had exercised little influence—and "what influence they did exert was bad!" He recalled in staccato Cantonese: "The Peking people told our Red Guards they were not enthusiastic enough. Those foreigners from the north demanded that we attack the 'local power-holders' more fervently and more determinedly."

The first target of the Cultural Revolution and its "shock troops" in Wu's school was the same butt set up throughout China—"the men in power within the Communist Party who follow the capitalist road." The school's Red Guards needed little encouragement from outsiders to

attack the most prominent local "power-holders." Two weeks after he
founded the Red Guards, the First Secretary of the Party Committee
was deposed. He was charged with "acting illegally by disobeying the
orders of the Party Center." His punishment was "corrective labor" in
the school's experimental fields. Wu explained:

> Everyone had long felt much resentment of the Party Secretary and
> his overbearing ways, his playing favorites, and his own self-indulgent
> manner of life. When the Cultural Revolution offered the opportunity,
> "the masses" attacked him. The school came, formally at least, entirely
> under the control of the new Revolutionary Committee, composed of
> "revolutionary teachers and students." Obeying the "revolutionary stu-
> dent" who became chairman of the Revolutionary Committee, the Red
> Guards then moved outward to "purify" the entire local Party apparatus.

Having "triumphed" in the school, the Cultural Revolution was "carried out thoroughly" in the neighboring People's Commune. The Party
Committee was broken up. Senior officials were condemned and paraded
through the Commune wearing their dunce caps and placards detailing
their crimes.

The Red Guards received unexpected, and somewhat mysterious,
assistance from outside sources. The Public Security Bureau kept a
dossier on every Chinese, including his "class background" and all his
activities, personal as well as political. Selected dossiers given the Red
Guard leaders provided "evidence" against local Party officials. They
were, the Public Security chiefs said, "members of the black gang of
bourgeois elements" who had somehow escaped the winnowing of all
previous "campaigns." The "class" enemy was wily and implacable. He
had not merely survived the relentless suppression of the preceding
17 years but had actually "usurped control of the Party machinery"—
from the highest to the lowest level.

"There was always something—some error or crime—they could find
to pin on anyone they chose," Wu explained.

The Red Guards reveled in their new authority and their unwonted
freedom. Nonetheless, they were uncertain of their specific duties and
skeptical of the individual indictments, supplied as often by the military
as by the police. Since they held no personal grudges against the officials
of the People's Commune, their attacks were frequently lackadaisical.
That lack of enthusiasm was roundly condemned by the Red Guards
from Peking. Still, the school's Red Guards, acting in substantial isola-
tion, "overthrew the men in authority"—at least in form.

But their offensive was generally distinguished more by slogan-shout-
ing than by effective "destruction" of the "power-holders." Dismayed

by the loyalty and protection the masses gave their local officials, the
Red Guards became confused and indolent. Through September 1966,
they self-consciously *played* the role they had been assigned, but they
did not live it. Like most southern Chinese, they were natural actors.
Dramatic posturing took the place of effective attacks.

Still the youths had, initially at least, responded with decisive enthusiasm to the tocsin of the Great Revolution. Why? Wu's answer, though
conditioned by his own apolitical attitude, was illuminating:

> We Chinese are thoroughly accustomed to special "movements."
> We've had so many "campaigns" over the years that we respond almost
> automatically to whatever new demands are made upon us. They pressed
> a button, and we immediately acted. Otherwise, we would be in big
> trouble. Even so, *they* had to mobilize the youth because adults were so
> skeptical. I think, though, that very few Red Guards were taking the
> Cultural Revolution or the Thought of Mao Tse-tung seriously. It was,
> really, a good holiday from school and a chance to see the country!

His own "class background" was tainted, for his father had been a
"rich peasant." Wu was, therefore, not admitted to the Red Guard until
early October. By that time the bars were down. The movement was no
longer selective in recruiting, since it required constant reinforcements to
crush growing opposition. Finding the school's Red Guards less than
effective in their own backyard, *they* dispatched the unit to Canton.

As strangers in the great southern metropolis, the rural Red Guards
were given a new assignment. After studying dossiers provided by the
Canton Public Security Bureau, the unit actively attacked "power-holders and bourgeois elements." Since they did not know their victims, their
task was easier. Since their enthusiasm was not restrained by familiarity,
their performance was highly effective. When they swept through a
condemned household, they searched for "anti-Mao writings, jewels,
money, and arms." The "surging revolutionary tide" was not only to
sweep away "all vestiges of the old civilization" but was to ensure that
"the wealth the bourgeoisie have stolen from the people" was returned
to the people.*

Wu Ming-shih gradually comprehended the strategy of the shadowy
leadership he alternately called *they* and "the men in Peking." He was,
after all, an intellectual—in Chinese terminology.

> The men in Peking *had* to turn to the young students. The older peo-
> ple, even university students, were all afraid that it was just another

---

* By early 1967, the curio shops of Hong Kong began to display a wide selection of newly arrived *objets d'art,* furniture, and jewelry.

Communist trick. Most of the younger students were enthusiastic—in the beginning. They thought that things would really change for them. Besides, as I said, they didn't have to attend classes, and they could ride trains without paying and get free room and board wherever they went.

Many, too, believed that they would be rewarded with good jobs if they showed great enthusiasm and diligence in "making revolution." At that stage, in October, 1966, everyone still looked upon Chairman Mao as a demi-god out of old Chinese mythology. But, even then, the Red Guards who were *really* dedicated were only a small number, and they berated the rest of us for hanging back.

From October through early January, Wu's unit undertook a "Long March" from Canton to Chingkangshan, where Mao Tse-tung had ruled his First Kiangsi Soviet Area in the early 1930s. The decision to commemorate the Long March of the Red Army was issued by the First Minister of Peace, Premier Chou En-lai, and later endorsed by the Disciple Lin Piao.

The "little Long Marches" were a device to bring the Red Guards under control. The banner of the Great Proletarian Cultural Revolution was flaunted throughout China; lackluster units like Wu's were removed from the cities; and the violent excesses of the hyperzealous were curbed. The Maoists called the Red Guards' peregrinations Long Marches to stimulate the "revolutionary spirit," but they were almost as important strategically as the original Long March. As they had by fleeing from Kiangsi to Yenan, the Maoists again sought to break out of encirclement—the unexpected mass resistance the Red Guards had encountered. They could only escape from the trap they had devised for themselves by reviving the crusading fervor of earlier days. Nostalgia for the simple verities of the heroic guerrilla period also moved them. Life had ben straightforward and uncomplicated during the years in Yenan when they were fighting to conquer a nation. It had become complex and irritating after that conquest.

"The common people," Wu remembered of his own little Long March, *"had* to act as if they were glad to see us. And they had to feed us—we were the 'guests of Chairman Mao.' But, underneath, I could sense, they were more glad to see us go. I don't think we inspired many revolutionaries."

Returning to Canton in early January 1967, Wu found the northern Red Guards objecting that the Cultural Revolution was "too cool and too sweet." There was a marked lull while the Maoists regrouped forces battered by opposition. His unit diverted itself with the routine work of changing the names of shops and buildings to make them "truly revolutionary"—and reprimanding pedestrians for affecting extreme styles or inability to recite the canonical *Quotations From Chairman Mao.* Wu recalled:

> But in late January, the atmosphere changed abruptly. The "foreign" Red Guards clashed time after time with the local Red Guards, who were supported by working-men. Those clashes, small at first, exploded into open battle in early February. The different sides were largely chosen by where people came from—southerners against northerners, Cantonese against "foreigners."
>
> The Red Guards from the Peking Institute of Administration and Law organized the All-Kwangtung United Revolutionary Committee and decided to "seize power" from the local Public Security authorities.
>
> The Public Security Police then organized their own Anti-Seizure Red Guards. For almost four days, the two groups fought each other at the main gate of the big, white-pillared Security Headquarters on the street renamed Uprising Road. A few were hurt, for the battle continued without stopping as both defenders and attackers changed shifts. But I got the impression that it was largely a mock battle. People's hearts didn't seem to be in it.

The Public Security Police appealed to the People's Liberation Army to drive away the besiegers, though the police were presumably anti-Mao and the military were presumably pro-Mao. Troops arrived in force, but then simply stood by, unwilling to intervene. Commanders had already received orders to "participate in the Cultural Revolution," but were reluctant to commit troops. Wu was himself vague on the ideological significance of the siege of the Canton Public Security Headquarters, an epochal moment in the Cultural Revolution. His confusion reflected the confused reality. Most Chinese, even the participants, were by that time as confused as he was.

"I simply couldn't tell who was really pro-Mao and who was really anti-Mao!" he said.

> Of course, both sides claimed to be pro-Mao. Both sides said they were fighting for the Thought of Mao Tse-tung and to defend Chairman Mao. There were, after all, *no* avowed anti-Maoists in China. But it looked to me more and more like a fight on straight regional lines, with hardly any deeper significance. I finally left Canton toward the end of February, 1967, to try to make my way to Hong Kong. The revolution had come to seem to me wholly destructive, and the issue was still not resolved. By that time, they were arguing again—instead of fighting!

Wu Ming-shih's matter-of-fact account of his personal experience glossed over major events beyond his knowledge. From December

1966 through February 1967, the Cultural Revolution was "undergoing great changes and shifts," as the Maoists themselves put it. Recounting his experiences in full has actually carried the narrative ahead of its strict chronological progression. In the crucial months of October and November 1966, the Red Guards were, on the one hand, "creating disorder and wreaking destruction," and, on the other, staging Long Marches "to exchange revolutionary experience."

While the Red Guards wrangled and marched, the nation's nominal rulers wrestled for the soul of China. Whatever had been fixed by the *coup d'état* of August 1966 was cast into flux by the growing resistance of the masses. They were rallied by "local representatives and agents of the black gang"— that is, the "working-level cadres" of the Communist Party of China. Whatever control the Maoists had imposed on the apparatus was, ironically, broken by the violent exertions of the Red Guards. Whatever power had been restored to Mao Tse-tung's palsied hands by the initial victories of his field commander, Lin Piao, was sapped by public apprehension of the new social order the Maoists promised—or threatened.

The Chairman was sanctified, but as one Red Guard said contemptuously, "He has as little to do with what is going on as a great statue of the Buddha!" Mao Tse-tung was hymned as "the red, red, sun in our hearts." But men knew that even the King of the South, Tao Chu, had asked, "Did you ever hear of sunspots? Even the sun sometimes has black spots on its face!"

Lin Piao had planned a swift "victory of annihilation" over an enemy paralyzed by the rampages of the Red Guards—and the threat of the People's Liberation Army. The precise timing presumably laid down in his meticulous plans is still obscure. But October 1, 1966, the seventeenth anniversary of the People's Republic of China, should certainly have found the Maoist forces on the verge of total victory. Their enemies should have been driven to surrender signaled by ritual, mass public confessions of error. As it was, the traditional ceremony in the Plaza of Heavenly Peace was not a victory celebration, but a mobilization for stronger attacks on the "class enemy."

That mass rally—not formally counted among the Great Rallies of the Cultural Revolution—was remarkable for two phenomena. The first was shockingly unconventional, though expected—Lin Piao's self-assertion. The second was normal, though surprising—Mao Tse-tung's continuing silence.

The Disciple cast off his cloak of humility to stand forth as the true ruler of China. Although his brief address ritually declared that he spoke "on behalf of Chairman Mao, the Communist Party, and the People's

Government," his demeanor conveyed a wholly different impression. *Only* Lin Piao, among all the hierarchs, spoke. His words were echoed by "Red Guard, worker, and peasant representatives"—as well as such luminaries of the International Communist Movement as E. F. Hill of the splinter Australian Communist Party (Marxist-Leninist) and Robert Williams, described as "the American Negro leader."

Behind Lin Piao on the Gate of Heavenly Peace still stood men he was attacking. Among them were Comrade Liu Shao-chi; the Organizer, Teng Hsiao-ping; the Bandit General, Ho Lung; and several others making their farewell appearances. The purge was, however, not yet complete.

The Chairman himself still did not address the throngs, though resounding choruses of Red Guards demanded, "Let Chairman Mao speak to us!" The First Minister of Peace, Premier Chou En-lai, remarked somewhat testily, "All the Chairman has to say is already in his writings. Go and read them!" Yet the bewildering Mao Tse-tung deliberately smiled upon his arch-rival, Comrade Liu Shao-chi, and chatted with him —before television cameras that carried the scene to a few thousand receivers in the Chinese capital.

While that strange by-play was performed, the Disciple called for renewed attacks on the men who stood just behind him, "the handful of men who have wormed their way into power in the Party and are following the capitalist road." He exhorted the Red Guards to even greater feats of heroism in "destroying the old civilization and the anti-Party, anti-Socialist black gang."

The next day, *Red Flag,* the Maoists' ideological journal, obliquely explained why October 1 had not been a joyous celebration of victory in the intra-Party war that had begun ten months earlier. Revealing indirectly that the Disciple's drive for personal power had aroused antipathy, fear, and resistance, a tortuous article exhorted: "We must attack the anti-Party, anti-Socialist faction within the Party even more strongly." Realizing that they were fighting not only for principle and political survival, but for their lives, the anti-Maoists had fallen back on new defensive positions. Calling upon the loyalty of the workers, peasants, and even disaffected generals and soldiers, the "power-holders" had actually strengthened their forces under the attack. *Red Flag* ordered the Liberation Army to "intensify vigilance against capitalist elements."

> The purpose of the Great Proletarian Cultural Revolution is to completely drag out the persons in power who take the capitalist road after having wormed their way into our Party. We must dig out, one by one, the time-bombs hidden within our Party in order to check counter-revolutionary subversion and to consolidate out impregnable proletarian

State. . . . The former exploiting classes are engaged in a comprehensive plot to assemble and use those cadres whom they have infiltrated into our Party as their secret agents. The battle between the two roads of Socialism and capitalism is by no means over. *In many areas and in many units of the Party, the struggle between the two lines is still sharp and complex.* *

The revealing article summed up: "Some such factions are adopting new devices in order to deceive the masses, to oppose the Party's policy, and to strengthen the capitalist, reactionary line. *They are inciting the masses to struggle against the masses* * in order to accomplish their own ends."

The non-Maoists had not yielded. Finally aware of its total peril, the Party apparatus was mobilizing its great resources against the Maoist usurpers. By rallying both "cadres and masses" around them in defiance of the Disciple and his Red Guards, the "old-line power-holders" were thwarting the blitzkrieg the Maoists had launched to reconquer power.

The battle had become a stalemate, and the Maoists were facing possible defeat. Since they were the aggressors, they would lose unless they captured—or destroyed—*all* the citadels of power held by their enemies within China and, particularly, within the Communist Party of China. If the moderates could hold out, it appeared they would win. The defense held the advantage. Merely intensifying attacks on individuals according to their initial strategy would *not* win the Maoists victory. The "power-holders" could only be "dragged out" by first destroying their "fortifications." Since their "entrenched positions" were integral parts of the structure of the Communist Party, the new assault was to be directed against the Party itself.

The battle was close. In Peking itself, the moderates rallied on November 12, 1966, to stage a public celebration of the one hundredth birthday of Sun Yat-sen, leader of the Revolution of 1911. Attended by Generalissimo Chu Teh, a vice chairman of the People's Republic, by Chou En-lai, and by Sun's widow, also a vice chairman of the People's Republic, the reception implicitly reaffirmed continuity with the past. Sun Yat-sen was also a hero to the Nationalists; paying him homage was hardly "destroying the old world." Because such resistance persisted even in Peking, the Maoists were forced to broaden their attack.

The new strategy altered the entire nature of the war. The Disciple was forced to display the Maoist blueprint for an entirely new China, which would, it appeared, function without either a Communist Party or a People's Government. Lin Piao needed a psychological atomic bomb

* Emphasis supplied.

to shatter the citadels of the "old civilization." On the morning of November 3, 1966, he exploded his nuclear bomb at the Sixth Great Mass Rally of Red Guards in Peking. Almost two million ardent youths —the largest number ever assembled—cheered his declaration that they fought to create a wholly new society under wholly new administration.

Lin's speech of that day was the climax of the last great fight between the extremists and those moderates who still possessed influence at the Party Center. The later celebration of Sun Yat-sen's birthday was anticlimactic. The intensity of the struggle in Peking had been publicly demonstrated by the Fifth Great Mass Rally. During that "silent rally" in late October, a million and a half Red Guards were only allowed to gaze upon their leaders riding through the Plaza of Heavenly Peace in a motorcade. Armed troops had formed cordons between the masses and the open limousines. Something was seriously wrong. The hierarchy had obviously been unable to agree on new instructions to the Red Guards —and the Maoists had obviously not yet beaten down resistance within the Party Center.

But by November 3, the Disciple had overcome the caution of the faint-hearted among the Maoists. He was ready to detonate his atomic bomb. The Communist leaders stood in their accustomed places on the Gate of Heavenly Peace as the morning sun warmed the cold air. Comrade Shao-chi and the Organizer were still among them, though their eclipse was fast approaching. Chen Po-ta, the Chairman's faithful Ghostwriter and director of the Task Force of the Cultural Revolution, acted as master of ceremonies.

The Plaza resounded to the heelbeats of phalanxes of Red Guards, "the revolutionary pathfinders who had suffered repression under the bourgeois reactionary line." Fresh from the provinces they came, proudly wearing the wounds of battle in the provinces "from the southern coast to the Tienshan Mountains [of Sinkiang] in the northwest, from the banks of Heilungkiang [Amur River] in the northeast to the Sikang-Tibet Plateau in the southwest," as Maoist organs boasted.

They were bitter at their failure to sweep all before them. They were frustrated by the opposition's stubborn refusal to concede its strongholds. And they were disillusioned by the failure of the masses to rise to their tocsin. The dispirited Red Guards were inspired with new hope and fresh devotion by gazing upon their demigod, Chairman Mao Tse-tung.

"What is the reddest thing in the world? The sun on the Gate of Heavenly Peace! [They cried as one, the Maoists reported.] Who is the dearest person in the world? The great Leader Mao Tse-tung! What is the greatest happiness in the world? To see the great commander Chairman Mao! What is the most glorious task in the world? To study, implement, propagate, and defend the Thought of Mao Tse-tung!"

The Disciple's fighting speech was intended to give the dispirited Red Guards new heart—like a half-time pep talk to a trailing football team. The undertone of desperation was audible only to a few keen ears. Most heard only the promise of imminent victory.

> Comrade Lin Piao has today put into words our common feeling which we ourselves knew not how to express. [The breathless official account reported the Red Guards' reaction.] A generation of men and women unique in all history has appeared—fighters who place "daring" before all else, fighters who accept Chairman Mao as their supreme commander and the People's Liberation Army as their brilliant example. They fear neither heaven nor earth. They dare to scale a mountain of swords and to brave a sea of flames. They are filling the world to over-flowing with youth and vitality.

Red Flag outlined the new ideal the dedicated two million sought:

> Taking all under heaven as their own responsibility, our young revo-lutionary fighters and the broad revolutionary masses . . . are creating the new . . . *extensive democracy* under the dictatorship of the pro-letariat. *Extensive democracy* means that the Party is not afraid to *sub-ject leading organizations and leaders of the Party and the State at all levels to criticism and supervision by the broad masses*—through full and frank expression of views and opinions by posting great-character posters, carrying on great debates, and engaging in extensive exchanges of revolutionary experience.
>
> The Great Proletarian Cultural Revolution movement has in the past several months fully proved that through *extensive democracy* we can truly arouse the masses, touch people in their very souls, and weed out the posisonous revisionist sprouts. . . . *Extensive democracy is a people's war without guns.* Not a single one of the ghosts and monsters will escape our sallies . . . *extensive democracy* is a revolutionary school without formal classes. Everyone can be educated and tempered.*

From Lin Piao's viewpoint the great ideological implications of "ex-tensive democracy" were secondary to tactical considerations. He had commanded a "people's war" against the Communist Party of China. The underlying ideological significance was to prove equally decisive to the final outcome of the Great Revolution—and the Maoist position in the world Communist movement. The Chairman and the Ghostwriter had declared a "people's war" against orthodox Marxism-Leninism.

---

* Emphasis supplied.

XVI

The Eunuch Intellectual

The Disciple's instructions to that largest Great Mass Rally of all on November 3, 1966, were brief and pungent. Crackling through the loudspeakers, his words were the most vehement since the Great Revolution's inception, despite—or, perhaps, because of—the undertone of apprehension. Lin Piao declared that he was foresaking authoritarianism, the only form of government he knew. "Extensive democracy" would create a new order of noncoercive harmony among all Chinese—and ultimately all mankind.

In order of rank behind the Disciple stood: the indispensable Minister of Great Peace, Premier Chou En-lai; the King of the South, Tao Chu, who would soon rebel against Maoist fantasies; and the architect of the new structure, the man who had given substance, form, and doctrinal justification to Mao's visions, the Ghostwriter, Chen Po-ta.

Proclaiming the dawn of a new era, Lin Piao appeared uncertain of what he specifically promised. He spoke not only briefly but allusively.

In the past two months or more, the correct line of Chairman Mao has been put before the broad masses and has been thoroughly comprehended. . . . The broad masses have truly translated into action Chairman Mao's call to "manage the great affairs of State yourselves!"

Guided by Chairman Mao's correct line, the broad revolutionary masses have passed through the new creative experience of developing extensive democracy under the dictatorship of the proletariat. By this *extensive democracy,* the Party is *fearlessly* permitting the broad masses to use the media of free airing of views, great-character posters, great debates, and extensive exchange of revolutionary experience to *criticize and supervise the leading Party and Government institutions and leaders at all levels.* At the same time, the people's democratic rights are being fully realized in accordance with the principles of the Paris Commune.

Without such *extensive democracy,* it would be impossible to initiate a genuine Great Proletarian Cultural Revolution; to stage a great revolution in the depth's of men's souls; to carry out the Great Proletarian Cultural Revolution thoroughly—and totally pluck out the roots of revisionism; to consolidate the dictatorship of the proletariat; and to guarantee the advance of our country along the road of Socialism and Communism.*

Lin Piao had spoken. But what had he said? What was "extensive democracy," and what were the "principles of the Paris Commune," which were to guide the future of China?

"Extensive democracy" ** was a new coinage describing direct rule by "revolutionary masses," theoretically granted unprecedented freedom and power. Physical and psychological coercion against "enemies of the people . . . the bourgeois and feudal remnants" would continue and intensify. But the "proletarian masses" were promised that their "management of the great affairs of State" would extend far beyond freedom of expression. When the Disciple promised to realize the people's rights "in accordance with the principles of the Paris Commune," he was pledging a wholly new form of intensively and universally participatory democracy the world had seen only once—and then most briefly.

The Commune that ruled Paris from March 26 to May 26, 1871, was hailed by Karl Marx as the first *"non-exploitive administration in the history of mankind."* Marx did not consider the Paris Commune a government, for he defined "governments" as mechanisms through which the dominant social class—be it the nobility, the bourgeoisie, or the proletariat—controlled, oppressed, and exploited all other classes. The author of Marxism saw a vision of the perfect future in the Paris Commune. He felt that the embattled people of Paris had transcended age-old exploitation through all-powerful assemblies made up of solid proletarians. Despite its brief span, the Paris Commune appeared "a perfect administration" to the romantic Karl Marx. Despite its failure, the Paris Commune exerted the same fascination on the even more romantic Mao Tse-tung.

Not the Chairman himself, but his faithful Ghostwriter Chen Po-ta

* Emphasis supplied.
** In Chinese, literally, "big or great democracy," officially translated by Peking as "extensive democracy." *Ta min-chu,* in the conventional transliteration, pronounced *dah min-joo,* the *ta* meaning "big" and *min-chu,* quite literally, "people's rule," the conventional term for democracy.

drafted the actual plan for applying to a vast and heterogeneous nation of more than 700 million an administration that had not succeeded in a homogeneous city of less than two million. Lin Piao's declaration that the Paris Commune was the model for China revealed not only the state of the power struggle, but the unique influence exerted by the Ghostwriter. Circumstances and their own errors had forced the Maoists to the desperate expedient of the Great Proletarian Cultural Revolution. Chen Po-ta, himself largely responsible for earlier grievous miscalculations, drafted not only the strategy, but the indispensable doctrinal rationale for that grand climacteric.

The stocky figure in the rumpled khaki Liberation Suit blinked nervously through the thick lenses of his black-rimmed spectacles at the shouting throng of students from the Peking Institute of Broadcasting early in August 1966. His movements were graceless and his demeanor awkward. His cheeks were chubby with good living above a broad, sensual mouth, and his neck was a plump column draped with slack flesh below his receding chin.

"My Mandarin is poor. Can someone act as my interpreter?" he asked, his standard Chinese heavily adulterated by the thick-tongued patois of Fukien Province. Comprehension was further impeded by his stammering.

The ardent students assembled to receive the Ghostwriter's instructions on the Great Revolution were shocked by his poor presence and by long pauses as he searched for words. Yet they were attentively silent— except when responding to rhetorical questions with deep-voiced approbation lightened by higher female voices.

An indefinable air of authority cloaked the 62-year-old writer and theoretician. Even if they had not known precisely *who* he was and *whom* he represented, they would have known that the veneer of diffidence covered a conviction of great power. Chen Po-ta might otherwise have been an aging academic whom professorial status had eluded—or, as the Chinese Nationalists described him, a clerk in the half-bankrupt general store of a remote market town.

His lackluster appearance and diffident manner but half-concealed his authority. In early August 1966, when the Cultural Revolution was emerging from the egg of his theories, Chen Po-ta was *the* most powerful man in China. At that instant in time, *true* power corresponded to the intellectuals' definition rather than the politicians'. With all things in flux, power was the ability to transform ideas into reality, rather than the ability to manipulate human beings. Chen Po-ta was truly realizing his abstract concepts, for his intimate relationship with the Chairman gave him almost absolute intellectual authority. He could actually force the leaders of China to take *his* path into the future—in part because there was no other path. *He* had conceived the total catharsis he called "the most penetrating proletarian revolutionary upheaval in man's history, far more sweeping than the Paris Commune or the Russian October Revolution!"

The ideological *alter ego* of Mao Tse-tung, Chen Po-ta, had long exercised unique influence in the secret councils of the Party. When he came to the guerrilla capital of Yenan in 1937, shortly after the Sino-Japanese War formally began, he was already a respected scholar and a well-known, semi-popular political commentator. He had written voluminously, always advancing the "progressive" line, and had helped sway both the Chinese intelligentsia and international public opinion toward the Communist cause. He had rendered his greatest service as ideologue, propagandist, and recruiter when teaching at China University in Peking, though his students had jeered in disbelief when he let it slip that he was the famous Chen Po-ta. It was hard to believe that their clumsy, stuttering professor, who called himself Chen Shang-yu, was the popular author celebrated for mordant wit and Marxist insight.

His original name was indeed Chen Shang-yu, while Chen Po-ta and the infrequently used Chen Chih-mei were his *nommes de plume et de guerre*. Hiding behind two pseudonyms was more than literary affectation or expression of the traditional Chinese penchant for many names. While teaching at China University, Chen was an "underground" activist. In the 1930s he worked directly under Comrade Liu Shao-chi and the Mayor Peng Chen, whom he crushed in the 1960s—as he had hastened the extinction of his two closest friends in the 1950s. Chen Po-ta had been well schooled in "revolutionary ruthlessness" at the Shanghai Workers' University and the Sun Yat-sen University in Moscow.

In Yenan, later, Mao Tse-tung drew Chen into close association, confirmed by his formal appointment as the Chairman's political secretary. He had first endeared himself by his attacking Chairman's enemies —Communist and Nationalist. Like an archbishop diverted from theological abstractions by his worldly responsibilities, Mao Tse-tung never quite commanded the intricacies of dialectical materialism. Chen Po-ta, therefore, filled a great need in the Chairman's entourage, functioning as his theological adviser.

Chen's command of the theological complexities of Marxism-Leninism forged the ideological weapons Mao wielded as skillfully as temporal weapons in his last fight against the powerful "Russian faction" in the late 1930s. Thereafter, all Mao's writings bore the stamp of Chen Po-ta's doctrinal adroitness. The forceful visions were Mao Tse-tung's, the polished apologetics were Chen's. Both in Mao's own works and in tracts signed by Chen Po-ta himself, it was all but impossible to distinguish their separate hands.

The Ghostwriter earned his nickname by his anonymity. Although he was known as Mao's ideological adviser and editor of the theoretical journal for cadres, *Study,* the Ghostwriter made few public appearances. Polemical tracts were his chief contribution until 1955, when the Chairman required an advocate for collectivizing the land he had given the peasants only a few years earlier. The Ghostwriter so effectively bore down on intra-Party opposition that the Chairman again called upon him to justify the Great Leap Forward and the Great People's Communes in 1958. In the same year, Chen founded *Red Flag* to preach the Maoist gospel within China—and to all "true Marxist-Leninists" throughout the world. *Red Flag*'s first assignment was creating the ideological rationale for the "imminent transition to true Communism" through the Great People's Communes.

"Men of 70 and even 80," the Ghostwriter promised in an access of enthusiasm, "will live to see true Communism."

The statement was undeniably excessive in view of the complex and protracted process Karl Marx had foreseen for attainment of the earthly paradise he envisioned. But Chen Po-ta was writing about his best-loved child. The People's Communes were not only the matrix of the new "collective life"; they were the precursors of the institutions that would transform all China into a single Great Commune. Chen had previously demonstrated his enchantment with the Paris Commune, while the Chairman's own works had mentioned the French experiment only in passing.

The Ghostwriter was the high priest of his own creation, the new cult of Mao Tse-tung. The Chairman's semi-deification and the codification of his canonical Thought were inspired by Chen Po-ta. Before Lin Piao commandeered the sacred vehicle of the Thought of Mao Tse-tung to carry him to power, Chen Po-ta had coined the term and exalted the Thought as "the apogee of human wisdom." He had hailed Mao Tse-tung as "the greatest living Marxist-Leninist . . . the greatest genius of modern times" and the Thought of Mao Tse-tung as the "peak of Marxism-Leninism, shaped by the concrete experience of the Chinese revolution."

This ideologue stood before the elite youth of Peking to proclaim the ultimate crusade in the summer of 1966. The annointed "revolutionary rebels" rendered respectful attention to his orders. The Ghostwriter possessed no independent following and no special practical competence —unlike the specialists in warfare, administration, intelligence, propaganda, and social control, who were his colleagues. But his skill in polemics and his command of Marxist theory, sustained by the Chairman's absolute confidence, commanded the highest respect and evoked a thrill of fear. He soon demonstrated why his master trusted him totally.

His style blended vicious insinuation against his opponents and abject sycophancy toward Mao Tse-tung. The Ghostwriter ordered the formation of a "Cultural Revolutionary Committee" to supplant the Communist Party Branch of the Peking Institute of Broadcasting. He further defended the Starlet against the students' muttered complaints.

"Some comrades have asked: If the Cultural Revolutionary Committee were given all power, would that not mean doing away with the leadership of the Party?" Chen Po-ta remarked, touching the heart of the new Cultural Revolutionary Movement:

"Is the person who asks this question a member of the black gang? Let me remind you that those who oppose this slogan are not necessarily revolutionary; no more are the advocates of the slogan counterrevolutionary! The slogan, POWER TO THE CULTURAL REVOLUTIONARY COMMITTEE! is itself revolutionary—and by no means counterrevolutionary!"

The intent students were still confused. They saw only vaguely the grand outlines of the *truly* revolutionary propositions the Ghostwriter was outlining for them.

Citing the Chairman for authority, Chen asserted that only two legitimate sources of power existed: the ineffable wisdom of the Chairman expressed in the Thought of Mao Tse-tung; and the will of the "revolutionary masses" loyal to Chairman Mao. He denied the Communist Party its unique position as the "vanguard of the proletariat." The Chairman, he indicated, stood above the Party which he could reform —or destroy—if it questioned his will.

"What we now advocate," he told the students, the vigor of his words remaining undiminished as he revealed the ultimate goal of the Great Revolution, "is that *all* power should go to Cultural Revolutionary Committees at *all* levels during the current Cultural Revolutionary Movement."

The Ghostwriter had dropped the veil of allusion. The Cultural Revolution, he had already said, would dominate *every aspect of life* in China under the slogan PUT POLITICS IN COMMAND! If *all* power at *all* levels was seized by the Revolutionary Committee, they would, quite simply, displace the Communist Party. The Ghostwriter spelled out his meaning clearly to avoid any possible misunderstanding. He was issuing commands to the students, but he was also pleading for their allegiance:

> *The inability of the Party to lead the Cultural Revolution demonstrates that there are deficiencies and defects in Party organizations and that their leadership has been usurped by the revisionists!*

Those words were the Ghostwriter's formal declaration of war against the Communist Party. Insurgent students and the new Revolutionary Committees, he stressed, must obey the "Party Center," which meant the Maoist clique. They must defy the conventional Party apparatus, which was "controlled by revisionists." Chen Po-ta seems to have been impelled largely by sincere idealism, kindled to incandescence by his personal vision of a new order of mankind and the urgent desire to reclaim power from the moderates. He therefore proposed to transform all China into one Great People's Commune, a nation-wide New England Town Meeting composed of all "true proletarians."

The strategists of power supported him fully, for they had need of a wholly new instrument. Chen Po-ta might dream of perfect participatory democracy, but his masters intended to control the new administration by democratic centralism.

The Ghostwriter believed that the masses were absolutely loyal to Chairman Mao. He therefore sought an alliance of the Chairman and the masses against the corrupt cadres. As chief of the Task Force of the Cultural Revolution, Chen Po-ta actually commanded a new Political Bureau charged to remake the nation in his own arcane new mold. If the Disciple Field Marshal Lin Piao was chief-of-staff to the enfeebled Mao Tse-tung in his last desperate attempt to create the China of his dreams, the Ghostwriter was deputy chief-of-staff for plans and operations.

The man who conceived history's single most audacious endeavor to transform the essential character of a nation, a society, and hundreds of millions of human beings was distinguished chiefly by the grandeur of his visions. Chen Po-ta was otherwise cast in the same mold as his activist comrades, the sons of middle-income farmers who had made the Communist revolution. His character is known primarily through his political career—in part because politics *was* his life and, in part, because of deliberate Communist concealment of the leaders' personal lives.

Physically unattractive and handicapped by his severe stammer, the Ghostwriter was born in 1904 to a poor family in Huian County of coastal Fukien Province. The grinding hardships of the barren land drove many of Fukien's sons into exile in Southeast Asia, where the unremitting industry that had provided bare subsistence at home made large numbers millionaires. Circumstances, as much as deliberate choice, apparently impelled Chen Po-ta to remain in China—and inspired him to transform the society that had exploited his ancestors for centuries.

Life in Huian on the rocky coast where the mountains lean into the sea, 60 miles north of the seaport of Amoy, was calculated to make a man of spirit either a millionaire-in-exile or a Communist-in-residence. Jagged hills yielded only meager crops to unceasing labor with primitive implements; the renowned teas of Fukien were expensive as much because of their scarcity as their quality. The turbulent sea yielded a meager harvest of fish to nets and lines trailed by battered, tung-oil-impregnated junks under patched sails. There were a few rich men in Fukien when Chen Po-ta was born just seven years before the dissolution of the Manchu Dynasty. The landlords, officials, and merchants wrung their wealth from the impoverished—and Chen's family was impoverished.

Still, he secured a fragmentary education at the village school, where he studied the Confucian classics. He owed his secondary education to a coolie who had fled Fukien to become a millionaire during the first Malayan rubber boom. Tan Kah-kee* was the first and greatest of the Chinese rubber barons, dominating the expanding trade throughout Southeast Asia. But he never forgot the Motherland. He was a fervent Chinese patriot and ultimately a Communist sympathizer. His first gesture was subsidizing the Chipmee Middle School in Amoy to offer free education to needy boys.

Chen Po-ta entered that middle school after establishment of the Republic in 1911. Forced by financial difficulties to leave school for a time, he finally returned to graduate as a qualified elementary school teacher. Like Chairman Mao in similar circumstances, he reportedly received assistance from a friendly neighbor. He was, moreover, probably granted a meager subsidy by the infant Marxist movement through a bourgeois sympathizer. The Chipmee Middle School was at the time a center of radical thought, partly because of its contacts with the outside world. In a China in transition, "radical thought" was generally nurtured by foreign inspiration. In practice, it could mean anything from mild liberalism to socialism or anarchism. Not innate rebelliousness but the successive failures of milder solutions to China's problems impelled intelligent young men to the radical solution of Marxist-Leninism during the decade from 1911 to 1921. When he came to Shanghai in the early 1920s to study at the Workers' University sponsored by the Communists, Chen Po-ta certainly received direct support from the burgeoning movement.

He was a serious, puritanical young man devoted to his studies—as much to compensate for his personal unattractiveness as to give sustenance to his inquiring intelligence. He neither drank nor smoked and

---

* *Chen Chia-kang* in Mandarin.

was notably shy; his severe stammer and his Fukien accent often made him half-intelligible to his schoolmates. But his brilliance attracted a senior professor, who sponsored his entry into the Communist Party in company with his closest friend, Jao Shu-shih, whom Chen would later denounce.

Upon graduation, the apparatus assigned the Ghostwriter as a staff officer and secretary to General Chang Chen, who commanded the 49th Division of the combined Nationalist-Communist "National Revolutionary Army" then campaigning to sweep the warlords from power. The Ghostwriter was invaluable; he composed orders and correspondence, while subtly preaching the Communist doctrine. Originally based in Changchou in Fukien, the 49th Division took part in the siege of Shanghai. Chen Po-ta was arrested after the Nationalist-Communist break in mid-1927, but his commander secured his release a few months later. With other discomfited Communists, he fled to Moscow.

His imprisonment was the 24-year-old intellectual's passport into Chinese émigré circles. He enrolled in the Sun Yat-sen University, a training academy for Asian agitators. But he erred tactically by joining a splinter faction amid the intricate intrigue of the Chinese Communist Party. The Sixth Party Congress of 1928, convened in Moscow and dominated by the "Russian faction," ignored him. In 1930 he was censured for "sectarianism."

Since Chen Po-ta was under a cloud when he returned to China in 1931, he lived on the fringes of the movement when he began teaching at China University in Peking. But he acquired a reputation as a theoretician, for he was one of the few members of the Party who devoted himhelf to mastering Marxism-Leninism. By 1936, he had joined the North China underground apparatus directed by Comrade Liu Shao-chi and the Mayor Peng Chen. Since they found him both useful and congenial, he played a major role in the December Ninth Movement, the peripatetic student demonstrations that pressed the Nationalist government to resist Japanese incursions. He was simultaneously recruiting new adherents among his students. No longer a mere theoretician, he had entered the mainstream of the Communist movement—and Comrade Liu Shao-chi was his sponsor.

Chen Po-ta's later enmity towards Chou Yang, the Backstage Boss, who was one of the first victims of the Cultural Revolution, was apparently kindled by the literary controversy already described. The Ghostwriter advocated "Masses' Literature for the National Revolutionary War," while the Backstage Boss championed "National Defense Literature." The first meant stressing Communist propaganda in all leftist writing; the second meant propagandizing, above all else, for resistance to the Japanese in cooperation with the Nationalists. The apparently abstruse controversy of 1935–36 became a major issue in the Cultural Revolution of 1966–69.

The Ghostwriter had lived down choosing the wrong side in Moscow. By 1937, Mao Tse-tung's "rural Chinese faction," ensconced in Yenan, had broken the "international Russian faction." Chen's previous "deviationism" became an advantage. Introduced by Comrade Liu Shao-chi, Chen Po-ta was warmly welcomed to Yenan by Mao Tse-tung himself. He was immediately put in charge of the Party's Research Section for Study of the China Problem and was appointed lecturer at the Lu Hsün Academy of Art, where he met the Starlet Chiang Ching. Shortly thereafter, he was made political secretary to the Chairman. He also wrote a play called *Song of the Villages* for the itinerant theatrical troupes of the Lu Hsün Academy. It was, curiously enough, a musical.

The Ghostwriter's talent for invective and contention was invaluable to the Chairman, who was determined to establish his doctrinal authority. Chen polished Mao's prose and imbued it with authority through extensive citations from the classical literature of Marxism-Leninism. The works he himself signed exalted Mao Tse-tung and denigrated Mao's enemies. His elementary tract entitled *Certain Proofs of Marxist Theory* was used as a manual for indoctrination by the Eighth Route Army. In addition, he refined and publicized the Chairman's unique doctrines in essays collected in 1951 in the volume *On the Thought of Mao Tse-tung*. Chen was the first to proclaim the Chairman's absolute ideological supremacy by exalting the Thought of Mao Tse-tung. The relationship was perfectly symbiotic; the Chairman had found an ideological mentor, and the Ghostwriter had found an all-powerful sponsor.

The Rectification Movement of 1942 in theory purged the Party of all non-Maoist thought. Chen Po-ta directed the campaign and prepared its handbook, *Documents on Ordering the Winds*. He subsequently paraded his loyalty in a 16-day-long attack on Wang Shih-wei, who had dared dispute Mao's dictum: "Literature and art may only expose the enemy's sins; they may not reveal the hidden errors of the proletariat." The Ghostwriter's virulent attack foreshadowed the vicious denunciations of the Cultural Revolution. He declared:

> Even speaking generally, it is clear that Comrade Wang's "ideal" comprehends anti-masses, anti-national, anti-Marxist elements. It serves the interests of the exploiting classes. It is, in reality, Trotskyism which toadies to Japanese imperialism and international Fascism. . . . Wang himself is plotting to utilize the weakness of youth in order to direct our younger comrades onto the dark paths of evil. Is he really *for* the Party? We can answer simply: He wishes to destroy the Party, working upwards from small groups to the Center itself. . . . Whom does Comrade Wang

love? He loves the Trotskyites, Trotskyism, and every kind of counter-revolutionary power. Whom does he hate? He hates the Communist Party, Marxism, and every kind of revolutionary power.

Wang Shih-wei had, further, denied the Maoists' claim to speak for the people and to serve the people, though they were actually a small, authoritarian group. The Ghostwriter's attack became more vicious and more personal. Like the enemies Chen Po-ta vilified during the Cultural Revolution, Comrade Wang had struck at the roots of the Chairman's power.

"Wang Shih-wei," the Ghostwriter went on, "claims to be a great 'hard bone' of the revolution. He is truly great—a great blubbery mass like a leech or a destructive locust. He has soft bones—or none at all. He is *not* a hard bone."

The debate recessed for a day. The Ghostwriter prepared himself well for its resumption.

"Wang Piss-stench!" he declaimed, changing the intonation of *Shih* to alter the name's meaning from "flavor of reality."

Wang Piss-stench, I can tell you, everyone's bones but yours are indeed hard and revolutionary. Only your bones are rotten! Your bones are dissolving. You have dared to utilize this meeting to undermine the position of Chairman Mao. You have strewn anti-Party rubbish all about and have vulgarly asserted: "Our Party has already become self-serving. The leading cadres have altered their basic character. They have deteriorated. Many prominent personalities use the name of the people and the power of their positions in the Party to deceive the public with false slogans and to establish personal dictatorship. They usurp the people's power and rape intra-Party democracy. They have transformed the entire Party into the slaves of a small, dictatorial group!"

That is what Wang Piss-stench dared to allege.

The Maoists prevailed—largely because Comrade Wang was right. They had already become a dictatorial faction that would tolerate no criticism.

The Ghostwriter had thus established his indispensability to the Chairman. During the next few years, he published widely circulated attacks on Chiang Kai-shek's credo, *China's Destiny,* thereby winning many wavering intellectuals to the Communist cause. He was notorious for his sycophancy. The ripe flavor of his flattery is conveyed by two typical excerpts:

Mao Tse-tung's *Report on the Peasant Movement in Hunan* is a major document which summed up definitively the struggles of the

Hunan rural masses. It is, even more, a *major document which definitively summed up the experience of the nation-wide masses' struggle in the revolutionary period from 1924 to 1927*. Indeed, the *Report* epitomizes the very essence of the entire era and all its history!

Another article advised: "If anyone wishes to study the history of the Chinese revolution and the correct line of the Party, he *must* diligently study the works of Chairman Mao." No other research, the Ghostwriter implied, was necessary.

The Ghostwriter was elected an alternate member of the Central Committee at the Seventh Party Congress in April 1945, attaining full membership in succession to a deceased member the next year. Thereafter, he rose rapidly, becoming vice director of the Party's Propaganda Bureau and sitting in councils ranging from the State Planning Commission to the Special Commission on Agricultural Reform, which directed collectivization. He was, above all, the Chairman's man, presenting the Chairman's views, which he had helped shape.

In 1950, he accompanied Mao Tse-tung to Moscow for protracted negotiations with the Russians. Officially still Mao's *personal* political secretary, he was elevated to alternate membership in the Politburo after the Eighth Party Congress of 1956. That appointment, like the senior academic posts he held, was a reward. He had championed the Chairman during the controversy over collectivization, which split the Party. He had cheerfully betrayed his two closest friends at the Shanghai Workers' University—Jao Shu-shih, First Secretary of the Shanghai Municipal Committee, and Kao Kang, the satrap of Manchuria, for both had directly defied Mao.

During the early days of the People's Republic, Chen Po-ta drove his pen in the service of the Chairman. In 1951, he published *On the Thought of Mao Tse-tung: The Synthesis of Marxism-Leninism and the Chinese Revolution*. He was prolific. *China's Four Great Families, Public Enemy Chiang Kai-shek,* and *The True Account of Chiang Kai-shek's Selling Out Manchuria* were violent attacks on the Nationalists that swayed undecided intellectuals because of the author's scholarly standing. *The Philosophy of Lao Tze* and *The Philosophy of Mo Tze* were, respectively, Maoist reinterpretations of the metaphysics of the founder of Taoism and China's first totalitarian thinker. Other works were tactical, like *Counter-revolution and Revolution in the Era of Civil War, Preserve the Enemy's Original Industrial Structure,* and *The Important Issue Is Skill in Study*. Those works that did not proselytize for the Communist cause provided philosophical justification for Mao's policies.

All were composed in close consultation with the Chairman. The

Ghostwriter's signed works tended to be more abstract, while material composed for the Chairman's signature treated immediate problems.

Chen Po-ta was a nervous author. The printers of the Communist publishing house complained that he demanded three or four sets of galley proofs—and reworked each so heavily that it required complete resetting. They lived in fear of hearing his heavy tread making for the composing room, even after the final version was locked on the stone.

From such agonizing emerged a major work entitled *Human Nature, Party Nature, and Individual Nature,* which asserted: "In a class society, the question of human nature is entirely a question of class nature. . . . Party nature and class nature are exactly the same phenomenon. Party nature is merely collective class nature. . . . The different character of the life of different societies [dominated by either the bourgeoisie or by the proletariat] determines all aspects of each man's individual nature." The Ghostwriter later declared flatly in *Red Flag:* "There is no such thing as human nature; there is only class nature."

The Ghostwriter was convinced that human beings were infinitely malleable, since they were molded entirely by the nature of the society in which they lived and by their positions in that society. His conviction that human beings could be deliberately molded by applying the techniques of I. P. Pavlov dominated Maoist thinking from the creation of the Great People's Communes in 1958 until the Cultural Revolution was muted in 1969. Even more single-minded than Mao Tse-tung, he was determined to force Chinese society to conform to his own theories—a mélange of literally interpreted Marxism-Leninism and the traditional Chinese concept of the individual as the unfeeling building block of society. Chen Po-ta was also more ruthless than Mao Tse-tung, for his arid, intellectualized passion considered humanity even less than did the Chairman's megalomania.

The Ghostwriter's blueprint of Utopia based on the Paris Commune was remarkably alienated from reality. The two theoreticians, who boasted of "reinterpreting Marxism-Leninism in light of the concrete experiences of the Chinese revolution," abandoned all they should have learned of politics and psychology. Two Marxist classics formed the theoretical basis of the new China: Karl Marx's *The Civil War in France,* written in 1871; and Vladimir Ilyich Lenin's *The State and Revolution,* written in 1917. They discussed a historical episode that was Chen Po-ta's obsession—the 72 days of the abortive Paris Commune of 1871.

The Paris Commune harked back to primitive *communal* life, distinguished by common ownership and unselfish cooperation, which the Marxists believed existed before private property bred antagonistic social classes. Since it appeared to re-create the golden age, Karl Marx hailed the Paris experiment as the mankind's first "non-exploitive, proletarian form of administration." Although it had been crushed before it could demonstrate either success or failure, the Paris Commune was the ideal prototype of the Great People's Communes imposed upon China in 1958—primarily by the Chairman and the Ghostwriter.

Forced to retreat from that experiment in the early 1960s by the concerted will of the Communist Party, Mao and Chen in 1966 proclaimed the Great Proletarian Cultural Revolution. Like a gambler quadrupling his stake on a losing number, the Maoists believed they could overcome the opposition of man and nature to their grandiose design by imposing that same design writ a hundred times larger. Convinced that "revolution always endures setbacks before winning victories," they were no more deterred by the failure of their own first experiment than they were by the short, unhappy life of the original Paris Commune, the literal model of the totally perfect society.

Even the "dictatorship of the proletariat," which preceded pure Communism, by Marxist definition meant that the proletarian *government,* acting through the Communist Party, "coerced and exploited" other social classes. The new non-exploitive *administration* the Maoist envisioned would not be an instrument of oppression because its appearance would signal the disappearance of classes, incidentally making both the Communist Party and the People's Government superfluous.

The ground plan of the Paris Commune displayed a simple symmetry that fascinated the hyperlogical Ghostwriter. Revolutionary Committees would administer social units called communes, while the State would disappear, becoming a great commune, a free federation of smaller communes. The Revolutionary Committees, exercising the functions of the executive, the legislative, and the judicial arms in one, would be composed of ordinary workingmen selected by their peers through universal "proletarian" franchise. The representatives of the proletariat would receive neither special privileges nor increased wages for service on the Revolutionary Committee. They would, moreover, continue their normal work in order to maintain their "proletarian world outlook." Further safeguards against the rise of a new bureaucratic caste were brief tenure for the Committees and their constant vulnerability to the referendum and the recall. Chen Po-ta's conditions for paradise on earth would thus realize both Confucian and Marxist visions of the Golden Age.

Since all functionaries were "members of the working class and representatives of the working class," both individual and social conflict arising from the clash of class interests would disappear. The Revolutionary Committees would be drawn from occupations as diverse as artists and professors, scientists and factory workers, accountants and weathermen—all good "proletarians" and all servants of the people receiving the same salaries as other workingmen. The institution of private property would cease to exist. All property would be held in common under the Revolutionary Committee, fulfilling the formal Marxist requirement for "ownership by the entire people" before true Communism could be attained. Each individual would work at his highest pitch, "according to his ability," and each would receive the requisites of life "according to his need." Diverse wages or specific material incentives would be unnecessary, since every man and woman, knowing neither material want nor personal envy, would labor joyously for the "collective" well-being. The State and its "coercive machinery" would "wither away."

The reasoning was absolutely logical—and quite unrealistic. It took no account of psychological conflict arising from "human nature," whose existence the Maoists denied. Since there was no private property, there would be neither economic competition nor social classes. Since there were no social classes, there would be no class conflict. Since there was no class conflict, there would be no need for police or armies. Since there were no coercive mechanisms to impose the will of one class upon others, there would be no State or government. It was all beautifully simple.

The Ghostwriter reaffirmed Karl Marx's prediction that the new order would "restore to the social body all the forces hitherto absorbed by the parasitic State feeding upon and clogging the free movement of society." Enacting the ideal system of the Paris Commune would, the Ghostwriter affirmed, automatically stimulate a "great upsurge of industrial, and agricultural production . . . by joyous, free labor."

It was magnificent, one is forced to admit, but one is forced to ask: Was it practical politics?

Confidently anticipating the spontaneous emergence of a new Great Leap Forward, the Maoists envisioned the appearance of the perfect new Communist man, his perfection guaranteed by indoctrination in the canonical Thought of Mao Tse-tung. Chen Po-ta did not note that Mao Tse-tung's constant appeal to class and national hatreds was a peculiar psychological foundation for a new order of humanity that would render extinct both classes and nations. He precluded hatred and conflict by precluding all distinctions among men. All differences between city and countryside would vanish, as would all distinctions between intellectual and manual labor. The perfect new man would be an "educated laborer and a laboring intellectual." The regular army would be absorbed by the militia, an entire people in arms. Other "coercive arms," like the police and the courts, would disappear when their reason for being vanished. The new order in China would, finally, be the model and precursor of a new order for all mankind.

Unfortunately, paradise was not destined to appear on earth.

On October 24, 1966, less than three months after his speech to the Broadcasting Institute, Chen Po-ta reviewed the progress of the Cultural Revolution without enthusiasm. Although the tide was still rising and Lin Piao waited until November 3 to proclaim extensive democracy "according to the principles of the Paris Commune," the shape of the future had become disturbingly unsatisfactory to the obsessed Maoists. The "old forces" would not depart the stage of history of their own free will—as the extremists would have known had they referred to the little red book of *Quotations From Chairman Mao,* their field manual as Oliver Cromwell's had been the Bible. The obstreperous Red Guards might "seize power" on behalf of the proletariat, but the officials of the old regime would hardly subscribe enthusiastically to their own demise. Most perplexingly to the theoreticians, the masses were siding with the old officials. Regional and personal loyalties prevented the creation of the perfect new order. Chen complained on October 24, 1966:

> There are many people who do not carry out the proletarian line, which is the will of the Party Center, the will of the revolutionary masses, and, above all, the will of Comrade Mao Tse-tung. The aberration arises because Chairman Mao's mass line is, from head to toe, at variance with the bourgeois outlook of many comrades who will not reform. The policy of the Cultural Revolution advocated by Chairman Mao calls upon the masses to educate themselves and to emancipate themselves. But representatives of the erroneous line oppose that process. They prefer the Nationalists' policy of "political tutelage." They consider the masses dullards and themselves the anointed leaders, and they distort the direction of the great movement. They are conducting a bourgeois, reactionary Cultural Revolution.

Chen Po-ta thus formally noted the massive resistance the Cultural Revolution had aroused. Ordered to give up their posts to the halfhatched Revolutionary Committees, the "representatives of the old order" replied forcefully—by word and by deed. The transition was "the will of the Party Center," but the old guard felt justified in disobeying because the Maoists had circumvented the legitimate Central Committee through trickery and coercion. Comrade Liu Shao-chi, they maintained, would have won a clear majority had the critical Eleventh Plenum of August 1966 met under normal conditions. The "power-holders" supported Comrade Shao-chi's argument that no individual's will—not even

Chairman Mao's—could set aside the constitutional processes of the Communist Party. Sustained by this legal basis and stimulated by normal human reluctance to surrender power, passive resistance to the *diktat* rose day by day. Instead of being terrorized or cajoled into compliance, the conventional apparatus of the Party stubbornly resisted the imposition of the new order of society.

From August through November 1966, the assaults of the Red Guards crystallized the resistance of the old guard. Instead of breaking, the men who had administered the Chinese People's Republic for nearly two decades coalesced into a new force that was determined to withstand the transformation of their world. They took their allies where they found them, chiefly among the peasantry and the workers and among those military officers who, conservative by nature, feared that the disruption attendant upon the Cultural Revolution would deliver China naked to her enemies. Proclaiming their vendetta against the "black gang of anti-Maoist reactionaries," the Maoists had almost succeeded in unifying the opposition—a remarkable feat.

Victory evaded the extremists. The battle continued through December 1966. The Ghostwriter commanded his Task Force, but men snickered at his deeds. Chen Po-ta, they said, was just another Li Lien-ying.

The analogy was deadly twice over. The court eunuch Li Lien-ying had been the favorite adviser of the Empress Dowager Tzu Hsi at the end of the nineteenth century. He had encouraged her to resist the encroachments of the West and the natural decay of the Manchu Dynasty by mass violence; consequent disruption had hastened the dynasty's eclipse. Like the Ghostwriter's, the eunuch's personal power had depended entirely upon his aging and enfeebled patron. Like Chen Po-ta, Li Lien-ying had attempted to avert the holocaust by intensifying the repression of the *ancien régime*.

To the history-obsessed Chinese the parallel was fascinating—and devastating. If Chen Po-ta was indeed another Li Lien-ying, men whispered, then was not Mao Tse-tung another Empress Dowager? Was the Maoist Dynasty not being hastened to destruction by the counsels of Chen Po-ta—as the Manchu Dynasty had been hastened to destruction by the counsels of Li Lien-ying?

XVII

Black Spots on the Sun

No such insidious whispers derogated the man chosen by the Maoists to operate the machinery that would transform China's society, administration—and every individual Chinese. Tao Chu, the King of the South, had proved himself an implacable executor of Peking's policy, who, nonetheless, won deep loyalty from his subordinates and, at least, tolerance from the masses. Since he was no theoretician but an intensely practical man of affairs, Tao Chu was the essential complement to the visionaries who surrounded the Chairman. He had governed China's most populous and most troublesome area with remarkable competence. The theoreticians—and even the administrators—of Peking were several levels removed from the daily "struggle" they incited; the King had mastered the immense problems of imposing Communist rule on the ground.

He was, therefore, placed above the Ghostwriter, who directed the Task Force of the Great Revolution. Tao Chu was first assigned to remake the Communist Party's Propaganda Bureau, "the center of the revolutionary storm." Shortly thereafter, he was given control of the entire Party organization and was raised to the fourth position in the hierarchy. Only Chairman Mao, the Disciple Lin Piao, and the First Minister of Peace Chou En-lai ranked above Tao Chu in the new order of precedence established in mid-August. The Ghostwriter was just one step below the man charged with realizing his ideological fancies. The Maoists had great need of the only great regional satrap who still served them, for he was the most effective satrap.

But Tao Chu was to be destroyed by the very qualities that had recommended him as executive officer of history's most ambitious attempt to transform society by "collective action." He had ruled his satrapy by balancing pressure, humor, and rewards. He had accomplished much, even imposing a degree of order on the contentious Cantonese. He had succeeded because he had not attemped the impossible—regardless of Peking's Utopian demands. He had sought only what he could attain. He personified the "local power-holders" the Cultural Revolution swore to destroy, for he had, as much as other Regional first secretaries, leavened ideological compulsions with respect for the realities of human nature and economic processes. Tao Chu was chosen to administer the new Maoist Utopia because he was bound to the Disciple by ties of long and close association and because of his demonstrated success as a regional ruler. He had, ironically, been successful because his policies diverged sharply from the Maoists' demands.

As his nickname, the King of the South, indicated, Tao Chu controlled the archetypical "independent kingdom" the Maoists sought to abolish. He had ruled his five provinces as a semi-autonomous fief. His successor as First Secretary of South Central China, Wang Jen-chung, (First Secretary of Hunan when he swam in the Yangtze River with the Chairman in July 1966) came under criticism as violent as that directed at Tao Chu himself when the King's stubborn attachment to reality made it impossible for him to play out Maoist fantasies. Nor was it coincidental that the subordinates who accompanied him to Peking were also purged. They were men of a kind—hard-headed and heavy-handed Communist administrators who strove for the welfare of the Chinese people and the Chinese nation, even when that purpose conflicted with the Chairman's visions. They all cared about human beings, although their concern had often been perverted by the doctrine that the end justifies the means. When the Cultural Revolution spilled over the edge of reality they therefore joined the King of the South in crying: "Halt!"

Tao Chu became the nucleus of systematic opposition to the *coup de main* in November and December 1966. That resistance was strongest in the provinces, for the moderates in Peking itself had been outmaneuvered. Tao Chu, a man from the provinces, was apparently entrenched in power in Peking. He truly understood the needs of the people and the limits of natural resources—both concepts the Maoists disdained. However hardened they might be, the "working-level cadres" still in the provinces also recognized realities and cared about human beings. They could not have maintained Communist rule if they had not. Since they considered Tao Chu willy-nilly *their* representative in Peking, they appealed to him. The local, provincial, and regional resistance to Maoist terror contrived Tao Chu's downfall and almost provoked Civil War. It may, however, have saved the regime from destruction by diverting the frenzy of the Great Revolution from total madness.

* * *

The King of the South was short, brusque, and casual. He disdained display and ceremony, and he knew that the Chinese people were human beings, not merely malleable "social units." The King of the South had, since October 1961, ruled the five provinces of the Central-South Region, with hard, but just, discipline. Although he had often tempered Peking's harsh policies with reason, Tao Chu's name evoked more fear than affection from the masses. He would, they knew, break any Party organ, any civilian "unit," or any individual that contested his will. Peking knew, in turn, that the King often bent the Center's directives to make their execution possible. But Peking invariably assigned him to cope with the most severe troubles in the constantly troubled South. Despite his local reputation, he was not considered a major national figure before the Great Proletarian Cultural Revolution.

Five months after the Great Revolution began, the caustic Chinese gave the King of the South an additional nickname. They called him *Won-ton* (Dumpling) because, they said, his career was like a dumpling dropped into a steaming soup pot. The small, dough-wrapped meatball falls to the bottom, swells up suddenly, and rises to the top—to be snared by adept chopsticks and devoured.

So it was with Tao Chu. Summoned to Peking in June 1966 to take over the Propaganda Bureau, he virtually displaced the Organizer when he was named Secretary of the Communist Party's Secretariat and number four in the hierarchy in mid-August. He was purged in January 1967, because the concerted resistance of pragmatic local cadres had coalesced around his own essentially reasonable position.

He courted his fate by sternly opposing the Maoists' foolhardy decision to destroy the last barriers against anarchy. Like others before him, the King of the South overestimated both his own adroitness and the Maoists' rationality. His own was actually the last clear voice of reason in the Maoist camp. Chou En-lai enjoyed a reputation for human pragmatism, but his own survival was his overriding concern. It was not Chou En-lai, but the King of the South, considered a careerist unmoved by either moral questions or human suffering, who in fact held the last barricade against extremism. When he fell, the "great waves and high winds" of the Cultural Revolution swept unrestrained over all China, casting the world's most populous nation into chaos.

He might have survived by acquiescing when the extremists declared total war on Chinese society by expanding their assault against the "bourgeoisie" and the Party into an invasion of agriculture and industry. But he protested the disruption of the economy and the civil strife he knew expanded Red Guard attacks would produce—and he was liquidated.

Until he was forced to choose, no one knew exactly where Tao Chu stood. Despite good personal relations with the Chairman and the Disciple, his personal convictions on critical issues were obscure, perhaps by intent. He had always been a faithful servant, but not a zealot.

He had, before the end of World War II, worked for Comrade Shao-chi in the subversive underground, serving terms in Nationalist jails, which excluded him from the epochal Long March of 1934–35. After victory against Japan, Tao had risen rapidly through service as a political commissar and logistical director for Lin Piao's armies. He held major posts in the South and, finally, the First Secretaryship of the Central-South Bureau. His territory included China's most troublesome, most productive, and most regionalistic provinces—Kwangtung, Kwangsi, Hunan, Hupei, and Honan—with a total population of more than 160 million. He had committed himself to neither ideological faction—the Utopia-intoxicated Maoists or the pragmatists.

Tao had, instead, enforced divergent policies, regardless of their strict ideological content. He had whipped faltering land reform in Kwangtung Province to meet the national norm; he had killed "landlords" and fired cadres. As a Hunanese, a "foreigner" himself to the xenophobic Cantonese, he had used thousands of northern cadres to drive the flagging southern cadres. He had apparently broken Cantonese regionalism within the Communist Party, even replacing the Cantonese governor of Kwangtung. An ardent amateur of the arts despite his own limited schooling, he had personally led the campaign in his region to enforce the sweeping reforms of the stage decreed by the Starlet. But he had also pointed out errors of the Great Leap Forward, and he had restored the Region's economic life by essentially pragmatic, nondoctrinaire measures. He had insisted upon absolute obedience, but had bound his subordinates to himself by rewards and affection.

In the beginning the Maoists exalted Tao Chu. They were apparently confident that he would continue to exercise his two paramount virtues: obedience and efficiency in carrying out orders. His record made it most unlikely that his obedience would fall, even under demands to enforce policies that were ultimately unenforceable.

As far as outsiders can judge, the King of the South shares with two other senior hierarchs the honor of having displayed dignity, courage, and decency during the power struggle: the Great General Peng Teh-huai and the Mayor Peng Chen. Many cadres also felt that the King's behavior was honorable and unselfish. The majority of his adherents followed him into obscurity rather than attempt to save their own careers by denouncing him. He had won loyalty by loyally supporting his subordinates—and by using words, however harsh, rather than harsh deeds whenever possible.

In 1953, the King addressed several thousand Cantonese cadres who had just been censured and degraded for dilatoriness in the Land Reform Movement. The cadres were depressed and apprehensive. They expected further abuse and perhaps further punishment from the "foreigner" who had virtually deposed them. But Tao Chu set out to conciliate the cadres and win them back to the service of the Party, resorting to gallows humor to his point. Even more than the mass of their rough-tempered and contentious Cantonese compatriots, the cadres appreciated the harsh humor with which Tao Chu offered them new hope. Nor did they miss the implied threat.

You have all just been severely reprimanded and reduced in rank. I know that your hearts are heavy. If it were I, Tao Chu, who had just been treated as you have been, I would not be merely resentful and unhappy. I would probably be pondering one question: Should I give up and quit? If I decided to quit, I would also be thinking of where I went from here. The answer would probably be to flee China.

My first thought would be getting to Hong Kong or Macao. But I have neither friends nor family in either of those places. They would, therefore, hardly be very comfortable or salubrious.

Therefore, I'd probably next think of smuggling myself to Taiwan. But I'm afraid that old Chiang Kai-shek would probably shoot me out of hand. That would, obviously, be no solution to my problems.

Perhaps, then, as a last resort, I'd think of hiding myself in the countryside. But, again, the prospects would be poor. After all, I've never worked the fields or even held a hoe in my hand.

As far as I'm concerned, I would have exhausted all possibilities. There would be only one thing to do. I wouldn't quit, but would take my punishment—and then get on with the job.

The King thus informed his unhappy subjects that obedience and hard work would be rewarded by reinstatement. He spoke with confidence because he commanded the confidence of his superiors. He had just completed the arduous Land Reform movement in neighboring Kwangsi and had broken massive resistance in Kwangtung. His confidence was sustained not only by his recent accomplishments, but by a record of "revolutionary struggle" that had begun in his late teens. If he carried himself like an errant revolutionary rather than a dignified official, there was good reason. He had been a professional revolutionary in the half-world of "illegal struggle" most of his days.

His early life was somewhat easier than that of most of his colleagues. Born in 1906 into a "rich peasant" family in Chiyang County of Hunan

Province, he attended a conventional middle school. He was not forced to struggle for education, nor apparently did he feel the fierce antagonism against a harsh father that created so many Communists. Instead, he came to Communism by his enrollment in the Whampoa Military Academy's Fifth Class, which began its studies in 1925.

Like most young men, the 19-year-old Tao Chu was inspired equally by desire for higher education—providentially free—and by determination to "serve the country." The youth of China had, above all else, learned the paramount power of military force from China's constant humiliation by the West and from the depradations of warlords aligned with foreign governments and firms. They had also learned that military weapons were only as good as the men who wielded them—while soldiers were only as good as their training and discipline. Soviet advisers guided organization and indoctrination for both Nationalist and Communist Parties, as well as their combined armies. Under that guidance, the Whampoa Academy trained an entire generation of Chinese leaders.

Tao Chu was still a cadet when the Northern Expedition marched out to wrest China from the "northern warlords" in June 1926. The unnatural alliance between Nationalists and Communists was already strained. In April 1927, Generalissimo Chiang Kai-shek struck at the Communists, and Communist cadets at Whampoa were commanded to leave their formations. Tao Chu duly stepped forward. He had no choice, since most Communist cadets—unlike Lin Piao—had not concealed their allegiance, for Whampoa was a joint Nationalist-Communist academy. The Communists' arrest was largely formal. Almost 80 cadets soon escaped loose security, assisted by secret sympathizers among the Nationalists. Tao Chu waited his chance to slip away alone to Hong Kong, some 90 miles southeast down the Pearl River. But foreign concessions and colonies were no longer the refuge they had been for Communists before Chiang Kai-shek came to terms with the powers. Tao Chu was traced through his friends in Hong Kong's Communist underground by the Special Branch of the Crown Colony's police force. Returned to Nationalist custody, he escaped again a few months later— buying his freedom, the Red Guards later charged, by revealing the names of secret Communist agents. The accusation seems contrived, since he remained in good standing with the Chinese Communist Party.

In December 1927, the Communists, reeling in defeat, staged the fourth of their "adventurous" and counterproductive revolts. Despite the failure of the Nanchang Uprising in August and Mao Tse-tung's Hunan Harvest Rising in September, the Party still hoped to seize power through popular uprisings backed by regular military units. Eager for victory in China to confound his domestic enemies, Joseph Stalin encouraged the ill-advised and ill-prepared revolts. Besides, the desperate activists could site one major "success." The dashing Peng Pai, more traditional brigand-rebel than disciplined *apparatchik,* had established a Commune in the Hailufeng district of coastal Fukien Province in November 1927. It would endure until the spring of 1928 when it was crushed by Nationalist troops. Peng Pai's apparent success in carving out a Communist area with bayonets encouraged the Communists to proclaim the ephemeral Canton Commune of December 1927.

Tao Chu had already made his way to the southern metropolis. His role in the bloody 10-day uprising was minor, for he was still only a junior cadre. He apparently served as a staff officer of the Municipal Military Committee, the headquarters of the fragmented regular Communist troops that had converged on the city where the Communist labor movement was strongest. Despite the assurances of the Soviet advisers and their own confidence, the Communists found that the "proletariat" did not rally to the Red flag. The Canton Commune briefly controlled the first metropolis the Communists held. It ended in a massacre of their troops and extinguished Communist power from all the cities of China for a decade—and from the metropolises for more than two decades. Tao Chu was lucky to surive in freedom, but he was once again a fugitive.

He gravitated to the single relatively secure base of Communist power still extant, Mao Tse-tung's First Soviet Area in the Chingkangshan Range of western Kiangsi. He was not given a particularly warm welcome, for he was tainted by his association with leaders Mao deemed both "adventurists" and rivals for power. Yet he was a trained, albeit inexperienced, officer and the rural military base urgently needed professional soldiers. Tao was accepted by the Chingkangshan Military Affairs Committee and assigned to duty as a political commissar. His first extended contact with Mao Tse-tung aroused no particular enthusiasm on either side. Tao Chu was soon detached for duties outside the First Soviet Area.

His movements during the next two years are obscured by Party reticence. Tao Chu clearly left Mao Tse-tung to serve the Moscow-approved legitimatist leadership of the Party at the "Shanghai Center," which certainly appeared more dynamic at the time. Tao Chu was young, impatient, and naïve enough to believe passionately in the quick Communist victory promised by the "activists."

Compelled by adverse circumstances as much as he was guided by reasoned strategy, Mao was committed to slowly building power bases among the backward peasantry. To Tao Chu the "rural strategy" must have seemed wearing down the mountain of Nationalist power with trickling drops of water. Besides, the autocratic Mao had chosen the "rural strategy" for reasons that transcended his own circumstances and the "objective situation." Since he was determined to be supreme, he would submit to the authority of neither the Shanghai Party Center nor the Moscow Communist International. On the other hand, the Shanghai group, dominated by the dynamic and persuasive Li Li-san, not only enjoyed legitimate sanction but appeared to be moving rapidly toward the conquest of power. Even after the mercurial Li Li-san was deposed, the new Shanghai leadership, still encouraged by Stalin, still believed it could seize power by seizing the cities. The strategy was as attractive as it was futile.

From 1928 to 1930, Tao Chu operated in Fukien Province under the aegis of the Shanghai Center, while maintaining a loose liaison with Mao Tse-tung's "rural faction." It was by no means unusual for an activist to have a foot in either camp. Since both Shanghai and Kiangsi cultivated the fiction that they were one force, it was possible and desirable—politically and personally—to maintain good relations with both. But Tao Chu's inspiration and orders came from Shanghai. The virtually nonexistent "self-conscious industrial proletariat, the natural revolutionary nucleus," was expected to rise in revolt so that the Communists could consolidate their military victories politically. The lessons of Nanchang, Canton, and the Fukien Commune were ignored. Even more remarkably, the chronically independent Chinese still behaved as if Big Brother in the Kremlin knew best.

Tao Chu ran operations in Fukien. He concentrated on "illegal struggle" in the cities of the coastal province that boasted a "strong revolutionary tradition," largely because many émigré sons and daughters had conveyed radical thought from the world outside. Despite the Shanghai Center's ascendancy, Fukien was also a secondary sphere of influence of the Maoists in neighboring Kiangsi. As the "responsible comrade" of the Party's Fukien Provincial Military Affairs Committee, Tao Chu did not restrict himself to the "underground" organization of workers and intellectuals. He also persistently sought to create the nucleus of an effective conventional military force. His personal prestige was greatly enhanced in March 1930 by his leading the daring raid that freed 18 Party members imprisoned in Amoy, Fukien's chief port. Emboldened by effusive praise from Shanghai, he planned his boldest stroke in August 1930. Haphazardly planned and executed, his attempt to seize Amoy from within, beginning with the vital Salt Administration Bureau, failed starkly.

As the "strategy of a multi-provincial offensive to seize power by seizing the cities" approached its spectacularly unsuccessful climax, neither Tao Chu nor Shanghai learned from the failure of his "adventurous" endeavor. Nor did they learn from Great General Peng Teh-huai's defeat at Changsha in the same month. They still believed that the "rotten, imperialist-dominated" Nationalist regime would collapse under their hammer blow against the cities.

Instead, the entire Communists' Amoy apparatus was crushed after the coup, and the Fukien apparatus was battered. Tao Chu directed a Military Affairs Committee that commanded *no* effective troops. Communist soldiers who had not been captured, killed, or crippled were drawn irresistibly to their single refuge, Mao Tse-tung's Workers' and Peasants' Red Army. Tao Chu was bereft, outflanked—on the left by Mao Tse-tung, on the right by Chiang Kai-shek—and virtually deserted. From 1931 to 1933, he doggedly applied himself to a largely unsuccessful effort to rebuild the Party's clandestine apparatus in Fukien from a tenuous base in the northern city of Foochow. Like many young Communist officers, he had sailed a swift course, but, during the early 1930s, he was marooned in the backwaters by the "great storm" of the Party's internal struggles.

The career begun so promisingly came to an abrupt—and almost total—halt in 1933. Reporting to the Shanghai Party Center, which still exercised nominal authority, Tao Chu was arrested because his contact man was known to the Nationalists' secret police. He was swiftly transferred from Shanghai to more secure confinement in the Military Prison of Nanking, the new Nationalist capital—and was summarily condemned to death. He had already consumed the bowl of noodles customarily served just before execution—and on birthdays—because the long strands symbolize longevity. That paradoxical ritual completed, the 27-year-old Tao Chu awaited death with what composure he could muster. The Secretary-General of the Communist Party had already been executed while singing the "Internationale." The Nationalist ring was tightening around Mao Tse-tung's First Soviet Area. It was the blackest moment the Communist movement had known since the terrible summer, autumn, and winter of 1927, when Chiang Kai-shek's assault fragmented the Communist Party.

But conservative Generalissimo Chiang still lived by the traditional Chinese virtues which Tao Chu and his comrades despised—and fought to destroy. The Generalissimo's impulse to display magnanimity in victory was strengthened by the responsibility he felt for men like Tao Chu, his own student when he had been commandant of the Whampoa Military Academy. Moreover, Chiang felt that the Communist officers were still not beyond redemption; there was ample precedent for the defeated to choose to serve China by serving the victor. Marked for arrest in 1927 because he was a Communist in the Whampoa cadet corps, Tao Chu was saved from execution in 1934 because he had been a Whampoa cadet. Chiang Kai-shek offered to commute his sentence if he confessed and repented his sins. Not only Chinese tradition, but specific Communist orders sanctioned Tao Chu's accepting Chiang's conditions. Comrade Liu Shao-chi, chief of operations in "enemy territory," had instructed prisoners to preserve themselves for later service to the cause by formally recanting. Accordingly, Tao Chu addressed to Chiang Kai-shek a letter renouncing Communism and pledging loyalty to the Nationalist regime.

"I, your pupil," he wrote, "have committed many errors. I have joined a foreign political party, and I have violated the laws of China. I have, however, now awakened to my sins. I am determined to quit the Communist Party and to give up my previous, erroneous political views."

His sentence was reduced to life imprisonment. Other Communists were released after recanting, but Tao Chu was confined until 1937, when Japanese invasion forced the second Nationalist-Communist alliance. With China apparently united against the Japanese, Tao Chu was released in the custody of General Yeh Chien-ying, the Communists' military representative in Nanking. Generalissimo Chiang Kai-shek appears to have taken his recantation no more seriously than had Tao Chu.

For the next seven years, Tao Chu was a guerrilla leader, often behind the Japanese lines, nominally coordinating his operations with Nationalist forces. After a brief tour in Hupei Province, he was assigned to the New Fourth Army commanded by General Yeh Ting, who had led the Nanchang Revolt in 1927. It was guerrilla warfare with a difference, for major Chinese units operated in the large "unpacified" areas that surrounded and intertwined conventional Japanese strongpoints.

For the first time, Tao Chu's talents found full expression, free of the circumscriptions previously imposed by power struggles within the Communist Party. Japanese invasion had *nominally* united Nationalists and Communists; it had *actually* united the Communists. Mao Tse-tung had, for all practical purposes, already taken control. The New Fourth Army in the central-south was distant from main Communist forces in the north and west, but it fought a concerted battle.

As director of the Civilian Work Section of the Army's Political Department, Tao Chu organized the farmers into anti-Japanese intelligence, propaganda, and "people's self-defense" militia units. It was not remarkable that he also recruited adherents to the Communist apparatus while nominally serving the Nationalist-Communist alliance against the Japanese. No more than Mao Tse-tung himself did he forget the ultimate purpose—the conquest of China for Communism. He did well for the cause—and for himself. He was unscathed by the bitter intra-Party struggle which followed major clashes between the New Fourth Army and Nationalist forces in 1941. Tao Chu had won such credit with the Party Center that he was ordered to Yenan in March 1945, as the war against Japan clearly approached its end. The real war was just beginning.

Both Nationalists and Communists had anticipated their later battle for control of China, even during ostensible cooperation against the Japanese. Tao Chu was assigned to the decisive theater of operations, for he had proved himself—politically, militarily, and personally—in the New Fourth Army. He accompanied the Disciple to the northeast to train the Manchurian Democratic Allied Armies. Their victory would precede the final campaign to conquer China. Having demonstrated his proficiency in rallying civilian support for the Communist troops, Tao Chu was appointed deputy chief political commissar of the Manchurian armies— with special responsibilities for recruiting and logistics. In 1947, he was rewarded for his service to Lin Piao by the First Secretaryship of the Party's Liaohsi Provincial Committee.

Tao had staunchly supported the Disciple in his struggle against the Mayor, whom Comrade Liu Shao-chi had installed as First Secretary of the Manchurian Region. The Mayor had stressed organizing the proletariat and the intellectuals of the cities, while the Disciple was determined to concentrate upon winning the rural masses in order to provide bases and recruits for his armies. Tao Chu had espoused the Chairman's strategy of first conquering the countryside and then enveloping the cities. He had missed the Long March because of his imprisonment, but his experience with the semi-guerrilla New Fourth Army had altered his perspective. He was, besides, personally loyal to the Disciple.

In 1948, a truly decisive battle took Shenyang and virtually guaranteed the Communists' conquest of Manchuria as the staging area for their subsequent conquest of China. Tao Chu was named deputy director of the Shenyang Military Control Commission. When Lin Piao's Fourth Field Army took the vital triplet industrial cities called Wuhan in Central China in the spring of 1949, Tao Chu was once again promoted. He was not only deputy director of the Political Department of the Fourth Field Army, but deputy director of the Wuhan Military Control Commission. After the proclamation of the People's Republic in October 1949, he finally entered upon the career his talents merited. Unlike many of his senior colleagues, who were anointed during the protracted struggle for power, Tao Chu did not come to fulfillment until after the establishment of the Republic, when he was 43. He owed his preferment to his proven ability and to the favor of the Disciple. Tao Chu's rapid progress after 1949 can best be demonstrated by listing the more important posts he held.

In November 1949, Tao Chu was appointed deputy director of the

Political Department of the Central-South Military Region and in December 1949 was elevated to membership in the Committee that ruled the Central-South Military and Administrative Region. All China had been divided into five Military and Administrative Regions, all but one, Manchuria, ruled by senior generals. The Central-South Region under Lin Piao was—marginally, but definitely—the most important. It included the Wuhan industrial complex and Hunan Province, the granary of Eastern China, as well as the southernmost province of Kwangtung, the nation's door to the outside world.

In March 1950, Tao Chu became a member of the Financial and Economic Commission of the Region and, shortly thereafter, Director of the Political Departments of the Fourth Field Army and the Central-South Military Region. Later that year he became political commissar of the newly created South China Military Region and the Kwangsi Military District. Kwangsi, a mountainous province, inhabited in good part by non-Chinese tribespeople, was appallingly poor and endemically rebellious. Tao managed to bring Kwangsi under effective control so rapidly that he was rewarded in 1952 with the Fourth Secretaryship of the Central–South China Regional Bureau of the Communist Party. In 1952, he was transferred to Kwangtung to break the fierce resistance to the Land Reform Movement offered by that province's assertively independent natives.

He was so successful in quelling "regional tendencies" that he rose rapidly from acting governor to become governor of Kwangtung in 1955. Assisted by circumstances, he had disposed of the men who blocked his way. He advanced within the Party hierarchy to Acting First Secretary of the Central-South Bureau as early as 1954. First Secretary Lin Piao was incapacitated by illness, while his immediate subordinate, General Yeh Chien-ying, was assigned elsewhere. When the Eighth National Congress of the Chinese Communist Party met in 1956, Tao Chu was elected to the Central Committee, though he was, until his abrupt elevation to fourth place in 1966, only eighty-sixth in the hierarchy. The Central–South Military and Administrative Region had been abolished in 1955, along with its parallel, but superior, organization, the Party's Central-South Bureau. Tao Chu was, nonetheless, established as First Secretary of Kwangtung Province and Political Commissar of the triprovincial Canton Military Region. In 1961, the Central-South Regional Bureau was re-created, along with the other five Regional Bureaus, to reimpose the Communist Party's authority on a nation restive after the fiasco of the Great Leap Forward. Tao Chu was First Secretary of that Bureau until he was called to Peking in June 1966 to apply his forceful administrative methods to the Great Revolution.

* * *

The vigorous official with the square, open face and the close-cropped, graying hair who arrived in the capital with his considerable personal entourage was outwardly a model *apparatchik*. Untainted by strong expression of any deep ideological commitment, he was an essential instrument for the Maoists, who were "struggling" against the majority of effective administrators in the Party. Half-careerist, half-civil servant, and beholden to Lin Piao for his advancement, Tao Chu would presumably do as he was told. Any doubts he might entertain would, presumably, be smothered by his own ambition and his loyalty to Mao Tse-tung. Moreover, he was at 60 still young enough to aspire to the summit, but not so young, it appeared, as to become the nucleus of a new center of power. The aging Mao Tse-tung, deeply suspicious of all associates who might claim equality with him, had gathered new personal adherents. All were either inherently subordinate or significantly younger. To this new Maoist group, the King of the South contributed his practical, administrative experience, which, the Maoists assumed, was not adulterated by inclination toward insubordination.

But the Disciple and the Chairman misassessed the man, just as they misassessed the "objective conditions" that would make him the nucleus of new opposition. Tao Chu was in 1966 truly the King of the South and no longer the obedient follower Lin Piao remembered. He had ruled a great region too long and too independently to submit absolutely to a pair whose motives he mistrusted because their policies flouted reality as he saw it. His period of ascendance in the Central-South Region had extended from 1961 to 1965, corresponding exactly with the moderates' effective administration of the Party Center. He had become accustomed to making his own decisions under the loose guidance of men who sought the same pragmatic ends he sought. During his long sojourn in the South, he had acquired not only the casual manners of the southerners but their contemptuous and almost automatic resistance to authority. He had, moreover, acquired a sense of his own power and a devoted cadre of followers.

Two chief impressions emerge from talks with Communist officials who worked with Tao Chu in Kwangtung.* He was jovial and relaxed to a degree that first shocked, but soon delighted the strenuously disciplined cadres. He was, moreover, a supreme realist who addressed himself to problems with remarkable concentration and without prejudgment.

His teeth stained black by the smoke of the cigarette perpetually

* Because he was for so long stationed in Canton, less than 100 miles from the British Colony of Hong Kong, I have had the opportunity to speak with a large number of men who knew Tao Chu with varying degrees of intimacy during extended periods of time.

hanging between his lips, the King was so casual in his dress as to be slovenly. His shirt was usually only half-buttoned, and he disdained the Liberation Suits, meticulously tailored of expensive cloth, that were the prerogative and delight of others of his rank—sharply divisive status symbols in the "classless society." Visiting a farm village accompanied only by a secretary, the sloppily attired Tao Chu was mistaken for a discharged serviceman returning to his home village. He was offered food and accommodation by solicitous farmers who believed they were welcoming one of their own.

He did not correct their misapprehension, for he enjoyed it. He prided himself on the versatility which made him at home with all the "people" —from peasants to professors. Indeed, he took on the manners and the language of the group in which he found himself. "Tao Chu," a former assistant recalled, "could talk with writers or farmers, with workers or physicists. And he always spoke their own language."

The King was, nonetheless, impatient of delay and occasionally severe with subordinates who he felt had transgressed the broad limits of forgiveness his tolerance normally extended. Though his mind was so well organized he could speak for three hours without notes, his hand-writing was so flowing as to be almost illegible to all but his practiced secretaries. He could always spare time to chat with visiting local officials and, like a proficient democratic politician, would delight them by remembering their names and asking after their families. Although he might inflict swift punishment, Tao Chu never vented his temper upon his subordinates, restraint unusual among the hard-driving and hard-driven senior cadres. Reveling in the rough humor that spiced his speeches, his subordinates were also pleasantly surprised by his courtesy in pouring tea for them, his lack of personal arrogance, and his failure to pursue "female comrades." A former secretary remarked with some wonder, "He was definitely never a voluptuary!" Again, such restraint was unusual enough to evoke comment.

The King's normal workday ran from seven in the morning to mid-night, though he might take an hour or two during the day to read for pleasure. "Most of his books, aside from the Marxist classics and the works of Mao Tse-tung," his former secretary recalled, "were Chinese history and Chinese or Russian novels. But few of the Chinese novels were published after Liberation." The King of the South thus displayed discriminating literary taste; the burgeoning Chinese literary renascence had been crushed after 1949 by Maoist insistence that all art must serve as "a weapon in the class struggle." Yet, like all successful *apparatchiks,* he subdued personal taste to the directives of Peking when necessary. Having already convinced the Disciple that he was a highly effective "docile instrument," he endeared himself to the Starlet in the early 1960s by vigorously enforcing the order to play her drastically revised "model Peking operas" throughout the Central-South Region. He was the only regional satrap who did so.

The King did not require his staff to share his protracted labors unless it was absolutely necessary. He also bound his subordinates by ties of tolerance. He overlooked their petty foibles—and even their using his name without authorization to obtain minor personal privileges or to enforce policy decisions. He was, above all, determined to get the job done, and a contented staff which exercised personal initiative was an essential instrument. Again, his attitude differed from that of many of his peers. The King not only delegated authority, but deliberately cultivated a reputation for absent-mindedness so that he could overlook trifling misdemeanors. His staff called him *Wu Lung,* literally, "the Blind Dragon," the Cantonese equivalent of "the absent-minded professor." They used that nickname to his face, and he laughed with them.

Some subordinates actually rejected promotion when he offered them direction of their own country or provincial offices. They not only felt themselves cherished by their somewhat eccentric master, but also considered themselves secure under his protection from the erratic purges that periodically swept the apparatus.

The Blind Dragon awed his secretaries with his nearly photographic memory. They would sit in his home library, the walls lined with eight bookshelves, each more than eight feet high and four feet wide. Challenged to place a passage, the man who paraded his absent-mindedness would cite volume, page, and paragraph.

The home life of the King's family, who were housed in a relatively modest dwelling in Canton, was also marked by good humor. His wife, Tseng Chih, was an attractive woman with the *matte* white skin the dark Cantonese particularly admire. She was eleven years his junior and, just five feet tall, some six inches shorter. Average in height for a Cantonese woman, she possessed a robust Cantonese sense of humor. One secretary recalled with innocent precision, "She was always cracking jokes, and their relationship seemed very close."

After serving as director of a section of the Canton Municipal Propaganda Bureau, Madame Tao rose rapidly through her husband's influence; nepotism was as firmly established under the Communists as it had been under the Nationalists or the Empire. She finally became alternate secretary of the Secretariat of the Kwangtung Provincial Committee, secretary of the Secretariat of the Canton Municipal Committee, and deputy director of the Municipal Propaganda Bureau. Despite her official duties, she gave the King one daughter, called Ming-ming, who was in her early twenties in 1966, and a younger son. They appear to have been a happy and close-knit family, for neither his wife nor his children joined the choruses of denunciation against Tao Chu after his fall. Their silence was unusual at a time when wives and husbands were regularly criticizing each other and children were vilifying their parents.

The King's pragmatism and concern for individuals manifested themselves most strikingly in his attitude toward the "high-level intellectuals." Like the Backstage Boss, Chou Yang, deputy director of the Propaganda Bureau of the Party Center, Tao Chu respected talent for its own sake. Very much aware of China's need for all the talent she possessed, he consistently championed men and women the Communists characteristically described as "human natural resources." He even risked his own position to succor such men and women who were trapped by the periodic ideological purges ordered from Peking.

A professor in the Engineering Department of the Kwangtung Branch of the Academia Sinica, China's foremost research institute, was denounced in 1955 during a campaign against "rightists" that began with criticism of an author called Hu Feng. The professor was a representative academic who valued a quiet life above all else. Hoping to preserve his personal and professional life from total destruction, he duly confessed his sins in a "public self-examination."

The matter ultimately came to Tao Chu's attention, in part because of the professor's rank, but in greater part because he was personally concerned with "human natural resources." The King called the professor into his office and went over the confession line by line. Finally he cast the document aside, exclaiming, "This is nonsense. There's no evidence at all. You've done nothing wrong."

Fearing another trap, the professor insisted that he had truly sinned and that his confession was valid. Tao Chu impatiently swept it off his desk and ordered, "You're cleared. Go back to work!"

In 1957, the Anti-Rightist Campaign followed the intellectuals' revelation of deep resentment through the free speech briefly permitted by the Hundred Flowers Movement. Tao Chu reprimanded the overzealous Party Secretary of the South China College of Engineering for filling his quota of "rightists" by denouncing the Dean of the Faculty of Physics, a specialist in electronics.

"Do you know how many electronics experts we have?" he asked. "Do you know the Party's attitude toward high-level intellectuals?"

The Party Secretary sat in silent misery.

"Well, I'll tell you," the King said. "We have very few indeed, and the Party is determined to cherish them. If we throw him out of work, we'll set our electronics development back years."

Although the Party Center's attitude was by no means as clear as Tao Chu intimated, the professor was rehabilitated and restored to work. The Party Secretary was punished in his place.

The King's high-handed reversal of the Party hacks' rote obedience to Peking's directives aroused their resentment. Tenacious bureaucrats waited hopefully for him to commit a major political error so that they could crucify him. Their opportunity came when the Cultural Revolution was a few months old and Tao Chu protected a diva of the classical Cantonese Opera called Hung Hsien-nü, literally, Red-line Girl.

The Red Guards attacked the actress, who had fled Hong Kong to avoid punishment for falsifying income-tax returns. She was, they said, really Hei Hsien-nü (Black-line Girl), since she not only lived in bourgeois luxury, but "spread the anti-Socialist, anti-Party black line." Tao Chu, already exercising great power in Peking, defended Hung Hsien-nü. She was, he said, a "great national treasure" because her films earned much foreign exchange. Besides, he admired her singing, having developed a taste for Cantonese Opera, which is quite different from Peking Opera.

The King was deeply involved in the Great Proletarian Cultural Revolution from the moment he reached Peking in June 1966. Under Comrade Liu Shao-chi's aegis, he initially directed the Work Teams of the Cultural Revolution, later denounced as anti-Maoist. He was notably fearful of excesses and hesitated to give "all power to the masses." In late June, he telephoned to order the First Secretary of the Party's Kwangtung Provincial Committee to begin the Cultural Revolution in the schools, but added that the Party would "maintain control." The student activists, he stressed, were *not* to be allowed to take command of the movement. His chief subordinate, Wang Jen-chung, First Secretary of Hupei Province and acting First Secretary of Central–South China, had already issued similar instructions. Wang told the Work Teams to "attack landlords, rich peasants, counterrevolutionaries, former Nationalist military and police officers, monks, nuns, and Taoists." He did not mention the "men within the Party taking the capitalist road."

Despite his new eminence, the King was apparently not aware of the vast potential scope of the Cultural Revolution in June and July. He did not foresee the climactic "movement" that would destroy the Communist Party. Even on August 2, 1966, when the Eleventh Plenum of the Central Committee was sitting in Peking under the guns of Lin Piao's soldiers, Tao Chu remained uncertain of the magnitude of the Great Revolution. He said as much in a speech to students of the People's University of Peking.

He had, he declared, carried out all previous campaigns ordered by the Party Center with dispatch because he had thoroughly understood their goals and tactics. But, he added, he did not feel that he fully comprehended the Cultural Revolution, particularly since he was not sure who were its targets. In some puzzlement, he passed vital questions back to the students. Mock submission to the "will of the masses" was at the moment the approved "work style" of Maoist leaders; Tao Chu, however, seems to have been sincere. He also showed imprudent concern for individual victims of the purge. He told the students:

> There exists a definite question of protecting the minority. Since your ranks and views are at present quite well balanced, there is no need for us to make our own attitude plain by applauding one side or the other. But we must clap our hands a few times when the minority speaks up. The minority may not necessarily be correct, but we should, nonetheless, protect the minority. The minority would be overwhelmed by the sheer weight of numbers of the majority in a debate if it were not protected— and there could then be no debate.

The King of the South had missed the point of the Great Proletarian Revolution—the destruction of all dissidents and the stifling of all debate. He finally paid with his political head for this failure of under-standing—and for his humanity toward victims. Still, several months passed before the Maoists realized that Tao Chu was not the subservient tool they had thought him. During that time, he made effective opposi-tion possible, in the provinces by his presence—and apparent power— in Peking.

On November 20, 1966, Tao Chu learned that the Cultural Revolu-tion was indeed different from all the previous violent "campaigns" that had purged the Communist Party and the State bureaucracy. No one, he found, was immune. Despite his new eminence, his control of the propaganda apparatus, and the Praetorian Guard of loyal subordinates surrounding him, he too was publicly vilified. The "bombardment" of Tao Chu was initiated by a student called Lu Jung-ken who emerged from a Shanghai junior middle school for the occasion and returned to that obscurity after he had served his masters' purpose.

Since Shanghai had never been under the King's administration, he could hardly have aroused strong personal antipathy in that great port. The "spontaneous protest" was clearly inspired, for "great-character posters" that suddenly appeared on the walls of Peking revealed both the source and the purpose of the attacks. Like the criticism of the playwright, Vice Mayor Wu Han of Peking, which opened the Cultural Revolution, the "great-character posters" commented exhaustively on the public and private statements Tao Chu had made over many years. Like the crescendo of attacks on the "literary black gang," they pur-ported to prove by extracts from his own writings that the King was an implacable foe of the Chairman and the sacrosanct Thought of Mao

Tse-tung. The style and the content of the "bombardment" revealed that Tao Chu had come under attack by the small group of "extreme leftists" gathered around Mao's wife. The thorough research and ingeniously twisted logic revealed that the criticism had not been produced by a junior middle-school student, but by the Starlet's professional character assassins.

The extravagantly ambitious extreme leftists were determined to destroy their rival, since he alone offered orderly government. Their extreme ruthlessness spared no man's character or life. The welfare of China did not enter into their calculations, for the King was obviously an obstacle to their ambition. Unless he were removed, their plans and ambitions would be blocked by the growing opposition of the provincial pragmatists. Tao's assailants were clearly opportunists, but it remains debatable whether desire for personal aggrandizement moved them more than did zealous dedication to the "new world" they were presumably building under the direction of the Chairman. But their tactics and their own later expulsion from the Maoist ranks support the former hypothesis. Lu Jung-ken, the amorophous "student" who had "fearlessly denounced" Tao Chu, conveniently "fell ill" as a result of his exertions. On February 12, 1967, he "died" in Shanghai—and no one outside the ultra-leftist cabal knew whether he had in truth ever existed.

The evanescent stalking horse had done his work well. Tao Chu's name began to drop out of the official name lists, that ever shifting *Who's Who* of Communist China. By mid-December 1966, it was apparent to external observers that the King of the South had been ambushed in Peking and, on December 28, he was conspicuously slighted at the last of the Great Mass Rallies of the Red Guards, where the Maoist leadership assembled to display a solid front against growing resistance within the Party.

Tao Chu played an active role in organizing that opposition, for he deployed his own Red Guards throughout China. Ostensibly utterly loyal to the Maoist Party Center, they really gave immediate allegiance to the King himself. The triplet industrial cities of Wuhan, the original seat of the Central–South China Bureau, were the rallying point of Tao's youth legions. Their detachments appeared in centers of power like Canton in the far south, Lanchow in the north, Chungking in the southwest, and even Manchuria in the northeast. Although no apparent center controlled the opposition, men who felt themselves and their accomplishments threatened came together in informal—and frequently tacit—alliances. The ruthless and destructive tactics of the ultra-leftists crystallized the opposition. Around the nucleus, a greater and more solid structure was forming.

Thwarted by passive resistance, the Maoists determined to invade the two areas of Chinese life that had been specifically excluded from the factional struggle in the original *Sixteen-Point Directive* that laid down the strategy of the Cultural Revolution. The Maoists, who had to win rapidly and totally if they were to win at all, abruptly realized that their restraint had ceded their enemies two nearly impregnable strongholds— the countryside and industry.

Labor had long been the redoubt of Comrade Liu Shao-chi, the Maoists' *bête noire,* while the self-consciously proletarian workers of ports, factories, mines, and railroads had remained highly independent. The farmers had experienced the disillusionment of the Great Leap Forward and the Great People's Communes. Having struggled back to a degree of well-being during the early sixties, they were determined to protect the privileges they had gained. A small bonus and a half-day's holiday for the workers, a plot of private land and an occasional party for the peasants—such small benefits, along with freedom from constant intrusion into their lives, meant more to the urban proletariat and the rural masses than all Mao's promises of Utopia. The old-line cadres, who had rebuilt the economy and restored confidence after the Great Leap Forward, were the natural rallying point for farmers and workers. The structure of the resistance was built on the massive foundation of China's working masses.

The evidence does not prove conclusively that the King broke with the Maoists on the decision to throw China's economic and social structures into turmoil by extending the Cultural Revolution to industry and agriculture. But the timing of his disaffection, sustained by general knowledge of his character, indicates that that issue was critical to the split. Accelerated by vicious personal attacks, Tao Chu's break with the Maoists was almost certainly precipitated by his conclusion that the dwindling band of zealots surrounding the enfeebled Mao Tse-tung were undertaking a campaign that would *not* break the opposition he half-favored and *would* create nation-wide chaos.

Striving to overcome the disastrous effects of the Great Leap Forward in his own region, the King had openly expressed himself forcefully on the Maoist dogmas that delivered China to the edge of catastrophe. In May 1961, summing up a symposium on industrial problems in his Central-South Region, he ascribed the nation's economic difficulties to "the violation of the law of planned and proportional development and the law of values . . . as well as giving no thought to economy or business procedure in casting the economic plans." He said China had suffered devastating reverses because of specific faults: "hastiness—too much speed; size—everything attempted on the same great scale; equality—Communist style; urgency—over-eagerness for accomplishment without first seeking to comprehend reality by examining facts; dispersion—manpower and material spread over too wide a front; and confusion—lack of proportion and balance in enterprises." Taken all in all, it was a formidable and woundingly accurate appraisal of the follies of the Great Leap Forward.

Those early comments were veiled criticisms of Maoism, however gauzy the veil. Later, Tao Chu discarded the veils. He had asked in a speech in 1962:

> Do we say the Long March was arduous and full of misery? The Long March was not as miserable as the Great Leap Forward. . . . We have been too drastic in changing the system of ownership of property. The general orientation of the establishment of People's Communes in 1958 was correct, but we had had no experience—and the concrete measures adopted were improper. The People's Commune should, it appears, grow by stages. The present [1962] stage is based upon a federation of cooperatives, and the next stage will be based upon ownership by the commune. This stage will, in time, pass into ownership by the whole people. But, in 1958, we wanted to reach Heaven in one leap and to introduce ownership by the entire people immediately. We have suffered deeply as a result of that impetuousness.

The King's remarks may seem abstract economic and philosophical observations to the non-Marxist. What, after all, does "ownership by the entire people" mean in reality? But his points would intrigue schooled Marxists—and horrify true Maoists. The ultimate goal of all orthodox Marxist-Leninists is the attainment of true Communism—when Utopia on earth is created by the spontaneous dissolution of the coercive agencies of the State, which successive ruling classes have employed to oppress subject classes. By the orthodox definition, an essential prerequisite to the creation of true Communism is the ill-defined condition known as "ownership of the means of production by the entire people."

The Maoists had asserted that "ownership by the entire people" was the outstanding accomplishment of the Great People's Commune—and Premier Nikita Khrushchev of the Soviet Union had scoffed at their claim. China, like Russia, Khrushchev had pointed out, was a long way from that idyllic state. The Chinese, he had added scornfully, advanced their claim solely to fulfill the technical requirements for the "transition to Communism." Tao Chu's remarks implicitly associated him with the hated Khrushchev—and derided all the Maoists' claims.

The King had also committed a greater sin, perhaps unwittingly.

"How can anyone say the sun has no faults?" he had written. "Of course, mankind cannot live without the sun . . . but the sun also starts great conflagrations or causes droughts . . . and its heat and brilliance are sometimes excessive. Besides, everyone knows well and—has remarked—that there are black spots on the sun." Since Mao Tse-tung was acclaimed as "the red, red sun in our hearts," the Red Guards cited those remarks as a direct attack on the Chairman.

The debris of the Great Leap Forward was thus the seedbed of the anti-Maoist movement. Springing from that soil, "poisonous weeds" had grown over the Communist Party and forced the Maoists to mobilize the Red Guards to clear them away. One of China's foremost professional economists, appalled by the Great Leap, had evolved a comprehensive new program to rebuild China. His plan was the theoretical cornerstone laid by the practical men who were gradually forced into active opposition to the Maoists. Sun Yeh-fang, director of the Institute of Economics of the Academia Sinica, ridiculed the Maoist slogan PUT POLITICS IN COMMAND! He characterized Maoist economic management in a few sentences:

"As soon as the Party lays hands on the economy, the economy dies—and the Party worries. When the Party worries, it relaxes its hold —and the economy falls into disorder. When the economy falls into disorder, the Party lays firm hands on the economy—and the cycle begins again."

Sun urged that fundamental economic processes be allowed to operate under central planning, but without political interference. Material incentives to work harder, he declared, were essential in a country that possessed a vast labor force, but limited capital equipment. Peasants and laborers would, under Sun's program, be rewarded for increasing production by bonuses and other benefits. At the same time, the central authorities would place primary responsibility for efficient performance upon local economic enterprises—and would grant their managers concomitant independence. When central authority ceased "binding the hands and feet of enterprises" and limited its taxes and other exactions to a fixed proportion of invested capital, agriculture and industry would produce efficiently. Since Sun's theories had proved themselves during the *laissez-faire* administration of 1961–65, they were anathema to the Maoists. They not only denied the commanding position of politics and deprecated the wisdom of the Party Center, but, further, implied that China could never become a major industrial power by her own efforts.

Moreover, small, immediate benefits were demonstrably much more stimulating to China's workingmen and farmers than was the promise of material abundance and national glory in the remote future. The working masses demonstrated that preference by their actions when Red Guards and other ideological zealots "invaded" industry and agriculture in late 1966 and early 1967. The intruders' instructions were appropriately elaborate and detailed, but their objective was relatively simple: break the anti-Maoist resistance by taking over its strongholds in the countryside and the factories.

The Maoists ordered the Red Guards to "carry the Cultural Revolution into mining, industry, and agriculture—and carry out the movement thoroughly." The economy, previously out of bounds, was to become the center of the struggle. The motivation was obvious. As *The Peking People's Daily* declared, the opposition "consider[ed] themselves the backbone of the Communist Party" and had organized their own "Red Guards," who were largely workers and farmers, to resist the directives of the Maoist Party Center. The traditional New Year's Day editorial of 1967 ordered all China "swept clean of the anti-Party, anti-Socialist men in power following the capitalist road."

A Red Guard report of a meeting in Peking on January 8, 1967, quoted the Chairman himself. Though apocryphal, it demonstrates how completely attitudes had changed. Mao Tse-tung, the Red Guards reported, said, "This man Tao Chu was introduced into the Party Center by [the Organizer] Teng Hsiao-ping, and I said from the start that this man Tao Chu was not trustworthy. . . . I did not solve the problem of Tao Chu, nor did the leadership. When the Red Guards rose in revolt, they solved the problem of Tao Chu."

The Red Guards also "solved the problem" of the political order they despised. They destroyed all functioning legal and administrative institutions. The total struggle for the future of China was met in the first weeks of January 1967, on the economic battlefield both sides had previously avoided for fear of devastating consequences. The reality exceeded their forebodings. The masses stood with their old cadres, and China was cast into a maelstrom of strikes, slowdowns, and sabotage that led to a major breakdown of transport, industry, and commerce, exacerbated, in turn, by armed skirmishes.

XVIII

The January Storm

Assessing their position as 1967 dawned, the extremists saw themselves further than ever from reclaiming power and imposing Utopia by fiat. A year had elapsed since *Red Flag* had demanded "total re-organization" of Chinese society on January 1, 1966—and 13 months had gone by since the Great Revolution opened with the vilification of the playwright Wu Han. Terror had forged a coherent opposition; the depredations of the Red Guards had performed the minor miracle of bringing together the masses and the working-level cadres. Mao Tse-tung's fear of the "recrudescence of capitalism" had proved as accurate as his prescription for the malaise was ineffective. Masses and cadres alike had, from 1961 to 1965, glimpsed the prospect of small luxuries like bicycles and radios, not to speak of an adequate and varied diet. During 1966, they had proved themselves more interested in "material incentives" than spiritual regeneration or world-wide "liberation."

If 1966 had been a bad year for all Chinese except the Red Guards, it had been shattering for the Maoists. Having mounted their counterattack to regain power in January 1966, they had been forced to the defensive by January 1967. The alliance of the Chairman and the Disciple had suffered a major defeat. Since they had neither broken their enemies' will nor destroyed the "strongholds of the men in power in the Party following the capitalist road," they were, in effect, losing. Time was running out. Unless they could win decisively in 1967, they might lose *all* power.

The Ghostwriter's *Red Flag,* echoed by *The People's Daily* and *The Liberation Army Daily,* proclaimed 1967 the year of "universal class struggle." Every Chinese was to be forced to a political decision for

288

the Chairman. Every Chinese was to prove his loyalty by "actively participating in the class struggle." Reluctance would automatically identify one as a "class enemy," for everyone who was not for the Maoists was implicitly against them. Except for scientists and technicians engaged in defense projects of "national importance," no one was exempt.

Though he had himself proclaimed the revolution in January 1966, the chief political commissar of the People's Liberation Army was purged. He was but an example of the testing and "rooting out" at all levels of the stratified society. At the top, Cabinet ministers and university presidents, provincial governors and directors of industrial complexes were to be removed if they did not surrender. The private in the ranks and the laborer on the construction site, the machinist at his bench and the farmer spreading nightsoil on his seedlings, the primary-school teacher and the overworked midwife at the lower levels were also to be torn from their tasks to "make revolution." "All revolutionary individuals," *The People's Daily* directed, "must assist our State organs of the dictatorship of the proletariat in safeguarding extensive proletarian democracy."

A vast network of informers and vigilantes was to enforce the new order. They were needed, Peking said, because the opposition had resisted the Red Guard with "murder, arson, poisoning, staged traffic accidents . . . traitorous relations with foreign countries [presumably the USSR and the Nationalist Republic of China], theft of state secrets, and sabotage." One man's crime was another's "just" resistance. The Maoist outcry proved the tenacity of the opposition the Disciple had aroused by imposing absolute conformity to the Thought of Chairman Mao—as interpreted by Lin Piao. *Red Flag* and *The People's Daily* directed: "We must make 1967 the year in which the proletariat launches a general offensive against the handful of individuals within the Party who are in authority and are taking the capitalist road—as well as against demons and monsters everywhere in our society."

It was quite a handful. The Maoist journals demonstrated the scope of the opposition by ordering: "Struggle against and overthrow all class enemies in factories, mines, and the rural areas. . . . Anyone who argues against thoroughly carrying out the large-scale Proletarian Revolution in factories, mines, and the rural areas is making a major error." Because labor, management, and the farmers opposed the Great Revolution, economic dislocation, for the first time, was candidly accepted as an unavoidable consequence of the overriding necessity to crush the opposition. Those who argued, "The Cultural Revolution will impede production!", were castigated for failing to PUT POLITICS IN COMMAND!

The Liberation Army Daily revealed obliquely that Defense Minister Lin Piao's control of the armed forces was imperiled by the military's distaste for Red Guard terror. Everyone from field marshal to private, the Army organ directed, must in 1967 redouble his concentration upon "political action and purifying his own thought." Absolute political reliability—that is, absolute obedience to Lin Piao—was the price of promotion, and the sole criterion for promotion. Many young officers, the Army was informed, would be advanced to higher ranks, while many older officers would be degraded. Senior officers were warned that they would be relieved if they did not display "revolutionary fervor" in thought, word, and deed. The Liberation Army was ordered to devote itself entirely to "politics and production." Both Great General Peng Teh-huai and Chief-of-Staff Lo Jui-ching, the Securityman turned "professional" general, had argued that diverting the armed forces to such nonmilitary tasks would radically reduce their effectiveness and make China vulnerable to foreign attack.

The extremists were fighting for their political lives. They could not allow themselves to be distracted from the mortal struggle by concern for effective national defense, public order, or economic needs. Their counterattack had met concerted resistance, and they were determined to break all resistance. *Red Flag* and *The People's Daily* stated unequivocally that 1967 would be "the year of the decisive victory of the Great Proletarian Cultural Revolution." The rump Party Center decided to cast the nation into total confusion rather than compromise with the moderates.

The executive officer of the Maoist cabal was caught on the wrong foot by the new and total offensive. The First Minister of Great Peace Premier Chou En-lai, the great compromiser, had joined the Maoists because he had no choice. His adherence was almost a reflex action, for his obsessive purpose through four decades of intra-Party struggle had always been survival. He had always set his course by the prevailing wind, rather than the destination. He could, of course, argue that he would lose all influence if he too were purged. Chou En-lai had therefore, quite consistently, joined the Maoist hue and cry, while still attempting to keep the Great Revolution within some rational limits.

Those limits were breached by the invasion of industry and agriculture, but the Minister of Peace showed no intention of following his close associate, the King of the South, into obscurity. Chou En-lai was strongly entrenched because he was the unique symbol of rational government to many Chinese and almost all foreigners; he was not identified with any single regional administration and therefore could not be held accountable for massive resistance in the provinces. Nonetheless, the new directives all compromised the First Minister.

He had repeatedly warned against allowing the Great Revolution to disrupt the economy, and the economy was deliberately cast into confusion. He embodied orderly administration, and orderly administration was specifically derided. He was the mentor of many of the senior generals of the Liberation Army, and those generals were to be sacrificed. He had told the Red Guards to halt their outrages, while returning "to make revolution" in their home places, and the Red Guards were invading areas from which they had previously been barred. He had used the Chairman's own words to instruct the Red Guards not to use force against "leading cadres," but the Red Guards were casting off the control of the Party Center. They had already "dragged out" the Mayor Peng Chen and the Securityman Lo Jui-ching for howling "mass trials."

Moreover, Chou En-lai had specifically told Red Guard leaders they must not "polarize" the conflict by "dragging out" the Campus Belle Wang Kwang-mei, who still lived with her husband, Comrade Liu Shao-chi, in their official residence in the Imperial City of Peking. But the Red Guards boasted of "entrapping" Wang Kwang-mei in a special issue of one of their tabloids. The style and content were both deeply revealing of the temper and the tantrums of the "little generals of disorder," who believed they were laying the foundation of a new society but were in fact, as subsequent developments have amply demonstrated, making all coherent social order impossible.

WANG KWANG-MEI CAPTURED BY RUSE
Foreword

As the notorious No. 1 "big pickpocket" of Chinghua University, Wang Kwang-mei should be subjected to examination and struggle. She should admit her guilt before 20 thousand revolutionary teachers, students, staff, and workers of Chinghua University.

However, on December 25—ten days after the delivery of our ultimatum—the slick and pretty "big pickpocket" did not show up. All our battle group were anxiously waiting for her to appear!

In order to protect Chairman Mao, boost the morale of the revolutionaries, prick the arrogance of the enemy, and comply with the eager demand of the vast numbers of revolutionary teachers, students, staff, and workers to have Wang Kwang-mei brought back for examination, we adopted the strategy of "drawing the snake out of its hole."

I. Prelude

At 2:30 p.m. on January 6, a jeep left the Chinghua Campus. An hour later, a big sedan car left the University compound. Passengers in the car sang lustily over and over these songs composed from *Quotations from Chairman Mao Tse-tung:*

"Resolute and unafraid of sacrifice, surmount
difficulties of all sorts to win victories."

"A revolution is not a dinner party, or writing
an essay, or painting a picture, or doing embroidery;
it cannot be so refined, so leisurely and gentle, so
temperate, kind, courteous, restrained and magnanimous.
A revolution is an insurrection, an act of violence
by which one class overthrows another."

That day, 40 persons of 6 combat groups of the Chinghua University
Battle Group . . . proceeded to three battlefields in preparation for
capturing Wang Kwang-mei by ruse.

The first car headed directly for the No. 1 Attached Middle School of
the Normal University, where Liu Ping-ping, Wang Kwang-mei's daughter, was conducting an open self-examination before the teachers and
students. The fighters then hit upon the idea of capturing Wang Kwang-
mei by detaining her daughter after she had finished her self-examination—and then informing her bourgeois mother that her daughter had
had a traffic accident on her way home—using this as a ruse to entice
Wang Kwang-mei to the hospital where her daughter was supposed to
be kept.

The second car took the fighters to the communications post and a
certain hospital. After the battle cry was raised, the fighters arriving at
the communications post immediately controlled the telephone switch-
board room to prevent Liu Shao-chi, the so-called "Model of the White
Areas," from telephoning the communications post to make inquiries
after he was told the bad news.

As the hospital was the center of the battle, complex class struggle
was to be unfolded there—a battlefield where Wang Kwang-mei, the
No. 1 "big pickpocket" of Chinghua Campus, was soon to be ensnared.

II. *The Curtain Rises on the Battle*

As dusk was gathering, the criticism rally in which Liu Ping-ping examined herself was concluded. Her schoolmates left the school compound one after another.

In one of the classrooms in that school, several fighters of Chinghua
University were talking things over with Liu Ping-ping.

As conversations slowly subsided, the ticking of the wall clock was
clearly audible. Three of the fighters muttered Chairman Mao's words of
exhortation: "Resolute and unafraid of sacrifice, surmount difficulties of
all sorts to win victories!"

"Start fighting!" The crisp battle cry was raised to break the prolonged
silence. The hands of the clock then indicated 18:10 hours.

"Hello, are you the parent of Liu Ping-ping? . . . This is the communications post calling. Your child Liu Ping-ping was knocked down by a car tonight near Hoping Gate. She suffered serious injuries. We have informed her school. She was taken to Peking XX Hospital. . . ."

"Hello, are you the parent of Liu Ping-ping? . . . This is the No. 1 Attached Middle School of the Normal University calling. We have just been informed by the communications post that Liu Ping-ping was knocked down by a car near Hoping Gate."

The two telephone calls sounded so increasingly urgent in tone that the first volley of capturing Wang Kwang-mei by ruse was fired successfully!

III. *Mobilizing Guards and Trying to Win Over*

Word that victory had been won in the first battle fought in the No. 1 Attached Middle School of the Normal University greatly cheered the spirits of those fighters who stood guard at the XX Hospital. With the help of the revolutionary comrades of that hospital, all 12 telephone instruments in the hospital were taken over by the fighters. Members of our Corps posted at the casualty ward were waiting for the "visitor" who was expected to come soon. Our men in plain clothes guarded all approaches to that hospital.

Quite contrary to our expectations, an Army man between 30 and 40 years old and a young girl of 14 or 15 entered the hospital hurriedly. The man was Comrade Li, one of Liu Shao-chi's guards, and the young girl was Liu's daughter, Liu Ting-ting. They were visiting Liu Ping-ping at the hospital.

"Has Ping-ping been taken here?" Liu Ting-ting asked.

"No," replied the nurse.

"Well. . . ." Both Ting-ting and the soldier appeared lost.

Turning around, the Army man quickly walked to the telephone, ready to inform Wang Kwang-mei. When he was dialing the last figure, one of our fighters who stood beside the telephone put his hand on the cradle, saying:

"This is for emergency only! You mustn't use it. Follow me to that side."

"Are you standing on the side of Chairman Mao or on that of Liu Shao-chi?" our fighter asked.

"Of course, I am standing on the side of Chairman Mao."

"Would you prefer to be a revolutionary in words only or in deeds as well?"

"A revolutionary in deeds."

"Well, then, prove yourself by action."

After discussing the matter for a while, we decided to detain him before trying to win over 14-year-old Ting-ting. Turning to Liu Ting-ting, we said:

"You should rebel against your father and mother, Ting-ting!"

After our persuading Liu Ting-ting to rebel against her parents, she ultimately yielded.

Lifting the telephone and dialing her house number, Liu Ting-ting talked to her mother:

"Mom, Ping-ping's left leg is injured, and the doctor says he has to operate on her."

"What has happened? How bad is the injury?" Wang Kwang-mei asked in anxious tones. Her sobbing was heard on the telephone. "Let me talk to the doctor, quick!"

Taking the telephone, our doctor said:

"Hello, she is in bad shape. The joint is broken. We are all set to take her to the operating room. Hospital regulations require the parent to sign his or her approval. . . ."

"Wouldn't it be all right for Ting-ting to sign?" Wang Kwang-mei said with a trembling voice.

The doctor handed the telephone to Ting-ting so she could say a few words.

"Mom, Mom," Ting-ting said. But Wang Kwang-mei was already gone.

From the other end of the telephone line came this startling news.

"Be prepared for combat action!"

IV. *Liu Shao-chi Hoodwinked and Wang Kwang-mei Captured*

At about 20:00 hours a small sedan came to a halt at the entrance to the hospital.

"What, Liu Shao-chi!" It hadn't occurred to the fighters' Corps that Liu Shao-chi—one who was "experienced in struggling against others in the White Area"—would fall into the trap. Then, Wang Kwang-mei alighted from the car.

Liu Shao-chi had swollen eyes and so had Wang Kwang-mei. She occasionally wiped her nose with a handkerchief. Perhaps she had cried bitterly over her daughter's injuries!

"Where is Ping-ping?" Liu Shao-chi asked bluntly.

"We have been hoodwinked! They want to seize Wang Kwang-mei!" The Soldier, Liu Ying-chen (Liu Shao-chi's son) who had come a little later, and another man, whom Ting-ting called uncle and who resembled Liu Shao-chi, said in loud voices almost simultaneously.

"No. 1 big pickpocket of Chinghua Campus Wang Kwang-mei is to stay, but all the others may go back!"

Tearfully, Wang Kwang-mei stepped forward and said in a pitiful manner: "Very well, I shall go with the Chinghua schoolmates, and you may all go back!"

In an angry but apprehensive mood, Liu Shao-chi turned back and left.

Knowing that she could not get away, Wang Kwang-mei collapsed onto the bench like a deflated balloon. Her left hand supporting her cheek, she said: "Let me calm down. . . ." Completely betraying her fears, she acted as if she wanted to ask forgiveness or to play new tricks.

"Follow us to Chinghua!"

After walking a few steps, Wang Kwang-mei sat on the muddy staircase, saying: "Let's talk terms. . . . Please sit down." Pointing to the staircase, she asked us to take a seat there too.

"Aren't you going to Chinghua?!" We knew that this was going to be a serious round of class struggle.

"Negotiations. . . . Let us study the supreme directives first . . ."

A really sly woman, Wang Kwang-mei stood pat and would not move an inch. At this moment, more and more people gathered around her to watch the antics of this "lady."

Wang Kwang-mei had committed towering crimes at Chinghua University. The more she wanted to deny them, the more irritated we became.

Chairman Mao teaches us: "Revolution is not a dinner party . . . it cannot be so refined . . ."

Therefore, our fighters protected her while urging her to rise and go to Chinghua University. With the help of other revolutionary comrades who were on hand, Wang Kwang-mei was eventually taken to the waiting jeep.

The car door closed with a bang. Almost at the same time, the jeep drove on.

V. *Finale*

As the jeep was speeding along the motor road, the "lady" who a moment ago was pulling a long face and insisted on not going to Chinghua University now said with a smile:

"In which department of the university are you people?"

"We are from a number of departments!" One of the unidentifiable fighters replied coldly.

"What about you, a bit frightened?" another fighter asked with a trace of scorn.

"Oh, no! You have done something very dramatic. But you made a slip in the hospital's telephone . . ."

"Then why did you still show up?"

"Well, as soon as I got word that Ping-ping had been knocked down, I couldn't care about anything else!"

At about 10:00 p.m. Wang was taken to the platform on the western campus of Chinghua University. Wearing the cotton-padded shoes of one of our schoolmates, she began to repay the debt to our revolutionary teachers and students of the school amid shouts of "Down with Liu Shao-chi!" and "Down with [the Organizer] Teng Hsiao-ping!"

Comrade Liu Shao-chi was still beyond the Red Guards' reach, but his wife was not. Although the Red Guards already flouted the orders of the official Party Center, they still dared not "seize" Comrade Shao-chi himself. But someone—probably the Starlet herself—had ordered the humiliation of the Campus Belle. Since the means, however foul, were justified by the end, however obscure, the "fighters" boasted of exploiting her maternal concern in order to win a pallid "victory." Wang Kwang-mei made a brief promise after ten hours of "persuasion."

Wang Kwang-mei's Four-point Pledge

First, out of their deep-seated hatred for the bourgeois reactionary line of the Liu-Teng group, some revolutionary teachers and students of Chinghua University have dragged me out for examination. This revolutionary action is very good and has my support.

Second, I am ready to remain at Chinghua to conduct repeated self-examinations before all revolutionary teachers, students, staff, and workers of the University until my self-examination is acceptable to them.

Third, I am willing to bring to light all that I know of Comrade Liu Shao-chi. Beginning January 10, 1967, I shall send over a copy of material based on my self-examination and exposure [of Liu Shao-chi] every ten days without delay. This chiefly concerns data exposing the bourgeois reactionary line espoused by Comrade Liu Shao-chi in the light of political and organizational lines. Things pertaining to his daily life and moral character will also be brought to light—and nothing will be held back.

Fourth, if I am taken to Chungnanhai [the official residence], I am ready to return to Chinghua any time revolutionary teachers and students there want me to.

Wang Kwang-mei (s)
5:00 a.m.
January 7, 1967

The incident of the night of January 6 and 7 was not Wang Kwang-mei's first ordeal. It was not to be the last. Her ultimate humiliation was reserved for April 1967, when her husband was also "dragged out." Nonetheless, the "exposure" of the Campus Belle was, in January 1967, still concealed from the outside world. Much greater events were in train. The workers and peasants of China had finally revolted against the "rebel revolutionary faction" of Chairman Mao Tse-tung and the Disciple, Lin Piao.

Shanghai, China's greatest port, was the center of the storm that rose in major cities and soon battered the countryside as well. Waves of general strikes, absenteeism, protest demonstrations, and sabotage led to widespread fighting between contending factions. The "January Storm" was so violent that the Maoists were forced to make fuller revelation than they had at any time in the past. Official statements, "great-character posters," and Red Guard tabloids reported the struggle in Shanghai in minute detail. The entire Shanghai Municipal Committee of the Communist Party turned against the Mao-Lin faction, as had the Peking Municipal Committee under the Mayor Peng Chen eight months earlier.

According to Chang Chün-chiao, later chief of the Shanghai "rebel* government," the opposition had organized the workers and cadres so well that their activists were as numerous as the "rebel revolutionaries" at the beginning of 1967. "The two factions were equally matched in strength," Chang reported subsequently, "explaining why massive armed clashes between them were rife." Actually, by Chang's own figures, the Workers' Rebels Headquarters was 50 to 60 thousand strong, while the opposition's Workers' Scarlet Sentinels claimed a following of 80 thousand. Chang Chün-chiao wrote:

> I recall going to Shanghai on January 4th [1967] with Comrade Yao Wen-yüan [the Literary Assassin]. The old Municipal Party Committee had been paralyzed. Many factories, including vital industrial plants, had stopped production. When the critical Kaohsiao Chemical Works halted work, many other plants stopped production. The piers and railways were also immobilized, causing severe dislocation. . . . Under these circumstances, the old Municipal Party Committee had resorted to "economism" to corrupt and split the rebels among the workers.

A new term had appeared in the Maoist lexicon: "Economism" was the deliberate appeal to the masses' self-interest offered by the resurgent opposition. The "old power-holders" did not exhort workers and farm-

* The terms "rebel," "rebel revolutionaries," and "leftists" all refer to the Maoists, even when they actually hold power. I have followed the Chinese usage, though it may occasionally confuse the reader, because any other usage would be even more confusing.

ers to toil for the Thought of Mao Tse-tung or incalculable benefits for future generations. Instead, the pragmatists offered the working masses a greater share of the fruits of their own toil. The attraction was almost irresistible to men and women whom the Maoists exhorted to ceaseless sacrifice to make China a great power, to consolidate the Maoist *imperium,* and to "emancipate" all mankind. Self-exploitation for such abstractions had lost all idealistic appeal to the "self-conscious proletariat" of Shanghai. Hope, deferred time and time again, had turned to sour cynicism. Therefore the urban proletariat and the rural masses responded with alacrity to the immediate material benefits they received from the opposition. They had already learned to expect more consideration from the "working-level" cadres who had presided over rehabilitation after the Great Leap Forward. In any event, the material incentives the Maoists called "sugar-coated bullets" effectively rallied the laboring masses against the adolescent Red Guards.

The strategy of the opposition was simple and obvious. Industrial and transportation workers were given higher wages, more holidays, shorter workdays, and increased fringe benefits, as well as bonuses for increased production. The purpose was, after all, economic as well as political. The moderates, damned as "conservatives" by the Maoists, felt that production would increase sharply if labor worked harder to win a greater share of increased production. Economist Sun Yeh-fang had advanced that thesis, only to be damned by the extremists for "encouraging the recrudescence of capitalism." The pragmatists realized that the State's share would initially decrease—absolutely as well as proportionally. But the moderates felt that exploitation of the people was self-defeating. While deliberately rallying the workers' political support by "economism," they confidently expected that the State would shortly benefit from greatly increased production.

The same inducements were offered to farmers, who were as angered as the workers by the induced frenzies of the Cultural Revolution. The intricate accounting, costing, and "work-point" systems of the decadent Great People's Communes made "economism" a highly complex process in the countryside. The Maoists had rendered the farmers highly receptive to the siren song by demanding that they labor unceasingly for the "collective good" without thought of personal benefit. In any event, the farmers were petty bourgeoisie by strict Marxist definition, for their dearest wish was to own their land, livestock, and tools. The opposition was not prepared to revert to the halcyon days just after Land Reform had distributed land to the peasants—and before collectivization had confiscated that land. Only rarely did they actually attempt to redistribute the land, although they often promised to do so. But they employed many other means to win the allegiance of the countryside.

Local cadres increased the farmers' "share-out" of Communal production, while reducing taxes and "contributions" to the State. The
Communes themselves retained a greatly increased proportion of their
crop—and used the wealth to improve living and working conditions.
"Private plots" allotted families during the relative *laissez-faire* of
1961–65 were confirmed and sometimes enlarged. The peasants were
permitted to sell their "private" produce in "free markets" for their own
profit. Infant "free enterprise" appeared. Not only farmers but small
merchants and handicraftsmen worked for their own gain. The results
were twofold: increased production and a tidal flow of loyalty toward
the moderates.

The Disciple was on the verge of decisive defeat. The tough longshoreman and railway workers of Shanghai, proud of their skill and
independence, led the resistance, and other workers followed. They and
their fathers had already proved their mettle—and their devotion to the
Communist cause—many times. In 1927, they had held the port for the
joint Nationalist-Communist Revolutionary Army marching against the
"northern warlords" and the "foreign imperialist capitalists"—until their
Workers' Militia was broken by Generalissimo Chiang Kai-shek. They
had organized the anti-Japanese boycott in the 1930s and had waged a
"fierce underground struggle" against the Nationalists until the Communist "liberation" in 1949. Once again in 1967, the workers swarmed
into the streets, backed by disillusioned students and commanded by
their own cadres. They seized key governmental offices and communications facilities; they took over transport and industrial complexes. For a
time, the old Shanghai Municipal Committee of the Communist Party
once again administered the restive metropolis.

The counterrevolt in the cities had been precipitated by the unrestrained Red Guards. The adolescent "generals of disorder" had ignored
instructions to return to their homes—defying even the imperative order
to all out-of-town Red Guards to leave the capital. In Shanghai in
mid-December, they had occupied newspaper and radio offices, vital
public utilities, and both Government and Party bureaus for a full week.
They had effectively destroyed all orderly administration in China's
largest city—and had aroused the hearty resentment of the proletariat.
They had, further, precipitated the break between extremists and practical administrators within the Maoist faction. Even in mid-December,
Red Flag, still nominally supervised by the King of the South, had
spoken with two voices. The journal had simultaneously pleaded for
reconciliation among factions and further attacks on the "handful of
men in power within the Party following the capitalist road." The King
had apparently been purged because he opposed violation of the tacit
agreement between the opposing factions to avoid widespread violence

and to leave the economy untouched. With the King's abdication, all limits had been abrogated.

A personal tale may serve better than detached narrative to describe the development of the Red Guard movement in Shanghai from its beginning to the violence of the January Storm. A highly intelligent and sensitive 25-year-old leader of the "little generals of disorder" was a student of physics at the Shanghai Normal University until the Great Revolution suspended all education. He told his tale in Hong Kong after he had been transformed from an ardent participant in the Maoist movement by the events he saw and the deeds he did.

When the Cultural Revolution began formally in Shanghai in August 1966, the target of struggle was neither the Municipal Party Committee nor officials of the Government's organs. The chief target was the city's cultural leaders.

About September 12, 1966, almost a million Red Guards from out of town arrived in Shanghai to "exchange revolutionary experiences." The first lot had letters of introduction from their own units, and the Party Center had instructed us to provide them with money, as well as accommodation in our schools. But many of the later ones had no letters of introduction, and they wandered aimlessly about the city in throngs, tying up traffic and creating a food shortage.

There was a fixed ration for each person, but those Red Guards had nation-wide ration cards, and they didn't care if no provision had been made to feed them in Shanghai. What they wanted to buy, they bought, creating a very tight situation and long queues. Some parents were unable to queue up and sent their student children—most of them Red Guards themselves—to buy food. When the out-of-town Red Guards wanted to buy things, the local Red Guards stopped them, demanding that they go to the Municipal Committee to work things out. They should not, the local Red Guards said, casually appropriate goods intended for the citizens of Shanghai.

These disputes led to arguments and fist fights.

Other out-of-town Red Guards just barged into hotels, like the Peace Hotel, which was reserved for foreign guests with admission only by order of the Overseas Chinese Affairs Commission. When the out-of-town Red Guards moved in and demanded food, the staff asked them to leave. They refused flatly, and the staff threw them out. Again, there were big fights when the local Red Guards came out to assist the staff of hotels against the out-of-towners. At the Peace Hotel alone, ten of a staff of 300 were severely injured.

In the beginning, violence was usually restricted to fights among the

Red Guards themselves. But, after a while, the Shanghai workers also reacted, largely because the traffic tie-ups prevented their getting to and from work.

The leaders of the Municipal Committee wanted to get the out-of-town Red Guards out of town. So they used "economism," sending a workers' delegation to Peking to ask for relief. The workers were given slips allowing them to finance their trips by drawing on the profits of their factories held in bank accounts. The banking regulations provided that deposits could be withdrawn only with permission of the Factory and Municipal Party Committees, so the Municipal Committee issued the proper documents, and money was drawn upon until it was exhausted. This prodigality created definite economic problems.

When the workers got to Peking, they found they couldn't get the interviews they sought. They reported their frustration to Shanghai, and the Shanghai Municipal Committee made representations. The workers paraded in front of the Cabinet Offices to ask that Chou En-lai come out and talk with them. Finally, Lin Piao himself came out to see them and promised to send a team to Shanghai to investigate the situation.

After the workers returned to Shanghai, the Party Center sent Chang Chün-chiao to Shanghai to investigate—and the Anting Incident followed. The workers' delegation to Peking had been made up primarily of men from the large Anting Radio Parts Factory.

The Shanghai Municipal Committee had a very bad impression of Chang Chün-chiao. They said he was a "political pickpocket" and an opportunist, who had no real knowledge or convictions.

When Chang Chün-chiao reached Anting, he should have been received with honors. But the workers were all opposed to him. He wanted to make a statement, but they gave him no opportunity. They felt that Chang's knowledge of Marxism was shallow and considered it insulting that a man like him had been sent to them as a representative of the Party Center to "solve their problems." They tore down the loudspeakers at the station to prevent his speaking, because, they said, his propaganda had nothing to do with the Rebel Faction. The women workers, who were rightists sympathizers, shouted insults at Chang Chün-chiao.

One small group belonging to the Mao-Lin faction later issued a statement saying that the treatment of Chang Chün-chiao was a Fascist, counterrevolutionary incident, but many workers and students opposed their statement. The extreme Red Guards said the reception was Fascist behavior, but we said the actions of the proletarian power-holders could not be called Fascist. The statement led to nearly two months of debate, but in the end the group that had issued the statement acknowledged that they had gone too far—and the consequences of the Anting Incident subsided.

Chang Chün-chiao remained in Shanghai, and every day hundreds of great-character posters attacked him. Two distinct groups spoke out, one against and one for Chang. Their essential composition was much the same. The most numerous were workers, administrative cadres, and people from academic and artistic circles. It was clear that those opposed to Chang were the majority. The regular Municipal Committee was not attacked.

Also, sometime in the first part of January 1967, the *Wen-hui Pao* and *The Liberation Daily* issued an Appeal to the People of Shanghai—and proclaimed the establishment of the Shanghai Revolutionary Committee and its seizure of power [from the regular Municipal Committee]. After the take over, the Shanghai Red Guards [in distinction to the out-of-town Red Guards] rose to oppose Chang Chün-chiao's intervention because he had on the evening of the seventh or eighth [of January 1967] issued a Proclamation in the name of the Municipal Committee directing them to return to their schools, while the Scarlet Sentinels were to go back to their factories, without returning home.

Therefore, on the day after the power seizure was proclaimed, the students and workers were extremely dissatisfied. They were particularly angry because they felt they had been deceived when Chang told them to wait a day for an important Central announcement—and then seized power himself. We felt we had witnessed a political farce in that take over.

Sometime after the tenth, one of the Red Guard groups, which called itself the Fighters for the Doctrine, published an article in a Red Guard tabloid urging an attack on Chang Chün-chiao's residence. On the evening of the fifteenth or the sixteenth, three of our schoolmates were in the groups who broke into Chang's house. Two were Overseas Chinese, and one was a student-cadre of the Physics Department. They had personally decided that Chang represented a problem and, in protracted discussions, they urged our Red Guard unit to oppose him. Then the entire unit rose, well organized after three days of preparation, and set up a mass rendezvous for eight in the evening at the Shanghai People's Park. They climbed into cars and set out to attack Chang Chün-chiao at his residence.

The weather was fine, clear, and cold that evening when they arrived at Chang's house in the vicinity of Sun Yat-sen Park at about nine o'clock. They first cut the telephone wires so that he couldn't call the Public Security Office. Then they attacked, determined to drag Chang Chün-chiao out, parade him through the streets—and remove him from his offices. After breaking in, they couldn't find Chang, so they just smashed his furniture, burst open every door in the house, and examined every document.

But one of his staff escaped and called the Public Security Office from an outside phone. When the Public Security Police arrived to control the demonstration, the Red Guards heard their sirens in the distance and fled. As a result, only 10 were arrested.

After the assault on Chang's house, one student of our Chinese Department and another of the Mechanical Engineering Department of Tungchi University wrote a report on the incident. Because they were highly critical and attacked the incident as a "counterrevolutionary manifestation," the students who had participated were infuriated! They said they had only acted for the benefit of the masses because Chang's activities were contrary to the people's wishes.

We decided to revenge ourselves in order to teach the students of Tungchi University not to talk nonsense. So we beat them up.

The Tungchi students felt they were activist elements because they stood with the Revolutionary Municipal Committee [which had displaced the regular Municipal Committee of the Communist Party]. That evening, our entire class went to the homes of the students who had offended. But the students of Tungchi were also holding a meeting in a primary school. We knew where and when they were meeting and decided to break it up. There were about 60 of them, and we were about 200, about 100 from the Physics Department. The rest were several score from our own school and a score or so from other schools.

We ourselves didn't want a fight, though some of the others did. About nine, when the meeting was just finishing, our preparations were complete. We waited for them to come out and jumped them without saying a word. Every time we struck someone down, we told him that he was engaging in counterrevolutionary activity and ordered him to change his ways. After we had beaten quite a number, some of the local people called the Public Security Force. The hundred-odd who had done the fighting thereupon fled, and the rest of us came out into the open to help the injured students by bandaging their wounds. When the police arrived, the battle was over. They asked what was going on, and we said we'd just arrived to help the injured. They asked what school had launched the attack, but we said we didn't know. Really it was peculiar. We started out to beat them up and ended by succoring them.

The confusion of loyalty and ideology among the Red Guards was duplicated among the workers. In each case, personal antagonisms arising from the "class struggle" beclouded the fundamental issues. Nonetheless, the sharp division into two camps became more pronounced as the struggle developed. The same student leader also described the fighting among the workers.

About November 1966, the first strike occurred on the railway line
from the North Station to the Woosung District because many of the
trains on that line were specials for workers of the Shanghai Number
Three Iron and Steel Works. Every day, great numbers of out-of-town
Red Guards decided to take trips to Woosung, and they crowded the
carriages far beyond the permitted number. Since they refused to alight,
the train couldn't start. So the workers went on strike—half because
they couldn't help it. In December, almost all the Shanghai Railway
workers went on strike. They refused to carry Red Guards to Shanghai,
saying they had to think of the well-being of the citizens.

From the 1st to the 5th of January, the fighting in Shanghai was
very fierce, primarily because of the reaction against the out-of-town
Red Guards. For instance, there was the incident when the out-of-town
Red Guards wanted the railway workers to return to work and the
workers refused. The out-of-town Red Guards thereupon marched upon
the new settlement that had been built for the railway workers. There
was a middle school there specially for the children of the workers, and
the Red Guards of that school naturally stood with their fathers. They
said: "You out-of-town types have created such turmoil in Shanghai
that the whole place is a mess—and even getting enough food has become a major problem."

Then there was a series of fights between the two groups of Red
Guards. Each time, several hundred were involved on each side, and the
fighting went on for about 10 days.

The Shanghai Waterworks Union went on strike to protest the sending
of Red Guards from Peking armed with orders from the Task Force
of the Cultural Revolution and the Party Center to suppress the workers'
movement. The Red Guards demanded first that the Workers' Self-
Defense Corps turn over its arms to them, and they pulled down the
Party Secretary of the Waterworks, who was supported by the great
majority of workers as a good and honest man. Although the workers
said the Party organization should not be touched, the out-of-town Red
Guards attacked the Party units the very first thing.

After the big strike started at the Waterworks, the workers of electric
generating facilities also went on strike. In part, they struck in sympathy
with the workers of the Waterworks and the railways. But, besides that,
the railways couldn't deliver coal for the generators. And, in addition,
the electricity workers wanted improvement in their working and living
conditions, which were the worst of all the workers' groups. Their allow-
ances were the lowest, and the time they had to devote to reading political works [i.e., the Maoist classics] was the greatest of all the workers.
They demanded that the number of political meetings be reduced and
that their compulsory study of politics be cut back. They struck for

about two days, starting about the eighth, and then Red Guards began arriving with representatives of the Revolutionary Committee to demand that they get back to work. But all the workers didn't resume their tasks, and a number of student and worker Red Guards had to do part of the job.

The Liberation Army and the Public Security Forces did not really interfere in the strikes. They didn't go to the workers' homes and force them back to work.

About January 6th and 7th, the workers marched on the headquarters of the new authorities of the Municipal Revolutionary Committee on Foochow Street to ask that their grievances be remedied. The Revolutionary Committee stalled them, and the language of both sides became violent. The workers took the National Constitution as their authority. They said the Constitution guaranteed the people's right of free assembly and free speech. Therefore, they argued, neither the strikes nor the assembly [before the Committee's offices] were illegal, but were, rather, quite legal and quite reasonable.

The Revolutionary Committee didn't merely reject those arguments, but put forward an entirely different point of view in order to suppress the workers. As a result, the workers became furious and swore at the Committee's spokesmen: "You claim you've seized power. Now we'll seize your power!"

The Revolutionary Committee had a detachment of about 50 or 60 security guards, who fired at the workers from inside the building. In the beginning, they didn't aim to hit, but shot at the ground in front of the workers' ranks. The Workers' Scarlet Sentinels also carried arms, and they fired into the air in order to warn the security guards and get them to cease fire.

As soon as the shooting stopped, the workers broke into the building, so that the security guards had to open fire again. They shot down five workers—and the Scarlet Sentinels returned the fire. The battle was fierce, and every window of the headquarters of the Revolutionary Committee was shattered.

The Public Security Force headquarters sent their men to surround the workers. But they didn't arrest anyone, because the Committee telephoned the Public Security Headquarters: "Just disperse the workers. Don't pursue them."

In all, during this period, at least 50 percent of the Shanghai factories and plants went on strike. Of the heavy industrial plants, almost all struck—and the economic consequences were grave.

By the end of January, Shanghai was almost entirely under military control, but there was no military administration, as such. The troops merely broke up the fights, moving in whenever they saw something starting. However, they didn't interfere with internal problems in the plants, nor did they touch the roots of the fighting.

The impressionistic, personal account was borne out by official statements. Public and private statements led to the same conclusions.

The first result of the opposition's counterattack was the Maoists' losing control of major centers of power—and finding even their possession of Peking was disrupted. For the first time, the word which was to become the obligato of the Cultural Revolution was prevalent. China was on the verge of true *anarchy*.* The Maoists had succeeded better than they dreamed—or desired—in "destroying the old world," and the new world of *extensive democracy* modeled after the Paris Commune was *not* taking shape. The enemy too, it was manifest, could use violence, insubordination, and disruption for his own purposes.

The opposition counterattacked with strikes and attacks on the same key centers the Red Guards had seized. In Nanking as well as Shanghai, the Communist Party organs supported the workers' revolt, when they did not lead it. Although cordons of armed troops maintained control of the essential radio stations for the Maoists, they were islands in a hostile sea. The military and, particularly, the Public Security Forces tended toward neutrality or cautious support of the old power-holders. The opposition in Shanghai responded to the Maoist attempt to suppress their "mass organizations" by a virtual general strike. From the fourth through the ninth of January 1967, communications and transport were paralyzed, while electricity and water supplies were available only sporadically. Industrial production dwindled to insignificance owing to strikes and the lack of both power and raw materials. The docks all but ceased functioning, though soldiers and Red Guards tried to do the work of the longshoremen. Railroad connections with the rest of the country were cut. Red Shanghai became White Shanghai.

The first appeal to return to work was issued by eleven *ad hoc* organizations hastily created by Chang Chün-chiao and the Literary Assassin Yao Wen-yüan. Those organizations, self-appointed to rule China's largest city, declared: "Recently in a great many factories, economic enterprises, and productive facilities, a number—indeed, a very great number—of Scarlet Sentinels have halted production . . ." The new Revolutionary Committee appealed to the "misguided workers" to return to their "production posts" and promised they would not be punished by their "class brothers" if they obeyed immediately. "But," the extremists warned, "the instigators will be uprooted and dealt the most severe punishment under proletarian dictatorship."

* In Chinese, highly evocatively rendered as *wu-cheng-fu-chu-yi*, literally, "no governmentism."

The appeal was broadcast to the entire nation on January 8, 1967, by the Central Radio Station of Peking. Shanghai was, quite clearly, the vanguard of a nation-wide movement, for Peking declared: "This is a matter of the greatest gravity, which could have profound consequences on the development of the Great Proletarian Cultural Revolution throughout East China—and, indeed, in every city and province of China." The Maoists had been driven to bay in almost every major city of the vast country.

In Fukien Province, opposite Nationalist-held Formosa, a local broadcast admitted that the Communist Party had split irrevocably into two hostile factions. "There is," Fukien admitted, "no effective control." The official press and radio were not quite as candid in reporting disorder in Nanking, 175 miles from Shanghai, the Southern Capital of the Empire and the Nationalists. But "great-character posters" and tabloids issued by both sides described major armed clashes in Nanking. More than 50 persons were killed, and several hundred were injured in fighting that lasted a full week. The opposition cut off all communication with the rest of the country and virtually ruled Nanking during the period. The *coup* was suppressed only by armed force. During the same period, the two factions fought for control of the Public Security Headquarters in Canton, the metropolis of the south.

Despite the Maoist counterattack, Shanghai itself remained in a state of internal siege, with pitched battles fought in the streets. On the eleventh of January, the Maoists issued three revealing statements. The first was the Urgent Proclamation of the Shanghai Workers' Revolutionary Rebel Headquarters, composed of 32 newly formed organizations —some as remote as the Shanghai Branch of the Peking Aeronautical Institute and all outside the normal structure of the Communist Party and the People's Government. The second was a nation-wide appeal issued by the Cabinet of the Central Government in conjunction with three Party groups: the Central Committee, the Military Affairs Commission, and the Task Force of the Cultural Revolution. The weight of those mighty institutions all applied to a single city, however important, was explained by the third document, a joint editorial of the Shanghai *Wen-hui Pao* and *Liberation Daily,* just "recaptured" by force from the "reactionaries."

The three statements, read in conjunction, depicted chaos. The Urgent Proclamation declared that the Party's Shanghai Municipal Committee was rallying for "fresh counterattacks on the economic front . . . after having been totally overthrown." The entire Municipal Committee, the Proclamation declared, was "stubbornly following the capitalist road." The Revolutionary Rebel Headquarters issued a 10-point directive for resistance to the Municipal Committee. "Revolutionary rebels" who had left Shanghai to "carry the revolution throughout the country" were ordered to return to fight for control of their native city. The Headquarters further appealed to "revolutionary rebels" elsewhere to march on Shanghai to join the struggle, while, at the same time, promising the workers that their economic grievances would be considered "once the struggle is over." The workers were ordered to vacate "within a week" all the premises they had occupied. All financial institutions were to be returned to "revolutionary rebel" control immediately, for they were sustaining the revolt by paying out vast funds to the workers. Finally, the Proclamation demanded that the Public Security Forces obey the orders of the Rebel Headquarters, rather than the opposition.

The nation-wide appeal from Peking endorsed the Shanghai proclamation. It further ordered "the entire nation . . . the Party, the Government, the Army, all citizens, the workers, the farmers, revolutionary students, and intellectuals . . . to unite and hurl back the counterattack mounted by the capitalist, counterrevolutionary, reactionary force."

The two Shanghai newspapers explicitly confirmed the extent of the struggle. "The influence of the bourgeois, reactionary line," they declared, "is far-reaching, and its poison has spread far and wide. . . . The reactionaries have suppressed the masses and mounted attacks on the revolutionary young Red Guards in the most sinister and venomous manner. They have demoralized both the masses and the Red Guards— and have hoodwinked them into collaborating [with the opposition]."

The Maoist pacification campaign was not successful. Shanghai continued confused and violent, as statements throughout January disclosed. Moreover, the example of Shanghai, presumably broadcast by Peking for hortatory purposes, instead evoked emulation. From Canton, from Foochow, and from Manchuria came fresh reports of proletarian uprisings against the Maoists. In Canton the pattern of Shanghai was repeated all but verbatim. On January 17, 1967, the Canton Red Guard Self-Defense Corps Headquarters issued an Urgent Proclamation exhorting "revolutionary workers, students, cadres, and farmers to be thoroughly alert to crush the new counterattack by the counterrevolutionaries." The Proclamation declared that anti-Maoist elements had "incited cadres of the Central-South Regional Bureau [the stronghold of Tao Chu, the King of the South], the Kwangtung Provincial Committee, and the Canton Municipal Committee of the Communist Party to desert their posts." Most "reception stations for Red Guards" were closed by force.

"The anti-Party group," the Canton Urgent Proclamation continued, "has also encouraged the masses to rob and burgle, to wreck vehicles belonging to the rebel faction, to wildly distribute handbills containing poisonous propaganda, and to assault the police. Workers have walked

out of factories, and have fought youth groups of the rebel faction."
Eyewitness reports from Canton confirmed the strikes and disorder.

On January 18, 1967, the nation-wide appeal from Peking revealed
that the struggle had spilled out of the cities into the countryside—and
was threatening the nation's food supplies. Not only thousands of cities
and provincial towns had become battlefields, but also the broad rural
areas, where more than half a billion peasants lived. The farmers not
only formed themselves into anti-Maoist organizations, but devoured
Communal food and spent Communal funds in an orgy of consumption.
Some deserted their work, leaving the winter crops standing unharvested
in the fields. Vegetables, pork, eggs, and chickens intended for the cities
piled up in the countryside—and rotted.

The Peking broadcast quoted a letter to the Shanghai *Liberation
Daily,* purportedly written by "the leading accountants of an agricultural
People's Commune" in the city's suburbs. The battle for Shanghai was
far from over, the letter revealed, because "revisionist, reactionary
elements are still strong in the city." The apocryphal accountants reported that the peasants had been "won over and seduced through
economism by the class enemy." The "year-end share-out" of the Commune's earnings was entirely divided among the peasants. Nothing was
saved for the State. The anti-Maoists adeptly used Maoist slogans. The
peasants were urged to practice "rebellion . . . extensive democracy
. . . and uniting with the masses." As a result, "the winter crop has
been destroyed and fertilizer distribution is at a standstill, as is movement of food to the city." The Maoist Appeal urged the "rebel revolutionaries" to unite against the "class enemy," because the opposition *was
uniting* throughout the country. If resistance in the rural areas had not
been a national problem, Peking would not have broadcast the Shanghai
appeal.

Confirmation of armed revolt in the countryside came on January 20,
1967, in a broadcast from Kiangsi Province which revealed a crisis as
immediately acute as Shanghai's—and potentially disastrous. The peasantry of that vital province rose against the Maoists and organized their
own army under the command of anti-Maoist "old-line" cadres. The
Kiangsi rising was revealed by an Urgent Proclamation calling on "rebel
revolutionaries" to rally to defeat the anti-Maoist forces. Sensational
enough in itself, it substantiated persistent unofficial reports of peasant
risings of varying intensity in other provinces. At the very least, similar
revolts occurred in Szechwan in the southwest, Sinkiang in the northwest, several provinces of Manchuria, and Fukien on the coast.

The Proclamation revealed that the revolt had been most efficiently
organized by the "local power-holders," the anti-Maoist cadres of the
regular Communist Party of Kiangsi. The majority of the county, munic-

ipal, and local Committees of the Party, under the leadership of the Provincial Party Committee, had set up their own East Is Red Struggle Corps to command the Workers' Scarlet Sentinels. They then organized the August First Battle Corps, made up primarily of discharged soldiers, already trained in the use of arms. From that Corps sprang the Peasants' Red Army, which numbered perhaps 60 thousand.

Reinforced by recruits from other provinces, the new Kiangsi Red Army spread across the province after seizing the capital, Nanchang. The Proclamation complained that the anti-Maoists had "inaugurated White terror" in Nanchang, "gravely disturbing all public order." The Public Security Corps, the police, and the law courts were ordered to impose the most severe penalties on the Peasants' Red Army, though, ironically, most of those "State instruments of coercion" were either anti-Maoist or neutral. Despite the threat, the peasant uprising "closed down factories and mines, shut all retail stores, barricaded roads, cut off electricity and water supplies, took over radio stations and newspapers by force, and broke into banks." Only Nanchang Radio was preserved by its normal cordon of regular troops of the People's Liberation Army. Otherwise, Kiangsi was largely in the hands of the outraged peasants.

The Maoists' grave peril was conveyed by threats against police and Public Security Forces, which refused to intervene. There was particular irony in the new *jacquerie* in Kiangsi. Nanchang was, after all, the site of the August First Rising in 1927, the official birth of the People's Liberation Army. Moreover, Chairman Mao had established his first successful Soviet Area in Kiangsi in 1928. The Kiangsi uprising was therefore as shattering a blow to the Maoists as would have been an armed revolt in Illinois to Abraham Lincoln in the darkest days of the Civil War. If the Maoists could not bring Kiangsi under control, their prospects were grim.

Toward the end of January 1967, it appeared that the so-called conservatives, who were the legitimately elected majority of the Communist Party, might reclaim their legal power. Only one major force in all China still remained largely aloof from the struggle, primarily because neither side wished to risk civil war. The People's Liberation Army had judiciously refrained from intervening in force on the Maoists' behalf, though it had held key installations like radio stations and had generally sought to conciliate contending factions. But the Maoists had come to the point where they must either acknowledge defeat or use the Liberation Army against the people and the Communist Party of China. They wondered, however, whether the Army was completely reliable.

XIX

Seize Power!

It is necessary to order the People's Liberation Army to help the left-wing and the revolutionary masses. The Army should extend its help wherever there are genuine revolutionaries and whenever they ask for such help. So-called non-interference is false non-interference. It has long since become interference. In this connection, I direct that a new order be issued and the former order be rescinded.

> Chairman Mao Tse-tung to
> Deputy Chairman Lin Piao
> January 21, 1967

In mid-January, when the Maoists still publicly exulted in their "great new victories in establishing proletarian organs of power" in cities like Shanghai, they knew full well the tide of battle was flowing strongly against them. The Maoists characteristically resorted to force, obeying the Chairman's *dictum:* "Power grows from the barrel of the gun!" They still quoted the holy word, though their immediate peril had rendered ideology a subsidiary concern. The issue was, quite starkly, *power,* epitomized by the Chairman's other simplistic epigrams: "Without a People's Army, the people have nothing!" "Political power is all!"

Peking ordered the Maoist clique and the armed forces: SEIZE POWER! SEIZE POWER!

Commanding the Liberation Army to intervene in the struggle was a desperate decision, for it risked complete civil war. Using the gun was, moreover, an admission of twofold failure—failure to win the proletariat or extirpate the influence of the "old power-holders within the Party

311

following the capitalist road." Much debate preceded the order, since the Army's response could not be predicted. Defense Minister Lin Piao could certainly not guarantee that the soldiers would fire on the Chinese masses and the local officials of the Communist Party.

Anticipating the necessity to use troops against workers, peasants, students, and cadres, the Maoist Party Center had earlier intensified the continuing purge of the Army. "Public fanfare" had proclaimed the civilian Task Force to Direct the Cultural Revolution in August 1966, but the existence of the Task Force of the Cultural Revolution for the People's Liberation Army was revealed only when that body was itself purged. On January 11, 1967, Peking announced appointment of a new chairman, Hsü Hsiang-chien, a People's Marshal until formal military rank had been abolished in 1965. Hsü was well qualified as an old associate of the Disciple and, somewhat paradoxically, the chief general during the 1930s of the Chairman's chief rival for power, Chang Kuo-tao. His loyalty to Lin Piao, presumably reinsured by appointing the Starlet "adviser" to his Task Force, was a *sine qua non*. His curious history had supposedly prevented his being totally enmeshed in the intricate network of personal relationships within the higher ranks. Until he was himself purged,* he was required to deal harshly with his fellow marshals and with senior generals.

Marshal Hsü's Task Force was ordered to "open fire on the small group of bourgeois reactionaries within the People's Liberation Army." Obvious divisions within the regionally oriented armed forces had been exacerbated by the invasion of agriculture and industry—and the consequent universal disorder. Until mid-January, the Liberation Army had conducted its "ideological remolding" in the privacy granted by the original *Sixteen-Point Directive on the Great Proletarian Cultural Revolution* issued in August 1966. But the military's new mission required immediate removal of anti-Maoist "bourgeois reactionaries" from its ranks. The moderates were still powerful within the People's Liberation Army which was ordered to prevent the victory of the moderates of the normal Communist Party apparatus.

The Liberation Army was still divided when it was thrown into battle at the end of January. *The Liberation Army Daily* acknowledged: "The struggle between the proletarian, revolutionary line of Chairman Mao and the bourgeois line not only exists within the armed forces, but is sharp and complex. . . . [The opposition] is hatching new plots and mounting new counterattacks!" Still tainted after seven years of unremitting purges, the Army was commanded to "support the left-wing and the rebel revolutionaries." The directive was issued on the authority of the

---

* Hsü Hsiang-chien was rehabilitated when the Army later took all power.

Central Committee, the Cabinet, the Military Affairs Commission, and the Task Force of the Cultural Revolution:

A) The order that the Army should not become involved in manifestations of the Cultural Revolution is rescinded.

B) The Army must dispatch troops to help any genuine revolutionary group that appeals for help.

C) The Army must attack any counterrevolutionary group that uses armed force.

D) The Army must not become an "air-raid shelter" for counterrevolutionary elements.

The troops were specifically directed to intervene in localities as widely separated as Shanghai and Canton, Manchuria and Sinkiang, Kweichow and Chinghai. There, as elsewhere, "counterrevolutionary elements" had virtually re-established the normal power of the Communist Party. Despite the sweeping order, the soldiers were remarkably restrained. They preferred to maintain order by breaking up fights, rather than aggressively "seize power" for the Maoists. The Mao-Lin faction was realizing that the entire Party structure must be destroyed, and Lin Piao told the troops to ignore directives of the 29 Provincial and Municipal Party Committees because "they are all rotten."

The Army's intrusion into civilian politics was justified by an elaborate pretext. The conventional Party apparatus, controlled by the "enemy," was to be destroyed and replaced with the "new structures of proletarian power." The Revolutionary Committees, conceived by the Ghostwriter after the pattern of the Paris Commune, were to become the new government of China, initially displacing both Government and Party organs. The new Revolutionary Committees were, however, wholly different from the original conception of "proletarian administrative bodies made up of representatives of the proletariat." The Maoists proclaimed a "three-way alliance," in part to camouflage the military's predominance. The "great alliance" was to be formed by representatives of the People's Liberation Army; the "mass organizations," which meant the Red Guards and other "rebel revolutionary" associations born of the Cultural Revolution; and the "loyal cadres," old administrative officials lured into the new structures.

The Maoist prevarication, "walking on two legs," normally described the simultaneous implementation of essentially contradictory policies. The Revolutionary Committees were, however, expected to perform the extraordinary feat of walking on three legs. Innumerable "internal contradictions," to use another Maoist term, lay behind the façade of the "three-way alliance." The Revolutionary Committees were required both to reconcile differences and to "suppress the class enemy." They were to justify the military's violent pacification of the Red Guards' battles, but they were to include Red Guard representatives. They were to supplant State and Party organs, but they were to include the archetypical representatives of conventional power, the old cadres. Only "irreconcilable enemies" were, ostensibly, still to be persecuted. The Committees were, in short, to be all things to all men: a conventional power structure and a "revolutionary new social organization"; a harmonious gathering of all true Maoists and an instrument of stern "proletarian dictatorship." The actual Revolutionary Committees, formed by the man of compromise, Chou En-lai, were utterly different from the idealistic conception of the ideologue, Chen Po-ta.

The First Minister's genius for conciliation was desperately needed. Disorder, rising in Shanghai, had become nation-wide. The Red Guards had thrice disobeyed instructions to return to their homes to "resume classes and continue to make revolution." Tens of thousands of Red Guards were defiantly marching on Peking. As many workers and Scarlet Sentinels were converging on the capital to oppose the "rebel revolutionaries." Unless the contending groups were reconciled—or suppressed—Peking would become a battlefield.

Red Flag exhorted Maoist loyalists: "Seize political power from the men in authority following the capitalist road, who still hold Party, Governmental, and financial power in the localities and organizations where they are entrenched. . . . The anti-Party group has used the State power it retains to suppress the rebel revolutionaries, actually imprisoning them and organizing the masses against the masses, while forming its own Army of the Defenders of Red State Power. . . . Rebel Revolutionary Headquarters must be established, one by one."

The People's Daily, the previously staid organ of the Central Committee, uttered Baroque effusions. "Everywhere in China, on both banks of the great Yellow River and both north and south of the Yangtze River, all the nation is in a state of frenzy. . . . Only one word can describe present circumstances. That word is—Anarchy!" declared an article reprinted from a Red Guard magazine, *Red Sun.* "Without anarchy, there can be no order! The revolution requires anarchy! Without anarchy, there can be no revolution!"

The extent of anarchy ultimately satisfied even the most rebellious "revolutionary rebels" as much as it finally horrified Peking.

The People's Daily announced—with more enthusiasm than accuracy—that Shansi in the north had been "retaken overnight" from the opposition, which had sought to make the province "a strategic base for restoring capitalism throughout China." The opposition had "organized their own intelligence network . . . first stockpiled and then used arms and ammunition. . . . They utterly disorganized the economy and corrupted the revolutionary mass organizations."

An Urgent Proclamation dismissed the Shansi Provincial Committee of the Communist Party, as well as the entire Provincial Government—and all Party and Government organs of Taiyüan, the capital. All were supplanted by the Shansi Rebel Revolutionary Directorate. The recalcitrant Public Security Forces were ordered—on pain of arrest and "severe punishment"—to obey only the new Directorate. Shansi was still too unruly to erect the façade of a Revolutionary Committee. Nor could the façade be raised in Kiangsi Province, where the peasant uprising still resisted in late January. "In Kiangsi," *The People's Daily* said, "there has recently been a *continuing and rising* development of *large-scale attacks* on the revolutionary faction by the deluded masses, who are manipulated by the class enemy. Those attacks have even reached the point of armed clashes."

The two essentially agricultural provinces displayed the new force the Maoists confronted, the awful wrath of the peasants. Having ridden to power on the aspirations of the stubborn Chinese peasantry, Mao Tse-tung was imperiled by the same angry peasants. Those few cities still under loose Maoist control were encircled by a hostile countryside. By the beginning of February 1967, the Maoists claimed to have "seized power" only in five scattered provinces and the two great "autonomous" metropolises, Shanghai and Peking. But the countryside was the true source of power in China, whether the peasantry were led by disciplined commissars or by outlawed gentry.

The cities of China had always been the centers of power: their glittering courts, dignified officials, and wealthy merchants—or in the Communist era: Party Committees, powerful cadres, and "economic enterprises." But the countryside had almost invariably decided the fate of dynasties, when exploited farmers left their small plots to form great armies. The peasants had won power for Mao Tse-tung in 1949 as the culmination of the greatest *jacquerie* the world has ever known. In the early spring of 1967, the peasants threatened to deprive the Chairman and the Disciple of power by stubborn resistance led by men who had learned from Mao Tse-tung himself how to arouse and organize the rural masses.

The Maoists had come to power by promising: "The tiller shall own his land!" Land reform had given each family its own small holding. Thereafter, various devices had deprived the peasant of his land. Cooperatives, collectives, and Communes all sought the same purposes—more efficient production by concentrating ownership and cultivation for the benefit of the State, rather than the individual. During relative *laissez-faire* rule from 1961 to 1965, the State's demands on the peasants were heavy, but they were not crippling. The peasants gradually emerged from despondency and deprivation of the Great Leap Forward. Although his holding was minute, the tiller felt that he was again working for himself, since he sold the produce of his private plot on "free" markets.

The Great Revolution was intended to create true Communism in a historical instant. The Maoists therefore wished to confiscate private plots and close the free markets. Private plots were actually "returned to the collective" in some areas during the early stages of the Great Revolution, and income from family handicrafts was appropriated by the Commune. The peasants feared that Peking would represss all individual freedom and repossess all individual property.

The opposition therefore found it easy to rally the peasants. "Economism" distributed a greater share of their produce to the farmers. "Social discipline" was deliberately relaxed. In some places, the "power-holders" broke up the Production Brigades and Production Teams, which were the basic units of the Great People's Communes. Communal funds and property were divided among individual farmers, who were promised restoration and expansion of both free markets and private plots. The peasants chose to follow the mildly benevolent devil they already knew, the old cadres, rather than the malevolent devil they did not know, the Maoist Party Center. In loose coordination with the insurgent workers, peasant resistance created the February Adverse Current—almost as violent as the January Storm and even more obstructive to the Maoists' attempt to "seize power" by creating Revolutionary Committees.

Shanghai, already in turmoil, was swept into anarchy by the February Adverse Current. The port was the chief battleground because it was a stronghold of anti-Maoists; the left exceeded the instructions of a suddenly cautious Party Center by proclaiming the People's Commune of Shanghai. The new government was in fact modeled directly on the Paris Commune of 1871, that so entranced the Ghostwriter. Although the experiment was soon countermanded by Peking, the formal proclamation of the Shanghai Commune intensified differences. Once again, fighting broke out in the streets. The same Red Guard chieftain who had described the January Storm recalled:

> After the seizure of power, power in the factories also fell into the hands of the Rebel Faction. Since that faction lacked technical skill, industry was all snarled up. The workers had no work, and production all but ceased. After several minor clashes, the opposition deliberately stirred up the peasants living on the outskirts of the city—and they marched into Shanghai to present their demands.

The peasants said they wished to improve their living conditions. The workers united with the peasants when they came to present their demands to the municipal authorities. But Chang Chün-chiao still replied: "I can't, for the moment, do anything about this problem, since it is a matter for the Party Center."

The peasants left the city peaceably. But the municipal authorities did absolutely nothing whatsoever about their demands—and they soon returned—ready to fight. Although Peking finally promised to consider the problem and pleaded with the farmers not to use arms, the municipal authorities still refused to change their attitude. After the Shanghai Commune was organized on the 5th and 6th of February, the crisis became acute. The farmers were the first target the new Commune attacked—and they responded in kind. Shanghai became even more tumultuous as the farmers marched in bearing arms. They also refused to work or send their produce to the city.

The Revolutionary Committee therefore decided to send Red Guard detachments to the countryside to convince the farmers that they *must not* "engage in armed struggle," while they *must* continue supplying the city with food.

The driver of the truck the People's Commune sent to pick us up was a man of few words. He advised us to return, since we could do no good by "working alongside the peasants" as we had been instructed.

"This is the slack season," he said. "But, if you truly want to know why our life is so miserable, you'll see when we get there."

When we heard his words, we were all very much afraid. We knew that particular Commune had sent the largest unit to fight in the city and that they were all expert marksmen. One People's Militiaman was particularly famous. People said that every time he fired, someone dropped. He was, incidentally, also a leader of the Public Security Force of the rural Commune.

A few days earlier, when they marched into the city, the armed farmers converged on Kiangsi Road, where the new Revolutionary Committee had its headquarters. There must have been 200, with about 20 rifles. They marched up to the Committee's offices to present their grievances. But the authorities stalled, saying: "We can't solve your problems for you. Besides, you are doing wrong by presenting your problems!"

The farmers didn't disperse. Instead, they marched toward the building. The Committee's security guards opened fire with sub-machine-guns. The guards fired in front of the farmers, and the peasant People's Militiamen demanded they stop. "Otherwise, we will shoot back," they shouted.

At that point, the guards shot again—and three farmers fell. The

People's Militia immediately returned the fire. The marksmen of the rural Commune shot three guards out of 30 or 40. The Committee thereupon telephoned the Public Security Force, which dispatched a unit to disperse the farmers. But the farmers' blood was up, and they joined battle with the police. The Liberation Army simply cordoned off the area, but didn't interfere. Only when the farmers' ammunition was exhausted did they finally withdraw.

We were naturally not very happy at being sent to calm such hotheads. Indeed, when we did arrive and tried to sing revolutionary songs, not a sound came out. Our throats were all too dry from fear.

The farmers, nonetheless, received the Red Guards not with force but with indignation and curiosity. They were anxious to describe their plight to the city boys and girls. The Red Guards were surprised by the peasants' legitimate grievances. They were startled to find that all the insurgent leaders were officials duly appointed before the Cultural Revolution. They spoke at length with the Commune's Party First Secretary and other cadres, including commanders of the People's Militia. When he talked with a common farmer named Liu, the Red Guard began to doubt his own convictions. He recalled:

I told him about my own dissatisfaction with the new Shanghai Revolutionary Committee. After all, the whole business of "seizing power" was really just an elaborate trick. First they tried to use the Red Guards, then they told the Red Guards to go back to school. Liberation Army soldiers seized all the vital points in the city. Where was the power of the masses?

Then old Liu began to open up to me. He said he was only a simple farmer and had not carried a gun into the city, but admitted proudly that he had accompanied the Militiamen. Then he told me about his own life.

"You know," he said, "working the fields is hard indeed—from sunrise to sunset. But our rations are worse than the city's, though they're supposed to be the same. We get unhulled rice. A hundred catties [133 pounds] make only 80 catties of edible rice. Why shouldn't we be as well fed as the cityfolk? If the working class are the big brothers and we are the small brothers, it's not right for them to exploit us. They should look after us. And what is your precious Party Center doing about our requests?"

He also had other complaints. The farmer added: "Compared to the city, it's a dull life out here. In the whole country, there's just one movie theater—and the films are all propaganda. After a full day of hard work, all we hear is quotations from Mao Tse-tung, political analyses, and political reports. If we want to see or hear a good old-fashioned story, we can't. Why can't you cityfolk, at least, print a few interesting books for us, instead of all this dry political stuff?"

The Red Guard was swayed by the farmer he had come to convert. But he felt impelled to warn, "Seizing power is not something you farmers can accomplish, since the Liberation Army doesn't support you. If the soldiers did support you, then you could seize power. But, as it is, you'll just have to put up with things."

When he interviewed a People's Militia leader named Tung, who acknowledged that he had fired at the security guards, the college student found himself on the defensive.

> Tung told me that the people who were seizing power were not true Marxists—and I had to agree, because I knew he was talking about Chang Chün-chiao. All I could do was plead with him not to lead his Militiamen into the city or cut off the supply of vegetables. All I could do was ask him to be patient until the Party Center, which, I admitted, had truly committed errors, could sort things out.
>
> When we got back to Shanghai, the Revolutionary Committee demanded that we give them lists of the ringleaders of the peasant resistance, but we got together and decided we would report that we had found no ringleaders. I think that was the beginning of my own decision to flee Shanghai—and China. I could no longer feel myself a true Red Guard of Chairman Mao Tse-tung.

Peasants and workers opposed the Maoists with arms. The Red Guards were splintering, and many were joining the opposition. The Maoist leadership knew that only the People's Liberation Army could save them from political extinction. Yet the generals were reluctant to order their troops to fire on workers or peasants. The Maoists were failing to "seize power." Only that master of compromise, the First Minister of Peace, Premier Chou En-lai, it appeared, could resolve the impasse. He temporarily transformed the militant movement to "seize power" into a conciliatory movement to create "revolutionary unity based on the three-way alliance" of soldiers, "rebels," and old cadres.

Never excessively concerned with the masses, except to manipulate them, Chou En-lai was not disturbed at their omission from the new Revolutionary Committees. He characteristically collaborated with the Liberation Army in the attempt to restore order and avert military predominance. During February, March, and April 1967, Peking spoke with the voice of Chou En-lai. During that period, all the grandiose goals of the Cultural Revolution were virtually repudiated. Despite the brief flowering of the People's Commune of Shanghai, "extensive democracy according to the principles of the Paris Commune," proclaimed by the Disciple in November 1966, was jettisoned. *The People's Daily* declared: "Extensive democracy is merely a means to an end—and that end is political power."

The First Minister was himself concerned with means, rather than ends. A professional administrator, he had always served whoever controlled the Communist Party. His superiors defined the goals, and he devised the means. Excessive idealism was never his failing, but he was by no means the perfect cynic. The single end he sought consistently was a functioning political and social order, *i.e.,* a workable means. It was no ignoble goal, though he was invariably frustrated by the obsessions of the Chairman and the internal tensions of the Party.

Chou En-lai was a professional revolutionary before he became a professional administrator. Except for his outstanding intelligence, he was the typical *apparatchik*. His remarkable resilience enabled him to survive and to rise, although the formal ideal of the Communist movement is the metallic—and rigid—vigor of the Iron Bolshevik. Chou was called the Elastic Bolshevik, as well as the First Minister of Great Peace, because his adaptability was hampered by neither excessive principle nor idealism. His agility maintained his position, as the Party juggernaut whipped around the corners of deviationism or shattered itself against the granite of purges. The First Minister was by no means immune to suspicion or criticism, either before or during the Great Revolution. But he survived many purges and even the manifest displeasure of Chairman Mao.

His most spectacular tightrope performance occurred early in his career. Chou En-lai was relieved as director of the Party Organization Bureau by the purge that swept the Li Li-san faction from power in 1930; he allied himself with the "Russian faction," led by Wang Ming in 1931, and was given charge of the Military Affairs Commission; but by 1933 he had deserted Wang Ming to follow the rising star of Mao Tse-tung. Like Talleyrand, his pliancy bred neither contempt in his colleagues nor humility in Chou himself. He was not only respected, but allowed himself displays of temper. Perhaps in his later years his irritability derived from a chronic liver complaint; despite everything, he demonstrated remarkable self-confidence.

The First Minister apparently felt himself secure because he was *the* indispensable man. He was shielded in the ceaseless power struggle as much by his unique ability as by his adroitness. Since he never aspired to supreme power, the reigning ruler could employ his services without fear of his ambition—just as the Confucian Emperor utilized the mandarin who could not aspire to his position. The tradition of such service was his heritage. Chou En-lai was set off from his colleagues not only by his unique abilities but by his origins. They were the sons of petty-bourgeois farmers, artisans, and merchants. His family had been officials of the Confucian Empire for generations.

Chou En-lai came to the certainties of Marxism by way of the certainties of Confucianism. When his father began his classical education with the traditional couplets of the *Three Character Classic* when En-lai was five in 1903, he was setting the boy's feet on the road to Moscow. From the Confucian classics, Chou En-lai learned not only his ideographs, but the conviction that the educated man must care for the masses. As a student at middle school and college during the turbulent second decade of the twentieth century, Chou was forcibly made aware of the flaws in the traditional Chinese political and social structure—the flaws that had made China easy prey to the West and brought about the collapse of the Empire. Still obedient to the Confucian ethos, which enjoined responsibility upon the educated, Chou and his contemporaries undertook the mission of restoring China to her pre-eminent place in the world. The instrument they considered best fitted to reshape China— and make her powerful—was Marxism. Since Confucianism was moribund, they required another absolute doctrine they could serve without question. They therefore followed an injunction of Confucius to bind themselves to Marxism—which sought the total destruction of the Confucian morality.

Chou En-lai had spent the early years of his life in Manchuria, rather than in the family's ancestral home, his own birthplace of Huaian, not too far from Shanghai. His mandarin father had been given an official post outside the Great Wall. After the Revolution of 1911, the elder Chou retired from government service, but chose not to return to Shanghai. He managed his business affairs from the mercantile port of Tientsin in the north. In that city's large foreign concession, the young Chou En-lai observed at first hand the forces that had destroyed the old China. In 1913, at the age of 15, he enrolled in the "modern" Nankai Middle School. He was determined to acquire the tools of Western learning. The elder Chou, a tolerant and intelligent man, supported his ambition. Chou En-lai was not tried by paternal harshness, unlike so many of his colleagues.

Although he later presented a cool, calculating face to the world, the young Chou En-lai too was moved by fierce passions of resentment and hatred against the West. Entering the collegiate department of Nankai, he was soon arrested for demonstrating against the reigning warlord. He had begun his career as an agitator. He attained the higher status of organizer after a year's sojourn in Japan, which offered a more salubrious climate for young Chinese rebels than their homeland. After learning how the Japanese had outwitted the West by adopting Western ways, Chou returned to Tientsin to found the Awaken Society. Like other student associations formed after Chinese youth learned its political power through the May Fourth Movement of 1919, the Awaken Society was a rallying point for young radicals. They were irresistibly drawn to Marxism because all other means had proved ineffective to "save the country."

The radical movement was also a matchmaking bureau. In 1920, Teng Ying-chao, a 20-year-old girl student, applied for membership in the Awaken Society. Her political views had been confirmed by a brief course at that finishing school for agitators, the Tientsin Municipal Jail. Like her sister students, Teng Ying-chao was actually more intensely political than their brothers. To the half-emancipated Chinese girl of good family, the brave new promises of equality and liberty were intensely personal, since they promised release from the formal subjection that bound Chinese women. The girls were, naturally, much maligned. The solid bourgeoisie whispered that the short-haired girl students changed their lovers more frequently—and more casually—than they did their dresses. Despite the sexual license preached in self-conscious defiance of bourgeois convention, most girls were still bound by Puritan inhibitions, almost as strong in the Marxist movement as in the Confucian tradition. There was little promiscuity but much intense political conversation.

Teng Ying-chao undoubtedly found the slim and intense Chou En-lai attractive, while he was attracted as much by her vivacious good looks as by her political dedication. There was nothing effeminate about the tough-minded agitator, although he had demonstrated the histrionic talent that would later serve him so well by playing a female role in the drama *Yi Yüan Chien,* presented by his middle-school class. But the couple was not married in Canton until five years later, when they began a virtual idyll of monogamy among the much-marrying Communist leaders.

In 1920, Chou En-lai had greater concerns, for he was planning the great adventure abroad that would endow him with his mystical reputation for knowledge of the outside world. Unlike Mao Tse-tung, who yearned to go but could not, Chou joined the leftist-sponsored Worker-Student Movement, which took Chinese radicals to Europe. Chou En-lai, who spent four years on that continent perfecting his knowledge of things Western, was for the next decade to be a more powerful figure in the Chinese Communist movement than the stay-at-home Mao Tse-tung.

The word "Worker" stood first in the movement's title with good reason. Although some of the young men enrolled in universities, their chief pursuit was studying the proletariat of the West by working alongside them. For most of the Chinese, formal study was no more than a diversion squeezed between long hours in silk mills, automobile factories, or coal mines. Some were employed as waiters, others in road-repair crews. Inevitably, they learned more in workshops and workgangs than in classrooms and libraries. That tutelage by labor was, after all, recommended by the European Communists, who sponsored their visits. All their bitterness was directed into political channels, though their ordeal was as much personal as social. Strangers in alien lands, they endured the twin trials of loneliness and young manhood.

Chou En-lai worked in the coal mines of the Rhineland and the Renault Automobile Works in Lille. He confirmed his hatred of the "capitalist system" which, he believed, imposed great suffering upon him —though he was supported in part by his capitalist father. He was apparently already marked for advancement by the Communist International, which allotted an allowance large enough to enable him to study in England and France, as well as Germany. In return he was more active in politics than in either work or study. In Berlin in late 1920, he organized a branch of the Socialist Youth Group of China. In the summer of 1921, he attended the founding meeting of the Paris Branch of the Chinese Communist Party, itself just formally established in Shanghai.

His four years abroad raised Chou En-lai to eminence in the Communist Party in China. Having won the approbation of the Comintern, he was the darling of Moscow's agents in China. He returned just as the Comintern forced an alliance between the Nationalists and the Communists. He was promptly appointed First Secretary of the Kwangtung Provincial Branch of the Communist Party, a major post because Canton was the power center of the new alliance, where the Revolutionary Army was built with Soviet financing and Soviet advice. Chiang Kai-shek, who had attended a Japanese military academy, was made commandant of the Whampoa Military Academy, founded in May 1924. The Comintern designated young Chou En-lai chairman of the Political Training Department. The Nationalists could not deny the Communists that vital position, since Moscow, which sponsored Chou, also paid the bills.

Following Soviet practice, each major unit in the Revolutionary Army was to possess a political commissar and a political section, charged equally with indoctrinating the troops and winning the civilian populace. When the joint Nationalist-Communist Revolutionary Army marched out of Canton in June 1926, Chou En-lai was Political Commissar of the crack First Army, its officer corps composed largely of Whampoa graduates. The most modern military unit in China, it was the first truly *national,* rather than *provincial* army the country had created.

After the early victories of the Revolutionary Army, Chou En-lai was detached for service in Shanghai in late 1926. Among the largest "proletarian" concentration in China, he organized the Workers' Militia to take the city from within. His chief collaborators were the Party's Secretary-General Chen Tu-hsiu—soon to be denounced as a Trotskyite —and Comrade Liu Shao-chi, the Party's chief labor organizer. The trio was so effective that Shanghai fell without a fight. The Workers' Militia disarmed the remnants of the warlord armies and patrolled the city until the Nationalist Army arrived to take the formal surrender. The regulars camped in the suburbs while Generalissimo Chiang Kai-shek conferred with the leaders of the Commune—and with bankers and secret-society leaders.

At four on the morning of April 12, 1927, secret-society thugs dressed as workmen joined General Pai Chung-hsi's Kwangsi divisions to attack the workers' strongholds. By noon the Shanghai Workers' Militia was fleeing through the streets pursued by regulars firing rifles and submachine guns. The only sustained resistance was mounted by the security guards of the Communists' headquarters in the offices of the Shanghai Federation of Labor. The overwhelming technical superiority of the regulars soon broke that resistance.

Chou En-lai, taken prisoner, was recognized by a Nationalist captain who had been his student at the Whampoa Academy. The master-student relationship prevailed over political differences, and Chou was taken secretly to Pai Chung-hsi's headquarters. The Kwangsi general owed the Communist leader a debt for having saved his brother's life. He deliberately failed to recognize the Communist leader. Chou was set at liberty in a China rapidly coming under Nationalist control in the late twenties.

Chou En-lai was a major figure in the Communists' last desperate struggle. He was a leader of the Revolutionary Committee that directed the military rising in Nanchang, the capital of Kiangsi Province, on August 1, 1927. He sat in the Emergency Session that relieved Chen Tu-hsiu as Secretary-General. He was a leader of the Revolutionary Committee that directed the catastrophic ten days of the Canton Commune in December 1927. Thereupon, he fled through British Hong Kong, reaching Moscow for the Sixth National Party Congress in June 1928. Chou En-lai became chief of the Organization Bureau and Comrade Liu Shao-chi chief of the Labor Bureau of a Chinese Communist Party that possessed little strength in its homeland. Chou fell into disfavor when his mentor, Li Li-san, forced the Party to sponsor new insurrections that failed completely. Although he exerted considerable influence in Moscow, which had tacitly supported the disastrous policy, Chou En-lai could not prevent Li Li-san's fall. The supple Chou made his own peace, first with the "Russian faction" of his Paris schoolmate

Wang Ming and, soon thereafter, with the rising "rural faction" of Mao Tse-tung.

With his sure instinct for survival, Chou En-lai picked the winning side. He was named vice chairman of the Kiangsi's Soviet Military Affairs Committee and in time became vice chairman of the Political Bureau of the Communist Party. There was little need for Chou's talents as a negotiator in the mountainous Soviet area. Except for smuggling, the Communists conducted foreign relations with shot and shell. Chou therefore became chief political assistant to Generalissimo Chu Teh. Having helped train the Nationalist armies, he trained the Workers' and Peasants' Red Army to counter their tactics.

When the Long March reached its goal in the autumn of 1935, Chou began to function more like a foreign minister. From their base in the Northwest the Communists were bound to clash with the Japanese invaders, but they could also resume closer communication with the Soviet Union. Besides, Moscow was urging a second alliance between Nationalists and Communists against the Japanese. Chou's first task as chief of the Foreign Affairs Office was coordinating the political life of semi-regular forces and guerrilla bands operating all the way from the far northwest to the Tibetan border in the southwest and Canton in the extreme southeast.

His strong features veiled by a jet-black beard, Chou would ride his thick-maned Mongolian pony through the arches of Yenan, the Communist capital, when he returned from his tours of inspection. Two fountain pens peeped from the breast pocket of his heavy, loose-cut jacket. They were his only badges of rank as he cantered through the yellow hills of Shensi or across the parched plains of Kansu to study the political and military situation for himself. The beard, grown as a partial disguise in his Shanghai days, would remain until he assumed more conventional diplomatic functions. He must still remember the pony, for he still carries his left arm awkwardly bent. It was badly set after he fell from the saddle.

Opportunity to exercise his talent for negotiation soon appeared. Chou En-lai conveyed the Politburo's decision that Chiang Kai-shek must be kept alive when the Generalissimo was imprisoned by his own restive troops. Sent to the northwest to fight the Communists, those troops were highly receptive to Communist propaganda, for they really wanted to fight the Japanese. Skillful agitation—and a virtual cease-fire —finally induced the Nationalist commanders to make common cause with the Communists—and brought Chiang Kai-shek to Sian, 480 miles from Yenan, to command a renewed offensive in December 1936. When the Nationalist generals were unable to persuade Chiang to turn them against the Japanese, they took him prisoner.

For five days, the captive Generalissimo wavered between despair and righteous indignation. Having heard the officers of his guard discussing his imminent execution, he was prepared for death when the door of his room opened one evening to admit a visitor he had last seen in 1926 when they pledged mutual loyalty on setting out from Canton to unify China. Chou En-lai had come from Yenan in the Nationalist commander's personal airplane. When he lifted his cap from his close-cropped hair, the light revealed his mobile actor's features: the heavy, precise eyebrows shading intense black eyes; the high cheekbones under olive skin; and the straight, long mouth, which could twist in either derision or laughter in an instant. Despite his heavy clothing, he moved with his accustomed grace.

"Mr. Chairman," the First Minister said, "I have come to sign the articles of betrothal for the remarriage of the Nationalist and Communist Parties."

The negotiations thus begun were to continue through the summer of 1937, though Chiang Kai-shek was released on Christmas Day of 1936 after agreeing in principle to the new alliance. On September 23, 1937, the new alliance was confirmed. The two parties, compelled by the open Japanese invasion that began in July 1937, pledged cooperation in implementing the Three People's Principles of Dr. Sun Yat-sen, founder of the Nationalist Party, whom both honored. The Communists agreed to reorganize their forces, call them the Eighth Route Army, and place them under the nominal command of Chiang Kai-shek's Central Government.

The Communists sent Chou En-lai to the Nationalist capital at Nanking as their chief representative in the new semi-coalition. He sat on the presidium of the Extraordinary National Congress of the Nationalist Party in Hankow in March 1938. He was, shortly thereafter, appointed vice minister of the Political Training Board, the conglomerate body that nominally ruled China during the war. After the two parties virtually split again in 1941, Chou's chief function was propagandist-in-chief for the Communists in the Nationalist capital-in-exile in Chungking in the deep southwest.

Accessible at all times and an attentive host at his weekly afternoon tea parties, Chou convinced many foreign diplomats and correspondents that the eminently reasonable Communists desired only a coalition government that would win the war and strive for the welfare of the Chinese people. He also convinced them that he was himself a most reasonable and charming person. He was, in truth, both reasonable and charming. Besides, most of his foreign guests deceived themselves. They were, with good reason, convinced that the Nationalists were so bad that they desperately wanted to believe that the dedicated Communists could save the nation the foreigners had come to love.

Having won great foreign sympathy, the First Minister of Peace exploited that sympathy brilliantly during the protracted negotiations with the Nationalists that started in 1944 and finally ended in 1947 with the outbreak of the Civil War. He was the Communists' chief negotiator at those talks, held under American sponsorship. The ultimate conclusion was, of course, a Communist military victory, which created the People's Republic of China in 1949—with Chou En-lai as Premier and Foreign Minister of the Central People's Government.

Since he knew that politics was the art of the possible, the First Minister of Peace proved an adroit administrator. He presided over the violent "campaigns" designed to change the essential character of Chinese society by eliminating the landlord and commercial classes. He protested, without effect, against the premature collectivization of 1955, which deprived the farmers of their land. He served through the Great Leap Forward and the subsequent period of *laissez-faire,* for his executive ability was always at the service of the men who determined policy. Although he took part in their councils, his voice was rarely decisive. But he always drove himself hard, whether impelled by the habit of power or love of China.

Whenever he could, the First Minister tempered the extremism of Chairman Mao—not necessarily because he was humane, but because he was practical. Chou could presumably understand—if not share—the soaring visions of the Chairman. But he was required to attain Mao's grandiose goals—a feat often beyond human power. Chou En-lai and his chief lieutenants, like Vice Premier and later Foreign Minister Field Marshal Chen Yi, consistently sought to attain the possible, rather than break the nation in pursuit of impossible goals. Chou was, therefore, from time to time attacked by the Maoists for deliberately sabotaging their transcendent programs. But he survived, primarily because he was *the* essential administrator and, secondarily, because he was *the* symbol of rationality.

When the Great Revolution broke, Chou En-lai initially allied himself with the Maoists, since it appeared they would win. He may also have grown weary of changing sides. As the Great Revolution continued, near-exhaustion was ever more discernible in his voice and movements. Although he tried to moderate the frenzies, he could not. He still carried himself with the arrogance of the indispensable man. He maintained his ties with the moderates and the military; he protected his vice premiers from attack; and he chided the Red Guards. In the spring of 1967, many observers, Chinese as well as foreign, expected Chou En-lai to emerge as the great peacemaker and the supreme authority in a China that required his particular talents for conciliation as never before.

The prophets were disappointed. Chou En-lai had been too long a subordinate, and he was too wise to attempt to seize supreme power which no longer existed. He was, instead, content to preserve his considerable authority by serving as the chief liaison between the Maoists and the increasingly disaffected senior generals and marshals. Those men had been given a task that was inappropriate to their means, beyond their capacity, and acutely distasteful. They were ordered to make China safe for Maoism by "seizing power" from the powerful opposition. They were also expected to maintain civil order and a functioning economy by preventing clashes between the opposing factions.

The assignment was manifestly impossible because it was inherently contradictory. Disorder could only be stimulated by the violence necessary to "seize power" from "power-holders" supported by the masses. The schizophrenic task would exacerbate divisions within the Liberation Army. Actually firing upon the masses might provoke mutiny in the ranks and civil war between regular army units. Most generals therefore proclaimed their absolute obedience to the Chairman, while ignoring his presumed orders. The Army was not willing to shoot its way into control of the civilian administration. If it did, however reluctantly, assume power, it was not prepared to act solely as an agent of the Maoists.

Only where disorder was most extreme did the troops use extreme force. They were then as likely to "suppress" the rebellious Red Guards as they were the opposition's "shock units." Forced to act as policemen, the troops adopted the policeman's pragmatic means of quelling violence —seizing ringleaders and agitators, regardless of their ideological coloration. Since the Red Guards were more often the "trouble-makers" than the Scarlet Sentinels, the Red Guards were more often "suppressed" than the Scarlet Sentinels. The mass of workers and peasants were formidable opponents the Liberation Army had no desire whatsoever to engage.

The generals instinctively supported the policy of the First Minister of Great Peace, Premier Chou En-lai, rather than the tactics of the Disciple, Defense Minister Lin Piao. They sought no "war of annihilation" against the Chinese people, but wished to restore harmony with the least possible force. They considered themselves conciliators, rather than the scourge of Chairman Mao. Nonetheless, they exercised power by default in the "three-way alliance," since no coherent nucleus of authority existed outside the Army. The "three-way alliances" were usually only façades behind which the factions struggled for power. The military, therefore, had no alternative but to accept responsibility.

The soldiers thus found themselves by default exercising influence that was, during the next two years, to be solidified by circumstances. The People's Liberation Army did not seek to impose military rule on China. It was given no real choice. The Army was forced to penetrate every major civilian organization—economic, social, and political—because no other force could either maintain a semblance of civil order or protect the economy from the severest derangement.

The "military representatives" accordingly moved into factories, rural Communes, schools, financial and trading agencies, and civic organizations—as well as Government and Party organs. Reality again differed from the image projected by Maoist-controlled organs of publicity. China's vast size and great population made it impossible for troops to control all organizations. Instead they concentrated on those areas where the two factions had fought pitched battles. Bewildered, semi-literate corporals crammed their knees under school desks to preserve order among Red Guards who used the schools as battlefields, rather than institutions of learning. Captains and majors moved into the offices of factories and banks, while sergeants and lieutenants stood on the assembly lines. Army propaganda teams pleaded with workers and managers alike to "push the revolution and advance production," rather than fight among themselves.

When it was necessary, the troops used force. In Harbin in Manchuria, troops broke up attacks by "counterrevolutionary elements" upon "rebel revolutionaries" who had "seized power," though the rebels confessed to "confusion within our own ranks." In Foochow, capital of coastal Fukien Province, troops turned back a mass assault on the headquarters of the Provincial Military District and the Assembly of Activists in Studying the Works of Mao Tse-tung. In Shanghai the struggle did not abate. Not only the peasants but the "hygiene workers" of the municipality went on strike. For a brief time neither food nor medical care was readily available. But armed soldiers ensured that trains rolled along the rails connecting the port with the hinterland. Yet the longshoremen's strikes on the docks kept some ships lying at their moorings for six to eight weeks waiting to be unloaded. There was obviously a limit to what the Army could do.

By mid-February, the Maoists claimed control of only six provinces and the municipalities of Shanghai and Peking. In Nanking, it was guardedly revealed, some military units had actually sided with the disgraced cadres of the King of the South Tao Chu. In Tibet, General Chang Kuo-hua refused to "press the Cultural Revolution," feeling he had enough problems with his endemically rebellious Tibetan subjects. In Sinkiang, the New Dominion in the northwest, General Wang En-mao forced Peking to formally suspend the Cultural Revolution. As the time for spring planting drew near, the Cultural Revolution was "temporarily suspended" in the entire countryside.

Despite the generals' restraint, China resembled a nation under military occupation—by its own People's Liberation Army. The slogan "military guidance and military control" described—and justified—virtual martial law. Vestigial central power existed only under the guns and bayonets of the People's Liberation Army, itself a regionally oriented force. Colonels and generals controlled the jerry-built Revolutionary Committees, for the "three-way alliance" of the First Minister of Peace was hardly more than a convenient slogan. Troops prevented some workers' and peasants' shirking, but they could not enforce Maoist conformity on the entire nation. The People's Militia, 20 million strong, was commanded by the regular forces, but the Militia was more often anti-Maoist than pro-Maoist. Even some regular units collaborated with the old "power-holders" they were ordered to destroy.

By the beginning of April 1967, the Maoists claimed to rule only eight provinces, plus the two autonomous municipalities. The troops were often hard-pressed to do more than "control" food warehouses and communications. The presumed representatives of the Party Center were surrounded by vast areas where no real authority functioned. The movement to "seize power" had failed, as had the First Minister's conciliation. The first phase of the Great Revolution, it appeared at the time, had closed with a stalemate. Hindsight reveals that the Great Revolution had itself come to an end. The bright ideals of Maoist zealots had proved beyond realization, while the control Peking had previously exerted over the nation was no longer operable. It was time to pick up the pieces—and attempt to reconstruct an effective machinery of authority for China.

That effort would occupy just two years. In the meantime the purge of the small group of enemies of the Chairman and the Disciple was to be pressed even harder. The Maoists were determined to revenge themselves for their great frustration by that small "victory." Whatever else happened, Comrade Liu Shao-chi and his close supporters were to be destroyed.

The practical end of the Great Revolution's striving to create the perfect society envisioned by the chairman had been graphically demonstrated by the last sunburst of idealism in Shanghai. The Shanghai People's Commune was climactic, and so decisive that it justifies departure from the chronological account to gaze upon its ephemeral splendor.

BOOK THREE

The Subsiding Waves

XX

A Stinking,
Rotting Heap of Garbage

In February 1967, it was Paris in Shanghai—for 17 days. The ultimate goal of the Great Proletarian Cultural Revolution—as both the Ghost-writer Chen Po-ta and the Disciple Lin Piao had proclaimed—was establishing "proletarian organs of administration" modeled upon the Paris Commune. On February 5, Shanghai, the turbulent "vanguard city" of the Great Revolution, formally enacted Utopia—amid a chaos of strikes and factional fighting.

The 17 days of the Shanghai People's Commune were not the dawning of a "new era for mankind," but the Götterdämmerung of all the romantic visions that had inspired the Maoist idealists. The Canton Commune, enduring for ten days in 1927, had been the death throes of the orthodox Stalinist strategy of conquering China by seizing the urban centers of power. Though sporadic Communist raids harassed the cities thereafter, two decades of laborious "struggle in the countryside" had been required to conquer China. The Shanghai People's Commune even more decisively destroyed Chairman Mao's dream of creating a perfect China. Thereafter, politics were indeed in command, but they were the practical, slightly grubby, and often violent politics of the possible, rather than Maoist politics of the ideal.

The Shanghai Commune was proclaimed with great fanfare, though it was, even at the moment of its creation, already obsolete. As if to calm the "great winds and high waves" of popular and Party resistance by incantation, the Maoist clique declared that the opposition's January Storm had in fact been its own January Revolution. Beset by violent resistance, they invoked authority by intoning yet another magic formula.

"Today was announced," proclaimed the Shanghai *Wen-hui Pao* under the massive red headlines reserved for proclamations of major triumphs, "the birth of the new Paris Commune in the sixties of the twentieth century, the Shanghai People's Commune! Under his attentive eyes and sustained by the ardent support of our dearly beloved and magnificent leader Chairman Mao, the people of Shanghai have been liberated for the second time!"

Printed in tens of thousands by the nocturnal labors of the pressmen of the Shanghai People's Publishing Firm, "great-character posters," "spontaneously" blossomed throughout a city in sullen revolt against all authority. ALL HAIL TO THE BIRTH OF THE SHANGHAI PEOPLE'S COMMUNE! ALL POWER BELONGS TO THE SHANGHAI PEOPLE'S COMMUNE! WHOEVER DARES OPPOSE THE TASK FORCE OF THE CULTURAL REVOLUTION IS A COUNTERREVOLUTIONARY!

The implicit assertion that the "revolutionary transformation of Shanghai" had been directed by the Task Force under the Ghostwriter was not wholly false; neither was it, by a long way, true. Peking was still considering the proper response to the opposition the initial intervention of the People's Liberation Army had aggravated, rather than suppressed. Nonetheless, the Shanghai Maoists behaved as if they enjoyed the full sanction of the Party Center, when they were actually creating an "independent kingdom." The "purified" Maoist Center was itself already split.

On February 6, 1967, Shanghai newspapers outdid themselves in voluminous and enthusiastic accounts of the ceremonies that had "given birth" to the "Paris Commune of the 1960s." The mass meeting that established the Commune at 2:00 P.M. the previous day had been attended by "rebel revolutionary groups, the revolutionary masses, including workers and farmers," *and,* of course, "the fighters of the Army, the Navy, and the Air Force," as well as "revolutionary students and cadres." Two leaders dominated the proceedings: the old administrator Chang Chün-chiao and his chief henchman, the Literary Assassin, Yao Wen-yüan, both members of the Central Task Force.

"According to the proposal of the Central Task Force of the Cultural Revolution," Chang told the crowd, "and with the consent of the rebel revolutionary groups who worked for the establishment of the Shanghai People's Commune, Comrade Yao Wen-yüan and myself will take part in the work of the temporary directing committee."

The Assassin lauded the "great victory for the Thought of Mao Tse-tung" and the demonstration that "living study and living use" of the Thought had entered a triumphant new stage. He was followed by the commander of the Shanghai garrison who warned the opposition that the military, faithful to Chairman Mao, would support the Shanghai People's Commune.

A "telegram of homage" to the Chairman from the new Commune implicitly assured him that it had acted under his direct inspiration. Addressed to the "red, red, red sun in our hearts," the telegram asserted: "You personally have supported the creative spirit of the Shanghai rebel revolutionary groups, the establishment of this new form of regional State organ of the proletarian dictatorship, the Shanghai People's Commune!"

The Shanghai group, claiming to lead the entire country, thus revealed both its insecurity and its lack of understanding of the Paris Commune. The principle of the Paris Commune was, of course, *not* consolidating the "dictatorship of the proletariat," but *transcending* such dictatorship. The two ambitious men of Shanghai were trying to convince the Chairman and the Central Task Force that their precipitate action was "the correct policy" by associating Peking with their "new form of regional State" authority. They were, to say the least, maladroit.

"The birth of the Shanghai People's Commune," the telegram continued, "is only one step in the Long March. Many difficulties still lie ahead of us. But we fear neither Heaven nor earth, and we do not tremble before ogres and monsters. We are following Your sage advice: 'Seize revolution and promote production!' "

The *Wen-hui Pao* strove even more audaciously to associate the Chairman with the new Commune when it declared: "The great vision of Chairman Mao has become reality in the Shanghai area with the birth of the Shanghai People's Commune."

Peking was ominously silent. While all Shanghai's organs of publicity celebrated the establishment of the "revolutionary new form" of administration, neither the New China News Agency nor *The Peking People's Daily* reported the dawning of the new era. Worse was to come. Wall posters in Peking said flatly that the Shanghai People's Commune had *not* been approved by the Central Task Force of the Cultural Revolution. The First Minister of Great Peace, Premier Chou En-lai, was quoted at length; he rejected the Commune as "premature." The men of Peking, who truly understood the concept of the Paris Commune, felt the time "was not ripe." The First Minister said that development of a Commune fashioned after the Parisian ideal required that 95 percent of workers, students, and soldiers should vote. Until that ideal was attainable, he suggested, Revolutionary Committees, rather than People's Communes should administer the few areas where the Mao-Lin faction actually exerted substantial influence.

On February 24, Chang Chün-chiao delivered a eulogy over the short-lived Shanghai People's Commune. Quite understandably, he withheld formal acknowledgment of the demise of the institution that had been intended to win him outstanding power. But his message was clear. "To seize power," he said, "we [Maoists] must find the best form of a great revolutionary alliance"—not a People's Commune. "The three-way alliance," he added, "is the proper road to power." He unctuously sought to placate the cadres, the workers, and students his own behavior had alienated.

> The Chairman has paid us high esteem, but, since the three-way alliance had not been realized when the provisional committee of the People's Commune was established, our signboard would have been smashed. . . . Were others not already preparing a second and third Commune?* Even the garrison company guarding the offices of the Commune had sought instructions from higher levels [*i.e.,* Peking] as to what action they should take if people marched to smash the signboard. For this reason, without the support of the People's Liberation Army, we could do nothing. . . . Some people always want to have a bash. Some previously opposed the Shanghai People's Commune. Some now are opposing the Shanghai Revolutionary Committee.

The three-way alliance was, above all, to be based upon compromise —enforced by the Liberation Army. It could not operate, Chang admitted flatly, unless the "working-level cadres" and the military cooperated. The wind had veered diametrically during the 17 days of the Commune. "More than 600 cadres rank as heads of bureaus and more than 6,000 as section-heads in Shanghai. How can we fail to find good candidates for the three-way alliance among so many cadres, most of them basically good men?" The revolts that had plagued Shanghai, Chang said blandly, were merely the result of certain high-ranking cadres' failure to transmit the instructions of the Party Center. He even blamed the same failure for his own humiliation at Anting, where workers had booed him off the stage. Compromise was the white flag run up by the romantic Maoists in full retreat. Asked Chang Chün-chiao:

> With the People's Commune inaugurated, do we still need the Communist Party? I think we do. We must have a hard core, regardless of what it is called. . . . I think, though, that names need not be changed. We should still convene the [old] National People's Congress, and the State Council [Cabinet] should still be called the State Council. Let the Shanghai People's Commune be changed to the Shanghai Municipal Revolutionary Committee again. Is the mere title, People's Commune, so important? Would you not feel isolated because Shanghai's was the only Commune in the country?

The men who had overreached themselves thus acknowledged defeat, made amends—and scuttled to cover. Regardless of how the Chairman

* An enigmatic reference still unexplained—like so many aspects of the Great Revolution.

himself might feel, neither the generals of the Liberation Army nor the administrators of First Minister Chou En-lai were prepared to give China over to mass popular rule. The romantics and the opportunists who had clustered around the Starlet had been forced to retract. When the time came to establish the "new administration" in Peking, after another two months of "struggle," there was no pretense of a People's Commune. Instead, a Revolutionary Committee under military control was installed in the capital. Although compromise with the old cadres was as essential in Peking as in Shanghai, the Party's Municipal Committee was swept aside—for the second time in a year.

The chairman of the Peking Municipal Revolutionary Committee was General Hsieh Fu-chih, a soldier who was also a vice premier and Minister for Security. The Starlet herself appeared to formalize military pre-eminence by proclaiming the new slogan soon to become dominant throughout China: RESPECT THE ARMY AND LOVE THE PEOPLE! The New China News Agency distributed a paean of praise of the Liberation Army, while the chief theme of the inaugural meeting was violent denunciation of the former Mayor Peng Chen. The Great Revolution had begun as a power struggle, with the contenders sharply divided by wholly different approaches to China's fundamental problems. It had briefly sought to create a terrestrial Utopia. Ideology and idealism were then set aside, but the power struggle would not end until the new men in power had totally discredited the old men in power.

First Minister Chou En-lai, speaking last, mused on the "difficulties of maintaining and exercising power" as compared with the relative ease of "seizing power." Determined to write *finis* to the romantic and turbulent phase of the Great Revolution, Chou stressed: "The chief present task is to stimulate production, both agricultural and industrial, while promoting scientific research." The Premier attacked the Mayor unmercifully, for the "opposition" was still strong. China could only restore orderly administration if the influence of the new Party Center were re-established by discrediting the chief symbols of the opposition. The Starlet had already admitted that "making revolution" was difficult and had warned, "The course of the revolution does not run in a straight line." She too attacked the Mayor for his "persistent attempts to restore capitalism since 1949." Such "traitors," she said, were the true "class enemy" against whom true "rebel revolutionaries" must struggle.

A greater target than the Mayor, however, was coming into the Maoists' sights. The rally declared: "We tell the people of China, we tell the people of the entire world that the biggest man in power within the Communist Party of China following the capitalist road, China's Khrushchev, has been overthrown!" The target was, of course, Comrade Liu Shao-chi, still formally Chairman of the People's Republic. He was not yet mentioned by name, but his total humiliation was approaching. As long as Comrade Shao-chi was not "destroyed," the Maoist *coup d'état* would be imperiled.

The same stalwart of the left who had fired the first shot of the Great Revolution was to be a leader in the attack on Liu Shao-chi. The Literary Assassin Yao Wen-yüan had already played a major role in the literary inquisition and the Shanghai Commune. His pen had transfixed the Backstage Boss on the Literary Front, Chou Yang. Besides, Yao was editor of the most extreme Maoist organ, the Shanghai *Wen-hui Pao*. He had also served as Deputy Leader of the short-lived Shanghai People's Commune and Deputy Secretary of its Party Committee. But he knew when to disengage. When it became clear that the Commune had gone too far, the Assassin scurried back to Peking to renew his pledges of loyalty to the Chairman and the Starlet. When the conservative "three-way alliance" under military tutelage became the chief instrument of the Revolution, he turned his unique powers of vituperation against Comrade Shao-chi. Although more gifted than most, the ever flexible and ever vitriolic Yao Wen-yüan typified the young opportunists the Starlet had gathered around her.

Having risen by the pen alone to the heights of the disintegrating Chinese Communist Party, the Assassin might have been expected to perish by the sword—or be crushed under the debris of the Party's collapse. Instead, he alone among the Starlet's bright and unscrupulous young men survived, perhaps because principle was incomprehensible to him and compassion despicable. He was among the first to denounce his henchmen and form a new alliance—however tenuous—with the military.

Yao Wen-yüan was the intellectual gray eminence of the extremists of the Great Proletarian Cultural Revolution. The critic, around 40 years old when the upheaval began, was both chief adviser and literary hatchetman to the Starlet. Chiang Ching, the ill-educated, semi-professional actress, needed Yao Wen-yüan, the professional intellectual, to provide aesthetic and theoretical authority for her extreme policies.

The Literary Assassin, whose given name—with no false modesty—means "chief in culture," himself fired the first shot of the Cultural Revolution. He was well rewarded for his vicious attack on Wu Han, the playwright-historian who spoke for the anti-Maoists—and for his continuing vitriolic assaults on the opposition, which finally included the entire intellectual and artistic establishment of Communist China.

Not even a member of the Central Committee in 1965, when he loosed the lightning, Yao Wen-yüan first appeared on reviewing stands in Peking in mid-August 1966, after the Maoists had purged the Politburo and the Central Committee. At the conclusion of the Great

Revolution, he was a full member of the Politburo in a hierarchy created by an ill-balanced compromise among the generals, the old cadres, and the extreme Maoists. He attained that precarious eminence by betraying his original collaborators and selling his pen to the generals. He had finally called a formal halt to the excesses of the Great Revolution, having abandoned his original position as literary dragoman to that obsessed amateur of the arts, Chiang Ching.

Shaken by the political kaleidoscope of the Great Proletarian Cultural Revolution, the so-called conservative faction—*i.e.,* the men trying to keep China from disintegration—undoubtedly took much pleasure in forcing Yao Wen-yüan to sound the retreat from the wilder excesses of the Revolution. Late in August 1968, the Assassin was directed to write a lengthy article which gave the rampaging Red Guards final notice that their days of violent feuding and undisciplined marauding were at an end. Called "The Working Class Must Exercise Leadership Over All!", the article proclaimed the determination of the new leadership to crush the anarchism that had engulfed China. By deliberate irony, Yao thus also sounded the knell of the obsessive, doctrinaire leadership of Chairman Mao Tse-tung, which had created chaos.

It was necessary that the Assassin himself issue the order for reimposition of discipline that signaled the formal end of the Maoist dream— already abandoned in practice when the Shanghai People's Commune was broken in February 1967. After all, he symbolized the wilder reaches of Maoism, having come to power by the same tactics that earned him the nickname the Literary Assassin among the writers of Shanghai in the 1950s. He had clambered over the political corpses of authors much better known than he, and much more productive artistically.

"Yao Wen-yüan was always a critic rather than a novelist, essayist, or descriptive writer," recalled a Chinese novelist who saw him frequently in meetings of the Shanghai Writers' Association when he was just beginning to claw his way upward. "But let's call him the Assassin. That nickname describes both his temperament and his method."

> The Assassin had two pet tricks. He never bothered with lesser figures, for he knew that his reputation as a "zealous Marxist-Leninist critic" could only grow from successful attacks against the big names. His unvarying method was to pick a few phrases or sentences out of context and launch an all-out attack on his opponents, using their own words —thus distorted and out of context—as his own weapon.

The Assassin displayed the physical and psychological stigmata that marked so many members of the Maoist clique. The aging Mao Tse-tung rarely spoke in public; Lin Piao, slight in build and chalky of skin, was accurately called the Invalid; and the Starlet was neither handsome nor healthy.

The Assassin's unrestrained ambition and viciousness probably stemmed in part from his own unprepossessing appearance. Buck-toothed, heavy-spectacled, and somewhat shorter than the average Chinese, he spoke Mandarin, the "national language," badly. Besides, his personality was far from winning, and the sickly rot of ambition that disfigured his character made his contemporaries reject him—even when he was but a youth.

His failure to win literary recognition rankled even more deeply because of his father, Yao Peng-tze, who was a leading figure in left-wing literary circles of the 1930s. The elder Yao was respected for his character and his artistic achievements. Though he was not quite in the first rank, his novels and essays were well reviewed and reasonably popular.

Yao Wen-yüan was born of an old Chekiang family of hereditary intellectuals, probably in 1927, but his formative years were spent far from that coastal province that also gave birth to Chiang Kai-shek. In the late 1930s, during the fight against Japan, he lived in exile in Chung-king, the capital of the Chinese Republic. His family returned to the metropolis of Shanghai at the end of the war in 1945. The Assassin was educated and shaped in Shanghai. His Mandarin bore the heavy imprint of the city's distinctive accent. He spoke a sibilant, sizzling "southern Mandarin," buzzing with the crackling *zzz* sounds of the Shanghai dialect.

His earliest critical article appeared in the *Wen-yi Pao* (*The Literary Gazette*) in 1951, when he was already a member of the Standing Committee of the Shanghai branch of the Communist Youth league. He began seeking fame in earnest through his frenzied orthodoxy in the literary-political controversy that attacked the liberal writers of the Hu Feng group in 1955 and was thereafter an ardent opponent of the "rightists." But Yao did not emerge as a public personage until the Anti-Rightist Movement of 1957 afforded him his first solid opportunity to elevate himself by treading on his fellows. In mid-1957, he first made his mark by attacking the chairman of the Shanghai Writers' Association in the *Shanghai Literary Monthly*. But he was far from a national figure.

So new was he before the Cultural Revolution that his personal life has remained obscure. Persistent rumor holds that during the Great Revolution he took a most useful wife—reportedly Mao Li-na, the eldest daughter of the Chairman and the Starlet. That alliance may explain his survival, for the Chairman's son-in-law would be protected by his own aura. If he is, in truth, married to Mao Li-na, the pair apparently have no children. She was so hectically busy as an "activist" of the Cultural Revolution under the *nomme de guerre* Hsiao Li that she had no time for childbearing. The marriage is not documented, though it would explain both his uncanny rise and his survival in a nation that has reverted to unabashed nepotism. It would be truly ironic if Yao Wen-yüan had acquired a father-in-law who outshone him infinitely more than had his own father. His vengeful character was, after all, largely shaped by his jealousy of his father's literary reputation and prestige.

Yao was, from the beginning of his ruthless career, feared for his violent attacks. But he was regarded with scornful contempt by other writers—until the Cultural Revolution. The Assassin's enormous influence in precipitating that cataclysm intensified both the fear and the contempt. Thus he had twice made himself an outcast among honest intellectuals.

Fame was the spur that drove him from the beginning. He confided to a colleague in 1955 that the writer he admired most in all the world was Honoré Balzac, "because Balzac with his pen made himself as great as Napoleon ever did with his sword!"

His acquaintances of that period (he had no intimate friends) are still struck by the divergence between his outward manner and avowed interests—and the career he subsequently carved out for himself. In the days when he was still seeking his own road to fame and power, Yao was shy and so abstracted he could not be bothered with formal etiquette. When he spoke to the Shanghai Writers' Association or to groups of worker-students, his eyes were invariably fixed upon a point somewhere in space.

"He never looked at his audience or at his notes," recalled a fellow writer who knew him well. "His attention always appeared to be fixed upon an imaginary fly crawling across the opposite wall or upon the pen he took from his pocket and clicked open and shut during his discourse."

Even among young men and women who self-consciously disdained niceties of manners to demonstrate their ardent dedication to the "proletarian" cause, the Assassin was remarkable for his uncouth ways. "I remember best of all the way he slurped his tea," recalled a novelist now living in exile in Hong Kong. Since the Chinese consider a certain gusto in feeding a sign of appreciation, that criticism implies extraordinary disregard of etiquette.

In addition to their feeling that he was obsessed by ambition, his colleagues were struck by Yao's lack of honest commitment to the Communist cause. " 'Was he an idealist?' you ask," remarked his former associate. "Anything but that, I'd say. He mouthed the proper slogans, but I never discerned even the slightest tinge of the sincerity most of us felt in those early days before everything went sour."

Aside from ambition, Yao's ruling passion was aesthetic. Curiously enough for the man who later sounded the clarion for the "total destruction of the old civilization," he was sincerely devoted to the traditional arts, culture, and graces of old China. His learning in those fields, particularly in classical literature, was quite profound, as even his detractors readily acknowledged. It was also pedantic. In an essay entitled "On Parallelism [in Literary Style]," published in the *Shanghai Literary Monthly* in 1955, he wrote with inspired fervor of the beauty of a maid's bosom as originally described in a classical work. "The breasts of snow glow in the mirror," he rhapsodized, "like fairy gems studding the foliage around the seraglio."

The passage contains an additional and untranslatable* double play on words that implies the utter harmony—or coupling—of man and woman, giving Yao his parallelism twice over. Intricately subtle play on words is not unusual for writers in a language that lends itself to such symbolism, strained though it may sound to Western ears. Such verbal play is not difficult in Chinese, but it is supremely difficult to perform well. Yao Wen-yüan performed with particular grace. An aesthete he was in truth. He wrote in another essay: "One can find the essence of all beauty even in the gestures of a beauty-parlor attendant shampooing a lady's hair."

Despite the grudging admiration of his more sophisticated associates, Yao's devotion to traditional aesthetics and classical literature did little to advance him in the utilitarian China of Mao Tse-tung. Nor did he evoke admiration by sheer literary power—or win advancement by writing propaganda homilies in fictional form. It therefore appears that he turned to his career of destructive criticism in frustration. All his former associates agree that Yao's governing passion was, from the outset, an overwhelming compulsion to "make his name" and demonstrate his superiority over both his colleagues and his father.

"When he mentioned the men of fame in the Party," the Chinese novelist recalled, "there was a catch in his voice. He spoke not as men speak of other men, but as they speak of demigods."

The Assassin's early writing displayed this single-minded passion. Inventing a new discipline, which he called "the study of name-lists," he wrote in 1955: "If an editor does not attend to the proper order of precedence in the table of contents of a magazine, there will be much grumbling behind his back. That's an open secret. I was originally a total amateur in 'the study of name-lists,' but since I've been doing editorial work, I've begun to understand its wonders!"

Chinese writers scratched their heads when they read the passage. No more than Westerners could they quite understand what Yao was getting at. They finally concluded that the words revealed a petty mind obses-

* Because of linguistic incompatability, not bad taste.

sessed by fixing *his* name high on lists indicating rank. There could be no other rational explanation.

In an essay on classical poetry, the Assassin was even more revealing. "The little student who would become Emperor," he wrote, "must first learn to cry with all his voice: 'May the Emperor live ten thousand times ten thousand years!" Yao did precisely that in his praise of the Chairman.

When Mao proclaimed in 1957, "Let all schools of thought contend! Let a Hundred Flowers Blossom!" the Assassin became useful. Regretting the torrents of criticism they had loosed by allowing free expression, the Maoists hastily decided to dam them. A sweeping campaign against "rightists" was proclaimed. The Assassin had found his metier.

His first major target was Hsü Chieh, chairman of the Shanghai Writers' Association. Referring to the Land Reform Campaign of 1950–53, Hsü had written a couplet describing his "day and night endeavors in land reform." The couplet also recalled "floating in a small boat" and "leaning on the railing while crossing a bridge." The Assassin's attack ignored the first part of the couplet. While the rest of the nation was engaged in the "heaven-moving and earth-shaking work of land reform," he charged, Hsü Chieh had proclaimed himself "superior to such mundane affairs . . . preferring to drift leisurely in a boat or stroll over bridges." Yao concluded, "Hsü was really notifying Chiang Kai-shek that he despised the Land Reform Movement."

Since any stick would do to beat Hsü Chieh, the absurd charge based on a distorted quotation helped disgrace him. The Assassin had made his first killing. He had added to his thirst for power a taste for blood.

The absurdities of the Cultural Revolution in the literary realm sprang from the fertile and perverted brain of Yao Wen-yüan. His unbridled distortions and illogical polemics also set the tone for the "struggle" in realms far from the world of letters. To non-Chinese it may appear peculiar, to say the least, that a literary critic commenting on plays, essays, and novels should have been a prime mover of the greatest upheaval of the Communist Party and its creature, the People's Republic of China. The Chinese, conditioned to consider the written word a sacred and powerful force, are themselves bemused by the Assassin's influence.

Yao owed his eminence to two factors. The Great Proletarian Cultural Revolution, though it became an elemental force sweeping across China, did actually begin in the sphere of culture. Moreover, the Starlet, who saw herself as the Czarina of all the arts, badly needed a professional intellectual to serve as her confidant, chief executioner, and cultural guide. The Assassin was delighted to play that complex role, scorned by most of his colleagues.

Avid for power and revenge, Yao became Chiang Ching's man. Both the Starlet and the Assassin were, initially, determined to remake a cultural milieu that rejected their talents. Both were, finally, determined to destroy the society that encapsuled that milieu. When the desperate Maoists felt in 1965 that they must strike back at their entrenched enemies or accept defeat, they charged the Assassin to break the reputation of Wu Han, vice mayor of Peking. Wu Han was the outstanding representative not only of the Maoists' intellectual opponents, but of the powerful group at the apex of the Communist Party that had rejected Mao's authority in the day-to-day administration of China. The Assassin led the Maoist pack against all intellectuals who retained any degree of independence. By attacking those writers, educators, and editors, the Maoists struck at their sponsors—the infamous "men in power within the Communist Party following the capitalist road."

The Assassin was both a major force in the Cultural Revolution and a tool in others' hands. His influence was truly enormous during the initial turmoil begun by his attack on Wu Han in the winter of 1965. For more than a year, he was the chief artistic authority of Communist China—and one of a handful of political powers. His enemies fell in windrows. His own decline began in mid-1967, although he survived the purge of Chiang Ching's ultra-leftist clique in early 1968. Finally, he became a willing instrument of a new group striving to pacify China in the name of the same Mao Tse-tung who had cast the country into turmoil.

Yao Wen-Yüan thus planned a major role even after the visionary phase of the Great Revolution ended in April 1967—a climax clearly seen in retrospect, though hardly obvious at the time. Developments after April 1967 were determined by the natural reluctance of the Chinese People's Liberation Army to murder great numbers of the Chinese people in order to force the remainder to live in the Chairman's vision of paradise. That reluctance ended the Utopian phase of the Great Proletarian Cultural Revolution. But Mao Tse-tung remained indispensable. If the generals and the new pragmatists were to "pacify" the country and impose their own authoritarian rule—which was all they knew of the government of men—the Chairman was an essential symbol of unity.

To preserve the Chairman's eroded prestige, Comrade Liu Shao-chi, the prime symbol of anti-Maoism, had to be "destroyed"—even if his policies were later enacted. Therefore in April the great attack began on the Chairman of the People's Republic of China. Their interests coinciding once again, Maoist and military publicists mounted a major campaign of vituperation. BEAT THE MAD DOG DROWNING IN THE STREAM! DESTROY THE HEAP OF STINKING, ROTTING RUBBISH! Under such slogans the propaganda legions marched against the man who had striven to preserve China from excesses at home and hazards abroad.

April was indeed the cruelest month. Beginning on the first, tens of millions flung themselves into hysterical demonstrations. Frantic Red Guards and bewildered soldiers swarmed into streets throughout China to denounce the "chief personage in the Communist Party following the capitalist road." With pounding of drums, fusillades of firecrackers, clanging of cymbals, and, of course, the constant blaring of loudspeakers, they "celebrated another great victory for the Thought of Mao Tse-tung." Although still not identified by name, Comrade Liu Shao-chi and the Organizer, Teng Hsiao-ping, *quondam* Secretary-General of the Communist Party, were being prepared for the ritual slaughter.

The attack had begun with "bombardments" by *Red Flag* and *The Peking People's Daily. The Liberation Army Daily,* which had a year earlier been the bellwether of the Maoist flock, was curiously silent in the beginning. It seemed the generals approved the Disciple's decision that Comrade Liu Shao-chi must perish to prevent civil war—but did not relish the mission of destruction.

The civilian organs, however, rejoiced in the last outburst of unrestrained Maoist rancor. Comrade Shao-chi and the Organizer were denounced as "traitors to China and Socialism . . . spies and agents of Soviet Revisionism and American capitalism . . . scabs and renegades." Liu's chief work, *How To Be A Good Communist,* was characterized as a "poisonous weed" that corrupted the Party. He had commended loyalty to a disciplined Party governed by encoded laws, rather than automatic obedience to the will of Chairman Mao. The pair were further denounced for "capitulationism" because they wished to cooperate with other nations, rather than destroy them. "We must," said *Red Flag,* "resolutely oppose the so-called patriotism (in reality, unabashed Quislingism) advocated by the handful of counterrevolutionary revisionists and the chief personage in authority in the Party taking the capitalist road." The "bombardment" was to continue for 18 months before Comrade Shao-chi was finally expelled from his offices and from the Communist Party by yet another rump plenum of the Central Committee. The inordinate length of time necessary to "destroy" Liu demonstrated that the opposition was indeed "strong and well entrenched."

The Maoists chose, somewhat deviously, to indict Comrade Shao-chi for deeds done decades earlier. One of the most curious was condemnation of his approval—17 years earlier—of a Hong Kong-made motion picture called "The Secret History of the Manchu Court," which was no more than a particularly well-produced historical epic with minor propaganda content. Liu Shao-chi, the Maoists said, had deliberately glorified the Reformer Emperor Kuang Hsü while denigrating his powerful aunt, the Empress Dowager Tzu Hsi, in order to denigrate Mao Tse-tung. The innumerable charges against the Chairman's chief lieutenant have already been outlined in previous chapters. In any event, a full accounting would be impossible because the campaign was so loud, so detailed, and so protracted—in public.

Not only Liu Shao-chi but his wife, the Campus Belle Wang Kwang-mei, were subjected to personal persecution—in private. Liu himself, still formally Chairman of the People's Republic, enjoyed some immunity from the more humiliating aspects of that persecution. When Red Guards marched on his home in Chungnanhai within the Imperial City to "drag him out to answer for his crimes," the Liberation Army turned them back. No such immunity, however, protected the Campus Belle. She was brutally forced to "answer for her crimes"—and her husband's—in public meetings that were even more frenzied and more violent than her mass interrogation in January 1967 when the Red Guards "captured her by ruse."

A full record of the "three trials of Wang Kwang-mei during the day and night of April 10, 1967," was subsequently published* by the "South Seas Battle Unit" of the Chinghua University Red Guard unit. The Introductory Remarks and excerpts from the "three trials"—one at 6:30 A.M., the second at 1:00 P.M., and the third from 5:30 to 10:00 P.M.—graphically demonstrate how she was harried. They also cast much oblique light on the earlier developments that had made the confrontation of the Great Revolution inevitable.

> On April 10, the Chingkangshan Corps of Chinghua University and the revolutionary masses of Peking, as well as those from other places now in the capital, *totaling several hundred thousand people,* waged a fierce struggle against Wang Kwang-mei, a member of the reactionary bourgeoisie and No. 1 pickpocket on the Chinghua campus.

> Before and after this struggle meeting, the fighters of our Chingkangshan Corps had tried pickpocket Wang Kwang-mei on three occasions.

> We are publishing here the records of these three trials. *This pamphlet is a very good set of teaching material by negative example that deserves to be read by everybody.*

> It can be seen clearly from the records of these three trials that Wang

* And translated by the Press Translation Unit of the American Consulate-General in Hong Kong with all its linguistic barbarisms retained intact.

Kwang-mei, that bitch in trouble, is still not reconciled to her defeat and is still playing tricks by all ways and means to pit her strength against the revolutionary people. Sometimes, she deliberately equivocated and resorted to chicanery. She denied the towering crimes committed by herself and Liu Shao-chi. Sometimes, she made accusations by insinuation, resorted to provocations to sow discord, laid the blame on other people, and attempted to bombard the proletarian headquarters. On other occasions, she assumed a pitiful look and practiced cajolery in a vain attempt to hoodwink others to show sympathy for her. Sometimes she was very ferocious, bared her teeth and claws, and shouted hysterically to cover up her fear and insecurity. She pictured exactly the ugly performance of a bitch struggling in the water.

Of course the barking of a dog in the water serves nothing more than to expose to a greater extent its nature. To those innocent people who think that those dogs "baptized in water have repented and will not come out to bite people again," this is a very good sobering dose. Because of this, it is really a very good thing to adopt in addition this rare set of teaching material by negative example in the onflow of irresistible revolutionary mass criticism and repudiation. All revolutionary comrades must make good use of this set of teaching material by negative example, hit the *new counteroffensive* of China's Khrushchev in the head, *break his spine, topple, discredit, and destroy him by criticism, and turn him into a heap of dog's dung spurned by mankind.*

THE FIRST TRIAL

PLACE:	Main Wing of the Chinghua Building, 7th Floor.
TIME:	About half past six early in the morning.
INTERROGATOR:	Why did Shao-chi say that *The Secret History of the Manchu Court* was patriotic?
WANG KWANG-MEI:	I have never heard Comrade Shao-chi say that this film was patriotic. It is definite that Comrade Shao-chi has said nothing of the sort. I have faith in Chairman Mao, and he will no doubt make an investigation to clear up things. (The students asked her to put on the dress she had worn in Indonesia for the struggle, but Wang Kwang-mei refused to do so.)
INTERROGATOR:	You must put on that dress!
WANG KWANG-MEI:	I will not!
INTERROGATOR:	You have no choice in this regard!
WANG KWANG-MEI	(drawing in her horns and pointing at the dress she wore): This is good enough for receiving guests.

INTERROGATOR	(sternly): Receiving guests? You are the subject of struggle today!
WANG KWANG-MEI:	I am not going to put on that dress. It is not presentable.
INTERROGATOR:	Why did you wear it then in Indonesia?
WANG KWANG-MEI:	It was summer at that time, and I wore it in Djakarta.
INTERROGATOR:	Why did you wear it in Lahore?
WANG KWANG-MEI:	I am not going to put it on, whatever you may say.
INTERROGATOR:	Let me tell you: You are the subject of struggle today. If you are not honest with us, beware!
WANG KWANG-MEI:	Even if I have to die, that does not matter.
INTERROGATOR:	Death? We want to keep you alive. Put it on!
WANG KWANG-MEI:	Would it not be better for us to discuss things seriously?
INTERROGATOR:	Who wants to discuss things with you? Let me tell you: You are the subject of struggle today!
WANG KWANG-MEI	(angrily): On no account can you encroach upon my personal freedom.
INTERROGATOR	(amidst the sound of laughter): You are the wife of a three-anti element, a member of the reactionary bourgeoisie and a class dissident. *You will not be given an iota of minimum democracy, let alone extensive democracy! Dictatorship is exercised over you today, and you are not free.*
WANG KWANG-MEI	(interrupting): Who says I am the wife of a three-anti element?
INTERROGATOR:	We do.
WANG KWANG-MEI:	I will not put the dress on, come what may. If I have committed mistakes, I am open to criticism and struggle.
INTERROGATOR:	You are guilty! You are the subject of struggle today and you will also be the subject of struggle hereafter. Put it on!
WANG KWANG-MEI	(evasively, pointing at the fur coat she was wearing): This is already good enough for receiving guests. It was a gift from Afghanistan. They had this in mind when they said that I was fashion-minded.
INTERROGATOR:	We want you to put on the dress that you wore in Indonesia.
WANG KWANG-MEI:	That was summer. There is winter clothing for

winter, summer clothing for summer, and spring clothing for spring. I cannot put on a summer dress now. If I must wear a dress for spring, I can send someone to bring me one.

INTERROGATOR: *Skip it. We know nothing about such bourgeois stuff as what is good for summer, winter or spring, for receiving guests or for travel.*

WANG KWANG-MEI: Chairman Mao has said that we must pay attention to climate and change clothing according to it.

INTERROGATOR (amidst laughter): What Chairman Mao has said refers to the political climate. According to your standpoint, even though you are wearing a fur coat, you will also freeze to death.

INTERROGATOR: Let me ask you: Didn't you wear that dress when you were in Lahore although it was colder at that time than it is now? Put it on! It will do so long as you will not freeze to death. Are you going to put it on?

WANG KWANG-MEI: No.

INTERROGATOR: All right! We'll give you 10 minutes. See what will happen at quarter to seven. Try to defy us by not wearing that dress. We mean what we say.

WANG KWANG-MEI: (keeping silence) . . .

INTERROGATOR: Wang Kwang-mei, what do you think of the unhorsing of Liu Shao-chi?

WANG KWANG-MEI: That is fine; there will be no revisionism in China.

INTERROGATOR: *We still want to drag out Liu Shao-chi for struggle. This will take place some day. Do you believe it?*

WANG KWANG-MEI: You are at liberty to struggle against him if you want to. . . . (silence)
People of the Chingkang Mountains are thoroughly revolutionary. The mode of struggle you are using is not very good. You can make use of a higher form of criticism and repudiation.

INTERROGATOR: Ignore her! In 10 minutes you will see.

WANG KWANG-MEI: You . . . I can ring someone up and ask for a spring dress.

INTERROGATOR: That won't do!

WANG KWANG-MEI: This dress is made of silk. It is too cold!

INTERROGATOR: Put it on and wear your fur coat on top of it.

INTERROGATOR: "Small wonder flies freeze and perish."

WANG KWANG-MEI:	If I were really opposed to Chairman Mao, I would deserve to freeze to death.
INTERROGATOR:	You are opposed to Chairman Mao.
WANG KWANG-MEI:	I am not against him now, and I will not oppose him in the future.
INTERROGATOR:	No more nonsense with her. Well, there are seven minutes left.
WANG KWANG-MEI:	How about my putting on that pair of shoes (pointing to the pair of pointed shoes she had brought with her)?
INTERROGATOR:	That is not enough! You must wear everything.
WANG KWANG-MEI:	You have not the right.
INTERROGATOR:	*We have this right!* You are the subject of struggle today. We are at liberty to wage struggle in whatever way we want to, and you have no freedom. *It is better for you to put away your notorious theory that "everybody is equal before truth." We are the revolutionary masses while you are a counterrevolutionary and notorious woman. You cannot confuse the class line!* (At the time limit set, the members of the ghost-catching detachment began to force her to put on the outlandish dress.)
WANG KWANG-MEI:	Wait a moment. (They ignored her. Wang Kwang-mei sat on the floor and refused to allow them to slip the dress on her. Later, she was dragged up, and the dress was slipped on her.)
INTERROGATOR:	Have you got it on now? (Wang Kwang-mei said that the dress was too small for her.)
WANG KWANG-MEI:	You have violated Chairman Mao's instruction of no struggle by force. (All recited Chairman Mao's words: *A revolution is not a dinner party, or writing an essay, or painting a picture, or doing embroidery; it cannot be so refined, so leisurely and gentle, so temperate, kind, courteous, restrained, and magnanimous. A revolution is an insurrection, an act of violence by which one class overthrows another.*)
WANG KWANG-MEI:	Opposition to Chairman Mao's instruction means . . . (She was interrupted as all recited: "Although the diehards of the world may be stub-

born and firm today, tomorrow and the day after tomorrow, yet they cannot remain stubborn and firm forever. . . . The diehards are actually stubborn but not firm, and eventually their stubbornness will change into dog's dung spurned by mankind."

(Wang Kwang-mei could do nothing else but to put on the transparent silk stockings and high-heeled shoes. They put on a specially made necklace for her, and she was photographed.)

WANG KWANG-MEI: I am a Communist and fear nothing. I am not afraid of death by a thousand cuts. . . .

INTERROGATOR   (shouting a slogan): Down with three-anti element Wang Kwang-mei!

WANG KWANG-MEI: Since you think in this way, I will one day . . .

INTERROGATOR   (revealing facts): Light a cigarette for Sukarno and bring disgrace to the Chinese people.

WANG KWANG-MEI: I am of the opinion I have nothing to be ashamed of. At the farewell banquet on that day, he sat next to me, and as the hostess . . . I should respect the Indonesian customs.

INTERROGATOR: To hell with you! *We know nothing of those foreign conventions.* You flirted with such a bad fellow as Sukarno.

WANG KWANG-MEI: At that time Sukarno was quite progressive . . . in diplomacy. . .

INTERROGATOR: Tell me, how many students have been branded as revolutionaries by you? Quite a number of us here have been so branded.

WANG KWANG-MEI: In any case, we have only made criticism, but have not branded anybody as counterrevolutionary.

INTERROGATOR: Who authorized you to oppose the "phoney left?"

WANG KWANG-MEI: Not Liu Shao-chi.

INTERROGATOR: What instructions had Liu Shao-chi given?

WANG KWANG-MEI: Liu Shao-chi seldom gave instructions in respect of Chinghua. . . . Chairman Mao asked Liu Shao-chi: "Why is it that Wang Kwang-mei does not live together, eat together, and work together with the masses now as she did during the Four Purification's days in the past?" The Chairman said: "She can participate in labor. . . . In this way she is able to accept criticism." I heard this and was moved. So I went to work.

INTERROGATOR: What is your view in regard to the criticism and repudiation of *How To Be A Good Communist Party Member?*

WANG KWANG-MEI: This book is an idealistic one and does not discuss the class struggle. I agree with what is said in the article of the *Red Flag* commentator already published. But I disagree with the claim that he [Liu] is subjectively opposed to the thought of Mao Tse-tung. He has not satisfactorily transformed his world outlook.

INTERROGATOR: What is your view in regard to Comrade Chi Pen-yü's article criticizing the film *The Secret History of the Manchu Court?*

WANG KWANG-MEI: This film is an out-and-out film of national betrayal, and Comrade Chi Pen-yü has made a most penetrating criticism of it. Liu Shao-chi has never described this film as patriotic. I saw the film together with him, and he only saw half of it. Later, at daybreak, the picture was not very clear. He did not say anything. I am definite that he did not say anything. I saw the picture together with him and I should know. He definitely did not say anything.

INTERROGATOR: According to your story, Liu Shao-chi has made no mistakes.

WANG KWANG-MEI: Liu Shao-chi has some responsibility. In 1952, Chairman Mao had told him that this picture was guilty of national betrayal. As a leader, it was a big mistake that he had not organized criticism and repudiation against it.

INTERROGATOR: This was not a big mistake, and he was only guilty of neglect of duty.

WANG KWANG-MEI: Neglect of duty or a bigger mistake. . . . Liu Shao-chi is responsible for some of them, but he has nothing to do with some problems.

INTERROGATOR: Then *Red Flag* is spreading a false report, and Liu Shao-chi is not a person in authority taking the capitalist road?

WANG KWANG-MEI:	I have faith in Chairman Mao and the masses. In the past I made mistakes because I had not enough faith in him. I have worked by the side of Liu Shao-chi for more than 10 years, and I feel that not everything is in agreement with facts. In any case, Liu Shao-chi has nothing to do with many things. It never occurs to me directly that he is the top Party person in authority taking the capitalist road.
INTERROGATOR:	What about his instructing the renegade group to surrender itself? *
WANG KWANG-MEI:	This was not his instruction. A responsible comrade made the suggestion, and he endorsed it.
INTERROGATOR:	Who was he?
WANG KWANG-MEI:	I won't tell you!
INTERROGATOR:	You are shielding him! Tell me at once.
WANG KWANG-MEI	(meditating for a while): The suggestion was made by Ko Ching-shih,** and Liu Shao-chi endorsed the idea.
INTERROGATOR	(indignantly): You are not allowed to vilify Venerable Ko! . . . Tell me, Wang Kwang-mei, how do you look at the allegation that Liu Shao-chi is the top Party person in authority taking the capitalist road?
WANG KWANG-MEI:	Subjectively I am still not up to this level in recognition. In any case, prior to the Eleventh Plenum of the Eighth CCP Central Committee, the Chairman entrusted Liu Shao-chi to deal with many things, and held him responsible when trouble occurred. *But he has now been told to stand aside. He has no responsibility and is no longer in authority*. When the reactionary line was in force, he did follow the capitalist road for a time.
INTERROGATOR:	Only the reactionary line?
WANG KWANG-MEI:	This is of course not all. Everyone committing mistakes in the line takes to the capitalist road for a while.

* The imprisoned Communists who were released by the Nationalists after recanting.
** Deceased Mayor of Shanghai.

INTERROGATOR: Do you mean to say that Liu Shao-chi is a person in authority taking the capitalist road, but with shortcomings and mistakes?

WANG KWANG-MEI: He subjectively wants to take the Socialist road, but his world outlook has not been satisfactorily transformed, and because he holds an important position, he could lead China toward capitalism. It is dangerous to let things develop in this way.

INTERROGATOR: Was Liu Shao-chi also subjectively taking the Socialist road by extolling the Red capitalists and speaking in favor of exploitation?

WANG KWANG-MEI: Liu Shao-chi said the wrong things on many occasions. You are referring to the speech he made in Tientsin in 1950. I know it because I was also present at that time. Many things he said were wrong. At that time Tientsin was disposed to be over "left," and a good many people wanted to wipe out the exploiting classes. He was sent by Chairman Mao to rectify the deviation, and some of the remarks he made were for the purpose of rectifying the deviation. The remarks now quoted in the wall posters are not exactly what he said.

INTERROGATOR: Do you mean in this way that it is correct to say "workers should be exploited"?

WANG KWANG-MEI: Some were wrong. Some were correct, but not properly presented. One cannot do anything without regard for the environment. For example, if you told a capitalist that exploitation is a crime, then one would commit a big crime by setting up a factory, and a bigger crime would be committed if one more factory were set up. Liu Shao-chi only said that so long as exploitation by factories was of advantage to the prosperity of the country and the people, such exploitation was necessary, and the workers also needed such exploitation. This observation was made under a specific condition, but some people now quote it out of context.

INTERROGATOR: Who then advocated a new stage of peace and democracy, disseminating blind faith in Chiang Kai-shek?

WANG KWANG-MEI: He also was not the only one. According to press reports, this was definitely not the responsibility of one person. The words "peace" and "democracy" were clearly written in the armistice agreement. Now he has assumed the responsibility—bravely assumed the responsibility. (Everyone laughed and said: In that case isn't he a hero?) He has bravely assumed the responsibility.

INTERROGATOR: Tell me then, who were the others?

WANG KWANG-MEI: Is it necessary for me to elaborate?

INTERROGATOR: This won't do! Those capitulating to Chiang Kai-shek must be located.

WANG KWANG-MEI: I am one working on the Central Committee and must keep secrets. You can look through the papers for those articles that have been made public. . .

INTERROGATOR: What about the gold buckle and gold shoehorn embezzled by Liu Shao-chi?

WANG KWANG-MEI: It is true that he owned a gold buckle and a gold shoehorn. Because he worked in the White Area, he ran the risk of being arrested at any time and he should carry something with him. Although I do not know Comrade Hsieh Fei,* I feel that she did the right thing in not taking anything with her when she left. Wang Chien* was not so good, and she took these two things with her. At that time, many persons were in favor of the divorce because Wang Chien hampered Comrade Liu Shao-chi's work. . .

INTERROGATOR: Have you ever said that that big capitalist Wang Kwang-ying** was good and should be made to join the Party?

WANG KWANG-MEI: Wang Kwang-ying was not a big capitalist, and was, at most, a member of the middle class or a national capitalist. It is true that he had something to do with exploitation . . . but you can make investigations to see if he is really able to play the role of a progressive capitalist. He was unwilling to work as a capitalist, saying that the name of a capitalist was too notorious. He ap-

---

* Both Liu's former wives, according to the Red Guards.
** Her younger brother.

plied for Party membership, and the Party assigned him a task and made him work as a capitalist.

INTERROGATOR: Which Party? Your Liu and [the Organizer] Teng Party! What do you think of your mother? Has she something to do with exploitation?

WANG KWANG-MEI: She ran a kindergarten, and this was not exploitation, but collective welfare and a commendable undertaking. The children she brought up were better than our own.

INTERROGATOR: Nonsense! What did she do with an orphan she hired? That orphan was tortured to death.

WANG KWANG-MEI: She did not exploit the orphan. That I know. There was no exploitation. When the orphan fell sick later, she was given good care. Has the Chairman not said that we should make earnest efforts? How many good deeds are described as bad ones. You must investigate things in real earnest.

(Comment: She still wanted to confuse black and white and bite back.)

INTERROGATOR: What is your opinion of Liu Shao-chi now?

WANG KWANG-MEI: I have insufficient data to show that he was opposed to the revolution but never against capitalism all his life.

(The students asked her to put on the necklace.)

INTERROGATOR: Tell me this! Comrade Chiang Ching had told you not to wear the necklace when you were abroad. Why must you wear it?

WANG KWANG-MEI: Comrade Chiang Ching only told me not to wear the brooch, but said nothing about the necklace. But the question is one and the same.

INTERROGATOR: You are talking nonsense! You are a three-anti element.

WANG KWANG-MEI: I am not!

INTERROGATOR: What do you think of the smashing of Wang Huai-ching's* tombstone?

WANG KWANG-MEI: I approve the action. It was a mistake for me to put up that tombstone.

INTERROGATOR: How shameless! You take pride in hoodwinking people. Now everyone has seen your essence as a reactionary bourgeois element.

* Her father.

WANG KWANG-MEI:	I am not a reactionary bourgeois element, but a member of Chairman Mao's Communist Party. Truth is truth. I might, however, have been influenced by the bourgeois reactionary line.
INTERROGATOR:	You are rejecting the revolutionary young fighters!
WANG KWANG-MEI	(hatefully, and peering at the people through narrowed eyes): One should call a spade a spade if one really cherishes the revolutionary young fighters. One cannot cherish the revolutionary young fighters by distorting facts. . . . (She was interrupted by someone crying "You are spreading poison!") If you want me to lay all facts on the table, let me finish what I am going to say. Chairman Mao said: "We should listen to the views of others, be they favorable or unfavorable to us, including those of the opponents, and let them have their say." If you don't want to lay the facts on the table and are unreasonable, then I have nothing more to say. Go ahead with your struggle.
INTERROGATOR:	We intend precisely to struggle against you—a reactionary bourgeois element, the big pickpocket of the Chinghua campus.
WANG KWANG-MEI:	I am not what you say; I am a Communist Party member.
INTERROGATOR:	Don't try to denigrate our Party. Haven't you done enough in spreading scandal? What did you do during the Four Purifications Movement at Taoyüan?*
WANG KWANG-MEI:	How much do you know about the material of the Four Purifications Movement? From whom did you get your information? *You have spent no more than five days at the grassroots level while I stayed there for almost one year.* I understand things better than you do. You must investigate things in real earnest.
INTERROGATOR:	*To hell with you.* Your Taoyüan experience is notorious enough. You'll soon hear of it.
WANG KWANG-MEI:	Taoyüan's experience is good and not a bad one. But there are shortcomings and mistakes.

* The Peach Garden Production Brigade, where she lived in 1963.

INTERROGATOR: How meritorious! Then the *Latter Ten Articles* [*on Agriculture*] are also good but with short-comings and mistakes.

WANG KWANG-MEI: On the basis of the *First Ten Articles,* many people went to the grassroots level to set up experimental spots for the purpose of feeling out the situation. [The Mayor] Peng Chen had set up experimental spots in a number of provinces, and on the basis of the conditions there, he delimited many policies. It seemed that there were too many taboos. When we went to the grassroots level, we worked on the basis of both *Ten Articles* as stipulated by the Central Committee. The *Latter Ten Articles* were revised by Liu Shao-chi. There were some taboos, but the spirit was good. It was Chairman Mao who told him to revise them.

INTERROGATOR: According to what you say, the *Latter Ten Articles* are simply wonderful!

WANG KWANG-MEI: The *Latter Ten Articles* are good in part, but there is metaphysics as well as scholastic philosophy.
(The masses were enraged, and they "dressed" her up for a photograph.)

WANG KWANG-MEI: Thank you. You should not insult me.

WANG KWANG-MEI: . . . you are making every effort to make me look ugly.

INTERROGATOR: This is what you have been all the time. Why feel shy over what you have carried out and done. This is done to restore your true identity.
(Wang Kwang-mei was ready to "go to prison" and she brought with her a towel, a toothbrush and other things.)

INTERROGATOR: Wang Kwang-mei! Are you afraid?

WANG KWANG-MEI: Why should I fear? I am not afraid. A Communist has nothing to fear.
(As she was about to go downstairs, she changed clothes and her shaky hands were unable to put things in the proper place.)

WANG KWANG-MEI: I want a glass of water. Where is the PLA comrade? Old Ma, I want a tranquilizer.

INTERROGATOR: Are you afraid?

WANG KWANG-MEI:	My mind is calm. I have to take medicine because I am sick. I am nervous. (She gasped for breath and her trembling hands were unable to put things away.)
INTERROGATOR:	Wang Kwang-mei's hands are trembling.
WANG KWANG-MEI:	There is some trouble with my hands. I am not afraid, and I am very calm in mind. (Wang Kwang-mei asked for two tranquilizer tablets, but the PLA comrade gave her only one.)
WANG KWANG-MEI:	All right. I'll take one as you say. (As she was dragged out, she became downcast and turned pale. She dragged her feet step by step, and again asked for a tranquilizer.)
WANG KWANG-MEI:	Where is the PLA comrade? I want some more medicine.
INTERROGATOR:	Didn't you say you were not afraid? Paper tiger!
WANG KWANG-MEI:	I am not afraid, and I am willing to go through with the meeting. I have been running a fever these few days. Liu Shao-chi is also sick, and I have nursed him a number of days. (She then pursed her lips, and the veins stood out on her hands.)

THE THIRD TRIAL

PLACE:	Room 803, Main Wing of the Chinghua Building.
TIME:	From 5:30 P.M. to 10:00 P.M.
INTERROGATOR:	Wang Kwang-mei, you have not been honest with us in the last two trials. This time you must make a true confession. First, tell us your family background!
WANG KWANG-MEI:	I came from a national bourgeois family, and I was a student. My family owned more than 40 houses and some shares in a certain Company and the Yengcheng Company. After the place was occupied by the Japanese. . .
INTERROGATOR:	Tell us the exact number.
WANG KWANG-MEI:	I cannot say, but the number was not a big one. In 1937, my family was not well off and had to sell houses to make ends meet. Why was it still classified as the national bourgeoisie? Because

the proceeds from the houses sold were deposited in banks, and this involved exploitation. My father was at first an office worker. Later he taught in a middle school. After that he went to study law at Waseda University in Japan. After his return to China, he was promoted as head of the Industry and Commerce Division.

INTERROGATOR: How did your father finance his studies in Japan?

WANG KWANG-MEI: My father and his elder brother saved up some money through teaching. He joined the Christian Church in Japan. . .

INTERROGATOR: Why was he able to climb so fast?

WANG KWANG-MEI: He had worked as an office worker a number of years!

INTERROGATOR: What did he do afterward?

WANG KWANG-MEI: After liberation, he suffered from hypertension and stayed home to take a rest. He grew vegetables in the courtyard. . .

INTERROGATOR: How "industrious"!

WANG KWANG-MEI: Not at all. He did this to kill time. His family was a down-fallen one, but should be classified as the national bourgeoisie. I had asked other comrades about this when I participated in agrarian reform work.

INTERROGATOR: So this was determined by you yourself?

WANG KWANG-MEI: No.

INTERROGATOR: Why was your father able to move up so fast?

WANG KWANG-MEI: This was not clear to me.

INTERROGATOR: What was the amount in fixed dividends he received after liberation?

WANG KWANG-MEI: He received fixed dividends for one or two years. I asked no question about the payment of fixed dividends. As to the amount he received, you can go to make inquiry. In the first two years, he received between 200 and 300* people's dollars each year. Judged by the fixed dividends he received, he really was unfit to be called a big capitalist.

INTERROGATOR: When did your father amass a fortune?

WANG KWANG-MEI: Probably in the days of the Northern warlords, when he was head of the Industry and Commerce Division. He himself said that he was on one

* About U.S. $100 to $150.

occasion Acting Minister of Industry and Commerce. A bureaucrat naturally would not describe himself as a corrupt official. At that time he was a reactionary bureaucrat, but because he later relied on capitalist exploitation, he should be classified as national bourgeoisie. My elder brother described him as "reactionary bureaucrat."

INTERROGATOR: In which year did your father pass away?

WANG KWANG-MEI: He died in 1956 according to the wall posters.

INTERROGATOR: What did you write on your father's tombstone?

WANG KWANG-MEI: I originally thought that he was a target of the united front, that he was not very bad, and that he wanted to make progress. I do not know in what year the tombstone was erected. I read in the handbills that it was smashed by you, the Chingkangshan rebels. I entirely support and approve the smashing of that tombstone.

INTERROGATOR: You were self-contradictory in what you said! What was your father's calling after all? Was he a "Red capitalist"?

WANG KWANG-MEI: He was a capitalist desirous of making progress. Liu Shao-chi never talked about "Red capitalists." He cultivated capitalists desirous of making progress in various big cities, and let them play the leading role. The reason was that we had not carried out any work among capitalists at that time, and the capitalists could carry out the work more efficiently than we could. He also said that the Women's Federation should take charge of work among the dependents of capitalists.

INTERROGATOR: Hereafter, you are required to submit a copy of self-examination every 10 days. In the next self-examination, you should state your family background, the amount of fixed dividends received, the amount obtained through exploitation after liberation. Otherwise, a struggle will be waged against you without mercy.

WANG KWANG-MEI: Good. But you are now in a more advantageous position than I in making investigations. It is better for you to investigate things yourselves.

INTERROGATOR: Don't talk nonsense. It is definite that your father was not from the national bourgeoisie but a re-

	actionary capitalist! Tell me about your brothers and sisters.
WANG KWANG-MEI:	I have six brothers and four sisters. My eldest brother Wang Kwang-te died long ago. He was blind, and was unable to do anything. My second elder brother Wang Kwang-chi is attached to the Information Research Center of the Foreign Trade Ministry.
INTERROGATOR:	When did he join that office?
WANG KWANG-MEI:	After the banks were brought together, Wang Kwang-chi was criticized and repudiated. After that he was transferred there. Before liberation, he was . . . in the office of the Tsingtao Bank. Later he joined the office of the Peking Bank. After that, he taught economics at Yenching University. His wife is the daughter of a Szechwan capitalist. He went to study in the United States. Because the bank paid all expenses, after he came home he still worked with the bank.
INTERROGATOR:	Who was the owner of that bank?
WANG KWANG-MEI:	. . . This was how things stood after he came back from Chungking. His father-in-law and the brother of his father-in-law were big capitalists in Szechwan. One escaped to Hong Kong and died there. Another went to Taiwan. . . . It was his father-in-law who introduced Wang Kwang-chi to Li Tsung-jen.* Li Tsung-jen left his child with our family in the second half of 1945. I saw Li Tsung-jen when he came to visit his child.
INTERROGATOR:	What about your third elder brother?
WANG KWANG-MEI:	My third elder brother is called Wang Kwang-chao. He was formerly with the Peiping Union Medical College Hospital. He stayed with the hospital after liberation. Later he was transferred to Peking University Hospital. Now he is in charge of the Department of Dermatology. His wife is Deputy Superintendent of the Hospital and concurrently Chief of the Department of Gynecology.
INTERROGATOR:	What about your fourth elder brother?
WANG KWANG-MEI:	He is Wang Kwang-chieh. He graduated from the

* Vice president and later acting president of the Nationalist Republic of China, who returned to Peking in 1965.

Wireless Department of Chinghua before liberation, and had participated in the December 9th Movement. After the July 7th incident,* Chinghua University moved southward, but he stayed behind and joined the underground Party as a wireless operator. Because the doings of the underground Party were kept secret, I do not know in which year he joined the Party. Later, he operated an underground radio station in Tientsin. In 1939 and 1940, he was in charge of wireless telegraphy. Now he is a deputy bureau chief of the 4th Ministry of Machine Building. The year before last, he went to Shensi to carry out the Four Purifications Campaign and was deputy commander of the Purifications Work Corps. I am not clear whether he has any part to play in the Great Cultural Revolution.

INTERROGATOR: What about the two others?

WANG KWANG-MEI: Wang Kwang-fu joined a rapid-course middle school. That school was subservient to the Nationalist Air Force. He left the same day he sat for examination. At the early stage of the war of resistance, he joined the Air Force in Sinkiang. Later he was a squadron leader of the Air Force at Hsüchow. Subsequently, he escaped to Taiwan. He wanted to join the Air Force because he was antagonistic to Wang Kwang-chieh. He did not understand that the *Kuomintang* was reactionary.

The sixth is Wang Kwang-ying. He was also a graduate of Fujen University. He graduated from that university in 1942. At first, he worked as a technician in his uncle-in-law's soap factory. After spending one year in post-graduate study, he set up a chemical engineering plant in Tientsin and became its engineer. This plant was operated as a partnership business with the other party putting up capital and Wang Kwang-ying contributing technical knowhow. I have no idea whether he himself also put up some capital. He

* The Marco Polo Bridge Incident which formally began the Sino-Japanese War in 1937.

was not a big capitalist at that time. When Japan surrendered, through the recommendation of a schoolmate, he also participated in the work of taking over factories. He was arrested once for corruption. Besides this, he also had been arrested for some other offense. . .

INTERROGATOR: Be honest with us!

WANG KWANG-MEI: I have told you everything. (She got up without permission and asked for water.) After liberation, Wang Kwang-ying owned some small factories. I had gone to take a look and gradually participated in the Federation of Industry and Commerce's work.

INTERROGATOR: What connection had you with the US side?* Be honest!

WANG KWANG-MEI: No connection at all! A diplomat of the US side gave me a box of candy, and I also gave him something in return. There was no political relationship. Apart from this, because of my impending departure for Yenan, the Division Chief of the US side invited me to a dinner. I had reported this to the Executive Headquarters. This had no political bearing. . . . Negotiations were also conducted at banquets at that time. . .

INTERROGATOR: Were you accompanied by anybody to dinner?

WANG KWANG-MEI: I went myself. It was not for negotiations purposes. On the US side was the Chief of the Executive Division Stanin and his wife. Another couple was also present.

INTERROGATOR: Was the Nationalist Party also present?

WANG KWANG-MEI: No. There were only five persons present.

INTERROGATOR: What did you people talk about?

WANG KWANG-MEI: The only undesirable remark made was: "Once you go to the liberated area, you will not come back." The rest was general conversation.

INTERROGATOR: Why was it only you who were invited?

WANG KWANG-MEI: That was a sort of farewell party, a friendly gathering.

INTERROGATOR: What kind of friendship? Were the aggressors on friendly terms with you?

* The conciliation mission of General of the Army George C. Marshall.

WANG KWANG-MEI: They had, of course, their objective. . . . At that time I was accompanied there by the chauffeur of the Executive Headquarters. I went there after I approached the leadership for instruction.

INTERROGATOR: What line did you carry out in the agrarian reform?

WANG KWANG-MEI: At first, I knew nothing, and knew only to read documents. . . . Naturally I failed to arouse the masses fully, and I also had no faith in the masses. . . .
(Wang Kwang-mei again asked the PLA comrade for medicine.)

INTERROGATOR: Don't be afraid of death. You won't die yet!

WANG KWANG-MEI   (angrily): I regard death as going home! (There was on her face a blank expression that reflected the aching void in her heart.) We should lay facts on the table and reason things out.
(She swallowed a green tablet and two white ones.)

INTERROGATOR: Tell me honestly: Was it Liu Shao-chi who pulled the strings to get you into the Party?

WANG KWANG-MEI: Liu Shao-chi would not do such a thing. My request was investigated by the leadership. I was not clear how they handled things. Liu Shao-chi suffered many setbacks on the question of marriage. He had my sympathy.

INTERROGATOR: You see, there were so many things for you to do in connection with joining the Party and getting married. How could you cope with them in a little more than 10 days?

WANG KWANG-MEI: . . . Liu Shao-chi did not pull strings to get me into the Party. If he thought that I was not good enough for membership, he would not have asked me to be his wife. I still hold the same view today. I am a Communist.

INTERROGATOR: You still call yourself a Party member!

WANG KWANG-MEI   (flying into a rage like a shrew): Don't you bully me!

INTERROGATOR   (angrily retorted): We want precisely to bully you! . . . Don't get frantic!

WANG KWANG-MEI: Prior to my marriage, some comrades came to talk with me, asking me to help Liu Shao-chi. Out of my expectation,* I had done him a disservice on some problems. For example, my incorrect reflection of the situation in Chinghua University caused him to make up his mind, and the shortcomings of my Taoyüan experience also rendered him ill service. . . . *It is too mild to say that I have corrupted him.* His *How To Be A Good Communist Party Member* was written in 1939. Since he had not married me then, this showed that he had not remolded well his questionable world outlook. It goes without saying that I have also not satisfactorily remolded myself.

INTERROGATOR: Do you think then that Liu Shao-chi's book is revisionist stuff?

WANG KWANG-MEI: It is all right to say that it is idealistic, but I cannot think of anything to justify the allegation that it rejects the dictatorship of the proletariat. . . . If Liu Shao-chi is not remolded, he could develop to become a person of the Khrushchev type. During the anti-Khrushchev campaign, Liu Shao-chi disagreed with Khrushchev's point of view in many respects.

INTERROGATOR: Is *How To Be A Good Communist Party Member* one and the same with Khrushchev?

WANG KWANG-MEI: They are the same in some respects, but there are also things which are in conformity with Marxism-Leninism.

INTERROGATOR: Ha! This is revisionism! She is waving a red flag to oppose the red flag. You have answered this question yourself. Who made the decision to print this book on a large scale in 1962?

WANG KWANG-MEI: This can be investigated. It was not Liu Shao-chi. I don't know.

INTERROGATOR: Is Chi Pen-yü's article in *Red Flag* very good or very bad?

WANG KWANG-MEI: It is very good when seen from the angle that it criticizes *The Secret History of the Manchu Court* and eradicates Liu Shao-chi's influence. But I have some reservations in respect of some facts. I have not come to know that he is a

* Presumably meaning "unintentionally."

	phoney revolutionary or counterrevolutionary. Liu Shao-chi has never said that the film is patriotic.
INTERROGATOR:	[The Backstage Boss] Chou Yang has attributed this to Liu Shao-chi in his confession.
WANG KWANG-MEI:	Chou Yang may try to pull your leg. I am waiting for Chairman Mao's words. . . . In any case, Liu Shao-chi is not a counterrevolutionary.
INTERROGATOR:	Did you cry?
WANG KWANG-MEI:	I shed some tears. They (referring to her children) should draw a clear line of demarcation with me. This should be done politically, ideologically, and also economically.
INTERROGATORS	You have said that Liu Shao-chi is not tantamount to Chiang Kai-shek. Is he tantamount to Khrushchev?
WANG KWANG-MEI:	I did not think of that. . . . If things develop . . .

Neither such public humiliation nor the nation-wide public diatribes against Comrade Shao-chi and the Campus Belle crushed either their influence or the personal respect they were tendered by both cadres and the military. A month later, in May 1967, Liu Shao-chi, still not "dragged out for struggle," still insisted on his innocence of the wild charges against him. According to the Red Guard publication, he told his daughter Liu Ping-ping: "I am not a counterrevolutionary. Notwithstanding my mistakes and shortcomings in the Great Cultural Revolution, I am a revolutionary. Wang Kwang-mei's work at Taoyüan and Chinghua should, in the main, be affirmed."

His daughter, of course, reported his remarks to her Red Guard chieftains. She had chosen her side, however unwillingly. But the mass of the cadres and the Liberation Army was not quite certain where lay either truth or the ultimate welfare of the Chinese people. Their doubts were to lead to a military insurrection that verged upon civil war before Comrade Shao-chi was finally deposed.

XXI

The Revolt of the Generals

The counterrevolution erupted into conventional battle when the People's Liberation Army joined insurgent, anti-Maoist workers in "Red" Wuhan, which had made the young Lin Piao a Communist. The triplet industrial cities at the great bend of the broad Yangtze River in Central China had consistently flaunted a "revolutionary tendency" that was anathema to the Chairman, but quite congenial to Comrade Liu Shao-chi. The "anti-feudal" Revolution of 1911, which destroyed the Manchu Dynasty, had begun with the premature explosion of a bomb in Wuhan. The Railway Unions' General Strike of 1923, suppressed by a massacre, was commemorated by a granite column surmounted by the hammer-and-sickle.

Urban strikes were not the style of Mao Tse-tung, nor was the hammer-and-sickle of the "revisionist" Soviet Union his emblem. The old labor leader, Comrade Shao-chi, displayed an obvious affinity for both the militant "urban proletariat" and the USSR. More congenial to the Chairman was Wuhan's Revolutionary Museum—a long, farm-style building with a gray-tiled roof supported by spindly red columns—which had been the Cadres' Training Academy of the Peasant Movement sponsored by the short-lived Hankow Government. But the Chairman also remembered that the Hankow Government, composed of left-wing Nationalists and moderate Communists, had collapsed in 1927 by obeying Moscow, while he was already rejecting Moscow. Even worse, Comrade Shao-chi had won glory before the final collapse by leading his militant unions in demonstrations which forced the British Concession in Wuhan to surrender to the Communists.

Wuhan was simply not the Chairman's city, though symbols of his own regime abounded in 1967 on the streets radiating from the central axis of the city, broad Liberation Boulevard. The spire-chimneys of the

Wuhan Iron and Steel Works laid a blanket of smoke over the surrounding "workers' quarter." The Iron and Steel Works had existed before "liberation," though they had been greatly expanded by the Communists.

Amid silver birches and flowering peach trees lay Wuhan University with its massive, medieval-looking buildings capped by pale green tiles and cupolas with upward-curling eaves. The university had, however, resisted the Maoist onslaught with particular vigor at the beginning of the Great Revolution. Nor did it console the Chairman to reflect that Wuhan possessed the chief connection across the muddy Yangtse which for millenia divided China into antagonistic northern and southern regions—and sometimes into separate nations. Still, the Maoists delighted in gaudily illuminating the only bridge across the "Long River," though it was as much a symbol of divisiveness as potential unity.

The Maoists were vulnerable—politically, economically, and geographically—in Wuhan. Since 1961, the cities had been the fief of the King of the South Tao Chu and the stronghold of a powerful, independent labor movement ultimately loyal to Comrade Shao-chi. Wuhan had been the command post for the Red Guards the King had deployed across China to carry out his own Cultural Revolution. His successor as First Secretary of the Central-South Regional Bureau had been Wang Jen-chung, the object of the Chairman's subsequent personal vendetta. Wang Jen-chung had shared Mao's finest moment, his 65-minute swim in the "Long River" amid the adoring "masses" on July 16, 1966, but Wang Jen-chung had subsequently followed his patron, the King of the South, rather than the Chairman. Even after he and the King were formally deposed in January 1967, Wang Jen-chung had lived in state in Wuhan under the protection of General Chen Tsai-tao, the Rebellious General. He had, furthermore, exercised significant influence, for Wuhan remained the "underground" command post of the opposition. Wuhan was simply not the Chairman's City.

Open revolt against the Maoists—blatant and destructive—erupted in Wuhan in mid-July 1967. It was preceded by an extended period when senior officers of the Liberation Army wavered indecisive. Less than 20 percent of the key commanders publicly affirmed their support of the Chairman and the Disciple. The Army's recalcitrance had begun in February, when it was ordered to "seize power" for the Maoists; reluctance to move was manifest in March. April through July passed in tumult, foreshadowing the irrepressible instability that would terrify the nation until the generals imposed a tenuous armistice by enforced compromise at the Ninth Congress of the Communist Party in April 1969.

The generals' and marshals' stubborn dedication to unity and civil order enabled China to survive; the basic conditions for survival were created during just four months: April through July of 1967. The generals often acted in concert with the anti-Maoist provincial cadres. From Canton in the far southeast to Sinkiang in the deep northwest, the generals, who were truly "independent princes," vigorously suppressed spontaneous Red Guard disorder originally incited by the extreme Maoists. They were not always successful. Indeed, the most violent fighting occurred from mid-1967 to late 1968. But the generals established a pattern of modified military rule. It was unimaginative and oppressive, but it was purposeful and—essentially—effective.

During the tumultuous first half of 1967, the tide of battle ebbed and flowed. Local commanders alternately supported and opposed "revolutionary rebels" or "conservative" workers and cadres, depending on which was more obstreperous at the moment. Peking issued bewildering directives, since civilian and military organs regularly contradicted each other, and often themselves. The Disciple's carefully planned guerrilla harassment, followed by his "battle of annihilation," had failed. The Maoists were themselves surrounded by political guerrillas as elusive and persistent as the forces Lin Piao had deployed against Japanese and Nationalists. Peking's utterances reflected and compounded indecision regarding purpose and means. Confusion was intensified by divergent appeals from local organs that were at cross purposes with each other— and with Peking.

By mid-April, clashes between the Red Guards and the Liberation Army were constant. The adolescents acted always in the name of the Chairman—as did their opponents, the Workers' Scarlet Sentinels. But it was impossible to read the true will of the Chairman, who had first exhorted them to "make disorder" and then, quite abruptly, ordered them to "maintain discipline." Freedom—not to speak of power—was a heady draught to an inhibited generation, and the Red Guards were beyond control by words and defiant of force. Local commanders' primary duty was to restore order and production by restraining the unruly adolescents. Inclination marched with duty. The generals were appalled by the spectacle of violent disobedience—which violated all their instincts, both as officers and as Communists.

The Liberation Army Daily in Peking, still isolated from the realities of the provinces, finally took note of the potentially catastrophic situation on April 11, 1967. Aware that military lines were buzzing with informal consultations on suppressing the Red Guards among the commanders of Military Regions and Districts, Peking used the most public medium to order them *not* to suppress the Red Guards—except, of course, when necessary.

"It is absolutely impermissible at any time or under any circumstances," Lin Piao's paper admonished, "to direct your spearhead at the revolutionary masses. . . . It is quite impossible for the young fighters [of the Red Guard] to be entirely free of shortcomings . . . and it is hardly avoidable that they should make mistakes of one kind or another. But, compared to their many magnificent deeds, their misdeeds are insignificant!"

Confusion among local commanders was reflected in this further admonition: "We should not fail to support all mass organizations which are *truly of the left* merely because they have evidenced some shortcomings or have made some mistakes. Among the revolutionary mass organizations, we should not arbitrarily support one faction in suppressing another."

The message was as clear as it could be under the circumstances. The Liberation Army and the Maoist "little generals of disorder" had clashed openly. Moreover, the "rebel revolutionary group" was splitting into opposing factions, each contending against the others for power. Since many generals had been inveigled into throwing their weight behind one group and against others, the Liberation Army was enmired in the factional struggle it was required to suppress. Though the isolated men of Peking believed the local generals could distinguish between "true leftist" and non-leftist organizations, it was, by mid-April, impossible to draw a clear distinction.

The generals therefore cooperated with representatives of the "old power-holders," who were themselves determined to stand off the Red Guards and preserve the "old order" they had given their lives to build. A bitter article in the Peking *Kwangming Daily* declared:

> The representatives of the old order use every possible means to prevent the birth of the new social phenomena [*i.e.,* "revolutionary mass organizations" and Red Guards]. They ruthlessly attack the new phenomena. . . . They pay lip-service to the revolution, but, as soon as the new phenomena display any shortcomings, the representatives of the old order act as if they were grotesque freaks and forcefully point out their flaws. . . . Thus do they seek to preserve—and revive—the old order!

By the end of April, the Maoist position had deteriorated sharply. The Liberation Army was most reluctant to "seize power" for the Maoists by "supporting the left"; while the truly rebellious Red Guards zestfully fought each other and the Army. A ceremonial communion with the Chairman revealed Peking's failure to install Revolutionary Committees sustained by the "three-way alliance." Out of China's 29 major administrative units, only six Revolutionary Committees sent representatives— Shansi and Shangtung, which, on the east and west, flanked the metropolitan province of Hopei, itself not represented; Kweichow, a sparsely populated, mountainous region in the deep south; Heilungkiang in Manchuria, where the "bombardment of Party headquarters" had begun in August 1966; and the municipalities of Peking and Shanghai, which could hardly be considered "pacified." Almost a year after deposing the Mayor Peng Chen, the Maoists exercised less effective power over China than they had before the Great Revolution began.

Red Guard factions fought a pitched battle for possession of a Peking department store, while Honan Radio declared that the "young generals" of their province just south of Peking had split into pro-Mao and anti-Mao factions and were fighting each other. *The Peking People's Daily* expanded: "At this critical moment, *anarchism* has again appeared to scatter the targets of our struggle and to divert the proper orientation of the struggle."

In Kiangsi, where the January peasant rising was still not suppressed, the commander of the Provincial Military District turned his back on political confusion to declare: "There is only one central task at this moment—getting on with farming!" The generals had received implicit sanction for the non-Maoist emphasis upon economic production. First Minister Chou En-lai had virtually instructed them to ignore the directive that POLITICS MUST COMMAND ALL! in order to get in the harvest.

On May 1, 1967, only 28 percent of the Central Committee appeared on the reviewing stand in Peking to celebrate the international workers' holiday with the Chairman. While some Maoist adherents were, of course, fully occupied in the provinces, a number of men already violently attacked by the extremists were present. Peking had endeavored to assemble all major leaders in order to demonstrate the unity of the leadership to a disintegrating nation. The sparse representation, nonetheless, indicated that, at most, one-third of the Central Committee supported the Maoist Party Center. Even that figure was perhaps overstated, for men who disapproved of the extremists displayed themselves in the greater cause of China's unity. One such personage was 81-year-old Generalissimo Chu Teh, the father of the Liberation Army. Chu Teh, was, of course, also inspired by personal loyalty to Mao Tse-tung, the man whose name had been intertwined with his own for four decades, however much he might disapprove of Mao's new campaign.

The generals were, in any event, assuming major power—and they bitterly detested the Red Guards. Vice Premier and Foreign Minister Chen Yi, himself a marshal, had revealed the Army's sentiments when he was publicly harried by the Red Guards. Always notably outspoken and protected by the First Minister Chou En-lai, Chen Yi had expressed the disgust felt by the generals and the marshals. The Foreign Minister was particularly bitter since, as he said, Red Guard harassment had made the Ministry of Foreign Affairs "a complete mess." The "little generals of disorder" had rampaged through the Ministry, terrorizing officials and scattering documents. When one anguished official protested that they were "revealing State Secrets," a Red Guard had asked with rough humor: "What's so great about State Secrets, anyway?" Chen Yi declared vehemently:

> You Red Guards say there are only six "clean" persons in all China— Chairman Mao, Lin Piao, Premier Chou En-lai, [the Ghostwriter] Chen Po-ta, [the Executioner] Kang Sheng, and Chiang Ching. You really believe, do you, that in a nation as vast as ours, there are only six clean persons? But, perhaps, you would be kind enough to include the five vice premiers—and make it 11 clean persons. Even if you were that kind, I don't think I would want to be considered a clean man under those conditions!

By early May, Peking feared that the Army might split into rival units fighting each other—or even turn *en masse* against the Party Center. Since the Disciple's claim to iron control over the "remolded" Liberation Army had proved unfounded, it was necessary to conciliate the generals. Peking flatly acknowledged that all China was under "military control." Notably shifting its emphasis, *Red Flag* exhorted all Chinese "to give urgent attention to the question of the correct treatment of the Liberation Army by the revolutionary masses, as well as the question of the correct treatment of the revolutionary masses by the commanders and fighters of the People's Liberation Army." Relations between civilians and soldiers had deteriorated to surly mutual distaste, often exacerbated by sharp clashes. Peking had obviously decided that the Liberation Army must be cosseted, lest the generals turn decisively against the Maoist clique and the "rebel revolutionary mass organizations"—and flatly assert their own, independent "military control of the nation."

The ideological journal plainly revealed the impotence of the Party Center by pleading for mutual understanding "at this moment, when we are organizing to seize power." By exhorting organization for a movement that had begun four months earlier, *Red Flag* admitted that Peking had made little or no progress. The military alone exercised whatever coherent authority still functioned. Since the generals had obviously decided neither to what extent nor on whose behalf to exercise their power, the Maoists were deeply worried.

By mid-May 1967, the situation was desperate—as revealed by both guarded official statements and the candid "great-character posters" the Maoists had once encouraged, but would, by that time, have liked to suppress because they revealed with fair accuracy reports that dismayed the Party Center. Violent and sanguinary clashes between pro-Maoists and anti-Maoists were commonplace, and the fighting drew in the Liberation Army on different sides at different times. Although narrowly averted by the First Minister's compromise "three-way alliance" in February, civil war was once again an imminent danger.

"Great-character posters" reported sensational events, later confirmed from other sources. Rising from low-grade, endemic antagonism, major clashes took place between troops and civilians, notably in Szechwan in the southwest, China's most populous and fertile province; Honan, just south of the home province of Hopei; and Sinkiang, the New Dominion, the strategic bastion with its nuclear facilities, its large non-Chinese population, and its 2,300-mile-long border with Soviet Central Asia and Outer Mongolia. *The Peking Daily,* organ of the city's new Revolutionary Committee, inveighed against mass clashes in both Peking and Shanghai.

By the beginning of June, the Maoists virtually admitted that Honan had been "seized" by "conservatives," backed by the local military. In the most candidly despairing statement since the Cultural Revolution had begun, Chengchou Radio appealed: "Halt the wild wind of armed struggle!" The broadcast of June 1, 1967, admitted: "Large numbers of the deluded masses have been misled into violent action by the class enemy and are turning their spearheads against the correct line of Chairman Mao." The appeal said "bloody armed clashes" had been incited by "the black gang of anti-Party power-holders," which meant, of course, the old officials of the Communist Party. The Honanese were "kidnapping soldiers of the Liberation Army, stealing military equipment, and attacking both commanders [officers] and warriors [soldiers]." Workers and farmers had "abandoned their places of work in order to indulge in a spree of looting and strife."

Chengchou Radio added in dismay that "anarchy has arisen from strife within the mass organizations." The broadcast explained: "All the evil elements have come out of hiding and are now determined to settle accounts with us and take their revenge upon us!" Chengchou declared flatly: "Only violent struggle can solve the problems of Honan!" It warned that a "nation-wide counterattack" was being launched by the anti-Maoists, emboldened by the "breakdown of discipline within our own ranks."

Shanghai Radio, making similar revelations in another Urgent Proclamation on June 9, 1967, again flourished the King Charles' Head of the Great Revolution. "The chief personage in authority within the Party following the capitalist road," said Shanghai, "is inciting armed struggle within our own ranks—and among the deluded masses." Comrade Liu Shao-chi, the "stinking heap of rotting garbage," whose "overthrow" had been proclaimed in April, was once again held responsible for all

China's ills. He was more than a convenient whipping boy. His influence was without question still pervasive and powerful, both among the masses and in the ranks of the Liberation Army. Indeed, the Proclamation specifically cited "shortcomings and errors" within the Army and added: "Our enemies have tried in every way possible to discover the weaknesses within our revolutionary ranks, to enlarge those splits, to incite armed struggle, to wreck State property, and to sabotage the new revolutionary order."

The opposition's campaign, which exploited inherent contradictions within the Mao-Lin clique, exacerbated three "evil tendencies": severe disagreements verging on open splits within the Party Center; growing disaffection within the Liberation Army; and popular revulsion against the Maoists.

The military, ostensibly obedient to the Disciple, were openly opposed to the young careerists typified by the Literary Assassin Yao Wen-yüan —and their sponsor Chiang Ching. The generals, by and large, wished to placate the non-Maoists and prevent destruction of "the leadership of the Communist Party." The extremists still pressed for the creation of a wholly new power structure. *The Peking People's Daily* declared hotly:

> Some comrades think they are perfect. When they show shortcomings or make mistakes, they do not make conscientious self-criticism or allow others to criticize them. Comrades in authority should particularly encourage democracy, and they should encourage others to criticize them. They consider their own comrades as displaying no shortcomings or mistakes whatsoever *before they are criticized*. But, *after those comrades have been criticized*, they shout that those comrades must be "overthrown."

Bitter personal disagreements split the Maoist clique. *Red Flag* said flatly: "It is wrong for some people to raise the slogan, COMPLETELY REVAMP THE DICTATORSHIP OF THE PROLETARIAT! Certain persons who have ulterior motives wish to negate *everything* accomplished in the past. They are determined to overthrow everything created in the past . . ." The extremists frightened even that zealous ideologue, the editor of *Red Flag,* the Ghostwriter Chen Po-ta.

At the end of June, Canton, the metropolis of the south, revealed major conflicts within the ranks of the military. For the first time, the official radio acknowledged that some units had not merely refused to support the Maoists, but had actually fought for their enemies. The situation was complex, for the military governor of Kwangtung Province had commanded a major drive to suppress Red Guard disorder. Soldiers arrested Red Guard chieftains who wished to organize a "people's march" against the British Crown Colony of Hong Kong, which was at the time shaken by uncoordinated Maoist strikes and riots. Canton Radio further implied clearly that Lin Piao was losing control of the military. Instead of marching, certain units "staged a great debate" when ordered into action. Even officers declared they would not "support a feudal lord." Other units offered arms and sanctuary to anti-Maoist activists. "Within the ranks of the People's Army," the broadcast said, "class struggle still persists, and there is a clique within the Army following the capitalist road. That clique, well entrenched in our ranks, is *the most dangerous time bomb in China."*

Some military units quietly defied orders. Civilians moved openly and violently against Maoists, Red Guards, and the Army. A series of urgent conferences of senior commanders and political commissars convened to discuss the strategy for quelling dissension within the ranks and halting civilian attacks. Maoist organs thundered in desperation: "The situation is so acute that our country will change color from red to white and our proletarian dictatorship will be succeeded by a bourgeois dictatorship— unless we reverse the present trend!" On July 4, "senior cadres of the directing organs of Peking's military units" warned: "Unless we reconcile conflicts among our supporters, we will not be able to utilize the positive force of the masses, and we will not be able to concentrate our strength for the assault on the implacable enemy—the small group of men within our own ranks who are following the capitalist road." The Air Force added: "The great numbers of the masses who have come under the influence of the bourgeois clique can be reclaimed. But this phenomenon must not be allowed to spread. It must be crushed—absolutely and rapidly—wherever it develops. Otherwise, the enemy will triumph!"

Sinkiang Province typified the military's recalcitrance and encouraged that recalcitrance. The New Dominion became a symbol of the "new trend" among the military because it was a vital strategic area and because of the character of Wang En-mao, the commander of the Military Region. He possessed great power, since the enormous province was one of the 13 paramount Military Regions. He used his influence to persuade other generals to demand that "Socialist legality" govern the Great Revolution. He could not openly champion Comrade Liu Shao-chi, but he could demand that the Chairman of the People's Republic be given an open hearing by his peers of the Central Committee, rather than being destroyed by "rumor and character assassination." He had even forced formal suspension of the Cultural Revolution in Sinkiang. The province and the general had mutually shaped each other's character.

The Chinese, essentially convinced that time and eternity were synonymous, called the area Sinkiang, the "New Dominion," because it was not conquered by China until the eighteenth century. In the nineteenth, Peking's rule was shaken by constant rebellion, while, throughout the twentieth, it had been an epicenter of violence and intrigue, a constant irritation to the capital, 1,500 miles away. Rarely had Sinkiang worried Peking more than it did during the Great Revolution. With Sino-Soviet tension rising, the area was—and has remained—an extremely valuable prize lying at Moscow's fingertips. The treasurehouse of natural resources jutted into Soviet Central Asia. It was not only vulnerable geographically, for its volatile mixture of races invited Russian meddling and made it one of the most obdurate provinces during the Cultural Revolution.

Sinkiang was, in one aspect, ultra-modern. Across its 636 thousand square miles were dispersed oilfields, uranium mines and processing plants, as well as testing ranges for nuclear weapons and missiles. Despite vast reclamation projects undertaken by forced labor, it still presented scenes out of the remote past: camel caravans struggling through dust storms across sand dunes toward sparse oases; nomadic tribes driving herds of sheep along the narrow rivers that nurtured meager strips of green grazing.

The compound of such elements was explosively volatile.

The only province in which the Cultural Revolution was officially suspended for a time, Sinkiang was also the last to form a provisional Provincial Revolutionary Committee—as late as December 1968. Sinkiang's creeping "pacification" was due to its protracted resistance, beginning in the spring of 1967. The façade of local Revolutionary Committees stood firm everywhere else in China by the early summer of 1969—after the Ninth Party Congress. But only in the spring of 1969 had local "alliances" of the People's Liberation Army, the old "power-holders," and the "revolutionary rebels," by that time much degraded, even begun raising those façades in the major towns of Sinkiang.

The trouble with the New Dominion was that it was not really Chinese. It remained, as it had been for centuries, foreign territory under primarily military colonization. The Chinese genius for assimilating minority races and cultures had signally failed to work its accustomed magic, largely because there were so few Chinese in Sinkiang. The Liberation Army was finally to operate like an occupation force in China proper, directly supervising all vital economic and political functions. But the Liberation Army *was* the Chinese presence in Sinkiang. Moreover, the Army units, primarily labor troops exiled for political errors, were riven by the cumulative bitterness of the Cultural Revolution even more deeply than were their fellows elsewhere.

Sinkiang's frontiers with foreign territory were actually longer than its boundary with Chinese-ruled territory. They extended for 3,000 miles, about 2,300 with Soviet Central Asia and Moscow-controlled Outer Mongolia, as well as 700 with Afghanistan, Pakistan, and India, against 1,500 with Chinghai and Kansu provinces and the Tibetan Autonomous Region. The obvious vulnerability of that exposed position was increased many-fold by sparse population and difficult communications. Divided north from south by the great range called Tienshan—"The Mountains of Heaven"—Sinkiang was traversed by seven major highways that generally followed the old caravan routes, the ancient Great Silk Road to the West among them. Tihua, also called Urumchi, was linked to Lanchow, China's chief center for production of nuclear weapons in Kansu Province, by a single-tracked railroad. Spurs extended to the oil center at Karamai to the north and to Chingho in the south. Projected links to the Trans-Siberian Railroad had been left uncompleted because of deteriorating relations between Peking and Moscow.

The diversity of terrain—mountains, deserts, oases, and small fertile basins—was matched by the racial diversity of a largely nomadic, pastoral population. The vast province, which comprised almost one-sixth of the total area of the People's Republic, had a population of approximately 8 million. Between 40 and 45 percent were Chinese, almost all recent, involuntary exiles—civilian and military. The region's alien character was recognized by its official name, the Sinkiang Uighur Autonomous Region. Chief among the "minority peoples"—perhaps 70 percent—were the different Uighur tribes, with whom the Chinese had made their first foreign alliance in the second century B.C. Others, like Tajiks, Uzbeks, Mongols, and Tatars, had closer emotional, economic, and social ties with their brethren across Soviet borders than with their Chinese overlords. The largely Muslim population had periodically rebelled. The greatest uprising had been put down in 1878 and the most recent in 1962.

Divided ethnically and geographically while lying at great remove from China proper, the New Dominion had attracted Russian ambition since the time of the Czars. Under the Nationalist Republic of China, the ruling Chinese general was more attentive to Moscow's wishes than Nanking's. Russian subversion in the remote march of the Chinese *imperium* intensified after the Sino-Soviet quarrel became a public scandal in 1960. So effective was Soviet subversion that Moscow's consulate-general in Urumchi was closed down late in 1962.

Moscow's interest was spurred by much more than the natural desire to expand its influence in Central Asia or the fact that Sinkiang was a salient aggressively thrusting deep into territories where the Soviet Union had its own problems with racial minorities. Nor was Moscow's interest titillated by the sheer grandeur of the heart of Central Asia, a land whose scattered oases were rich with the memories and the artifacts of ancient civilizations older, even, than Alexander the Great. Sinkiang evoked intense Soviet attention because it was a rich source of uranium —and Moscow was not liberally endowed with fissionable ores. At least three significant deposits were worked: one in the southwest at Puli, a second in the west near Paicheng, and a third in the northeast near Yüanhu. Other sources of uranium were undoubtedly known, though not publicized. Besides, the new city of Shihhotze in the Dzungaria Basin in the north was built around a plant that refined uranium ore for shipment to Lanchow.

In addition to possessing one of China's three major oilfields, the Karamai (Black Sands) Field in the extreme north near the Soviet border, Sinkiang was rich in other minerals. Sketchy geological surveys revealed gold, copper, iron, tungsten, molybdenum, antimony, sulfur, gypsum, and jade. Some of those resources were worked, though by no means intensively, while still uncharted resources probably exceeded known resources several times over. All China's nuclear tests had taken place around Lop Nor, the "Great Salt Lake," an ancient eastern terminus of the Great Silk Road. Peking had also created an alternate proving ground at Hotien in the south to test intermediate-range and intercontinental ballistic missiles.

Because of its barren and vast expanse the New Dominion was sparsely defended against the attacks the Russians would certainly mount if they came into conflict with China. But the inhospitable terrain and the terrible caprices of nature—fantastic ranges of temperature and great storms—somewhat limited possible invasion routes. Still, aircraft were not seriously hampered by such factors, nor was inciting revolt among the discontented minority races. Peking therefore feared that Moscow could divert China's drive toward nuclear great-power status by cutting off uranium supplies and curtailing production of weapons. Nowhere else was China quite so vulnerable—and hardly anywhere else could attack hurt her so badly. Yet her defenses were ravaged by the Cultural Revolution, and, equally, by the alienation of both Chinese settlers and native minorities against Maoist repression.

Some 500 thousand troops were stationed in Sinkiang. They were divided into two distinct groups, which came under a curiously divided command as a result of the Great Revolution. North of the Mountains of Heaven, the Sinkiang Military Region Headquarters at Urumchi (Tihua) commanded the front-line troops that would counter Russian attack from the north. South of the range, troops guarding the western and southern frontiers were commanded directly from Liberation Army Headquarters in Peking.

About 10 divisions, between 100 and 150 thousand men, were front-line combat troops. In addition to service units, they were supported by a single "division" of the Chinese Air Force, which mustered perhaps 400 aircraft, chiefly fighters. The remainder were in the same anomalous status as approximately two million young men and women, chiefly from the Shanghai region, who had been involuntarily resettled in Sinkiang "to open the frontier regions." Like those civilians, the troops of the Production and Construction Corps were essentially unsympathetic to the regime. They consisted, in part, of former Nationalist soldiers and, in greater part, of men sent to Sinkiang as labor troops in punishment for political crimes of varying gravity. They were armed with hand weapons and small artillery pieces.

Sinkiang was China's Siberia. Neither prisoners undergoing "reform through labor" nor their guards were in high favor with Peking. They reciprocated the sentiment. Only in February of 1969 did the Production and Construction Corps finally begin to establish its own Cultural Revolutionary Groups. Until that late date, neither the neo-Stalinist generals nor the Maoist "rebel revolutionaries" had dared tamper with the Corps for fear of provoking even greater violence.

Because of the complex array of factors—geographic, demographic, and political—Sinkiang long evaded much of the rigor of the Cultural Revolution. Because of the same factors, Commander-in-Chief Wang En-mao long acted as spokesman of the moderate generals from his secure base.

Although Wang En-mao was finally relieved as commander of the Military Region late in 1968, he remained a force even the Maoists respected. Most troops and officers owed no particular loyalty to Lieutenant General Lung Shu-chin who came from Hunan in Central China in the autumn of 1968 with no more than a division of his own to take over the Military Region. Most were still basically committed to General Wang En-mao—commander from 1957 until his relief. The practice of stationing troops in a single area for decades made Wang En-mao a major power, for the troops tendered him great personal loyalty. Allegiance to Peking was further vitiated by the residual personal influence of the former marshals of the Liberation Army who had been utterly degraded.

Former Minister of Defense Great General Peng Teh-huai was the first ruler of the Northwest Region, which included Sinkiang. His chief troop commander was the amiable, semi-literate Bandit General, Ho Lung, who became a bemedaled Communist marshal from his start as a robber chieftain sponsored by extra-legal secret societies. Giving their primary loyalty to Ho Lung, who was degraded in 1966, and still in awe of Peng Teh-huai, who fell in 1959, the troops of Sinkiang as late as 1970 still listened to Wang En-mao. He had acted as a major moderating influence since the Liberation Army entered the fray in early 1967.

The slim figure with the horn-rimmed glasses, the high, balding forehead, and the prominent, angular cheekbones above a stubborn jaw looked like a professor. Wang En-mao might appear a particularly tough-minded intellectual. But he still resembled an intellectual, rather than a professional general with almost four decades of combat experience, a remarkably successful colonial administrator, the warden-in-chief of one of the world's largest forced-labor camps, a pioneer of new frontiers, a tenacious political strategist, a practical administrator of great ability, a ruthless suppressor of rebellion, and the custodian of the nuclear resources of the world's largest nation. Yet Wang En-mao, 55 years old in 1967, still—or had—filled all those jobs. He was also a man of stubborn principle who consistently resisted the purge called the Great Proletarian Cultural Revolution and, somehow, survived without sacrificing principle.

Though almost all his personal associations and his political inclinations were, to say the least, unfortunate, Wang En-mao survived bitter personal attack and calumny to retain a significant position of power. He was ultimately degraded from full to alternate membership in the Central Committee, but the strength of his character and his adroit use of his advantages made it more than likely that he would rise again. Wang En-mao survived, in good part, because he was all but indispensable. Peking knew that it might urgently require his services to hold the vast treasurehouse called Sinkiang. Wang was one of the few men—if, indeed, not the only man—who could both withstand Soviet incursions and maintain Chinese control over the disparate racial and religious groups of the New Dominion.

Because of his unique qualifications and experience, as well as his own stubborn integrity, Wang En-mao had played a remarkable role during the most turbulent period of the Great Revolution in 1967. He not only isolated Sinkiang from the worst excesses, but felt secure enough to leave his own power base unattended during extended absences for negotiation with the authorities in Peking. On behalf of the practical generals, Wang En-mao repeatedly demanded an end to the violent contention and persecution of the Cultural Revolution. He did not endear himself to the Disciple Lin Piao, who had briefly been his schoolmaster, by opposing the vilification of Comrade Liu Shao-chi. But his insistence that the Communists convene a National Party Congress won the respect of his peers, who valued courage and common sense even above principle.

Wang En-mao enjoyed a peculiar advantage because he came to the movement so young. His adherence to the Communist cause and his combat record began at the same time. Unlike many of his contemporaries, Lin Piao among them, he did not attend military schools or join the

Communist Youth League. He "learned fighting by fighting," as Mao Tse-tung himself advised. Wang was a 19-year-old middle-school graduate when he joined Communist guerrillas in his native Kiangsi Province. He enlisted in the Workers' and Peasants' Red Army of the First Soviet Area in company with his father and two brothers. His father, Wang Nan-mei, was a farmer from Yunghsin, a poor district in western Kiangsi bordering Mao's native province, Hunan. The elder Wang had been all but ruined by the constant fighting attendant upon the Nationalist Government's attempt to crush the Communist stronghold centered on the mountain range called Chingkangshan, 32 miles away.

The father and his three sons had no alternative but to earn their rice by joining the fighting that had broken their rice bowls. Their only choice lay between joining the Communists or the Nationalists. The Wangs chose the Communists, perhaps because they hoped to keep their small land holdings. The Communists, at that point, still wooed small proprietors. Equally important, they hoped to remain in their native district, which the Red Army controlled. In their own isolated world of 1931, the Communists appeared the likely winners. They were the only visible authority, and they carefully avoided offending potential supporters like the Wangs, who were almost as poor as their meager, rocky-seamed fields.

The choice determined the course of his life, though it did not keep Wang En-mao near the sacred graves of his ancestors. In 1934, when he had begun his rise in the Red Army because, as a middle-school graduate, he was an "educated intellectual," the Communist forces were driven out of Kiangsi. Attached to the Eighth Army Group under Political Commissar Liu Shao-chi, Wang En-mao set out at 24 on the Long March of eight thousand miles, which brought the Communists to sanctuary in Shensi Province in the northwest a year later. His combat experience was varied, abundant, and instructive. He crossed the Chinsha (Golden Sands) River on the suspension chains of a shattered bridge. He was briefly trapped by the internal conflict between forces loyal to Mao Tse-tung and those of the Chairman's chief rival for power, Chang Kuo-tao. He traversed the hostile lands of fierce mountain tribes and was harried by Tibetan Khampas riding heavy-bodied ponies on the edges of the high plateau.

It was invaluable training for the young combat officer who was also making his reputation as an organizer and political commissar. He served General Wang Chen, who had been his immediate superior since he joined the guerrillas. He remained in the service of Wang Chen until he attained independent command of Sinkiang. In 1954, Wang Chen, the former labor agitator who had begun his working life as a mechanic in the railway yards of the Wuhan industrial complex, turned his command over to his young protégé.

The only advanced education Wang En-mao received was a brief tour of study in 1937 at the Communists' Anti-Japanese Military and Political Academy. Lin Piao was the principal, but he and Wang did not become friends. The young officer's allegiance was bestowed elsewhere. After Wang Chen, Wang En-mao gave his loyalty to the Bandit General Ho Lung, who had come to Communism from the conspiratorial realm of Chinese secret societies. It was an unfortunate association during the Cultural Revolution. Ho Lung commanded the troops of the First Field Army of Great General Peng Teh-huai, who had run the Northwest Military and Administrative Region. Both were purged.

Wang En-mao survived his mentors' downfall because he had founded an independent reputation in the late 1930s. When the Nationalists blockaded their Communist allies in the early 1940s, he was detached for service with the 359th Brigade, a special unit assigned to produce its own food and other necessities while guarding a vital border of the Communist enclave in the northwest. That experience was invaluable in 1949, when he was ordered to oversee the reclamation of the deserts of Sinkiang by the Production and Construction Corps, composed primarily of former Nationalist and disaffected Communist troops. He was also, over the ensuing years, responsible for keeping peace among two million-odd youths transported from the Shanghai area to "open the frontier regions."

Wang En-mao progressed steadily until, by the early 1960s, he was First Secretary of the Communist Party Committee of the Sinkiang Uighur Autonomous Region, political commissar of the Production Corps, and commander of the Sinkiang Military Region. He had proved his worth during the 1950s by crushing a series of Muslim revolts and, equally, by winning some confidence from the restive minority races. Unlike his counterparts in more settled regions, Wang En-mao was constantly campaigning against one dissident group or another. He maintained the delicate balance between Chinese and Soviet influence in Sinkiang by a combination of force and guile. The Russian ally—and later enemy—never relaxed his efforts to penetrate the vital region.

It was, therefore, not remarkable that he would not comply when ordered to cast his carefully cultivated realm into disorder by allowing the Red Guards free rein. Instead, he resisted so successfully that Peking did not dare relieve him as commander of the Sinkiang Military Region until the fall of 1968. He remained political commissar of the Military Region, a post hardly less important. His retention was due to his major influence in the area, rather than to his "background and performance," which were obviously highly flawed in the eyes of the Party Center. He was also saved by the informal council of senior generals and People's Marshals which virtually ruled China from mid-1967 until the Ninth Party Congress confirmed the predominant authority of the military in April 1969. Indeed, he would not have survived the Wuhan Revolt of July 1967 had he not been powerfully established in both the New Dominion and the capital, for Wang En-mao was a champion of resistance to extremism by the Liberation Army. Without the encouragement of colleagues like Wang En-mao, Chen Tsai-tao, the Rebellious General, could not have been maneuvered into countenancing a virtual military revolt against Peking in "Red" Wuhan that summer.

The heroes and villains of political mythology depend, of course, upon who tells the tale, as do assessments of the favorite theme of Communist myths, "epic struggles." If the militant anti-centrists had won decisively, the "Wuhan Incident" might have ranked with the Nanchang Rising among the legends of Chinese Communism.

All the irony of the Great Proletarian Cultural Revolution was, in any event, encapsulated by events in Wuhan from July 14 to July 23, 1967. The highpoint of anti-Maoist resistance made ultimate Maoist victory impossible, though the Center won the immediate battle. Thereafter, the Great Revolution was military-dominated, for the proletariat—pro-Mao or anti-Mao—had been defeated.

The Wuhan Rising was the mirror image of the Canton Commune of 1927. In both cases, the urban working class seized and held power until the proletariat was suppressed by central military forces—in Canton Nationalist, in Wuhan Communist.

Military historians relish the phrase "the fog of war." It justifies imprecision in their accounts, as much as it confuses the combatants. The "fog of war" still obscures the Great Revolution, for all the firsthand accounts are by no means available from participants patently bewildered by illogical and uncontrollable events. Since the chief accounts of the Wuhan Incident stem from ostensible pro-Maoists, they are voluminous, but one-sided. Besides, Maoists, non-Maoists, and anti-Maoists all lacked coherent strategies after the Revolution had been diverted from its original channel by the mass resistance of January and February 1967. Since both sides improvised and reacted thereafter, the "fog of war" lay heavy over all China.

The origins of the revolt in Wuhan can, nonetheless, be clearly discerned in the struggles that began everywhere in China at the beginning of the year. The "rebel revolutionaries" and the "power-holders" struggled for supremacy, restrained—and, occasionally, abetted—by the military. In Wuhan, as in many other places, the commander of the Wuhan Military Region, which included Hupei and Honan provinces, was inclined toward the anti-centrist forces.

The anti-Maoist force was actually organized by an amorphous cabal grandiloquently self-called the Million Heroes. Those motley, armed workingmen, old cadres, and students were allied with a military detachment cryptically known as the 8201 Unit, a division-size formation composed of regular soldiers of both the People's Liberation Army and the paramilitary Public Security Force. The Million Heroes, at full strength, numbered approximately 50 thousand while the 8201 Unit was about 12 thousand strong. They were ultimately opposed by the Wuhan-based 8119 Division of the Liberation Army, by a flotilla of ten gunboats of the Eastern Seas Fleet, by paratroops, and by Air Force bombers. Despite their energy and determination, the anti-centrist forces were ill-organized and badly led. They lacked either a strong commander or a unifying doctrine. Wuhan was, nonetheless, so firmly in their grasp from April through mid-July 1967 that Peking dispatched no less a figure than Premier Chou En-lai to reassert Central authority.

The Million Heroes and its satellite bodies had come into existence in conscious opposition to the Maoists. One organizer, a textile worker expelled from the Communist Youth League, embodied the resentment against Maoist repression that inspired the proletariat to revolt. He had been recruited while a patient in a Canton Hospital and sent to Peking for indoctrination, according to his later "confession." As early as December 1966, he declared, officers of the 8201 Unit had sent him to Wuhan in the uniform of a colonel of the People's Liberation Army to "sway public opinion and mobilize the masses" by exhorting mass meetings and distributing leaflets. The discontented working class was highly receptive, for it feared a breakdown of public order and intensification of exploitation like the Great Leap Forward. The organizer "confessed":

> The second thing I did was to recruit followers, expand our ranks, set up a core, form groups, and seek outside aid. Early in January [1967], a five-man core and a 17-man Standing Committee were formed, while a command post was set up. . . . The "3905" of Hankow was the main group, while the big cotton-mills of Wuchang were the centers of operations. . . . We were further backed by two "fortresses." One was the provincial shipyard, where 200 former midshipmen [presumably discharged from the People's Navy] had made contact with their former superiors to set up an armed force. . . . Our headquarters also established contact with the *Hung-yeh* [Red Field Army], whose leaders and members were discharged veterans of the Red Army and cadres.

Cells were established in all the main plants of the great industrial complex, including the Wuhan Iron and Steel Works, later the center of the revolt. While the January Storm raged throughout China, the workers of Wuhan demonstrated and cut off power supplies. Infiltrators were inserted into the "rebel revolutionary groups," while arms and vehicles were assembled, many drawn from sympathetic Liberation Army units. Nevertheless, those initial demonstrations in Wuhan were limited in comparison with action elsewhere.

From April through June, the Million Heroes expanded rapidly. General Chen Tsai-tao remained neutral—in their favor. A later Maoist Urgent Appeal reported:

> The Million Heroes set up strongholds everywhere and carried out extensive training. This group of bandits, wearing steel and plastic helmets, waving iron spears and daggers, and armed to the teeth, attacked by night and by day. They used fire-fighting equipment, gasoline, insecticide poisons, and gas shells. . . . They encircled and attacked revolutionary rebels from Hanyang to Hankow and from Hankow to Wuchang, inciting the June 6th bloody incident, the June 8th bloody incident, the June 13th tragedy, the June 15th tragedy, the June 17th massacre, and the June 19th massacre [all clashes among rival factions resulting in heavy casualties].

> June 17th was a particularly bitter day. The Million Heroes dispatched many trucks loaded with fully armed bandits against the Chungshan Hostel in order to destroy the People's Park of Culture, a red stronghold. . . . When the revolutionaries rushed reinforcements, the bandits used military trucks to intercept them. . . . The first truck of revolutionaries was halted and surrounded by bandits who attacked the 37 reinforcements with blood-stained steel bars, pitchforks, and axes. Only three of the 37 escaped after fierce resistance, the rest all laying down their lives. Thus began the massacre at 1:00 P.M. which lasted till the early morning of June 18th. More than a hundred were killed by the bandits, while many others were injured.

The Million Heroes' resistance to a Maoist takeover became more audacious through June and into July. By the middle of the month, the entire city was divided into two hostile camps, with the opposition preponderant. The two regular units, the 8201 Division and the 8199 Division, were encamped so near each other their pickets clashed from time to time. Civil war appeared imminent, if "civil war" is defined as fighting between armed regulars. Despite Peking's orders to crush the Heroes, the Rebellious General Chen Tsai-tao still refused to attack the people of Wuhan. The Great Revolution had become a counterrevolution against the Maoists. Wang Jen-chung, acting First Secretary of the Central-South Regional Bureau of the Communist Party, formally in disgrace, was a powerful figure behind the scenes. He joined the Military Region's political commissar in urging General Chen Tsai-Tao to ignore Central Directives, such as that of the twenty-sixth of June which ordered all factional fighting put down. The equivocating Rebellious

General was himself a former subordinate of the Bandit General Ho Lung. He had served the Disciple for some time, but had never transferred his fundamental allegiance.

On June 14, the Million Heroes seized the Yangtze Bridge, cutting north-south communications. Central China's most important industrial complex had already been half-paralyzed by a series of strikes beginning with the sit-down strike of 2,500 workers of the Wuhan Iron and Steel Works. Regular military officers were "advising" the Million Heroes and providing them with equipment ranging from sound-trucks to machine guns. Maoist propaganda and political directives were suppressed, and the opposition's publicists issued their own pamphlets. The anti-centrists apparently planned to proclaim a "three-way revolutionary alliance," as the basis of a Revolutionary Committee under their complete control. The Million Heroes prepared to prevent a Maoist "power seizure" by "seizing power" themselves. A fearful Peking already inveighed against "*sham* power seizures" elsewhere.

But the Wuhan leadership was indecisive. General Chen Tsai-tao could not steel himself to break totally with the Party Center by proclaiming a Revolutionary Committee to rule Hupei Province. The opposition stopped just short of that final defiance, after taking all the preliminary steps. More than 300 "rebel revolutionary organizations" were declared "counterrevolutionary," and their arms were sequestered. The Million Heroes were well armed, while even "vehicles were confiscated from the "rebel revolutionaries." Technically, none of those actions violated the Peking directive to "support the left in seizing power"—if the Million Heroes were indeed the left. The Wuhan Command's action did not even violate the directive not "to support one faction of the left against another faction of the left"—again, if the Million Heroes were indeed the left, and their opponents the right. The Command's most decisive action did, however, explicitly violate Peking directives. In the name of suppressing counterrevolutionary activities and restoring order, the Wuhan Command allowed the Million Heroes to occupy the strategic strong points of the city.

All railway stations, communications facilities, piers, and most "rebel revolutionary" headquarters were "seized" by armed units. Major buildings, which commanded the city from their heights, were taken over, as were radio stations and the "liaison stations" the Liberation Army had established to receive "outside revolutionary rebels." Wuhan University was partially occupied, as were a number of middle schools. Nonetheless, factional fighting continued, largely because the military command was either too timorous or too crafty to suppress the clashes. The "great-character posters" of Peking reported: "Between June 4th and June 15th, more than 80 scattered, small-scale fights killed or injured

500-odd. From the 16th to the 24th, there were 50-odd clashes which killed approximately 350 and injured more than 1,500. From the 16th to the 30th, when the Party Center ordered cessation of all fighting, there were six major clashes, which killed eight and injured 25."

By July 13, Peking decided to dispatch Premier Chou En-lai to Wuhan. He was expected to employ his accustomed skill in conciliation and his great personal authority to mediate differences. If compromise proved impossible, Chou was to compel the military command to suppress fighting by direct force. According to the wall posters, Chou spent only one day in the city. Discovering that bringing order to Wuhan would be a long and complex process, he sent a message to Kunming, the troubled capital of Yünnan Province in the far southwest. Two circuit-riders of the Maoist clique had just succeeded in enforcing an uneasy armistice on feuding factions in that walled city. Though the first truce was short-lived, the pair were ordered to work their magic in Wuhan. They were Hsieh Fu-chih, Minister of Security, and Wang Li, one of the Starlet's bright not-so-young men who held high rank in the Task Force directing the Cultural Revolution under the Ghostwriter Chen Po-ta. The pair arrived on July 14, and Chou En-lai departed for Peking.

The Minister of Security and the ultra-leftist stalwart busily received delegations and issued instructions, confident that they would soon bring order to Wuhan. They visited Wuhan University to command both factions to lay down their spears and knives; they conferred with General Chen Tsai-tao; they designated certain factions true "rebel revolutionaries" and others "counterrevolutionary"; and they encouraged the "true revolutionaries" to stage a welcoming parade.

On July 15, the procession formed up on the university campus. About two thousand Red Guards escorted Wang Li from Wuchang to Hankow across the Yangtze Bridge while "the masses cheered," according to a Maoist account. But, the account added:

. . . when we approached Hanyang [the third of the triplet cities], 12 trucks suddenly sped into our route. They carried bandits of the Million Heroes, all brandishing long spears. . . . The bandits dispersed when they saw our resolution . . . but they lay in ambush near the Hanshui Bridge, waiting to attack our procession when it returned. . . . Suddenly, the Million Heroes bandits hiding in the Tram Company attacked us, throwing stones and bottles. . . . When our entire procession had entered the main road, the bandits rushed out from the Liberation Building and the Tram Company building. . . . Several hundred bandits with swords and spears debouched from two side-streets into the main road and cut off our fighters from the rest of the procession. We fought bravely as more bandits attacked, but, overwhelmed by their superior numbers, we were surrounded. . . . Although they dared not attack our chief revolutionary stronghold [a Maoist island within the city], reinforcements came in an unending stream to the street battle. Dressed uniformly in yellow jackets and blue trousers, they had been trained in killing. The bandits on the south threw stones, quicklime, and smoke-bombs. The white smoke [of phosphorous grenades (?)] was suffocating. The inhuman bandits used their long spears to pierce the bodies of our fighters. . . .

The street battle ended when the "rebels" withdrew to the First Middle School. They were surrounded by the enraged Heroes, who stormed the building. Several hundred "rebel revolutionaries" were captured, and others were killed. The rest finally withdrew to their "revolutionary base," where Wang Li and Minister of Security Hsieh Fu-chih visited them at 11:00 that evening. Thus ended the "bloody 15th of July," the opening engagement of the Wuhan Revolt.

The next day was quiet, for it was the first anniversary of the Chairman's "heroic swim" in the Yangtze. But on the nineteenth, the two men from Peking felt they knew enough to "solve the situation." They told the military: "The Million Heroes are a reactionary, royalist clique, and the Wuhan Command has committed serious errors. The Command must acknowledge its errors to the masses and make a self-confession." The "four-point directive" ordered the Rebellious General Chen Tsai-tao to "rectify his errors, suppress the Million Heroes, and liberate the rebel revolutionaries." White with anger, the Political Commissar of the 8201 Division slipped out of the room to rally his forces. Soon the streets of Wuhan resounded with broadcasts from sound-trucks: "Wang Li is a criminal rascal who seeks to incite the masses to fight the masses! Hsieh Fu-chih is not competent to represent the Party Center!" The July 20th Incident, the high-water mark of the Wuhan Revolt, had begun.

Scrupulously sparing the Minister of Defense, the Million Heroes, backed by the 8201 Division, "dragged out" Wang Li. General Chen Tsai-tao had already told the men from Peking. "The problem is now in your hands. I don't know what to do!" Many of his troops either stood by or participated as the Million Heroes baited Wang Li in his hotel, paraded him in mockery through the streets, and subsequently attacked all "rebel headquarters." Red Guard accounts reported:

After Comrade Wang Li was seized, the Million Heroes and other detachments trained by the Wang [Jen-chung]-Chen [Tsai-tao] clique for special operations—supported by the rotten eggs of the 8201 Unit—moved swiftly, mounting machine-guns on trucks and tall buildings, loading their rifles and unsheathing their swords. Brandishing pistols, the killers rampaged through Wuhan. The sirens of fire-engines mingled with the rumble of more than a thousand vehicles carrying detachments of the Million Heroes. Loudspeaker-trucks blared reactionary slogans, and the entire Wuhan area was cast into the horror of war.

After the military deliberately withdrew their sentries, their posts were seized by the Million Heroes. All the neighborhoods of the Military District Headquarters were under the control of the mutineers. . . . Both the Yangtze River and the Chianghan Bridges were closed; navigation on the river was halted; communications routes, main thoroughfares, and major buildings were occupied; the airfields were surrounded; and railway stations were seized. The "liberated areas" where the rebels outnumbered the mutineers were thus imperilled. . . . Wuhan was under the complete control of the *coup,* and White terror reigned.

Wang Li was subjected to the same gentle "public examination" his enemies had endured. Displayed on the balcony of Regional Command Headquarters, he was violently indicted as a "counterrevolutionary." He strove in vain to appeal for the support of the troops. The crowds shouted, "Hang Wang Li!" He was punched in the face, and tufts of hair were torn out. The Million Heroes were planning a "mass trial" at a football stadium, like the "trials" anti-Maoists had endured in Peking. But he evaded that final humiliation by escaping amid the confusion with the help of a few soldiers of the 8199 Division. So complete was the opposition's control that the divisional political commissar and Wang Li were forced to spend the night of July 20 hiding in the underbrush of a small hill before a jeep could carry them to the one airfield still under the control of the loyal Maoists. As the plane with Wang Li and Security Minister Hsieh Fu-chih took off, the Million Heroes surrounded the airport—and the troops allowed them in. Only a handful of officers, it appeared, were "true rebel revolutionaries"; most were neutral or anti-Maoist.

Despite the subsequent vilification of Wang Jen-chung, the disgraced First Secretary of the Central-South Region, and the Rebellious General Chen Tsa-tao, commander of the Wuhan Military Region, there had obviously been no coordinated plan to establish a new, anti-Maoist regime. Even the Red Guard account revealed the lack of direction as the Wuhan Revolt entered its most violent and least coordinated stage.

Whipped by gusts of the evil wind, the cloud hung ominously over Wuhan. Hundreds of trucks carrying mutineers dashed everywhere through the streets. . . . On the morning of July 21, hundreds of trucks massed in the vicinity of the University [still held in part by Maoists], with the troops in the vehicles shouting and agitating. Military vehicles also surrounded all the middle schools around the campus and mounted guard on the approaches. . . . Look, the convoys of the 8201 Division and the Million Heroes rattle up. Look, more than 30 trucks carrying peasants with weapons force their way onto the campus. Look, mutineers carrying submachine guns, rifles, revolvers, and spears march into the University. Look, mutineers, shouting "Hang Wang Li!" . . . battle the masses. Look, young revolutionary fighters and masses fall to the ground in puddles of blood, shouting: "Long Live Chairman Mao!"

After the university fell, other buildings were also surrounded and the "liberated areas" [of the Maoists] were taken one by one . . . The Wuhan Iron and Steel Works was also taken over completely—and the mutineers occupied the entire city. . . . Counterrevolutionary *coups* erupted throughout Hupei Province.

Victory seemed to lie with the Million Heroes, the 8201 Division, and their many supporters among regular Liberation Army Units, as well as the old apparatus of State power—the entire legal structure, the Public Security Force, the Procurator's Office, and the Courts. It appeared on July 21 that majority action had retaken power from the Maoists.

On the same day, Wang Li and Hsieh Fu-chih were given a heroes' welcome in Peking. First Minister Chou En-lai had once again flown to Wuhan, but was forced to land at an outlying airport. Nonetheless, he coordinated both the demonstrations in Peking and the military action at Wuhan, which broke the coup. Under the threat of infantry, artillery gunboats, paratroops, and bombers, the Military Region Command retracted its support of the "mutineers." Wuhan was reoccupied by Central military forces to "suppress rebellion."

The Liberation Army had prevented China's splintering into a congeries of "independent kingdoms." It had put down the gravest popular uprising against the Maoist Party Center—one that might have founded a new popular government, unique in China. The Liberation Army had not saved the Maoists. It had only ensured that the continuing violence of succeeding years would not again overtly create "independent kingdoms."

Minister of Security Hsieh Fu-chih was to survive in the end, and General Chen Tsai-tao was to be severely censured in Peking. But Wang Li, the hero of Wuhan, was soon purged for opposing military domination under the slogan DRAG OUT THE REACTIONARY POWER-HOLDERS FROM THE LIBERATION ARMY! The revolt at Wuhan, while failing to establish popular government, had thwarted the extremists' attempt to impose their will. It had laid the basis for a virtual military government, harassed by constant factional fighting, which would thenceforth seek to rule China. It had also, paradoxically, ensured that, in time, the policies of the derided moderates would be re-enacted, and the policies of the Maoists discarded.

XXII

Rebrevs and Revcoms
of the Cultrev

The Wuhan Revolt of July 1967 destroyed hope of restoring orderly, conventional government to China. Thereafter, even a military regime could not enforce its will on the unruly "mass organizations" of the left or the right—and certainly not a military apparatus that was itself deeply divided.

The glorious promise of a wholly perfect human society had been foreclosed when the ideological phase of the Great Revolution ended in February 1967. The Revolutionary Committees based on the "three-way alliance" of the Liberation Army, "loyal" officials, and "mass organizations" were the blatant antithesis of the communal, "proletarian" administration envisioned by the Chairman and the Ghostwriter. Hierarchical "discipline" would thenceforth be enforced by a small elite through formal "government," rather than "extensive democracy's" being exercised by an "all-people administration." The ideal "participatory democracy" of Chairman Mao Tse-tung had yielded to the practical policies previously advocated by Chairman Liu Shao-chi—implemented by the revived "dictatorship of the proletariat acting through the Communist Party." But the unavoidable preponderance of the Army, the "chief coercive instrument of the State," was to make even these modestly reactionary aims unattainable—as was the new spirit of the Chinese people, particularly the irrepressible "new intelligentsia."

The Shanghai People's Commune had been peremptorily abolished, while the proposed Peking People's Commune had been aborted at mid-term. The romantic idealists failed to "seize power" from the vested bureaucratic, economic, and military interests—the establishment created by 18 years of Communist rule. First Minister Chou En-lai and the generals had canceled Utopia in favor of structures jerry-built to control the populace and maintain economic activity. The Great Proletarian Revolution could not be summarily declared null and void. Since it was never Peking's way to admit error or retract policies, another expedient was necessary. The Cultural Revolution, which had promised to "touch the souls of all men," was reduced to a purge of the "small group of men in power in the Party following the capitalist road."

The Wuhan Incident had made it impossible to operate the burgeoning Revolutionary Committees by a reasonably equal balance of the three forces. The old officials were timorous and frustrated; the headstrong "rebel revolutionaries" refused to subordinate themselves to "revolutionary discipline"; and only the military possessed any power of decision or execution—however attenuated.

The Rebellious General Chen Tsai-tao had actually given the "working masses" their head, perhaps because he misunderstood his orders, perhaps because he actually sought "independent power" as the Party Center charged. The final result had been brutal suppression by the Liberation Army; for the first time the military had struck in force against the Chinese masses. Thereafter, the military was not merely the preponderant, but the *sole* effective authority. The logic of events dictated that, a few months later, General Chen Tsai-tao would be largely exculpated. The generals were in command, and he was one of their own. The restoration of the battered Establishment thus began, and all functioning authority in China became inherently "revisionist." Thereafter, the sacred writings of Mao Tse-tung justified policies that totally rejected his goals. The Great Revolution to perfect mankind had become at once, a vendetta and police action conducted by harassed generals.

There were still Maoists in China, utterly dedicated Maoists utterly devoted to the visions of Mao Tse-tung. The Chairman's ideals were taken quite literally by his best disciples. They were not the opportunistic and hubristic Lin Piao, but tens of thousands of youths who earnestly believed that Utopia could be spontaneously created by the simple expedient of "destroying the class enemy." The true believers were equally opposed to the "bourgeois liberalism" they attributed to Comrade Shao-chi and to the "bureaucratic, military dictatorship" developing around them. They impartially denounced the old power-holders and the new power-holders.

Premier Chou En-lai was a chief target of the passionate Maoists' attacks on "Red bureaucrats, capitalists, and militarists." The impassioned youths felt that Chou En-lai had preserved the Establishment by his "three-way alliance." In January 1967, they said, power had actually been held by the masses, while the bureaucrats had "been reduced to zero." After February, they argued, the situation had once again been reversed. Indeed, the new "rebel revolutionaries" impartially directed their continued public assaults at all the luminaries of the Great Revolution except the Chairman, the Disciple, and the Starlet, who were sacrosanct. Even the Holy Trinity was derided verbally—and in clandestine publications—for "betraying" the ideals they had themselves so eloquently expressed, the ideals that had inspired the youth of China to rise in the revolt to make a new world. Since they defamed the inviolable demigods, few of those pamphlets reached the outside world, the only significant omission in the innumerable Red Guard publications that voluminously documented the Great Revolution.

The idealists' obdurate refusal to relinquish "popular power" was the spark that set China aflame for the next 20 months. In the name of "extensive democracy," the insurgents seized arms, suborned military units, established their own "liberated areas," sabotaged the Revolutionary Committees, and precipitated conflicts they themselves described as "limited revolutionary civil war." Their ideological justification was derided by the Party Center as the New Thought Trend or, more simply, the Evil Trend. Still, the insurgents enjoyed much support. Not only the freedom-intoxicated provincial "rebel revolutionaries" rallied, but also the discontented extremists clustered at the Center around the Starlet, who were later purged as the May Sixteenth Evil Group. Even some local "power-holders" of the military and conservative factions tacitly encouraged their opposition to Peking.

The New Thought Trend had deep roots. A precursor association, most active in 1966 and early 1967, had called itself the United Action Group. Composed primarily of the children of senior Central cadres, the United Action Group was, somehow, to survive all repression, though much battered. In late 1967, the Group made common cause with the new "left" opposition arising throughout the country.

The new opposition rationalized the confusing terminology of the Great Revolution by its existence, while further confusing actual conditions. Fortuitously, reality and description achieved a rough correlation. The "rebel revolutionaries" (shortened in Chinese into *tsao-fan pai*), which can conveniently be rendered as the English acronym "rebrevs," were truly in revolt against *all* authority. They felt betrayed by the Cultural Revolutionary Committees, usually shortened from *Wen-hua Ko-ming Wei-yuan-hui* to *Ko Wei Hui,* or, in English, "revcoms." The rebrevs considered the Committees merely new forms of the oppressive "State machinery" of the old, *i.e.,* Communist, regime. They wished to "carry through to the end" the Great Proletarian Cultural Revolution, the *Wu-chan-chieh-chi Wen-hua Ta Ko-ming,* usually reduced in speech to *Wen Ko,* quite literally, "cultrev." The abbreviations were the constantly circulating verbal currency for which men hazarded liberty and life.

The United Action Group, characteristically shortened to *Lien Tung,* "Uniact," demonstrated clearly in January 1967 that the Cultural Revolution had escaped Peking's control ideologically, as well as organizationally. The militant sons and daughters of high-ranking officials rapidly attracted a following that extended, however thinly, over most of the nation. Uniact was the first to demand that China's leaders actively pursue the grandiose ideals they espoused and actually carry out their glowing promises to the Chinese people. Uniact not only attacked the Ministry of Public Security, the spearhead of the purge, but dared demand: "Drag out the backstage boss of the Task Force of the Cultural Revolution!" They presumably meant the Chairman himself. They disrupted rallies while displaying two slogans: "Resolutely criticize the new bourgeois reactionary line represented by certain persons in the Task Force of the Cultural Revolution! The Task Force of the Cultural Revolution of the Party Center is following an opportunist policy, appearing leftist at one moment and rightist the next!" Convinced that the Starlet was using the "leftist" line to attain personal power, they criticized her unmercifully. A satirical couplet, annotated "Words and deeds are not consistent!", declared:

> He who recalls the past remembers that she came when called
>   and was a docile servant.
> He who contemplates the present sees that she rejects a
>   hundred summonses.

Leaflets making specific charges were distributed throughout Peking by Uniact. A later orthodox report, which piously omitted the details of those charges, nonetheless noted: "On January 4 [1967], Uniact broke into a meeting according to a well-laid plan. They smashed windows, distributed leaflets, and set off firecrackers. They shouted wildly, forcibly took over the microphone, beat the chairman, and tore clothes off members of the audience."

The movement spread outward from Peking during the early months of 1967. Uniact appeared in Canton, the metropolis of the south, to fight other Red Guard factions. Never quite clear where it stood, Uniact was the predecessor of an organization that knew exactly what it wanted. The Hunan Provincial Proletarian Revolutionaries Great Alliance Committee was called the *Sheng Wu Lien,* which abbreviates assonantly, but cacaphonically to "Provprolal."

The Provprolal, who attained great intellectual and political influence throughout the country, were unreconstructed Maoists of the most idealistic strain. Despite their revolutionary romanticism, they were also highly sophisticated in their interpretation of Marxism-Leninism and the Thought of Mao Tse-tung. Their lengthy manifestos are outstanding among the voluminous outpourings of the Great Revolution for their intellectual vigor. Their goal was the People's Commune of All China, and their means were founding their own Ultra-Left People's Commune to control the root province of Hunan. In the beginning they were ostentatiously deferential to the Chairman. He was the symbol of their aspirations, and his writings were their guide. But later charges that the Provprolal became "anti-Mao" were correct. Ideologically, they were utterly Maoist, but they became anti-Mao Tse-tung because the Chairman failed to pursue the Revolution. Their "Great Leader," they felt, had sold them out. He had become no more than another defender of the *status quo* of "Red bureaucratic capitalism and privilege"—himself a Liuist rather than a Maoist, by his own *original* definition.

The possibility of attaining Utopia once accepted, the intellectual structure and the political course of the Provprolal were rigorously logical. They issued two major manifestos. The first, drawn in mid-1967, stated their program: 1) continuous revolution; 2) violent action by which one class overthrows another . . . the proletarian revolutionaries overthrowing the newborn, yet decadent privileged stratum of the bourgeoisie (headed by [Comrade] Liu Shao-chi and [the Organizer] Teng Hsiao-ping), since the majority of the cadres have become capitalist . . . and a privileged class has emerged . . . while the principal components of the State machinery—the Army, the prisons, the courts, and the police . . . have become totally decadent; 3) the Cultural Revolution has, so far, touched neither the class roots of the reactionary line nor the bureaucratic organs serving the reactionary line; 4) not reform [through Revolutionary Committees], but revolution that will place power in the hands of the masses; 5) Hunan must thoroughly smash the old State machinery, for the Preparatory Group for the Provincial Revolutionary Committee [itself not yet established] is a carbon copy of the old political power; 6) breaking the bonds imposed by leaders corrupted by bourgeois opportunism; and 7) further concentration on theoretical study.

By late 1967 the disillusion of the Provprolal with the Establishment was overwhelming, but their dedication was even more intense. A long article entitled "Whither China?" revealed both desperation and determination to create the People's Commune of All China. Still striving to retain their faith in the Chairman, the Provprolal rationalized as "tactical moves in the struggle" Peking's sweeping concessions to the "decaying bureaucratic class which impedes the movement of history." Chairman Mao, they affirmed, had *not* abandoned his ultimate goal, though that goal might give "some people a Utopian impression." The Provprolal declared that the January Storm had given power to the people, while the February Adverse Current had restored power to the "corrupt State machinery." Their own task, they affirmed, was to create the Ultra-Left People's Commune as "the embryonic form of the new society modelled upon the Paris Commune." Rejecting the Revolutionary Committees, they declared that true communes could not be established until the Liberation Army itself had been conquered. "The vital problem of all revolutions must be solved—the problem of the Army." No longer did they praise "the great Deputy Commander-in-Chief Lin Piao," for they had concluded that the Liberation Army was a reactionary force, defending the old order and "Red capitalism."

Discussing the widespread violence of August 1967, which rose from the Wuhan Revolt, the tract said:

> It is now clear that a revolutionary civil war is necessary if the revolutionary masses are to overcome the armed Red capitalist class. . . . Capitalist fellow-travellers are power-holders in the Army, and parts of the armed forces have not merely altered the flesh-and-blood relation with the people that prevailed before Liberation, but have even become tools for suppressing the revolution. . . . Large-scale seizure of arms, such as has already occurred, is a historical necessity. Local civil wars of varying magnitude in which the Army has taken a direct part have erupted. . . . The people, instead of lamenting the fall of the Command of the Military Region [*i.e.,* General Chen Tsai-tao] should rejoice.

The ultra-left suffered a major reverse in September 1967. Peking formally forbade attacks on troops or "seizing" their arms—and ordered the Liberation Army to shoot anyone who molested soldiers. The Starlet herself attacked a mysterious "counterrevolutionary organization," called the May Sixteenth Group, which was largely made up of her own followers. That group had promulgated the slogan SEIZE POWER FROM THE SMALL GROUP OF CAPITALIST POWER-HOLDERS IN THE ARMED FORCES! But their sponsor repudiated them to preserve her own position.

"Without the Liberation Army," she said on September 5, 1967, "would it be possible for us to sit at this conference? You can not treat the Army in this fashion. When you seized their guns, some fighters wept. They knew you were going to seize their guns, but they could not open fire because they, like you, were part of the revolutionary masses." She acknowledged that "guns are being seized everywhere in the nation," but asserted most culprits were the "evil rightists." She further declared: "At present, a gust of evil wind is blowing. Apart from being directed at the Party Central Committee headed by Chairman Mao and at the People's Liberation Army—it is directed at the Revolutionary Committees." The Starlet spiritedly defended the Revolutionary Committees her followers attacked, and she formally promulgated the Party Center's order prohibiting "gun-seizing" and attacks—verbal or physical—on the Liberation Army and the Revolutionary Committees.

Within the next six months, all the Starlet's coterie fell from power, including Wang Li, the "hero of Wuhan." The sole survivor was the Literary Assassin Yao Wen-yüan, who characteristically adapted himself to the new line. His colleagues were attacked as "counterrevolutionaries, class enemies, bourgeois renegades, and agents of imperialism." The left had become almost indistinguishable from the right, for both were opposed to military rule, which was descending over China like a fog.

The Provprolal openly deplored "the setback in September" and abruptly ceased its praise of the Starlet. Never abashed by a mixed metaphor, they declared that the bourgeoisie had "seized the fruits of the August storm." They called for a "revolutionary storm in the rural areas," but cautioned against the "infantile leftist error" of demanding the immediate replacement of Revolutionary Committees with Communes. They still placed their faith in the Chairman—or pretended to do so. Attempting to reconcile the contradiction in their own position, they explained that the "capitalist, bureaucratic class in the Liberation Army" was sabotaging the Cultural Revolution. While endorsing the "extensive concession" of allowing old cadres to return to limited power as a temporary means of placating the administrators, they lamented the failure of the "bombardment of Chou En-lai," the chief administrator. Nor could they avoid denouncing the Starlet's order of September 5— because "It completely nullified the call to 'arm the Left'; the working class was disarmed, and the bureaucrats, came back to power."

The "proletarian strategy," the Provprolal said, was clear. It was necessary to found a "revolutionary party," not, obviously, the "bureaucratic-controlled Communist Party," but a truly revolutionary party, in order to complete the revolution. "The Revolutionary Committees," they stressed, "are a product of bourgeois reformism." They rejected criticism of themselves as Utopia "extreme leftists" and added: *"The nation must necessarily move towards the new society of the People's Commune of All China. If dictatorship by the Revolutionary Committees is regarded as the ultimate objective of the Great Cultural Revolution, China will inevitably go the way of the Soviet Union—and the people will fall under the Fascist, bloody rule of the capitalists."*

The leftist position was quite clear—and its appeal great. The Provprolal was powerful in its own right, and a hundred other Red Guard factions supported its purpose. Curiously, even liberals by Western definition agreed with its immediate purposes. Although the liberals could not share the left's Utopian aspirations, they too felt that the

Revolutionary Committees were creating a military dictatorship. Both groups were, of course, reviled and vilified, individually and collectively. The Party Center accused them of "spreading anarchism and anarchy." The charge was absolutely correct, for the ultra-left rejected *all* constituted authority. They were truly romantic anarchists who believed, as Mao Tse-tung had told them, that "destruction" of the old society, by which they meant the Communist society, would prepare China for a perfect new society. The liberals, on the other hand, actually sought an ordered hierarchy of ideas and authority—within a framework of basic freedoms. One youth cried out, "Only let them enforce their own constitution! That is all we ask!" Both groups of idealists, of course, hoped in vain. The new order was built with bayonets, rather than upon ideas or the popular will.

Despite Peking's orders—and the bayonets—the resistance continued. Having released the genie of youthful aspiration, the authoritarian Party Center could neither entice nor force it back into the bottle. While outside observers were criticized by the tender-minded for "exaggerating" disorder, Peking continued well into 1970 to utter a stream of denunciation of such phenomena as "anarchism, armed clashes, capitalist tendencies, corruption, speculation, bourgeois restorationism, indiscipline"— and such splendidly graphic faults as "mountain-topism and wind-headism." The struggle within the Mao-Lin faction was also confirmed by the purge of the "extreme leftists" originally sponsored by the Starlet.

That purge was complete by the spring of 1968, and the limited purge of the Liberation Army by early summer of the same year. Peking sought another uneasy compromise by eliminating acting Chief-of-Staff Yang Cheng-wu, the same Yang the Gun who had displaced the Securityman Lo Jui-ching and had commanded the original military *Putsch* in Peking—on behalf of Lin Piao. His successor was the commander of the Canton Military Region, General Huang Yung-sheng, whose name felicitously meant "Huang the Ever Victorious." Since Huang had suppressed the dissident Red Guards of Canton with remarkable alacrity and enthusiasm, no major shift of policy was implicit in his appointment. Like Yang the Gun, Huang the Ever Victorious was a loyal subordinate of Lin Piao. It, therefore, appeared that Yang the Gun had been sacrificed to the spirit of Party amity, just as had the Starlet's "extreme leftists." They had criticized the military and cried, "Seize power from the small group within the Liberation Army following the capitalist road." Yang the Gun had, perhaps, been somewhat tactless in his assertion of military control.

The balance struck by the mutual sacrifice did not endure long. In August 1968, the Literary Assassin Yao Wen-yüan published a remarkable article in *Red Flag,* denouncing the "anarchism and indiscipline" that had overwhelmed China and demanding that the "mass organizations" manifest "revolutionary discipline" and absolute obedience to the Thought of Mao Tse-tung. He excoriated his former companions of the extreme left and the "phenomenon of extreme democracy" he had so clamorously praised earlier.

Another entirely new force was created to impose order—Workers' Thought of Mao Tse-tung Propaganda and Investigation Teams. "Under the direction of the Liberation Army," those armed groups were to put down disorder by Red Guard factions of the left, the center, and the right. The conservative workers took on the task with zest, for they had too long been harassed by the adolescents. The Workers' Teams signaled a new turn in the course of the Cultural Revolution. But two major divisive tendencies were hardly affected: accumulation of political and economic power in the hands of the generals; and the continuing violent protest of the ideological dissidents, called the New Thought Trend.

Throughout 1969 and well into 1970, the Party Center continued to rail against "indiscipline by mass organizations." The term "rebel revolutionaries" had vanished from general usage—for obvious reasons. Shanghai admonished the remaining rebrevs:

> There are still comrades in our ranks who have idiotic ideas. They say: "We wrought the victory of the revolution. We took power without the leadership of the Party, and everything went well! . . ." That manner of talking is utterly wrong. We must study the new Party Constitution and reject the ultra-leftist bourgeois reactionary trend [sic]. We must maintain vigilance against the class enemy, who uses factionalism to undermine the reconstruction of the Party. The revolutionary mass organizations at all levels must accept the leadership of the Party organization. *The proper relation between the Party and mass organizations is that between rulers and subjects.**

Authority had by no means successfully reasserted itself against the pernicious New Thought Trend. Intellectual anarchism, romantically seeking a perfect new civilization free of all coercion, had become total anarchy. In Kweichow, one of the first provinces to establish a Revolutionary Committee, both the Liberation Army and the "masses" were instructed in the differences between "freedom and discipline."

> Some muddle-headed people cannot cope with proletarian freedom and discipline as two sides of the same coin. . . . They do not understand that observing revolutionary discipline on their own initiative

* Emphasis supplied.

consolidates the dictatorship of the proletariat. They say, "To hell with discipline. I have my own freedom. . . . We are now living in an entirely new Socialist system under the dictatorship of the proletariat. Everyone enjoys extensive democracy and freedom. . . ." Those who have no sense of responsibility and just talk about freedom, but neglect revolutionary discipline and entertain ultra-leftist, extreme-democratic ideas are preaching petty-bourgeois freedom.

Workers in Honan Province were taking the same attitude according to the provincial press: "The class enemies* in the Honan Mining Bureau, not reconciled to their defeat, spread anarchism and other 'ultra-democratic ideas.' They said the eight-hour work system was only a framework, while obeying the leadership was 'manifesting slave-mentality.' They even peddled Liu Shao-chi's theory of 'bonuses in command,' causing a drop in production."

In Outer Mongolia, the people were urged: "We must thoroughly encourage the masses to develop deep revolutionary criticism in order to counter the erroneous tendency of the anarchistic reactionary thought trend and to advance and strengthen the instruction of our ranks in revolutionary discipline, while attacking all counterrevolutionary indiscipline. . . . Otherwise, contradictions among the masses can become mortal antagonisms."

It was left to *The People's Daily* to offer the finest example of Maoist acrobatics on the intellectual highwire:

Many people are saying: "Chairman Mao teaches that the masses must educate themselves. We are the masses, so what we do is nobody else's business!"

This, of course, is merely a pretext contrived by the extremely democratized faction [*i.e.,* the Provprolal and its allies]. Chairman Mao's instructions are the exact opposite of Liu Shao-chi's Theory of the Backwardness of the Masses. The masses' teaching themselves means: They must love Chairman Mao without limit; they must assume the correct responsibility for the revolution and production; and they must display a revolutionary, disciplined consciousness. They must use the Thought of Mao Tse-tung to overcome all *non-proletarian thought trends,* while ceaselessly elevating their own political consciousness.

Democracy is protection, while centralization is dangerous!" A number of members of leadership circles speak in that way. In such thinking *fear* is the dominant element, and *fear* encourages the tendency toward extreme democratization.

---

* By 1970, the "leftists" and the proletariat.

When the proletariat makes revolution, there must be authority and high-level centralization. Otherwise, the proletariat will not be able to seize political power or hold political power.

The Party Center, still presumably Maoist, had come a long way from the days of "extensive democracy . . . the people managing the great affairs of State according to the principles of the Paris Commune." Although Comrade Liu Shao-chi had been read out of the Communist Party in the fall of 1968, the chief organ of that Party was in 1970 asserting his views, rather than those of Chairman Mao.

What had happened? The tumultuous year and a half between the total—though not formal—end of the Cultural Revolution, from August 1967 and the Ninth Party Congress in April 1969, can best be conveyed episodically. This is what happened, usually as recounted by participants.

AUGUST 11, 1967:

Peking was cut off from direct land communication with much of the great south. The Maoists could only exhort their followers to look to better days and await the "inevitable" victory that would be theirs because they moved with the "wheel of history."

Honan Province, with its 55 million inhabitants just south of Hopei and Peking, had been conceded to the anti-Maoists administratively two months earlier. Honan, said private reports, had subsequently become a military base for the anti-Maoists.

Minister of Security Hsieh Fu-chih told a secret Red Guard meeting that the anti-Maoist generals of Wuhan had withdrawn the core of their military forces into Honan. Hsieh had briefly been held captive during the Wuhan Revolt of mid-July. Thereafter, Wuhan was savaged by constant fighting among factions.

Security Minister Hsieh's admission that the Maoists could not move troops from their presumed stronghold of Peking to Wuhan through Honan demonstrated the Center's desperate position. Honan virtually blockaded Peking from South China, since all major communications lines ran through that province.

Battles among organized factions were fought against a background of widespread violence throughout China, producing widespread disruption of normal communications and economic life. Almost every major city was deserted by large numbers of refugees. They fled clashes between pro-Mao and anti-Mao activists, marked by mass killing and atrocities like gouging out eyeballs with hollow bamboo rods.

Railroad communications along the main north-south and east-west axes were slow, uncertain, and often cut completely. Traffic on the Yangtze River ceased for days on end.

"The stubborn opposition elements will never recognize their defeat," a Peking statement said. The opposition "are trying to create a small typhoon in their areas," the article continued. "They are surrounding and destroying the proletarian revolutionary faction. . . . We cannot relax for an instant."

The Maoists reminded their followers in the most vigorous language they had ever employed that they faced "great difficulties and enormous vicissitudes." Promising total amnesty to enemies who came over to their side, the Maoists admitted that the "bulk of the masses are deluded by the enemy."

SEPTEMBER 3, 1967:

The Maoists acknowledged their enemies' strength by asserting: "The enemy's appearance of total superiority is illusory." Self-contradictory again, they warned further that the struggle would be protracted and bitter because the anti-Maoists were by no means in a state of "anarchy."

The Central Political Department of the People's Air Force described the opposition as "a kind of government of its own." To an outsider, that analysis might appear to overstate both the power and the cohesiveness of the anti-Maoist camp. But the Maoists' estimate of their enemies' power commanded serious consideration, tempered by recognition of their propensity for alternately exaggerating and deprecating the enemy for propaganda purposes.

At the very least, events and the Maoists' own statements showed that anti-Maoist or neutralist officials exercised a high degree of power in most of the 29 provinces, special administrative areas, and autonomous municipalities into which China was divided. The anti-Maoist and neutral authorities were in communication, and their actions, as well as their responses to Maoist pressure, were coordinated, albeit loosely.

The force that bound those local authorities was not only dedication to common purposes but the only functioning nation-wide structure in China—the People's Liberation Army. The Liberation Army was necessarily Maoist in philosophy, but the great majority of generals in the provinces were, without question, non-Maoist in action. Since Maoist pressure insisted upon dividing all China into unquestioning supporters and outright foes, the generals were almost compelled to make common cause with the anti-Maoist or neutralist civilian officials in their localities.

NOVEMBER 6, 1967:

China entered the winter of 1967–68 devoid of even the effective pretense of a functioning central authority. The single unifying force still operating in the world's largest nation was unacknowledged by Peking's propagandists: a loose, almost tacit alliance of senior generals that strongly influenced—though it did not control—the virtually autonomous chiefs of the 13 military districts, who were China's true government.

The generals' group used persuasion and moral force and worked in tenuous, arm's-length understanding with Premier Chou En-lai, who still strove to preserve the vestiges of central administration and central government that his own adherence to the Maoist "revolutionary rebels" had earlier ravaged.

The Maoists had surrendered the grandiose objectives of the Cultural Revolution. They had not proceeded to the formal degradation of Comrade Liu Shao-chi, Chairman of the People's Republic of China, and his inner "small group" of adherents whom they called "the real enemy." The Maoists pleaded with the "men in power within the Communist Party," who were the broad initial target of the Cultural Revolution, to join with them in a "grand alliance" designed to restore a functioning structure of authority. They strove to regain a vestige of power by placating the men whose "usurpation of power" originally induced them to proclaim the Cultural Revolution.

The Maoists declared that the "great majority" of officials of the Communist Party and the People's Government were "basically good." Yet those same men were the "structure of authority" the extremists originally had sworn to destroy.

The Maoists exhorted unwilling Red Guards to return to their school desks and "to make revolution by studying." The Red Guards were further told, "The great majority of teachers are basically good." That was a remarkable statement, since the chief initial ideological thrust of the Cultural Revolution was against "bourgeois academic savants" who sought "restoration of capitalism throughout China."

Like the Emperor of a decaying dynasty frantically seeking to bolster his authority, Mao Tse-tung made a hurried—almost clandestine—tour of five troubled provinces before the Maoists offered their tactical surrender. His failure to rally support, combined with the Disciple's realization that he was losing control of those few troops still loyal to him, appear to have precipitated the sweeping decision.

Soldiers were ordered to use their weapons to suppress disorder. They had previously been forbidden to resist even when Red Guards stole their arms. The Maoists were forced to give in or see the nation explode into a total civil war they knew they could not win.

The Maoists had formally established Revolutionary Committees in only 8 of China's 29 major administrative divisions, the latest coming into existence in Inner Mongolia a week earlier.

Each of the commanders of the country's 13 military districts ruled in the name of Maoism. But each administered his area in accordance with local needs and in loose alliance with the "local power-holders"—from the township to the provincial and regional levels. Those men still exercised effective influence among the civilian population. Despite directives from Peking, the farmers once again possessed private plots of land and sold a substantial portion of their produce for their own profit.

NOVEMBER 19, 1967:

The People's Liberation Army cut down the corpses that hung from the lamp posts in Canton, where 2.5 million southern Chinese had been living amid terror for three months. The systematic maneuvers of newly confident troops broke the armed bands that had turned the city into a private battlefield. The feuding gangs of pro-Maoists, anti-Maoists, and opportunists in the middle were scattered and deprived of most of their weapons.

An apprehensive peace lay over the city, and ordinary citizens once more dared venture forth after dark—*if* their business was pressing. Foreign merchants arriving for the Canton Autumn Trade Fair, postponed for exactly a month from the scheduled opening on October 15, found a jittery after-the-battle atmosphere. The precarious truce owed as much to the Communists' desire to make the city fit for the Trade Fair as it did to the renewed confidence of a Canton garrison that had finally been authorized to use its full strength to put down civil disorder.

As if to celebrate the new but tenuous imposition of order, Canton staged a curious spectacle. A "mass rally" of 100 thousand cheered the establishment of the Preparatory Committee for the Canton Workers' Revolutionary Great Alliance. It was the first step, Canton Radio explained, toward the establishment of a Provisional Structure of Power that could in time become the Canton Revolutionary Committee. That latter body, when established, would presumably rule the city on behalf of the Maoist faction. Radio Canton, presumably speaking for the Maoists, hailed its establishment as "a great victory for the Thought of Mao Tse-tung!"

The reality behind the Canton Preparatory Committee was better illuminated by the Premier. Still balancing between pro-Maoists and anti-Maoists in the hope of preserving a semblance of ordered unity— and his own position—Chou En-lai had in mid-October offered a veiled confession of the Maoists' great frustrations in a major speech. Among resounding and bellicose Maoist clichés and inevitable claims of "great victories" ran an unmistakable thread of candor. The Maoists, Chou said, had "not yet even begun" to re-establish their power.

Chou spoke at Wuhan, and his theme was a quotation attributed to Mao Tse-tung himself: "Bad things can be turned into good things." But the First Minister failed to prove his case—perhaps deliberately.

Contradicting an earlier assertion by the Disciple, the First Minister admitted that the Great Proletarian Cultural Revolution had seriously disrupted the economy:

> Such a world-shaking revolutionary movement exacts a certain price in production in certain places and in certain departments. *We took this into account in advance.* Production is affected to a certain extent, especially in places where disturbances occur. But this is only a transient thing. As soon as disorder is turned into order, production can quickly resume and swell. The revolutionization of the thinking of the people is bound to be transformed into a tremendous material force.*

Chou added:

> United and forming a mighty revolutionary army, the proletarian revolutionaries will then carry out the revolutionary mass criticism and repudiation of the handful of Communist Party men in authority taking the capitalist road, headed by China's Khrushchev [Mao's arch-enemy, Comrade Liu Shao-chi] to still greater depth. You must carry out well struggle-criticism-transformation [self-purging] in your own units, realize revolutionary three-way alliances, and carry the Great Revolution through to the end. . . . It is a very arduous task to completely discredit the handful of Party persons in authority taking the capitalist road and to carry to success the struggle-criticism-transformation in various units. The latter task, especially, it can be said, has not even yet begun.

DECEMBER 1, 1967:

Expanding military rule was graphically demonstrated by the new shape of government in Kansu Province in the remote northwest. Although "Revolutionary Committees" were initially described as the "new organs of power" through which the Maoists would exercise their authority, the Preparatory Committee in Kansu was made up of anti-Maoist generals who had, only a few months earlier, been assailed by the Red Guards. The pattern demonstrated that the handful of Revolu-

* Emphasis supplied.

tionary Committees represented anti-Maoist or neutralist rule. Although the Maoists did control the Revolutionary Committees of a province or two, most Committees were set up by what the Maoists themselves labelled "sham seizures of power." Anti-Maoists had, as the Chinese say, "put on a Maoist hat" and continued to act as they had before changing the forms of power.

In most provinces where anti-Maoists or neutralists were winning formal power, the established military high command, which controlled the local garrison before the Great Proletarian Cultural Revolution disrupted all China, remained in power. The most dramatic example was Kansu, where the political commissar of the garrison, the commander, and the deputy commander were the chief figures in the rally announcing the formation of the Preparatory Committee. The three also held the key offices in the committee.

All three had previously been accused of bloody suppression of the "revolutionary movement" by Red Guards. They had reportedly suppressed a Maoist student rising in Lanchow in the spring of 1967—with several hundred killed and wounded, including 97 students dead.

The reappearance of those men in pseudo-Maoist guise was as remarkable as the survival of the commander of Honan Province, who had previously been bitterly attacked by Red Guards as a "butcher" for the vigor with which he put down disorder. A survey of China's provinces revealed a remarkable preponderance of military men effectively exercising power, most of them distinctly non-Maoist—if not in every case identifiably anti-Maoist.

DECEMBER 14, 1967:

The Army was still in the process of bringing tumultuous Canton under control by forcefully supressing unruly Maoists—behind a smokescreen of Maoist words. Events in Canton and Kwangtung, the country's southernmost province abutting Hong Kong, demonstrated most dramatically and most significantly the new direction taken by the Great Proletarian Cultural Revolution. It was in sum: no longer cultural in emphasis, but total; no longer a revolution, but re-establishment of conventional power; no longer proletarian, but military; and, finally, a phenomenon China's effective rulers, the generals, were striving to make small, rather than great.

Lengthy statements from the "responsible leaders" of Canton's Small Group of the Preparatory Commission for the Revolutionary Committee, all only recently denounced as anti-Maoist, indicated conclusively that the prevalent generals were not ideologically motivated. They were concerned with establishing order out of the welter of violent factions brought forth by the Cultural Revolution—and with bringing the country's fragmented economic machinery back into full operation as rapidly as possible.

The critical issues of the Cultural Revolution had been focused on two vital groups: the "old cadres" and the "rebel revolutionaries." From the Maoist standpoint, old cadres were bad and rebel revolutionaries good. The Canton Small Group reversed the emphasis.

Its report enjoined the masses of Canton City and Kwangtung Province to seek to "protect" cadres—rather than unseat them. The report further advised that the "verdict" on an individual cadre "must not be based upon isolated actions, but upon the sum of his service to the people." The "men in power," who had been denounced for specific offenses against the Maoist "young generals of disorder," were to be restored to office and honor.

The Canton report condemned in the severest terms the "phenomenon of extreme leftism" for creating disorder. Resistance to constituted authority was denounced as a "petty bourgeois tendency which violates Marxist discipline." The generals boasted in a most "economist and bourgeois" manner that essential services were rapidly being restored in the Province and the city. The catalogue demonstrated the previous total disruption, for it included gold shops, electrical generators, running water, radio facilities, transport, and chemical and textile industries.

JANUARY 1, 1968:

Although the Maoists had persisted in their vendetta against only a handful of their opponents, sweeping concessions had failed to bring even the semblance of peace. By year's end 1967, the clashes that began as a political and ideological struggle had been transformed into civil strife that could not be described as "civil war" only because no organized armies faced each other along conventional battle lines.

In Canton, peaceful citizens locked themselves in their homes each evening behind makeshift barricades. Criminals and political dissidents roared through the streets in commandeered trucks, sometimes breaking into arsenals to steal their stocks of arms. Foreign captains lying off major ports in North China like Dairen and Tientsin were kept awake by fusillades from rifles and automatic weapons. In Huhehot, the capital, and other chief cities of Inner Mongolia, the Maoists complained of a wave of crime including arson, racial clashes between Chinese and Mongols, shoot-outs, clandestine murder, violent robbery, burglary, and sabotage of communications. Chungking, in the southwestern province of Szechwan, was beset by thousands of armed peasants who had sworn to "wash Chungking clean with blood." Within the city, the crump of grenades, the thunder of artillery, and the rattle of small arms mocked the Liberation Army's efforts to safeguard essential stores of foodstuffs and gasoline.

In Anhwei Province, the new wave of violence shattered the "provisional alliance" of Maoists and anti-Maoists that was intended to bring order to that troubled area in Central China. In Hunan Province, the birthplace of Chairman Mao himself, the new Preparatory Revolutionary Committee was declared in peril from "misguided elements within the masses." Yet Hunan was apparently better off than neighboring Hupei and Kiangsu Provinces. Scheduled visits to Wuhan and Nanking in Kiangsu by touring foreign students were canceled, and Changsha, the capital of Hunan, was substituted.

Peking Radio, ostensibly speaking on behalf of Chairman Mao and the Disciple Lin Piao, ordered: "The two contending factions should talk much less about each other's shortcomings and faults. Let each side discuss its own shortcomings and faults. Self-criticism, rather than mutual criticism, is the need of the day. The two factions should seek harmonious common ground on major issues, and they should reserve their differences* on minor issues for subsequent discussion."

JANUARY 10, 1968:

General Huang Yung-sheng, Huang the Ever Victorious, titular ruler of Kwangtung Province, denounced "fighting, killing and looting."

Honan, lying between the key industrial center of Wuhan and Peking, suffered a particularly virulent outbreak of armed factionalism. According to *The Honan Daily,* local chieftains had organized their own guerrilla forces, "gathering recruits, reoccupying mountainous areas, using mountain caves as headquarters, and sallying forth to make armed raids."

Honan had long been a center of anti-Maoist activity. After the mutiny in Wuhan in July 1967, 30 thousand veterans, students, and soldiers fled into Honan to continue the anti-Maoist struggle. *The Honan Daily* castigated some "chieftains who distort and reject the meaning of Mao's doctrines." Other leaders "practice counterrevolutionary economism," the Maoist term for wooing the common people by appealing to their material interests with higher wages, shorter hours, and promises of fringe benefits. The same men also "incite work stoppages and cut communications lines" in order to harass the Maoists.

The object of the widespread attacks in Honan was the new Revolu-

* The Mayor Peng Chen had likewise pleaded in his *February Theses* of 1966 for rival groups to "reserve unreconcilable differences for later discussion."

tionary Committee that strove to create a workable administration and to bring order to the province in the name of Mao. Although that Committee was dominated by generals who were often anti-Maoist, or at least neutralist, it was unable to halt the waves of "armed anarchism." "The province," Honan Radio said, "is falling into a new tumult of contention for power!"

MARCH 8, 1968:

They called him "01," the previously obscure clerk who for almost a year swayed the lives of the 40 million people of Communist China's southernmost province, Kwangtung. His real name, known only to a few in his headquarters, was Chang Chun. He was the chieftain of the August First Struggle Regiment of 160 thousand ardent and armed "revolutionary rebels."

Linked with other "rebel revolutionary" groups throughout the country, "01" was among the few hundred most powerful men in China during the turmoil. Finally, a new spin of the wheel cast him back into the bitter obscurity from which he had come.

Chang Chun epitomized the ill-educated proletarian leader who arose when Chairman Mao decided to supplant the conventional apparatus of the Communist Party and the People's Government with a new "revolutionary structure of power." He represented the local chieftains whose intransigence cast China into a state *The Peking People's Daily* described as "anarchism and factionalism." Entrenched amid China's 700 million or more citizens, each with his own band of devoted followers, hundreds of men like Chang Chun were the greatest obstacle to the restoration of public order.

In the beginning they probably fought for principle and the common welfare. In the end they fought to retain and enlarge their individual power. They attacked anyone who appeared to be consolidating his power, regardless of whether he was a moderate sanctioned by the new authorities or another "rebel" chieftain.

A youth who worked in the message center of the August First Regiment until he fled to British-ruled Hong Kong explained:

> We started out on one side, but, at the end, it was hard to tell where we stood. We were with Chairman Mao and his Deputy Commander Lin Piao and against the old-line officials—the men in power in the Communist Party following the capitalist road. But then everything became topsy-turvy! Peking told us the old-line officials were really good and that we ought to cooperate with them. That was nonsense, but it left us without a policy except to go on fighting for the people!

Chang Chun, a man in his mid-thirties, was a disgruntled clerk in a district public health clinic in Canton in 1966 when the cataclysm called the Cultural Revolution gave him his great opportunity. He had served as a private in the People's Liberation Army and had been assigned to the clinic on discharge. He felt that he had been ill-rewarded for his service to the cause. His application for membership in the Communist Party had not been accepted, and he had been given work he considered demeaning at a salary he considered ridiculously low—40 people's dollars, officially, less than $25 U.S. a month.

Nursing his resentment of the men in high places he felt had oppressed him, Chang was an ideal recruit to the ranks of the "rebel revolutionaries" when the Maoists proclaimed the Cultural Revolution. The abstruse ideological aspects evaded him to a great extent. But Chang Chun welcomed with uncomplicated glee the opportunity to revenge himself on the old-line officials—and to exercise power himself. The stocky former private with the high forehead and the hesitant, almost diffident, manner of speech became an urban guerrilla chieftain in China's great southern metropolis. The influence of the band of veterans he commanded extended throughout Kwangtung Province. He was in constant communication with men of the same faction in places as far away as Sinkiang in the northwest and Szechwan in the southwest. "01" ran a well-administered machine with four operating sections: "propaganda, organization, struggle, and finance." He had been liberally endowed with arms, vehicles, equipment, and funds by the Maoists who originally enfranchised him.

In time, the August First Struggle Regiment—named to commemorate the uprising at Nanchang that gave birth to the Communist Army on August 1, 1927—became a self-contained community within Kwangtung Province. Although it operated its own factories and published its own newspaper, it basically sought two chief goals: to destroy the old structure of rule and all rivals; and to protect its own members. It was joined in its raids on arsenals and armed demonstrations by other Kwangtung "struggle units" totaling 250 thousand persons who made up the so-called Red Flag of the Thought of Mao Tse-tung Battle Group.

The Red Flag Group was opposed by the equally large East Wind Group of "struggle units." Both groups included veterans, former officials, workers, and university and middle-school students. In the beginning, the East Wind Group tended to support the old-line officials—and the Red Flag Group to oppose them.

The original darling of the Red Flag Group was General Huang the Ever Victorious, the personal protégé of both Mao and Lin, who then was commander of the Canton Military Region. In time, however, Huang made common cause with the East Wind Group for the sake of order—and became the hated enemy of the Red Flag Group. Each group insisted that it was the only true "revolutionary rebel faction" and the only faithful adherent of Chairman Mao. Each was, on the surface, bitterly opposed to Mao's arch-enemy, Liu Shao-chi, Chairman of the People's Republic.

The career of "01" was almost as confused as the shifts in the position of the August First Regiment. Men who observed him closely felt that he was really a convenient mouthpiece for his subordinate leaders, who were too shrewd to expose themselves by assuming the chieftainship. Those subordinates wrote his orders, composed his speeches, and manipulated him for their own purposes.

The men in his headquarters did not believe the charge by his enemies that "01" was devoting himself to a career of pleasure on the sealed-off fifth floor of the hotel the Struggle Regiment had commandeered in downtown Canton. They were puzzled at his reluctance to show himself even to them until they remembered that they themselves were always muffled to the ears and wore dark glasses when they went out to "fight the enemy." Everyone shared a deathly fear of being photographed and identified by their enemies.

When the end came, it came quickly. The August First Regiment was ordered dissolved by Chou En-lai because of "left-wing extremism." The order would not have meant much, for the factions were almost wholly independent, except that the regiment had failed to provide itself with an adequate financial base. Its members were dispersed among other factions of the Red Flag group.

Chang Chun, no longer "01," was offered work in a factory. The wheel had come full circle, for he felt the work beneath his dignity. His former followers, irritated by his inefficiency, refused to have anything to do with him. Chang Chun escaped arrest, since he had become unimportant. Meanwhile hundreds of other Chang Chuns were still preventing the imposition of order on China.

May 28, 1968:

Nanning, the chief railway center in southern China, was terrorized by constant and costly factional fighting. Inhabitants who could, fled. Train services were disrupted.

A letter from a daughter in Nanning to her father in Hong Kong dramatically conveyed the "oppressive atmosphere of armed struggle." Nanning was like a bacterial culture suddenly blighted. The tiny beings scurried frantically about to avoid the violent death that visited their fellows. The young lady's letter spoke first in general terms of "large-scale armed fighting which kills and wounds many many people." She said inhabitants avoided as best they could the sudden attacks "mounted by landlords, counterrevolutionaries, and the evil elements, but their belongings are destroyed, and many cannot escape."

In Wuchow, an idyllic town that straddles the Kweissu River on the border between Kwangtung and Kwangsi provinces, recent clashes destroyed five full blocks. Two thousand dwellings were burned out or heavily damaged, leaving "tens of thousands homeless." Some of the instigators were "arrested" by their opponents, though it was almost impossible to tell who was the legitimate authority amid the total political confusion. In the breakdown of public order, many of the arrested were severely beaten and some died of their injuries.

"Many people," the letter observed, "take advantage of the so-called 'class struggle' to take revenge on old enemies." The young lady pointed out that the "political struggle between Communists and anti-Communists" often became no more than a pretext for savage and often mortal grudge fighting. Moreover, bandits and habitual criminals used the disorder as a cover to loot and kill.

The political significance of events seemed even less precise in Nanning, the capital of Kwangsi Province, 200 miles from Wuchow. *Nanning* means "Southern Tranquillity." There the chief assaults were mounted by People's Militia rallied by the "old men in power." Fighting was general but particularly concentrated on the area marked by New China Street and Liberation Road. At the worst times, when the trains could not carry the anxious refugees, the streets of Nanning were impassable all day long. At all times, the remaining inhabitants locked themselves behind front doors no later than 8:00 P.M., shutting off darkened roads where street lamps no longer functioned. Only the looters and the contending factions ventured into the Nanning night. Schools, closed about 18 months earlier, had opened briefly in March, but disorder soon forced their reclosure.

"The deeds these people do," the letter declared, "are more fierce and ruthless than those we saw when the Japanese devils were here. One can think of many things one might do, but there is only one thing for me to do—flee as everyone else is trying to flee."

JUNE 26, 1968:
Violent street fighting between rival factions once again transformed Canton into a city under internal siege, where the police retreated into barricaded station houses guarded by armed troops.

Officials of the Revolutionary Committee all but abandoned attempts to maintain order. The occasional policeman still abroad and soldiers of the People's Liberation Army confined themselves primarily to rescuing innocent individuals. They dared go no further than attempting to contain the most virulent clashes between the Red Flag and East Wind factions in order to prevent their engulfing the entire city. Determined efforts failed to break up battles waged with homemade grenades, Molotov cocktails, clubs, knives, improvised metal spears, and a few small arms.

Official Radio Canton lamented disorder: "Evil elements and class enemies are aiming their spearheads at the proletariat's headquarters, the newborn Revolutionary Committee, and inciting the masses to fight the masses. . . . Some are fanning reactionary, anarchistic ideas and wrecking Socialist labor discipline."

The Red Flag and the East Wind factions still fought in the name of Chairman Mao. But each, numbering approximately a quarter of a million, sought primarily to establish its own supremacy. The "great alliance" of different factions, blessed by Peking in the name of peace, had broken down. The "legitimate" Revolutionary Committee had become a thin façade that hardly disguised official impotence. The continuing struggle obscured political, and even practical, objectives. Young workers and students attacked each other largely because pointless struggle had become a conditioned reflex, a normal way of life during the Great Revolution.

Despite tightened security measures along China's border with the Portuguese and British colonies of Macao and Hong Kong, refugees dared death to escape. Many evaded land patrols by swimming the Pearl River Estuary. Grim confirmation of the struggle's violence and the refugees' anxiety was washed up on the islets of Hong Kong. During one week in June 1968 at least 18 unidentifiable bodies were found in Hong Kong waters—all obviously executed or murdered. Some had been decapitated and others strangled. Almost all had bound wrists.

Where they could, the authorities sought to suppress the springs of disorder—regardless of whether they were Maoist or non-Maoist, terms which had lost almost all meaning amid the turmoil. The swarm of newspapers published by the Red Guards were no longer allowed to be sold on the streets. Army patrols, supported by "youth propaganda teams," marched through the city in the daytime trying to discourage struggle, although the Liberation Army in general avoided excessive interference. Commanders obviously feared that direct intervention would splinter their commands or provoke sporadic fighting between regular units like that reported from Yünnan and Kwangsi provinces to the west.

The common people, however, took a hand. The red brassards bearing the legend "Red Guard," previously flaunted, were now rarely seen in Canton. Citizens were so angry at the "little generals of disorder" that anyone wearing the brassard was a target for attack. The authorities, ostensibly promoting Mao's Cultural Revolution, also discouraged the brassards. They called them a violation and "disruption of the great alliance of all factions" that was supposed to bring internal peace.

Spectacular incidents dominated the news: A tram driver is killed, and the resultant battle for revenge leaves 30 dead and dying on the tracks. Workers attack students holed up in the chemistry building of Sun Yat-sen University, and the students retaliate by hurling acid and homemade explosives.

The effect on the daily lives of uninvolved citizens was profound. A few primary schools were open for two hours each morning and afternoon, their only subject of study the Thought of Mao. Middle schools and universities, officially reopened in the spring, were all closed again. Electricity supplies were available only in spurts, with day-long cessations not uncommon. Some bus and tram routes were entirely suspended. Others operated sporadically in a city where private transport was practically nonexistent. The few vehicles running were so crowded that passengers swarmed through the windows. Workers went on half pay because factories operated only intermittently. They had to scrounge desperately for food on the black market, where a pound of rice cost the equivalent of five days' work. Refugees from turmoil elsewhere increased the pressure on sparse supplies of food. An unofficial curfew operated, enforced by fear.

JULY 4, 1968:

A sporadic but fierce civil war, involving elements of the People's Liberation Army, was waged in southern China. Yünnan and Kwangsi, the two mountainous provinces bordering on North Vietnam, were the locus of heavy fighting that caused many casualties and much material damage. The armed conflict, primarily between the countryside and the cities, was also waged in three additional provinces—Szechwan, Kweichow, and Kwangtung—which with Yünnan and Kwangsi made up the populous (170 million persons) southern tier of China.

In Yünnan and Kwangsi, units of the regular People's Liberation Army attacked each other with weapons including artillery, tanks, machine guns, small arms, and grenades. Particularly in Kwangsi, army units laid siege to major cities and devastated large areas in capturing them.

In both Yünnan and Kwangsi, the implicitly anti-Maoist forces, the "men in power," swung the bulk of the army to their side and held the edge in battle. They mobilized anti-Maoist rural People's Militia units and angry peasants to attack cities—in many cases with the active support of Liberation Army soldiers. The violent confrontation raged in Szechwan for several months. Intelligence further reported that in early July the anti-Maoist "power-holders" in the countryside of Kwangtung were organizing a march of rural armed units against Canton, the metropolis 90 miles from Hong Kong.

With the avowedly pro-Maoist forces in the cities retaliating when they could, there was acute danger that the flames of total civil war would spread to rural areas of southern China that had heretofore avoided large-scale disorder. The situation was so volatile in Kwangsi and Yünnan that the Maoists still withheld recognition of the military-dominated Revolutionary Committees, which claimed to rule the two provinces. Elsewhere, the dwindling Maoist leadership in Peking granted recognition to its barely veiled enemies in order to minimize conflict. Details of the fighting in Yünnan were obscure because the province was remote from the heavily populated eastern seaboard, but it was clear that local Liberation Army units and regular forces from outside the province had clashed in bloody battles.

Acknowledging "the class struggle is still acute and complicated," the official Kunming Radio exhorted: "The rapid establishment of a revolutionary three-way power alliance organ cannot be delayed in Yünnan Province, which is at the front line of national defense and is responsible for the heavy task of aiding Vietnam and resisting America."

The civil war in Kwangsi, a province of 23 million, filled major rivers with the slain. More than 50 bodies floated into the waters of Hong Kong, 200 miles away. Not only quasi-official radio broadcasts and newspapers but a large volume of Red Guard publications, as well as private letters, confirmed the extent and the violence of the struggle. A Kwangsi youth in Hong Kong offered an eyewitness account.

The conflict was met between the inherently anti-Maoist group called the Kwangsi United Revolutionary Command Rebels and the urban, Maoist-inclined April 22nd Revolutionary Rebel Army. The United Command was controlled by Wei Kuo-ching, former First Secretary of the Provincial Communist Party Committee and subsequently Chairman of the Preparatory Revolutionary Committee. Wei, an anti-Maoist "old-line power-holder," had won the support of most major units of the Liberation Army, as well as rural workers, former ranking cadres, and the old Public Security Bureau. The April 22nd Army was directed by Wu Chin-nan, a former member of the Provincial Party Committee. It consisted largely of urban students and their sympathizers among the working class.

The major cities of Kwangsi were attacked by the United Command and severely damaged. They included Wuchow, Liuchow, and Nanning, as well as Kuaichi in Kwangtung Province, just over the Kwangsi border.

In Liuchow—and some other cities—the local garrisons fought on the side of the April 22nd Army. Kweilin, like Liuchow, a major American air base during World War II, was the only city still under the undisputed control of the April 22nd Army. The pro-Maoists called it the "liberated city."

"The April 22nd Army is rich in polemicists," explained the youth from Kwangsi, "but the United Command has the guns and the numbers." Fighting started after emissaries from Peking had arranged a truce between the two factions in April. Adhering to the pact, the April 22nd Army turned in almost all of its guns, many looted from shipments to North Vietnam. The United Command broke the agreement by turning in only a few weapons. When places on the Preparatory Revolutionary Committee were allotted, the April 22nd Army considered itself flagrantly underrepresented. Open fighting then began, and the Liberation Army, contrary to its established policy, took sides.

With the gradual defeat of the April 22nd Army, massacres occurred throughout the province. Bodies of the defeated were bound with bamboo strands and hurled into the West River to drift out to sea. The families of the April 22nd adherents fled for their lives, and packed into Canton. A kangaroo court called the Kwangsi People's Revolutionary Supreme Tribunal meted out sentences indiscriminately.

JULY 19, 1968:

The nominal government of China's most volatile southern province, Kwangtung, launched a desperate drive to prevent the civil war in neighboring provinces from engulfing the entire area. It threatened execution for disobedience.

The provincial authorities thus obliquely—but unmistakably—repudiated the central purpose of the Maoists' Great Cultural Revolution. They declared that public order was essential, while the "constant revolution" the Maoists preached was undesirable. The ruling Revolutionary Committee issued orders to "suppress the enemy by all possible measures." It threatened penalties ranging from jail terms to execution for members of feuding "factions" who disobeyed the directive to lay down their arms and end the civil strife. The strongest threats ever used against the "revolutionary rebels," who claimed the sanction of Chairman Mao for their violent contention, were expressed in the highly emotional language of an editorial in The Southern Daily, the official organ of the Provincial Revolutionary Committee.

Backed by the regular units of the People's Liberation Army, the pragmatic—therefore implicitly "rightist" and anti-Maoist—leaders who controlled the Revolutionary Committee announced their determination to put down "lawlessness and anarchy."

Fighting between armed groups struggling for power—each claiming to be the "true rebel revolutionary faction"—spread throughout the Kwangtung countryside. Violence had spilled over from the sporadic civil war in the neighboring province of Kwangsi and from the metropolis of Canton, where inhabitants had known hardly a moment of tranquillity for 15 months.

Although the "class" enemy was identified in ritual fashion as "the right," *The Southern Daily*'s charges made it absolutely clear that the real enemy was the unrestrained "leftist, revolutionary rebels," armed with machine guns, hand grenades, rocket-launchers, and light artillery pieces. The sound of rifle fire was heard intermittently throughout the day in Canton, and palls of smoke hung over contested areas of the city.

The charges directed at the feuding factions by *The Southern Daily* demonstrated that the "left" was trying to destroy the institutions of authority recognized, under duress, even by the Maoists of Peking. The "rebels" were accused in startling detail of "turning the masses against the cornerstone of the revolution, the People's Liberation Army; disrupting communications and the economy; and distorting the directives of Chairman Mao for their own benefit."

If the factions refused to make peace, only one course remained, said *The Southern Daily*. "The way to deal with the class enemy is simple: *Suppression! Suppression! Suppression!* To crush them eternally is the only possible way of fundamentally protecting the masses." The most extreme language ever used by any of the new Revolutionary Committees against self-styled "popular mass organizations," which the Maoists had encouraged, followed: "If the masses violate the law, they too must be punished by being sent to jail or, even, by execution. . . . There must be freedom within the ranks of the masses, but there must also be discipline. There must be democracy in the ranks of the masses, but there must also be obedience to central authority."

AUGUST 8, 1968:

Amid the extraordinary turmoil, pork and shrimp and fish sometimes did more than polemics could to clarify events.

Anyone who took the utterances of China's official and nonofficial news sources literally would have been well along toward galloping schizophrenia. One day, Peking Radio would announce that all was "not merely going well, but going very well indeed!"—and further assert that the Maoists were well on the way to reconquering power from their enemies. The next day, a half-dozen provincial newspapers presumably controlled by the Maoists would warn bitterly that factional jealousy and even "armed strife within our own camp is rising dangerously."

A letter from a housewife in Chengtu in Szechwan Province in the southwest probably gave a clearer idea of what was really going on, though it deliberately avoided discussion of politics. The lady's account of her shopping for fish and shrimp and pork laid bare a fundamental social and economic pattern prevalent through China.

The housewife might be called Mrs. Wu, but wasn't because it would do her no service to reveal her name. She asked her cousin in Hong Kong not to worry because parcels of food and clothing mailed from the British Crown Colony had consistently failed to arrive in Chengtu. There was, she said, no need to send any more parcels. "Never," she wrote, "in the past 18 years [since the Communists took China] have we eaten as well as we have in the past few weeks. All sorts of delicacies have appeared that we haven't seen in many, many years. There is shrimp, pork, and fresh fish—even frogs legs and eel. The green vegetables are particularly fresh and good."

It sounded like no more than a gossipy letter from one housewife to another. But Mrs. Wu added, "There is much available, but prices are high because there are so many eager buyers. The farmers from the surrounding countryside have set up their own 'collective markets' where all those things are available."

In the topsy-turvy world of Maoist dogma and the Cultural Revolution, Mrs. Wu's letter revealed a situation that was in fact anathema to the Maoists. It was *not* remarkable that parcels were not delivered all the way from Hong Kong to Chengtu. Lines of communication had been severed by disorder like an eel under a cleaver. But it *was* remarkable that the peasants of China had dared set up their own markets to peddle their own produce for their own profit. It was even more remarkable that they could openly operate those markets without interference. The Maoists were still fighting under the slogan "Extirpate selfishness and exalt the common good!" As they interpreted that slogan, it meant that no man should deal for his private profit, while all men should strive only for the collective welfare—as the Maoists defined that "welfare."

Farmers tilling their own plots and selling their own produce flagrantly violated that principle. Besides, the institutional basis of the Maoist system was the agricultural People's Commune in which no man was permitted to own his land or sell his own produce for his own profit.

AUGUST 18, 1968:

A nation-wide network of illegal underground enterprises not only mocked China's strict formal prohibition on private ownership and corrupted Communist cadres but also did a thriving business with State-owned firms and even military units. The trend was exemplified by an "underground" welding factory in the metropolis of Canton. A workman who escaped to Hong Kong described the procedures of his factory, only one among thousands in Communist China.

Stimulated by red tape, widespread unemployment, and shortages of raw materials, foodstuffs, and consumer goods, while blessed by the calculated disregard of "rightist" officials, the "underground" free enterprises were linked to each other—and to complaisant functionaries—by a web of personal relationships in the traditional Chinese manner. They survived, and grew because they were efficient and because they appealed to the desire to get as much as possible for one's work—a "bourgeois tendency" the Communists could not crush.

The doctrinaire Maoists called the development of such primitive private enterprise "the evil wind of economism." More realistic Communist officials, concerned primarily with increasing production and keeping the people happy, often encouraged the trend.

The enterprises took many forms, ranging from the illicit conversion of State-owned shops or factories into functioning cooperatives whose workers shared profits to firms actually owned by an individual or individuals who had put up the original capital. Besides marketing foodstuffs grown by peasants on their tolerated private plots, the various firms produced and sold a variety of goods, including mattresses, tools, gloves, shoes, combs, simple musical instruments, suits, bicycles and thermos bottles. Such private enterprises flouted all authority and stimulated corruption and black-marketeering.

In Canton, the metropolis inhabited by individualistic southerners with strong local loyalties, it was easy to set up in business as "underground" welders. One of the chief covers for the illegal factory were the Service Centers established by the authorities to give work to the city's unemployed—30 to 40 percent of Canton's total work force. Those Service Centers subcontracted work from legal factories, which almost always lagged behind their production schedules. State-owned factories were harried not only by shortages of raw material and fuel, but by the lackadaisical attitude of their employees, who knew they would be paid —regardless of whether they worked. The Service Centers, paradoxically, employed men for 30 to 50 people's dollars (about $15 to $25 U.S.) a month to do the same work for which factory hands received more than 100 people's dollars.

The enterprising founder of the illegal welding establishment that finally employed 70 men had "good relations" with the directors of several such Service Centers. The directors would issue official receipts of the Service Centers to the legal factories, which actually subcontracted their work to the "underground" factory. Without such receipts, the manager of the legal factory could not account for his expenditures. The amount was, of course, adjusted to allow for the factory manager's personal cut. The "underground" welding crews could make as much as 60 thousand people's dollars a month.

"The boss was a good talker and well-connected," his former employer explained, "even though he was illiterate."

Allowing for a squeeze along the line, his workers could take home as much as 300 or 400 people's dollars a month, much more than they could make elsewhere.

Business went well for some time. The underground factory not only produced more efficiently, but was able to obtain raw materials unavailable to legal establishments. Methods of procurement were unorthodox. Many goods were purchased on the black market, after being looted from legal factories. In other cases, cadres in charge of procuring materials were bribed to divert their supplies.

The founder-owner finally overreached himself. After landing a big job with the naval authorities on Hainan Island, he decided to fly his work crew down. When their papers were checked on the plane, they were arrested. "If he hadn't decided to fly," the former workman explained, "my old boss would still be in business. We'd done lots of jobs for the military before, but we'd always gone by ship or bus—where no one checks papers anymore."

The entrepreneur was sent to jail, and his workshop was broken up. The workmen caught with him were held for only 20 days. The workman observed:

> The Communists figure there are so many "underground" workmen, they don't bother giving them real sentences. Lots of times, the authorities actually helped us.
>
> All you need is a few good workmen. They're easy to get because the "underground" wages are so much higher—or because they can't work in legal factories because they are released "criminals" and, therefore, "enemies of the State."
>
> Then you need some capital. Particularly in Canton, a lot of people get money from relations living abroad—or a few men will get together and pool their money.

Unconsciously expressing the capitalist creed that he had never heard, he concluded: "If you can do a good job, there's always work—and money."

AUGUST 25, 1968:

Life in most of Communist China, particularly the rural areas, was quite different from the outsider's picture of a tightly regimented society terrorized by the erratic marauding of Red Guards. The Great Proletarian Cultural Revolution had massively eroded authority and permitted a relapse into the old ways.

A Chinese from a major city described life in the small southern fishing port of about four thousand where he stayed while planning his escape to Hong Kong. The fisherfolk hardly lived joyously, but neither did they groan under rigid oppression. The cadres of the Communist regime had given up attempting to impose intellectual, economic, and social uniformity on the country people.

The small town was a revelation when the city dweller arrived to see an acquaintance who had promised him help in escaping. He found everyone from simple fishermen to the commander of the local People's Militia company and a purged senior cadre happily engaged in black-market transactions. All showed great interest in helping him organize his escape. He felt they wished him well—and he knew they would all get a share of the 400 people's dollar's (about $200 U.S.) the escape would cost him.

Most of the people in town went barefoot, he found, even in cold weather. Wearing shoes, usually of rubber, was a sign of higher social status—the black-marketeers, the factory hands, and those aristocrats who owned bicycles, which were the chief means of transport. They carried fertilizer and other goods to places where the goods commanded higher prices. Selling State fertilizer was a grave crime, but the cadres were happy to take their cut and close their eyes.

For 10 people's dollars (about $5 U.S.), he found a week's board and lodging with a cadre who had been purged for corrupt practices years earlier. The official's sin had been cheating on his "work-points" so that he obtained a pound or two more of rice a week for his wife and seven children. This year, still a member of the Communist Party, the former cadre was getting 44 pounds of rice a month for his entire family. In the old days, that would have been ample—for one person. Still, he could supplement the family diet by raising yams, chickens, and pigs—as well as doing a little fishing. Such private economic activities were officially forbidden. All produce was supposed to go to the State. But the old cadre managed to get along, although he could find no doctor, and had only herbs he picked himself when his children fell ill.

"Hygienic conditions in the house were bad," the fastidious city man observed. "Even on cold days, flies and fleas swarmed, while the two pigs slept under the beds."

When discovered by the commander of the People's Militia company, the city dweller was not arrested. Instead, the officer spent much time chatting with the would-be escapee and volunteered, "I can guarantee that you will not be disturbed." He too would get his cut of the escape money.

The black market was the main economic activity of the small port. Artisans in the town did so well black-marketeering that they had rice twice a day, supplemented by fish and vegetables. A ration coupon for a foot of cotton cloth was worth one people's dollar (roughly 40¢ U.S.), compared with 60 people's cents last year. Since new coupons had not yet been issued, the poor sold theirs for food money. Kerosene, officially rationed to two ounces a month at five people's cents an ounce, sold for 20 people's cents an ounce. Rice was supposed to sell for 13 cents a catty (1⅓ pounds) but brought 45 cents on the "free market." The black market was obviously not officially sanctioned. "But the cadres of the Market Control Committee would not dare to interfere for fear of being beaten up," the visitor said.

A housewife who visited the government shop to buy fish was told that there was no stock. The manager explained, "This shop is Chairman Mao's, so we have no fish. Why don't you go to Comrade Liu Shao-chi's shop? He may have some." Such irreverence was widespread —and practiced with impunity—as was the black market to which the manager recommended his customer.

Gambling was, for instance, strictly forbidden by the Communists. But everyone played a pokerlike game in which each player gets three cards. Heaping insult on disobedience, the players called the game "studying the three old pieces." In Maoist jargon, the "three old pieces" were sacred articles written by Mao Tse-tung that everyone was supposed to study constantly.

Returning to the worship of their old gods, the people pasted religious pictures and excerpts from the Buddhist and Taoist scriptures over portraits of Mao and Communist slogans. Asked how she dared do such things, one housewife answered, smiling, "Last year was the lucky year of Chairman Mao, and the Old Man in Heaven and the God of Wealth were chased away. This year, Chairman Mao is collapsing, so the gods have come back to their proper places!"

SEPTEMBER 6, 1968:
Li Liu-mang was flotsam on the high waves of the Proletarian Cultural Revolution. A great fighter for the Thought of Mao Tse-tung in the early days of that Revolution, he sat at home, teaching himself to paint

and wondering what future the turmoil of China held for him. He could not even find reading matter, he complained. Since he could not find employment either, the 20-year-old Li lived on the earnings of his mother, a 63-year-old midwife.

"My youth is passing as a leaf adrift on the broad Pacific," he wrote from his home in Fatshan near Canton. "Each day is as empty as the preceding one—and I can see no end to these aimless days." Li's dilemma was typical of almost 30 percent of the urban youth of Kwangtung Province. Denied work because of their "impure class backgrounds," or, more simply, because the pace of normal commercial and industrial life had slowed and the schools were closed, they sought to fill their days by various expedients.

Young Li, the son of "bureaucratic capitalist" parents, was luckier than most. The Red Guard faction with which he had campaigned before his disillusionment came to him for propaganda posters, and he could put in hours each day drawing pictures of heroic Vietnamese "fighters for freedom" and villainous "American imperialist butchers"— all embellished with ringing slogans.

But his heart was not really in that work for which, in any event, he received no payment. An island of tranquillity—and futility—amid the "great winds and high waves" of the Cultural Revolution. Li Liu-mang finally conceived a plan to fill his days. "I already have some goldfish and some tropical fish," he wrote his cousin in Hong Kong. "Now I'm building a pigeon loft and planning to get a dog.

"At least, then I'll have something to do. I'll be the commander of the three forces: the fish—the navy; the pigeons—the air force; and the dog—the army."

The tragedy of young Li was particularly poignant because he was an active, happy youngster before the Cultural Revolution swept across China in 1966. He finally withdrew into himself, in part because he had no choice, and in part because he could no longer believe in the future—either his own or his country's.

"When the Cultural Revolution began," he wrote, "Chairman Mao said we should use persuasion, rather than violence. But now the two factions fighting each other are both true 'mass organizations.' Why should they be fighting each other? As for me, I shall have nothing to do with either faction!"

Li Liu-mang could not even find work in the special projects set up to alleviate widespread unemployment. The Labor Service Centers, which paid a bare living wage to unemployed workers over 30, would not have him. The Youth Labor Brigades intended for his age group had long waiting lists. He lacked the special influence necessary to obtain dole. In any event, the authorities told him that 12 people's dollars (about $6

U.S.) a month was a good enough living wage for anyone. Since his mother made 45 people's dollars a month, the family was considered well provided for.

The spectacle of talent wasted in a country that desperately lacked trained men and women was driving many of Li's contemporaries from disillusionment to—still inchoate—desperation. The spectacle of machinery lying idle in a country that desperately lacked consumer products was reinforcing their contempt for the feuding Communists. Unlike Li Liu-mang, most of his contemporaries did not even have the consolation of the "command of three forces" or the talent to teach themselves painting. But like him they were inclined to cry out, "My youth is passing in a vacuum. Life seems so hopeless! It is hard to believe that a universe so large has no place for me!"

SEPTEMBER 27, 1968:

Gory anarchy gradually came to an end as an alliance of senior generals, administrators, and Party leaders forced the extremist faction to admit defeat and formally endorse the end of the Great Revolution. The extremists were compelled to acknowledge the supremacy of the "conservatives" and submit to their relatively moderate policies because the "conservatives" enjoyed popular support—and controlled the People's Liberation Army.

The attempt to create a Utopia by direct rule was declared a failure. The main problem confronting the leadership, itself divided by personal and regional differences, was the re-creation of a viable nation. The conservatives tried desperately to impose order on a China in tumult and to prevent total disintegration of the splintered nation. In the process the unruly Red Guards were harshly repressed and the basically conservative working class exalted. Even *Red Flag* attacked the Red Guards and gave Chairman Mao's personal sanction to the restoration of the old structures of authority under new names. The Maoist era was coming to an end. The struggle for succession at the presumed center of power in Peking was secondary to the stark necessity for holding together a nation that was in peril of splitting into regional groupings.

Mao himself was a virtual figurehead. He would continue to be paid extravagant honor until his death, but his Utopian policies had been repudiated and his influence had been all but destroyed. The new leaders in Peking, possessing little actual control over the provinces, strove to restore authoritarian rule throughout China. But their first task was, quite simply, to make China a functioning nation again—a task that would take some time, perhaps years.

Peking also attempted to restore the "normal" relations with other nations that had been shattered by the Cultural Revolution. Support for Hanoi's attempt to conquer South Vietnam was markedly less vehement or enthusiastic than it had been, since the conservatives wished neither to take the excessive risks nor to pay the increasing costs of Ho Chi-minh's war.

Internally, from Sinkiang and Inner Mongolia in the far northwest to Kwangsi and Kwangtung in the southeast, one major theme dominated all official statements of the Revolutionary Committees seeking to re-establish order over the defiance of the anarchic factions originally given sanction for total disorder by Mao. That theme was: "A single, established authority must be obeyed implicitly!" *The Inner Mongolian Daily* admonished:

> We must point out with the utmost severity that the only legal Workers' Propaganda Teams are those Thought of Mao Tse-tung Workers' Propaganda Teams which are directed from above by the Provincial Revolutionary Committee and organized by the United Workers' Assembly. We will absolutely *not* permit certain self-seeking groups using the pretext of political necessity to defy the Revolutionary Committee and incite the misguided masses to raise up other workers' propaganda teams to sabotage the proper leadership of the working class. . . . All such self-appointed workers' propaganda teams are illegal, and must immediately be dispersed!

The Thought of Mao Workers' Propaganda Teams were the new strong-arm organizations created in the late summer of 1968 to suppress feuding Red Guard factions in collaboration with the People's Liberation Army. They succeeded the Red Guards as the official heroes of the Great Revolution. *Red Flag* itself remarked: "Not *all* Red Guards are bad!"

The stress upon legality and unswerving obedience to orders from above struck a wholly new note in a country where the Cultural Revolution had given license to riot to all. That stress expressed the determination of the military conservatives to assert their total authority. The 180-degree reversal of the course of the Cultural Revolution was justified by the slogan PLACE ALL LEADERSHIP IN THE HANDS OF THE PROLETARIAT!—the urban working class originally allied with Mao's arch-rival, Chairman Liu Shao-chi.

From Shanghai came an equally significant assertion: "The proletariat must not only rely on the machinery of the State like the Army, the courts, and the prisons to resist invasion of imperialism from abroad and to suppress the opposition of class enemies at home. It must also exercise proletarian dictatorship wherever bourgeois ideology is found. . . ."

In Kwangtung Province, the leaders of the extreme Red Flag faction were denounced as "agents of the Nationalist enemy." The people were told to accept all their old leaders "except for a stubborn handful." All "mass organizations" were being purged of "troublemakers." In Kwangsi where 50 thousand and 100 thousand had died in civil war a few months earlier, the tightest controls were imposed upon travel by individuals in order to suppress the Maoist opposition.

Workers in the southern provinces, as elsewhere, were ordered to "go into all schools and all other institutions including factories" to suppress disorder. Ideological instruction was the pretext employed by the conservatives, who used the worker vigilantes to assert their control over every aspect of life. In Canton the schools were still not functioning. But the conservative Revolutionary Committee finally imposed sufficient order on the turbulent city to issue the cloth-ration tickets for 1968 that should have been distributed in January. Factories were once again ready for work, but were severely handicapped by lack of raw materials.

Most revealing of the depressed state of the extreme leftists was the speech delivered by the Starlet at a workers' rally in Peking. Having already seen with chagrin her chief spokesman, Yao Wen-yüan, the Literary Assassin, transformed into a mouthpiece of the conservatives, Chiang Ching confessed that she had learned of the crucial meeting only that morning. Acknowledging that she had been "instructed" to speak, apparently to cast the aura of Mao's direct authority around the new trend, Chiang Ching said her assigned piece—however reluctantly. She did not initially hail the "leadership of the working class," but instead pleaded for mercy for her Red Guards.

"We must not forget that the revolutionary youth and the young Red Guard fighters made tremendous contributions during the initial and middle stages of the Cultural Revolution. . . . Now a small number of young fighters have committed mistakes of various kinds." Admitting the necessity to "correct those mistakes," the Starlet tried to minimize the factional clashes as "merely ludicrous." She begged "the leading class, the working class, to protect the young Red Guard fighters . . . to help them and educate them."

The termagant of the Cultural Revolution thus acknowledged that the attempt to change the nature of China by mass, spontaneous violence had failed.

OCTOBER 1, 1968:

Speaking in a hesitant voice that reflected either exhaustion or illness, Deputy Chairman Lin Piao affirmed that the Great Proletarian Cultural Revolution had already ended. He spoke in Peking at rather pallid celebrations of the nineteenth anniversary of the founding of the People's Republic of China. The heir-presumptive to Chairman Mao declared: "The Cultural Revolution *has already* attained its great victory."

In a 15-minute speech delivered, he said, "on behalf of Chairman Mao, the Communist Party, and People's Liberation Army," the 60-year-old Disciple laid the greatest stress on "rebuilding" the country and the Communist Party. He hailed the creation of Revolutionary Committees throughout continental China, specifically endorsing them as instruments of the will of Mao Tse-tung, despite the fact that almost all those committees were under conservative leadership. He made no reference to establishing the "totally new systems of government based on the model of the Paris Commune," which he had originally declared to be the purpose of the Cultural Revolution. He made no reference to the "extensive democracy," which he had explained on November 3, 1966, was the new device for "placing all power in the hands of the people."

The new policy enunciated by both Lin Piao and Chou En-lai was "consolidation." The Communist Party, both declared, must be rebuilt as the country's major instrument of power.

OCTOBER 11, 1968:

China was tending toward a loose association of semi-independent regions governed by local rulers, moved primarily by their own, rather than national interests. The "central power" for which politicians in Peking hotly contended was rapidly dwindling as regional and provincial rulers asserted their autonomy by disregarding and reinterpreting instructions from the Party Center. Avowed Maoists and skeptical non-Maoists alike were agreed that the chief task before them was the restoration of the structures of authority destroyed by the Great Proletarian Cultural Revolution. They therefore concentrated upon rebuilding and "consolidating" the Chinese Communist Party, which had been destroyed by Red Guard rampages. Two chief tendencies were in conflict in that consolidation.

The men of Peking sought to re-create the highly centralized and highly intrusive system of government that had ruled China before Chairman Mao proclaimed the Cultural Revolution. The men who held actual power in most of China's 29 major administrative divisions helped re-create local Communist Party structures as the basis of their own individual authority. Since it was obviously necessary to rebuild the Party from the ground up, the local satraps possessed an overwhelming advantage in the bitter competition for power. Without an effective Communist Party operating in the provinces, the Party Center in Peking would be quite powerless. The process of reconstituting the local Party apparatus obviously enhanced the power of local authorities, who chose new officials and admitted numerous recruits to the Party ranks.

Local administrative power in individual provinces was established by quashing hyper-Maoist and anarchistic Red Guard factions with the guns of the People's Liberation Army, backed by militant Workers' Thought of Mao Tse-tung Propaganda Teams.

China's new satraps could not accurately be described as "warlords." Not only would they work together upon many occasions, but they would give their ostensible loyalty to Mao—and their true loyalty to the Liberation Army because most were generals. China appeared to be moving toward a loose federation of such rulers.

The ceremonies marking the nineteenth anniversary of the founding of the People's Republic of China were *not* attended by the chairmen of ten of the most important Provincial Revolutionary Committees—nor by General Wang En-mao. Wang was still the real ruler of Sinkiang Province with its concentration of nuclear facilities, though he was titularly only Deputy Chairman of the province's Revolutionary Committee and Political Commissar of the Sinkiang Military Region. Wang had been a chief strategist of the military's campaign to force the "ultra-leftists" to acknowledge reality and the Army's authority.

When the Albanian delegation to the October 1 Celebrations arrived in Sinkiang, first to greet them at the airport was Wang En-mao, who also delivered the keynote speech at the banquet tendered the visitors. He made all the proper quasi-Maoist statements, attacking the "Soviet revisionists" and swearing "to defend the motherland" against any attack by his Russian neighbors. He said little else. It was, of course, the settled policy of the provincial satraps to quote Mao and to swear eternal fealty to their "Great Leader" and his canonical Thought, while acting generally as they wished. By so doing, they not only protected themselves against criticism, but also used the words of Mao to crush the ultra-leftist, dissident factions that had once been the Chairman's "revolutionary vanguard."

There was no overt evidence that the 11 key leaders stayed away from Peking either in direct defiance of orders from the Party Center or because they were afraid to venture into the enemy camp. Most likely they were so fully occupied at home that they could not be bothered to pay their ceremonial calls at Peking—even for a day. The more probable and less dramatic likelihood also supported the hypothesis that regional power had become dominant. Previously local leaders would not have dared reject orders to come to Peking—nor would they have missed the opportunity to consult their friends and consolidate their influence at the center.

Some observers cite evidence that an influential group had suggested that China might best exist as a federation rather than a tightly controlled, highly centralized state—at least until the damage of the Cultural Revolution could be repaired. That conclusion arose out of the violent attacks against the concept of "polycentrism" that Peking had loosed a month earlier in early fall 1968. Characteristically, local rulers seized upon the Center's opposition to "polycentrism" to order new attacks against stubborn local Maoists who had insisted upon their own freedom of action and revolt within the individual satrapies.

"Only one authority," local organs thundered, "can exist—the authority of the Revolutionary Committee." The Chairman's instructions to old cadres to "go down to the people" were presumptuously reinterpreted by *The Peking People's Daily,* no longer controlled by hard-core Maoists. They were, characteristically, recast to suit local convenience.

"New cadres, in particular," the newspaper said, "should go down to the masses in groups, since they, too, need to revolutionize their thinking." The comment was a transparent justification for disposing of some of the troublesome "new cadres" who might still be too Maoist and too centrist.

Nanchang Radio of pivotal Kiangsi Province in Central China made a further revelation. Rural leaders, a broadcast said, were afraid that cadres "sent down" to the countryside might attempt to "seize their power." Their apprehension presaged not only further local struggles, but the expulsion of "new cadres" at the lowest levels. Installed during the Cultural Revolution, those new cadres might oppose the conservative satraps of the Provincial Revolutionary Committee.

The struggle for mastery of China was by no means over. Still, it was clear that the ascendant provincial and regional power-holders were determined to consolidate and extend their control—almost inevitably further sapping the central power of Peking.

NOVEMBER 25, 1968:

The disruptions, violence, and "anarchy" of the Great Proletarian Cultural Revolution refused to subside in Chekiang. The Revolutionary Committee, titular rulers of the coastal province of 31 million, for the first time anywhere in China, specifically identified former Red Guards as the "class enemy" that sought to break newly established authority and "set up watertight, independent kingdoms."

The "little generals of disorder" who had initiated the violent Cultural Revolution were accused of forming a new alliance between "ultra-left" forces and the "extreme right," presumably supporters of Comrade Liu Shao-chi. Chekiang alleged that the two disparate groups were allied in opposition to the neo-Stalinist generals trying to restore order in the embattled province.

Chekiang, a starkly beautiful region of mountain peaks just north of Nationalist-held Formosa, was once noted for three chief assets: Fenghwa, the birthplace of Generalissimo Chiang Kai-shek; Hangchow, the resort on the West Lake, which displayed in wood, stone, and flowering trees the quintessential beauty of traditional Chinese civilization; and Shaohsing, which produced the best yellow-rice wine and the most gaudily histrionic operatic troupes of all China. Chekiang was remarkable, too, for the continuing irrepressibility of the forces unloosed upon it by the original command of Chairman Mao. "Dare to make revolution. . . . Disorder is a very good thing. . . . Let the people manage the great affairs of state."

The bitter resentment felt by every class in Chinese society, but pent up by more than a decade and a half of authoritarian rule, had been released in 1966. Every vigorous man had become his own Machiavelli and his own Napoleon in a sweeping and increasingly violent parody of the "extensive democracy" the Maoists had sought to create. Instead of an enormous New England Town Meeting, the Maoists had contrived anarchy. Among its remarkable features were the shifting alliances of groups that in all logic should have been bitterly opposed to each other.

Chekiang publications railed bitterly against "counterrevolutionary elements" who strove "by tricks and violence" to break the authority of the Revolutionary Committee. Most remarkable was the open identification as a *major* center of resistance of the Red Guards and other "mass organizations," known in Maoist jargon as "the rebel faction." An editorial of *The Chekiang Daily* condemned the men who plotted to destroy the Revolutionary Committee and who denounced its members as "opportunists, plotters, and counterrevolutionaries." It charged that the followers of Liu Shao-chi, "on the extreme right" were in league with elements of the "extreme left"—a grouping "left in appearance, but rightist in reality."

The editorial asked rhetorically: "Why otherwise are certain people in units and areas where the *rebel faction has the sole hold on power* adopting an attitude of disagreeing with, refusing to participate in, and not supporting the recently established Revolutionary Committee?"

The attitude most prevalent in Chekiang was: "I don't care about the orders of the Revolutionary Committee." Arguing, with much justification, that there was really "no rebel faction and no conservative faction," the independent-minded leaders of Chekiang's numerous power factions were pursuing their own courses. The fight was no longer ideological, but merely a battle for survival and for naked power.

NOVEMBER 28, 1968:

The practical men who ruled China's provinces refused to turn back their powers to the Communist Party, despite central orders to purge and rebuild the Party. Seven weeks had elapsed since the Disciple ordered the simultaneous "rectification and reconstruction" of the Communist Party organization, which had virtually ceased functioning. After paying casual lip service to the Party-rebuilding campaign for a few weeks, the military-dominated Revolutionary Committees stolidly refused to negate their influence or, in effect, abolish themselves by reconstructing a Party apparatus that would exercise *real* power.

Except for the inherent contradiction of trying simultaneously to purge and to re-create an apparatus, Peking's order appeared fairly simple. It proved unenforceable. Only two provinces, Hunan and Kwangtung, held Provincial Congresses for the purpose of "rectifying and rebuilding" the Communist Party. Elsewhere, the original acclamation of the order and promises of immediate obedience dwindled into highly significant silence.

The "conservative men in power" in the provinces were a new vested interest—much like the vested interest of the Party apparatus the Maoists had originally attacked. They were simply not prepared to relinquish their power to nominees of the theoretical central authority who were armed neither with guns nor with economic control but only with the "latest directives and the Thought of Mao Tse-tung." Those abstractions no longer counted for much in the naked power struggle.

There was only superficial compliance. Cadres were being "sent down to the countryside to perform manual labor and re-educate themselves." In most cases, those cadres were the extremists whom the Maoists had attempted to install in power. Despite Peking's call for "an infusion of new blood," there were no reports of mass inductions of "rebel revolutionaries" into the Communist Party, which was presumably being "reborn." Indeed, there were no significant reports of the resumption of Party activity, much less Party dominance—except, of course, within the People's Liberation Army. The Army remained the only nation-wide functional structure of authority. The Party Committees within the Army had never been broken up.

The Party Central Committee commanded: "We must carry out Chairman Mao's directives . . . and conscientiously perform the work of Party consolidation and Party building! We must expel from the Party proven renegades, enemy agents, diehard capitalist-roaders . . . and take into the Party fresh blood from the proletariat—above all, advanced elements with Communist consciousness from among industrial workers. . . ."

The response was widespread passive resistance. The nature of that resistance was explained by an article in *The Hunan Daily* on the situation in Chuchow city where the local "Support-the-Left Leadership Group"—that is, the military—and the local Revolutionary Committee dutifully established a special Office for Party Rectification after the order went out.

"It was found," the newspaper reported, "that a number of Party members [on the right] who had made mistakes during the Cultural Revolution were disaffected. They grumbled and complained because they feared 'severe rectification' [punishment]. Some of the revolutionary rebels [on the left] said: 'Conditions are not yet ripe for rectifying the Party. We should go slowly!' "

Neither the right nor the left, each occupying separate positions of power taken during the Cultural Revolution, was prepared to abandon its stronghold. Neither group was willing to submit itself to the uncertain authority of a new Communist Party structure. "The Liberation Army took power reluctantly," one Chinese authority observed. "After the manner of all generals, it is likely to surrender power even more reluctantly!"

DECEMBER 1, 1968:

The generals solved their major problem of youthful dissent by deporting hundreds of thousands to the countryside and remote border areas to "reform themselves through manual labor."

From Canton, a letter written by a girl student named Wang Mei-kwei reported, "All senior high school students are being sent to the countryside—and 80 percent, at least, of junior high scool students. . . . There is nothing voluntary about it. My choice is as narrow and my vision as limited as a frog's at the bottom of a well."

The day of reckoning had arrived for China's New Left.

The hardheaded men who ran the Revolutionary Committees were concerned neither with youthful sensibilities nor with abstract ideology. They wished only to get on with the job of putting the pieces back together—and, equally important, solidifying their own power.

Each day, thousands of young students and workers streamed reluctantly out of China's great metropolises—Shanghai, Tientsin, Peking, Wuhan, and Canton, as well as the lesser cities. Their destinations were varied. Some went to nearby farms to "learn from the peasants"; others traveled thousands of miles to Sinkiang, the barren New Dominion on the edge of the Central Asian steppes. All were sent to places where they could make no more trouble for the tough bureaucrats and generals. Neither youthful idealism nor the spirit of mischief was tolerated.

Officially all participants in the exodus were "volunteers." If a young man or woman "selected" for transportation resisted, his parents received a visit from the "persuaders" of the Workers' Investigation Corps, the club-carrying vigilantes who "assisted the People's Liberation Army in restoring order." If refusal persisted, armed soldiers called upon the household—and the "volunteer" departed the next day. "We no longer have any freedom of choice whatsoever," young Miss Wang wrote. "It's no longer a matter of how one feels, because that's simply the way it is. Such is the new 'thrust of the movement!' "

Previously, girls could escape deportation by marriage, but that was no longer a valid excuse. Husbands and wives were deported separately, given no choice as to their different destinations. Previously, good connections with Red Guard "mass organizations" had enabled youths to evade exile. No excuse was subsequently acceptable.

Mei-kwei reported on the fate of Li Liu-mang, who had led a life of idleness and managed to evade transportation because he had formerly been a leader of a major Red Guard faction. Liu-mang had just been sent to a remote county in rural Kwangtung, separated from the dogs, cats, and fish upon which he had concentrated his attention and affections during the summer. His fiancée was also, as Mei-kwei wrote, "not going to get away with it any longer."

"We have no course but to obey," Mei-kwei commented bitterly.

Internal travel was totally restricted in Kwangtung, as elsewhere. For a time the Red Guards had wandered anywhere they wished at government expense. But restoration of the system of internal passports—and visas—prohibited even visits to close relations a few score miles away without special permission. That permission was almost impossible to obtain.

Canton Radio reported that the students of the South China Technical Academy had requested the resumption of classes "because the general criticism movement is just about finished!"

The report continued, "Although the attitude of most students and teachers toward educational reform is highly positive, the Workers' Thought of Mao Tse-tung Propaganda Team [which ran the school] saw clearly that the old thought patterns, the old ideology, and the old style of work of the intellectuals could not be reformed in a single day or night. They must emerge from the school gates and go among the masses."

As a result, "three roads" were prescribed:

—Going to the Huang Shan Tung Independent Production Brigade to study the Thought of Mao Tse-tung while working in the fields.

—Going to the Whampoa Docks to "work in producton."

—Going to factories, communes, and construction sites, or to farms run by Liberation Army units.

The reforms accomplished were remarkable, as attested by one example: "A woman teacher educated in the Soviet Union had never been in the countryside in her life . . . but the peasants demanded that she carry her share of their burdens. She can now tote 75 pounds . . . and she says: 'After many years of study in the Soviet Union, I couldn't lift a thing and my brain was all confused. Now by going among the masses, I have overcome my evil tendency toward revisionism.'"

DECEMBER 10, 1968:

The newly constituted conventional authority of the Revolutionary Committee of Honan Province sought to destroy the "independent kingdoms" of the "rebel revolutionary" Red Guards with weapons ranging from persuasion under threat to executions.

"You set up mountain-top strongholds," the Chengchow military authorities told the Red Guards, "rally people of your own kind, and try to establish independent kingdoms. You are stumbling blocks to the cleaning up of the class ranks. . . . We must drag out the people who have wormed their way into the mass organizations, knock them down, and deal with them according to the law."

The Maoists had based their drive for destruction of the conventional institutions of power on the thesis that "Socialist legality" was merely a "set of stilted preconceptions," while the will of Chairman Mao was supreme. But Honan implicitly repudiated the divine right of the Chairman. "The masses were launched to carry out checkups on every production team, every household, and every individual," an official report declared.

Why the need for such intensive investigation—and suppression—in the province which had once been a model, chosen as the site of the very first People's Commune?

The answer came in a long diatribe by the Honan Provincial Military District, the organization whose leaders really ruled the province. It first rebutted the charge that the Army was "suppressing the rebels," but continued with the flat admission:

> As for those who are clamorous, ambitious, and in favor of setting up independent kingdoms, seizing power and gaining profit, there is nothing wrong in suppressing them. As for those who regard enemies as friends, and shield bad elements, there is nothing wrong in suppressing them. As for those who, *with their many contacts and wide connections,* plot to overthrow the Revolutionary Committee, do we do wrong if we suppress them? We say it is right and proper to suppress them.*

* Emphasis supplied.

They distort public opinion to oppose the Revolutionary Committees, the People's Liberation Army, and the Workers' Mao-Thought Propaganda Teams. They have brought about a chaotic state of public opinion in their attempts at counter-seizure of power by their shout: "Do you want to beat us to death?"

It could hardly have been more obvious that it was the "rebels" the military were determined to suppress. No longer was there more than the gossamer-thin pretense that the main enemy was the right, rather than the left. A conference of the provincial, city, and county Revolutionary Committees admitted that their enemies had accused them of "restoring the old ways."

The remedy: "We must absolutely and resolutely deal with the masses. We must not countenance the support of one faction and the suppression of another. We certainly must not permit those factions to attack the masses for their own vengeance." So much for Chairman Mao's fundamental thesis of "unceasing class struggle." Not struggle but harmony was the new goal.

DECEMBER 15, 1968:

China's Central Radio Station broadcast an appeal for obedience to Peking's authority which dramatically illustrated the profound schisms dividing the country's nominal rulers. Appeals against divisiveness and the "theory of many centers of power" had become common. But the early December broadcast was the first to inveigh specifically against disobedience and disregard of orders issued by the Center.

The editorial urged all Chinese to "resolutely implement the policies of the proletarian revolutionary headquarters"—meaning Chairman Mao Tse-tung and the group surrounding him in Peking.

"Some people adopt an irresponsible attitude toward implementing State [national] policies on the pretext that such implementation is the responsibility of their superiors," the broadcast said. It called for struggle against "sectarianism, liberalism, mountain-topism, and small-group mentality, all of which are reflections of bourgeois mentality. . . ."

The appeal underscored the accelerating decay of Peking's influence; the bitter struggle among the leaders who had survived continuous purges; and local defiance of orders issued by both Peking and provincial capitals. Bitter divisions among his closest followers left Chairman Mao isolated and practically powerless. The men and women who had launched the Great Proletarian Cultural Revolution fought bitterly among themselves, while their national authority dwindled away. Mao's heir-presumptive, the Disciple, was in direct opposition to Mao's wife, the Starlet, Deputy Chairman of the Task Force of the Cultural Revolution and "chief adviser" to the military's Cultural Revolution Group. The fundamental split was created not only by basic differences on policy, but by fundamental divergences of interests. Each having purged a number of the other's chief followers, the two antagonists finally found themselves largely isolated.

Lin Piao could control only part of the People's Liberation Army and could not be wholly certain of the loyalty of even his own units. Chiang Ching's Red Guard "rebel revolutionaries" were systematically harried throughout the country—primarily by the Liberation Army reinforced by worker vigilantes. Peking itself was rapidly losing its residual power to influence events in the provinces effectively. The bitter feud in the capital occasioned by the growth of regional and provincial authority offered further opportunity for the "local power-holders" to extend their sway and further assert their independence.

The decline of central authority became the chief factor provoking dissension within Peking itself. The shadowy Task Force of the Cultural Revolution, whittled down by successive purges, was obviously in conflict with the local military authorities, who were determined to impose a modicum of civil order on the factious nation in order to re-create a functioning economy. That fundamental division between the Starlet's faction and the Liberation Army forced the split between herself and the Disciple.

If Lin were to sustain his drive for supreme power he would find it necessary to: 1) maintain his control over scattered and dissident military units; and 2) compromise with the self-assertiveness of local authorities. He could do neither without repudiating both the Utopian social schemes and the "unceasing revolution" which the Starlet urged upon her "rebel revolutionary group."

A series of conferences of military officers in areas as widely separated as Yünnan in the southwest, Wuhan in Central China, and Honan in the north attempted to enforce unitary discipline on Chinese soldiers —and generals. Most of those men, brought up in the tradition of guerrilla autonomy, found it onerous to accept and execute the orders of the Center unquestioningly. They were burdened with the enormous responsibility of ending anarchic chaos—and they would do so in their own way.

The generals' way, almost invariably, was "suppressing the rebel, revolutionary faction." Both implicitly and explicitly, such tactics defied the authority of Peking. When Peking reluctantly assigned the mission of pacification to the local military commands, it had effectively abdicated its own authority—and formally endorsed the effective decentralization of power already occurring.

Under the influence of a group of essentially conservative senior generals in Peking and the provinces, official statements became increasingly conciliatory. The constant emphasis lay upon harmony and unity rather than the "unceasing class struggle . . . unmasking, criticism, and transformation," that had been the theme of Chiang Ching. The Disciple was mending fences with the powerful, informal council of senior generals whom he had originally defied and humiliated. The immediate beneficiary of the new policy at the center was Premier Chou En-lai, the only man who commanded a bare minimum of trust from the two contending sides—both for his adroitness in avoiding absolute commitment and for his undoubted administrative efficiency. It was unlikely, however, that Chou would emerge in the end as the man wielding major power over the entire nation. First, he was an executive rather than a policymaker. Second, not even Chou could marshal nation-wide power that had ceased to exist.

DECEMBER 29, 1968:

The Great Proletarian Cultural Revolution, which sought to create a new and perfectly selfless human being, had begun in Shanghai, China's greatest metropolis. It died gradually in Shanghai with the corruption of high-ranking officials by bribes ranging from a pair of shoes to an evening with a lady of pleasure.

Shanghai on the surface was the "Reddest" area in China, for its ruling Revolutionary Committee was by far the most fervent in carrying out extremist policies. The city was also the "greatest bourgeois center" in puritanical, proletarian China, for the people of Shanghai could not forget their gaudy, cosmopolitan—and corrupt—past.

The Shanghai *Liberation Daily,* the organ of the Revolutionary Committee, complained bitterly of "arrogance, corruption and complacency" among high-ranking officials. The editorial charged that "senior cadres willingly fell into traps set by the class enemy." Those traps were baited with varying "material pleasures."

The editorial asked: "Are there not many people in our ranks who feel they can relax because 'power has been won and the revolution is over'? Are there not many cadres who no longer study the Thought of Mao Tse-tung, who don't even read newspapers, and who have simply stopped seeking to advance the cause?"

The answer was a resounding "Yes!" The "proletarian revolutionaries" of Shanghai were being corrupted by the "sugar-coated bullets" of the opposition. Quite as remarkable as the triviality of the pleasures that could turn members of the Revolutionary Committee from their duty in austere and materially deprived China was the "class enemies' " access to such means. The editorial continued:

> Some people change their viewpoint entirely and expose themselves to the enemy for just a cup of tea, a simple meal, a handkerchief, or a pair of shoes. Gradually they fall into the enemy's trap and become captives of the enemy. Our comrades, particularly those comrades who carry the heavy responsibility of exercising leadership, must be constantly on the alert against becoming a privileged class. . . . They must remain united with the laboring masses.

The enemy thus employed "the tactics of the exploiting class to divide, corrupt, attack, and break up our revolutionary ranks. . . . Their secret agents in our midst are conducting a mortal struggle. Theirs are extremely venomous techniques."

The enemy went further: "He selects many comrades at every level of the different Revolutionary Committees, especially the new and youthful cadres, as special points to attack. . . . The enemy gives you cars, houses, money, and ladies of pleasure to pull you into deep waters. . . ."

JANUARY 15, 1969:

The task of re-creating effective government in Kiangsi Province, which occupies a unique place in the folklore of Chinese Communism, exemplified the problems besetting the titular rulers of nearly all China's provinces. The generals who ran the Central China province were trapped between increasing popular resistance and a nominal central authority in Peking which became ever more petulant as its impotence became obvious.

Peking ordered: "Root out the class enemy!"—the generic name for any opponent of the men who sought, however ineffectively, to wield power. The Kiangsi Revolutionary Committee, the gauze curtain behind which the Kiangsi Military District operated, sought to comply, since it literally knew no other means of administration than "suppression and constant struggle." The result was invariably the creation of new "class enemies." The people were no longer deluded by Maoist rhetoric or frightened by the bayonets of the Army. At the same time the Great Revolution had smashed the old structure of the Communist Party in Kiangsi, it had broken the patience of the masses.

The struggle to impose authority was fought on three distinct battlefields: the schools, where students rebelled at the compulsory study of the sacrosanct Thought of Mao Tse-tung—and worried about their personal futures; the factories, where the workers simply wanted to end the ceaseless "class struggle and purges," pressed in the guise of the "three investigations"; and the farms, where the People's Liberation Army was trying to restore at least the form of the old People's Communes and to reconsolidate Production Brigades, which had virtually broken down into pre-Communist rural villages.

In every case, "great victories" were announced with the "total defeat and weeding out of all class enemies." In every case, a few months later the horrified discovery occurred: "The diabolically cunning class enemy has gathered all his strength again; evil men and plotters exist in great numbers in our midst."

The students had been hailed only two years earlier as the vanguard of the Cultural Revolution. But the ever present class enemy "takes advantage of students' concern about their post-graduation assignments to spread rumors and shoot poisoned arrows." As a result, "the students turn their spears against Chairman Mao . . . the Kiangsi Revolutionary Committee . . . and the Liberation Army."

In the countryside the struggle was more serious, but equally futile. Not because they were doctrinaire Maoists, but because they were determined to reassert their control, the military authorities sought to restore the old People's Communes and Production Brigades of the pre-Cultural Revolution period. The Commune was, after all, the only administrative unit in the countryside. Besides, the Kiangsi authorities badly needed their share of the crop—whether in the guise of taxes or "contributions" to the State. Unless greater control was exerted over the farmers, the military could not finance their rule.

The military authorities attempted to reimpose the repression of the early 1960s. Private plots were to be radically reduced in size, if not wholly abolished. The farmers had undoubtedly taken large slices of public land for private use. It would not be easy to force them to disgorge—particularly when local leaders encouraged their resistance.

Finally, the factories. The story was much the same in the Kiangsi Shipyard and the Nanchang Hand-Tractor Works. Time after time, the "class enemy" had been rooted out. Time after time, the factories' Revolutionary Committees had been accused of arrogance and complacency and had been ordered to root out new "class enemies"—initially from their own ranks.

Before the Cultural Revolution began, the people of Kiangsi were reasonably happy under the fairly mild rule of the group within the Communist Party denounced by the Revolution. At the beginning of 1969, the people of Kiangsi were fed up with endless "class struggle." Passive resistance combined with outward compliance—the technique the Chinese masses practiced so skillfully—taught the Kiangsi military that in truth "you can do anything with bayonets except sit on them!"

MARCH 4, 1969:

In the spring of 1969 the battle for the future of China was being fought in the countryside, though the combatants had previously skirted that ultimate battlefield. The struggle was pressed by all sides in the name of the deified Chairman Mao Tse-tung; but no clearly identifiable Maoist faction was involved. The Great Revolution in China had been divested of its ideological trappings—and revealed as a naked power struggle.

Having failed first to control the students and intellectuals and then the urban working class, China's would-be masters now attempted to bring the farmers to heel. The jerry-built, military-dominated Revolutionary Committees, which nominally ruled the nation, were matched against the old rural leadership, now bolstered by dissident intellectuals and officials "sent down" to be "re-educated" by the peasants. The peasants themselves rallied around the old leaders they knew, rather than bow to the new "revolutionary authorities," and peasant resistance had already forced significant retreats by local and provincial Revolutionary Committees.

The battle was fought with many weapons—from social pressure, arrests, mass meetings and "propaganda teams" to bayonets and rifles. The stake was control of China's rural population of approximately 550 million and the country's chief source of wealth, the produce of its vast fields. Understanding only one way of governing, generals, colonels, and majors who dominated the Revolutionary Committees at every level were intensifying pressure on the peasantry. Their first goal was totalitarian rule. Their second was transformation of the peasantry into "willing, docile oxen of the revolution"—the source of the raw materials that would enable China to industrialize and build her military strength.

The "masses" of the countryside had other ideas. They rallied under their old officials, as well as the new leadership unintentionally provided by the "mass transfer to the countryside" of 10 million to 20 million disaffected Red Guards, officials, and intellectuals. The peasants, as the controlled press delicately described it, were "creating difficulties and extensive difficulties." Widespread resistance had already forced the military to retract the more ambitious and more repressive aspects of the rural policies spelled out at the beginning of 1969. They unsuccessfully set out to "remodel the People's Communes."

The new, hard-line authorities originally sought to deprive the peasants of the private plots they farmed for their own profit. Once again, all work was to be performed directly for the benefit of the state. But an editorial of *The Peking People's Daily* directed a tactical retreat. Affirming that agriculture was to take precedence over industry, a significant softening of the previous position, the editorial further enjoined officials to "consult with the masses and learn from the masses."

For once, the ritual formula meant exactly what it said. The men administering the new hard line were being ordered to moderate their policies whenever they encountered firm opposition. The "Flying Leap Forward" in the countryside was by no means to be abandoned, but it was to be significantly modified. Their chief difficulty, official Communist sources constantly reiterated, was "the problem of the leadership group." That statement indicated that the new hard-line leaders were rejected by the "rural masses," while the old-line leaders, who had retained the confidence of the peasants, were directing resistance to renewed exploitation.

The peasants devised many tactics to oppose the new wave of repression. In Hupei Province in the north, the Communists revealed both their purposes and their frustrations when they boasted, not quite truthfully, that the new policy "has steadily reduced the private domain [individual profit] and enhanced the rule of the collective [the State's and Communes' share of the crop]." But, the same broadcast continued, certain groups of leaders had resisted the new "communalization" and had sought to "go it alone in a disguised form of co-operatives."

In Shensi Province in the northwest, "leadership comrades . . . have underestimated the activism of the poor and the lower-middle peasants and the revolutionary basic-level cadres and are incapable of leading the campaign. . . . In some places, they even do as they please."

In Honan in North-Central China, the military formed their own Thought of Mao Tse-tung Propaganda Teams, formally under the people's own control. The teams were in reality a perversion of the Maoist ideal of "extensive democracy." The "elected team members" could be dismissed by the Revolutionary Committees, just as they could be elected only with the approval of the Committees.

The Maoist ideal, the original goal of the Cultural Revolution, was to create all-powerful Revolutionary Committees, themselves elected by mass, popular franchise and subject to recall at any time. The words and the outward form of that ideal were reportedly in existence, but the reality of "extensively democratic" and popular rule was wholly absent. The Revolutionary Committees were *not* elected, while even low-level propaganda teams required approval from on high.

The most radical divergence from Maoist ideals was exhibited in a long editorial from *The Shensi Daily*. It was evoked by the peasants' adept employment of the technique adopted universally: Quoting the sacred Thought of Mao Tse-tung to prove one's own point—however anti-Maoist it might be.

The peasants, *The Shensi Daily* complained, refused to throw themselves into the new production campaign "because we are too busy with the struggle-criticism-transformation campaign" that had been commanded to "totally alter their thinking." "This is the wrong attitude!" the newspaper fulminated. "It is wrong to set revolution against production."

The Cultural Revolution had itself begun with the baldest assertion: "Revolution—and spiritual transformation—are more important than material production!" As the Maoists were forced back, the slogan had been adapted to read: "Grasp revolution and promote production!" But *The Shensi Daily* declared: "If we only grasp struggle-criticism-transformation, but neglect production, soil and water conservation, and capital construction, production is bound to be affected adversely—and the overall victory of the Great Proletarian Cultural Revolution will also be seriously impaired."

The wheel had come more than full circle. In the name of Mao Tse-tung, the hard-line military were advocating the same concentration on material production for which the Maoists had most vehemently denounced their enemies. At the same time, the materialistic peasants, determined to keep their gains of the past eight years, were quoting Mao against the Revolutionary Committees.

The battle in the countryside would pass through many phases. Above all else, the struggle for control of the great mass of China's population centered around one objective—power. "Too many people advocate the theory of many centers of power, which means in reality no center of power," the Revolutionary Committees reiterated. The Revolutionary Committees were determined to control that still nonexistent "single center of power." The hundreds of millions of Chinese peasants, workers, and intellectuals were fighting to control their own lives.

MARCH 16, 1969:

A broadcast declared ominously: "The waves that float the boat can also rise and overturn it!"

The mode of expression was characteristically allusive and indirect, but the meaning was wholly clear from the context. The Red Guards were the boat, and the waves were the power of the new military-dominated establishment in China. The fate of 20 million adolescent Red Guards epitomized the Great Proletarian Cultural Revolution. Less than three years ago they rose like rockets in the clouded Chinese political firmament. Instead of entering orbit, the Red Guards fell back to earth.

The Great Revolution had scorned and humiliated its children. The Red Guards—"pure" of heart and class background, wholly free of "bourgeois taint"—were the weapon chosen by the Chairman to destroy the old Communist bureaucracy. But the least idealistic or imaginative segment of the old bureaucracy, the generals, in 1968 and 1969 denounced the Red Guards as "the class enemy . . . the exemplars of petty bourgeois thinking, who are striving to restore capitalism."

All the while, the great smiling face of Chairman Mao, the demigod of the discontented youth, looked on beaming—still silent, as it had been from the beginning. All the while, Mao's "best disciple and closest comrade-in-arms," the pale and haggard Lin Piao, Deputy Chairman of the Communist Party, gazed unmoved upon a revolution that had reversed its course. Neither would say more for the dedicated, violent, and devout Red Guards than: "At the beginning and during the middle stages of the Cultural Revolution, they did a good job and performed useful functions, but now . . ."

The Red Guard was created in 1966 and was assigned one simple mission consistent with the inclinations of naturally resentful youth: "Destroy every vestige of the old world!"

Aroused youth was the weapon the ostensible idealists surrounding Mao used to destroy their enemies within the Communist Party and the government of China. It was the "iron broom which would sweep away the rotten old society, clearing the ground for the brilliant new proletarian society." In the spring of 1969, the Red Guards were excoriated by the spiritual twins of the bureaucrats they had attacked. The Red Guards were shipped off to remote country towns to "learn from the peasants" and "transform their thinking through manual labor."

Yet their function had remained, remarkably and consistently, the same throughout the Cultural Revolution. They attacked the Establishment, which they considered with much justification to be oppressive, decadent, and exploitive. They continued to play the same role, even when they had officially been stripped of both power and honor by the Establishment. Making common cause with the workers, the peasants, and old local officials, they fought against the reassertion of the authority of the military—with wile and with guns.

The Red Guards had set out to fight an unjust Establishment in a spirit of bounding enthusiasm, exalted by florid oratory. They were still fighting an unjust Establishment, but from the shadows and for reasoned motives. They had recognized the deceit and hypocrisy of an Establishment that cynically used their youthful idealism to overthrow its relatively moderate opponents—and then abandoned them.

The Red Guards had hoped for a new era free of exploitation and suppression. They finally entered into armed opposition because the "extensive democracy" they were promised had become a repressive military bureaucracy. A commentary by *The Kiangsi Daily* summed up the confrontation: "A small group of unrepentant class enemies is utilizing the non-proletarian tendencies [*i.e.,* the New Thought Trend] within our society to disrupt and wreck the Proletarian Cultural Revolution, attacking from both the right and the left. . . . Once they [the Red Gaurds] were themselves emancipated, they became content with the *status quo*. . . . They surrendered to the rightist bourgeoisie and to the extreme left; they conducted wrecking operations on the broadest scale."

The commentary's climax was a plaint: "Round after round teaches us the meaning of the old maxim: 'The trees yearn for calm, but the wind will not subside.' "

The irony was perhaps unintentional. At the beginning of the Great Revolution the same slogan had been used by writers later denounced as extreme leftists to praise the Red Guards, the "wind" that shook the "trees" of the old Establishment. The wind continued to blow, and the trees of the new Establishment yearned for calm.

The Red Guards had learned a bitter lesson. One representative summed up his conclusions for all would-be revolutionaries without definite purpose: "First, we learned that it may be easy to change some officials, but the system endures—and gets worse. Second, we learned that change for the sake of change is meaningless, unless you know where you are going. And finally, we learned the most bitter lesson of all —we were just tools in a fight between ambitious opportunists on both sides." He concluded: "But we shall fight on!"

Despite their own disarray and continuing resistance "from the left and the right," the generals felt by April 1969 that they had built the spare provincial foundation of a new national structure of authority. Since Revolutionary Committees existed in all 29 of China's major administrative divisions, the Liberation Army had presumably established a certain minimal influence. But the Party Center remained weak and divided, while purges had reduced the Central Committee to a third of its original membership. The factions at the Center contended for power almost as fiercely—and much more cunningly—than the "ultraleft and the extreme right" in the provinces. Even the Liberation Army was still divided. The Disciple's following had dwindled, while the senior generals and marshals were united primarily by opposition to Utopianism and belief in the necessity to re-establish civil order.

Although the foundaton was weak, the generals decided in consultation with the Chairman and the Disciple, advised by First Minister Chou En-lai, that they could finally convene the Ninth National Congress of the Communist Party of China. The Eighth Congress had elected the gutted Central Committee in May 1956. Since the Party Constitution, soon to be superseded, provided for a National Party Congress every four years, the Ninth Congress was long overdue. Even though it could not possibly represent a united Communist Party, the Ninth Congress was therefore convened. It was, it appeared, necessary to create the semblance of new unity at the Center before the nation could itself be reunited.

XXIII

The Generals' Congress— and Beyond

The most enigmatic figure of the Cultural Revolution was its prime mover, Chairman Mao Tse-tung. He had presumably commanded the cataclysm. The "latest instructions" attributed to him had periodically altered its direction—at least in form. But the Chairman had made not a single public statement during the entire Revolution. Only when the Ninth National Congress of the Communist Party of China convened in Peking in April 1969 did Mao Tse-tung finally utter a few sentences the people heard in his own voice on the radio and in films. The burden of his message was his hope that "This will be a Congress of unity!"

Mao Tse-tung, alone among the leading figures of the Congress, was wholly composed in his demeanor at the conference. The Disciple fidgeted wanly, while Chou En-lai frequently betrayed irritation. The Chairman beamed soporifically as he accepted the constant plaudits of 1,512 delegates. He walked repeatedly through the cavernous Hall of the People's Congress waving to the delegates—most, like himself, wearing the Liberation Army uniform. He repeatedly shook hands with eager "representatives of the proletariat," neither wincing nor withdrawing when an enthralled farmer jerked his arm up and down for two full minutes like the handle of a balky village pump. He was, it appeared, either inspired or sedated.

Still, the Chairman finally spoke at the Big Nine, as the Congress was called. While he beamed, generals and old-line officials exalted his person and his Thought—and methodically undid all his policies. The Chairman had sought to create a new and perfect world by giving power to the masses. His professed disciples sought to re-create a functioning system of government, however imperfect. The council that formally

447

celebrated the victory of the Thought of Mao Tse-tung actually repudi-ated his ideals and rejected his visions.

The Ninth National Congress, much like the Sixth held in Moscow in 1928 after an earlier upheaval, strove to build a new structure of authority. The method was compromise, and the goal was coalition. The Great Revolution had splintered the Communist Party into factions, each claiming independent power and asserting its own special interests. The delegates were nominally representative of all the divergent inter-ests, having been chosen by an ostensibly nation-wide consensus that disdained the "bourgeois superstition" of elections. They included repre-sentatives of the "proletarian masses, the good cadres, the People's Liberation Army, and the rebel revolutionaries of the mass organiza-tions." The "revolutionary great alliance" First Minister Chou En-lai had sought so long in vain was formalized—largely in vain.

The preponderance of the military was immediately apparent, as was the degradation of the Red Guards. More than 40 percent of the 176 members of the Presidium that directed the Congress came from the Liberation Army, while the few representatives of the "rebel revolution-aries" were ignored. The same preponderance of a group no more than 3 million strong in a nation of more than 700 million was displayed when the new Central Committee and Political Bureau were elected at the end of the Congress. The generals sought a coalition based on compromise among rival policies and personalities, and they could argue with some justification that they were entitled to their overwhelming representation. The coalition was based not upon representation according to number, but according to power. The People's Liberation Army was the *only* functioning structure of power in China.

The goal of the Big Nine was a coalition that would create some functional harmony out of the universal contention Chairman Mao implicitly acknowledged by expressing his "hope" for unity. Like the Sixth Congress in Moscow, the Ninth was convened in an atmosphere of desperation. In 1928, a small political faction contending for power by subversion and force had been shattered. The Sixth Congress had sought to put the fragments together. In 1969, the administrative machinery of a vast nation had disintegrated, and the populace had splintered into contending factions. The Ninth Congress sought to heal the nation's wounds by allaying bitterness and outlawing rebelliousness. While the Sixth Congress had produced formal unity in Moscow, the open power struggle in China had continued for at least a decade, until Mao Tse-tung finally destroyed his chief rival, Chang Kuo-tao, in 1938. The disunity facing the Ninth Congress was greater by several magnitudes. The obvious prognosis was, therefore, violent contention for power—perhaps lasting a decade. Neither coalitions nor the "collective leadership" subsequently proclaimed had ever operated effectively for any length of time in any nation committed to the Leninist principle of strong unitary leadership.

The Ninth Congress left one fundamental question unanswered. Did the generals and marshals truly desire a coalition of interests or were they creating a façade behind which they planned to exercise absolute power?

Though the Great Revolution was in many respects unique in the human experience, it shared one characteristic with most major historical movements. Actual events may be described with some clarity, but the motivations of the protagonists have remained obscure. Even memoirs are more often written to justify great men's actions than to reveal their sources. In this case, absolute assertion would be foolhardy, although a variety of evidence supports the tentative conclusion that the generals truly desired a functioning coalition of divergent interests—and not a military dictatorship. They might wish to exercise predominant influence, but they did not appear to seek sole or absolute power.

Besides, the generals knew they could not attain absolute power, even at the Center, while they certainly could not exercise absolute power in the provinces. Moreover, the Chinese tradition, ancient Imperial or modern Communist, differed from the conventional despotism of Moscow. The Chinese had ruled by consensus from the time of the Han Dynasty (206 B.C.–A.D. 220), when local officials had been instructed neither to interfere with established "village democracy" nor to intrude into the people's daily lives, but merely to maintain order and collect taxes. Mao Tse-tung's compulsion to remake the entire nation and remold men's souls had progressively violated that tradition, thereby evoking the ever rising resistance that made the Cultural Revolution necessary. The generals wished to avoid committing the same error whose consequences they were striving to remedy. Their actions demonstrated that they sincerely sought consensus—within the formally authoritarian structure of power—rather than absolutism. They hoped to win popular sanction by relative lenience. Besides, they could not dispense with the spiritual authority of the Chairman, however tattered, or the organizational genius of the First Minister, however frustrated. They were, moreover, eager to re-create the Communist Party as *the* instrument for enforcing the will of the Center on the nation.

Central power had been virtually destroyed in China by April 1969. The Communist Party had been shattered, and the People's Government was the gaping façade of a gutted edifice. Neither agency could agree on policies at the Center, much less execute those policies in the provinces. The feebleness of the Party Center persisted into mid-1970—and seemed likely to persist for some time thereafter. Whatever central authority still existed resided in the informal council of senior generals and field marshals who commanded the loyalty of the local generals. The council's resolution and stabilizing effect permitted convocation of the Ninth Congress—and dominated its proceedings.

Members of the council were not necessarily present in Peking at most times, if indeed the council's membership was fixed. Its power derived from its influence on the somewhat junior generals who controlled all the Provincial Revolutionary Committees. China was, in effect, ruled by the informal interaction of personal and professional loyalties the British call "the Old Boy net." If interrelations had been precisely defined, China's Old Boy net could not have operated. The council was effective insofar as it was amorphous. If it had proclaimed a formal center of authority, it could not have operated. Its purpose was to conciliate and pacify—not to assert a new, alternate seat of power.

Discretion nurtured a certain authority in a nation that preferred vagueness to constricting precision and allusion to explicit definition. An earlier—and more comfortable era—was implicitly reborn. The true power of the senior generals and marshals derived directly from the peculiarly Chinese relationship between superior and subordinate, a bond often stronger than that between father and son. Stemming from the Confucian injunction to honor one's master, the relationship had over the centuries provided for the subordinate's security and his advancement. In turn, his loyalty enhanced his superior's prestige and power. Despite Lin Piao's effort to destroy the overriding influence of such personal and regional relationships within the People's Liberation Army, ingrained reverence and obedience toward one's commander remained a cardinal virtue of the Chinese officer. Senior officers therefore exercised enormous influence over their juniors—and that influence was greatly enlarged when it became manifest that only the People's Liberation Army could save China from anarchy and, perhaps, dissolution.

The Liberation Army had itself survived because it was both an outgrowth of Chinese society and a semi-autonomous entity within that society. A Chinese army—Nationalist or Communist—was a true subsociety, a community in arms. Giving battle was, perhaps, its most important attribute, but only one of many attributes. The military were concerned not only to defend the nation, but to provide for the welfare of their community—from the wife of the newest recruit to the field marshal. Since the Liberation Army possessed its own communication and transportation networks, as well as its independent Communist Party organization and its own factories and farms, the military were autonomous —economically, politically, and socially.

The Army's unique position enabled the generals to resist the destructive Great Revolution—as could no other group. The people's marshals were, for example, protected. Only two of the ten created in 1955 fell during the ten years of contention that began in 1959 at Mount Lu. Great General Peng Teh-huai had invited formal degradation by his premature public opposition to the Chairman; the Bandit General Ho Lung was apparently directly implicated in plots aimed specifically at the Chairman. However, neither was executed, and both exercised "underground" influence. The Disciple Lin Piao was of course most visibly eminent; and one marshal had died. The remaining six all returned to power in the Party hierarchy and the Government, some formally advanced and others slightly degraded, though all had been vigorously attacked by the extremists.

Nieh Jung-chen remained chairman of his semi-autonomous fief, the Scientific and Technological Defense Commission, which directs rocketry and nuclear development. Shielded by the original provision that "scientists and technicians" were not to be disturbed at their "work of national importance," he had sat aloof from the turmoil. But Marshal Nieh, too, had been attacked when the irrepressible Revolution briefly invaded his realm. Vice Premier and Foreign Minister Chen Yi had been violently denounced and forced to submit to "criticism meetings" because of his outspoken advocacy of a rational foreign policy. He was a chief lieutenant of Chou En-lai, and his sphere had been largely civilian, though defense policy could not be separated from foreign policy. Marshal Chen Yi retained close connections with his peers and with serving generals. Both Nieh and Chen were dropped from the Politburo and— promptly and ostentatiously—appointed vice chairmen of the Military Affairs Commission after the Congress.

Generalissimo Chu Teh, the father of the People's Liberation Army, retained formal power, though he was, at 83, no longer active. The affection he inspired among all ranks meant that he simply could *not* be degraded, although he had been swingeingly denounced by the extremists. Marshal Liu Po-cheng, the One-Eyed General, startled observers when he too was appointed to the Politburo. He had devoted himself to quiet obstruction during the Great Revolution. His name had hardly been heard, but he had apparently protected the insurgent First Secretary of the Southwest Regional Bureau from the Maoists' assaults. His protection was withdrawn when the generals decided the Liberation Army must forcefully remove civilian leaders who provoked contention —and the First Secretary fell.

Marshal Yeh Chien-ying, the political general who had induced the Campus Belle to come to Yenan in 1947, ranked with the One-Eyed General when the new Politburo was announced. He had—in public at least—done nothing in particular throughout the Great Revolution, but he had obviously done it very well. Yeh Chien-ying appears to have been one of the chief conciliators. Besides, he was close to Premier Chou En-lai.

The final and most unlikely survivor was Marshal Hsü Hsiang-chien, who had briefly been chairman of the Task Force of the Cultural Revolution Within the Armed Forces. His record was flawed not only by his adherence during the 1930s to Chang Kuo-tao, the Trotsky of the Chinese revolution, but by his equivocal performance during the Great Revolution. He had earned the enmity of the right by his early commitment to the "rebel revolutionaries," while the left despised him for his lack of zeal. Nonetheless, Marshal Hsü survived.

The Disciple Lin Piao, 61 in 1969, was the youngest, the most ambitious, and the most prominent of the marshals. Although he was formally annointed by the new Party Constitution as "Chairman Mao's successor," his true power was almost as obscure as his master's. He was at best, first among the equals of the council of generals, whatever trappings of absolute power he displayed in public. Although he strove to seize absolute power, the Disciple was not chairman of the board of the generals' council, but an emissary of the Chairman. He had, it seemed, alienated his peers by his blatant display of ruthless ambition.

The council also rejected his militant thesis that "people's war" conducted by Chinese protégés abroad was the best defense of China. Aware of the weakness of their forces, the generals considered the "forward strategy" provocative. They were inclined toward the defense in depth, sustained by modern antiaircraft weapons, advocated by disgraced Chief-of-Staff Lo Jui-ching, the Securityman. All obviously agreed on the necessity to develop a formidable nuclear arsenal and to mobilize effective defenses to deter or counter a pre-emptive Soviet strike at China's nuclear facilities in the north.

The tasks of controlling China's restive millions and defending the nation fell to the generals in direct command in Peking and the provinces. Foremost was the Chief-of-Staff appointed in 1968, Huang Yung-sheng, Huang the Ever Victorious. Among the first to suppress the Red Guards when he commanded the Canton Military Region, Huang enjoyed the confidence of his conservative subordinates. But they were all strong men.

Most contentious and most controversial was Wang En-mao of Sinkiang, the New Dominion abutting Soviet Central Asia. Although he was not one of the 176 members of the Presidium of the Ninth Congress and had been relieved as commander of the Sinkiang Military Region in late 1968, Wang En-mao was hardly a spent force. He remained deputy commander and Political Commissar of the Military Region, and he reappeared as an alternate member of the Central Committee selected by the Congress. Wang's retention, albeit in a position formally degraded, demonstrated the power of the generals. They would make formal obeisance to Chairman Mao and Deputy Chairman Lin Piao, but they would not sacrifice the man who had most loudly demanded that "Socialist legality," rather than "proletarian violence," guide the Great Revolution.

Other generals had also defied the Maoists, including Lung Shu-chin, who replaced Wang En-mao in Sinkiang. Notable was Chang Kuo-hua of the southwest. General Chang had for a time made his Tibetan redoubt virtually autonomous. He had not then been degraded, but had instead been given greater responsibility. He was Political Commissar of the Chengtu Military Region, including strategic Yünnan and Szechwan, China's most populous and fertile province with its 72 millions and its great fields watered by ancient irrigation works. He was also chairman of Szechwan's Revolutionary Committee. In Central China, General Hsü Shih-yu exercised enormous influence as commander of the Nanking Military Region, which included the key provinces of Anhwei, Chekiang, and Kiangsu, the latter encompassing the autonomous municipality, Shanghai.

Other strong men, like Chen Hsi-lien, commander of the Shenyang Military Region, which controlled Manchuria, also rose in the new Party hierarchy because of their power in the provinces. The military's survival rate was remarkable at the regional and provincial levels. Of the 13 multiprovincial Military Regions, 5 lost their commanders, some through transfer like Huang the Ever Victorious, who became Chief-of-Staff. The regional political commissars suffered greater attrition, with only three surviving. The commissars were, of course, quasi-civilian in function and intimately associated with the local Party apparatus, the initial target of the Cultural Revolution. Some commissars were also prematurely enthusiastic in supporting the Great Revolution. But the 22 Military Districts, most controlling a single province, lost only two commanders.

Despite the purge that destroyed the machinery and the personnel of the two leading civilian organizations, the Communist Party and the People's Government, the generals retained their positions at the rice roots, the roots of power. Their power was the ultimate strength of the council of generals. It was also the cement that kept China from disintegrating amid the shocks of the Great Revolution—and bound the slightly cracked foundation of the Ninth Congress.

Red banners fluttered from the drably monumental buildings of Peking, and illuminated signs exhorted CELEBRATE THE BIG NINE. "The Ninth General Meeting of the Representatives of the Chinese Communist Party from the Entire Nation" had convened. In reality, the meeting was neither a congress nor a meeting of representatives. Even by the lax standards of the eight preceding congresses, the Big Nine was distinctly unrepresentative—and beset by dissension. Congresses of the Communist Party customarily discussed and ratified decisions already taken by the senior hierarchs. The largely ceremonial bodies functioned "by democratic centralism" according to the previous Party Constitution drafted by Comrade Liu Shao-chi. The lengthy intervals between Congresses further demonstrated their ceremonial character. The Big Eight had met in 1956 and the Big Seven in 1949. It would obviously be impossible to manage a nation, or even a political party, if the Congress were in truth the supreme policy-making body. Only in times of acute crisis were Party Congresses actually forums of debate and compromise.

The Big Nine was quite unlike most Party Congresses, except others that met amid crises, because of its duration alone. Negotiations lasted from the 1st to the 24th of April 1969.

The Ninth Congress was, moreover, a mirror image—not of other National Party Congresses, but of the Ninth Party Congress of the Fourth Red Army, which met in Kutien in Fukien Province in December 1929. At Kutien, Mao Tse-tung, then one of many contenders for supremacy over the Communist movement, imposed his will on the Red Army. After some resistance, the soldiers accepted his leadership—and the occasion was solemnized by the execution of more than 100 dissenters. Chen Yi, later Foreign Minister, reluctantly presided over the killing to prove his own loyalty.

In Peking in April 1969, the military asserted their supremacy over Mao Tse-tung. The indiscriminate killing of the Great Revolution the Big Nine sought to halt had already slain its thousands; in the times following the Congress, the leaders would revert to the selective execution of hundreds. As the authorities sought to re-establish their power, they were forced to use the tactics they had employed during the Land Reform Campaign of 1950–1952, when they sought to break the old society. Chinese society was, once again, in opposition to the Communists. At Kutien, Mao had forced the professional officers to endorse his conception of a guerrilla force, its strategy shaped by political rather than military considerations. In Peking, the professional officers reasserted their own strategy. China was to build conventional forces and pursue a cautious foreign policy, seeking limited rapprochement with both the United States and the Soviet Union, while avoiding undue provocation to either great power. The transition would, however, require much time.

Apparent paradox emerged, for the generals honored the forms while totally altering the substance. The forms of Maoism were not merely preserved, but actually expanded in the new Party Constitution. The

Thought of Mao Tse-tung was declared the official doctrine of the Communist Party, and Lin Piao was confirmed as the Chairman's successor, as well as sole Deputy Chairman—in contrast to the previous five vice chairmen. Both measures were unprecedented, though Mao Tse-tung had been much praised in one earlier Party Constitution.

As if to demonstrate their contempt for statutes, the Communists had changed their Constitution at almost every Congress. The Constitutions produced by the Big Seven and the Big Eight, both drafted by Comrade Liu Shao-chi, had liberalized qualifications for membership, internal administration, and the Party's external and internal policies. The Constitution ratified by the Ninth Congress was retrogressive. It was at once more rigid and more vague than its predecessors—and significantly shorter.* Its harshness, its specific elevation of both the Chairman and the Disciple, and its brevity all demonstrated that the Constitution was an interim document. It was convenient to reaffirm Maoism, but the generals quite obviously did not consider that the new Party Constitution prescribed fundamental principles which could guide China's course for an extended period.

After hallowing the Thought and the Disciple, the new Party Constitution discussed mundane matters. The Party machinery was remarkably simplified so that the Center could control the Party directly. The pretense of consulting the general membership was virtually abandoned, as were elections already denounced as "bourgeois superstition." Thus the new Constitution affirmed the Party's devotion to the Thought of Mao Tse-tung and simultaneously flouted the Chairman's principles. There was to be not even a pretense of the Party's masses participating in major decisions, much less the extra-Party masses. Glossing over the details of administration, the Constitution by omission sanctioned harsh, neo-Stalinist control of the Party Center and the entire country. The military-dominated Party Center had first to perform the successive Herculean feats of re-creating a responsive and effective Party apparatus in the provinces and bending the "masses" to their will with that apparatus.

When the Party Constitution was announced in mid-April 1969, the first—and most interesting—of three brief and Delphic utterances of the Chairman was also made public. Mao Tse-tung reportedly delivered "two important speeches" to the Congress, but only extracts were released.

"I hope," the Chairman told the delegates in a hoarse, low voice rendered but half-intelligible by his furry Hunan accent, "that the present congress will be a congress of unity and a congress of victory—and

* No more than 3,000 words, in contrast to the 15,000 words of the Eighth's.

that, after its conclusion, still greater victories will be won throughout the entire country."

The tentative statement hardly exuded confidence. Mao Tse-tung hoped for unity; he did not proclaim unity. He stated the need for more and "greater victories," rather than asserting that victory had already been won. His motivation is difficult to read. He may have been giving the military the bare minimum they demanded. He may, on the other hand, have been registering his distaste for the entire proceeding. His manner was as remarkably disengaged as were his words. Even in carefully edited films, his placid, immobile features truly resembled a "man attending his own funeral," as he had complained of his role during the ascendancy of Comrade Liu Shao-chi. The Big Nine was at once a political funeral and a canonization. The chief participant had apparently accepted with fatalism the fact that he could "struggle" no more.

The true character of the coalition and the projected future course of China were revealed as the Congress closed on April 24. The new Central Committee was larger than ever with 170 full and 109 alternate members, 279 in all. The previous record had been the 193 full and alternate members of the Central Committee elected by the Eighth Congress in 1956. Of that earlier total,* only 51—36 full members and 15 alternate members—were seated in either capacity in the new Central Committee. The preponderance of the military was blatant. At least 141 men and women were identified with the People's Liberation Army, a shade over half the total of 279. Among the 170 full members, 96 were from the Army, as were 45 of the 107 alternates. If there had been any question that the Big Nine was a generals' congress, the list of the new Central Committee closed discussion.

It was also an ecumenical conference, which attempted to produce a coalition under military "guidance" by including "representatives of all groups." The Starlet's favorite musician, who had scandalized all China by accompanying Peking Opera on a piano, was not included, although he had been among the 176 members of the Presidium of the Congress. The generals would go only so far to convey the impression of placating the Maoists. Although the list was padded with "workers' and peasants' representatives," only two Red Guard chieftains were included in the Central Committee, both as alternate members. They were an obscure Shanghai figure and Nieh Yüan-tze, the lady philosophy teacher who had composed the first "great-character poster." She was one of only 14 women. Madame Nieh was the only survivor of the five Red Guard chieftains of Peking who had dominated the early stages of the Cultural Revolution. Deliberately rubbing the salt into the lacerated

* Eighteen had died.

wounds of the Red Guards, the communiqué listed the "representatives of the mass organizations" last.

First among the members were "the old generation of proletarian revolutionaries and leading cadres on the Party, government, and military fronts." Much of the remainder of the list was intended to prevent those dominant categories from being excessively obtrusive. How, in any event, did one distinguish between the despised "old power-holders following the capitalist road" and the exalted "old generation of proletarian revolutionaries"? The answer, presumably, was that the latter had survived. As the Disciple had threatened at the Eleventh Plenum in August 1966, there had been many reassignments, promotions, demotions, and expulsions, but the new Central Committee was aptly described by the old Chinese epigram "Changing the water, but not the essence!" The Party Congress attempted to create the impression that all possible groups and all possible opinions were represented—a sharp departure, to say the least, from previous determination to "destroy all the representatives of the old civilization."

Peking also made a point of minutely describing the laborious, nine-day process that selected the Central Committee. Names were first put in nomination by the various delegations. They were then "collated" by the Presidium and returned to the delegations, which drew up the final list of candidates. Finally a "secret ballot" chose the new elite, each of 1,512 delegates dropping his ballot into a sealed box while the Chairman watched benevolently. The "bourgeois superstition" of elections had been revived in the cause of ecumenicism.

But the Political Bureau elected by the Central Committee after the close of the Congress further demonstrated forcibly that there was to be no nonsense about equal representation. Of the 21 full members and 4 alternates, 13 were from the military, including Yeh Chün, wife to Lin Piao. Only Mao Tse-tung and Lin Piao were identified by their specific ranks of Chairman and Deputy Chairman. Even the remaining three members of the Standing Committee of the Politburo were listed "according to the number of strokes" in the characters for their family names, the Chinese equivalent of alphabetical order. But the ranking had clearly not changed. Although some of his followers had been degraded, First Minister of Great Peace Chou En-lai was first, followed by the Ghostwriter Chen Po-ta, and the Lord High Executioner Kang Sheng. They were the civilian façade.

The rank of the rest of the Politburo was obfuscated by the same quasi-alphabetical device that had concealed rank within the Central Committee. Eliminating the three members of the Standing Committee left 15 full members of the Politburo, 11 unmistakably military. The Starlet was, perforce, among the civilians included, as were her protégés:

the Literary Assassin Yao Wen-yüan, who had proved that his pen would serve whatever cause served his self-interest; and the chairman of the Shanghai Revolutionary Committee, Chang Chün-chiao, who had taken the precaution of making his separate peace with the Army by becoming a political commissar. Thereafter, it was, with a few exceptions, soldiers all the way.

They were, even more pointedly, the commanders of large numbers of troops, except for the venerated marshals—the One-Eyed General, Liu Po-cheng, the Political General, Yeh Chien-ying, and the Generalissimo Chu Teh. They did not command troops. But Huang Yung-sheng, Huang the Ever Victorious, was Chief-of-Staff, while Chiu Hui-tso, a "black element" to the Red Guards, as chief of the Rear Area Command controlled the massive logistic apparatus with its production and transport facilities. General Hsieh Fu-chih, Minister of Public Security, commanded the Public Security Corps, perhaps 800 thousand strong, while Wu Fa-hsien was Commander-in-Chief of the People's Air Force, the technological arm that had served the Center throughout the struggle. Li Tso-peng was Political Commissar of the People's Navy, which had given Peking only occasional twinges. Chen Hsi-lien and Hsü Shih-yu commanded the bulk of troops in Manchuria and Central China respectively. Filled out with other regional commanders, the Politburo directly controlled approximately two-thirds of China's armed forces. From the direct command of troops flowed the political power of the generals.

Nonetheless, they indicated that they wished peace and not a sword in the lengthy Political Report delivered to the Big Nine by the Disciple on their behalf. Like the Party Constitution itself, the 24 thousand-word Political Report was fervently Maoist in its ritual expressions, but non-Maoist in essence. Above all, the Disciple declared that the new leadership was willing to give both domestic and foreign enemies "a way out." In effect, he told both groups that Peking would not trouble them if they did not trouble Peking. Although Lin Piao draped himself in the cloak of Mao Tse-tung's doctrinal authority, for the first time since the Great Revolution began in 1966 he did not assert in a major public declaration that he spoke "on behalf of Chairman Mao." That subtle restraint was not a signal that the Disciple was claiming independent power, but that he spoke for the "collective leadership." He implicitly repudiated the fundamental Maoist doctrines of "ceaseless revolution" at home and "people's wars" abroad. He explicitly reaffirmed the ecumenical theme of the Big Nine—at home and abroad.

Lin Piao promised amnesty to those "who have made mistakes" if they "reformed," meaning, presumably, if they no longer struggled against authority exercised by the People's Liberation Army and personified by himself. He promised "emancipation" to both old and new forces that had transgressed during the Great Revolution. Those who repented, he said, "will be given a way out." It was a most Chinese way of declaring—officially but imprecisely—that the Great Revolution had indeed ended.

The Deputy Chairman further promised to "rebuild the Communist Party," but was vague on details. He ritually spoke of "continuing struggle," but stressed the necessity for reconstructing the authority of "the organs of State power." Those organs were, presumably, the jerry-built Revolutionary Committees, though the Disciple did not identify them specifically. Lin Piao boasted of economic progress resulting from the Cultural Revolution—though there had been not progress, but retrogression. He ordered concentration upon restoring agricultural and industrial production. Although politics were presumably to remain the determining factor, the Disciple eschewed the sweeping Maoist slogan that had justified all excesses against persons and property: PUT POLITICS IN COMMAND!

The Political Report several times referred to the Red Guards, the Disciple's original "shock troops of the Cultural Revolution," but always in passing and always without enthusiasm. The Disciple reserved his enthusiasm for the People's Liberation Army. Voluminous citations from the canonical works of V. I. Lenin justified the imposition of military rule. Calling the Liberation Army "the strong pillar of the dictatorship of the proletariat," the titular ruler of China sought to vindicate his non-Marxist emphasis upon armed power in politics by quoting the Marxist classics for at least a third of his Report. He knew the Chinese people considered him the leader of a military *coup d'état* which had not yet been crowned by absolute authority. Despite his generally conciliatory tone, he spiritedly denounced "the theory of many centers of power, which means *no* center of power." The persecuted of the Great Revolution were required to earn amnesty by making submission to the centrally ruled unitary State the generals were determined to build on the foundation of the People's Liberation Army.

Speaking of China's few friends and many enemies abroad, Lin Piao set practical proposals against compulsory ideological liturgy. He denounced the Soviet "modern revisionist clique" for imposing a "social-fascist dictatorship" at home and pursuing "social imperialism" abroad. He predicted that the Soviet leadership would be overthrown by a "people's revolution," and he warned Moscow that China was well prepared for any Soviet military attack. He reiterated facts no one but the Soviets could deny: all the agreements demarking the Sino-Soviet border were "unequal treaties" imposed by force and subsequently renounced by the great Lenin himself. But, the Disciple said, Peking was considering Moscow's offer to negotiate the border dispute—on the basis of those unequal treaties.

He dealt similarly with other nations from Burma to the United States. He abstractly pledged support to insurrections in Asia, but he also suggested that the threatened nations' "State disputes" with China should be settled by negotiation, as had been the Sino-Burman border question. Ritually predicting that world-wide revolution would destroy the United States, he pledged specific support to neither North Vietnam nor North Korea. He actually mentioned neither of the two Communist countries that directly confronted the United States, though he did pledge continuing support to "the people of South Vietnam." He thus mouthed the obligatory revolutionary slogans, but indicated in no wise what they meant in practice. Behind the slogans, the Disciple implicitly endorsed the views of generals who had protested against Maoist policies as adventurous, provocative, and hazardous. Peking might promise support to revolutionary movements, but Peking was determined to avoid precipitating any confrontation that would involve the Chinese nation in war.*

"The formal culmination was startling," remarked one of the most acute observers of the Chinese scene, "though the trend had been clear for almost two years. The Mao-figure was already enshrined in the Chinese pantheon, and his ideology was venerated. But all the purposes, practices, and institutions Mao Tse-tung had advocated were virtually abandoned. Liu Shao-chi was damned to the furthest depths of the lowest hell. But his essentially moderate and conservative policies were revived."

Chairman Mao did not retreat to the hills to raise the Red Flag and lead a new guerrilla insurrection. He had threatened to provoke such a violent schism if the Party rejected him at Mount Lu in 1959—even if the People's Liberation Army turned against him. He had, in truth, launched his personal revolt against the Communist Establishment in 1966, but he had not prevailed. In 1969, he accepted the blasting of all his ideals without protesting loudly enough to be heard outside the Party's inner circle. The Army had made him a virtual puppet, and the demythologization of Mao the man soon began. His doctrines were exalted as abstract principles, but discarded as practical guides to action. while the hyperadulation rendered his person was gradually reduced. It was a slow and subtle process, but it was unmistakable. Mao Tse-tung

* Within six months, Peking and Moscow would be negotiating on their border disputes—without much success. Within ten months, the Sino-American talks, suspended in 1968, would be resumed intermittently.

was no longer the ruler of China, and the era of militant Maoism had ended.

"Whither China?" then, as the Hunan Provincial Proletarian Alliance had asked.

The Great Revolution's course—from its departure to its extraordinary landfall—has already been plotted in a necessarily impressionistic manner, deliberately omitting some elements not wholly pertinent to the flow of the main narrative. That method obviates a detailed account of events after the Revolution's obvious though unformalized conclusion in April 1969. But certain major currents continued to flow—and were likely to flow for some time to come.

The compromise sought by the generals was not successful. As the preceding chapter has indicated, the passions and aspirations released by the Great Revolution were too strong and too pervasive to be quelled by either fiat or conciliation, formal or informal. The "mass organizations," with their Red Guard nuclei, were denounced as the new "class enemy," but they continued to resist reimposition of central ideological or political authority. The industrious and ingenious Chinese people continued to operate an "underground" economy. Peking first experimented with leniency and compromise, but soon felt compelled to combine repression with conciliation.

The winds of resistance were, however, so high and so gusty that Peking steered a zigzag course. Moderate economic policies, still denounced, were actually enacted. Peking attempted to bring the farmers under absolute control by re-creating the People's Communes; altered that impossible direction; and, subsequently, tried again. Agriculture was, in any event, recognized as the "basis" of the economy, though heavy industrialization was still the ultimate aim. In the interim, Peking stressed production of consumer goods, farm implements, and fertilizer to stimulate agricultural production. Industry was to be decentralized—even more to harmonize with economic reality than to meet defense needs. Though the Center sought to retain overall control, much autonomous responsibility was given to individual managers, as Comrade Liu Shao-chi had proposed. Disentangling all the complex ideological and practical motivations was almost hopeless, but it was manifest beyond probable error that Peking had ordered primary concentration upon restoring the economy.

Economic decentralization, itself rational and unavoidable, accelerated the tendency toward regionalization of political and social power. Although the real threat of Russian attack was utilized to stimulate national spirit—rather than local spirit—people and leaders remained more concerned with immediate, local interests. The future was, therefore, obscure. No one could confidently anticipate the end of prevalent disorder. Neither could one foresee when a permanent government would take the place of the transitional structure, nor what form such government would take, nor who would rule the nation. An impressionistic, tentative projection, however, indicated that China might in time become a federation of regions rather than a centrally administered State.

The complex Great Revolution had clearly displayed another failure to create a modern, unitary nation effectively ruled from a single capital. The Maoist vision of the great federation, the People's Commune of All China, was even less likely of attainment. China remained a state of mind rather than a political state in the modern sense. Except for the brief episodes of the Chin Dynasty (221–206 B.C.), the Sui Dynasty (A.D. 589–618), and the Mongol Dynasty (c. A.D. 1280–1368), the Central Kingdom had never been a unitary nation before the Communist "liberation." For millennia, China had been a world in miniature. Encompassing all manners and conditions of men, the Central Kingdom felt no need for the centralized rule, the popular consensus, and the rapid communications that make human groups true nations. The rulers were united by the common State ideology of Confucianism, but the people were heterodox and diverse. Until its self-satisfied seclusion was destroyed by Western intrusion, China was content—and proud—to remain a world in miniature.

Only since the mid-1800s had the chief purpose of politically conscious Chinese been to transform China into a modern, unitary nation. Many obstacles impeded the road to that goal: a multiplicity of dialects; strong local prejudices, customs, and loyalties; inefficient communications; and, above all, inability to comprehend the fundamental concept of allegiance to a modern, unitary state. Yet the Central Kingdom could not take an equal place in the world—or reassert its previous supremacy —until it had become a unitary state. Creation of such a state had, therefore, been the conscious purpose of every responsible Chinese government since the Manchu Dynasty was overthrown in 1911 and the Confucian ideology, which had fostered a loose, federal unity, was progressively destroyed.

The turmoil immediately following the Revolution of 1911 made attainment of that goal impossible. The Nationalists, who came to power in 1928, for a time appeared to be approaching the same goal. But they were in turn frustrated—as much by their own inadequacies as by Communist insurrection and Japanese invasion.

Establishment of the People's Republic in 1949 appeared finally to bring the goal within reach. Until 1957, it seemed that the Communists were forcing the arduous metamorphosis that had eluded their predecessors. The process was most methodical: internal order was restored;

primarily regional loyalties were—apparently—reduced; communications were greatly improved; a new State ideology replaced discredited Confucianism; extra-legal clan and fraternal societies, usually clandestine and often criminal, were broken; and a strong national government in the old capital of Peking was controlled by a highly centralized Communist Party, sustained by the powerful People's Liberation Army. Seemingly, Peking ruled all China most effectively, and a unitary nation was being shaped.

But, after 1957, that appearance was progressively revealed as deceptive. The Communists had ruled effectively as long as they had not ruled too intrusively. Either the abrupt attempt to remake China in 1958 through the Great People's Communes had suddenly halted gradual progress toward creating a unitary nation or that progress had itself been illusory. In either event, the stubborn Chinese people demonstrated by their massive resistance how deeply rooted was the "old civilization." *Laissez-faire* rule from 1961 to 1965 unavoidably—and perhaps desirably—allowed the recrudescence of local interests, loyalties, and power. The Great Proletarian Cultural Revolution was, somewhat paradoxically, the next spasmodic attempt to create a centrally ruled unitary nation, though its avowed purpose was to transcend nationhood—and government—by realizing the great federation of semi-autonomous popular administrations described as the People's Commune of All China.

However, as it actually developed, the Great Revolution sought many objectives beyond the Utopia of Mao Tse-tung's vision. A chief purpose was destruction of the tenacious "old civilization" that had prevented creation of a unitary nation. The Revolution in the end became so complexly inverted, politically and ideologically, that it accomplished the opposite of what it had sought. The "old civilization" was actually strengthened. China reverted to the localism and defiance of central power characteristic of the decadent phase of each previous Imperial dynasty. All authority deteriorated, and anarchy supplanted the *laissez-faire* tolerance that had enabled both commissars and emperors to rule effectively—within reasonable limits—when their power was at its height. Rather than creating a modern, unitary state, the Communists had rent the loosely woven fabric of the nation.

Only two forces still preserved the simulacrum of a coherent, functioning political organism, though Peking's boast of a highly centralized "proletarian dictatorship" was totally dispelled. Still feeling themselves Chinese, the people recoiled from total fragmentation. United by professional interests, personal loyalties, and generalized adherence to Marxism-Leninism, the People's Liberation Army cast a loose net of authority around the nation and prevented utter disintegration. Both those unifying forces were, however, flawed. In a time of crisis, pride in being

Chinese was less significant to the people than the immediate security offered by local loyalties and associations. The people of Kwangtung and Kwangsi provinces in the deep south—once the vice royalty of the two Kwangs—were not greatly disturbed by the Russian threat to Sinkiang, Inner Mongolia, and Manchuria in the far north. The Liberation Army itself reflected the divisive tendencies of the Chinese society from which it sprang. It was still unbalanced by internal contention for power, even though the Ninth Congress had imposed much subordination. Civilian and military morale had been severely battered, while dissension not only split Peking, but wracked the entire country.

The Great Proletarian Cultural Revolution had proved to most Chinese that the ideal People's Commune of All China was an unattainable Utopia. Apparently imminent threats—from the Soviets in the north and the Americans in the south—had disproved reliance upon "people's war" abroad as an instrument for either effective defense or extending Chinese influence. Complemented by some prospects of establishing amicable relations with other nations, the same threats had stimulated the quest for a foreign policy truly suited to China's national interests and capabilities. With militant Maoism discredited, the hyper-independent Chinese had gone so far as to declare that they would not be averse to foreign aid—under appropriate conditions. Though it had been impeded by the Great Revolution, development of nuclear weapons and delivery systems proceeded rapidly. China orbited an earth satellite in the spring of 1970, proudly displaying her capability of deploying intercontinental ballistic missiles within a reasonable time. A nuclear-armed China, shorn of Maoist illusions, could well become less, rather than more, bellicose because she felt more secure—so long as obvious weakness in Southeast Asia did not again encourage the oldest continuous movement in human history, spontaneous Chinese expansion southward. China was seeking a new place in a world which she gradually recognized could be altered only slowly—if at all significantly —by Chinese initiative.

The Great Revolution had been a great catharsis of the Chinese soul. Many illusions had been half-dissipated, and many truths had been tentatively redefined. Both the Chinese people and the remaining three-quarters of mankind were, however marginally, better for the experience. China was not likely to fall under a centralized military dictatorship, since the People's Liberation Army was an inherent part of a nation with strongly regionalistic tendencies, rather than an integral, separate entity. Moreover, the traditional Chinese *ethos,* still powerful despite all endeavors to "destroy the old civilization," deeply opposed a military dictatorship like that in Greece or Burma. Nonetheless, a feeble administration supported by bayonets was an unsatisfactory and ephemeral solution of the overwhelming problem of re-creating an effective government. That problem remained *the* overriding concern of the Chinese nation.

It was tempting to conclude that China was displaying movement—in a direction that could not be plotted precisely—*despite* the persistence of that primary problem. Actually, movement was occurring *because* of that persistence. Alternation of limited conciliation and measured repression was, obviously, not a true solution, but only a means of maintaining a degree of stability during a transitional period. Peking was searching for an effective new foreign policy while striving to create effective internal administration. Both quests were circuitous and, largely, random. The intellectual, social, and political debris left by the devastation of the Great Revolution has impeded the endeavor made possible—and imperative—by the partial destruction of the "old civilization"—bourgeois and Communist. The two quests were, of course, essentially one. China was seeking a new appreciation of her own nature and a new relationship to the outside world based upon that new self-knowledge.

The final creation of a viable nation would depend upon general acceptance of a new, unifying State ideology to replace discredited Confucianism and Maoism. The Chinese, it appeared, were almost incapable of existing as a nation without such an ideology. They had never done so. Predicting with any precision the specific form that ideology might finally take was hazardous—if, indeed, that ideology should appear in final form before the end of the twentieth century. Almost 400 years had, after all, elapsed between the chaotic decline of feudalism, when Confucius taught, and the Han Dynasty's final institutionalization of his doctrines as the basis of government and morality in 150 B.C. Moreover, Confucius' original teachings were liberally altered by practical needs and even more liberally adapted to concepts and practices advocated by philosophers and statesmen who had stood in formal opposition to the supreme sage.

In the modern world of geometrically accelerated change, the formulation of a new State ideology was unlikely to require a comparable period of time. Nonetheless, developments in China have been remarkably attenuated. Traditional Chinese historiography viewed 21 years of Communist rule as the modern equivalent of the 15 years of the Chin and the 29 years of the Sui. Both those vigorous, innovating dynasties succeeded extended periods of disorder and themselves perished after laying the bases for the long-lived dynasties that followed, the Han and the Tang, respectively. In a more modern context, it took 67 years from the Boxer Rising of 1899, which doomed the Manchu Dynasty, until the Great Revolution sought to create a new China in a historical instant.

Comparisons with the French Revolution or the October Revolution also indicate that events in China take much longer to work themselves out because of the essential conservatism of the Chinese people and the stubborn resilience of traditional Chinese culture. Nonetheless, China lives in a world where all change is vastly accelerated by new techniques of production and communication. Once she accepts the fact that she is an equal part of that world, change in China, too, should be rapid.

If China does not break up into a congeries of separate entities—formally related by a common written language, embodying the great tradition, and the consciousness of being Chinese—a new system might, therefore, appear with relative rapidity. That system and its underlying State ideology are certain to embody many Communist concepts and practices liberally adapted to the demands of reality and the ideas of other thinkers. Internal administration might take the form of a federation of regions. Such a federation has been the basic pattern throughout most Chinese history, though Chinese pride would deny that assertion. The new form might yet be a unitary state based upon a greater degree of mutual tolerance—once a unifying ideology has been formulated and accepted. The prognosis can be stated with no greater clarity in mid-1970, but the prognosis is, by the slightest margin, more hopeful than grave.

Foreign policy will be integral to the internal solution, since the chief tension of Chinese history for the past 200 years has been adjusting to the existence of other nations—equal in certain respects, and, in other respects, more powerful than the Central Realms. China's southward drive, an involuntary movement, will undoubtedly continue. No outside power can, ultimately, prevent great Chinese influence over Southeast Asia. The nations of that area are, quite flatly, incapable of sustaining themselves—economically or socially, politically or militarily—under the great pressure of China. But outside powers like the United States, Japan, and the Soviet Union could limit China's hegemony, and they could, above all, assist in changing the nature of a nuclear-armed Chinese state.

American intervention in South Vietnam helped destroy the basis of Messianic Maoism, which proclaimed the "liberation of all the oppressed of the world through people's wars of revolution." Maoism was discredited by its failures—the domestic failure to create Utopia and the international failure to "drive capitalism back to its lair," where it would be destroyed by its "internal contradictions." Despite massive external assistance, the internal revolution has singularly failed in South Vietnam, which Peking called "the focus of the world-wide liberation movement." China is, therefore, looking to her own defenses, rather than to expansion—ideological and economic—abroad.

But a failure of the American will as the Vietnam conflict moves toward a conclusion could revive Peking's illusions. Involuntary Chinese expansionism, made purposeful by revived Maoism and armed with nuclear weapons, could resume its interrupted march. A nuclear war might yet follow. Much depends on the manner of the American disengagement from Vietnam—and a continuing American presence in Asia. If freedom of choice for the South Vietnamese people is not preserved and the Communists triumph by force, such a revival of Maoism would be an imminent danger.

Only a balance of powers can prevent the alienation of Southeast and southern Asia. In the short run, that balance requires the presence of American, Japanese, and Soviet power—all equally important. In the long run, the optimum solution would be a new China's participating equally with the other powers in the affairs of the region, her predominant interests clearly recognized. As long as the new China is truly *new* and *not* a reprint of Maoism, the long-term prospects are good.

Should Messianic Maoism revive, the prospects would be grim. A clash between China and Japan over Southeast Asia would not be unlikely, even if it were preceded by a temporary alliance of expediency, which would exclude other powers and subjugate the native peoples. Aside from the transcendent importance of preventing nuclear war, the rest of the world—and the United States, in particular—has a most real and immediate interest in developments in southern Asia. Chinese domination of the area through proxy governments would split the world along a north-south axis. It would not only deny Southeast Asians the opportunity to develop their own societies, but would sunder world trade routes. Japan would be able to transport her vital raw materials, above all petroleum, only by the favor of China—an intolerable situation Tokyo could not permit. The trading nations of Europe, as well as the United States, would be denied certain raw materials and markets, as Mao Tse-tung predicted. The entire world system of political and economic relationships, which has kept the nuclear peace, would begin to break down. Outside Asia, such Chinese hegemony would have wide, incalculable consequences. It would lead to instability not only in Asia, Latin America, and Africa, but, finally, in Western Europe and the United States. The world is, to recoin a truism, one.

Stimulated by apparently widespread resistance within the United States to the raids on the Cambodian sanctuaries of the Vietcong and the North Vietnamese, Maoism began to stir again in Peking in May 1970. The ideologues ignored the fact that the student protesters were isolated, since both the American "proletariat" and the blacks, theoretically the nucleus of the American revolution Mao Tse-tung predicted, were dissociated from the protest. Reading the protest movement as they wished, the Chinese once again began to talk in terms of world-wide liberation.

But Peking's actions were extremely cautious thereafter. Even a statement attributed to Mao Tse-tung made it clear that China would not involve herself as a nation, but would only serve as the "great rear area of the world-wide liberation movement." Mao himself has half-repudiated his previous thesis that World War III was inevitable. Even at that *most* ideologized level, great changes in Chinese thinking are apparent. While the change in internal policy is irreversible, foreign policy might still alter radically. If an essentially opportunistic Peking regime, compelled beyond its conscious will by the historical inclination toward expansion, were to conclude that the United States was, after all, a "paper tiger," about to perish amid "people's wars" abroad and revolution at home, China might yet move directly.

The peace and stability of the world teeters on the knife edge of Chinese psychology. But the prognosis is, again by a slight margin, more favorable than unfavorable. Above all, China is studying her true strengths and her true weaknesses. When they have finally learned to know themselves, the Chinese could learn to know other peoples better. With their national interests acknowledged by other nations through pressing invitations to participate fully in the peaceful evolution of the community of mankind in the United Nations, as well as through universal diplomatic relations and trade, China could become a beneficent—rather than a disruptive force—in the comity of nations. Much depends upon the actions of other nations, particularly the United States. Ultimately, all depends upon the changing "world view" of the Chinese themselves.

Index

About the Author

After more than two decades of specialization on Asia, Robert S. Elegant is now foreign affairs columnist for the *Los Angeles Times;* his commentaries are published in more than 300 newspapers in the United States and abroad. Long recognized as one of America's most distinguished foreign correspondents, he is also the author of three authoritative works on the Far East, as well as two widely acclaimed novels.

Born in New York, Mr. Elegant received a B.A., Phi Beta Kappa, from the University of Pennsylvania and an M.A. in Chinese and Japanese, as well as an M.S. in journalism, from Columbia University.

Mr. Elegant first went to Asia in 1951 and has lived in Asia and Europe since that time. He was married to Moira Clarissa Brady of Sydney, Australia, in New Delhi, India, in 1956. The Elegants now live in Europe with their daughter, Victoria Ann, their son, Simon David Brady, and their four dogs: Oliver, Pommerey, Flora, and Ptolemey.

Mr. Elegant, who travels throughout the world for the *Los Angeles Times,* received the Edgar Allan Poe Award for his novel of suspense, *A Kind of Treason,* set in Vietnam, whereas *The Seeking,* set in Central Asia in 100 B.C., was hailed as a remarkably poetic evocation of an age past. His first work, *China's Red Masters,* published in 1951, has just been reissued, as has been *The Center of the World,* originally published in 1964.

For his journalistic work, he has received three major awards from the Overseas Press Club, another from Sigma Delta Chi, the professional journalistic association, and a number of other prizes. Besides his thrice-weekly column, he is now concentrating upon writing fiction.